Abraham Ibn Ezra Latinus: Henry Bate's Latin Versions of Abraham Ibn Ezra's Astrological Writings

Études sur le Judaïsme Médiéval

Fondées par
Georges Vajda

Rédacteur en chef
Paul B. Fenton

Dirigées par
Phillip I. Lieberman
Benjamin Hary
and Katja Vehlow

TOME XCIII

The titles published in this series are listed at brill.com/ejm

Abraham Ibn Ezra Latinus: Henry Bate's Latin Versions of Abraham Ibn Ezra's Astrological Writings

With English Translation and a Collation
with the Hebrew and French Source Texts

*Abraham Ibn Ezra's Astrological Writings,
Volume 8-1*

Edited, translated, collated and annotated by
Shlomo Sela

BRILL

LEIDEN • BOSTON
2022

The Library of Congress Cataloging-in-Publication Data is available online at https://catalog.loc.gov
LC record available at https://lccn.loc.gov/2022035833

Typeface for the Latin, Greek, and Cyrillic scripts: "Brill". See and download: brill.com/brill-typeface.

ISSN 0169-815X
ISBN 978-90-04-52488-0 (hardback, set)
ISBN 978-90-04-52258-9 (hardback, volume 1)
ISBN 978-90-04-52388-3 (hardback, volume 2)
ISBN 978-90-04-52260-2 (e-book, volume 1)
ISBN 978-90-04-52389-0 (e-book, volume 2)

Copyright 2022 by Shlomo Sela. Published by Koninklijke Brill NV, Leiden, The Netherlands.
Koninklijke Brill NV incorporates the imprints Brill, Brill Nijhoff, Brill Hotei, Brill Schöningh, Brill Fink, Brill mentis, Vandenhoeck & Ruprecht, Böhlau and V&R unipress.
Koninklijke Brill NV reserves the right to protect this publication against unauthorized use. Requests for re-use and/or translations must be addressed to Koninklijke Brill NV via brill.com or copyright.com.

This book is printed on acid-free paper and produced in a sustainable manner.

*To my beloved wife, Leah, without whom
I could not have produced this volume*

TABLE OF CONTENTS

VOLUME 1

Preface	xiii
Abbreviations	xv
General Introduction	1
Abraham Ibn Ezra Latinus	1
Henry Bate's Life	4
The Henry Bate–Abraham Ibn Ezra Connection	6
1. The French Translations	7
2. The Treatise on the Astrolabe	8
3. The Treatise on the Equatorium	9
4. *Tabulae Machlinienses*	9
5. The Latin Translation of Ibn Ezra's Lost *'Olam* III and of the Two Kindian Treatises	10
6. The Astrological Autobiography	13
6.1. Nativities	13
6.2. World Astrology	14
6.3. Introductions to Astrology	15
6.4. Elections	16
6.5. Interrogations	17
6.6. Medical Astrology	18
7. Bate's Treatise on the Critical Days	18
8. The Philosophical and Scientific Encyclopedia	20
Earlier Research on Bate's Translations	20
Bate's Complete Translations	22
1. *Liber Abrahe Avenerre introductorius ad astronomiam*	22
1.1. The Contents and Sources of *Reshit Ḥokhmah*	23
1.2. The Manuscripts	25
1.3. Title, Authorship, and Place and Date of Composition	26
1.4. The Structure of *Introductorius*	27
1.5. The Source Text of *Introductorius*	29
1.6. The Source Text of *Commencement*	33

2.	*Liber causarum seu rationum*	33
	2.1. The Contents of *Ṭeʿamim* I	34
	2.2. The Manuscripts	35
	2.3. Title, Authorship, and Place and Date of Composition	35
	2.4. The Structure of *Rationes* I	37
	2.5. The Source Text of *Rationes* I	37
3.	*Secunda pars libri rationum*	40
	3.1. What is *Ṭeʿamim* II?	41
	3.2. The Manuscripts	42
	3.3. Title, Authorship, and Place and Date of Composition	42
	3.4. The Structure of *Rationes* II	44
	3.5. The Source Text of *Rationes* II	44
4.	*Liber introductionis ad iudicia astrologie*	46
	4.1. The Contents of *Mishpeṭei ha-Mazzalot*	46
	4.2. The Manuscripts	47
	4.3. Title, Authorship, and Place and Date of composition	48
	4.4. The Structure of *Iudicia*	53
	4.5. The Source Text of *Iudicia*	55
5.	*Liber de mundo vel seculo*	59
	5.1. The Contents and Sources of ʿ*Olam* I	59
	5.2. The Manuscripts	61
	5.3. Title, Authorship, and Place and Date of Composition	62
	5.4. The Structure of *De mundo*	63
	5.5. The Source Text of *De mundo*	64
6.	*Liber Abrahe Avenesre de luminaribus*	64
	6.1. The Contents of *Meʾorot*	64
	6.2. The Manuscripts	66
	6.3. Title, Authorship, and Place and Date of Composition	67
	6.4. The Structure of the *De luminaribus*	68
	6.5. The Source Text of *De luminaribus*	68
Bate's Modus Operandi as a Translator	69
1.	Henry Bate and the Art of the Doublet	69
	1.1. The Zodiac, the Ecliptic, and the Zodiacal Signs	71
	1.2. Astronomical Terms	75

	1.3. Astronomical Terms derived from ישר "Straight" and שווה "Equal"	77
	1.4. Astrological Terms derived from ישר "Straight"	78
	1.5. Planets and Fixed Stars	81
	1.6. The Use for the Planetary Conditions of the Latin Translations of Abū Maʿshar's *Great Introduction*	83
	1.7. The Dignities	85
	1.8. The Components of the Horoscope	86
	1.9. The Strongest Planet	88
	1.10. The Lots	90
2.	How much Hebrew did Bate Know?	93
	2.1. Translations "de Hebreo in Latinum"	93
	2.2. "Secundum quod iacet in Ebraico"	94
	2.3. Hebrew Words that Hagin Left Untranslated	95
	2.4. Biblical Stars, Hebrew Names of Planets, Stars and Constellations	98
	2.5. Translation of Hebrew Idioms	99
3.	Bate, Commentator and Supercommentator on Ibn Ezra	102
	3.1. Glosses in *De mundo*	102
	3.2. Glosses in *De luminaribus*	104
	3.3. Glosses in *Introductorius*	104
	3.4. Glosses in *Rationes* I	105
	3.5. Glosses in *Rationes* II	106
	3.6. Glosses in *Iudicia*	107
4.	Bate's Trajectory as a Translator of Ibn Ezra's Astrological Writings	109

Aims, Methodology and Editorial Principles	114
1. The English Translations	114
2. Notes Explaining Technical Terms, Glossaries and Lists of Authorities and Sources	115
3. The Collation	116
4. Divergent Readings	117
4.1. *Introductorius* Follows *Commencement* and Diverges from *Reshit Ḥokhmah*	117
4.2. Bate's Six Latin Translations Diverge from All their Source Texts	118
5. Doublets and Triplets	118
6. Omissions	118
6.1. Omissions in the Two-tiered Translations	118

  6.2. *Introductorius* and *Commencement* Omit Words
    Found in *Reshit Ḥokhmah* 119
  6.3. Omissions in *Introductorius* but not in
    Commencement 119
 7. Glosses 120
 8. Stylistic Alterations 121
 9. Additions from Lost Hebrew Manuscripts 121
10. Special Categories of Translation in *Introductorius* 121
  10.1. Translations of Names that Hagin Transliterates 121
  10.2. Calques of Hebrew Idioms 122
  10.3. Transliterations of Hebrew Words in *Introductorius* 122
  10.4. Reliance on a Lost Manuscript of *Commencement* .. 123
11. Notes 123

Part One: *Liber Abrahe Avenerre introductorius ad astronomiam*:
 Latin Text and English Translation 127

Part Two: Notes to *Liber Abrahe Avenerre introductorius ad
 astronomiam* 361

Part Three: *Liber causarum seu rationum*: Latin Text and English
 Translation 483

Part Four: Notes to *Liber causarum seu rationum* 581

VOLUME 2

Abbreviations xiii

Part Five: *Secunda pars libri rationum*: Latin Text and English
 Translation 631

Part Six: Notes to *Secunda pars libri rationum* 713

Part Seven: *Liber introductionis ad iudicia astrologie*: Latin Text and
 English Translation 769

Part Eight: Notes to *Liber introductionis ad iudicia astrologie* 873

Part Nine: *Liber de mundo vel seculo*: Latin Text and English
    Translation 933

Part Ten: Notes to *Liber de mundo vel seculo* 997

Part Eleven: *Liber Abrahe Avenesre de luminaribus*: Latin Text and
    English Translation 1029

Part Twelve: Notes to *Liber Abrahe Avenesre de luminaribus* 1063

Plates 1087

Part Thirteen: Appendices 1095
    1. Abraham Ibn Ezra's Astrological Corpus 1097
    2. MS Leipzig, Universitätsbibliothek, 1466 1101
    3. MS Limoges, Bibliothèque municipale, 9 (28) 1104
    4. Technical Terms in *Introductorius* and their counterparts in
        Commencement and *Reshit ḥokhmah* 1107
    5. Names of persons, authors, and sources in *Introductorius*
        and their counterparts in *Commencement* and *Reshit
        ḥokhmah* 1150
    6. Technical Terms in *Rationes* I and their counterparts in
        Ṭeʿamim I 1157
    7. Names of persons, authors, and sources in *Rationes* I and
        their counterparts in *Ṭeʿamim* I 1175
    8. Technical Terms in *Rationes* II and their counterparts in
        Ṭeʿamim II 1184
    9. Names of persons, authors, and sources in *Rationes* II and
        their counterparts in *Ṭeʿamim* II 1201
    10. Technical Terms in *Iudicia* and their counterparts in
        Mishpeṭei ha-Mazzalot 1207
    11. Names of persons, authors, and sources in *Iudicia* and their
        counterparts in *Mishpeṭei ha-Mazzalot* 1229
    12. Technical Terms in *De Mundo* and their counterparts in
        ʿOlam I 1235
    13. Names of persons, authors, and sources in *De Mundo* and
        their counterparts in *ʿOlam* I 1249
    14. Technical Terms in *De luminaribus* and their counterparts in
        Meʾorot 1256

15. Names of persons, authors, and sources in *De luminaribus* and their counterparts in *Me'orot* 1268

Bibliography 1270
Index 1277

PREFACE

Twenty years ago I started to research Abraham Ibn Ezra's astrological corpus. To date I have published the results of this research in seven volumes, divided into two parts. The first comprises five volumes that completed the research and publication of Ibn Ezra's extant Hebrew astrological writings, according to the branches of Greek and Arabic astrology into which Ibn Ezra's corpus is divided. The title "Abraham Ibn Ezra Latinus" fits the volumes of the second part, signaling that they look at the same cultural phenomenon: Abraham Ibn Ezra's renaissance in the Latin West, starting in the last decades of the thirteenth century, as a result of several almost simultaneous translation projects.

Ibn Ezra's Latin astrological corpus may be divided into three categories: (a) Latin translations whose Hebrew source texts are extant today; (b) Latin translations that have no surviving Hebrew counterpart but are obviously translations of texts by Ibn Ezra; and (c) Latin translations that have no surviving Hebrew counterpart in Ibn Ezra's astrological corpus and whose affiliation with Ibn Ezra is unclear. The first two volumes of *Abraham Ibn Ezra Latinus* presented specimens of the second and third of those categories, with parallel Latin-English critical editions, accompanied by a commentary, of Ibn Ezra's astrological writings whose Hebrew text is lost and which are extant today only in Latin translation, or Latin translations assigned to Ibn Ezra whose affiliation to him is unclear. In this volume we turn to Latin translations of the first category, which embodies the bulk of Ibn Ezra's Latin corpus.

In the present volume I focus on Henry Bate of Mechelen (1246–after 1310), the first scholar to bring Ibn Ezra's astrological work to the knowledge of Latin readers and the most prolific of all the Latin savants who produced various collections of Ibn Ezra's astrological writings. The volume has two main objectives. The first is to offer as complete and panoramic an account as possible of Bate's translational project. Therefore, instead of scrutinizing only one specimen and extrapolating from it to the other translations, which would offer only a partial picture, I decided to publish critical editions of all six of Bate's complete translations of Ibn Ezra's astrological writings. All of them, with one exception, are *editiones principes*.

A preliminary examination showed that these Latin translations are markedly different from their Hebrew source texts: they include numer-

ous divergent readings, alternative readings, omissions, stylistic alterations, glosses of various lengths, and additions from lost Hebrew manuscripts. Therefore, the second objective is to accompany Bate's Latin translations with literal English translations and to offer a thorough collation of the Latin translation (with their English translations) against the Hebrew and French source texts.

This methodology was selected for the following two reasons. First, because offering "literal English translations" is the best way to make readers aware of the special flavor, peculiarities, and minutiae of the Latin texts. Second, because "thoroughly collating" the Latin translations and their corresponding English translations against the Hebrew and French source texts is the best way to discover the main features of Bate's modus operandi as a translator and his attitude towards Ibn Ezra, and to convey these to the reader.

I wish to express my sincere gratitude to a number of people who have contributed toward the realization of this volume. Charles Burnett assisted me in solving many Latin paleographical puzzles. Carlos Steel, too, was very helpful regarding the edition of some part of the Latin texts. Although the responsibility for establishing the Latin texts is entirely mine, their aid has been essential to overcoming obstacles in the way; Jean-Patrice Boudet assisted me in understanding problematic Old French words; David Juste provided me with kind access to manuscript copies of some of Bate's Latin translations; I shared with Charles Burnett, Gad Freudenthal, David Juste, and Carlos Steel a preliminary version of the methodology used in this volume for collating the Latin translations and their corresponding English translations against the Hebrew and French source texts; their opinions were fundamental for determining the final shape of this methodology. Lenn Schramm revised the translations and the English sections of this book; he also made helpful suggestions about the translation of the Latin and Hebrew texts. The Israel Science Foundation (Grant No. 289/17) provided a generous grant. My warmest thanks to all of them.

Sh.S.

Sadly, Shlomo Sela passed away during the production of this book. His family wants to acknowledge Niran Garshtein who has corrected and revised the proofs and produced the index. They express their sincere appreciation for his work in bringing the volume to completion.

ABBREVIATIONS

⟨⟨...⟩⟩	omissions
⟨⟨...⟩⟩^μ	*Introductorius* and *Commencement* omit words found in *Reshit Ḥokhmah*
⟨⟨...⟩⟩^ν	Omissions in *Introductorius* that do not occur in *Commencement*
Bate's Latin translations	Henry Bate's complete Latin translations of Ibn Ezra's Hebrew astrological writings
collation	collation of Bate's translations with their source texts
Commencement	*Li livres du commencement de sapience*; Hagin le Juif
De diebus creticis	*De diebus creticis periodorumque causis*; Henry Bate
De luminaribus	*Liber Abrahe Avenesre de luminaribus*
De luminaribus, § 20:2	*De luminaribus*, section 20, passage 2
De mundo	*Liber de mundo vel seculo*; Henry Bate
De mundo, § 12:2	*De mundo*, section 12, passage 2
De nativitatibus	*Liber Abraham Iudei de nativitatibus* (assigned to Abraham Ibn Ezra)
De nativitatibus, II vi § 6:4, 314–315	*De nativitatibus*, ed. Sela (2019), part II (the twelve horoscopic houses), section vi (addressing the sixth horoscopic house), section 6, sentence 4, on pp. 314–315
De rationibus tabularum	*Liber de rationibus tabularum*; assigned to Abraham Ibn Ezra
E	Erfurt, Universitäts- und Forschungsbibliothek, Amplon. O.89
Electiones	*Liber electionum* (Book of elections), Latin translation of the third version of *Sefer ha-Mivḥarim*; Abraham Ibn Ezra
Elections	*Le livre des elections Abraham*; Hagin le Juif
Epitome	*Epitome totius astrologiae*
gloss at § 10.9:4 → 3	sentence 3 of the gloss at chapter 10, section 9, sentence 4 of Bate's relevant translation

Introductorius	*Liber Abrahe Avenerre introductorius ad astronomiam*; Henry Bate
Introductorius, § 2.7:2	*Introductorius*, chapter 2, section 5, passage 2
Introductorius, § 2:3	*Introductorius*, section 2 of the introduction, passage 3
Iudicia	*Liber introductionis ad iudicia astrologie*; Henry Bate
Iudicia, § 31:2	*Iudicia*, section 31, passage 2
Liber Electionum, II vi 1:5, 106–107	*Electiones*, ed. Sela (2020), part II (the twelve horoscopic houses), section vi (addressing the sixth horoscopic house), section 1, sentence 5, on pp. 106–107
Me'orot	*Sefer ha-Me'orot* (Book of the Luminaries); Abraham Ibn Ezra
Me'orot, § 25:4, 472–473	*Me'orot*, ed. Sela (2011), section 25, passage 4 on pp. 472–473
Mishpeṭei ha-Mazzalot	*Sefer Mishpeṭei ha-Mazzalot* (Book of the Judgments of the Zodiacal Signs); Abraham Ibn Ezra
Mishpeṭei ha-Mazzalot, § 38:7, 522–523	*Mishpeṭei ha-Mazzalot*, ed. Sela (2017), section 38, passage 7 on pp. 522–523
Mivḥarim I	First version of *Sefer ha-Mivḥarim* (Book of Elections); Abraham Ibn Ezra
Mivḥarim I, § 5.4:2, 66–67	*Mivḥarim* I, ed. Sela (2011), chapter 5 (addressing the fifth horoscopic house), section 4, sentence 2, on pp. 66–67
Mivḥarim II	Second version of *Sefer ha-Mivḥarim* (Book of Elections); Abraham Ibn Ezra
Mivḥarim II, § 1.5:2, 152–153	*Mivḥarim* II, ed. Sela (2011), chapter 1 (addressing the first horoscopic house), section 5, sentence 2, on pp. 164–165
Mivḥarim III	Third version of *Sefer ha-Mivḥarim* (Book of Elections); Abraham Ibn Ezra
Moladot	First version of *Sefer ha-moladot* (*Book of nativities*); Abraham Ibn Ezra
Moladot II	second version of *Sefer ha-Moladot*; Abraham Ibn Ezra
Moladot, I 9: 4, 88–89	*Moladot*, ed. Sela (2013), part I, section 9, sentence 4, on pp. 88–89
Moladot, III vi 8:4, 152–153	*Moladot*, ed. Sela (2013), part III (the twelve horoscopic houses) chapter 6 (addressing the

	sixth horoscopic house), section 8, sentence 4, on pp. 152–153
Nativitates	*Liber nativitatum*, Latin translation of second version of *Sefer ha-moladot*; Abraham Ibn Ezra
Nativitates, I i 2:6–7, 82–83	*Nativitates*, ed. Sela (2019), part I (introduction), chapter i, section 2, sentence 6–7, on pp. 82–83
Nativités	*Livre des jugemens des nativités*; Hagin le Juif
'Olam I	First version of *Sefer ha-'Olam* (Book of the World); Abraham Ibn Ezra
'Olam I, § 45:1, 82–83	*'Olam* I, ed. Sela (2010), section 45, sentence 1, on pp. 82–83
'Olam II	Second version of *Sefer ha-'Olam* (Book of the World); Abraham Ibn Ezra
'Olam II, § 28:3, 174–175	*'Olam* II, ed. Sela (2010), section 2, sentence 1, on pp. 174–175
'Olam III	Third version of *Sefer ha-'Olam* (Book of the World); Abraham Ibn Ezra
P	Paris, BnF, fr. 24276, fols. 1a–66a
P[1]	Paris BnF, fonds français, 1351, fols. 1a–66a
Questions	*Le livre des questions*; Hagin le Juif
Rationes I	*Liber causarum seu rationum*; Henry Bate
Rationes I, § 2.10:1	*Rationes* I, chapter 2, section 10, passage 1
Rationes II	*Secunda pars libri rationum*; Henry Bate
Rationes II, § 5.5:6	*Rationes* II, chapter 5, section 5, passage 6
Reshit ḥokhmah	*Sefer Reshit ḥokhmah* (Book of the Beginning of Wisdom); Abraham Ibn Ezra
Reshit ḥokhmah, § 9.1:6, 234–235	*Reshit ḥokhmah*, ed. Sela (2017), chapter 9, section 1, passage 6, on pp. 234–235
Speculum divinorum	*Speculum divinorum et quorundam naturalium*; Henry Bate
α	Divergent readings following *Commencement* and diverging from *Reshit Ḥokhmah* in *Introductorius*
β	Doublets and triplets in all the translations
γ	Divergent readings from the source texts in all the translations
δ	Bate translates names which Hagin transliterates
ε	*Introductorius* transliterates Hebrew words

ABBREVIATIONS

θ Hebrew idioms in all the translations
π lost manuscript of *Commencement*

GENERAL INTRODUCTION

The bulk of Abraham Ibn Ezra's (ca. 1089–ca. 1161) literary career played out in the Latin West. Born in Muslim Spain, he left his homeland at the age of 50 and began a nomadic life in Italy, France, and England. His reputation rests on his outstanding biblical commentaries, but his intellectual interests extended to the sciences,[1] especially astrology. Ibn Ezra's most significant contribution in this field is the creation of the first comprehensive corpus of Hebrew astrological textbooks that address the main systems of Arabic astrology. His astrological achievement has never been repeated.[2] Thanks to recent discoveries, today we know of twenty treatises by him, covering the main genres of Greek and Arabic astrological literature.[3] This relatively large number reflects the multiple versions or recensions of each individual work he produced. This phenomenon is typical of his literary career: he would set down a new version of an old work for a new patron when he arrived in a new town, thereby continuing to stimulate the attention and curiosity of readers all along his itinerary through Latin Europe.

Abraham Ibn Ezra Latinus

There are strong indications that Ibn Ezra had direct relations with Christian scholars during his peregrinations, and that some of his works became known to Christian scholars shortly after his death and were then translated or elaborated for Latin readers. This is supported by codicological evidence: most of the Latin works ascribed to Ibn Ezra, supposed to have

---

[1] For a chronological listing of Ibn Ezra's scholarly writings, see Sela and Freudenthal 2006, 13–55. For a general evaluation of Ibn Ezra's scientific contribution, see Steinschneider 1880, 59–128; Steinschneider 1925, 327–387; Millás Vallicrosa 1949, 289–347; Levey 1971, IV, 502–503; Goldstein 1996, 9–21; Levy 2000, 60–75; Sela 2003, 17–92.

[2] For lists of and studies on Ibn Ezra's astrological writings, see Steinschneider 1870, 339–346; Steinschneider 1880, 124–128; Steinschneider 1897, 136–150; Levy 1927, 11–57; Smithuis 2006.

[3] For a list of these astrological treatises, sorted according to the main genres of Greek and Arabic astrological literature to which they belong, accompanied by references to editions in which these treatises are available today, and by the abbreviations used throughout this volume to refer to each of Ibn Ezra's astrological writings, see Appendix I, Abraham Ibn Ezra's Astrological Corpus, pp. 1097–1100.

been written with his participation, or based on material derived from his work survive in manuscripts from the twelfth century. Five specimens of this type, associated with Ibn Ezra but without a Hebrew counterpart in his extant oeuvre, survive. (i) *Epitome totius astrologiae* (henceforth *Epitome*), a popular astrological work that consists of an introductory book, the *Ysagoge in astrologiam*, and the *Liber quadripartitus*, which addresses the four main subdivisions of Arabic astrology. *Epitome* evinces striking resemblances to Ibn Ezra's astrological works, employs literal Latin translations of Ibn Ezra's Hebrew neologisms, and is dated in one locus to 1142, shortly after Ibn Ezra arrived in the Latin West.[4] (ii) *Liber Abraham Iudei de nativitatibus* (Book on nativities by Abraham the Jew; henceforth *De nativitatibus*), which displays striking resemblances to Ibn Ezra's *Moladot*,[5] employs literal Latin translations of Ibn Ezra's Hebrew neologisms, includes substantial Jewish material, and incorporates explanations of astrological doctrines that are virtually identical to those found in other Hebrew works by Ibn Ezra on nativities.[6] (iii) A Latin treatise on the astrolabe, which bears striking resemblances to Ibn Ezra's Hebrew works on that instrument.[7] The author of this treatise writes explicitly: "Ut ait philosophorum sibi contemporaneorum Abraham magister noster egregius, quo dictante et hanc dispositionem astrolabii conscripsimus" = "We have written down this arrangement ⟨describing a figure⟩ of the astrolabe, as ⟨according to what⟩, of ⟨among⟩ his contemporary philosophers, Abraham, our illustrious master, says, ⟨and⟩ whilst he was dictating."[8] (iv) *Liber de rationibus tabularum* (Book of the reasons behind astronomical tables; henceforth *De rationibus tabularum*), a treatise explaining the astronomical rationale behind astronomical tables.[9] *De rationibus tabularum* begins *Dixit Abraham Iudeus* (Abraham the Jew said) and mentions a certain "Abraham" several times.[10] The author of *De rationibus tabularum* says that he compiled a set of astronomical tables according to the meridian of Pisa, which he adapted

---

[4] *Epitome*, ed. Heller (1548); see Burnett 2002, 75–77; Burnett 2008, 219–265; Burnett 2010, 70–75; Smithuis 2004, Ch. III, 169–199; Sela 2020, 9–10.

[5] For the meaning of this and other abbreviations of Ibn Ezra's works, see Appendix 1.

[6] *De nativitatibus*, ed. Ratdolt (1485); see Sela 2018, 313–348; Sela 2019, 49–71.

[7] *Astrolabio*, ed. Millás Vallicrosa (1940); Sela 2003, 31–36.
Sela 2003, 31–36. See London, British Library, MS Cotton Vesp A II, fols. 37v–40v; Arundel 377, fols. 63r–68v.

[8] *Astrolabio*, ed. Millás Vallicrosa (1940), 28. I am grateful to Charles Burnett for assisting me in the translation of this sentence.

[9] *De rationibus tabularum*, ed. Millás Vallicrosa (1947); Birkenmajer 1919, 147–155; Birkenmajer 1950, 237–249; Sela 2003, 22–27, Samsó 2012.

[10] *De rationibus tabularum*, ed. Millás Vallicrosa (1947), 73, 156, 159.

from the tables of al-Ṣūfī.[11] (v) *Ptolomeus et multi sapientum*, a text that comments on astronomical tables with structural features similar to those of the Pisan tables mentioned in *De rationibus tabularum*, and states that the tables were compiled in 1143,[12] a year that coincides with Ibn Ezra's residence in Lucca.[13]

It seems, though, that Ibn Ezra never went beyond sporadic contacts with Christian scholars. In contrast to the quick diffusion of his Hebrew astrological work among Jews,[14] and the transmission of Arabic astrological literature to Christian readers via Latin translations,[15] Ibn Ezra's astrological writings remained outside the mainstream of Latin astrological literature until the last decades of the thirteenth century.[16] Soon after, though, Ibn Ezra was "reborn" in the Latin West, thanks to almost simultaneous translation projects carried out then.

One extensive project, which included seven items, transmitted in a large number of manuscripts, was carried out by the Italian philosopher, astrologer, and professor of medicine Pietro d'Abano (ca. 1250–1316), during his years in Paris (1293–1307).[17] Another translation project was organized in the second half of the thirteenth century by Pierre de Limoges (c. 1240–c. 1306), who went to study in Paris and was probably a master of arts. Pierre commissioned, and perhaps himself carried out, one complete and two incomplete translations of Ibn Ezra's astrological writings.[18] Three more Latin translations of astrological treatises by Ibn Ezra were the work of Arnoul de Quincampoix (d. before 1336), physician to Philip IV the Fair (r.

---

[11] *De rationibus tabularum*, ed. Millás Vallicrosa (1947), 87: "Tabulas medii cursus solis secundum Azofi composui ... Et he tabule composite sunt secundum meridiem Pisanorum." Ibn Ezra was in fact acquainted with al-Ṣūfī (See '*Olam* I, § 17:10–11, 62–63) and in his astrological work evinces some familiarity with Pisa. See '*Olam* II, § 15:24, 166–167; *Nativitates*, I ii 2:7, 82–83.

[12] Fitzwilliam Museum, McClean 165, fol. 70v: "Tabule autem nostre, composite scilicet anno Christi 1143, habent secundum annum bissextilem."

[13] Nothaft 2018 (a), 145–210, esp. pp. 153–154.

[14] Leicht 2012, 262–273; Sela 2012, 296–299; Sela 2014, 189–241.

[15] Juste 2016, 173–194; Boudet 2006, 35–82.

[16] This emerges from the fact that neither Ibn Ezra's name nor references to any of his works are found in the catalogue of astrological writings in the *Speculum astronomiae* (Mirror of astronomy), probably composed around the middle of the thirteenth century, and in the *Liber astronomicus*, the most important astrological work of the thirteenth century, written by Guido Bonatti around 1270. See *Speculum astronomiae*, ed. Caroti et al. (1992); *Liber astronomicus* (1550); Thorndike 1923–1958, vol. II, ch. 67, 825–835, esp. 826–827.

[17] Sela 2019 (d), 1–82.

[18] Sela 2019 (b), 9–57.

1285–1314).[19] There are at least twelve more anonymous Latin translations of astrological treatises by Ibn Ezra.[20]

But the place of honor is reserved to Henry Bate (1246–after 1310), who, through his extensive translation project, was the first to bring Ibn Ezra's astrological work to Latin readers. This volume, the eighth installment of Ibn Ezra's complete works on astrology, offers the *editiones principes* (with the exception of one Renaissance edition recently redone in a critical edition) of Henry Bate's complete Latin translations of Ibn Ezra's Hebrew astrological writings (henceforth Bate's Latin translations). These six Latin translations, which, as will be shown in due course, are markedly different from their Hebrew source texts, are presented in this volume accompanied by "literal" English translations. In addition, the texts of the Latin translations and their corresponding English translations are thoroughly collated against their Hebrew and French source texts. The rationale behind this methodology and the principles of its implementation in this volume will be explained in detail below.[21]

The following introductory study is divided into six parts: (i) Bate's biography; (ii) the main stages of the Henry Bate–Abraham Ibn Ezra connection; (iii) earlier research on Bate's translations; (iv) a study of the main features of Bate's six Latin complete translations; (v) Bate's modus operandi as a translator of Ibn Ezra's astrological writings; and (vi) the aims, methodology, and editorial principles of the present volume.

Henry Bate's Life[22]

Henry Bate was born to a well-to-do aristocratic family in the city of Mechelen (= Malines), Flanders, on March 24, 1246. His family's comfortable situation allowed him to travel to Paris for his studies. In the colophons to the translations of Ibn Ezra's astrological works Bate is referred to as *magister*,[23] which indicates that he obtained at least a master's degree from the Paris arts faculty. Bate refers to himself as a philosophy teacher and secre-

---

[19] Sela 2020 (a), 16. They are preserved in a single manuscript, Ghent, MS Univ. 5 (416), copied in the fifteenth century, which contains four items related to Ibn Ezra's astrological writings.

[20] For a list see, Sela 2020 (a), 17–18.

[21] See below, p. 114 and following pages.

[22] The following biographical sketch is based, inter alia, on Steel and Vanden Broecke 2018, 31–43.

[23] See below, p. 27, 36, 48, 63, 67.

tary to princes,[24] a function we know he fulfilled for Guy of Avesnes, brother of John II of Avesnes, Count of Hainaut (1247–1304). Bate dedicated his philosophical encyclopedia, *Speculum divinorum et quorundam naturalium* (Mirror of the divine substances and some natural things; henceforth *Speculum divinorum*) to Guy of Avesnes.[25]

Little is known about Bate's intellectual circle in Paris, but it seems very likely that he was connected to the thriving local community of celestial practitioners, which included Pierre of Limoges, who was dean of the faculty of medicine between 1267 and 1270, and William of Saint-Cloud (1285–1292).[26] Bate completed his studies before 1273, when we find him back in Mechelen, ready for an ecclesiastical career. Bate certainly knew Thomas Aquinas (1225–1274), who taught in Paris between 1268 and 1272. Often, however, Bate criticizes Thomas's Aristotelian views, particularly on the intellective soul and its capacity to know intelligible objects, and defends a more Platonic view instead.[27]

Bate obtained his first ecclesiastical prebend in his 28th year (i.e., in 1273), when he was living in Mechelen.[28] In 1274, Bate participated in the council of Lyons (March 7–July 17), where he established a solid friendship with the famous translator William of Moerbeke, whose translation of Ptolemy's *Tetrabiblos* he used in his own work.[29] It was to Moerbeke that Bate addressed his treatise on the astrolabe.[30] It was also in Mechelen that Bate composed his treatise on the equatorium and his own astronomical tables, the *Tabulae machlinienses*.[31] Bate received a second and more substantial ecclesiastical benefice near the end of May 1276, when he was in his 31st year.[32] The earliest explicit evidence connecting Bate to Liège comes from the colophon of his translation of Ibn Ezra's *'Olam* I, which states that he began the translation in Liège, but finished it in Mechelen in 1281.[33] A third benefice was the position of cantor in the cathedral chapter in

---

[24] See *Nativitas*, ed. Steel et al. (2018), lines 2507–2508; 1129–1130; 2522. This edition is used for all quotations from or references to *Nativitas*, in the following format: *Nativitas*, 160 = *Nativitas*, ed. Steel et al. (2018), line 160.
[25] Van de Vyver 1960, pp. xiv–xv, 3.
[26] Juste 2018 (b), 68–80.
[27] Wallerand 1931; Guldentops 2005.
[28] *Nativitas*, 280–281.
[29] Wallerand 1931, 11.
[30] Wallerand 1931, 19–20; Poulle 1972.
[31] Steel and Vanden Broecke 2018, 35.
[32] *Nativitas*, 286, 314–315, 1017–1023, 290.
[33] See, below, p. 63.

Liège.³⁴ We find this title in the colophon of Bate's Latin translation of Ibn Ezra's *Reshit Ḥokhmah*.³⁵

Early in 1292, Bate accompanied Guy of Avesnes to Orvieto to help him defend his interests at the papal court. The occasion was a dispute about the succession to the episcopal see of Liège, which Guy was hoping to obtain following the death of prince-bishop John II of Dampierre (1282–1292). But Pope Nicholas IV (1288–1292) died on April 4, not long after their arrival. The deliberations about the election of a new pope were drawn out and only Bate stayed on, probably to keep an eye out for his patron's interests.³⁶ Bate benefited from this prolonged stay to complete five of his complete Latin translations of astrological works by Abraham Ibn Ezra. The last of them was dated October 29, 1292.³⁷

After returning to the Low Countries, Bate probably returned to Mechelen rather than Liège. Late in life he devoted himself to writing the philosophical encyclopedia *Speculum divinorum*, dedicated to Guy of Avesnes, who became bishop of Utrecht in 1301. The work was completed between 1301 and ca. 1305.³⁸ It is clear that Bate owned an extraordinarily large collection of scientific and philosophical works.³⁹ In an addition to Part XXII, chapter 18 of the *Speculum*, written some years after the work was completed, Bate refers to a solar eclipse he observed on the last day of January 1309, which, in his opinion, confirmed the astronomical tables he had composed and corrected. This is Bate's astronomical testament. He clearly took great pride in his astronomical tables and considered them superior to others.⁴⁰

The Henry Bate–Abraham Ibn Ezra Connection

The following stages and encounters illustrate the connection between Henry Bate and Abraham Ibn Ezra.

---

[34] The cantor was the second in dignity after the dean of the chapter, and a fat prebend was usually attached to such a position.
[35] See, below, p. 27.
[36] Steel and Vanden Broecke 2018, 38.
[37] See, below, p. 48.
[38] Poulle 1972; Van de Vyver 1960, xiv–xv.
[39] For a list of books available to Bate in 1280, see Steel et al. 2018, 269–285.
[40] Steel and Vanden Broecke 2018, 39–40. Steel and Guldentops 1996, 347–348 (*Additio*, 51–66).

1. *The French Translations*

In 1273, when Henry Bate was a student at the University of Paris and well before the composition of his first known book, he commissioned a Jewish scholar named Hagin le Juif to translate a collection of Ibn Ezra's astrological works from Hebrew into French: (1) *Li livres du commencement de sapience* (henceforth *Commencement*); (2) *Livre des jugemens des nativités* (henceforth *Nativités*); (3) *Le livre des elections Abraham* (henceforth *Elections*); (4) *Le livre des questions* (henceforth *Questions*). These versions of (1) *Reshit Ḥokhmah*; (2) *Moladot*; (3) *Mivḥarim* II; and (4) *She'elot* II[41] are preserved in two manuscripts:

(i) Paris, BnF, fr. 24276, fols. 1a–66a (henceforth P), a vellum manuscript written in the thirteenth century, is the earliest surviving version of Hagin's four French translations of Ibn Ezra's astrological writings. P was copied by a professional scribe, with the text and scholia in clear characters in two columns, and space left for rubricated initials at the beginning of each text. Its margins contain glosses in the hand of Pierre of Limoges, who, as was his custom, wrote comments in the manuscripts he owned. This indicates that P, too, belonged to him and was commissioned by him, or was given to him for his own use.[42]

(ii) Paris BnF, fonds français, 1351, fols. 1a–66a (henceforth P¹), a vellum and paper manuscript from the fifteenth century with the same four French translations of Ibn Ezra's astrological writings as P. As we shall see later, Bate did not use P, but a lost earlier manuscript of Hagin's French translation on which both P and P¹ were based.[43]

We have substantial bibliographical information only for *Commencement*, from whose colophon we learn that the Hebrew source text of this translation was composed by Abraham Ibn Ezra, translated orally by Hagin from Hebrew into French, and written down in French by a certain Obers de Mondidier in Bate's house in Mechelen (= Malines), Flanders, at the end of 1273.[44] A recently identified charter reveals that Hagin was still alive in

---

[41] For the meaning of these and other abbreviations of Ibn Ezra's works, see Appendix 1.
[42] See Sela 2019 (b), 9–36, and Juste 2018 (b), 68–80.
[43] See below, pp. 33, 123.
[44] P, fol. 66rb: "Ci define li livers de Commencement de Sapience que fist Abraham Even Aze ou Aezera qui est interpretes maistre de aide que translata Hagins li Juis de ebrieu en romans et Obers de Mondidier escriboit le romans et du fait a Malines en la meson sire Henri Bate et fu fines l'en de grace 1273."

1288 and living in Mechelen, a few meters from Henry Bate's home. Given that they were neighbors, Bate could have consulted his Jewish translator then whenever his astrological interests made it necessary.[45] Hagin's French versions exerted a great influence on later Latin translations of Ibn Ezra's astrological writings: Bate, Pierre de Limoges, Pietro d'Abano, and Arnoul de Quincampoix, as well as two anonymous translators, all used them as their source texts.[46]

2. *The Treatise on the Astrolabe*

Bate completed the *Magistralis compositio astrolabii*, describing the construction and uses of an astrolabe especially designed for astrological purposes, on October 11, 1274, at the request of William of Moerbeke. *Magistralis compositio astrolabii* follows immediately the *Liber Abraham Iudei de nativitatibus*, ascribed to Ibn Ezra, in the 1485 Venice Ratdolt edition, and is extant in five manuscripts copied from the 1485 edition.[47] This text mentions a certain "Abraham" together with Ptolemy, Jābir ibn Aflaḥ, al-Battānī, Abū Maʿshar, and unnamed "magistri probationum" (= masters of the observations).[48] Bate probably took the name "Abraham" from the aforementioned *De rationibus tabularum*, a treatise that explains the rationale behind the astronomical tables and was commonly ascribed to Ibn Ezra: the name "Abraham" appears in it several times,[49] together with very frequent references to the "magistri probationum"[50] and to the same Arabic astronomers and astrologers mentioned in *Magistralis compositio astrolabii*.[51] Moreover, this "Abraham" speaks *in propria persona* in *De rationibus tabularum*, offering his own opinions and explaining diverse features of the astronomical tables.[52]

---

[45] Sela 2021, 77–78.
[46] Sela 2021, 55–82.
[47] *Magistralis compositio astrolabii*, ed. Ratdolt (1485), sigs. C5r–D4r; Juste 2018 (a), 44.
[48] *Magistralis compositio astrolabii*, ed. Ratdolt (1485), sigs. C7v–C8r. *Magistri probationum* (= masters of the observations) is the name given in *De rationibus tabularum* (*De rationibus tabularum*, ed. Millás Vallicrosa (1947), 77, 78, 80 et passim), as well as in other works influenced by *De rationibus tabularum*, to the *aṣḥāb al-mumtaḥan* (= authors of the verified tables), astronomers who contributed to the development of the *tabule probationum* (*De rationibus tabularum*, ed. Millás Vallicrosa (1947), 77), which appear to be a calque on the *zīj al-mumtaḥan* (= verified tables) created by Yaḥyā ibn Abī Manṣūr (d. 830). On the identity of the *magistri probationum*, see Samsó 2012, 193–195. Bate repeatedly mentions the *magistri probationum* in his traslations; see, for example, *Iudicia*, preface → 2, 28, 40; §1:4.
[49] *De rationibus tabularum*, ed. Millás Vallicrosa (1947), 74, 148, 156, 159.
[50] *De rationibus tabularum*, ed. Millás Vallicrosa (1947), 77, 78, 80, 81, 82 *et passim*.
[51] *De rationibus tabularum*, ed. Millás Vallicrosa (1947), 75, 76, 77, *et passim*.
[52] *De rationibus tabularum*, ed. Millás Vallicrosa (1947), 78, 80, 82, 86, 87, 88, 89 *et passim*.

3. *The Treatise on the Equatorium*

Bate composed a short text, untitled and undated, describing the uses of an equatorium, an instrument to find the position of the planets mechanically and without calculations. This text, which follows immediately the *Magistralis compositio astrolabii* in the 1485 Venice Ratdolt edition, is extant in five manuscripts copied from it.[53] In this treatise Bate mentions a certain "Abraham Iudeus," together with prominent astronomers such as Ptolemy, Jābir ibn Aflaḥ, al-Battānī, al-Ṣūfī, and unnamed "magistri probationum" and "orientales astronomi." In all likelihood Bate took this "Abraham Iudeus," a term commonly assigned to Abraham Ibn Ezra, from the aforementioned *De rationibus tabularum*, which in most manuscripts begins "Dixit Abraham Iudeus" (Abraham the Jew said), and, as noted above, mentions a certain "Abraham" several times. In the same breath Bate refers to "Abraham's tables of Pisa and Winchester" as well as to the astronomical tables of Ptolemy and al-Battānī, as examples of tables cast for longitudes "in the ninth sphere," that is, for tropical longitudes. Ibn Ezra's tables for Pisa are mentioned in *De rationibus tabularum*; those for Winchester are referred to in Bate's recently identified translation of Ibn Ezra's *'Olam* III.[54] Bate also claims in his treatise on the equatorium that his own astronomical tables (i.e., the tables of Mechelen) are based on the motion of the planets according to the ninth sphere and expressly associates his own tables for Mechelen with Ibn Ezra's tables for Pisa and Winchester with regard to their reliance on longitudes "in the ninth sphere."[55]

4. *Tabulae Machlinienses*

Bate compiled a first version of the *Tabulae Machlinienses* (Tables of Mechelen) before 1280 and used them to cast his own nativity.[56] Throughout his

---

[53] *Equatorium planetarum*, ed. Ratdolt (1485), sigs. D4r–D6r; Juste 2018 (a), 44–45.

[54] *De rationibus tabularum*, ed. Millás Vallicrosa (1947), 87–88; *'Olam* III, ed. Sela et al. (2020), 276, 277.

[55] *Equatorium planetarum*, ed. Ratdolt (1485), ed. Ratdolt (1485), sig. D4r–D4v: "Est enim instrumentum hoc super motus planetarum ad octavam speram relatos ingeniatum et radicatum ... Ptholemeus vero et Geber, Albategni, Abrahamque Iudeus et Açophius, ceteri quoque magistri probationum et maxime orientales astronomi motus planetarum secundum nonam speram considerantes radices suas super hoc fundaverunt, et hoc patet in tabulis Ptholomei, Albategni et Abrahe in tabulis Pisanis, Wintoniensibus" = "This instrument has been devised and based on the motion of the planets in relation to the eighth sphere ... But Ptolemy, Jābir ibn Aflaḥ, al-Battānī, Abraham, the Jew, and al-Ṣūfī, as well as the other masters of the observations, and especially the eastern astronomers who scrutinized the motions of the planets according to the ninth sphere, based the radix (of the astronomical tables) on this [i.e., according to the ninth sphere], and this is evident in the tables by Ptolemy, al-Battānī, and Abraham in the tables of Pisa and Winchester."

[56] *Nativitas*, 347–352 and 417.

life he continued to correct them on the basis of his own observations, as he tells us in the *Speculum divinorum*.[57] Although in his treatise on the equatorium Bate associates the Tables of Mechelen with Ibn Ezra's Pisa and Winchester tables regarding their reliance on the ninth sphere for the calculation of planetary motions,[58] the Tables of Mechelen were not an adaptation of Ibn Ezra's Pisan Tables: they employ values for mean planetary motion that are not attested in any potential source and that are indeed likely to have been derived from observation, as he states.[59] The three known manuscripts present essentially the same material with varying parameters, probably reflecting Bate's own corrections. This material is restricted to planetary tables (mean motions) and contains no canons. According to one of the manuscripts, the last table bears the following title: "Argumentum Mercurii secundum Abraham Evenzare in annis Christi ad meridiem Machlinie" = Argument of Mercury according to Abraham Ibn Ezra in years of Christ according to the meridian of Mechelen.[60]

5. *The Latin Translation of Ibn Ezra's Lost 'Olam III and of the Two Kindian Treatises*

A tripartite Latin text on world astrology is preserved in a single manuscript: Vatican City, Biblioteca Apostolica Vaticana, Pal. lat. 1407, fols. 55r–62r (14th/15th century). Whereas the first part (fols. 55r–58r) of this tripartite text incorporates Bate's incomplete Latin translation of Ibn Ezra's lost 'Olam III, the other two parts (fols. 58r–594; 59r–62r; henceforth Part II and Part III) are Bate's Latin translations of two treatises on world astrology ascribed to Ya'qūb ibn Isḥāq al-Kindī, the "father of Arab philosophy" (d. after 866). The colophon of Part III, a Latin translation of al-Kindī's *Liber de iudiciis revolutionum annorum mundi*, says unambiguously that it was executed by Henry Bate of Malines in 1278 "ex Hebrayco in Latinum."[61] That

---

[57] Steel and Guldentops 1996, 347. Juste 2018 (a), 46.
[58] See above, note 55.
[59] Nothaft 2018 (b), 280–282.
[60] MS Paris, BnF, lat. 7421, fol. 220r.
[61] Sela et al. (2020), 267, 287: "Explicit liber de iudiciis revolutionum annorum mundi quem compilavit Iacob filius Ysaac Alkindi. Expletus est libellus iste ascendente Cancro, in quo Luna coniuncta Iovi, die tertia Septembris anno domini 1278° in Mechlinia, translatus ex Hebrayco in Latinum per Henricum Bate ad preces Iohannis de Milana." = "This ends the Book on the judgments of the revolutions of the world-years compiled by Ya'qub, the son of Isaac al-Kindī. This book was completed when Cancer was raising, and when the Moon was in conjunction with Jupiter in it, the third of September in the year of the Lord 1278, in Mechelen, translated from Hebrew into Latin by Henry Bate, at the request of Iohannes of Milana."

Bate was also the Latin translator of the other two parts is indicated by the fact that all three parts bear the hallmark of Bate as translator of Hebrew texts: double Latin translations of single underlying Hebrew terms.[62]

The following points demonstrate that the first part of the Vatican manuscript is a Latin translation of *'Olam* III:

(i) The text evinces striking similarities with ideas on world astrology developed by Ibn Ezra elsewhere in his astrological oeuvre.[63]
(ii) A complete list of the 28 lunar mansions appears in the middle of text (fols. 56r–56v), and each item is accompanied by a graphical representation of the asterisms of the corresponding lunar mansion. This list of mansions is the target of a cross-reference in *Liber electionum* (the Latin translation of Ibn Ezra's lost *Mivḥarim* III).[64]
(iii) The account of the lunar mansions in this Latin translation is followed by a note in which Bate explicitly assigns part of the account of the lunar mansions in this text to Ibn Ezra.[65]
(iv) New evidence first presented in this volume shows without a shadow of doubt that the first part of the Vatican manuscript is Bate's Latin translation of *'Olam* III. One of the doctrines put forward in this text is the ascription of numbers to the planets.[66] Ibn Ezra explains this theory, ascribes it to Ptolemy, and assigns a number to each of the seven planets in both versions of *Sefer ha-Ṭe'amim*,[67] which were translated by Bate into Latin and are included in this volume. Bate begins his translation of the section of *Ṭe'amim* II on this theory as follows: "Ptolomeus rex ait: Sol est in numero .18., Mercurius et Venus in numero .16." = "King Ptolemy said: the Sun is in the number 18; Mercury and Venus are in the number 16."[68] Then Bate interpolates

---

[62] Sela et al. (2020), 226.
[63] Sela et al. (2020), 195–200.
[64] *Liber Electionum*, II vi 1:5, 106–107.
[65] Sela et al. (2020), Part I, § 5:4, 250: "Nota quod sex sunt mansiones humide principaliter, secundum quod testatur Alkindus et illas ennarat Avenezre solum pro humidis, licet alique alie sunt humide mediocriter et sunt ille que hic sunt significate." = "Note that there are six mansions that are principally humid, according to the evidence provided by Al-Kindī, and Ibn Ezra enumerates only those as humid, and they have been indicated here."
[66] See Sela et al. (2020), Part I, § 2:4, 245, 269. These numbers depend on the theory, of Pythagorean origin, that each of the seven planets has numbers that correspond to the musical tones produced by the rotation of their orbs.
[67] See *Ṭe'amim* I, § 4.1:1–3, 68–71 and *Ṭe'amim* II, § 5.5:6, 230–231. I am not aware of other astrological treatises which apply this theory to explain the natures of the planets.
[68] *Rationes* II, § 5.5:6. For this method of reference, see below, note 199.

the following gloss: "in Libro revolutionis Abrahe, 14" = "in the *Book of the revolution* by Abraham, 14."[69] Now, in his two versions of the *Book of reasons* Ibn Ezra ascribes to Mercury and Venus the number 16,[70] but in chapter II, section 4 of the first part of the Vatican manuscript we read "Veneris et Mercurii sicut 14" = "⟨The number⟩ of Venus and Mercury is 14".[71] We see, then, that in this gloss Bate was correcting the number of Mercury and Venus he found in *Teʿamim* II (= 16) with the number of Mercury and Venus he found in *Liber revolutionis Abrahe*, (= 16). Ibn Ezra never refers to this theory in the first and second versions of his *Book of the world*. This proves that Henry Bate took the first part of the Vatican manuscript to be one of the versions of Ibn Ezra's *Book of the world* and called it the *Book of the revolution by Abraham*.

As said above, Part II and Part III of BAV Pal. lat. 1407 are Bate's Latin translations of two treatises of world astrology ascribed to Yaʿqūb ibn Isḥāq al-Kindī; but the colophon of Part III says that Bate produced this translation "ex Hebrayco in Latinum." Was Ibn Ezra the Arabic into Hebrew translator who executed the two Arabic into Hebrew translations from which Bate, in 1278, produced his Latin translations? Several links between the content of the two Kindian treatises and Ibn Ezra's work point in this direction:

(i) A list of the signs of cities in Part II has counterparts in *ʿOlam* I, *ʿOlam* II, *Nativitates*, *Epitome*, and *Tractatus pluviarum*.[72] Remarkably, all these lists include references to Lucca and Pisa, two cities we know Ibn Ezra to have passed through during his peregrinations in Italy. (ii) A list of countries and regions under the charge of a pair consisting of a planet and a zodiacal sign, ascribed to Enoch in Part II, has a parallel in *ʿOlam* I.[73] (iii) A list of planets and types of human beings under their charge in Part II finds its match in *ʿOlam* I.[74] (iv) *ʿOlam* I includes a long quotation from al-Kindī's

---

[69] Gloss at *Rationes* II, § 5.5:6.
[70] See *Teʿamim* II, § 5.5:6, 230–231; *Teʿamim* I, § 4.1:1, 68–69.
[71] See Sela et al. (2020), Part I, § 2:4, 245, 269.
[72] See Sela et al. (2020), Part II, § 6:1–5, 259; cf. *ʿOlam I*, § 38:1–24, 76–79; *ʿOlam* II, § 15:1–25, 164–167; *Nativitates*, I i 2:6–7, 82–83; *Epitome*, ed. Heller (1548), I:8, sig. G4r; *Tractatus pluviarum*, ed. Burnett, (2008), 246. *Tractatus pluviarum*, which survives in 12 manuscripts, is attributed to John of Seville, and is a portion of *Epitome*, similarly attributed to John of Seville. See *Tractatus pluviarum*, ed. Burnett, (2008), 221–222.
[73] See Sela et al. (2020), Part II § 4:1–7, 258; cf. *ʿOlam* I, § 37:1, 76–77.
[74] See Sela et al. (2020), Part II § 3:1; cf. *ʿOlam I*, § 36:1, 76–77. There is also a similar list in *Epitome*, ed. Joachim Heller (1548), I:5, sig. F3v.

Book of the revolution,⁷⁵ a title that is similar to that of the second Kindian treatise in the colophon of Part III: *Book on the judgments of the revolutions of the world-years*; however, we find no verbatim match of this quotation in Part III.

From these links it seems plausible that Ibn Ezra translated the two Kindian treatises from Arabic into Hebrew, although at present we do not have compelling evidence in this regard.

6. *The Astrological Autobiography*

In 1280, seven years after he commissioned Hagin's French translations, and one year before he carried out his first complete Latin translation, Bate composed an astrological autobiography, commonly known as *Nativitas*.⁷⁶ To ground the astrological interpretation of Bate's life *Nativitas* incorporates at least 140 paraphrases, translations, and quotations from twelve treatises written by or attributed to Abraham Ibn Ezra. These are the earliest known references to Ibn Ezra the astrologer in the Latin West. Let us review them according to the branch of astrology to which they belong.

6.1. Nativities

Three works on nativities were written or attributed to Ibn Ezra. In *Nativitas*, Bate assigned them to three different authors—all of them "Abraham," but with different cognomens.⁷⁷

(i) Bate's first Abraham is "Abraham Avenezra," to whom he assigned a *Liber nativitatum* that is identical with *Moladot*, the only extant complete Hebrew text by Ibn Ezra on nativities. As stated above, Bate commissioned Hagin to produce *Nativités*, a French translation of *Moladot*, which is extant in two manuscripts,⁷⁸ but did not produce a complete Latin translation from it. However, *Nativitas* does include at least 52 references to passages in *Moladot*.⁷⁹ The overwhelming majority are only a few words; but in one notable exception *Nativitas* offers a complete and precise translation of a passage from the introduction to *Moladot*.⁸⁰

---

⁷⁵ *'Olam* I, § 44:1–6, 82–83.
⁷⁶ See *Nativitas*, 127–267.
⁷⁷ For an analysis of this phenomenon, see Sela 2017a, 163–186.
⁷⁸ P, 66rb–100va; P¹, 66rb–102ra.
⁷⁹ For a list see *Nativitas*, ed. Steel et al. (2018), 269–270.
⁸⁰ See *Nativitas*, 1874–1883; cf. *Moladot*, I 9:4–5, 88–89. For an analysis of these passages, see Sela 2020 (b), 157–159.

(ii) The second Abraham is "Abraham Princeps," to whom Bate in *Nativitas* assigned a *Liber nativitatum*. The latter is the Latinized name of and identical in content with *Moladot* II (second version of *Sefer ha-Moladot*), whose Hebrew original is lost but which survives in an anonymous complete Latin translation designated *Liber nativitatum*. Bate's *Nativitas* has at least 24 references to passages in *Moladot* II; none of them is identical to its counterpart in the Latin translation of *Moladot* II.[81] This indicates that Bate did not have access to *Liber nativitatum* and must have relied on a French into Hebrew translation of *Moladot* II or on a now-lost Hebrew copy of *Moladot* II.

(iii) The third Abraham is "Abraham Compilator," to whom Bate in *Nativitas* assigned a *Liber nativitatum* that is identical with the aforementioned *De nativitatibus*,[82] a Latin work on nativities assigned to Ibn Ezra that survives in 16 manuscripts and three print editions. A close look at the manuscript and print witnesses of *De nativitatibus* reveals that this work was transmitted in four very different versions.[83] Bate's *Nativitas* includes no fewer than seventeen references to the so-called fourth version of *De nativitatibus*.[84] Particularly striking is that nine of these seventeen passages are verbatim quotations from the fourth version of *De nativitatibus*.[85] Of all the references in *Nativitas* to works by Ibn Ezra quoted in *De nativitatibus*, these are the only verbatim quotations from a text that appears in the manuscript or print tradition. For this and other reasons, it has been argued in a separate study that Bate was possibly the originator of the fourth version of *De nativitatibus*, which he then quoted in *Nativitas*.[86]

6.2. World Astrology

As we shall see, in 1281 Bate produced a complete Latin translation of Ibn Ezra's 'Olam I, entitled *Liber de mundo vel seculo*.[87] But the previous year Bate had already included in *Nativitas* two references to 'Olam I, which are

---

[81] For a list see, See *Nativitas*, ed. Steel et al. (2018), 272–273. I have myself compared each of the items of this list and their match in *Liber Nativitatum*.
[82] See above, p. 2.
[83] See Sela 2018, 328–337; Sela 2019, 49–59.
[84] For a list of these references, see *Nativitas*, ed. Steel et al. (2018), 272.
[85] For a list of these references in *Nativitas* and their match in the fourth version of *De nativitatibus*, see Sela 2019, p. 59 n. 364.
[86] See Sela 2019, 59–65.
[87] For this title, see below, p. 62.

attributed to "Avenezre in *Libro coniunctionum*" = "Ibn Ezra in the *Book of conjunctions*."[88] A third reference in *Nativitas*, addressing the signs of the cities, is attributed to "Abraham in *Libro revolutionum mundi*" = "Abraham in the *Book of the revolutions of the world*." This reference could mean either *'Olam* I or *'Olam* II.[89]

6.3. Introductions to Astrology

(i) Twelve years before Bate finished his complete Latin translation of *Reshit Ḥokhmah*, in 1292, *Nativitas* incorporated no fewer than 17 references to *Reshit Ḥokhmah*.[90] A third of them translate passages from Ibn Ezra's work; none are identical with their counterpart in Bate's complete Latin translation of *Reshit Ḥokhmah*.[91] Rather than *Liber Abrahe Avenerre Introductorius ad astronomiam*, the title assigned to *Reshit Ḥokhmah* in the complete translation, in *Nativitas* Bate always writes *Liber initii sapientie*, which renders the Hebrew title.[92] Bate also uses *Liber initii sapientie* when he translates cross-references to *Reshit Ḥokhmah* in his other Latin translations.[93]

(ii) *Nativitas* contains one implicit reference to *Mishpeṭei ha-Mazzalot*, another introduction to astrology by Ibn Ezra, and assigns it to Abraham Princeps.[94]

(iii) *Nativitas* contains no fewer than nine references to *Ṭeʿamim* I. In contrast with the doublet used to refer to *Ṭeʿamim* I in the incipit of the complete Latin translation (= *Liber causarum seu rationum*), *Nativitas* always has *Liber rationum* and generally mentions Avenezre as its author (= Avenezre in *Libro rationum*).[95] In some cases *Nativitas* specifies the chapter in *Ṭeʿamim* I from which the reference was taken, particularly when *Nativitas* translates from *Ṭeʿamim* I.[96] Some of the references consist of a few words and are intended to sum-

---

[88] See *Nativitas*, 2049–2051; cf. *'Olam* I, § 22:1, 66–67; *Nativitas*, 380–382; cf. *'Olam* I, § 23:1, 66–67.
[89] See *Nativitas*, 233–235; cf. *'Olam* I, § 38:1–25, 78–79; *'Olam* II, § 15:2–5, 164–167.
[90] For a list see, See *Nativitas*, ed. Steel et al. (2018), 270–271.
[91] For the analysis of one example, see Sela 2020 (b), 150.
[92] *Nativitas*, 250, 615, 821, 984, 3109.
[93] See *Rationes* II, § 1.1:1; gloss at § 4.1:2, *De luminaribus*, § 35:2; *De mundo*, § 64:2.
[94] *Nativitas*, 694–697; cf. *Mishpeṭei ha-Mazzalot*, § 29:1, 512–513.
[95] For a list see, See *Nativitas*, ed. Steel et al. (2018), 271.
[96] See, for example, *Nativitas*, 619–624; cf. *Ṭeʿamim* I, § 6.2:4, 86–87; *Nativitas*, 767–769; cf. *Ṭeʿamim* I, § 9.1:6, 92–93.

marize an entire idea or theory expressed in *Ṭeʿamim* I.[97] In other cases, though, *Nativitas* purports to offer translations of passages from *Ṭeʿamim* I.[98]

(iv) *Nativitas* contains 15 references to *Ṭeʿamim* II.[99] In contrast with the doublet used in the prefatory canticle of the complete Latin translation (= *Liber rationum seu causarum*), *Nativitas* always has *Liber rationum* and generally refers to Avenezre as its author. When *Nativitas* offers a translation of a passage from *Ṭeʿamim* II, the latter work is designated *Liber rationum, secunda parte* or *particula*.[100] In the overwhelming majority of cases, references to *Ṭeʿamim* II in *Nativitas* consist of short paraphrases or translations of a few words, cited by Bate to strengthen some argument. In one case, though, *Nativitas* incorporates a translation from *Ṭeʿamim* II.[101]

6.4. Elections

Ibn Ezra wrote three different versions of *Sefer ha-Mivḥarim* (Book of elections). Bate commissioned Hagin to produce a French translation of *Mivḥarim* II, entitled *Le livre des elections Abraham*, extant in two manuscripts.[102] Bate never produced a complete translation of any of the three versions of *Sefer ha-Mivḥarim*, but left translated passages and references to *Mivḥarim* II and *Mivḥarim* III, assigning the two works to two different Abrahams.

(i) There are two references to *Mivḥarim* II in Bate's *Nativitas*. One is a short reference to "Avenezre in *Libro electionum*," accompanied by a brief paraphrase.[103] The other begins, "Dicit enim Avenezre in suo *Libro electionum*" = "Ibn Ezra says in his *Book of elections*," followed by a short translation of a passage from *Mivḥarim* II, which appears verbatim in Bate's *De diebus creticis*, right before Bate's *De diebus*

---

[97] See, for example, *Nativitas*, 1637–1640. This refers to a Ptolemaic theory, detailed in *Ṭeʿamim* I, that assigns a number to each of the seven planets and explains that a planet is considered to be benefic if its number has a "noble" or harmonious ratio to the number of another planet. See *Ṭeʿamim* I, § 4.1:2–4, 68–71, and note on pp. 154–156.

[98] See *Nativitas*, 619–624; cf. *Ṭeʿamim* I, § 6.2:4, 86–87. *Nativitas*, 767–769; cf. *Ṭeʿamim* I, § 9.1:6, 92–93. For an analysis of these passages, see Sela 2020 (b), 152–154.

[99] For a list see, See *Nativitas*, ed. Steel et al. (2018), 271–272.

[100] See, for example, *Nativitas*, 160; cf. *Ṭeʿamim* II, § 6.1:1, 234–235. *Nativitas*, 593–595; cf. *Ṭeʿamim* II, § 4.1:3, 206–207.

[101] See, *Nativitas*, 593–595; cf. *Ṭeʿamim* II, § 4.1:3, 206–207. For an analysis of this passage, see Sela 2020 (b), 155–156.

[102] P, 104ra–107rb; P¹, 102ra–110va.

[103] See *Nativitas*, 605–607; cf. *Mivḥarim* II, § 10.2:1–2, 172–173.

creticis and *Nativitas* present the same translation of a passage from *Moladot*.[104]

(ii) The Hebrew original of *Mivḥarim* III is almost completely lost but survives in an anonymous Latin translation, designated *Liber electionum*. *Nativitas* contains four brief references to *Mivḥarim* III, all of them assigned to Abraham Princeps. The first is a reference to "Abraham Princeps in suo *Tractatu de electionibus*," with regard to corrections that should be made to the *trutina Hermetis*.[105] The second reference to Abraham Princeps also concerns the *trutina Hermetis*.[106] The third is a reference to "*Liber electionum* Abrahe Principis" regarding the power of a planet when it is in the domain of combustion or in Leo and Aries.[107] The fourth is a reference to Abraham Princeps regarding two combatants, a typical topic in elections.[108]

6.5. Interrogations

Ibn Ezra composed three versions of *Sefer ha-She'elot* (Book of interrogations). Bate commissioned Hagin to produce a French translation of *She'elot* II, entitled *Le livre des questions*, extant in two manuscripts,[109] but did not produce a full Latin translation of *She'elot* II based on it.

(i) *Nativitas* includes four references to *She'elot* II, which is always attributed to Ibn Ezra.[110] These are not translations of passages from *She'elot* II but rather loose paraphrases that combine elements of passages of *She'elot* II in order to flesh out some point in Bate's astrological autobiography.[111]

---

[104] See *Nativitas*, 562–563. Cf. *Mivḥarim* II, §1.5:2, 152–153; *De diebus creticis*, ed. Dell'Anna (1999), vol. 2, p. 113; *Elections*, P, 111rb. For an analysis of this passage, see Sela 2020 (b), 162–163.

[105] See *Nativitas*, 106–107; cf. *Electiones*, II v 3:1–2, 106–107. The *trutina Hermetis* is a procedure assigned by Ibn Ezra to Enoch or Hermes and used in the doctrine of nativities to determine the ascendant of the natal horoscope on the basis of the duration of pregnancy when the time of birth is not known (the usual situation). For the role of Ibn Ezra in the creation and diffusion of the *trutina Hermetis*, see Sela 2019 (c), 79–106.

[106] See *Nativitas*, 86–87; cf. *Electiones*, II v 1:1 through II v 2:5, 104–105. Note that there is nothing in *Mivḥarim* I and *Mivḥarim* II about the *trutina Hermetis*, but that *Liber electionum* allots the bulk of the chapter on the fifth horoscopic house to a detailed account of the *trutina Hermetis* (without using this name).

[107] See *Nativitas*, 603–604; cf. *Electiones*, II vii 5:5–6, 120–123.

[108] See *Nativitas*, 1919–1920; cf. *Electiones*, II vii 4:5, 120–121.

[109] P, 113va–125ra; P¹, 110va–123rb.

[110] For a list see, see *Nativitas*, ed. Steel et al. (2018), 271.

[111] For an analysis of these passages, see Sela 2020 (b), 164–165.

6.6. Medical Astrology

(i) Twelve years before the completion of the Latin translation of Ibn Ezra's *Me'orot* Bate had already incorporated five references to this work into his *Nativitas*. Four of them are loose references to various loci in *Me'orot*; one actually translates a passage from this work.[112] Bate attributes all these references to Ibn Ezra and in most of them mentions the *Liber luminarium* (Book of the luminaries), in the genitive and not the ablative plural (*Liber luminarium*, not *Liber de luminaribus*). Bate used this title for *Me'orot* in three places in *Nativitas*.[113]

7. Bate's Treatise on the Critical Days

At some point after 1280, Bate composed a work entitled *De diebus creticis periodorumque causis* (On the critical days and the causes of the periods; henceforth *De diebus creticis*).[114] This work, like Ibn Ezra's *Me'orot*, is concerned exclusively with the critical days when there are marked changes in the symptoms of a disease. *De diebus creticis* incorporates seven references to Ibn Ezra's astrological treatises.

As may be expected from their common subject matter, *De diebus creticis* refers to *Me'orot* and mentions "Abraham Avenesere in *Libro luminarium*" = "Abraham Ibn Ezra in the *Book of the luminaries*,"[115] in relation to the timing of the critical days and their dependence on the Moon's motion. Note here the use of *Liber luminarium*, in the genitive and not the ablative plural (*Liber luminarium* and not *Liber de luminaribus*). Bate used this title for *Me'orot* in three places in *Nativitas*, written in 1280.[116]

De diebus creticis also mentions Ibn Ezra in relation to the astrological aspects[117] in two adjacent references to *Ṭeʿamim* I and *Ṭeʿamim* II. The first, to *Ṭeʿamim* I, mentions "*Liber causarum seu rationum* Avenesare, capitulo 3o, prime partis" = "*Book of causes or reasons* by Ibn Ezra, third chapter, first

---

[112] For a list see, See *Nativitas*, ed. Steel et al. (2018), 269. For an analysis of the translation from *Me'orot*, see Sela 2020 (b), 165–166.
[113] *Nativitas*, 2978, 3022, 3131.
[114] See *De diebus creticis*, ed. Dell' Anna (1999), vol. 2, pp. 97–127; David Juste, Juste 2018 (a), 46–48.
[115] *De diebus creticis*, ed. Dell' Anna (1999), vol. 2, 106; cf. *Me'orot*, § 4:2–3, 456–457.
[116] *Nativitas*, 2978, 3022, 3131.
[117] The aspects (Hebrew מבטים, Arabic مناظرات) are four astrologically significant angular relationships (180°, 90°, 120°, and 60°) between planets, zodiacal signs, and other celestial objects. The aspect of trine (120°) is considered to be harmonious or fortunate; sextile (60°) is also harmonious or fortunate, but to a lesser extent; opposition (180°) is disharmonious or unfortunate; and quartile (90°) is also disharmonious or unfortunate, but to a lesser extent.

part."[118] The second, to *Ṭeʿamim* II, mentions *"Liber causarum seu rationum Avenesare, secunda parte, capitulo de aspectibus"* = *"Book of causes or reasons* by Ibn Ezra, second part, in the chapter on the aspects."[119]

Most interesting is the mention of "Avenesare" in relation to the aspects of the Sun with the Moon in two adjacent precise translations from *Mivḥarim* II and from *Moladot*:

> Dell' Anna, *Dies creticis*, vol. 2, cap. 8, p. 113:[120] Unde Avenesare in suo *Libro electionum* dicit quod omnes aspectus Solis ad Lunam boni sunt. Item quoque ait in *Libro nativitatum*: scito quod aspectus Solis ad Lunam, sive sextilis sive tertius aut quartus, melior est quam aspectus Iovis et Veneris, quamvis nam ambe infortune, Saturnus scilicet et Mars, coniuncte essent Lune, fortitudo aspectus Solis impedimenta repellet ambarum.

> Therefore Ibn Ezra says in his *Book of elections* that all the aspects of the Sun with the Moon are good. Likewise, he also says in the *Book of nativities*: know that an aspect of the Sun with the Moon, whether trine, sextile, or quartile, is better than an aspect of Jupiter and Venus, although because the two unfortunate ⟨planets⟩, namely Saturnus and Mars, are conjoined to the Moon, the power of the Sun's aspect will repel the impediment of both.

Strikingly, the same reference to "Avenesare" and the same translations of the same two passages from *Mivḥarim* II and from *Moladot* appear verbatim in *Nativitas*.[121] This demonstrates two main things: (i) Bate composed *De diebus creticis* after 1280 (= the year he wrote *Nativitas*), perhaps not long; (ii) no complete Latin translations of *Mivḥarim* II and *Moladot* by Bate survive, but when he wrote *De diebus creticis* and *Nativitas* he did have Latin versions of *Moladot* and of *Mivḥarim* II (either complete or incomplete) to hand, and quoted an excerpt from each in *De diebus creticis* and *Nativitas*.

De diebus creticis also mentions "Avenezre" in two adjacent references to *"Liber rationum*, prima pars et secunda," that is, *Ṭeʿamim* I and *Ṭeʿamim* II on the planets' periods or years.[122]

---

[118] *De diebus creticis*, ed. Dell' Anna (1999), vol. 2, 102; cf. *Ṭeʿamim* I, § 3.2:1–12, 60–63.

[119] Cf. *Ṭeʿamim* II, 4.6:1–5, § 4.7:1–8, § 4.8:1–3, 210–213.

[120] See Dell' Anna, *Dies critici*, vol. 2, cap. 8, p. 113; cf. *Mivḥarim* II, § 1.5:2, 152–153; *Elections*, P, 111rb; *Moladot*, III vi 11:4, 154–155.

[121] *Nativitas*, 562–567: Dicit enim Avenezre in suo *Libro electionum* quod omnes aspectus Solis ad Lunam boni sunt quia lumen suum a Sole recipit: scito quod aspectus Solis ad Lunam, sive sextilis sive tertius aut quartus, melior est quam aspectus Iovis et Veneris, quamvis nam ambe infortune, Saturnus scilicet et Mars, coniuncte essent Lune, fortitudo aspectus Solis impedimenta repellet ambarum.

[122] Dell' Anna, *Dies critici*, vol. 2, cap. 16, p. 125: "quod testatur Avenezere in *Libro rationum*,

8. *The Philosophical and Scientific Encyclopedia*

As already stated, *Speculum divinorum* is a philosophical and scientific encyclopedia composed by Bate between 1301 and 1305 and dedicated to his patron, Guy de Hainaut. The name "Abraham Iudeus," which occurs in Bate's treatise on the equatorium and in *De rationibus tabularum* and is commonly associated with Ibn Ezra, also appears in *Speculum divinorum*. However, in that case it is crystal clear that Bate took it from *De rationibus tabularum*. This is because in *Speculum divinorum* "Abraham Iudeus" is sometimes mentioned in a quotation from and sometimes in a paraphrase of *De rationibus tabularum*, which in *Speculum divinorum* is designated *Liber de opere tabularum* (Book on the use of ⟨astronomical⟩ tables). Here are the reference to "Abraham Iudeus" and the quotation from *Liber de opere tabularum*, accompanied by its counterpart in *De rationibus tabularum*:

> *Speculum divinorum* 1996, 337, 38–44: Hinc etenim Abraham Iudaeus in *Libro de opere tabularum* dicit se duos fratres Bensechit invenisse qui duo composuerant instrumenta seu astrolabia quorum utriusque diameter novem palmorum fuit. Et hi distinxerant gradus quadrantis altitudinis Solis per minuta et per 5. Et cum isti duo simul Sole intrante caput Arietis sumerunt altitudinem Solis, inventa est inter haec duo instrumenta differentia duorum minutorum.
>
> *De rationibus tabularum*, ed. Millás Vallicrosa (1947), 81, 7–12: Nam invenimus quod duos fratres Beni Sequir duo astrolabia composuerant quorum utriusque dyameter novem palmorum faciebat. Hi distinxerant gradus quadrantis altitudinis Solis per minuta et ipsa minuta per 5. Et cum isti duo simul, Sole intrante arietis caput, sumerunt altitudinem Solis, inventa est inter duo astrolabia differentia duorum minutorum.

Earlier Research on Bate's Translations

These eight encounters illustrate the long and strong association between Ibn Ezra and Henry Bate, running from the start of Bate's career until his death. But the most significant component of the Ibn Ezra–Henry Bate connection is the six complete Latin translations of Ibn Ezra's astrological writings produced between 1278 and 1292. Before we turn to scrutinize Bate's Latin translations, we should review the earlier research on this topic.

Raphael Levy allotted an entire section of *The Astrological Works of Abraham Ibn Ezra*, published in 1927, to Bate's oeuvre. In addition to mentioning

---

prima parte et secunda, ubi de peryodis determinat planetarum." Cf. *Ṭeʿamim* I, § 4.2:11, 72–73; *Ṭeʿamim* II, § 5.3:13, 224–225.

Bate's translations of Ibn Ezra, he also highlighted the frequent references to Ibn Ezra in *Nativitas*, Bate's astrological autobiography.[123]

Twenty years later, Lynn Thorndike published a landmark article with a list of all the Latin translations of astrological treatises by "Abraham Avenezra" (the Latinized form of Abraham Ibn Ezra) known to him, including the manuscripts. These included ten manuscripts containing five of Bate's six Latin translations of Ibn Ezra.[124] Thorndike's aim was to identify manuscripts and texts and to examine their titles, incipits, and colophons; hence he did not describe the contents or try to identify the Hebrew source texts.

Recently, David Juste updated this list with a catalogue of virtually all manuscripts of Bate's translations currently available in European libraries and identified the versions of Ibn Ezra's writings behind Bate's translations.[125] Juste also sketched the main contours of the intellectual circle at the University of Paris, where Bate presumably became acquainted with Ibn Ezra's astrological oeuvre. Juste asserted that Bate was part of a thriving local community of celestial practitioners, which included Pierre of Limoges, who was dean of the faculty of medicine between 1267 and 1270, and William of Saint-Cloud (1285–1292).[126]

I have studied special features of Bate's translations in two articles. The first focuses on the surprising fact that when Bate refers to astrological treatises that we now know were written by Ibn Ezra he assigns them to one of three different authors: all three are "Abraham," but they have distinguishing cognomens. The article determines which astrological treatises Bate assigned to each of the three Abrahams, tries to identify the historical figure behind each of them, and explains Bate's reason for trisecting Abraham Ibn Ezra.[127] The second article is a preliminary study that examines both Bate's translations of individual passages from Ibn Ezra's astrological writings and Bate's complete translations of Ibn Ezra's astrological writings.[128]

To date, only one of Bate's six translations of Ibn Ezra's astrological writings has been printed, and this was done twice. First, in the Renaissance, the Latin translation of *'Olam* I was included as the seventh item in the print

---

[123] Levy 1927, 24–32.
[124] Thorndike 1944: 293–302.
[125] Juste 2018 (a), 50–54.
[126] Juste 2018 (b), 68–80.
[127] Sela 2017a, 163–186.
[128] Sela 2020 (b), 103–201.

edition of Pietro d'Abano's translations of Ibn Ezra astrological writings, produced by Petrus Liechtenstein in Venice in 1507.[129] Then, in 2019, Carlos Steel published a complete critical edition of Bate's Latin translation of *'Olam* I, without English translation, but with a detailed description of the work's rich manuscript tradition.[130] In 2020 Steel also published a critical edition of Bate's prologue to his Latin translation of *'Olam* I, accompanied by an English translation and by a study of Bate's attitude towards Ptolemy and Ibn Ezra.[131] My edition of Bate's Latin translation of *'Olam* I in this volume is based on both of Steel's works.

Bate's Complete Translations

We turn now to scrutinize Bate's six Latin translations, in six separate sections. These translations are presented in descending order according to the number of words in their Hebrew source texts, not according to the order of their dates of composition. In each section, information is provided about the following elements: (i) the Hebrew source text behind the Latin translation; (ii) a brief account of the contents and sources of the Hebrew source text; (iii) the manuscripts used for the critical edition, the families into which these manuscripts are divided, and the criteria used to select the base text for the critical edition; (iv) the title or titles, authorship, and place and date of composition of the Latin translation; (v) structural and quantitative data related to the following features: the length of the translation (in words); alternative or divergent readings from the Hebrew source text; omissions in the Latin translation from the Hebrew source text; glosses in the Latin translation; stylistic alterations in the Latin translation with respect to the Hebrew source text; additions in the Latin translation from lost Hebrew manuscripts; (vi) information about the French source text of the Latin translation.

1. *Liber Abrahe Avenerre introductorius ad astronomiam*

The only complete translation with a counterpart in Hagin's Hebrew-to-French translations, the third part of Bate's translation project, and the longest of Bate's Latin translations of Ibn Ezra is *Liber Abrahe Avenerre introductorius ad astronomiam* (The introductory book to astrology by Abraham

---

[129] *De mundo* (Bate), ed. Liechtenstein (1507), sig. LXXVIIv2–LXXXVr1.
[130] *De mundo* (Bate), ed. Steel (2019), 227–278.
[131] Steel 2020 (a), 245–281.

Ibn Ezra; henceforth *Introductorius*).[132] This is a Latin version of *Sefer Reshit Ḥokhmah* (Book of the beginning of wisdom; henceforth *Reshit Ḥokhmah*), an introduction to astrology that is the longest of Ibn Ezra's astrological treatises and that with the widest circulation among Jews in the Middle Ages and after. *Reshit Ḥokhmah* runs to about 27,000 words and is extant in at least 70 Hebrew manuscripts.[133]

1.1. The Contents and Sources of *Reshit Ḥokhmah*

Reshit Ḥokhmah begins with the statement that a person can be delivered from the decrees of the stars on condition that he fears the Lord, which is the beginning of wisdom.[134] Next Ibn Ezra promises to compose a commentary on *Reshit Ḥokhmah*, supposedly because it presents raw astrological concepts without introducing their *reasons*, that is, their rational explanations.[135] Finally, the introduction presents a table of contents, a rarity in Ibn Ezra's astrological corpus, and a brief presentation of the cosmos.[136]

Reshit Ḥokhmah is divided into 10 well-defined chapters. Chapter 1 presents the 48 Ptolemaic constellations, with a succinct and preliminary account of the astrological features of the signs and the seven planets, or, as put in the table of contents, their "powers, motions, and dignities."[137] Chapter 2, the longest in the work (12,000 out of 27,000 words), gives the impression of being a treatise within a treatise. The information about the signs and their planetary dignities is organized in 12 sections, one for each sign. At the heart of each section, *Reshit Ḥokhmah* lists the *paranatellonta* of the decans of the corresponding sign[138] in what is wholly a translation from the sixth part of the Abū Maʿshar's *Kitāb al-mudkhal al-kabīr*.[139] After the 12 sections on the 12 signs, chapter 2 has three sections on "the mixture of the stars in the ecliptic and in the northern and southern constellations,"

---

[132] For this title, see below p. 26. References to the Latin text and the English translation of *Introductorius* are in the formats: *Introductorius*, § 2:3 = *Introductorius*, section 2 of the introduction, passage 3; *Introductorius*, § 2.7:2 = *Introductorius*, chapter 2, section 5, passage 2.

[133] Sela 2017, 635–638.

[134] See *Reshit Ḥokhmah*, § 1:1–2, 48–49.

[135] See *Reshit Ḥokhmah*, § 1:4 , 48–49.

[136] See *Reshit Ḥokhmah*, § 2:1–11 , 48–49; § 3:1–11, 50–51.

[137] See *Reshit Ḥokhmah*, § 1.1:1–3 through § 1.12:1–2, 50–59.

[138] The *paranatellonta* are the constellations, portions of constellations, or stars that co-ascend, co-culminate, or co-descend together with the three decans of the relevant sign. The decans are three equal divisions into which each of the twelve zodiacal signs is divided.

[139] For Ibn Ezra's reliance on Abū Maʿshar, see Sela 2019 (e), 345–380.

most of them asterisms but also some individual fixed stars, all of them accompanied with their planetary mixture.[140]

Chapter 3 describes the division of the zodiac into aspects and quadrants and addresses the twelve horoscopic houses and their astrological indications.[141] Chapter 4 gives an account of the astrological properties of the seven planets—or, according to the table of contents, "everything they signify for all the creatures on Earth"—each in its own section.[142] Chapter 5 defines the planets' good fortune, misfortune, power, and weakness: "when their power waxes and when it wanes."[143] Chapter 6, according to the table of contents, is "on the power of the planets themselves, and with respect of their being before and after the Sun."[144] Chapter 7 names and describes 30 planetary conditions: "everything related to the mixing of their power and everything signified by them."[145] Chapters 5, 6, and 7 of *Reshit Ḥokhmah* consist of translations of discontinuous excerpts from chapters 1, 2, 4, 5, and 6 of the seventh part of Abū Ma'shar's *Kitāb al-mudkhal al-kabīr*.[146]

Chapter 8 presents 120 aphorisms summarizing the implementation of the conditions described in Chapter 7 in the various branches of astrology.[147] Nearly a third of the 120 aphorisms are translations or paraphrases from Sahl ibn Bishr's *Nawādir al-qaḍā* (Maxims of judgment), a work organized in 50 aphorisms that is part of Sahl's introduction to astrology.[148]

Chapter 9 describes the lots[149] associated with each of the seven planets and with each of the twelve horoscopic houses, supplemented by a description of four additional categories of lots related to historical and meteorological astrology. It concludes with a theoretical explanation of the rationale behind the concept of astrological lots and the way they are cast.[150] While the bulk of this account is a translation from the eighth part of Abū Ma'shar's *Kitāb al-mudkhal al-kabīr*, the categories of lots related to historical and meteorological astrology were translated from the fifth part

---

[140] See *Reshit Ḥokhmah*, § 2.13:1–2 through § 2.16:1–14, 132–138.
[141] See *Reshit Ḥokhmah*, § 3.1:1–9 through § 3.16:1–2, 138–147.
[142] See *Reshit Ḥokhmah*, § 4.1:1–2 through § 4.7:1–29, 146–183.
[143] See *Reshit Ḥokhmah*, § 5.1:1–18 through § 5.8:1–12, 182–189.
[144] See *Reshit Ḥokhmah*, § 6.1:1–16 through § 6.8:1–14, 188–197.
[145] See *Reshit Ḥokhmah*, § 7.1:1 through § 7.33:1–8, 196–211.
[146] See Sela 2019 (e), 345–380.
[147] See *Reshit Ḥokhmah*, § 8.1:1–3 through § 8.8:1–12, 210–235.
[148] See Sela 2019 (e), 345–380.
[149] The lots are imaginary ecliptical points that are influential in the horoscope and whose calculation is based on three horoscopic entities. The distance between two of them (place of the planets, cusps of horoscopic houses, etc.) is added to the position of the third, usually the ascendant.
[150] See *Reshit Ḥokhmah*, § 9.1:1–7 through § 9.25:1–4, 234–267.

of al-Qabīṣī's *Kitāb al-mudkhal*.[151] Chapter 10 addresses the "projection of rays" and the "directions"[152] and their application in world astrology and to a lesser extent in nativities.[153] The diverse types of cycles and directions described in this chapter have their counterpart in Abū Maʿshar's *Kitāb al-ulūf*.[154]

1.2. The Manuscripts

Introductorius is extant in the following manuscripts:

L Leipzig, Universitätsbibliothek, 1466, fols. 2ra–23va, copied around 1300 or in the first quarter of the 14th century in northern France, includes a complete copy of *Introductorius*. For a detailed description of this manuscript, see below, Appendix 2, pp. 1101–1103.

W Wolfenbüttel, Herzog August Bibliothek, 81.26 Aug. 2° (2816), fols. 84r–111v; a fifteenth-century manuscript with a complete copy of *Introductorius*.

V Vatican, Biblioteca Apostolica Vaticana, Pal. lat. 1377, fols. 21ra–37va; a fifteenth-century manuscript with a complete copy of *Introductorius*.

G Gloucester, Cathedral Library, 21, fols. 37r–68r; a fifteenth-century manuscript with an incomplete copy of *Introductorius*, lacking the translation of the first chapter of *Reshit Ḥokhmah*.

B Berlin, Staatsbibliothek, lat. fol. 192 (963), fols. 152ra–163ra; a fifteenth-century manuscript with an incomplete copy of *Introductorius*, containing only chapters 4–9 of *Reshit Ḥokhmah*.

U Prague, Národní Knihovna České Republiky, III.C.2 (433), second half of the 15th century, 217 folios, with a collection of astrological (particularly related to weather forecasting), astronomical, and medical texts. For the contents of this manuscript, see Truhlář 1906, codex 433, 167–168. This codex contains an incomplete and discontinuous

---

[151] See Sela 2019 (e), 345–380.
[152] The astrological technique of "projection of rays" assumes that a planet or zodiacal object "projects its rays" on another zodiacal object when the two are at an angular distance that is equivalent to one of the astrological aspects: trine (120°), sextile (60°), opposition (180°), and quartile (90°). In the procedure of "directions," a number of indicators are launched from specific zodiacal positions and moved at various speeds along the zodiac. Applying "directions" in the framework of the "projection of rays" means that these indicators are continuously checked while being directed in their course through the zodiac, degree by degree, to find out whether they form aspects (trine; sextile; opposition; quartile) with other celestial astrological objects.
[153] See *Reshit Ḥokhmah*, § 10.1:1–9 through § 10.3:1–7, 266–271.
[154] See Sela 2019 (e), 345–380.

copy of the bulk of *Introductorius*: fols. 98ra–117rb → §1.2:1 up to §7.33:8; fols. 117rb–117va → §8.7.1 up to §8.8.12; fol. 117va (from the middle of the column to the end of the column → subtitle "de pluviis," §9.19.1–§9.19.4); fols. 118rb (middle of column)–118vb (line 10) → §9.1.2–§9.3.10 (lots of the planets).

We see, then, that of the six extant manuscripts of *Introductorius*, one, L, is from the 14th century, and the others from the 15th century: **WVGBU**. Only three of the manuscripts have complete copies of *Introductorius:* **LWV**. Of the remaining three, one (**G**) includes an almost complete copy that lacks only the first chapter; the others (**BU**) have only sections of some of the chapters of *Introductorius*.

All in all, two families of manuscripts can be identified: L, and **WVG**.[155] Both families seem to come from the first copy of *Introductorius* in Bate's library, a lost manuscript earlier than L. A preliminary collation of all six witnesses led me to take L, the earliest complete copy, as the base text. The critical edition started by collating L, first with **W**, which provides a rather divergent text from L, and then with **V**, which in rough lines follows **W** but not L. **G**, a clear but slightly incomplete manuscript, was helpful to establish obscure readings of the other witnesses; its readings followed in rough lines **W** but not L. The readings of the markedly incomplete **BU** turned out to be unhelpful and are ignored in the apparatus. Although L served as the base text, it was not followed slavishly for establishing the text of the critical edition. For example, in loci where **WVG** provide a divergent reading, their consensus was preferred over L, particularly where L is defective.[156]

1.3. Title, Authorship, and Place and Date of Composition

Of all the manuscripts, only the earliest provides a title for Bate's translation of *Reshit Ḥokhmah*: *Liber Abrahe Avenerre introductorius ad astronomiam* (The introductory book to astrology by Abraham Ibn Ezra).[157] The explicits of the three complete copies (**LWV**) and of one of the incomplete copies (**G**) provide significant information about this work. The fullest is the earliest:

> L, 23va (= *Introductorius*, explicit): Complete sunt .10. partes libri huius quem compilavit Magister Abraham Avenezre, quod interpretatur Magister Adiu-

---

[155] See, in the apparatus, among many others, note 43, at §2.2:13; note 47, at §2.2:14; note 56, at §2.2:37; note 59, at §2.2:45; note 60, at §2.2:46.

[156] See, in the apparatus, among many others, note 37, at 2.1:47; note 47, at §2.2:14; note 56, at §2.2:37; note 59, at §2.2:45; note 60, at §2.2:46; note 82, at §2.4:25.

[157] See note 1, in the title of the critical edition, at p. 128.

torii; et Magister Hynricus de Malinis, dictus Bate, cantor Leodiensis transtulit, translationemque complevit in Urbe Veteri, anno Domini MCCXCII, in octava Assumptionis Beate Marie Virginis Gloriose; laudationes illi Domini qui extendit aera sive celos et qui scientiam ampliavit. Amen.[158]

> The ten chapters of this book, which Master Abraham Ibn Ezra, ⟨a name⟩ whose translation is Master of Help, compiled, are completed; Master Henry of Malines, called Bate, cantor of Liège, executed the translation, which he completed in Orvieto, in the year of the Lord 1292, on the eighth day after the Assumption of the Glorious Virgin Mary; praised be the Lord who extended the Heavens and augmented wisdom. Amen.

According to the explicits of the three complete copies of *Introductorius*, all of which identify Bate as the cantor of Liège,[159] he finished working on this translation in Orvieto, on the eighth day after the Assumption of the Glorious Virgin Mary, i.e., August 22, the eighth day counting from the feast on August 15, 1292. This means that *Introductorius* was the second of the five complete Latin translations Bate executed in the same place and around the same time. Inasmuch as Bate's previous translation, *Liber Abrahe Avenesre de luminaribus* (the translation of *Me'orot*), was completed in Orvieto on June 4, 1292, he seems to have spent a maximum of four months (111 days) on *Introductorius*. Below we will explore why this explicit renders "Master Abraham Ibn Ezra" as "Master of Help."

1.4. The Structure of *Introductorius*

At approximately 34,900 words, *Introductorius* is by far the longest of Bate's Latin translations of Ibn Ezra. Like *Reshit Ḥokhmah*, *Introductorius* is divided into 10 chapters, each of them headed by a title bearing the name of the corresponding chapter in the Hebrew. *Introductorius* is a complete translation of *Reshit Ḥokhmah*, but with no fewer than 1,980 divergent or alternative readings (mainly phrases but also words) it is remarkably different from its Hebrew source. Here and elsewhere the expression "alternative readings" means double or triple translations for a single word or locution, that is, readings reflecting Bate's uncertainty about what Latin term best represents the Hebrew or French source. By contrast the expression "divergent readings" means different translations deviating from the souce text. These divergent or alternative readings may be divided into three types:

---

[158] See this colophon in the critical edition, at pp. 356–358. For the colophons of **WVG**, see note 1 in the critical edition, at p. 358.

[159] See above, p. 6.

(a) 1060 of them (53.5%) diverge from both *Reshit Ḥokhmah* and Hagin's French version of that text, *Commencement*;[160] (b) 406 of them (20.5%) are doublets or triplets;[161] (c) 514 of them (26%) diverge from *Reshit Ḥokhmah* but follow *Commencement*.[162]

Some 203 words or phrases that occur in *Reshit Ḥokhmah* are omitted from *Introductorius*.[163] They fall into two categories: (a) 108 of them (53.2%) are words or phrases found in *Reshit Ḥokhmah* that are omitted in both *Introductorius* and *Commencement*—meaning that in these loci Bate was following the text of *Commencement*.[164] (b) 91 of them (44.8%) are words or phrases in *Reshit Ḥokhmah* that are left out of *Introductorius* but appear in *Commencement*. Bate was entirely responsible for these omissions; In other words, he was not following the text of *Commencement*.[165]

Introductorius has 206 short glosses, consisting of a few words,[166] which will be briefly described in the next chapter.[167] Unlike other translations by Bate, there are no medium-length or extensive glosses here. *Introductorius* also features at least 800 stylistic alterations.[168] Other than these depar-

---

[160] Cases of this type are marked in bold in the critical edition of *Introductorius* and its corresponding English translation, and are accompanied at the end by a superscript γ. See below, p. 118.

[161] Cases of this type are marked in bold in the critical edition of *Introductorius* and its corresponding English translation, and are accompanied at the end by a superscript β. See below, p. 118.

[162] Cases of this type are marked in bold in the critical edition of *Introductorius* and its corresponding English translation, and are accompanied at the end by a superscript α. See below, p. 117.

[163] Omissions are presented in all the Latin editions of Bate's translations as an ellipsis enclosed by double angle brackets, i.e., ⟨⟨...⟩⟩. Instead of the ellipsis, all the corresponding English translations of Bate's Latin translations bring the text of the omissions enclosed by double angle brackets, i.e., ⟨⟨the Woman⟩⟩. See bellow, p. 118.

[164] In the Latin edition of *Introductorius*, the ellipsis enclosed by double angle brackets that signals an omission of this type is accompanied at the end by a superscript μ. In the English translation of *Introductorius*, the text of the omission enclosed by double angle brackets that signals an omission is accompanied at the end by a superscript μ and by a note documenting the omission. See bellow, p. 119.

[165] In the Latin edition of *Introductorius*, the ellipsis enclosed by double angle brackets that signals an omission of this type is accompanied at the end by a superscript ν. In the English translation of *Introductorius*, the text of the omission enclosed by double angle brackets that signals an omission is accompanied at the end by a superscript ν and by a note documenting the omission. See below, p. 119.

[166] Glosses of any size, in all the editions of Bate's Latin translations as well as in all their corresponding English translations, are marked in italics. See below, p. 120.

[167] See below, p. 104.

[168] For the concept of "stylistic alterations," see below, p. 121. Stylistic alterations are enclosed in single curly brackets = { }, in both the critical edition and the English translation of *Introductorius*.

tures, *Introductorius* follows *Reshit Ḥokhmah* rather closely, as can be seen from the critical edition and English translation.

1.5. The Source Text of *Introductorius*

As noted, in 1273 Bate commissioned Hagin's French translation of *Reshit Ḥokhmah, Commencement*, which survives in two manuscripts.[169] *Introductorius* is the only one of Bate's complete Latin translations that has a counterpart in Hagin's Hebrew-to-French translations. It stands to reason that Bate used Hagin's translation for his own Latin version of *Reshit Ḥokhmah* nearly two decades later, in 1292. Indeed, we have already seen that 108 (53.2%) of the 203 words or phrases from *Reshit Ḥokhmah* that are omitted in *Introductorius* are also omitted in *Commencement*, which means that here Bate followed the French text. Moreover, 514 (26.3%) out of the 1,574 divergent readings in *Introductorius* follow *Commencement*.

Among the 510 cases of this type, here I offer only one example, from the description of the tenth horoscopic house in the third chapter of *Reshit Ḥokhmah*:

Reshit Ḥokhmah, § 3.14:1–2, 146–147:

הבית העשירי יורה על האם, ועל המלוכה, ועל השם, ועל כל אומנות. ובעל השלישות ראשונה יורה על האם, והשני על מעלתו, והשלישי על אומנותו.

The tenth house indicates the mother, kingship, reputation, and every ⟨human⟩ craft. The first lord of the triplicity indicates the mother, the second ⟨lord of the triplicity indicates⟩ his [the native's] rank, and the third ⟨indicates⟩ his craft.

P, 34va (*Commencement*): La 10ᵉ meson enseigne sur rois, et oevres, et hautece, et essaucement, et roiaume, et memoire, et vois .1. [sic] de commandement, et sur maistries, et sur les meres, et gloire, et loenge, et chose emblee ou ostee, et les juges, et les princes et les prelas, et enseigne sur la moitié des ans de la vie. Et dit Alendezgoz que le sires de la triplicité premiere enseigne sur oevre et essachement, ch'est hauté de siege, et mansion tres haute; le secont enseigne sur vois de commandement et hardiece en cele; li tiers senefie l'estableté et la durableté.[170]

Introductorius § 3.14:1: Decima domus super reges significat, et opera, sublimationes, ac exaltationes, regna, et famositates, et auctoritatem; item super magisteria, et matres, et gloriam, et laudem, et res furatas aut sublatas, adhuc super iudices, et principes, et prelatos, et significat super medium annorum

---

[169] See above, p. 7.
[170] The section of this description of the tenth house assigned to Al-Andarzagar corresponds exactly to *The Introduction to Astrology* by Al-Qabīṣī (Alcabitius). See *Introduction*, ed. Burnett et al. (2004), I, section 66, 55.

vite. Dominus autem triplicitatis primus super omnia opera significat, et exaltationes, et mansiones altissimas; secundus super auctoritatem et audaciam in ea; et tertius stabilitatem et durabilitatem.

The tenth house indicates kings, works, being raised to a higher rank, and promotion, kingdoms, fame and authority; likewise, crafts, mothers, glory, praise, something taken away or stolen, as well as judges, princes, prelates, and it indicates half of the years of life. But the first lord of the triplicity indicates every work, promotions, and very high mansions; the second ⟨indicates⟩ authority, and boldness in it; the third ⟨lord of the triplicity indicates⟩ stability and longevity.

In addition, the following points demonstrate that Hagin's *Commencement* was without doubt the source text of *Introductorius*:

(1) As stated above, chapter I of *Reshit Ḥokhmah* includes a complete list of the 48 Ptolemaic constellations.[171] Ibn Ezra as a rule shuns transliteration of Arabic and translates their names into Hebrew. Hagin follows suit and translates these Hebrew names into French. A distinctive feature of P (i.e., Paris, BnF, fr. 24276) is that Latin translations of some of the names of constellations appear in the margins of the relevant parts of *Commencement*, in the same hand that copied the French translation. Proof that Bate followed this French translation and was using a manuscript of the family of P is that Bate incorporates *all* the Latin constellation names found in the margin of P into his Latin translation, together with a Latin translation of the French names of constellations and stars. See Table 1.

(2) A second proof emerges from a comparison of the explicits of *Reshit Ḥokhmah* (in one manuscript), *Commencement*, and *Introductorius*:

Reshit Ḥokhmah, § 10.3:6, 270–271: נשלם ספר ראשית חכמה לראב״ע ז״ל. = This ends the book *Beginning of Wisdom* by R.A.B.E (= Rabbi Abraham ben Meir Ibn Ezra), his memory for a blessing.

P, 66rb (*Commencement*): Ci define li livres de Commencement de Sapience que fist Abraham Even Azre ou Aezera qui est interpretés Maistre de Aide. = Here ends the book *Beginning of Wisdom*, which was composed by Abraham Ibn Ezra, or Ibn Eezera, ⟨a name⟩ whose translation is "Maistre de Aide" (i.e., Master of Help).

L, 23va (= *Introductorius* §10.3:5): Complete sunt .10. partes libri huius quem compilavit Magister Abraham Avenezre, quod interpretatur Magister Adiutorii. = The ten chapters of this book, which Master Abraham Ibn Ezra, ⟨a name⟩ whose translation is Master of Help, compiled, are completed.

---

[171] See *Reshit Ḥokhmah*, § 1.2:1–3 through § 1.5:1–23, 50–54.

TABLE 1

Reshit Ḥokhmah (ed. Sela, 2017), §1.4:2–§1.5:16, 52–53	Commencement P, 2ra–2va	Margin of P	Introductorius L, 2rb–2va (= Introductorius §1.4:2–§1.5:16)
§1.4:2: ארי הים, ויש שקורין אותו דוב = the Sea-Lion, some call it the Bear	le Lion de la mer, et tel i a qui l'apelent Ours	Cetus	§1.4:2: Leo maris quem quidam vocant ursus et est Cetus
§1.4:3: הכלב הגבור = the Mighty Dog	le Chien le fort	Orion	§1.4:3: Canis fortis et est Orion
§1.4:9: החיה = the Beast (meaning the Snake)	la Biche	Ydra	§1.4:9: Bestia et est Ydra
§1.4:12: נושאת האריה = the Lion Carrier	cele qui porte le Lion	Centaurus	§1.4:12: portans Leonem et est Centaurus
§1.5:5: בעלת הלהב = the Lady of the Flame	la Dame de la flambe	vel Flaminatus vel Cepheus	§1.5:5: Domina flamme alibi vocatur Flaminatus vel Cepheus
§1.5:6: הכלב הנובח = the Barking Dog	le Chien abaiant	Boetes	§1.5:6: Canis latrans alibi notatur ululans cuius intentio est vociferans vel Boetes
§1.5:12: הנושא את ראש השטן = the Carrier of the Devil's Head	celi qui porte le Chief du Diable	Perseus	§1.5:12: portans Caput Dyaboli et est Perseus
§1.5:13: הרועה = the Shepherd	le Pasteur	Agitator	§1.5:13: Pastor seu Agitator
§1.5:14: עוצרת החיה = the One who Holds the Beast (meaning the Snake)	celi qui retient la Biche	Serpentarius	§1.5:14: retinens Bestiam et est Serpentarius
§1.5:15: החיה = the Beast (meaning the Snake)	la Biche	Serpens	§1.5:15: Bestia sive Serpens
§1.5:16: השטן = the Devil	le Nuiseur	Sagitta	§1.5:16: Nocumentivus et est Sagitta

We see that the Latin explicit is a translation of its French counterpart, which is itself a translation of the explicit of one of the manuscripts of *Reshit Ḥokhmah*. It also emerges that the mysterious "Magister Adiutorii" of the Latin explicit is simply a translation of "Maistre de Aide" in the French explicit. That is, the Latin "magister" renders the French "maistre," which is a translation of the Hebrew abbreviation ר׳, which stands for "rabbi," but in this context means "teacher." The Latin *adiutorium* accurately translates the French *aide*; both mean "help." But the two explicits take "Magister Adiutorii" or "Maistre de Aide" to be a translation of "Avenezre," which is Ibn Ezra's Latinized surname. Is this correct? The response is definitely in the affirmative: Hebrew עזרא *'ezra* means "help." Hagin, who knew this, rendered the second element of Ibn Ezra's Latinized name as "aide" and created the name "Maistre de Aide." Subsequently, Bate, following Hagin, turned this into "Magister Adiutorii."[172]

(3) *Commencement* includes a number of Hebrew transliterations. Evidently these represent words that Hagin did not know how to translate into French. Solid proof that Bate relied on *Commencement* is that Bate incorporates these Hebrew transliterations into his Latin translation in the same loci as they appear in *Commencement*. Table 2 illustrates this phenomenon:

TABLE 2

Reshit Ḥokhmah (ed. Sela, 2017), 52–53	*Commencement* (P)	*Introductorius*
§ 2.1:28: תרפים = terafim (magical instruments)	5ra: terafim	§ 2.1:28: terafim
§ 2.5:16: רחמה = raḥamah (bustard)	13vb: raihema	§ 2.5:16: raihena
§ 2.10:8: החרוב = ha-ḥarob (carob)	24rb: le harobe	§ 2.10:8: orobe
§ 2.16:10: כסיל = kesil (the star Suhail)	31vb: kescil	§ 2.16:10: kesil

---

[172] The same occurs in the explicit of Pietro d'Abano's Latin translation of *Reshit Ḥokhmah*: Paris, Bibliothèque de la Sorbonne, MS 640, fol. 94rb: "Explicit *Liber Principium sapientie* intitulatus, editur ab Abrahae Nazareth vel Aezera Iudeo, qui Magister Adiutorii est appellatus" = "Here ends the book called *Beginning of Wisdom*. It was composed by Abraham Ibn Ezra, or Ibn Eezera the Jew, who is called Magister Adiutorii [i.e., master of help]." See Sela 2019 (d), 19–21, 25–26.

TABLE 2 (*cont.*)

Reshit Ḥokhmah (ed. Sela, 2017), 52–53	*Commencement* (**P**)	*Introductorius*
§ 4.1:11: רחם = raḥam (bustard)	35rb: *raihem*	§ 4.1:11: rachem
§ 4.1:13: חרוב = ḥarob (carob)	35va: harrobe	§ 4.1:13: harobe
§ 4.1:13: בלוט = balot (gum)	35va: balot	§ 4.1:13: balot
§ 4.1:16: נטף = nataf (storax)	35va: nathaf	§ 4.1:16: nataf
§ 4.4:8: הכרים = ha-carim (a biblical word for sheep)	39va: les carim	§ 4.4:8: carim

1.6. The Source Text of *Commencement*

As stated, Hagin's Hebrew-to-French translations of Ibn Ezra's astrological writings are preserved in two manuscripts: (i) Paris, BnF, fr. 24276 (= **P**), copied in the thirteenth century, with the earliest available version of Hagin's four French translations; (ii) Paris BnF, fonds français, 1351 (= **P¹**), copied in the fifteenth century with the same four French translations. Although it stands to reason that Bate used **P**, the collation of *Introductorius* against *Commencement* and *Reshit Ḥokhmah* carried out for this volume shows somewhat surprisingly that the manuscript of Hagin's *Commencement* used by Bate for *Introductorius* was neither **P** nor **P¹** but a lost manuscript earlier than either of them.[173]

2. *Liber causarum seu rationum*

The fourth component of Henry Bate's translation project is *Liber causarum seu rationum* (Book of causes or reasons; henceforth *Rationes* I),[174] his Latin translation of the first version of *Sefer ha-Ṭeʿamim* (Book of reasons; henceforth *Ṭeʿamim* I). As shown above, Ibn Ezra announced his intention to write such a work in the introduction to *Reshit Ḥokhmah*, in order to offer

---

[173] These 9 instances correspond to the π-type of special cases. For this category, see below, 123. See *Introductorius*, § 2.6:30,32; § 2.7:34; § 2.5:19; § 2.9:20; § 2.10:43; § 2.14:5; § 6.1:4,5; § 6.3:2.

[174] For this title, see below, p. 35. References to the Latin text and the English translation of *Rationes* I are in the format: *Rationes* I, § 2.10:1 = *Rationes* I, chapter 2, section 10, passage 1.

טעמים—"reasons," "explanations," or "meanings"—of the raw astrological concepts presented in his introduction to astrology.[175] *Teʿamim* I, which runs to 11,400 words, is extant in at least 32 Hebrew manuscripts.[176]

2.1. The Contents of *Teʿamim* I

That *Teʿamim* I is a close commentary on *Reshit Ḥokhmah* is borne out by the fact that it is divided into the same 10 chapters as *Reshit Ḥokhmah*, to such an extent that the survey of the contents of *Reshit Ḥokhmah* carried out in the previous section can serve to describe the contents of *Teʿamim* I. Moreover, *Teʿamim* I is full of quotations from *Reshit Ḥokhmah*, presented in the order they appear in the longer work. These quotations can be readily identified by a comparison of the two texts, but also by means of certain formulas, such as the peculiar use of the third person plural that often introduces verbatim quotations from *Reshit Ḥokhmah* in *Teʿamim* I.[177]

Teʿamim I also includes relatively long digressions spurred by brief quotations that quickly develop into independent discussions. For example, *Teʿamim* I expands considerably on the relatively short first chapter of *Reshit Ḥokhmah* and offers digressions about (a) the names and sizes of the signs; the motion, number and names of stars and constellations; the orbs of the planets and their relative height;[178] (b) the nature of the signs;[179] and (c) the nature of the planets.[180] For the second chapter of *Reshit Ḥokhmah*, *Teʿamim* I offers digressions about (a) the four seasons and the beginning of the solar year;[181] (b) the pains of the planets in the signs;[182] (c) the planetary houses;[183] (d) the beginning and length of the solar year, the motion of the stars of the eighth orb, and the division of the zodiacal signs;[184] (e) the exaltations.[185] *Teʿamim* I also expands significantly on the short tenth chapter of *Reshit Ḥokhmah* and offers a long digression about the calculation of the aspects, the directions, and the astrological houses.[186]

---

[175] See *Reshit Ḥokhmah*, § 1:4 , 48–49.
[176] See Sela 2007, 365–366.
[177] See, for example, *Teʿamim* I, § 1.1:1,3.4.6, 28–29. Bate, in his Latin translation, follows suit and also uses the third person plural to introduce verbatim quotations from *Reshit Ḥokhmah*. See *Rationes* I, § 1.1:1,3.4.6.
[178] *Teʿamim* I, § 1.2:1–6, 28–31; § 1.3:1–12, 30–33.
[179] *Teʿamim* I, § 1.4:1–7, 32–33.
[180] *Teʿamim* I, § 1.5:1–17, 32–35.
[181] *Teʿamim* I, § 2.1:2–6, 36–39.
[182] *Teʿamim* I, § 2.3:3–7, 40–43.
[183] *Teʿamim* I, § 2.4:1–12, 42–45; § 2.5:1–12, 44–47.
[184] *Teʿamim* I, § 2.12:1–15, 50–53.
[185] *Teʿamim* I, § 2.16:1–14, 54–57.
[186] *Teʿamim* I, § 10.1:1–5 through § 10.9:1–4, 94–107.

2.2. The Manuscripts

Rationes I survives in two manuscripts from the fourteenth century:

L   Leipzig, Universitätsbibliothek, 1466, fols. 60vb–73va, copied around 1300 or in the first quarter of the 14th century in northern France, contains a complete copy of *Rationes* I. For a detailed description of this manuscript, see below, Appendix 2, pp. 1101–1103.

M   Limoges, Bibliothèque municipale, 9 (28), fols 24r–44r, copied in the 14th century, contains an almost complete copy of Bate's translation of *Ṭeʿamim* I: it lacks a fragment at the beginning of the translation from *Rationes* I, § 1.1:1 up to § 1.4:2. For a detailed description of this manuscript and its contents, see below, Appendix 3, pp. 1104–1106.

L, the earlier of the two extant manuscripts, served as base text of the critical edition, but was not followed slavishly. L and M have many divergent readings and seem to have split from the first copy of the Latin translation of *Ṭeʿamim* I in Bate's library. In not a few cases M, the later, improves over L, the earlier: M offers many correct readings against defective readings of L;[187] moreover, M includes important phrases or glosses that L omits altogether,[188] relegates to the margin,[189] or brings incomplete.[190]

2.3. Title, Authorship, and Place and Date of Composition

Let us look first at the incipit of the complete manuscript of *Rationes* I:

> L, 60vb (= *Rationes* I, incipit): Incipit *Liber causarum seu rationum* super hiis que dicuntur in Introductorio Abrache Avi⟨nezra⟩, incipit ⟨Initium⟩ sapientie timor Domini
>
> Here begins the *Book of causes or reasons* for what is said in the Introduction by Abraham Ibn ⟨Ezra⟩, ⟨which⟩ begins "the beginning of wisdom is the fear of the Lord."

According to the incipit, the source text of *Rationes* I is entitled *Liber causarum seu rationum* (Book of causes or reasons). This title, which in-

---

[187] See, in the apparatus, note 4 at §1.4:7; note 9 at §1.4:7; note 11 at §1.5:11; note 13 at §1.5:16; note 18 at §2.1:14; note 19 at §2.1:14; note 34 at §2.16:4; note 50 at §3.2:10, *et passim*.

[188] See, in the apparatus, note 20, gloss at §2.2:19; note 23, at §2.2:19; note 25, at §2.4:8; note 26, at §2.4:12; note 65, at §4.2:11, *et passim*.

[189] See, in the apparatus, note 17, at §2.2:12; note 28, at §2.8:1; note 29, at §2.10:14, *et passim*.

[190] See, in the apparatus, note 3, gloss at §1.3:4.

cludes a double translation of the Hebrew name of the source text, *ṭeʿamim*, "reasons," makes perfect sense. The doublet "rationes seu causas" or "rationes et causas," in plural or singular, occurs three times in *Rationes* I, independent of the title of the translation,[191] and four times in Bate's other translations,[192] as a disambiguation of the Hebrew טעם, which may mean "reason," "cause," "meaning," "taste," or "flavor." The first paragraph of *Introductorius* employs a similar title—*Liber explanationis rationum et causarum* (Book of the explanation of causes and reasons)—to refer to *Ṭeʿamim* I.[193] By contrast, *Nativitas*, written 12 years before the completion of *Rationes* I, always has *Liber rationum* (Book of reasons) and generally mentions Avenezre as its author (i.e., "Avenezre in *Libro rationum*").[194]

The incipit also reports that this book presents the causes and reasons for what is said in an "Introduction" by Abraham Ibn Ezra, which begins "the beginning of wisdom is the fear of the Lord." The last words of the incipit, i.e., "⟨Initium⟩ sapientie timor Domini," are identical with the first words of *Introductorius*, and in fact render the opening words of that work.[195] This means that the "Introduction by Abraham Ibn Ezra" referred to in the incipit of *Rationes* I must be *Reshit Ḥokhmah*. That the incipit of *Rationes* I is not identical with the incipits of any of the manuscripts of *Ṭeʿamim* I that I have checked means that Bate had independent knowledge that *Ṭeʿamim* I is a commentary on *Reshit Ḥokhmah*. This is noteworthy, because Bate also translated Ibn Ezra's second version of *Sefer ha-Ṭeʿamim*, which is not a commentary on the *Reshit Ḥokhmah* to which *Ṭeʿamim* I is a pendant. Here is the explicit of the complete manuscript of Bate's translation of *Ṭeʿamim* I:

> L, 73va (= *Rationes* I, explicit): Explicit *Liber rationum* et completus est, cuius translatio perfecta est a magistro Hynrico de Malinis, dicto Bate, in Urbe Veteri anno Domini .1292°. in octavis nativitatis Beate Marie Virginis.
>
> Here ends and is completed the *Book of reasons*, whose translation was finished by Master Henry of Malines, called Bate, in Orvieto, in the year of the Lord 1292, on the eighth day after the ⟨Feast of the⟩ Nativity of the Blessed Virgin Mary.

According to this text, which is almost identical to the explicit of the second extant manuscript,[196] Bate finished his translation of *Rationes* I on

---

[191] See *Rationes* I, § 2.4:2; § 2.6:2; § 4.1:1.
[192] See *Introductorius*, § 1.1:4, § 10.2:1; *Ṭeʿamim* II § 5.1:11, § 8.5:1.
[193] See *Introductorius*, § 1.1:4.
[194] See *Nativitas*, 2161, 2332, 2387.
[195] See *Introductorius*, § 1.1:1.
[196] M, 44r: Completus est hic liber, cuius translatio perfecta a magistro Hynrico de Malinis,

September 15, 1292 (the Feast of the Nativity of the Blessed Virgin Mary falls on September 8). This makes *Rationes* I the third translation completed during Bate's stay in Orvieto and the fourth component of his translation project. Note too that he finished work on *Rationes* I only 25 days after he completed *Introductorius*, the translation of Ibn Ezra's *Reshit Ḥokhmah* (on August 22)—seemingly quite an achievement!

2.4. The Structure of *Rationes* I

At approximately 16,100 words, *Rationes* I is Bate's third-longest translation of Ibn Ezra's astrological writings.[197] It is a complete translation of *Ṭeʿamim* I, but differs significantly from its Hebrew source. The prefatory canticle in *Rationes* I does not occur in *Ṭeʿamim* I, which indicates that the former was based on a Hebrew text that is not identical with any of the Hebrew manuscripts of *Ṭeʿamim* I that I checked.

Rationes I has no fewer than 757 divergent or alternative readings, of which 523 (69%) are divergent readings, and 234 (31%) are double or triple translations. There are also some 552 stylistic alterations, at least 74 omissions from the Hebrew source text, and 118 glosses: (a) 110 short glosses, consisting of a few words; (b) 6 medium-length glosses consisting of a few lines; (c) two long glosses. These glosses will be briefly described in the next chapter.[198]

Except for the aforementioned departures, *Rationes* I follows *Ṭeʿamim* I rather closely, as can be seen in the critical edition and English translation of *Rationes* I. As noted, *Reshit Ḥokhmah* is divided into 10 chapters, introduced in the Hebrew text by the corresponding subtitles: Chapter One, Chapter Two, and so on. The same subtitles reappear in *Ṭeʿamim* I; *Rationes* I follows suit for all 10.

2.5. The Source Text of *Rationes* I

Rationes I is the only extant Latin translation of *Ṭeʿamim* I, and no French translation of *Ṭeʿamim* I has been found to date. At this stage, what can be said regarding the source text of *Rationes* I is that in some places the wording of this translation (as found in the two available manuscripts) diverges considerably from *Ṭeʿamim* I (as found in the available Hebrew manuscripts). This suggests that Bate based *Rationes* I on a Hebrew-to-

---

dicto Bate, in Urbe Veteri anno domini .1292°. in octavis nativitatis beate Marie virginis gloriose. Explicit Liber rationum Abrahe.

[197] The translation of *Mishpeṭei ha-mazzalot* with 16,300 words is very slightly longer than that of *Rationes* I.

[198] See below, p. 105.

French translation based on a Hebrew manuscript different from those available today.

Clear evidence pointing in this direction is found in the very first sentence of *Rationes* I, which, as mentioned, incorporates a prefatory canticle not found in any of the Hebrew manuscripts of *Ṭeʿamim* I that I checked. Additional evidence is provided by several loci in *Rationes* I, where the Latin text departs considerably from the Hebrew source. Here are seven examples of this (the differences between the Latin and Hebrew are in bold):

(1) *Ṭeʿamim* I, § 2.14:2, 54–55:

והוא יורה על כל גבוה **כמו השמים** בעבור שהוא תולדת האויר.

*It indicates everything that is high, **like the heavens**, because its nature is airy.*

L, 64vb (*Rationes* I, § 2.14:2): Significat **autem** super omnem sublimitatem **et principes, duces et prophetas legislatores**, eo quod est de natura aerea.

But it indicates every highness, **and princes, dukes, prophets and law-givers**, because it is of airy nature.

(2) *Ṭeʿamim* I, § 2.16:5, 54–55:

והנה יהיה מעלת **קלון** השמש תשע עשרה ממאזנים, ומעלת **קלון הלבנה השלישית מעקרב**; על כן אמרו מתשע עשרה מעלות ממאזנים עד המעלה השלישית מעקרב הוא מקום השריפה.

*Now the degree of the **shame** [i.e., dejection] of the Sun will be Libra 19°, **and the degree of the shame of the Moon Scorpio 3°**; hence they called from Libra 19° to Scorpio 3° "the place of burning."*

L, 65ra (*Rationes* I, § 2.16:5): Et erit **casus** Solis in .19. gradu Libre, ⟨⟨...⟩⟩, et hinc ⟨⟨...⟩⟩ usque ad tercium gradum Scorpionis est **locus combustionis seu via combusta**.

The **fall** [dejection] of the Sun will be at Libra 19°, ⟨⟨**and the degree of shame of the Moon will be Scorpio 3°**⟩⟩; hence ⟨⟨they called from Libra 19°⟩⟩ to Scorpio 3° **the place of burning or the burnt path**.

(3) *Ṭeʿamim* I, § 2.17:4, 56–57:

ושמו מאדים שותף עמהם בעבור כי הוא יורה על **רוח דרומית ומזלות העפר הם דרומיים**, והוציאו כוכב חמה ושבתאי בעבור שאין להם כח **ברוחות הדרומיים**.

*They put Mars as their partner because it indicates the southerly **wind and ⟨because⟩ the earthy signs are southern**; they excluded Mercury and Saturn because they have no power **over the southerly winds**.*

L, 65rb (*Rationes* I, § 2.17:4): Posueruntque Martem participem cum illis, eo quod super **partem** significat meridianam, ⟨⟨...⟩⟩; et repulerunt Mercurium ac Saturnum, quia fortitudinem **in angulo meridiano** non habent.

They made Mars their partner, because it indicates the southern **part**, ⟨⟨**and the earthy signs are southern**⟩⟩; and they excluded Mercury and Saturn, because they have no strength **over the southern corner**.

(4) *Ṭeʿamim* I, § 4.2:3–4, 70–73:

ובחלקו מהארץ המערות וכל מקום חושך בעבור כי בעל המרה השחורה תולדתו להתבודד ושלא יעמוד במקום מיושב. ויורה על כל חיה גדולה בעבור היותו עליון, ומכוערת בעבור כי המרה השחורה לא תעשה צורה יפה. ואילן העפצים בחלקו בעבור תולדתו, וכל דבר שיש בו סם המות בעבור כי הוא יורה על מות.

Its portion of the Earth is caves and any dark place, **because it suits a melancholy nature to be in solitude and not to stay in an inhabited place**. *It indicates any animal that is big because it is uppermost, and* ⟨*any animal*⟩ *that is ugly* because black bile does not shape any handsome image. **The gall-oak is in its portion on account of its nature**, as well as anything that contains a **deadly poison**, because it indicates death.

L, 67rb (*Rationes* I, 4.2:3–4): Et est in parte eius omnis locus tenebrosus et turpis ⟨⟨...⟩⟩. ⟨⟨...⟩⟩ quia **pulchram figuram et formosam** non efficit melancolia; et **significat arborem seu plantam *kenesesin*, et omnem rem toxicam et pocionem mortiferam**, eo quod super mortem significat.

And in its portion is every dark and ugly place ⟨⟨because it suits a melancholy nature to be in solitude and not to stay in an inhabited place⟩⟩. ⟨⟨It indicates any animal that is big because it is uppermost, and any animal that is ugly⟩⟩ because black bile does not produce any **beautiful or handsome form**; it indicates the tree or plant *kenesesin*, as well as any **toxic thing or deadly poison**, because it indicates death.

(5) *Ṭeʿamim* I, § 4.8:2–3, 80–81:

בחלקה הגבול השביעי כי ככה גלגלה לגלגל שבתאי, ומן הארצות אל צאביה בעבור היות מזלם סרטן שהוא ביתה. ומבני אדם המלחים בעבור שהיא תורה על הים, שהיא קרה ולחה.

The seventh **climate** *is in its portion, because like that is its orb to Saturn's orb; of countries, al-Ṣabia* ⟨*is in its portion*⟩, *because their sign is Cancer, which is its house. Of human beings, sailors* ⟨*are in its portion*⟩, *because it* **indicates** *the sea, which is cold and moist.*

L, 68vb (*Rationes* I, § 4.8:2–3): In eius {autem} divisione est **clima** septimus, hoc enim modo circulus eius respectu circuli Saturni se habet; **de animalibus** {autem}, pisces; ⟨⟨...⟩⟩ quia signum eorum Cancer est, qui est domus eius. De hominibus {autem}, naute, eo quod ipsa mari **preest**, {quia} frigidum est et humidum.

{But} in its portion is the seventh **climate**, because that is the relationship of its circle to Saturn's circle; {and} **of living beings, fish;** ⟨⟨**of countries, al-Ṣabia**⟩⟩ because their sign is Cancer, which is its house. Of human beings, {however,} sailors, because **it rules over** the sea, {because} it is cold and moist.

(6) *Ṭeʿamim* I, § 8.1:2, 90–91:

וטעם לשום ללבנה שותפות עם המזל העולה בעבור **שהיא קרובה אל הארץ**.

*The reason for making the Moon the partner of the sign of the ascendant is that **it is close to the Earth**.*

L, 71ra (*Rationes* I, § 8.1:2): Ratio **autem** quare Luna particeps ascendenti ponitur hec est quia **similitudinem habet cum signo ascendente**.

{But} the reason why the Moon was made partner to the ascendant is because **of its resemblance to the ascendant sign**.

(7) *Ṭeʿamim* I, § 1.5:5, 34–35:

ואני אברהם, המחבר, אומר כי זה הספר לא חברו בטלמיוס, כי יש שם דברים רבים בטלים משיקול הדעת והנסיון, כאשר אפרש בספר המולדות.

*And I, Abraham, **the author**, say that this book was not written by Ptolemy, because there are many things in it that have in them nothing of rational thought or experience, **as I shall explain in the** Book of nativities.*

L, 61vb (*Rationes* I, § 1.5:5): Et ego, Abracham **compilator**, dico quod librum illum non compilavit Ptolomeus, quia in eo multi sunt sermones otiosi scientie et experientie contra pensationem, **prout in Libris explanabo iudiciorum**.

But I, Abraham **the compiler**, say that Ptolemy did not compile this book, because there are in it many statements devoid of science and against the weight of experience, **as I shall explain in the Books of judgments**.

3. *Secunda pars libri rationum*

The fifth item in Henry Bate's project is *Liber rationum seu causarum* (Book of reasons or causes) or *secunda pars Libri rationum* (second part of the Book of reasons; henceforth *Rationes* II).[199] This is a complete translation of the second version of *Sefer ha-Ṭeʿamim* (Book of reasons; henceforth

---

[199] For these titles, see below p. 43. References to the Latin text and the English translation of *Rationes* II are in the format: *Rationes* II, § 5.5:6 = *Rationes* II, chapter 5, section 5, passage 6.

Ṭeʿamim II), which runs to approximately 10,700 words and is extant in at least 25 Hebrew manuscripts.[200]

3.1. What is *Ṭeʿamim* II?

In the opening sentence of *Ṭeʿamim* II Ibn Ezra writes, "I wish to lay the foundation of the *Book of the beginning of wisdom* (i.e., *Reshit Ḥokhmah*)."[201] Nevertheless, even though *Ṭeʿamim* II includes obvious quotations from an underlying text and many parts of *Ṭeʿamim* II do not make sense unless one assumes that they are commenting on quoted passages, it is virtually impossible to find explicit and obvious quotations from *Reshit Ḥokhmah* in *Ṭeʿamim* II. Moreover, some parts of *Ṭeʿamim* II address a variety of concepts related to nativities, which are never touched on in *Reshit Ḥokhmah*.[202] And in the many cases where similar topics are discussed in *Reshit Ḥokhmah* and *Ṭeʿamim* II, they are treated in a different order. What text is *Ṭeʿamim* II commenting on, then?

It turns out that Ibn Ezra wrote *Ṭeʿamim* II in order to explain the reasons behind the astrological concepts employed in his lost second version of *Reshit Ḥokhmah*, a fragment of which was recently discovered and has been published in a separate study and edition.[203]

Despite the differences between them, *Ṭeʿamim* I and *Ṭeʿamim* II were both written by Ibn Ezra as commentaries on another book; therefore, they share a similar interpretative methodology: digressions that expand on brief quotations from an underlying text. For example, *Ṭeʿamim* II includes long digressions on (a) the nature of the signs;[204] (b) the planetary houses;[205] (c) the exaltations;[206] (d) the indications of the horoscopic houses;[207] (e) the aspects.[208] Although the wording of these digressions is rather different from their counterparts in *Ṭeʿamim* I, in no few cases *Ṭeʿamim* I and *Ṭeʿamim* II share common ideas and explanations. However, *Ṭeʿamim* II includes a number of digressions on topics not dealt with in *Ṭeʿamim* I. This refers to the interest of *Ṭeʿamim* II in the doctrine of nativities, as reflected in the

---

[200] See Sela 2007, 367.
[201] *Ṭeʿamim* II, §1.1:1, 182–183.
[202] See *Ṭeʿamim* II, §6.1:1–5, 234–235; §6.2:1–11, 236–239.
[203] See *Reshit ḥokhmah* II, ed. Sela (2010).
[204] *Ṭeʿamim* II, §2.1:1–13, 184–187.
[205] *Ṭeʿamim* II, §2.5:1–10, 194–197; §2.6:1–7, 196–197.
[206] *Ṭeʿamim* II, §2.7:1–14, 198–201.
[207] *Ṭeʿamim* II, §3.1:1–12, 202–205; §3.2:1–6, 204–207; §3.3:1–7, 206–207.
[208] *Ṭeʿamim* II, §4.6:1–6, 210–213; §4.7:1–8, 212–213; §4.8:1–3, 212–213.

digressions addressing the rectification of the nativity[209] and the selection of the *haylāj*.[210]

3.2. The Manuscripts
Rationes II survives in the following manuscripts:

L   Leipzig, Universitätsbibliothek, 1466, fols. 49vb–60vb, copied around 1300 or in the first quarter of the 14th century in Northern France. Incorporates a complete copy of *Rationes* II. For a detailed description of this manuscript, see Appendix 2, pp. 1101–1103.

M   Limoges, Bibliothèque municipale, 9 (28), fols 1r–23v, copied in the 14th century, contains an almost complete copy of *Rationes* II, lacking a fragment at the end that corresponds to the segment from § 8.6:2 to § 8.7:11. For a detailed description of this manuscript and its contents, see Appendix 3, pp. 1104–1106.

L, the earlier of the two extant manuscripts, served as the base text of the critical edition of *Rationes* II. L and M have many divergent readings and seem to have split from the first exemplar of *Rationes* II in Bate's library. Besides the fact that L incorporates a complete copy, which M does not, as a rule L has better readings than M. M displays many significant omissions[211] and errors[212] which are corrected by readings of L. Nevertheless, L was not followed slavishly: M gives better numeric values than L[213] and corrects many omissions and errors of L.[214]

3.3. Title, Authorship, and Place and Date of Composition
Neither of the two extant manuscripts has an incipit, but we learn the title of this translation from the prefatory canticle found only in the earlier of the two manuscripts:

---

[209] *Ṭe'amim* II, § 6.1:1–5, 234–235. The term "rectification of the nativity" designates a variety of procedures to determine the ascendant of the natal horoscope when the time of birth is not known (the usual situation).

[210] *Ṭe'amim* II, § 6.2:1–11, 236–239. For the term *haylāj*, see below, p. 89.

[211] See, in the apparatus, note 2, § 1.1:1; note 67, § 3.3:3; note 73, gloss at § 4.1:2; note 167, § 6.2:1; note 186, § 6.5:5. *et passim*.

[212] See, in the apparatus, note 102, § 4.10:5; note 115, § 5.1:7, *et passim*.

[213] See, in the apparatus, note 90, § 4.5:2; note 173, § 6.3:1; note 173, § 6.3:1; note 174, § 6.3:3; note 191, § 6.9:2; *et passim*.

[214] See, in the apparatus, note 5, § 1.1:2; note 18, § 2.2:3; note 33, § 2.4:14; note 38, § 2.5:3; note 53, § 2.8:12; note 104, § 4.10:5; note 108, § 4.12:6; note 117, § 5.1:13; note 130, § 5.2:10; *et passim*.

> L, 49vb (= *Rationes* II, prefatory canticle): In nomine Dei manentis in excelsis incipiam *Librum rationum seu causarum*.
>
> In the name of God, who dwells in the Heavens, I begin the *Book of reasons or causes*.

This prefatory canticle, from which we learn that the translation of *Ṭeʿamim* II is called *Liber rationum seu causarum* (Book of reasons or causes), is found in at least one of the Hebrew manuscripts of *Ṭeʿamim* II that I examined.[215] As in the case of *Rationes* I, the double translation of the Hebrew name of the source text, *ṭeʿamim*, "reasons," is not unexpected. The doublet "rationes seu causas" or "rationes et causas," plural or singular, occurs twice in *Rationes* II in isolation from the title of the work,[216] and four times in Bate's other translations,[217] as a disambiguation of the Hebrew טעם, which may mean "reason," "cause," "meaning," "taste," or "flavor." Bate's *Nativitas*, which contains 15 references to *Ṭeʿamim* II and was written 12 years before the completion of *Rationes* II, offers two additional titles. It usually refers to *Liber rationum* (Book of reasons) and to Avenezre as its author (i.e., "Avenezre in *Libro rationum*").[218] But when *Nativitas* offers a translation of a passage from *Ṭeʿamim* II, its author is "Avenezre" and *Ṭeʿamim* II is designated *Liber rationum, secuna pars or particula* (Book of reasons, second part or element).[219]

More information is given in the explicit of the only manuscript of the complete translation of *Ṭeʿamim* II:

> L, 60vb (*Rationes* II, explicit): Translatio partis huius perfecta est .23. die mensis septembris anni Domini .1292.
>
> The translation of this part has been completed on the 23rd day of the month of September in the year of the Lord 1292.

The names of the translator, the translation, and the place where the translation was completed may be inferred from the explicits of the previous and next translations carried out by Bate in Orvieto in 1281. Bate wrote "translatio partis huius" = "translation of this part" because he considered *Liber rationum seu causarum* to be divided into two parts, the first identical with

---

[215] Vatican, Biblioteca Apostolica Vaticana, MS ebr. 47 (IMHM: F 00686), fol. 44v.
[216] See *Rationes* II, § 5.1:11; § 8.5:1.
[217] See *Introductorius*, § 1.1:4, § 10.2:1; *Rationes* II, § 5.1:11, § 8.5:1.
[218] See *Nativitas*, 593, 704, 965–966, 990, 1108–1109, 1279, 1683–1684.
[219] See, for example, *Nativitas*, 160; cf. *Ṭeʿamim* II, § 6.1:1, 234–235. *Nativitas*, 593–595; cf. *Ṭeʿamim* II, § 4.1:3, 206–207.

Teʿamim I and the second identical with *Teʿamim* II. This is confirmed by the fact that, as said above, in *Nativitas* he calls *Teʿamim* II "Liber rationum, secunda pars." Because *Rationes* I was completed in Orvieto on September 15, 1292, and *Rationes* II on September 23, 1292, Bate appears to have translated *Teʿamim* II in the span of eight days, seemingly quite an achievement for a text of approximately 14,100 words.

3.4. The Structure of *Rationes* II

Unlike *Teʿamim* I, *Teʿamim* II is not divided into chapters, but the various topics are headed by brief rubrics, which in the Hebrew text are commonly represented by one word, in the singular or plural. Bate frequently translates these one-word rubrics by means of doublets and triplets,[220] in some cases conveying their meaning by means of variant names;[221] he also adds rubrics that do not appear in the Hebrew text.[222]

At approximately 14,100 words, *Rationes* II is a complete translation of *Teʿamim* II, but markedly different from its Hebrew source text. *Rationes* II has 707 alternative or divergent readings from *Teʿamim* II, of them 517 (73%) are simple deviations and 190 (27%) are double or triple translations. *Rationes* II incorporates seven phrases that Bate took from a lost Hebrew manuscript of *Teʿamim* II, as we shall see in the next section.[223] There are 127 short glosses in *Rationes* II, which will be briefly described in the next chapter.[224] There are also 57 omissions from the Hebrew source text and at least 453 stylistic alterations. Apart from these departures, *Rationes* II follows *Teʿamim* II rather closely, as illustrated in the critical edition and English translation of *Rationes* II.

3.5. The Source Text of *Rationes* II

So far, no French translation of *Teʿamim* II has been found. Other than *Rationes* II, the only Latin translation of *Teʿamim* II known today is *Liber de rationibus* by Pietro d'Abano, produced in Paris after 1293.[225] The collation of *Teʿamim* II against *Rationes* II, as well as the comparison of Bate's and Pietro d'Abano's translations of *Teʿamim* II, reveals three noteworthy features:

---

[220] See *Rationes* II, § 2.4:5; § 2.4:6; § 2.4:13; § 2.7:1; § 4.2:1; § 7.2:27; § 7.2:28; § 8.7:1.
[221] See *Rationes* II, § 2.4:12; § 2.4:14.
[222] See *Rationes* II, § 8.4:1.
[223] See below, p. 45.
[224] See below, p. 106.
[225] See Sela 2019 (d), 1–82.

GENERAL INTRODUCTION 45

(i) There are at least seven phrases worded similarly in Bate's *Rationes* II and in Pietro d'Abano's *De rationibus* but not found in the critical edition of *Ṭeʿamim* II.[226]
(ii) There are at least five phrases omitted from Bate's *Rationes* II and Pietro d'Abano's *De rationibus* that do occur in the critical edition of *Ṭeʿamim* II.[227]
(iii) There are at least 53 phrases worded similarly in Bate's *Rationes* II and Pietro d'Abano's *De rationibus* that occur with a divergent reading in the critical edition of *Ṭeʿamim* II.[228]

These three features demonstrate without doubt that Bate and Pietro d'Abano based their parallel Latin translations on a lost Hebrew manuscript of *Ṭeʿamim* II. Was this lost Hebrew manuscript their source text? Or did they use a French intermediary that was based on this lost Hebrew manuscript of *Ṭeʿamim* II?

At present we cannot identify this source text, but given that Pietro says explicitly that he found the source text of his first translation of Ibn Ezra's astrological writings in French,[229] that Bate commissioned Hagin le Juif to produce French translations of Ibn Ezra's astrological writings, and that Bate and Hagin were neighbors in Mechelen, it is plausible to assume that the source text of *Rationes* II is a lost Hebrew-to-French translation by Hagin le Juif, commissioned by Bate.

---

[226] For these seven phrases, and for the parallel texts in Bate's *Rationes* II and Pietro d'Abano's *De rationibus*, see *Rationes* II, § 2.4:9, p. 723, note 23; § 2.4:16, p. 725, note 40; § 5.4:7, p. 748, note 11; § 5.5:12, p. 752, note 24; § 8.1:1, p. 763, note 1; § 8.4:1, p. 765. note 1; § 8.7:3, p. 767, note 5.

[227] For these five phrases, see *Rationes* II, § 2.7:3, p. 728, note 9; § 2.7:14, p. 729, note 32; § 2.8:7, p. 730. note 9; § 2.8:10, p. 730, note 12; § 5.5:6, p. 750, note 14.

[228] For these 53 phrases in Bate's and Pietro d'Abano's translations, and for their divergent readings in *Rationes* II, see *Rationes* II, § 2.1:11, p. 718, notes 15–16; § 2.3:8, p. 720, note 12; § 2.3:23, p. 721, note 40; § 2.4:4, p. 722, notes 9, 12; § 2.4:5, p. 723, note 13; § 2.4:10, p. 724, note 28; § 2.4:12, p. 724, note 31; § 2.4:14, p. 724, note 37; § 2.4:20, p 725, note 46; § 2.7:6, p. 728, note 19; § 2.8:7, p. 730, note 7; § 2.8:11, p. 730, note 14; § 2.8:12, pp. 730–731, note 15; § 5.1:10, p. 741, note 16; § 5.2:4, p. 742, note 5; § 5.2:7, p. 743, note 14; § 5.2:8, p. 743, note 16; § 5.2:9, p. 743, note 17; § 5.2:10, p. 743, note 19; § 5.2:16, p. 744, note 24; § 5.2:17, p. 744, note 25; § 5.3:6, p. 745, note 6; § 5.3:10, p. 746, note 22; 5.3:19, p. 747, note 38; § 5.4:4, p. 748, note 3; § 5.4:8, p. 748, note 13; § 5.4:9, p. 749, note 17; § 5.4:12, p. 749, note 19; § 5.6:1, p. 752, note 4; § 6.2:9, p. 756, note 21; § 6.2:10, p. 756, note 22; § 6.4:3, p. 757, note 3; § 6.5:2, p. 757, note 6; § 6.5:2, p. 757, note 8; § 6.8:3, p. 759, note 3; § 7.1:5, p. 761, note 11; § 7.1:5, p. 761, note 12; § 7.1:7, p. 761, note 14; § 7.2:14, p. 762, note 10; § 7.2:26, p. 763, note 21; § 8.2:4, p. 764, note 4; § 8.3:3, p. 765, note 6; § 8.7:5, p. 767, note 10; § 8.7:7, p. 768, notes 14, 15; § 8.7:9, p. 768, note 19; § 8.7:11, p. 768, note 22.

[229] See Sela 2019 (d), 19.

4. *Liber introductionis ad iudicia astrologie*

The sixth constituent of Henry Bate's translation project is *Liber introductionis ad iudicia astrologie* (Book of the introduction to the judgments of astrology; henceforth *Iudicia*).[230] This is a complete Latin version of *Sefer Mishpeṭei ha-Mazzalot* (Book of the judgments of the zodiacal signs), another introduction to astrology by Ibn Ezra, which runs to roughly 9,700 words and is extant in at least 25 Hebrew manuscripts.[231]

4.1. The Contents of *Mishpeṭei ha-Mazzalot*

Mishpeṭei ha-Mazzalot is arranged in sections or groups of paragraphs, headed by rubrics, addressing typical topics of introductions to astrology. Some of them, however, are typical of the doctrine of nativities, or characteristic of astronomical treatises, as we shall see.

Following an introduction devoted to a quadripartite division of the universe (the eighth orb; the zodiac, the seven orbs of the seven planets, and the sublunar domain),[232] the second long paragraph of *Mishpeṭei ha-Mazzalot* lists a bewildering variety of categories of signs and enumerates the signs in each category.[233] This is followed by a section of nine paragraphs on the essential dignities and other properties of the planets in the signs (planetary house, detriment, exaltation, dejection, joys, triplicity, term, face, novenaria, and duodenaria).[234] Next comes a discontinuous discussion of the horoscopic houses and their indications.[235]

At this point, the text turns to a typical topic of the doctrine of nativities: the "rectification of the nativity."[236] This is followed by two paragraphs addressing the doctrine of melothesia[237] and explaining the rationale behind the distribution of the pains of the planets among the zodiacal signs.[238]

Mishpeṭei ha-Mazzalot has significant astronomical content, which includes two astronomical tables (an extraordinary occurrence in introductions to astrology) and several discussions related to these tables. The first

---

[230] For this title, see below p. 48. References to the Latin text and the English translation of *Iudicia* are in the format: *Iudicia*, § 31:2 = *Iudicia*, section 31, passage 2.
[231] See Sela 2017, 638–639.
[232] *Mishpeṭei ha-mazzalot*, § 1:1–9, 488–489.
[233] *Mishpeṭei ha-mazzalot*, § 2:1–21, 488–491.
[234] *Mishpeṭei ha-mazzalot*, § 3:1 through § 11:1–4, 490–499.
[235] *Mishpeṭei ha-mazzalot*, § 12:1–7 through § 14:1–6, § 18:1–6, 498–505.
[236] See *Mishpeṭei ha-mazzalot*, § 15:1–5 through § 17:1–4, 500–505. For the term "rectification of the nativity," see above note 209.
[237] This doctrine distributes the parts of the body among the zodiacal signs.
[238] *Mishpeṭei ha-mazzalot*, § 19:1–3, § 20:1–12, 504–507.

table, displaying Venus's and Mercury's greatest eastern and western distance from the Sun, is identical to a table in *Luḥot ha-nasi'*, Abraham Bar Ḥiyya's astronomical tables.[239] The second table displays "how many degrees each planet retrogresses and approximately how many days it retrogresses," and presents values identical with those in a table included in the Toledan Tables.[240]

In a concluding section, *Mishpeṭei ha-Mazzalot* devotes several paragraphs to the calculation of the astrological aspects;[241] the natures or astrological properties of the seven planets;[242] the five places of dominion or *haylāj*,[243] a topic typical of the doctrine of nativities; the astrological lots;[244] the projection of the planets' ray and the directions;[245] and the correction of the horoscopic houses.[246]

4.2. The Manuscripts

Iudicia survives in three manuscripts, of which the earliest, from the fourteenth century, is complete; the other two, from the fifteenth century, are incomplete.

L   Leipzig, Universitätsbibliothek, 1466, fols. 37rb–49va, copied around 1300 or in the first quarter of the 14th century in northern France, contains a complete copy of *Iudicia*. For a detailed description of this manuscript, see Appendix 2, pp. 1101–1103.

U   Prague, Národní Knihovna České Republiky, III.C.2 (433), second half of the 15th century, 217 folios, incorporates a collection of astrological (particularly related to weather forecasting), astronomical, and medical texts. Folios 123ra–125rb are an incomplete text of *Iudicia*, corresponding to *Mishpeṭei ha-Mazzalot* from the beginning up to § 11:3.

V   Vatican, Biblioteca Apostolica Vatican, Pal. lat. 1377, 194 folios, a paper and parchment manuscript copied in the fourteenth century that incorporates a collection of astrological and astronomical texts.[247] Folios 37vb–43vb are an incomplete text of *Iudicia*, corresponding

---

[239] See *Mishpeṭei ha-mazzalot*, § 27:1–2, 510–513. See Sela 2017, 26–27.
[240] See *Mishpeṭei ha-mazzalot*, Mm § 31:1–5, 514–517. See Sela 2017, 27.
[241] *Mishpeṭei ha-mazzalot*, § 35:1–5 through § 37:1–5, 518–521.
[242] *Mishpeṭei ha-mazzalot*, § 38:1–15 through § 44:1–9, 520–531.
[243] *Mishpeṭei ha-mazzalot*, § 45:1–4, § 46:1–5, 530–533.
[244] *Mishpeṭei ha-mazzalot*, § 51:1–3 through § 64:1–3, 538–545.
[245] *Mishpeṭei ha-mazzalot*, § 65:1–10 through § 75:1–7, 544–555.
[246] *Mishpeṭei ha-mazzalot*, § 76:1–9, § 77:1–2, 554–555.
[247] For the contents of this manuscript, see Schuba 1992, 103–107.

to *Mishpeṭei ha-Mazzalot* from § 21:1 through the end. Other parts of *Iudicia* are missing as well, such as the complete section on the lots.[248]

L, the earliest copy, was again selected to serve as the base text for the critical edition. L was not followed slavishly, however, and the readings of U and particularly of V were occasionally preferred in the parts of *Iudicia* where the readings of these two manuscripts are available.[249]

4.3. Title, Authorship, and Place and Date of composition

We begin with the explicit of *Iudicia* as found in the earliest manuscript:

> L, 49va (= *Iudicia*, explicit): Explicit *Liber introductionis ad iudicia astrologie*. Deo gratias et laudes, cuius nomen magnum et per quem opera sunt numerata. Perfecta quidem est translatio libri huius in Urbe Veteri, a magistro Hynrico de Malinis dicto, anno Domini 1292 in crastino apostolorum Symonis et Iude etc.
>
> Here ends the *Book of the introduction to the judgments of astrology*. Thanks and praises to God, whose name is great and through whom works are counted. The translation of this book was completed in Orvieto, by the aforementioned Master Henry of Malines, called ⟨Bate⟩, in the year of the Lord 1292, on the day after ⟨the feast of⟩ the Apostles Simon and Jude [i.e., October 29, 1292], etc.

The Latin title *Liber introductionis ad iudicia astrologie* (Book of the introduction to the judgments of astrology) is somewhat similar to that of the original Hebrew (*Sefer Mishpeṭei ha-Mazzalot* = Book of the judgments of the zodiacal signs). According to the date in this explicit, *Iudicia* was the last of Bate's translations of Ibn Ezra executed in Orvieto, completed on October 29, 1292 (the feast of the Apostles Simon and Jude is celebrated on October 28), only 36 days after Bate had finished working on *Rationes* II (September 23).

A note in the upper margin of the first folio of *Iudicia* in the earliest manuscript provides an alternative title and reveals, surprisingly, that according to Bate Abraham Ibn Ezra was not the author of the source text:

---

[248] *Mishpeṭei ha-mazzalot*, § 51:1–3 through § 64:1–3, 538–545.
[249] For preferences of U, see, in the apparatus, note 5 at § 1:7, and note 2 at § 10:5, *et passim*. For preferences of V, see note 8 at § 25:11; note 9 at § 41:8; note 1 at § 42:7; note 1 at § 46:5, *et passim*.

GENERAL INTRODUCTION 49

L, 37rb: Ysagoge magistri Abrahe Ducis seu Principis vocati Hebrayce Nati Hezkia.

Introduction by Master Abraham the Duke or the Prince, called in Hebrew Bar Ḥiyya.

Abraham Bar Ḥiyya (ca. 1065–ca. 1136) was known to medieval Jewish society as *Abraham ha-Naśi'*, Abraham the Prince. It is therefore understandable that Henry Bate might have identified Abraham Princeps with the historical figure we know as Abraham Bar Ḥiyya. In the prologue to *De mundo*, the Latin translation of Ibn Ezra's *'Olam I*,[250] Bate twice ascribes to Abraham Princeps "5° Redemptionis Israel,"[251] (the fifth chapter ⟨of the book⟩ on the Redemption of Israel), that is, the fifth chapter of Abraham Bar Ḥiyya's *Megillat ha-Megalleh* (Scroll of the revealer), which is a Jewish and universal astrological history and an astrological prognostication of the coming of the Messiah. In the same prologue to *De mundo*, Bate also says that Abraham Princeps was Abraham Ibn Ezra's "magister" and that Ibn Ezra himself admitted this.[252] This explains why the note in the upper margin of the first folio in the earliest manuscript of *Iudicia* makes Abraham Dux or Princeps a "magister." But why is "Master Abraham the Duke or the Prince, called in Hebrew Bar Ḥiyya," given as the author of the source text of *Iudicia*?

The earliest manuscript of *Iudicia* ends: "Hec Abraham Princeps" = Abraham, the Prince, ⟨said⟩ these things.[253] This is followed immediately by a gloss written by an anonymous Hebrew scholar that Bate found and translated from a now-lost Hebrew manuscript of *Mishpeṭei ha-Mazzalot* and appended to *Iudicia*.[254] This is borne out by the Hebrew idiom and doublets (a frequent feature of Bate's translations) found in the Latin text of the gloss.[255] Bate may have been led to translate this gloss because it refers to the "aspects of the directions" or "projection of rays,"[256] the same topic covered at the end of *Iudicia*.[257] The gloss written by the anonymous Hebrew scholar is immediately followed by another long gloss with Bate's own commentary

---

[250] For this title, see below, p. 62.
[251] See *De mundo*, prologue → 2,26.
[252] See *De mundo*, prologue → 2, 26. For an explanation of these passages, see Sela 2017a, 175–180.
[253] gloss at the end of *Iudicia*, → 1.
[254] See gloss at the end of *Iudicia*, → 1–29.
[255] See gloss at the end of *Iudicia*, → 2 (numerus seu quantitas); → 5 (in oculis meis); → 8 (longitudo seu differentia); → 19 (diversi vel inequales; superfluum seu excessum; appropinquatio sive successio).
[256] For this term, see above, note 152.
[257] *Iudicia*, § 65:1–10 through § 75:1–9.

(a) on the gloss by the anonymous Hebrew scholar and (b) on the last section of *Iudicia*, both of which address the "aspects of the directions."[258] At the beginning of the anonymous Hebrew scholar's gloss, according to Bate's Latin translation, there is a reference to Abraham the Prince and to Abraham Ibn Ezra with regard to the "aspects of the directions":

> Passage A (= gloss at the end of *Iudicia*, → 5): Quoniam igitur aspectus directionum *Abrahe Principis* et *Avenerre* michi occulti sunt et absconditi, ideo sermones *Albumasar* explanabo diffusius quia recti sunt in oculis meis.
>
> Therefore, since the aspects of the directions put forward by *Abraham the Prince* and by *Ibn Ezra* are hidden and concealed from me, for that reason I will explain *Abū Maʿshar*'s statements at length because in my eyes they are right.

Note the Hebraism "recti sunt in oculis meis" ישרים בעיני, and the doublet "occulti sunt et absconditi," a clear sign that Bate was translating a Hebrew Vorlage. The Hebrew glossator's "aspectus directionum Abrahe Principis" mentioned in Passage A certainly refers to chapter 20 of Abraham Bar Ḥiyya's *Ḥešbon Mahalakhot ha-Kokhavim* (Calculation of the stellar motions), whose contents are very similar to the last section of Ibn Ezra's *Mishpeṭei ha-Mazzalot*.[259] What is more, the Hebrew glossator's "aspectus directionum Avenerre" in Passage A refer to the last chapter of Ibn Ezra's *Ṭeʿamim* I, which deals with the aspects of the directions.[260] However, whereas the anonymous Hebrew glossator was acquainted with chapter 20 of Bar Ḥiyya's *Ḥešbon Mahalakhot ha-Kokhavim*, Bate was not, and consequently took "aspectus directionum Abrahe Principis" to be a reference to the last section of *Iudicia*, which addresses the "aspects of the directions." This is supported by two passages in Bate's own gloss at the end of *Iudicia*. First, its beginning:

> Passage B (= gloss at the end of *Iudicia*, → 30): Dicit translator: quia sermones *Abrache Ducis* de planetarum aspectibus equandis in hac parte glossator iste obscuros aut insufficientes et imperfectos esse asserit, propter quod et sermonibus *Albumasar* magis adherendum esse decernit, eo quod illos in oculis suis clariores et planiores et rectiores forte iudicat.

---

[258] See gloss at the end of *Iudicia*, → 30–56.
[259] *Ḥeshbon*, ed. Millás Vallicrosa (1959), 108–117 (Hebrew section); 100–106 (Spanish section).
[260] *Ṭeʿamim* I, § 10.1:1–5 through § 10.9:1–4, 94–107.

The translator [i.e., Bate] says: because this glossator maintains that the statements of *Abraham the Prince* about the equation of the aspects of the planets in this part [i.e., in the last part of *Iudicia*] are obscure, insufficient, and imperfect, therefore he [the glossator] decided that it is more appropriate to adhere to *Abū Ma'shar*'s statements, because he judges that in his eyes they are clearer, plainer, and perhaps more correct.

In other words, Bate takes the "aspectus directionum Abrahe Principis," whose meaning is "hidden and concealed" from the Hebrew glossator (referred to by the Hebrew glossator in Passage A), to be identical with "sermones Abrache Ducis de planetarum aspectibus equandis in hac parte" (referred to by Bate, the translator, in Passage B), that is, the statements by Abraham the Prince about the calculation of the aspects of the planets in the last part of *Iudicia*, which Bate finds equally obscure, insufficient, and imperfect. Then Bate adds, several lines later in his own gloss:

> Passage C (= gloss at the end of *Iudicia*, → 51): Porro, licet in equandis planetarum aspectibus documentis *Abrache Ducis* et *Avenesre* in *Libro rationum* huius non accidant inconvenientia, nichilominus insufficiencia sunt ut prelibatum est et obscura nec non et vacillancia circa radiorum inventionem seu aspectuum et presertim ea que documentis *Abrache Ducis* et *Avenesre* superaddit in *Libro rationum* versus finem.
>
> In addition, although there are no inconsistencies in the equations of the aspects of the planets ⟨put forward⟩ in the texts by *Abraham Princeps* and by *Ibn Ezra* in his *Book of reasons*, nevertheless they are insufficient, as has been mentioned above, and there are obscure things as well as uncertainties about finding the rays or the aspects, and particularly about things that *Ibn Ezra*, towards the end of the *Book of reasons*, added to the texts of *Abraham, the Prince*.

We learn from Passage C that according to Bate "there are no inconsistencies in the equations of the aspects of the planets ⟨put forward⟩ in the texts by Abraham Princeps, and by Ibn Ezra in his *Book of reasons* (i.e., in the last chapter of *Ṭe'amim* I[261])" (= "in equandis planetarum aspectibus documentis Abrache Ducis et Avenesre in *Libro rationum* huius non accidant inconvenientia"). We also learn from Passage C that according to Bate the last chapter of Ibn Ezra's *Ṭe'amim* I is a sort of commentary on Abraham the Prince's *Iudicia* ("ea que documentis Abrache Ducis et Avenesre superaddit in *Libro rationum* versus finem" = "things that Ibn Ezra, towards the end of the *Book of reasons*, added to the texts of Abraham, the Prince"). That here

---

[261] *Ṭe'amim* I, § 10.1:1–5 through § 10.9:1–4, 94–107.

Bate makes Ibn Ezra a commentator on Bar Ḥiyya further explains why he considered Abraham Princeps to be Abraham Ibn Ezra's "master." This interpretation is supported by a gloss that Bate appended to *Rationes* I:

> Passage D (= gloss at the end of *Rationes* I, → 1–3): Dicit translator: advertendum quod etsi per documentum actoris huius in hac parte satis rationabiliter inveniri possit veritas in aspectibus equandis, et nihilominus vacillans additionis ac diminutionis per quam operandum esse docet, incertitudo regulari⟨s⟩ non est arti conveniens quale esse docet in hoc proposito. Preterea, quod, ad habendam equationem aspectuum planete distantia ab angulo, per partes horarum gradus ipsius planete dividendum esse, dicit Actor, in hoc error est secundum quod notum est ac satis declaratum in glossa quadam super *Introductorium Abrahe Ducis*, capitulo de aspectibus. Quapropter ad huiusmodi defectus ad implendos erroresque vitandos et aspectus ipsos artificiosius equandos, ac regularius ibidem regulare, quoddam et artificiosum ac breve tradidimus documentum.

> The translator says: Attention should be directed to the fact that although it is possible to find a sufficient and reasonable truth for the equation [i.e., correction] of the aspects by means of the text by this author [Ibn Ezra] in this part [i.e., the end of *Teʿamim* I], nevertheless, the uncertainty of the rules about addition or subtraction that he [Ibn Ezra] teaches should be used does not correspond to what the art should be in this case, as he [Ibn Ezra] teaches. Moreover, there is an error regarding what the author [Ibn Ezra] says, ⟨namely,⟩ that to equate [i.e., correct] the aspects of a planet by the distance from the angle, the degrees of the planet should be divided by the minutes of this planet, as has been noted and sufficiently explained in a certain gloss on the *Introduction by Abraham, the Prince*, in the chapter on the aspects [gloss at the end of *Iudicia*, → 1–29, written by an anonymous Hebrew scholar and translated by Bate]. Therefore, to overcome defects of this kind, to avoid errors, to equate [correct] these aspects more skillfully, and more in accordance with the rules, we have transmitted a document that is skillful and brief [the gloss reflecting Bate's own opinion at the end of *Iudicia*, → 30–56, after the gloss by an anonymous Hebrew scholar translated by Bate].

We see, then, that just as the marginal note on the first folio of *Iudicia* invokes "Ysagoge magistri Abrahe Ducis seu Principis" (= "the Introduction by Master Abraham the Duke or the Prince"), Passage D refers to *"Introductorium Abrahe Ducis"* (= "the Introduction by Abraham the Prince"). In the same breath Passage D also refers *in the past tense* ("tradidimus documentum" = "we have transmitted a document") to the two glosses at the end of *Iudicia*, that is, (a) the gloss translated by Bate but written by an anonymous Hebrew scholar, as well as to (b) the gloss reflecting Bate's own opinion. We also see that just as Passage C refers to *"Liber rationum* versus finem," (= "towards the end of the *Book of reasons*"), so Passage D refers to "documen-

tum actoris huius in hac parte" (= "the text by this author [Ibn Ezra] in this part [i.e., the end of *Te'amim* I]").

Let us summarize our findings so far:

(i) The "*Ysagoge magistri Abrahe Ducis seu Principi*" mentioned in the marginal note on the first folio of *Iudicia* is identical with "*Introductorium Abrahe Ducis*" mentioned in Passage D.

(ii) The Hebrew glossator's "aspectus directionum Abrahe Principis," mentioned in Passage A, refers to chapter 20 of Abraham Bar Ḥiyya's *Ḥešbon mahalakhot ha-kokhavim*, but Bate took the same "aspectus directionum Abrahe Principis," mentioned in Passage A, to be a reference to the last section of *Iudicia*, which addresses the "aspects of the directions."

(iii) The Hebrew glossator's "aspectus directionum Avenerre" in Passage A refer to the last chapter of Ibn Ezra's *Ṭe'amim* I, which deals with the aspects of the directions.

(iv) According to Bate, the last chapter of Ibn Ezra's *Ṭe'amim* I is a sort of commentary on Abraham the Prince's *Iudicia*. Bate wrote the gloss appended to *Rationes* I in order to send readers to the detailed gloss appended to *Iudicia*, where they would find Bate's remarks and instructions for correcting the defects and avoiding the errors related to the calculation of the aspects, found both in the last section of *Ṭe'amim* I, which according to Bate was by Abraham Ibn Ezra, and in the last section of *Mishpeṭei ha-Mazzalot*, which according to Bate was by Abraham Bar Ḥiyya. But note that whereas Bate finished *Rationes* I on September 15, 1292, in Orvieto, he completed *Iudicia* on October 29, 1292, in Orvieto. This means that Bate already had a draft version of *Iudicia* before he completed *Rationes* I. We will return to this point at the end of the next chapter.

4.4. The Structure of *Iudicia*

At approximately 16,300 words, *Iudicia* is Bate's second-longest translation of Ibn Ezra's astrological writings. It is an almost-complete translation of *Mishpeṭei ha-Mazzalot*—"almost" because the two manuscripts that contain the last part of *Iudicia* lack the sentences that correspond to §76:5–10 and §77:1–2, the last sentences in the print edition of *Mishpeṭei ha-Mazzalot*. Among all of Bate's translations, *Iudicia*, as we shall see, differs most radically from its Hebrew source text as we have it today.

Iudicia has 757 alternative or divergent readings from *Mishpeṭei ha-Mazzalot*—523 (69%) simple deviations and 234 (31%) double or triple trans-

lations. There are at least 74 omissions from the Hebrew source text, usually short phrases but occasionally whole sentences[262] or even a entire section of 180 words.[263] *Iudicia* incorporates at least 427 stylistic alterations and at least 74 phrases, sentences, and sections that Bate obtained from a lost manuscript of *Mishpeṭei ha-Mazzalot*, as we shall see in the next section. There are 160 glosses: 146 short, 9 of moderate length, and five long glosses. These glosses will be briefly described in the next chapter.[264]

There are strong indications that the organization and text of *Mishpeṭei ha-Mazzalot*, as we have it today, are the result of interpolations made either by Ibn Ezra in different stages of its composition or by copyists in the early stages of the transmission of the original text.[265] This is also reflected in the organization of the paragraphs in *Iudicia*, which usually follows that of *Mishpeṭei ha-Mazzalot*. A notable example relates to the indications of the twelve horoscopic houses, which both *Mishpeṭei ha-Mazzalot*, in all manuscripts I checked, and *Iudicia* organize into three discontinuous and illogical parts, as we shall see now.

The first part has the indications of the first through sixth horoscopic houses.[266] At this point, the sequence is unexpectedly interrupted and both *Mishpeṭei ha-Mazzalot* and *Iudicia* turn to Enoch's approach to the "rectification of the nativity," the so-called *trutina Hermetis* (Hermes' balance).[267] This account, too, is divided into three discontinuous parts: the first describes Enoch's *trutina Hermetis* and reports the author's own experiences with it;[268] the second part interrupts the account of the *trutina Hermetis* and discusses the distribution of the months of gestation among the planets, in the Ptolemaic order of their orbs;[269] and the third part resumes the discussion of the *trutina Hermetis* and presents is application.[270] At this point, both texts resume the account of the horoscopic houses and survey the indications of the seventh through twelfth houses.[271]

---

[262] See *Iudicia*, § 10:2; § 14:6; § 25:7; § 31:5; § 47:2.
[263] See *Iudicia*, § 5:1–3.
[264] See below, p. 107.
[265] See Sela 2017, 9–10.
[266] See *Mishpeṭei ha-mazzalot*, § 14:1–6, 500–501; cf. *Iudicia*, § 14:1–6.
[267] According to this doctrine, the position of the Moon at the moment of birth is the ascendant at the moment of conception, and vice versa. See Sela 2019 (c), 79–106.
[268] See *Mishpeṭei ha-mazzalot*, § 15:1–5, 500–503; cf. *Iudicia*, § 15:1–5.
[269] See *Mishpeṭei ha-mazzalot*, § 16:1–6, 502–503; cf. *Iudicia*, § 16:1–6.
[270] See *Mishpeṭei ha-mazzalot*, § 17:1–4, 502–505; cf. *Iudicia*, § 17:1–4.
[271] See *Mishpeṭei ha-mazzalot*, § 18:1–6, 504–505; cf. *Iudicia*, § 18:1–6.

Except for the departures noted previously, *Iudicia* tends to follow *Mishpeṭei ha-Mazzalot* rather closely, as can be seen from the critical edition and English translation of *Iudicia*.

4.5. The Source Text of *Iudicia*

So far, no French translation of *Mishpeṭei ha-Mazzalot* has been found. But folios 5r–19v of Erfurt, Universitäts- und Forschungsbibliothek, Amplon. O.89 (henceforth E), a paper and parchment manuscript from the second quarter of fourteenth century manuscript with an important collection of anonymous Latin translations of Ibn Ezra's astrological writings,[272] is the only extant copy of an anonymous Latin translation of the bulk of *Mishpeṭei ha-Mazzalot*, running from § 12:1 to the end of this work.

The collation of *Iudicia* against *Mishpeṭei ha-Mazzalot*, and particularly the comparison of *Iudicia* and E show that *Iudicia* incorporates at least 75 phrases, sentences, and entire sections whose counterpart can be found in E but not in *Mishpeṭei ha-Mazzalot*; that is, phrases, sentences and whole sections that are not Bate's alternative or divergent readings, or glosses in *Iudicia*.[273] This demonstrates that Bate's ultimate Hebrew source text for *Iudicia* was a lost manuscript of *Mishpeṭei ha-Mazzalot*, different from any of those extant today.

As noted, E is not a complete translation of *Mishpeṭei ha-Mazzalot*. However, that extensive passages of this lost manuscript of *Mishpeṭei ha-Mazzalot* are represented by long sections of *Iudicia* that do not have a counterpart in E or in *Mishpeṭei ha-Mazzalot*[274] may be extrapolated from the large number of phrases, sentences and entire sections of *Iudicia* that do have

---

[272] Besides the alternative Latin translation of *Iudicia* (fols. 5r–19v), Erfurt, UFB, Amplon. O.89 incorporates *Liber interrogationum*, an anonymous translation of *She'elot* III (fols. 19v–30r); *Liber interrogationibus ab alio editus*, an anonymous translation of *She'elot* II (fols. 30r–39v); *Liber electionum*, an anonymous translation of the lost *Mivḥarim* III (fols. 39v–46v); *Liber electionum ab Abraham Evenezre*, an anonymous translation of *Mivḥarim* II (fols. 46v–52v); *Liber nativitatum*, an anonymous translation of the lost *Moladot* II (fols. 53r–68v); *Liber revolucionum*, an anonymous translation of *Tequfah* (fols. 69r–72r); *Hec est Nativitas quedam ad instruenudum te, et est de iudiciis Abraham*, a work on nativities ascribed to Ibn Ezra (fols. 73r–76r).

[273] All these phrases, sentences and sections, whose counterpart can be found in E, are documented in the corresponding notes that accompany the English translation of *Iudicia*. In these notes the reader may also find the text of E (Latin and English translation) that corresponds to these phrases, sentences and sections.

[274] That is, in the part of *Iudicia* that corresponds to *Mishpeṭei ha-mazzalot* from its beginning up to § 12:1, where E begins.

a counterpart in E but not in *Mishpeṭei ha-Mazzalot*.[275] This conclusion seems safe because virtually none of these long sections found in *Iudicia* but with no counterpart in E or in *Mishpeṭei ha-Mazzalot*[276] incorporates the typical material of Bate's glosses, that is, explanation of terms, clarification of the Hebrew source text, or completion of what Bate took to be fragmentary phrases by Ibn Ezra.

By contrast, these long sections incorporate eight lists, typical of introductions to astrology:[277] The first, a table of the lords of the faces [decans] in each sign, from Aries to Pisces, deserves special attention.[278] *Mishpeṭei ha-Mazzalot*, as we have it today, organizes a parallel list of the lords of the faces in non-tabular form and into three completely illogical and discontinuous parts: the first begins with the lords of the three faces of Cancer (not Aries, as expected) and ends with the lords of the faces of Pisces;[279] the third part (not the second) begins with the lords of the three faces of Aries and ends with the lords of the faces of Gemini;[280] while in the middle of the section, between these two lists, we encounter the rubric "Lords of the faces" (which we would expect to find at the very beginning of the section), followed by a short explanation of how the lord of the face is determined for some specific horoscopic chart.[281] Thus, we receive the impression that while the list of lords of the faces in *Iudicia* reflects the original version of *Mishpeṭei ha-Mazzalot*, the list of lords of the faces in *Mishpeṭei ha-Mazzalot*, as we have it today, is the result of interpolations made by copyists in the early stages of the transmission of the original text.

The remaining seven lists that occur in *Iudicia* but have no counterpart in *Mishpeṭei ha-Mazzalot* as we have it today[282] are: (i) a list of the lords of the *novenaria* and their positions in each of the zodiacal signs; (ii) a list of the positions in the zodiacal signs of dark and bright degrees, pits, as well as smoking, shining, empty, and full degrees;[283] (iii) a list of the

---

[275] That is, in the segment of *Iudicia* from 12:1, where E begins, up to the end of *Iudicia* and E.

[276] That is, in the part of *Iudicia* that corresponds to *Mishpeṭei ha-mazzalot* from its beginning up to § 12:1, where E begins.

[277] All these lists are enclosed by double curly braces in the edition of *Iudicia* and its corresponding English translation.

[278] The first list follows a gloss by Bate on the lords of the faces [decans] after *Iudicia*, § 9:1.

[279] See *Mishpeṭei ha-mazzalot*, § 9:1, 494–495.

[280] See *Mishpeṭei ha-mazzalot*, § 9:3, 494–497.

[281] see *Mishpeṭei ha-mazzalot*, § 9:2, 494–495.

[282] These seven lists, one after the other, follow a gloss by Bate after *Iudicia*, § 10:7.

[283] These degrees are endowed with special astrological significance in the zodiacal signs. They are also mentioned in *Reshit Ḥokhmah*. See, for example, *Introductorius*, § 2.1:47–50.

positions of masculine and feminine degrees in the zodiacal signs; (iv) a list of the positions of pits in the constellations corresponding to the zodiacal signs; (v) a second list of the positions of the pits in the constellations corresponding to the zodiacal signs (accompanied by a gloss by Bate); (vi) a list of the positions of degrees called *azemena*[284] or defects in Taurus, Cancer, Leo, Scorpio, and Aquarius; (vii) a list of the positions of degrees increasing good fortune in the zodiacal signs.

Three of these lists are immediately followed by notes. They are significant because they include the hitherto-unknown date of composition of *Mishpeṭei ha-Mazzalot*, which does not occur in *Mishpeṭei ha-Mazzalot* as we have it today. First the note that accompanies the list of the lords of the faces [decans]:

> L, 38ra (= *Iudicia*, after gloss at § 9:1): In quodam libro scriptum inveni quod a terminis et faciebus ac ab aliis gradibus subtrahendi sunt .9. gradus in anno .921. secundum Iudeos.
>
> In a certain book I found written that 9 degrees should be subtracted from the terms and faces and from the other degrees, in the year ⟨4⟩921 [i.e., 1160/61 CE] according to the Jews.

That this note comes ultimately from an Hebrew source is supported by the use of the Hebrew calendar to specify the year in question. Also the formula "in a certain book I found written ...," without specifying the book, is typical of Ibn Ezra.[285] The second note accompanies the first list of positions of the pits:

> L, 38vb (= *Iudicia*, fourth list after gloss at § 10:1): Et omnibus hiis puteis addendi sunt 8 gradus perfecti in anno Christi 1160, secundum Iudeos autem in anno 921, ad sciendum loca eorum hiis diebus.
>
> Eight complete degrees should be added to all these pits in the year of Christ 1160, but according to the Jews in the year ⟨4⟩921 [i.e., 1160/61 C.E.], to know their positions in these days.

As in the previous note, that the present note comes ultimately from an Hebrew source is supported by the use of the Hebrew calendar to specify

---

[284] *Azemena* is a transliteration of الزمانة, used in al-Qabīṣī's *Introduction to Astrology* to denote a category of zodiacal degrees that indicate chronic diseases. See *Introduction*, ed. Burnett et al. (2004), 44–45.

[285] For similar cases, see, for example, *'Olam* I, § 38:24, 78–79; *'Olam* II, § 32:3, 176–177; *Interrogationes*, I:8, 174–175; *De nativitatibus*, II vi § 6:4, 314–315.

the year in question, although it seems to have been reworked by Bate, who added the parallel year on the Christian calendar. The third note accompanies the list of the positions of degrees called a *azemena* or defects:

> L, 38vb (= *Iudicia*, sixth list after gloss at §10:1): Pro hiis autem, id est, pro quolibet horum, subtrahendi sunt a locis in qua planetarum octo gradus hiis diebus, anno, *inquam, Christi .1160.*, quia sunt gradus qui permanent tamquam descripti et conservati in ymaginibus que sunt in spera.
>
> But for them, that is, for any of them, eight degrees should be subtracted from the places of the planets in these days, *I say, in the* YEAR OF CHRIST *1160*, because they are degrees that are still assigned to and contained in the images that are in the sphere.

In contrast to the previous note, here the year according to the Jewish calendar is omitted, but Bate adds a gloss with the year according to the Christian calendar. That this note belonged to the lost manuscript of *Mishpeṭei ha-Mazzalot* is also borne out by the fact that immediately after this note *Iudicia* has a gloss in which "the translator," that is, Henry Bate, refers to this note as written by "the author," that is, Abraham Bar Ḥiyya, and compares the content of this note with that of the two aforementioned notes:

> L, 38vb (= *Iudicia*, following the note after the sixth list): Translator inquit: notandum quod idem est id quod hic dicit actor de subtractione .8. graduum et quod prius dixit de additione eorumdem.
>
> The translator says: note that what the author [Abraham Bar Ḥiyya] says here about the subtraction of 8 degrees is the same as what he said above about their addition.

Moreover, that all three notes provide the same year (⟨4⟩921 according the Jewish calendar or 1160–1161 according to the Christian calendar) and Bate refers to them as "what the author [Abraham Bar Ḥiyya] says here about the subtraction of 8 degrees and what he said above about their addition," strongly indicates that all three notes, as well as the lists they accompany, were originally part of the same text; namely, the lost Hebrew manuscript of *Mishpeṭei ha-Mazzalot* that served as source text for *Iudicia* and for E.

As already mentioned, the Hebrew text of *Mishpeṭei ha-Mazzalot*, according to the surviving manuscripts, does not provide an explicit date of composition. But terminological links with Ibn Ezra's other astrological writings and the report of an astronomical observation suggest that it was written late in Ibn Ezra's career, when he was living in Rouen or in Eng-

land.²⁸⁶ The three notes just quoted fit well with this and now allow us to establish a specific date for the composition of *Mishpeṭei ha-Mazzalot*: Anno mundi 4921 according to the Hebrew calendar, which corresponds to AD 1160–1161 on the Christian calendar.

5. *Liber de mundo vel seculo*

The first component of Henry Bate's translation project is *Liber de mundo vel seculo* (Book of the world or the age; henceforth *De mundo*).²⁸⁷ This is a complete Latin translation of Ibn Ezra's first version of *Sefer ha-ʿOlam* (*Book of the world*, henceforth *ʿOlam* I), approximately 6,400 words and extant in at least 34 Hebrew manuscripts.²⁸⁸

5.1. The Contents and Sources of *ʿOlam* I

ʿOlam I deals with world astrology, that is, the prognostication of future events as well as the reconstruction and interpretation of past political, historical, and religious events. *ʿOlam* I also addresses weather forecasting. This is done by means of methods such as the interpretation of solar and lunar eclipses, the analysis of horoscopes cast in years of Saturn-Jupiter conjunctions, and the use of a great variety of periods, indicators, and cycles.

In the very first sentence of *ʿOlam* I Ibn Ezra unleashes a harsh attack on Abū Maʿshar, the most prominent astrologer of the Middle Ages.²⁸⁹ After that, the "120 conjunctions of the seven planets" is the first topic addressed.²⁹⁰ The content of *ʿOlam* I, like that of all medieval treatises on world astrology, is an accumulation of sources and doctrines that go back to the very beginnings of the astrological literature.

Antiquity is represented by Enoch, a legendary figure who derives from the god incarnate Hermes Trismegistus and was taken over by the Muslim

---

²⁸⁶ See Sela 2017, 28–29.
²⁸⁷ For this title, see below, p. 62. References to the Latin text and the English translation of *De mundo* are in the format: *De mundo*, § 12:2 = *De mundo*, section 12, passage 2.
²⁸⁸ Sela 2010, 295–296.
²⁸⁹ Ibn Ezra enjoins readers neither to like nor to trust Abū Maʿshar's *Book on the conjunction of the planets*, because it relies on the mean motion for the planetary conjunctions. Moreover, readers are warned not to trust Abū Maʿshar's book because a certain prediction regarding rain was not borne out by experience. *ʿOlam* I, § 1:1–3, 52–53; § 61:1–5, 92–93.
²⁹⁰ That is, the sum of the combinations of two, three, four, five, six, and seven planets. Ibn Ezra borrowed this numerical-cosmological pattern from the fiftieth aphorism of Pseudo-Ptolemy's *Centiloquium*. The lengthy explanations of the 120 conjunctions in *ʿOlam* I constitute Ibn Ezra's original attempt to provide a mathematical demonstration of each of the partial combinations of two, three, four, five, six, and seven planets. See *ʿOlam* I, § 2:1–4, 52–53; § 3:1–3, 52–53; § 4:1–7, 52–55; § 5:1–20, 54–55; § 6:1–7, 54–55. See Sela 2003, 313–323.

world as divided into the triple Hermes. Ibn Ezra follows this tradition closely and refers to the triple Enoch—the "Ancient Enoch," "Enoch the First," and "Enoch the Egyptian"—in three separate sections of *'Olam* I.[291] The common denominator of Ibn Ezra's three Enochs is that they produced "lists" of correspondences between planets or pairs consisting of a single planet and a single zodiacal sign, on the one hand, and various groups of people or geographical zones, on the other. *'Olam* I also invokes "Enoch," with no accompanying epithet.[292]

The Hellenistic period is represented by two authorities. The first is the astrologer Dorotheus of Sidon, referred to as King Dorotheus, who quotes from Enoch's *Book of secrets*.[293] The second and far more important source from the Hellenistic period is Claudius Ptolemy. The most prominent tool from the Hellenistic period for making world predictions, and the main astrological doctrine for which Ibn Ezra is indebted to Ptolemy, is the astrological theory of solar and lunar eclipses, covered in two sizeable sections of *'Olam* I.[294]

Ibn Ezra is also aware of a Persian layer in world astrology. The most prominent Persian doctrine received by the Arabic world and later bequeathed to Hebrew and Latin culture is the use of the cycles of the conjunctions of Saturn and Jupiter for world predictions or historical analysis. Ibn Ezra devoted four substantial sections in *'Olam* I to the exposition of the tripartite model of conjunctionalism.[295] As a rule, in *'Olam* I, the Saturn-Jupiter conjunctions play the relatively modest role of shaping the history of cities, signifying war, high or low prices, famine, and drought or plenty.[296] But in *'Olam* I we also read that the great conjunction "signifies that a prophet will come to found a nation."[297]

In *'Olam* I Ptolemy is credited with an astronomical theory (elaborated, in Ibn Ezra's account, with the collaboration of Indian, Egyptian, and Per-

---

[291] See *'Olam* I, § 36:1–2, 76–77; § 37:1–2, 76–77; § 56:1–15, 88–89;

[292] See *'Olam* I, § 32:1, 72–73. This is how Enoch is frequently referred to in Ibn Ezra's oeuvre, usually in an approving tone.

[293] See *'Olam* I, § 32:1, 72–73.

[294] See *'Olam* I, § 19:1–2, 64–65; § 29:1–8, 70–71; § 30:1–6. 70–73; § 31:1–2, 72–73.

[295] In its standard form these conjunctions are divided into three types or cycles: the "small" conjunction, with a period of 20 years between two successive conjunctions; the "middle" conjunction, with a period of 240 years between two shifts from one triplicity to another; and the "great" conjunction, with a period of 960 years between two conjunctions in the head of Aries. *'Olam* I, § 7:1–4, 56–57; § 8:1–4, 56–57; § 9:1–6, 56–57; § 10:1–2, 56–57.

[296] *'Olam* I, § 25:1–5, 68–69 (cities); § 32:1–8, 72–75 (cities); § 39:1–9, 76–77 (wars, cities); § 40:1–3, 78–79 (famine and plenty, high/low prices); § 42:1–7, 80–81 (cities, high/low prices of wheat); § 43:1–4, 80–81 (price of olive oil); § 57:1–4, 88–91 (drought/plenty in cities).

[297] *'Olam* I, § 10:2, 56–57.

sian scientists, as well as Dorotheus) which holds that, because it is impossible to determine the sign of the ascendant at the hour of the conjunction of Saturn and Jupiter, the astrologer should observe the moment of the luminaries' conjunction or opposition, whichever occurs last before the Sun enters Aries.[298] Ibn Ezra also explicitly mentions the Persian contribution apropos of the *fardār*,[299] a Persian term which appears in Arabic, Hebrew, and Latin texts and is used in both historical astrology and nativities as a period of 75 years.

Regarding weather predictions, Ibn Ezra speaks in *'Olam* I of a planet that is a "key" (מפתח) to another: "the lord of the seventh house ⟨counting⟩ from the ⟨house of an⟩ upper planet is always its key."[300] In addition, *'Olam* I offers a full account of the "12 keys of the Moon"—12 phases of the Moon that are considered to have influence on the weather, particularly on rain—and connects them to the aforementioned procedure for forecasting rain, in which a planet is a "key" to another.[301] In addition, *'Olam* I ascribes the 28 mansions of the Moon to the scientists of India.[302]

In *'Olam* I, as a rule, Ibn Ezra speaks about the contributions of Arab astronomers in highly favorably terms.[303] He also refers approvingly to the astronomical tables compiled by Arab astronomers—referring to them collectively as "scientists who rely on experience"[304]—or specifically to the tables of al-Battānī,[305] and does not fail to mention the contribution of Arab builders of astronomical instruments, such as the Banū Shākir.[306]

5.2. The Manuscripts

De mundo is the most widespread of Bate's translations: it was published in the Renaissance[307] and is extant in no fewer than 39 complete and incomplete manuscripts—two from the thirteenth century, nine from the fourteenth century, and the rest from the fifteenth century.[308] *De mundo* is

---

[298] *'Olam* I, § 11:1–5, 58–59; § 18:2, 62–65.
[299] *'Olam* I, § 23:1, 66–67; § 24:1, 68–69.
[300] *'Olam* I, § 47:1–2, 82–83.
[301] *'Olam* I, § 47:4, 84–85; § 48:1–14, 84–85.
[302] *'Olam* I, § 62:1–5, 92–93; § 63:1–2, 92–93. The lunar mansions is a division of the zodiac into 28 parts that are relevant to weather forecasting and astrology. Because the lunar month has approximately 28 days, each lunar mansion was taken to be the place where the Moon "lodges" on one day of the lunar month.
[303] See *'Olam* I, § 14:9, 60–61.
[304] *'Olam* I, § 11:3, 58–59.
[305] *'Olam* I, § 17:5; § 63:3.
[306] *'Olam* I, § 13:4–5, 58–59.
[307] *De mundo* (Bate), ed. Liechtenstein (1507).
[308] For a list of 34 manuscripts and editions, see Juste 2018 (a), 51. In addition to the

also the only one of Bate's six complete translations of Ibn Ezra's astrological writings that has received a critical edition, by Carlos Steel.[309] Steel also recently published a critical edition, accompanied by an English translation and detailed and insightful notes, of Bate's prologue to *De mundo*.[310]

Steel's edition of *De mundo*, based principally on a collation of the two earliest complete manuscripts (Paris, BnF, n.a.l. 3091, 13th century, fols. 107vb–113rb; and Leipzig, UB, 1466, 14th century, fols. 24ra–30va) is excellent. With his permission I have included it in the current volume, without the corresponding critical apparatus.[311] However, because my approach to translating the Latin text is rather different than Steel's, my English translation of Bate's prologue to *De mundo* is rather dissimilar from his.

5.3. Title, Authorship, and Place and Date of Composition

There is no consensus in the manuscripts of Bate's translation of *'Olam* I regarding the title of this work. The incipits and explicits employ a bewildering variety of names, but the most frequent is *Liber de mundo vel seculo* (Book of the world or the age; henceforth *De mundo*).[312] This name, which includes a double translation of the Hebrew title עולם, "world," is logical: the doublet "mundus vel seculum" occurs at least nine times in three of Bate's other translations,[313] unconnected to this translation, and as a disambiguation of the Hebrew term עולם, which can mean both "world" and "eternity."[314]

---

manuscripts mentioned in this list, fragments of *'Olam* I are found in the following five fragmentary manuscripts: Berlin, SBPK, lat. fol. 246, s. XV, f. 113ra–113vb; London, BL, Sloane 702, s. XV, f. 10v; Oxford, BL, Digby 161, s. XIV, f. 1r; Prague, NKCR, III.C.2 (433), s. XV, f. 117va–118rb; Vatican, BAV, Pal. lat. 1380, s. XIV, f. 85r–86v. I thank David Juste for this additional list. See also *De mundo* (Bate), ed. Steel (2019), 230–231.

[309] *De mundo* (Bate), ed. Steel (2019), 227–278.

[310] Steel 2020 (a), 245–281.

[311] Readers interested in the critical apparatus of this edition are invited to consult the relevant parts of Steel's critical edition of *De mundo*. See *De mundo* (Bate), ed. Steel (2019), 245–278.

[312] This name is used in the incipit of the earliest manuscript (Paris, BnF, MS n.a.l. 3091, fol. 107vb), as well as in the incipit of Ghent, UB, MS 2 (417/152), fol. 45v. The same name occurs in the explicits of the following manuscripts: Limoges, BM, MS 9 (28), fol. 143v; Paris, BnF, MS lat. 7336, fol. 109r; Paris, BnF, MS lat. 10269, fol. 99rb; Zurich, Zentralbibl., MS B.244 (769), fol. 87ra; Oxford, Bodleian, MS Canon. Misc. 190, fol. 72r; Ghent, UB, MS 2 (417/152), fol. 54r; London, BL, MS Sloane 312, fol. 96v.

[313] See *Rationes* II, § 2.2:1; § 2.4:6; § 2.4:8; § 2.7:1; § 6.2:1; *Introductorius*, § 2.4:34; § 10.2:7; § 10.2:10; *Iudicia*, § 1:9.

[314] For an explanation of this doublet, see note on *Introductorius*, § 2.4:34, s.v., "sign of the age or of the world."

Significant information about the author of *De mundo* and its source text, as well as about its place and date of composition, is given in the explicits, which exist in short and long versions. Most of the specimens of the short version mention the author of the translation and the language of the source text, but not the year of composition and the author of the source text.[315] More information is provided in the long version of the explicit found in three manuscripts and in the 1507 Venice edition by Liechtenstein:

> Oxford Digby 212, fol. 52v: Explicit *Liber de mundo vel seculo*, completus die Lune post festum Beati Luce hora diei quasi 10, anno Domini 1281, inceptus in Leodio, perfectus in Machlinia, translatus a magistro Henrico Bate de Hebreo in Latinum.[316]

> Here ends the *Book of the world or the age*, completed on the Monday after the Feast of Saint Luke, at about the tenth hour, in the year of the Lord 1281, started in Liège, completed in Mechelen, translated by Master Henry Bate from Hebrew into Latin.

According to this explicit, *De mundo* was finished on October 20, 1281, the Monday after the feast of St. Luke (October 18, which fell on Saturday in 1281). The use of the ecclesiastical calendar is typical of Bate. Despite the great diversity of the explicits, virtually all of them agree that *De mundo* was translated "de Hebreo in Latinum." We will return to this point later.

5.4. The Structure of *De mundo*

At approximately 9,800 words, *De mundo* is a complete Latin rendering of '*Olam* I, but markedly different from its Hebrew source text. *De mundo* has 414 alternative and divergent readings from '*Olam* I: 386 (93.2%) simple deviations and 28 (6.8%) double or triple translations. There are also at least 69 omissions from the Hebrew source text and at least 234 stylistic alterations. There are a total of 69 glosses: (a) 57 short glosses, consisting of a few words;[317] (b) two of moderate length (a few lines);[318] and (c) two long glosses; the first, which constitutes Bate's prologue to *De mundo*, runs

---

[315] See, for example, the explicit in Paris, BnF, MS n.a.l. 3091, fol. 113rb (quoted below, on p. 93) and Limoges, BM, 9 (28), fol. 143v.

[316] See Oxford, MS Digby 212, fol. 52v; Vienna, ÖNB, Cod. 5309, fol. 264r; Basel, UB, MS F.II.10, s. fol. 90rb; and the print edition, ed. Petrus Liechtenstein, Venice, 1507, sig. LXXXVra.

[317] All the glosses are marked in italics in the critical edition and English translation of *De mundo*.

[318] See *De mundo*, gloss at § 6:6; and gloss at § 13:8.

to 1700 words (17% of the entire work); the second is 190 words.[319] These glosses will be briefly described in the next chapter.[320]

Other than these departures, *De mundo* follows '*Olam* I rather closely, as illustrated in the critical edition and English translation of *De mundo*.

5.5. The Source Text of *De mundo*

De mundo is the only extant Latin translation of '*Olam* I; no French translation of that work has been found to date. By contrast with all the other five translations, however, virtually all the explicits of the available manuscripts agree that *De mundo* was translated "de Hebreo in Latinum." Since Bate never informs us that he had studied Hebrew, despite this assertion it is extremely unlikely that Bate himself directly translated '*Olam* I from a Hebrew manuscript.[321]

6. *Liber Abrahe Avenesre de luminaribus*

The second item in Henry Bate's translation project is *Liber Abrahe Avenesre de luminaribus* (Book of the luminaries by Abraham Ibn Ezra; henceforth *De luminaribus*),[322] a complete Latin version of *Sefer ha-Me'orot* (Book of the luminaries; henceforth *Me'orot*); its 4,300 words are extant in at least 35 Hebrew manuscripts.[323]

6.1. The Contents of *Me'orot*

Me'orot deals with medical astrology according to the Greek theory of the critical days; namely, that the course of acute diseases is determined by "crises" or "critical days" when marked changes in the symptoms take place and the disease reaches a climax, whether for good or evil. The Moon's position with respect to its position at the onset of the disease was thought to be connected to the time and character of these "critical days."

Me'orot starts with a cosmological preface on the source of the light of the Sun and Moon, in a cosmology that divides reality into "three domains": the supernal domain, the domain of the stars and orbs, and the sublunar domain.[324] The rest of the introduction to *Me'orot* is devoted to a defense

---

[319] See *De mundo*, prologue → 1–54; gloss at § 24:7 → 1–10.
[320] See below, p. 102.
[321] This point is expanded below, at p. 93.
[322] For this title, see below, p. 67. References to the Latin text and the English translation of *De luminaribus* are in the format: *De luminaribus*, § 20:2 = *De luminaribus*, section 20, passage 2.
[323] Sela 2011, 532–533.
[324] *Me'orot*, § 1:1–11, 452–455. In this framework, Ibn Ezra places the orbs of Mercury and

of the astrological theory behind the critical days, conveyed as a debate between a proponent and an opponent.[325] Then *Me'orot* is divided into four parts.

The first, subdivided into ten chapters, addresses the prognoses that may be indicated by various astrological and astronomical configurations at the onset of the disease, or by the Moon's being in quadrature or opposition with respect to its position at the onset of the disease.[326]

The second part is concerned with three technical definitions: conjunction, opposition, and quadrature. They are relevant to the main subject of *Me'orot* because they refer to the positions of the Moon and of any planet aspecting it on the critical days. Conjunction and opposition are defined according to the extent to which the Moon's testimony is valid; quadrature and opposition are defined by placing the Moon and the conjoining or aspecting planet in the framework of the cardines and the horoscope taken at the time of the onset of the disease.[327]

The third part, a single long "chapter of the conjunctions," consists of eleven sections that describe the prognosis of a disease, based on the conjunctions of the Moon with a planet, set of planets, or a fixed star, at its onset. As a rule, the prognosis depends on the nature of the star that conjoins the Moon. A disease is cured or alleviated by an astrological effect whose nature is the opposite of the disease's cause, and vice versa.[328]

The fourth part consists of two brief "chapters." The first deals with the conditions that must be satisfied for the astrological indications of the critical days to be valid—namely, that the Moon be aspected by the same planet at the onset of the disease and on the critical day. The second "chapter" is the only substantial section in *Me'orot* that deals exclusively with prognoses of diseases related to the Sun's annual path. Hence the cycle of critical days takes a full year to be completed, as against one month for acute diseases.[329]

Venus above that of the Sun, and the orb of the Sun above that of the Moon. This is the only locus in his entire oeuvre where he does so. See *Me'orot*, § 1:3, 452–453.

[325] *Me'orot*, § 3:3–7 through § 9:1–9, 454–461.
[326] *Me'orot* § 10:1–2 through § 19:1–3, 462–462.
[327] *Me'orot*, §§ 20–22, 466–469.
[328] *Me'orot*, §§ 23–33, 468–481.
[329] *Me'orot*, §§ 34–35, 480–483.

6.2. The Manuscripts

Bate's translation of *Me'orot* is the second most widespread of his translations: it was published in the Renaissance[330] and at the beginning of the modern era[331] and is extant in no fewer than 10 manuscripts, eight of them complete—three from the fourteenth century, six from the fifteenth century, and one from the sixteenth century.[332]

A preliminary collation of all eight complete witnesses led to the choice of three to be used for the critical edition, because, as we shall see, they belong to two rather divergent families and fill lacunae in the oldest manuscript:

L   Leipzig, Universitätsbibliothek, 1466, fols. 30va–34rb, copied around 1300 or in the first quarter of the 14th century in northern France, incorporates a complete copy of *De luminaribus*. For a detailed description of this manuscript, see Appendix 2, pp. 1101–1103.

M   Limoges, Bibliothèque municipale, 9 (28), fols 66r–71v, copied in the 14th century, contains a complete copy of Bate's translation of *Me'orot*. For a detailed description of this manuscript and its contents, see Appendix 3, pp. 1104–1106.

U   Prague, Národní Knihovna České Republiky, III.C.2 (433), second half of the 15th century, 217 folios, is a collection of astrological (particularly related to weather forecasting), astronomical, and medical texts. Folios 118vb–123ra are a a complete copy of Bate's translation of *Me'orot*.

These three manuscripts were found to fall into two families: LU in one and **M** in the other. This is reflected by that fact that LU have the same readings in 43 cases, against a divergent reading in **M**, while LM have the same readings in only two cases against a divergent reading in U. As in the cases of the other translations, both families seem to come from the exemplar of Bate's translation of *Me'orot* in his own library, a lost manuscript earlier than L.

L, the earliest of the extant manuscripts, served as the base text of the critical edition. Nevertheless, it was not followed slavishly. This refers particularly to cases where **M** follows the Hebrew text while filling lacunae

---

[330] Padua, [Matthaeus Cerdonis] 7 Feb. 1482/1483; Lyons, Johannes Trechsel, 1496, sig. f6v–f8r.
[331] Lyons, Johannes Cleyn, 1508, sig. h1rb–h3rb; Lyons, 1614.
[332] For a list of these manuscripts, see Juste 2018 (a), 52.

in LU,[333] and to cases where **M** is closer to the Hebrew than LU or offers readings that are more correct grammatically or logically than that of LU.[334] U was also preferred in a few cases because its readings are closer to the Hebrew than that of LM.[335]

6.3. Title, Authorship, and Place and Date of Composition

In the manuscripts, the title most frequently assigned to Bate's source text as well as to his translation of *Me'orot* is *Liber Abrahe Avenesre de luminaribus* (Book of the luminaries by Abraham Ibn Ezra; henceforth *De luminaribus*), which is a literal rendering of the Hebrew title (*Sefer ha-Me'orot* = Book of the luminaries);[336] the second most frequent title is *Tractatus/Liber Abrahe Avenare de luminaribus seu/et diebus creticis* (Book of the luminaries and/or the critical days by Abraham Ibn Ezra), which adds words referring to the book's main content.[337]

The translator of *De luminaribus* and the date and place of completion of the translation are stated in only two of the surviving manuscripts. This is the most complete:

> M, 71v (= *De luminaribus*, explicit): Explicit *Liber de luminaribus*. Pulcherrimas laudes habeat ille qui omnes creat creaturas. Perfectus 4 die iunii, anno Domini 1292, die Mercurii, Sole occidente in Urbe Veteri, translatus in Latinum a magistro Henrico de Malinis, dicto Bate, pro reverendo patre domino A, presule Aversano.[338]

> Here ends the *Book of the luminaries*. Glorious praises to Him who created all creatures. Completed on June 4, in the year 1292 of the Lord, on Tuesday, when the Sun was setting in Orvieto, translated into Latin by Master Henry of Malines, called Bate, on behalf of the reverend father Lord A⟨dam⟩, bishop of Aversa.

Thus, *De luminaribus* was the first in a series of five Latin translations of Ibn Ezra's astrological writings carried out by Bate in the same place and around

---

[333] See, for example, in the apparatus, note 52 at § 24:8; note 53 at § 24:9; note 58 at § 29:4; note 52 at § 24:8; note 60 at § 30:1.

[334] See, for example, in the apparatus, note 17 at § 4:2; note 27 in gloss at § 10:2; note 28 at § 11:2; note 46 at § 20:2; note 56 at § 29:1.

[335] See, in the apparatus, note 19 at § 5:2; note 30 at § 13:2.

[336] See M, 66r, 71v; L, 34rb (in the margin); Paris, BnF, lat. 16195, 5ra, 6vb; Glasgow, UL, Hunterian Museum 461, 114r.

[337] See L, fol. 30va; MS Praghe, NKCR, VI.F.7 (1144), fol. 147r; Vicenza, Bibl. Civica Bertoliana, 208, fols. 95r, 103v.

[338] The explicit of M renders this name as "N presule Aversano" but Glasgow UL 461, 114r, renders this name as "A presule Aversano." This is a reference to Adam, bishop of Aversa.

the same time. The dedicatee, the "reverend father Lord A⟨dam⟩," is Adam of Bray, bishop of Aversa between 1276 and 1293, a native of Picardy, who with the support of Charles I of Anjou (1226/7–1285) served as bishop of Aversa until his death in 1293. Adam probably stayed in Orvieto for some time during the prolonged conclave after the death of Nicholas IV. It is there that he may have become acquainted with Bate, with whom he could converse in Picardian on matters of common interest. Given Adam's interest in medical matters, it is possible that Bate also composed his *De diebus creticis* for him.[339]

6.4. The Structure of the *De luminaribus*

At approximately 5,500 words, *De luminaribus* is by far Bate's shortest translation of Ibn Ezra's astrological writings. Although a full translation, *De luminaribus* is markedly different from its Hebrew source text. There are 260 alternative and divergent readings from *Me'orot*: 205 (78.5%) are simple deviations and 55 (21.5%) double or triple translations. There are also at least 45 omissions from the Hebrew source text and at least 172 stylistic alterations. *De luminaribus* has nine phrases and omissions that derive from a lost manuscript of *Me'orot*, as we shall see in the next section. There are 66 glosses, 52 of them consisting of a few words, and 14 that are entire sentences. These glosses will be briefly described in the next chapter.[340] There are no long glosses in *De luminaribus*.

Besides these departures, *De luminaribus* follows *Me'orot* rather closely, as can be seen from the critical edition and English translation of *De luminaribus*.

6.5. The Source Text of *De luminaribus*

Apart from Bate's *De luminaribus*, we know of two additional Latin translations of *Me'orot*: *Liber de luminaribus* by Pietro d'Abano, extant in at least nine manuscripts and one print edition;[341] and *Liber Abraham de terminatione morborum* (Book by Abraham on the imposition of the boundary of the diseases), in whose production was involved Pierre de Limoges and extant in two manuscripts.[342] The collation of *Me'orot* against Pietro d'Abano's *Liber de luminaribus* and Pierre de Limoges' *Liber Abraham de*

---

[339] For this work by Bate, see above, p. 18; for the contact between Bate and Adam, bishop of Aversa, see Steel and Vanden Broecke 2018, 38–39.
[340] See below, p. 104.
[341] See Sela 2019 (d), 1–82, esp. pp. 66–70.
[342] See Sela, Sela 2019 (b), 15–20.

terminatione morborum revelas that there are at least nine phrases worded similarly in the translations by Bate, Pietro d'Abano, and Pierre de Limoges, but not found or with a different form in *Me'orot*. All these cases are documented in the corresponding notes to the English translation of Bates *De luminaribus*.[343]

This demonstrates that the three translators ultimately relied on a lost Hebrew manuscript of *Me'orot*. No French translation of *Me'orot* has been found so far, but the existence of so many Latin translations which agree among themselves but disagree with *Me'orot*, as we have it today, also suggests that the same lost manuscript of *Me'orot* that served Bate, Pietro, and Pierre was also used by Hagin le Juif to produce a lost French version. It should be taken in consideration not only that Bate commissioned Hagin to produce French translations of Ibn Ezra's astrological writings and that they were neighbors in Mechelen,[344] but also that Pietro says he found a copy of Ibn Ezra's astrological writings in French[345] and the earliest manuscript with Hagin le Juif's French translations of Ibn Ezra's astrological writings is full of marginal notes in Pierre's handwriting.[346]

BATE'S MODUS OPERANDI AS A TRANSLATOR

In this part of the introduction we study the most salient features of Henry Bate's *modus operandi* as a translator of Ibn Ezra's astrological writings. First we examine his use of double or triple translations for a single word or locution, a feature that readers of his translations will agree is his signature. Then we investigate Bate's familiarity with Hebrew and how he applied this knowledge in his translations. Next we review the additions and glosses Bate incorporated into the translations and seek his motives for proceeding in this way. Finally, we summarize Bate's trajectory as a translator of Ibn Ezra's astrological writings.

1. *Henry Bate and the Art of the Doublet*

The most conspicuous stylistic feature of Bate's *modus operandi* in his Latin translations is the frequent double and sometimes triple translations of a single word or expression in his source text, reflecting Bate's uncertainty

---

[343] See *De luminaribus*, § 10:2 note 6; § 22:3 note 2; § 23:6 note 4; § 24:3 note 1; § 24:4 note 2; § 25:4 note 2; § 29:1 note 2; § 30:1 note 1; § 33:3 note 5; § 33:4 note 8.
[344] Sela 2021, 77–78.
[345] Sela 2019 (d), 19–20.
[346] Sela 2019 (b), 30, 38.

about what Latin term best represents the Hebrew or French source. A study of the words or expressions rendered as doublets or triplets, an examination of their contents, and scrutiny of Bate's motives for multiple translations of specific words or expressions, highlight the details of this conspicuous stylistic feature and reveal his linguistic approach to the art of translation, his wide general knowledge, and his acquaintance with the Latin technical astrological and astronomical vocabulary in vogue in his time.

Let us begin with the quantitative aspect. Other Latin translators produced double or triple translations of a single word on occasion,[347] but not with the frequency found in Bate's translations of Ibn Ezra. Table 3 displays his fondness for this method (in descending order):

TABLE 3

Latin translation	Hebrew source text	Words	Divergent and alternative readings	Doublets & triplets	Per cent
Introductorius	Reshit Hokhmah	34,900	1,980	406	20.5%
Rationes I	Teʿamim I	16,100	757	234	31%
Rationes II	Teʿamim II	14,100	707	190	27%
Iudicia	Mishpeṭei ha-Mazzalot	16,300	757	234	31%
De luminaribus	Meʾorot	5,500	260	55	21.5%
De mundo	ʿOlam I	9,800	414	28	6.8%

We see, then, that with the exception of De mundo, Bate's first complete translation, in all the others between one-fifth and almost one-third of the alternative and divergent readings in the corresponding translation are dou-

---

[347] One example is the Latin translation of Kelal qaṭan, a Hebrew work on medical astrology based on Ibn Ezra's Meʾorot, where we find, inter alia, the following doublets: "flebotomari vel flebotomiam facere" for להקיז דם "bloodletting"; "motus vel cursus" for הליכה "motion"; "mala vel impedimenta" for רעות "calamities." See Charles Burnett's critical edition of this text in Kelal Qaṭan, ed. Bos et al. (2005), 64–71.

blets or triplets—indeed a large number. We also see that Bate's fondness for doublets became stronger as his translational experience increased, reaching its peak in his last translations (*Rationes* I, *Rationes* II, and *Iudicia*).

I now focus on doublets and triplets strictly related to astrology and astronomy that Bate used (i) more than once in a single translation; (ii) in more than one of his translations, and (iii) only once, but which render important astrological or astronomical terms. To make the content more comprehensible, they are divided below into the astrological and astronomical categories to which they pertain. In what follows, when with regard to some term or phrase a footnote points to a specific locus in one of Bate's Latin translations (i.e., "see *Introductorius*, § 1.10:4"), the reference is to the contents of the note that documents the term or phrase in the locus specified.

1.1. The Zodiac, the Ecliptic, and the Zodiacal Signs

The zodiac is a narrow strip, inclined with respect to the celestial equator, that divides the celestial sphere in half and in which the planets are confined and travel. It is conventionally divided into 360 degrees. The zodiacal signs are twelve equal divisions of the zodiac, 30° each, beginning from the vernal equinox. The ecliptic is the apparent path that the Sun follows through the zodiac over the course of the year. Astrological tradition groups the zodiacal signs in various categories and usually assigns them metaphorical names. To denote these and other elements related to the zodiac Ibn Ezra usually uses Hebrew terms that are literal translations from the Arabic. In his translations, Bate sometimes clarifies these names by means of doublets or triplets, as in the following examples:

(i) To denote the zodiac Ibn Ezra frequently writes גלגל המזלות, "circle of the signs," translated by Hagin as "cercle des signes" and subsequently by Bate in *Introductorius* as "circulus signorum" = "circle of the signs."[348] In *Introductorius* Bate takes the liberty to translate Hagin's "cercle" or "orbe," which in their turn, translate גלגל, "circle," as "zodiacus."[349] But In *Rationes* I and *Rationes* II Bate uses "zodiacus" to translate גלגל המזלות, circle of the signs.[350] In a gloss in *Iudicia*,

---

[348] See, for example, *Introductorius*, § 3:1; § 1.10:4 *et passim*; cf. *Reshit Ḥokhmah*, § 3:1, 50–51. See also, *Iudicia*, § 1:7; § 12:1; *Rationes* I, § 1.3:7; § 10.2:2; § 10.3:1 *et passim*; *Rationes* II, § 1.2:5; § 4.4:1 *et passim*.

[349] See *Introductorius*, § 1.11:1; § 8.7:1; § 10.1:8.

[350] See *Rationes* I, § 2.12:7; § 5.3:3; *Rationes* II, § 1.2:6.

though, Bate uses the doublet "obliquus circulus vel zodiacus" even when not translating.[351]

(ii) To denote the ecliptic, Ibn Ezra uses the biblical expression חשב אפודת הגלגל, "the girdle of the vest of the circle."[352] Hagin renders this expression, which appears several times in *Reshit Ḥokhmah*, as "ceint dil ymaginacion du cercle"; Bate, as "cingulum ymaginationis circuli signorum" = "the girdle of the imagination of the circle of the signs"[353] or "cingulum orbis signorum" = "girdle of the orb of the signs"[354] or "linea cinguli signorum" = "line of the girdle of the orb of the signs"[355] In *Rationes* I, though, Bate twice employs the doublet "cingulum orbis signorum sive ecliptice linee" = "girdle of the orb of the signs or line of the ecliptic,"[356] and in *De mundo* "linea ecliptica" or "ecliptica" tout court[357] to translate the same expression חשב אפודת הגלגל, "the girdle of the vest of the circle."

(iii) For the bicorporal signs (Gemini, Virgo, Sagittarius, and Pisces), *Reshit Ḥokhmah* has שתי צורות, "two figures," and יש לו שני גופות, "it has two bodies." In Hagin's French these become ".2. figures," and "et a .2. cors." Bate, in *Introductorius*, renders the first expression by means of the triplet "duarum figurarum seu bicorpor vel duas habens figuras" = "of two figures or double-bodied or having two forms" and the second expression as "duorum corporum sive bicorpor" = "of two bodies or bicorporal."[358] Bate's *Rationes* II and *Iudicia* represent the second Hebrew expression by means of the same doublet as he uses in *Introductorius*.[359] We see that in both cases one component of the doublet or the triplet is a literal translation of the Hebrew and the other is the common Latin technical term.

(iv) For Ibn Ezra, the tropical signs (Aries, Cancer, Libra, Capricorn) are מתהפכים, "turning ⟨signs⟩," or "reversing direction." Hagin, in his translation of *Reshit Ḥokhmah*, renders this as "s'est trestournans"; Bate's

---

[351] See gloss at *Iudicia*, § 22:1.
[352] The expression חשב אפדתו appears in this context in the poem *Keter malḥut* (Royal crown) by Solomon Ibn Gabirol (ca. 1021–ca. 1057); see Rodriguez Arribas 2009: 323.
[353] See *Introductorius*, § 1.10:5; cf. *Reshit Ḥokhmah*, § 1.10:5, 56–57. For an explanation of why Hagin and Bate uses these peculiar translations, see note on *Introductorius*, § 1.10:5, s.v., "in the girdle of the imagination of the circle of the signs."
[354] See, for example, *Introductorius*, § 2.14:1; cf. *Reshit Ḥokhmah*, § 2.14:1, 132–133.
[355] See, for example, *Introductorius*, § 6.3:2.
[356] *Rationes* I, § 1.2:1 and § 1.3:3; cf. *Ṭeʿamim* I, § 1.2:1, 28–29 and § 1.3:3, 30–31.
[357] See *De mundo*, § 21:4.
[358] See, respectively, *Introductorius*, § 2.1:11, and § 2.9:2; cf. *Reshit Ḥokhmah*, § 2.1:11, 58–59; and *Reshit Ḥokhmah*, § 2.9:2, 108–109.
[359] See *Rationes* II, § 2.3:4 and *Iudicia*, § 2:4; cf. *Ṭeʿamim* II, § 2.3:4, 188–189.

Introductorius uses the doublet "mobile seu tropicale" = "changeable or tropical."³⁶⁰ Bate's *Iudicia* and *Rationes* II, too, clarify the term by means of the doublet "mobilia seu tropica";³⁶¹ *Rationes* I offers the triplet "mutabile seu tropicum et mobile" = "mutable or tropical and changeable."³⁶² As in the previous case, one component of the doublet or triplet is a literal translation of the Hebrew and the other is the common Latin technical term.

(v) *Reshit Ḥokhmah* describes a fixed sign (Taurus, Leo, Scorpio, Aquarius) as עומד על דרך אחד, "standing in one way;" Hagin renders the expression literally as "il est sur une voie"; in *Introductorius*, Bate offers a doublet that omits a literal translation and instead provides the Latin technical term plus an explanation: "fixum sive non mutabile" = "fixed or not changeable."³⁶³ A similar denomination, מזל עומד, "standing sign," is found in both versions of *Teʿamim*; in *Rationes* I and *Rationes* II Bate writes "stabile seu fixum" = "stable or fixed."³⁶⁴ For the same category of signs, *Mishpeṭei ha-Mazzalot* and *Meʾorot* use נאמנים, "enduring." In *Iudicia* Bate opts for the triplet "firma seu fixa vel stabilia" = "firm or fixed or stable"; in *De luminaribus* he has the doublet "firma seu fixa" = "firm or fixed."³⁶⁵

(vi) The "long signs," from Cancer to Sagittarius, divide the zodiac according to their rising times or ascensions.³⁶⁶ Ibn Ezra designates them מזלות ארוכים, "long signs." In *De luminaribus* Bate uses the doublet "signa longa seu longarum ascensionum" = "long signs or of long ascensions."³⁶⁷

(vii) Ibn Ezra designated the "terminal sign" as בית הסוף, "terminal house."³⁶⁸ Bate renders it by the same doublet three times, once in *De*

---

³⁶⁰ See *Introductorius*, § 2.1:4; cf. *Reshit Ḥokhmah*, § 2.1:4, 58–59.
³⁶¹ See *Iudicia*, § 2:2; *Rationes* II, § 2.3:1; cf. *Mishpeṭei ha-Mazzalot*, § 2:2, 488–489; *Teʿamim* II, § 2.3:1, 188–189.
³⁶² *Rationes* I, § 2.2:1; cf. *Teʿamim* I, § 2.2:1, 38–39.
³⁶³ See *Introductorius*, § 2.8:2; cf. *Reshit Ḥokhmah*, § 2.8:2, 102–103.
³⁶⁴ See *Rationes* I, § 2.13:1; and *Rationes* II, § 2.3:3; cf. *Teʿamim* I, § 2.13:1, 52–53; *Teʿamim* II, § 2.3:3, 184–185.
³⁶⁵ See *Iudicia*, § 2:3; *De luminaribus*, § 17:1; cf. *Mishpeṭei ha-Mazzalot*, § 2:3, 488–489; *Meʾorot*, § 17:1, 466–467.
³⁶⁶ The term "rising times" or "ascensions" refers to how many degrees of the equator cross the horizon of a given locality simultaneously with the consecutive zodiacal signs.
³⁶⁷ See *De luminaribus*, § 23:3; cf. *Meʾorot*, § 23:3, 468–469.
³⁶⁸ Ibn Ezra's *Sefer ha-Tequfah* (§ 6:1, 374–375) explains this term as follows: "מזל הסוף, והטעם שתתן במעלות ישרות לכל מזל שנה אחת, ובהשלים י״ב שנה, יחזרו חלילה." = "the terminal sign, this means that you assign, in equal degrees, one year to each sign, and repeat the cycle when 12 years are up." *Teʿamim* II (§ 8.5:1, 252–253) explains as follows the rationale behind

Mundo and twice in *Rationes* II: "domus finis sive signum profectionis" = "terminal house or sign of profection."[369] Here too one component of the doublet translates the Hebrew term literally, while the other is the common Latin technical term.

(viii) The "signs of deformities" (Taurus, Cancer, Scorpio, Capricorn, and Pisces) are referred to throughout Ibn Ezra's astrological oeuvre as מזלות המומים, "signs of deformities." Hagin translates literally as "signes les mehaignans"; Bate, in *Introductorius*, clarifies the term by means of the triplet "signa impedimentorum, orbationum seu mutilationum" = "signs of defects, maimings or mutilations."[370] The same category occurs in *Ṭeʿamim* II as המומים, "deformities," which Bate translates by means of the doublet "orbationes seu *azemena*" = "defects or *azemena*."[371] The second component of this doublet is a transliteration of الزمانة, used in al-Qabīṣī's *Introduction to Astrology* to denote a category of zodiacal degrees that indicate chronic diseases.[372]

(ix) The zodiac is divided into groups of degrees that are taken to have astrological influence on specific portions of the signs. Ibn Ezra calls one of them חשוכות, "dark." Hagin translates literally as "oscurs," which Bate expands in *Introductorius* into the doublet "obscuri vel tenebrosi" = "dark or tenebrous."[373]

(x) Following Arabic sources, Latin astrology calls the interval of the zodiac between Libra 19° and Scorpio 3° "via combusta," "the burnt path." A planet is said to be weak there. *Mishpeṭei ha-Mazzalot* and *Ṭeʿamim* I employ מקום השריפה, "the place of burning." Bate's *Iudicia* and *Rationes* I clarify this expression by means of a doublet that includes a literal translation of the Hebrew and the common Latin technical term: "locus combustionis seu via combusta" = "place of burning or the burnt path."[374] *Ṭeʿamim* II, though, uses דרך החושך, "the path of darkness," which Bate expands into another doublet that consists of

---

this instruction: "טעם לתת לכל מעלה שנים עשר יום ועוד שתי שעות ושלישית שעה שבכן יתחלקו כל ימות השנה על שלשים מעלות ישרות, שהם בית הסוף." = "The reason for assigning '12 days plus two and a third hours to each degree' is that in this manner all the days of the year are divided into 30 equal degrees, which is the terminal house."

[369] See *De mundo*, § 57:3; *Rationes* II, § 6.4:1; § 8.5:1; cf. *ʿOlam* I, § 57:3, 88–89; *Ṭeʿamim* II, § 6.4:1, 238–239; *Ṭeʿamim* II, § 8.5:1, 252–253.

[370] See *Introductorius*, § 2.8:30; cf. *Reshit Ḥokhmah*, § 2.8:30, 106–107.

[371] See *Rationes* II, § 2.3:17; cf. *Ṭeʿamim* II, § 2.3:17, 190–191.

[372] *Introduction*, ed. Burnett et al. (2004), 44–45.

[373] *Introductorius*, § 2.4:42; cf. *Reshit Ḥokhmah*, § 2.4:42.

[374] See *Iudicia*, § 4:3; *Rationes* I, § 2.16:5; cf. *Mishpeṭei ha-Mazzalot*, § 4:3, 492–493; *Ṭeʿamim* I, § 2.16:5, 54–55.

a literal translation of the Hebrew and the common Latin technical term: "via obscuritatis seu via combusta" = "path of darkness or burnt path."[375]

1.2. Astronomical Terms

Ibn Ezra's introductions to astrology (and to a lesser extent his treatises on other branches of Greco-Arabic astrology) incorporate extensive astronomical content. Ibn Ezra's astronomical terms are usually literal translations from his Arabic sources, although there are also Hebrew coinages derived from the Bible or the Talmud. Bate clarifies these terms by means of doublets, which as a rule include the common Latin technical counterpart, as follows:

(i) The common Latin technical term to denote the distance along the zodiac between two planets is "longitudo." To denote this concept, Ibn Ezra always writes מרחק, "distance," even though this term may apply to the distance of a planet from the Sun, from the Earth, etc. In seven places Bate's *Iudicia* disambiguates the Hebrew term by means of the doublet "distantia seu longitudo" = "distance or longitude."[376] The same doublet appears five times in *Rationes* I and once in *Introductorius*.[377]

(ii) By contrast, the common Latin technical term to denote the distance between a planet and the Sun is "elongatio." To denote the distance between a planet and the Sun, Ibn Ezra again uses the equivocal מרחק, "distance." Bate's *Introductorius* and *Rationes* I disambiguate the Hebrew term by means of the doublet "distantia seu elongatio" = "distance or elongation."[378]

(iii) The common Latin technical terms to indicate that a planet has northern or southern latitude with respect to the ecliptic are "septentrionalis" or "meridionalis." To denote these two concepts Ibn Ezra, influenced by his Arabic sources, uses the biblical שמאל and ימין, whose primary sense are "left" and "right," which Hagin renders literally as "senestre" and "destre," "left" and "right." Bate disambiguates them as "sinister vel septentrionalis" and "dexter vel meridionalis" = "left or

---

[375] See *Rationes* II, §2.7:5; cf. *Ṭeʿamim* II, §2.7:5, 194–195.
[376] See *Iudicia*, §35:3–4 *et passim*; cf. *Mishpeṭei ha-Mazzalot*, §35:3–4, 518–519 *et passim*.
[377] See *Rationes* I, §9.2:2 *et passim*; *Introductorius*, §9.18:3; cf. *Ṭeʿamim* I, §9.2:2, 92–93; *Reshit Ḥokhmah*, §9.18:3, 260–261.
[378] See *Introductorius*, §1.10:1; *Rationes* I, §6.3:5; cf. *Reshit Ḥokhmah*, §1.10:1, 56–57; *Ṭeʿamim* I, §6.3:5, 86–86.

northern" and "right or southern." These doublets are found at least five time in *Introductorius*, three times in *Rationes* I, three times in *Rationes* II, and once in *Iudicia*.[379]

(iv) To denote the nodes, the points where a planet crosses the ecliptic, Ibn Ezra always employs the talmudic word תלי, "Dragon." *Reshit Ḥokhmah*, for example, refers to ראש התלי, "the head of the Dragon," and Hagin translates "le chief du Dragon." Bate's *Introductorius* clarifies this by means of the doublet "caput Draconis seu *genzaar*" = "the head of the Dragon or *jawzahar*."[380] The second component of the doublet is the transliteration of the Arabic-Persian term جوزهر *jawzahar*, which Latin scholars used for the nodes.[381]

(v) To denote the perigee, the point in the orbit of a planet where it is closest to the Earth, Latin scholars use "oppositum augis," that is, "the opposite of the apogee," the point in the orbit of a planet where it is furthest from the Earth. Ibn Ezra uses שפלות or מקום שפלות, "lowness" or "place of lowness." *Reshit Ḥokhmah*, for example, has מקום שפלות, which Hagin renders literally as "le lieu de la baisseté." This is translated by Bate in *Introductorius* by means of the doublet "depressio seu appositum augis" = "depression or the opposite of the apogee," which combines a literal translation of the Hebrew term with the common Latin technical term. The same doublet is found twice in *Introductorius*, three times in *Iudicia*, and once in *Rationes* I.[382] In another passage in *Introductorius*, though, Bate translates the same term as "depressio seu humiliatio" = "depression or humiliation."[383]

(vi) To denote the concept that one planet eclipses another, in *Teʿamim* II and *Mishpeṭei ha-Mazzalot* Ibn Ezra employs the verb הסתיר, "hide." In *Rationes* II Bate uses the doublet "occultat seu eclipsat" = "hides

---

[379] See *Introductorius*, § 1.10:2 *et passim*; cf. *Reshit Ḥokhmah*, § 1.10:2, 56–57 *et passim*; *Rationes* I, § 1.4:3 *et passim*; cf. *Teʿamim* I, § 1.4:3, 32–33 *et passim*; *Rationes* II, 2.2:1 *et passim*; cf. *Teʿamim* II, § 2.2:1, 186–187 *et passim*; *Iudicia*, § 44:5; cf. *Mishpeṭei ha-Mazzalot*, § 44:5, 530–531.

[380] *Introductorius*, § 2.12:35 *et passim*; cf. *Reshit Ḥokhmah*, § 2.12:35, 130–131 *et passim*.

[381] Pietro d'Abano, for example, in his translation of *Reshit Ḥokhmah*, § 5.5:6–7, 186–187, writes: "Aut sint cum capite suorum *genazahat* Draconis aut cauda, aut cum capite *genazahat* Lune, sitque inter eos minus .12. gradus." See Bibliothèque de la Sorbonne 640, fol. 89va.

[382] See *Introductorius*, § 2.3:25 *et passim*; cf. *Reshit Ḥokhmah*, § 2.3:25, 74–75 *et passim*; *Iudicia*, § 21:3; cf. *Mishpeṭei ha-Mazzalot*, § 21:3, 506–507; *Rationes* I, § 2.6:3; cf. *Teʿamim* I, § 2.6:3, 46–47.

[383] See *Introductorius*, § 2.1:40; cf. *Reshit Ḥokhmah*, § 2.1:40, 62–63.

or eclipses,"[384] and in *Iudicia* the doublet "eclipsare seu occultare ab oculorum visione" = "eclipse or hide from the vision of the eyes."[385]

(vii) In Greek astronomy, the "eccentric circle" is one whose center is not the Earth but some point slightly offset from it. It is also called "deferens," "carrying," because the epicycle is carried by the eccentric circle. To denote this, Ibn Ezra uses הגלגל המוצק, "the circle of the center," which incorporates his neologism מוצק, *muṣaq*, *lit.* "solid, stable, or strong," for "center.[386] In *Rationes* II, Bate avoids a literal translation of Ibn Ezra's expression and instead uses the doublet "circulus ecentricus sive deferens" = "eccentric or carrying circle."[387]

1.3. Astronomical Terms derived from ישר "Straight" and שווה "Equal"

Ibn Ezra uses words derived from ישר and שווה, literally "straight" and "equal," for several astronomical terms. Bate found these terms rather confusing and clarified them by means of doublets. Usually, one component of the doublet is the literal translation of the Hebrew word and the other is the common Latin technical term:

(i) To denote the "mean motion of the planets," in contrast to the "variable motion" of the planets, *'Olam* I uses המהלך השווה, "the equal motion." *De mundo* renders this as "medius cursus vel equalis" = "mean or equal motion."[388]

(ii) To denote "equal degrees," that is, degrees measured along the zodiac, Ibn Ezra frequently uses מעלות ישרות, "straight degrees." *Introductorius* clarifies this term, rendered by Hagin as "grés droits" = "straight degrees," as "gradus recti seu equales" = "straight or equal degrees."[389] The same doublet, translating the same Hebrew expression, is found in *Rationes* I.[390]

(iii) For the "straight signs," those from Cancer to Sagittarius (in contrast to the "crooked" signs, from Capricorn to Gemini), which divide the zodiac according to their rising times, Ibn Ezra uses מזלות ישרים,

---

[384] See *Rationes* II, § 1.2:3; cf. *Ṭeʿamim* II, § 1.2:3, 182–183.
[385] *Iudicia*, § 32:1; cf. *Mishpeṭei ha-Mazzalot*, § 32:1, 516–517.
[386] For this neologism, see Sela 2003, 113–116.
[387] See *Rationes* II, § 2.5:1; cf. *Ṭeʿamim* II, § 2.5:1, 194–195.
[388] See *De mundo*, § 1:1; cf. *'Olam* I, § 1:1, 52–53.
[389] See *Introductorius*, § 1.1:3; cf. *Reshit Ḥokhmah*, § 1.1:3, 50–51.
[390] See *Rationes* I, § 10.5:2; cf. *Ṭeʿamim* I, § 10.5:2, 98–99.

"straight signs." *Rationes* I has the doublet "equales signa aut recta" = "equal or straight signs."³⁹¹

(iv) Ibn Ezra uses מישור, "plane," derived from the root ישר, in the expression גלגל המישור, "plane circle" or "straight circle," for "sphaera recta," which refers to the situation when calculations are transferred from the ecliptic to the celestial equator. Bate hesitated about the meaning of this expression and produced three different translations in three different loci of *Iudicia*: (a) "circulus equalis sive rectus" = "equal or upright circle";³⁹² (b) "circulus equalitatis sive spera recta" = "circle of equality or upright sphere";³⁹³ (c) "rectus circulus seu linea equalis" = "upright circle or equal line."³⁹⁴

(v) Ibn Ezra uses יושר, "straightness," another word derived from ישר, in the expression קו היושר, "line of straightness," to denote the equator. *Rationes* I translates and explains this expression by means of the doublet "linea equalis sive spera recta" = "equal line or upright sphere."³⁹⁵

1.4. Astrological Terms derived from ישר "Straight"

Ibn Ezra employs the same Hebrew terms ישר "straight" and יושר "straightness" to represent the adjective "temperate" and the noun "temperament" as they apply to the physical nature of planets, signs, and the human body. In many cases, as we shall see in this section, Bate clarifies the term by means of doublets or triplets. No doubt Bate became aware of the alternative meaning of these words as a result of the context in which they appear and not as a result of French intermediaries, which usually offer literal translations of the Hebrew text. To highlight the latter point, here are Bate's doublets or triplets (underlined), together with their context.

(i) The following five examples relate to the nature of the planets:

(a) *Reshit Ḥokhmah*, § 7.14:1, 204–205:

שיביט כוכב אל כוכב ... אז יהיה ממסך שניהם ישר.

When one planet aspects ⟨another⟩ planet ... in which case the mixture of both is straight [tempered].

---
³⁹¹ See *Rationes* I, § 3.3:2; cf. *Ṭeʿamim* I, § 3.3:2, 62–63.
³⁹² See *Iudicia*, § 1:7; cf. *Mishpeṭei ha-Mazzalot*, § 1:7, 488–489.
³⁹³ See *Iudicia*, § 65:9; cf. *Mishpeṭei ha-Mazzalot*, § 65:9, 546–547.
³⁹⁴ See *Iudicia*, § 71:5; cf. *Mishpeṭei ha-Mazzalot*, § 71:5, 550–551.
³⁹⁵ See *Rationes* I, § 2.4:4; cf. *Ṭeʿamim* I, § 2.4:4, 42–43.

GENERAL INTRODUCTION

P, 49vb (Hagin): Regarde estoile a estoile ... adonc sera le mellement de eus .2. droit.

Introductorius, § 7.14:1: Ut aspiciat planeta planetam alium ... tunc erit eorum commixtio eorum <u>equalis</u> <u>seu</u> <u>temperata</u>.

When one planet aspects another planet ... then their mixture is <u>equal or tempered</u>.

(b) *Reshit Ḥokhmah*, § 7.28:5, 208–209:

והכוכב הטוב יקבל הטוב בעבור היות תולדתו ישרה.

A good planet receives a good one because of its straight [balanced] nature.

P, 51rb (Hagin): L'estoile bone reçoit la bone pour ce que est leur nature droite.

Introductorius, § 7.28:5: Planeta benevolus recipit benevolum eo quod natura ipsorum <u>equalis</u> <u>est</u> <u>seu</u> <u>temperata</u>

A benevolent planet receives a benevolent one because their nature is <u>equal or tempered</u>.

(c) *Ṭeʿamim* I, § 2.17:7, 58–99:

צדק, שהוא ישר בתולדתו.

Jupiter, which is straight [temperate] in its nature.

Rationes I, § 2.17:7: Iovem ... eo quod <u>equalis</u> <u>seu</u> <u>temperatus</u> est in sua natura

Jupiter ... because it is <u>equal or temperate</u> in its nature.

(d) *Ṭeʿamim* II, § 5.4:10, 38–39:

והוא כוכב אמת כי כן התולדת הישרה.

It is a star of truth because such is the straight [temperate] nature.

Rationes II, § 5.4:10: et itaque planeta veritatis similiter enim est et eius natura <u>equalis</u> <u>sive</u> <u>iusta</u> <u>et</u> <u>temperata</u>.

Therefore, it [Jupiter] is a planet of truth, because it is similar, and its nature is <u>equal or just and temperate</u>.

(e) *Ṭeʿamim* II, § 5.7:2, 232–233:

כוכב חמה ... על כן משתנה מהרה לכל תולדת בעבור היותו ישר.

Mercury ... for this reason it quickly changes to any nature because it is straight [temperate].

Rationes II, § 5.7:2: Mercurius ... et ideo confestim mutatur ad qualibet naturam eo quod <u>equalis</u> <u>est</u> <u>seu</u> <u>rectus</u> <u>vel</u> <u>temperatus</u>

Mercury ... for this reason it quickly changes to any nature because it is <u>equal</u> or <u>straight</u> or <u>temperate</u>.

In all these cases Bate uses both "equalis," the literal translation of ישר, as well as "temperata," which conveys the meaning. In the two last examples Bate uses triplets, which, in addition to "equalis" and "temperata," include synonyms for the literal translation of ישר: "iustus" and "rectus." The first two examples here present Hagin's French translation, on which Bate relied to produce his *Introductorius*. Given that in both examples Hagin opted for a literal translation of ישר: "droit," it follows that Bate must have become aware of the alternative meaning of ישר as a result of the context.

(ii) The next two examples relate, respectively, to the nature of zodiacal signs and of the human body:

(a) *Reshit Ḥokhmah*, § 2.4:9, 80–81:

סרטן ... והוא יורה ... על כל ממסך קר ולח במעט יושר.

Cancer ... indicates ... any mixture of cold and moist that is somewhat straight [balanced].

P, 11rb (Hagin): La Creveice ... et il enseigne ... sur tout mellement froit et moiste en un petit de droiture.

Introductorius, § 2.4:9: Cancer ... et significat ... super omnem complexionen frigidam et humidam <u>in</u> <u>equalitate</u> aliquantula <u>seu</u> <u>temperamento</u> existentem.

Cancer ... indicates ... any mixture of cold and moist that appears <u>equal</u> to a slight extent or somewhat <u>balanced</u>.

(b) *Reshit Ḥokhmah*, § 2.12:26, 128–129:

והנולד בו מבני אדם יהיה ישר גופו ממוסך.

A person born in it, will be straight, his body will be mixed.

P, 28va (Hagin): Et celi qui est nés en li d'enfans d'ome sera son cors droit

Introductorius, § 2.12:26: Qui natus fuerit in hoc signo, erit corpus eius <u>rectum</u> <u>et</u> <u>temperatum</u>

One born in this sign, his body will be <u>straight</u> <u>and</u> <u>temperate</u>.

In these two examples, related to the nature of the signs and the human body, we note the same features as in the five previous examples related

to the nature of the planets: the use of "temperamentum" or "temperatus" to clarify the meaning of "equalitas" and "rectus," which translate יושר and ישר. In addition, we see that in these cases Hagin opted for a literal French translation of the Hebrew—"droiture" and "droit"—so Bate must have based his alternative translation on the context.

1.5. Planets and Fixed Stars

(i) Ibn Ezra uses two words for "planets." One is משרתים, "servants," perhaps Ibn Ezra's most frequent and distinctive biblical neologism.[396] Inasmuch as this Hebrew term refers unequivocally to the planets, Bate translates it everywhere as "planete," with no need for a clarifying doublet. The other Hebrew term, though, כוכבים, "stars," may refer to the planets or to the fixed stars. Hagin translates it as "estoiles," but given the ambiguity, Bate frequently employs the doublet "stelle seu planete."[397] The same doublet occurs frequently in *De luminaribus*,[398] *Rationes* I,[399] *Rationes* II,[400] and *De mundo*.[401]

(ii) Ibn Ezra often writes העליונים, "the uppermost ⟨stars⟩," meaning either the three uppermost planets, Saturn, Jupiter, and Mars, or the fixed stars. In *De luminaribus*, Bate twice resolves the ambiguity by means of the doublet "stelle supreme seu fixe" = "highest or fixed stars."[402]

(iii) Following his Arabic sources, Ibn Ezra uses צורה, "shape" or "figure," for a constellation. Hagin translates "figure"; Bate, in *Introductorius*, clarifies the terms by means of the doublet "figura seu ymago" = "figure or image."[403] The same doublet, clarifying the same Hebrew term, is found in *De mundo*.[404]

(iv) The planets are assigned various appellations related to their motions, indications, and positions. Ibn Ezra, following his Arabic sources,

---

[396] For this neologism, see Sela 2003, 129–130.
[397] See *Introductorius*, § 2.1:32; § 3.2:4; § 7.2:1; cf. *Reshit Ḥokhmah*, § 2.1:32, 62–63; § 3.2:4, 140–141; § 7.2:1, 196–197.
[398] See *De luminaribus*, § 1:2; § 1:5; § 10:1; § 23:5; § 29:1; § 34:2; cf. *Me'orot*, § 1:2, 452–453; § 1:5, 452–453; § 10:1, 462–462; § 23:5, 469–469; § 29:1, 474–475; § 34:2, 480–481.
[399] See *Rationes* I, § 1.3:2; § 3.2:11; § 4.5:6; § 5.2:6; cf. *Ṭe'amim* I, § 1.3:2, 30–31; § 3.2:11, 60–61; § 4.5:6, 76–77; § 5.2:6, 84–85.
[400] See *Rationes* II, § 4.3:1; § 6.5:3; cf. *Ṭe'amim* II, § 4.3:1, 208–298; § 6.5:3, 240–241.
[401] See *De mundo*, § 64:2; cf. *'Olam* I, § 64:2, 94–95.
[402] See *De luminaribus*, § 34:5; § 35:1; cf. *Me'orot*, § 34:5, 480–481; § 35:1, 482–483.
[403] See *Introductorius*, § 2.6:21; cf. *Reshit Ḥokhmah*, § 2.6:21, 94–95.
[404] See *De mundo*, § 62:5; cf. *'Olam* I, § 62:5, 92–93.

often calls the slow planets כוכבים כבדים, "heavy planets." Bate clarifies the term with the doublet "stelle graves seu tarde" = "heavy or slow stars."[405]

(v) Ibn Ezra is in the habit of calling the beneficent and maleficent planets טובים ורעים, "good and bad," Bate clarifies the term with the doublet "boni et mali, seu benefici et malefici" = "good and bad or benefic and malefic."[406]

(vi) *Reshit Ḥokhmah* designates a planet that is located in the "straight signs" as הנגיד, "the governor," and one that is located in the "crooked signs" as העבד, "the slave." Hagin translates these two terms as "siegneur" and "serjant," respectively. *Introductorius* clarifies these metaphors by means of doublets: "dominus seu principans" and "servus seu subiectus" = "lord or ruler" and "slave or subject."[407]

(vii) A planet is said to be "peregrine" when it is not in its planetary house, exaltation, or triplicity. *Reshit Ḥokhmah* calls such a planet as גר במקומו, "stranger in its position." Hagin translates "etrange en son lieu"; and Bate clarifies the metaphor with the doublet "peregrina seu extranea in loco suo" = "peregrine or strange in its position."[408]

(viii) *Reshit Ḥokhmah* uses the verb התחבר "conjoin" when the distance between two planets is less than 15° and they are moving closer, and not only for two planets that are in conjunction.[409] Hagin translates literally as "se conjoint a autre estoile." Bate, though, disambiguates the term by means of a doublet that includes the verb "applicare," the common Latin technical term for the approach of planets: "applicet seu coniungatur" = "applies or conjoins."[410]

(ix) The planets are said to emit "rays," a metaphor for a certain number of degrees in the zodiac, ahead of or behind the planet, where its influence is still felt.[411] For this concept, *Teʿamim* I and *Teʿamim* II use אור "light," in both the singular and the plural. Bate clarifies the term three times in *Rationes* I and four times in *Rationes* II by means of the doublet "lumen seu radius" = "light or ray."[412]

---

[405] See *De mundo*, §7:1; cf. *ʿOlam* I, §7:1, 56–56.
[406] See *Introductorius*, §1.9:2; cf. *Reshit Ḥokhmah*, §1.9:2, 54–55. In addition, because Ibn Ezra uses the same adjectives for the zodiacal signs, Bate clarifies the term with the same doublet. See *Rationes* I, §2.2:2; *Teʿamim* I, §2.2:2, 38–39.
[407] See *Introductorius*, §3.2:4; cf. *Reshit Ḥokhmah*, §3.2:4, 140–141.
[408] See *Introductorius*, §5.4:14; *Reshit Ḥokhmah*, §5.4:14, 184–185.
[409] For this condition, see *Introductorius*, §7.2:1–4; cf. *Reshit Ḥokhmah*, §7.2:1–4, 196–197.
[410] See *Introductorius*, §7.6:3; cf. *Reshit Ḥokhmah*, §7.6:3, 200–201.
[411] For this concept, see Sela 2017, 592–593.
[412] See *Rationes* I, §2.16:4; §2.16:5; §4.2:12; cf. *Teʿamim* I, §2.16:4, 54–55; §2.16:5, 54–55;

(x) The planets are said to indicate "pains" when located in specific signs.[413] *Ṭeʿamim* I denotes this concept by כאב "pain," which *Rationes* I translates by means of the doublet "dolor seu passio" = "pain or suffering."[414] *Mishpeṭei ha-Mazzalot* designates the same concept by מכאוב כל כוכב, "pain of any planet," which *Iudicia* translates by means of the doublet "planete dolores et passiones" = "pains or sufferings of the planets."[415]

1.6. The Use for the Planetary Conditions of the Latin Translations of Abū Maʿshar's *Great Introduction*

Chapter 7 of *Reshit Ḥokhmah*, which is a Hebrew translation of several sections of part 7 of Abū Maʿshar's *Great Introduction*, names and describes several planetary conditions.[416] Ibn Ezra's names for these planetary conditions are usually literal Hebrew translations of Abū Maʿshar's metaphorical Arabic names. Hagin, as is his wont, offers French literal translations of Ibn Ezra's Hebrew. Bate, in his Latin translations, translates the French terms but also seems to rely on the Latin versions of Abū Maʿshar's *Great Introduction*, particularly that by Hermann of Carinthia. This applies for places where Bate employed doublets and others where he did not (see Table 4).

TABLE 4

Ibn Ezra[417]	Hagin[418]	Bate[419]	Hermann[420]	John[421]
הקירוב = approach	l'aprochement	applicatio	applicatio	coniunctio
החיבור = conjunction	la conjunction	coniunctio	conventus	coniunctio

---

§ 4.2:12, 74–75. See *Rationes* II, § 4.2:1; § 4.2:3; § 4.9:3; § 5.2:15; cf. *Ṭeʿamim* II, § 4.2:1, 208–209; § 4.2:3, 208–209; § 4.9:3, 214–215; § 5.2:15, 220–221.

[413] For this concept, see Sela 2017, 589–590.
[414] See *Rationes* I, § 2.3:4; cf. *Ṭeʿamim* I, § 2.3:4, 40–41.
[415] See *Iudicia*, § 20:1; cf. *Mishpeṭei ha-Mazzalot*, § 20:1, 504–505.
[416] *Reshit Ḥokhmah*, § 7.1:1 through § 7.3:8, 196–211 and notes on 438–457.
[417] *Reshit Ḥokhmah*, § 7.2:1 through § 7.32:1, 196–211.
[418] P, 47va through 51vb (*Commencement*).
[419] *Introductorius*, § 7.2:1 through § 7.32:1.
[420] *Kitāb al-mudkhal al-kabīr*, ed. Lemay (1996), vol. VIII (Traduction latine de Hermann de Carinthie), VII:5–7, pp. 135–141.
[421] *Kitāb al-mudkhal al-kabīr*, ed. Lemay (1996), vol. VII:5–7, pp. 292–307.

TABLE 4 (*cont.*)

Ibn Ezra		Hagin	Bate	Hermann	John
המסך = mixture		li mellemens	commixtio	permixtio	complexio
המבט = aspect		le regars	aspectus	respectus	aspectus
הפירוד = separation		le departement	separatio	separatio	separatio
הילוך בדד = solitary motion		aler seul	solitudo	solitudo	vacuatio cursus
השומם = desolate		l'ataisement	alienatio	alienatio	feralitas
השבת האור = reflecting the light		le retournement de la clarté	redditio luminis	redditio	redditus luminis
הבטול = cancellation		le destorbement	refrenatio seu contradictio	contradictio	refrenatio
המקרה = accident		l'accident	accidens seu eventus accidentalis	inpeditio	accidens
האבוד = loss		la deperdicion	frustratio seu evasio	evasio	frustratio
כריתות האור = cutting of the light		le taillement de la clarté	abscissio luminis seu interceptio	interceptio	abscissio luminis
הנועם = pleasantness		la sovantume	compassio seu largitio	compassio	largitio
הנדיבות = generosity		la volentivité	benevolentia sive liberalitas		
הדמיון = similitude		la samblance	similitudo sive haiz sive esse in suo limite	haiz	alhaiz
האמצעיות = intermediacy		la miloennetes	obsessio	obsessio	obsessio

That Bate used the Latin translations of Abū Maʿshar is particularly evident in the two last items in the table. In the penultimate line, Bate opts for a triplet: the first component is a literal translation of Hagin's French (similitudo); but the second (haiz) is a transliteration of حيّز, which he could have found in Hermann of Carinthia's or John of Seville's translations of the *Great Introduction*.[422] Most interesting is the last item in the table, where Abū Maʿshar wrote حصار, "siege." In this particular case Ibn Ezra avoided a literal translation and rendered the planetary condition as אמצעיות "intermediacy," which is a technical description of the astrological or astronomical condition.[423] Hagin translated Ibn Ezra's Hebrew literally, as "miloennetes." But here Bate completely diverged from the French and wrote "obsessio," "siege," which he could have found in Hermann's or John's translations of Abū Maʿshar's *Great Introduction*, and corresponds precisely to Abū Maʿshar's Arabic.

1.7. The Dignities

The dignities (house, exaltation, triplicity, term, decan) are five distinct zodiacal positions (a whole sign, a degree in a sign, or an interval of degrees in a sign) where a planet is said to acquire strength in the horoscope, for good or for evil, according to its nature.

(i) *Mishpeṭei ha-Mazzalot* denotes the concept of dignity by means of פקידות, "lordship." In *Iudicia* Bate clarifies the term by means of the doublet "dignitas seu potestas" = "dignity or government."[424]

(ii) The second of the planets' five essential dignities is "exaltation." Ibn Ezra, following his Arabic sources, used the Hebrew כבוד "honor."[425] Hagin turns this into "oneur"; *Introductorius* sometimes explicates what would strike his readers as a curious term by means of the doublet "honor seu exaltatio" = "honor or exaltation."[426] Because כבוד meaning exaltation is extremely frequent in Ibn Ezra's astrological corpus, the doublet "honor seu exaltatio" appears frequently in Bate's translations of Ibn Ezra: at least twelve times in *Introductorius*, five times in *Rationes* I, four times in *Iudicia*, three times in *Rationes* II, and once in *De luminaribus*.

---

[422] See *Reshit Ḥokhmah*, § 7.31:1–2, 240–241 and note on p. 456.
[423] See *Reshit Ḥokhmah*, § 7.32:1, 240–241 and note on pp. 456–457.
[424] See *Iudicia*, § 38:14; cf. *Mishpeṭei ha-Mazzalot*, § 38:14, 520–521.
[425] For this concept, see Sela 2020, 242.
[426] See *Introductorius*, § 1.11:1; § 1.11:3; cf. *Reshit Ḥokhmah*, § 1.11:1, 56–57; § 1.11:3, 56–57.

(iii) A planet is said to be in its "house of dejection" if it is in the house opposite its exaltation. The common Latin technical term for this astrological concept is "casus," "falling," or "domus casus," "house of falling." To denote this concept, Ibn Ezra coined קלון "dishonor," being the antonym of כבוד "honor." Hagin renders קלון as "honte"; *Introductorius* sometimes makes the sense clear by means of the doublets "casus vel dedecus" or "domus casus sive dedecoris" = "fall or shame" or "house of fall or shame."[427]

(iv) A planet is said to be in its "detriment" if it is in the house opposite its planetary house, which is the first of the planets' five essential dignities. In all of the components of the astrological encyclopedia he composed in Béziers in 1148, Ibn Ezra used שנאה or בית שנאה, "hate" or "house of hate."[428] Hagin wrote "meson de la haine." Bate seems to be bewildered by this expression; in *Introductorius* he attempted both "odium seu domus dedecoris" = "hate or house of shame"[429] and "domus exilii vel odiii" = "house of banishment or hate."[430]

1.8. The Components of the Horoscope

The horoscope is the main tool used by astrologers from antiquity to the present to make their prognostications. Bate invested much of his translational energy in efforts to clarify the meaning of some of its components:

(i) The common Latin technical term for the first, fourth, seventh, and tenth horoscopic houses, which are taken to be highly influential in the interpretation of the horoscope, is "anguli" or "cardines," that is, "angles" or "hinges." Following his Arabic sources, Ibn Ezra employs יתדות whose primary sense is "pegs," which Hagin renders literally as "chevilles." Rather than translating this, Bate frequently writes "anguli"; but several times in *Introductorius* he uses the doublet "anguli vel cardines" = "angles or cardines."[431] The same doublet is also found in *Iudicia*[432] and twice in *Rationes* I.[433]

---

[427] See *Introductorius*, § 2.4:36; § 2.12:35; § 9.20:3; cf. *Reshit Ḥokhmah*, § 2.4:36, 82–83; § 2.12:35, 130–131; § 9.20:3, 262–263.
[428] This includes *Reshit Ḥokhmah, Teʿamim* I, *Moladot, Mivḥarim* I, *Sheʾelot* I, *ʿOlam* I.
[429] See *Introductorius*, § 2.5:32; cf. *Reshit Ḥokhmah*, § 2.5:32, 90–91.
[430] See *Introductorius*, § 5.4:11; cf. *Reshit Ḥokhmah*, § 5.4:11, 184–185.
[431] See *Introductorius*, § 3.4:2; § 3.4:5; § 5.3:5; cf. *Reshit Ḥokhmah*, § 3.4:2, 142–143; § 3.4:5, 142–143; § 5.3:5, 184–185.
[432] See *Iudicia*, § 12:6; cf. *Mishpeṭei ha-Mazzalot*, § 12:6, 498–499.
[433] See *Rationes* I, § 3.1:4; § 3.5:5; cf. *Teʿamim* I, § 3.1:4, 60–61; § 3.5:5, 64–65.

(ii) Ibn Ezra refers to the third, sixth, ninth, and twelfth horoscopic houses as חלשים "weak." In *Introductorius* Bate employs the doublet "debiles seu cadentes" = "weak or cadent," where the second component derives from the idea that these four horoscopic houses are "falling/cadent from the cardines." In this particular locus, though, Bate was following Hagin, who employed a doublet in his French, "foibles ou cheans."[434] The same doublet occurs also in *Iudicia*.[435]

(iii) In *Ṭeʿamim* I Ibn Ezra designates the cusp of the fourth house, which is the lowest place of the horoscope, as קו התהום, "the line of the abyss." Bate twice turns this into the doublet "abyssi linea seu angulus terre" = "line of the abyss or angle of the Earth."[436]

(iv) Virtually all the elements and celestial objects that play a role in the horoscope are said to have "power." This is an extremely frequent term in Ibn Ezra's astrological writings, always expressed by the word כח "power." Hagin always renders this as "force," but Bate frequently employs the doublet "virtus seu fortitudo" = "power or strength." This doublet appears at least ten times in *Rationes* II,[437] seven times in *Iudicia*,[438] six times in *Rationes* I,[439] and three times in *Introductorius*.[440]

(v) In horoscopes related to the doctrine of interrogations, the person who poses the question to the astrologer is represented by some component of the horoscope. *Reshit Ḥokhmah* designates this person as השואל, "the one who asks a question." Hagin translates this term as 'le demandeur," and *Intoductorium* uses the doublet "querens seu interrogator" = "querent or interrogator."[441]

Bate's motive for doublets such as "dolor seu passio," "virtus seu fortitudo," "querens seu interrogator," "obscuri vel tenebrosi," etc. remains a puzzle. In these cases the two components are near synonyms, and not a literal translation plus the common Latin technical term. Probably Bate deemed that by providing near synonyms he was clarifying obscure terms: one component of the doublet is a rare Latin term that Bate took as a literal

---

[434] See *Introductorius*, § 3.4:4; *Reshit Ḥokhmah*, § 3.4:4, 142–143; P, 33rb (*Commencement*).
[435] See *Iudicia*, § 12:6; cf. *Mishpeṭei ha-Mazzalot*, § 12:6, 498–499.
[436] See *Rationes* I, § 3.6:2; § 10.5:2; cf. *Ṭeʿamim* I, § 3.6:2, 66–67; § 10.5:2, 98–99.
[437] See *Rationes* II, § 3.3:2 *et passim*; cf. *Ṭeʿamim* II, § 3.3:2, 206–207 *et passim*.
[438] See *Iudicia*, § 42:12 *et passim*; cf. *Mishpeṭei ha-Mazzalot*, § 42:12, 528–529 *et passim*.
[439] See *Rationes* I, § 3.4:6 *et passim*; cf. *Ṭeʿamim* I, § 3.4:6, 62–63 *et passim*.
[440] See *Introductorius*, § 6.6:6 *et passim*; cf. *Reshit Ḥokhmah*, § 6.6:6, 192–193 *et passim*.
[441] See *Introductorius*, § 8.2:3,4; cf. *Reshit Ḥokhmah*, § 8.2:3,4, 212–213.

translation of what he found in his source text, the other component, a near synonym of the former, is the Latin term in vogue in Bate's time.

1.9. The Strongest Planet

The strongest planet in a horoscopic chart is usually the one that has the most dignities (house, exaltation, triplicity, term, and decan) in the ascendant or in other zodiacal locations. The common Latin technical term for this concept is "almutaz," a transliteration of the Arabic المبتزّ (*al-mubtazz*).

(i) Ibn Ezra, who shuns transliterations of Arabic terms, uses at least four different Hebrew words to mean the strongest planet. Bate turns all of them into doublets.

(a) הממונה, literally "the overseer." In *De mundo*, Bate uses two different doublets for this, whose common feature is the inclusion of "almutaz": "prepotens sive almutaz" and "almutaz vel dominum" = "very powerful or *al-mubtazz*" and "*al-mubtazz* or lord."[442] But in *Rationes* II the same Hebrew term (הממונה) becomes "banilus seu presul" = "*banilus* or ruler,"[443] and in *Rationes* I "presul seu prepositus qui vocatur almubtaz" = "ruler or chief, which are called *al-mubtazz*."[444]

(b) הפקיד, "the one in charge," translated in *Iudicia* as "presul seu almubtaz" = "ruler or *al-mubtazz*."[445]

(c) המושל, "the ruler, translated in *Iudicia* as "presul seu dominus" = "ruler or lord."[446]

(d) השליט, "the governor," translated in *Rationes* II as "prepositus sive presul" = "chief or ruler."[447]

(ii) Ibn Ezra coined new Hebrew names for the same concept when it applies to the strongest planet in the natal chart; Bate renders them by means of new doublets:

(a) *Ṭeʿamim* II, in one locus, refers to הממונה על המולד, "the one that is in charge of the nativity." *Rationes* II translates this as "presul nativitatis

---

[442] See *De mundo*, § 24:1, § 42:3; cf. *ʿOlam* I, § 24:1, 68–69; § 42:3, 80–81.
[443] See *Rationes* II, § 7.2:23; cf. *Ṭeʿamim* II, § 7.2:23, 244–245. A "banilus," "ballivus" or "bajulus" is a royal minister or governor.
[444] See *Rationes* I, § 3.3:3; cf. *Ṭeʿamim* I, § 3.3:3, 62–63.
[445] See *Iudicia*, § 47:3; cf. *Mishpeṭei ha-Mazzalot*, § 47:3, 534–535.
[446] See *Iudicia*, § 48:7; cf. *Mishpeṭei ha-Mazzalot*, § 48:7, 536–537.
[447] See *Rationes* II, § 7.1:4; cf. *Ṭeʿamim* II, § 7.1:4, 244–245.

seu ille qui nativitate preest" = "the ruler of the nativity or the one that is in charge of the nativity."[448]

(b) *Teʿamim* II, in another locus, refers to כל נולד שיהיה הפקיד עליו, "any native whose ruler is ...." *Rationes* II has the triplet "cuicumque nato presul sive almutaz aut significator" = "the ruler, or *al-mubtazz*, or significator."[449]

(c) In *Meʾorot*, Ibn Ezra employed the expression הפקיד הממונה על מולד, "the ruler who is in charge of the nativity." *De luminaribus* has a Latin triplet: "dux vel presul seu almutaz super nativitate" = "the commander, or the ruler, or *al-mubtazz* over the nativity."[450]

(iii) A related concept is that of the "strongest planet in the five places of dominion."[451] In Arabic astrology these "five places of dominion" are known as الهيلاج (*al-haylāj*), and the strongest planet over one of these five places is كدخداه (*kaddudhah*). The common Latin technical terms for them are transliterations of the Arabic: "*hillej*" (or some variation) and "*alcochoden*" (or some variation). Ibn Ezra, who avoided transliterations of Arabic words, coined new Hebrew terms for the five places of dominion and for the strongest planet in these places. Bate, as is his wont, turned them into doublets:

(a) *Teʿamim* II designates the "five places of dominion" by המושלים, "governors." *Rationes* II translates this Hebrew term by means of the doublet "presules seu duces" = "rulers or commanders."[452]

(b) *Teʿamim* II calls the *kaddudhah* השרש שילקח ממנו החיים, "the root from which ⟨the length of⟩ life is taken." Bate understood Ibn Ezra's metaphor and opted for the doublet "princeps seu presul a quo sumpta est vita" = "the prince or ruler from which ⟨the length of⟩ life is taken."[453]

(c) *Mishpeṭei ha-Mazzalot* refers to the *kaddudhah* as הפקיד על חמשה מקומות השררה, "the one in charge over the five places of dominion."

---

[448] See *Rationes* II, § 2.1:5; cf. *Teʿamim* II, § 2.1:5, 184–185.
[449] See *Rationes* II, § 2.4:20; cf. *Teʿamim* II, § 2.4:20, 194–195.
[450] See *De luminaribus*, § 8:4; cf. *Meʾorot*, § 8:4, 460–461.
[451] The five places of dominion, which play a significant role in the prediction of the native's lifespan, are (1–2) the positions of the two luminaries, (3) the position of the conjunction or opposition of the luminaries, whichever occurred last before the native's birth, (4) the degree of the ascendant, and (5) the lot of Fortune. For an account of the selection of the strongest planet in these five places, see Sela 2013, 45–57.
[452] See *Rationes* II, § 6.2:1; cf. *Teʿamim* II, § 6.2:1, 236–237.
[453] See *Rationes* II, § 8.6:2; cf. *Teʿamim* II, § 8.6:2, 252–253.

Again, Bate understood Ibn Ezra's expression and offered four alternative translations, one of which transliterates the Arabic *al-haylāj*: "presul super quinque loca dominium seu dignitatis aut principatus quod est hilles" = "the ruler of the five places of dominion, or dignity, or governance, that is, the *haylāj*."[454]

(4) The concept of "strongest planet" is also applied to the planet in the natal chart that is in charge of the native's spiritual and physical makeup.

(a) *Mishpeṭei ha-Mazzalot* refers to הפקיד על הנשמה, "the one in charge over the soul," which *Iudicia* translates as "prepositus seu presul super animam" = "the chief or ruler of the soul."[455]

(b) *Ṭeʿamim* I mentions הממונה על דבר הגוף, "the one that is in charge of the body," which *Rationes* I turns into "presul seu almubtaz super res corporis" = "the ruler or *al-mubtazz* of something related to the body."[456]

1.10. The Lots

(i) To denote the concept of astrological lot, *Reshit Ḥokhmah*, *Ṭeʿamim* I, and *Ṭeʿamim* II always employ the biblical term גורל, whose original sense is "destiny," "stone, pebble," used to allot the territories to the tribes (Daniel 12:13 *et passim*). By contrast, to denote the same astrological term, *Mishpeṭei ha-Mazzalot* usually uses the Hebrew word מנה (plural: מנות), which is a literal translation of سهم, "portion," (the customary technical term used in Arabic astrological literature for the concept of astrological lot); but in a some cases *Mishpeṭei ha-Mazzalot* employs גורל. This ambiguous approach is noticeable in Bate's translations of Ibn Ezra's introductions of astrology. In *Iudicia*, in the loci where *Mishpeṭei ha-Mazzalot* uses מנה Bate employs "pars" = "part," and in the loci where *Mishpeṭei ha-Mazzalot* uses גורל Bate employs "sors" = "lot."[457] In *Introductorius*, *Rationes* I and *Rationes* II, Bate sometimes uses "pars" (plural: "partes"), sometimes "sors" (plural: "sortes"), and sometimes he clarifies the term by means of the doublet

---

[454] See *Iudicia*, §43:9; cf. *Mishpeṭei ha-Mazzalot*, §43:9, 528–529.
[455] See *Iudicia*, §22:4; cf. *Mishpeṭei ha-Mazzalot*, §22:4, 506–507.
[456] See *Rationes* I, §5.2:6; cf. *Ṭeʿamim* I, §5.2:6, 84–85.
[457] See *Iudicia*, §55:1, §57:1; cf. *Mishpeṭei ha-mazzalot*, §55:1, §57:1, 542–543.

"sortes sive partes" = "lots or parts."[458] The same ambiguity occurs in the description of the lot of the Moon in *Rationes* I ("sors Lune vera est ... et hoc est pars Lune" = "the lot of the Moon is true ... and this is the part of the Moon")[459] and in *Introductorius* ("sors Lune, que vocatur pars fortune" = "the lot of the Moon, which is called the part of fortune").[460] Another reason for this inconsistent approach seems to be that, despite the fact that *Reshit Ḥokhmah* always uses גורל, in the first instance of this word Hagin translates *pars*[461] but usually he employs *sort*.[462] Another reason seems to be that the common Latin technical term for lot is "pars," a translation of one meaning of سهم, "portion," the standard Arabic term for "astrological lot."[463]

(ii) Ibn Ezra's introductions to astrology, all of them translated by Bate, present lists of lots and how they are calculated. In many cases, Bate glosses the names of these lots by means of doublets, sometimes using *sors* and sometimes *pars*. In the doublets, one component is usually a literal translation of the Hebrew and the other the common Latin technical name, sometimes incorporating a transliteration of the Arabic term. This is illustrated in Table 5.

TABLE 5

Reshit Ḥokhmah[464]	Mishpeṭei ha-Mazzalot[465] Ṭeʿamim I,[466] Ṭeʿamim II[467]	Hagin le Juif[468]	Henry Bate[469]
הגורל הטוב = lot of fortune		le sort le bon	sors bona sive sors fortune
גורל התעלומה = lot of the secret		le sort du reçoilement	sors secretorum sive celati animi

---

[458] See *Introductorius*, § 2:10; cf. *Reshit Ḥokhmah*, § 2:10, 48–49; *Rationes* II, § 7.1:3; cf. *Ṭeʿamim* II, § 7.1:3, 244–245.
[459] *Rationes* I, § 9.1:1; cf. *Ṭeʿamim* I, § 4.2:10, 92–93.
[460] *Introductorius*, § 2.13:1; cf. *Reshit Ḥokhmah*, § 2.13:1, 132–133.
[461] See note on *Introductorius*, § 2:10, s.v., "lots and parts."
[462] See note on *Introductorius*, § 9.1:1, s.v., "parts."
[463] See *Introduction*, ed. Burnett et al. (2004), Differentia Quinta, 350–363.
[464] See *Reshit Ḥokhmah*, § 9.1:2 through § 9.16:10, 234–235.
[465] See *Mishpeṭei ha-Mazzalot*, § 45:1, 530–531.
[466] See *Ṭeʿamim* I, § 9.1:2, 92–93.
[467] See *Ṭeʿamim* II, § 7.2:21 through § 7.2:28, 246–248.
[468] See P, 57vb–62rb (*Commencement*).
[469] See *Introductorius*, § 9.1:2 through § 9.16:10; *Iudicia*, § 45:1; *Rationes* I, § 9.1:2; *Rationes* II, § 7.2:21 through § 7.2:28.

TABLE 5 (*cont.*)

Reshit Ḥokhmah	Mishpeṭei ha-Mazzalot Ṭeʿamim I, Ṭeʿamim II	Hagin le Juif	Henry Bate
	גורל התעלומה = lot of the secret (*Ṭeʿamim* I)		pars secretorum sive celati
	מנת התעלומה = lot of the secret (*Mishpeṭei ha-Mazzalot*)		pars celati animi seu secretorum
גורל המומין = lot of the deformities		le sort des mehains	sors impedimentorum seu axemena
גורל צניעות האשה = lot of the woman's chastity		le sort de la simpleté a la fame	pars simplicitatis seu pietatis femelle
גורל ערמת הזכרים = lot of the cunning of men		le sort de l'engin des malles	sors ingenii seu fallacie virorum
גורל ההליכה במים = lot of travel by water		le sort de l'aller par l'iaue	sors eundi per aquam sive navigandi
	גורל על דרך המים = lot of travel by water (*Ṭeʿamim* II)		pars navigationis seu iteneris per aquas
גורל הענוה = lot of humility		le sort de la simpleté	sors simplicitatis seu pietatis
גורל הדעת = lot of knowledge		le sort du savoir	sors sapientie et scientie
גורל המלוכה = lot of kingship		le sort de la roiauté	sors regni seu regnandi
גורל הנצוח = lot of subjugation		le sort du vainquement	sors vincendi seu victorie
גורל הנדיבות = lot of generosity		le sort de la volentivité	sors benevolentie seu liberalitatis
גורל הרעים = lot of friends		le sort des compaignons	sors sodalium seu consortium

TABLE 5 (*cont.*)

Reshit Ḥokhmah	Mishpeṭei ha-Mazzalot Ṭeʿamim I, Ṭeʿamim II	Hagin le Juif	Henry Bate
גורל המום בגוף = lot of physical deformity		le sort du mahing ou cours	sors inpedimentum seu azemena
גורל העָקָב = lot of reward		le sort de l'agait	sors retributionis vel insidiationis
גורל הגבורה = lot of courage		le sort de la force	sors fortitudinis et audacie
גורל ההריגה = lot of killing		le sort de l'ocision	sors feritatis vel occisionis
	גורל הזנות = lot of prostitution (*Ṭeʿamim* II)		pars incestus seu violentus coitus ac ingenii et fallacie
	גורל הכבוד = lot of dignity (*Ṭeʿamim* II)		pars honoris seu exaltationis et dignitatis
	גורל החן = lot of beauty (*Ṭeʿamim* II)		pars gratie et acceptabilitatis

2. *How much Hebrew did Bate Know?*

We do not know whether Henry Bate ever studied Hebrew. There is, however, evidence that he could parse at least some Hebrew words and passages and even translate Hebrew texts with the assistance of a Hebraist.

2.1. Translations "de Hebreo in Latinum"

All the explicits of the numerous manuscripts of *De mundo vel seculo* agree that Bate's translation of *ʿOlam* I was made "de Hebreo in Latinum" (see above, p. 63). The best representative is the explicit of the earliest available manuscript:

> Paris, BnF, MS n.a.l. 3091, fol. 113rb:[470] Explicit *Liber* Avenesre *de mundo* translatus de Hebreo in Latinum a magistro Henrico Bate anno Domini 1281.

---

[470] See also the explicit in Limoges, BM, 9 (28), fol. 143v.

> Thus ends the *Book of the world* by Ibn Ezra, translated from Hebrew into Latin in the year of the Lord 1281.

Note, however, that such a remark does not occur in the explicits of any of Bate's other translations of Ibn Ezra. Since Bate never writes that he ever studied Hebrew, it is highly implausible that Bate himself directly translated *'Olam* I from a Hebrew manuscript. Rather, two scenarios are conceivable.

One is that "de Hebreo in Latinum" means that the translation of *'Olam* I was carried out without a written but with a oral French intermediary, that is, *à quatre mains*: one scholar, probably Hagin le Juif, would read the Hebrew text and translate it orally into French; Bate then translated what he heard into Latin and wrote it down. The second possibility is that *De mundo* was produced in the same manner as *Introductorius*: Hagin le Juif translated orally from Hebrew into Old French, another scholar (like Obers de Mondidier in the case of *Introductorius*) wrote down the text in French, and Henry Bate translated the French into Latin.

Regarding Bate's translational career, this occurrence is not unique. As mentioned above, the first section of a tripartite Latin text on world astrology incorporates a hitherto unknown incomplete Latin translation of *'Olam* III (see above, p. 10). The colophon of the last component of this tripartite text, which includes a Latin translation of al-Kindī's *Liber de iudiciis revolutionum annorum mundi*, says unambiguously that this translation was carried out by Henry Bate of Malines in 1278 "ex Hebrayco in Latinum."[471]

2.2. "Secundum quod iacet in Ebraico"

Ibn Ezra opens *'Olam* I with a lengthy, detailed, and original mathematical explanation of the 120 planetary conjunctions, a numerical-cosmological pattern borrowed from pseudo-Ptolemy's *Centiloquium*.[472] Henry Bate appears to have had trouble understanding this section, because at the end of his translation of this section he added the following gloss:

> *De mundo*, gloss at §6:7: Inquit translator: hic est itaque sermo Avenesre secundum quod iacet in Ebraico, sed visum est nobis aut truncatam fuisse litteram in exemplari aut salvis bene dictis eius doctrinam nimis confusam tradidisse et minus artificiosam.

---

[471] See Sela et al. (2020), 191–303, esp. p. 267.
[472] See *'Olam* I, § 2:1–4 through § 6:1–7, 52–55; cf. *De mundo*, § 2:1–4 through § 6:1–7.

The translator [Bate] says: This is therefore Ibn Ezra's account according to what is stated in the Hebrew ⟨text⟩, but it seems to me that either the writing has been cut off in the ⟨manuscript⟩ copy or, while the words are sound and well, its sense has been transmitted in an exceedingly confused manner and with little skill.

Here Bate states explicitly not only that he had a Hebrew manuscript of ʿ*Olam* I in front of him, but also that part of the Hebrew text was illegible or its meaning unclear to him. Again, since Bate never informs that he had studied Hebrew, it is highly unlikely that this statement means that he was translating by himself from a Hebrew manuscript. Rather, it seems that Bate's statement is transmitting the embarrassment he felt because his Hebrew assistant, Hagin le Juif, could not properly understand and translate from Hebrew into French, and hence he [Bate] could not adequately translate into Latin, Ibn Ezra's abstruse mathematical explanation of the 120 planetary conjunctions. Note that no fewer than eight consecutive sentences of Ibn Ezra's mathematical explanation of the 120 planetary conjunctions are left untranslated in *De mundo*.[473]

2.3. Hebrew Words that Hagin Left Untranslated

Bate knows the meaning of numerous Hebrew words that Hagin transliterated instead of translating and translates them into Latin. This applies to names of stars, animals, plants, countries, diseases, stones, etc. It is plausible that Bate gained this knowledge from Hagin, who completed or corrected his original text of *Commencement* when he was face to face with Bate. The Latin-French-Hebrew collation of *Introductorius*, *Commencement*, and *Reshit Ḥokhmah* found at least 26 cases like this.[474] It is noteworthy, however, that in nine places Hagin transliterated Hebrew words instead of translating them, and Bate followed suit, transliterating rather than translating them into Latin.[475] Table 6 illustrates this phenomenon:

---

[473] See the omissions in *De mundo*, § 5:10 through § 5:17.
[474] Cases of this type are marked in bold in the critical edition of *Introductorius* and its English translation, and accompanied at the end by a superscript δ. See below, p. 121.
[475] See *Introductorius*, § 2.1:28; § 2.5:16; § 2.10:8; § 2.16:10; § 4.1:11; § 4.1:13 (2 instances); § 4.1:16; § 4.4:8.

TABLE 6

Locus (*Introductorius, Commencement* & *Reshit Ḥokhmah*)	Latin	French	Hebrew
§1.3:3	Pleiades	*kima*	כימה = *kimah*
§1.5:2	Ursa Minor	עיש = *ʿayish* (In Hebrew in the French text)	עיש = *ʿayish*
§1.5:7	Corona Septentrionalis	la corone senestre	הנזר השמאלי = the northern crown
§2.1:13	Egyptus	*Miseraim*	מצרים = *Miṣerayim*
§2.2:27	Pleiades	*kima*	כימה = *kimah*
§2.3:34	sortilegii ac artifices magici	les seigneurs de *terafim*	בעלי התרפים = masters of *terafim*
§2.4:21	mirtus	*hezasz*	הדס = myrtle
§2.5:10	adamas	*alaas*	אלמאס = *al-mās* [diamond]
§2.5:24	canis feri	*sevohacim*	הצבעים = hyenas
§2.7:17	liber scripturarum	le livre de *kessuvim*	ספרים כתובים = *sefarim ketubim*, meaning written books
§2.7:30	utriusque (of one sex as well as the other)	*tumtum*	טומטום = *tumtum*, a person of uncertain sex.
§2.7:30	hermafroditus	*endroginos*	אנדרוגינוס = *androginos* (meaning an androgyne)
§2.8:28	neutrus sexus	*tumtum*	טומטום = *tumtum*, a person of uncertain sex.
§2.8:30	fistulas	et sur mehaing qui est apelé *sereten* (a transliteration of סרטן "*sartan*," the Hebrew word for cancer)	ועל המום הנקרא סרטן = the deformity called cancer.

TABLE 6 (*cont.*)

Locus (*Introductorius, Commencement* & *Reshit Ḥokhmah*)	Latin	French	Hebrew
§ 2.9:9	ventus orientale	vent de *ruahih* (a transliteration of רוח, the Hebrew word for wind)	רוח קדים = *ruaḥ qadim*, "wind of *qadim*," meaning east wind.
§ 2.9:20	caput canis feri seu lupi	*scevoa*, a transliteration of צבוע "hyena"; in margin: canis ferus	צבוע = hyena
§ 2.9:23	canis feri	*scevoa* (a transliteration of צבוע "hyena")	צבוע = hyena
§ 2.14:3	Pleiades	*kima*	כימה = *kimah*
§ 2.16:13	lupus vel bestia	*scevoe* (transliteration of צבוע = *ṣavua'*)	הצבע = the hyena
§ 4.3:10	lupus	*scevoe* = transliteration of צבעים, meaning hyenas	הצבועים = hyenas
§ 4.3:16	scarlatice seu in grana	en *alcarmeze*	באל כרמז = in *al-karmez* (meaning with carmine)
§ 4.4:6	adamas	*alaas*	אלמאס = *al-mās* [diamond]
§ 4.4:9	strutio	*aozeniia* = transliteration of העזניה	העזניה = *ha-o'zniah* (meaning black vulture)
§ 4.5:8	mirti	*hezasim* = transliteration of הדסים	הדסים = myrtles
§ 4.6:4	Indi	les homes de *Hodu* = the people of *Hodu*; (*Hodu* is the transliteration of הודו, meaning India)	אנשי הודו = the people of *Hodu*, meaning the people of India

TABLE 6 (cont.)

Locus (Introductorius, Commencement & Reshit Ḥokhmah)	Latin	French	Hebrew
§ 4.6:12	Anglia	Engleterre = a transliteration of אינגלאטירא	אינגלאטירא = Ingleterra (England)

Other names that Hagin frequently transliterates and Bate recognizes and translates into Latin, are ארץ כוש, transliterated by Hagin as "terre de Cus" and translated by Bate as "terra Ethyopie";[476] and ארץ אדום, transliterated by Hagin as "terre de Edom" and translated by Bate by means of the gloss "terra Edom, id est Christianorum" or by means of the doublet "terra Edom sive Christianorum."[477]

2.4. Biblical Stars, Hebrew Names of Planets, Stars and Constellations

Bate knows the Latin counterparts of the Hebrew names of biblical stars and constellations and presumes to understand their meaning. (i) Ibn Ezra always refers to the Pleiades as כימה (Kimah). Hagin always transliterates "Kima," which Bate always turns into "Pleiades."[478] (ii) Ibn Ezra refers to Suhayl as המאיר הנקרא כסיל, "the bright star called Kesil." Hagin translates "le cler qui est apeles Kescil." Bate expands this into "lucida que est in pede Orionis, in hebrayco vocata est Kesil, id est ignis vel lucida vel fortuna" = "the bright ⟨star⟩ in the leg of Orion, called in Hebrew Kesil, that is, fire, or bright, or fortune."[479] (iii) Ibn Ezra refers to Ursa Minor as עיש ובניה (Job 38:32), "'ayish and her sons." Hagin, according to P, brings 'ayish in Hebrew letters but in reverse order, שיע, and then adds "et ses enfans." Bate, for his part, knows the meaning of the Hebrew word and translates "Ursa Minor cum fetibus suis" = "the Lesser Bear with Her Sons."[480]

---

[476] See Introductorius, § 2.2:13; § 2.7:13; § 2.10:9; § 2.11:11; cf. Reshit Ḥokhmah, § 2.2:13, 66–67; § 2.7:13, 98–99; § 2.10:9, 116–117; § 2.11:11, 122–123; P, 18rb (Commencement).

[477] See Introductorius, § 2.7:13; § 2.10:9; § 4.4:4; § 4.5:3; cf. Reshit Ḥokhmah, § 2.7:13, 98–99; § 2.10:9, 116–117; § 4.4:4, 164–165; § 4.5:3, 168–169; P, 18rb (Commencement).

[478] See Introductorius, § 1.3:3 et passim; cf. Reshit Ḥokhmah, § 1.3:3, 50–51 et passim; P, 2ra (Commencement) et passim.

[479] See Introductorius, § 2.16:10; cf. Reshit Ḥokhmah, § 2.16:10, 50–51; P, 31rb (Commencement).

[480] See Introductorius, § 1.5:2; cf. Reshit Ḥokhmah, § 1.5:2, 52–53; cf. P, 2rb (Commencement).

As noted above, *Reshit Ḥokhmah* includes a complete list of the 48 Ptolemaic constellations. Ibn Ezra, as a rule, shuns transliteration of Arabic and translates their names into Hebrew. Hagin follows suit and translates these Hebrew names into French. Bate, in his turn, often offers the Latin names of these constellations.[481] What is more, many of the 206 short glosses incorporated into *Introductorius* comment on Ibn Ezra's Hebrew names of stars and constellations and provide literal translations of Arabic names of stars and constellations. The most frequent cases are "Hydra," used in *Introductorius* no less than eight times, and "Orion," used in *Introductorius* no less than six times.[482]

Bate not only knows how to pronounce the Hebrew names of the planets, but also their literal non-astronomical meanings. In *Nativitas*, Bate writes "ab Hebreis vocatus est Mercurius stella Solis," that is, "Mercury is called by the Hebrews the 'star of the Sun.'" Indeed, Mercury is כוכב חמה (*kokhav ḥamah*), which, because *ḥamah* can mean Sun, could be parsed (albeit incorrectly) as "the star of the Sun."[483] In *Iudicia*, Bate describes Jupiter and Saturn in a gloss as follows.

> *Iudicia*, § 41:5: Clavis autem et summa est quod est planeta veritatis, *et ideo vocatus est in hebrayco Cedec, id est, iustus, nam et Saturnus etiam in Hebrayco vocatus est Sabtay, id est, quiescens, eo quod servit die Sabbati, id est, quietis.*

> But the key and essence is that it is a planet of truth, *therefore in Hebrew it is called Ṣedek, that is, "just"; Saturn, too, is called in Hebrew Shabbetai, that is, being at rest, because it serves on the day of Sabbath, that is, ⟨the day⟩ of rest.*

2.5. Translation of Hebrew Idioms

All of Bate's complete translations of Ibn Ezra's astrological writings offer literal Latin renderings of Hebrew idioms. Their number is more or less proportional to the length of the translation. Thus, *Introductorius* has 18 translations of this type, *Rationes* I also has 18, *Rationes* II has 12, *Iudicia* 10, *De mundo* 6, and *De luminaribus* 3.[484]

The notes in the English translation of *Introductorius* accompanying the 18 translations of this type bring the Hebrew and French counterparts of

---

[481] See above, p. 31.
[482] See, below, p. 104.
[483] *Nativitas*, ed. Steel et al. (2018), 614–615.
[484] Cases of this type are marked in bold in the critical editions of Bate's complete translations and their corresponding English translation, and are accompanied at the end by a superscript θ.

the Hebrew idiom.[485] They show clearly that Bate's literal Latin translations of Hebrew idioms are a replica of the French translations of the Hebrew idioms found in *Reshit Ḥokhmah*. Here are three examples: (i) in *Reshit Ḥokhmah*, § 2.2:4, Ibn Ezra uses the Hebrew idiom "פריה ורביה" = "fertilization and increase"; Hagin le Juif in *Commencement* translates "fructisement et acroisement," and Bate in *Introductorius*, § 2.2:4 translates "fertilitas et habundantia" = "fertility and abundance;" (ii) in *Reshit Ḥokhmah*, § 2.3:26, Ibn Ezra uses the Hebrew idiom "בני אדם" = "sons of man," meaning human beings; Hagin le Juif in *Commencement* translates "enfans d'ome;" and Bate in *Introductorius*, § 2.3:26 translates "filii hominum" = "sons of men," meaning human beings; (iii) and in *Reshit Ḥokhmah*, § 2.13:1, Ibn Ezra uses the Hebrew idiom לא עלתה על לב אדם = did not ascend in the heart of a man; Hagin le Juif in *Commencement* translates "non montera sur cuer d'ome;" and finally Bate in *Introductorius*, § 2.3:26 translates "nec in corde hominis ascendit" = "does not ascend in the heart of a man," meaning no one ever imagined.

It seems that Bate translated this way because in *Introductorius* he was closely following Hagin le Juif's *Commencement*, to such an extent that he did not pay attention that his Latinizing of Hebrew idioms did not always adequately convey their meaning to the reader. However, scrutiny of the literal Latin translations of Hebrew idioms in Bate's other five translations leaves a totally different impression. This is illustrated in Table 7, which displays cases where Bate accompanies his literal Latin translations of Hebrew idioms with explanations (presented in italics).

TABLE 7

Reference	Hebrew Idiom	Bate's translation and explanation of the Hebrew idiom
Iudicia, § 2:12	עמי הארץ = people of the land	*communia* seu illa que sunt gentis terre = *common people* or those who are people of the land
Iudicia, § 22:4	על ידי המשרת = through the hands of the servant	*a planeta* seu per manum planete = *from the planet* or through the hands of the planet

---

[485] See notes to *Introductorius*, § 2.2:4; § 2.3:26; § 2.3:34; § 2.4:4; § 2.4:10; § 2.5:25; § 2.6:24; § 2.9:26; § 2.13:1; § 3.6:1; § 4.2:3; § 4.2:19; § 4.5:2; § 4.6:14; § 6.6:14; § 7.4:9; § 8.3:5; § 9.3:10.

TABLE 7 (*cont.*)

Reference	Hebrew Idiom	Bate's translation and explanation of the Hebrew idiom
Iudicia, § 32:1	יסתיר למראה העין = will hide from sight	*eclipsabit* seu occultabit ab oculorum visione = *eclipses* or hides from sight of the eyes
Iudicia, § 52:5	חסרון כיס = deficiency of the pocket, meaning lack of money	diminutionem burse *et divitiarum* = decrease of the purse *and* ⟨decrease⟩ *of riches*
Rationes II, § 5.2:6	יתיר הקישור = will loosen the knot. Cf. Job 38.31	nodum dissolvit, *id est, coagulatum liquefacit* = it loosens the knot, *that is, it liquefies what is solidified*
Rationes II, § 5.4:8	בעל מטבע = lord of the coin, meaning operator of a mint	monetarum dominos *seu monetarios* = lords of coins, *or operators of the mint*
Rationes II, § 8.2:4	והם חוזרים חלילה = and they return again	percurrentes et revertentes *tamquam in circulo* = running through and returning *as in a circle*
Rationes I, § 2.2:20	עלה בידם = came up in their hands	*veraces* inventi sunt in manibus eorum = came up in their hands *to be correct*
Rationes I, § 2.8:3	חוזרים חלילה = return again	revertantur iterum *sive circulantur* = return back again *or form a circle*
Rationes I, § 2.13:2	פריה ורביה = reproduction and multiplication	*luxuriam* aut prolis generationem = *lust* or generation of offspring
De luminaribus, § 11:2	לא עלה על לב = did not ascend to the heart.	in cor non ascendebat *sive ignorabatur prius* = did not ascend to the heart *or was ignored before*
De luminaribus, § 15:3	לא עלה על לב = did not ascend to the heart	in cor non ascendebat *sive non suspicabatur* = did not ascend to heart *or was not suspected*
De luminaribus, § 16:4	והדין עמו = he has logic on his side	*et verum dicit* et ius habet = *and he says the truth* and he is right
De mundo, § 23:1	חוזרים חלילה = return again	revertuntur *secundum circulationem* = come back *according to the circular movement*

According to this table, in 14 cases in *Iudicia, Rationes* I, *Rationes* II, *De luminaribus* and *De mundo*, Bate accompanied literal translations of Hebrew idioms with brief explanations, either as glosses or as doublets. This certainly entails that Bate understood the meaning of the Hebrew idioms. Where could Bate have learned this? As stated above, the most plausible answer, given that Bate never writes that he studied Hebrew, is that he was assisted by his Hebrew into French translator, Hagin le Juif. This implies that Bate did not translate only from a written copy of a French translation, as surely was the case for *Commencement*, but, at least for *Iudicia, Rationes* I, *Rationes* II, *De luminaribus*, and *De mundo*, that Bate translated in the presence of, or frequently consulted with, Hagin le Juif, who was his neighbor in Mechelen.

3. Bate, Commentator and Supercommentator on Ibn Ezra

A notable feature of Bate's *modus operandi* is that he does not confine himself to the role of translator, but takes on the task of commentator and even supercommentator. This is noticeable in the fairly frequent and sometimes lengthy glosses in some of his complete translations of Ibn Ezra's astrological writings. Here I look at these glosses in chronological order and limit myself to a quantitative account and a brief review of their contents.

3.1. Glosses in *De mundo*

There are 61 glosses in *De mundo*.

(i) Of them, 57 are short, consisting of only a few words to explain terms and names, make the meaning of the Hebrew source text clearer, or complete what Bate took to be a fragmentary phrase by Ibn Ezra.[486] For example, he glosses the "intersection of the two circles" by adding "which are the circle of the signs and the circle of equality;"[487] and a "small circle" by adding, "which is the epicycle;"[488] *De mundo* refers to the year ⟨4⟩908 according to the Hebrew calendar, and Bate explains that this is "from the creation of the world according to the Jews, in truth 1147 from the incarnation of the Lord;"[489] and where *De mundo* refers to "Enoch, the Ancient," Bate glosses "that is, Hermes."[490]

---

[486] All the glosses, in *De mundo* and in the other complete translations, in the critical editions and their English translations, are marked in italics.
[487] See *De mundo*, gloss at §13:2.
[488] See *De mundo*, gloss at §21:2.
[489] See *De mundo*, gloss at §24:1.
[490] See *De mundo*, gloss at §36:1.

(ii) *De mundo* has two glosses of moderate length—a few lines. In one of them "the translator," i.e., Henry Bate, mentions Ibn Ezra's account of the "120 conjunctions of the seven planets" in Hebrew;[491] the other presents the "masters of the observations" and touches on the discrepancies in their observations.[492]

(iii) The first of the two long glosses in *De mundo* is spurred by the opening sentence of *ʿOlam* I, in which Ibn Ezra unleashes a harsh attack on Abū Maʿshar.[493] This led Bate to write a long prologue of 1700 words in order to refute Ibn Ezra's criticism of Abū Maʿshar.[494] Bate begins by expressing his indignation and disbelief and insists that Ibn Ezra should have been more tolerant in his reading of Abū Maʿshar. Next he shows how Ibn Ezra manipulates Ptolemy's authority. Rather than defending Ptolemy against Ibn Ezra, Bate wonders where in Ptolemy's oeuvre Ibn Ezra could have found the argument he attributes to the astronomer. Finally, Bate discusses Ibn Ezra's main arguments in support of his conclusion, namely, that the incertitude of observations results both from errors in the manufacture of the instruments and from the different ideas about the length of the year because of the discrepancies in the observations of the masters of the observations. A second long gloss in *ʿOlam* I is occasioned by a digression in which Ibn Ezra, on the authority of *Sefer Yeṣirah*, seems to reject the hypothesis that there is a perfect cyclical regularity of the celestial motions.[495] Here Bate tries to reveal what Ibn Ezra only hinted at:[496] Ibn Ezra did not really reject the cyclical regularity of the celestial motions, but wanted to say only that one could never calculate exactly when a certain relation between celestial bodies would return, given the infinite possibilities of combination. But, he adds, admitting the difficulty of calculating the exact return of a celestial configuration does not lead to the conclusion that the celestial motions will continue to infinity without ever returning to a certain configuration.[497]

---

[491] See *De mundo*, gloss at § 6:6; see above, p. 94.
[492] See *De mundo*, gloss at § 13:8.
[493] See *ʿOlam* I, § 1:1–3, 52–53; cf. *De mundo*, § 1:1–3.
[494] For an analysis of this prologue, see Steel 2020 (a), 245–261.
[495] See *ʿOlam* I, § 24:3–6, 68–69; cf. *De mundo*, § 24:3–6.
[496] In the middle of the gloss Bate writes: "Et hoc forsan est quod hic innuit actor iste" = "This is perhaps what this author hinted at"; See *De mundo*, gloss at § 24:8 → 2.
[497] See *De mundo*, gloss at § 24:8 → 1–10. For an analysis of this gloss, see Steel 2020 (a), 261–265.
See Steel, "A Discussion on Ptolemy's Authority."

3.2. Glosses in *De luminaribus*

There are 66 glosses in *De luminaribus*.

(i) Fifty-two of them are short. Where the text mentions "the luminous stars," Bate correctly glosses "namely, the planets" (not the fixed stars);[498] he glosses "the host of heaven" as "that is, the fixed stars;"[499] "the intersection of the circles" is explained as "that is to say, from the equinoctial points;"[500] to "the upper ⟨stars⟩" he adds "that is, the fixed ⟨stars⟩".[501]

(ii) There are 14 glosses that consist of whole sentences.[502] Some of them are also divergent readings. For example, where *De luminaribus* has, "if this happened in a bad mixture," Bate glosses "when they are mixed with bad ⟨planets⟩;"[503] and where *De luminaribus* has "if the illness persists," Bate glosses "when it is eclipsed, because its eclipse will prolong the illness or sickness."[504]

There are no long glosses in *De luminaribus*.

3.3. Glosses in *Introductorius*

Introductorius has no fewer than 206 short glosses, consisting of a few words. Many of them offer the Latin names of stars, to elucidate Ibn Ezra's Hebrew names, which are literal translations of the Arabic designations of stars and constellations.[505] The most frequent case is "Hydra" (the eighth southern constellation in Ptolemy's star catalogue), which Bate interpolates eight times to gloss Ibn Ezra's "the Beast," or "the Fighting Warrior."[506] Another frequent case is "Orion" (the second southern constellation in Ptolemy's catalogue), which Bate supplies six times to gloss Ibn Ezra's "the Mighty Dog," "the Dog," or "the Mighty One".[507] Other cases are "Perseus" (the eleventh northern constellation in Ptolemy's catalogue), which glosses

---

[498] See *De luminaribus*, gloss at § 1:2; cf. *Me'orot* § 1:2, 452–453.
[499] See *De luminaribus*, gloss at § 1:4; cf. *Me'orot* § 1:4, 452–453.
[500] See *De luminaribus*, gloss at § 15:2; cf. *Me'orot* § 15:2, 464–465.
[501] See *De luminaribus*, gloss at § 35:1; cf. *Me'orot* § 35:1, 482–483.
[502] See glosses at § 1:9; § 8:1; § 8:3; § 9:7; § 10:2; § 13:2; § 15:1 (2 glosses); § 15:3; § 16:2; § 16:3; § 24:8; § 32:3; § 34:3.
[503] See *De luminaribus*, gloss at § 8:1; cf. *Me'orot* § 8:1, 460–461.
[504] See *De luminaribus*, gloss at § 13:2; cf. *Me'orot* § 13:2, 462–463.
[505] See particularly *Introductorius*, § 1.4:1–16; § 1.5:19.
[506] See *Introductorius*, § 1.4:9; § 2.4:25; § 2.5:17; § 2.5:20; § 2.5:23; § 2.5:43; § 2.7:19; § 2.16:9.
[507] See *Introductorius*, glosses at § 1.4:3; § 2.3:19; § 2.3:22; § 2.3:53; § 2.16:4; § 2.18:10.

GENERAL INTRODUCTION 105

Ibn Ezra's "the Devil's Head,"[508] "Cetus" (the first southern constellation in Ptolemy's catalogue), which glosses Ibn Ezra's "the Sea-Lion,"[509] and "Flaminatus or Cepheus" (the fourth northern constellation in Ptolemy's catalogue), which glosses Ibn Ezra's "the Lady of the Blazing Fire."[510]

As a rule, these short glosses explain terms and names and make the meaning of the Hebrew source text clearer. For example, Bate glosses *terafim* as "that is, magical devices;"[511] he explains that "the present time, which is the year 4908 from the creation of Adam," means "according to the Hebrew truth, which is in the year 1147 from the Incarnation of our Lord Jesus Christ;"[512] and "the land of *Alhind*" and "the land of *Edom*" are clarified as "that is, the land of India" and "that is, the land of the Christians."[513]

3.4. Glosses in *Rationes* I

There are 118 glosses in *Rationes* I.

(i) Almost all of them—110—are short. For example, where *Teʿamim* I instructs the reader "⟨from⟩ the result extract seven and seven," Bate adds "or divide by seven";[514] where *Teʿamim* I mentions "our master Abraham," in a clear reference to Abraham Ibn Ezra, Bate glosses "called the Prince," as if the reference were to Abraham Bar Ḥiyya;[515] where *Teʿamim* I states that "it is necessary to make only three ⟨aspects⟩," Bate explains that this is so "because you can specify the right aspects opposite the facing signs."[516]

(ii) *Rationes* I also has six glosses that consist of a few lines, where Bate identifies himself as the translator, mentions Ibn Ezra as the author of *Teʿamim* I, criticizes Ibn Ezra, alludes to Abū Maʿshar's opinions in his *Great Introduction*, and prefers what Abū Maʿshar writes there to Ibn Ezra's opinions in *Teʿamim* I.[517] For example, according to *Teʿamim* I, "Aries is hot and dry because the image of the stars resembles a ram; and this is the explanation for Leo and also for the sign of Sagittarius, which are like images of heat or of hot things." Bate takes exception:

---

[508] See *Introductorius*, § 1.5:2.
[509] See *Introductorius*, § 1.4:2.
[510] See *Introductorius*, § 1.5:5.
[511] See *Introductorius*, gloss at § 2.1:28.
[512] See *Introductorius*, gloss at § 2.1:40.
[513] See *Introductorius*, gloss at § 2.10:9.
[514] See *Rationes* I, gloss at § 2.8:4.
[515] See *Rationes* I, gloss at § 3.4:8.
[516] See *Rationes* I, gloss at § 10.6:1.
[517] See *Rationes* I, glosses at § 1.4:4; § 1.4:7; § 2.2:19; § 6.3:5 and § 10.7:5 (2 glosses).

"The translator says: if the truth is to be taken into consideration, Abū Ma'shar gives a much better explanation in his *Great Introduction*, namely the second book, seventh chapter."[518]

(iii) *Rationes* I has two long glosses. The first, running to 890 words, fleshes out Ibn Ezra's middle-ground opinion about the power of a planet when it attains its apogee by offering new perspectives on the problem: the motion on the epicycle, that is, direct motion and retrogradation, as well as what Bate takes to be the opinions of the Philosopher (Aristotle), al-Biṭrūjī, Plato, and "the astrologers."[519] The second, of 200 words, criticizes Ibn Ezra's approach to the calculation of the aspects and refers to another gloss, not by Bate but by a Jewish scholar, who turns out to be Abraham Bar Ḥiyya. This gloss can be found at the end of Bate's translation of *Mishpeṭei ha-Mazzalot*.[520]

3.5. Glosses in *Rationes* II

There are 127 short glosses in *Rationes* II. Here are some examples. With regard to Cancer as the "sign of the world," *Ṭeʿamim* II offers a succinct description of the horoscope of the creation of the world: "If we place the Sun at the beginning of Aries, where its power is strengthened, then the ascendant sign is Cancer." Here Bate adds, after "Aries," "at midheaven," and after "Cancer," "at the upright sphere or under the upright circle."[521] With regard to Venus, *Ṭeʿamim* II states that it indicates "quarrels and dishonor, which are the end of all pleasures," but also that it indicates "singing." Bate glosses both statements: regarding the first, Bate adds that this is "because lamentation takes possession of joy"; regarding the second, he writes that this is "because Venus indicates melody and pleasures."[522] Regarding the "science of the images," *Ṭeʿamim* II states that it is forbidden by the law of God. Bate glosses that this is "because the image of a cross is there, but according to another reading, because it resembles a foreign rite or religion."[523]

Three other short glosses deserve special mention; one proves that Bate was the translator of a hitherto unknown version of Ezra's *Book of the world*;[524] another is a significant cross-reference to another part of Ibn Ezra's

---

[518] See *Rationes* I, gloss at § 1.4:4.
[519] See gloss at § 5.2:8.
[520] See gloss between the end of *Rationes* I and the explicit of *Rationes* I.
[521] See *Rationes* II, gloss at § 2.4:9.
[522] See *Rationes* II, glosses at § 5.4:6 and § 5.4:8.
[523] See *Rationes* II, gloss at § 8.3:2.
[524] See *Rationes* II, gloss at § 5.5:6.

astrological corpus;⁵²⁵ and the third is the only one in which the fact that it is a "gloss" is explicitly acknowledged.⁵²⁶

3.6. Glosses in *Iudicia*

There are 160 glosses in *Iudicia*.

(i) Of them, 146 are short and consist of only a few words. In the four following examples, Bate added a gloss because he thought that this wording of *Mishpeṭei ha-Mazzalot* is not precise or clear enough. In one locus, *Mishpeṭei ha-Mazzalot* asserts that Aries is the beginning of the signs, because when the Sun enters it day and night are equal "in all the countries;" this is glossed by Bate who adds "in all the climates of the Earth."⁵²⁷ In a second locus *Mishpeṭei ha-Mazzalot* says that there is a distance of "120 degrees" between two planets; Bate adds, by way of explanation, "and they comprise four signs, which are the third of the circle."⁵²⁸ In a third locus *Mishpeṭei ha-Mazzalot* asserts vaguely that the circle is divided into only two equal parts "because any circle has two diameters"; Bate adds that this is so because "in any circle there are two diameters that cut themselves mutually at a right angle."⁵²⁹ In a fourth locus *Mishpeṭei ha-Mazzalot* refers to "synagogues"; this is glossed by Bate who adds "temples, monasteries or assembly halls of chapters where prayers are ⟨offered⟩."⁵³⁰

(ii) There are nine glosses consisting of a few lines, in which Bate expands significantly on a topic covered in *Mishpeṭei ha-Mazzalot*, provides examples or illustrations, expresses his reservations or makes corrections regarding some doctrines, occasionally mentioning the author of *Mishpeṭei ha-Mazzalot* and explicitly referring to the addition as a "gloss."⁵³¹

(iii) There are also five long glosses:
   (1) The first, of 130 words, expands on the *novenaria* and mentions Ibn Ezra explicitly (as a source, not as the author).⁵³²

---

[525] See *Rationes* II, gloss at § 4.1:2.
[526] See *Rationes* II, gloss at § 6.7:1.
[527] See *Iudicia*, gloss at § 1:7.
[528] See *Iudicia*, gloss at § 35:4.
[529] See *Iudicia*, gloss at § 36:1.
[530] See *Iudicia*, gloss at § 38:13.
[531] See glosses at *Iudicia*, § 2:4; § 8:2; § 9:2 (2 glosses); § 10:7; § 41:5; § 41:10; § 73:2; § 74:1.
[532] See *Iudicia*, gloss at § 10:7.

(2) The second, 160 words long, is on how many degrees should be added or subtracted from astronomical tables to calculate the positions of special zodiacal degrees endowed with astrological significance. This gloss refers both to the ostensible author of *Mishpeṭei ha-Mazzalot* (i.e., Abraham Bar Ḥiyya) and, twice, to Ibn Ezra in his *Book of reasons*.[533]

(3) The third (240 words) brings the opinion of the "translator," i.e., Henry Bate, who relies primarily on Aristotle's *De generatione et corruptione* and comments on the statement in *Mishpeṭei ha-Mazzalot* that "the Ancients said that when a planet is at its apogee, then it is very good, and the contrary at the opposite of the apogee."[534]

(4) The fourth (180 words) presents diverse opinions about the testimonies of the horoscopic houses and the planets: (a) the opinion of "the *Book of nativities*" that is, Ibn Ezra's second version of *Sefer ha-Moladot*, which Bate assigns to "the author," that is, Abraham Bar Ḥiyya, regarding the testimonies of the first horoscopic house; (b) the opinion of Māshā'allāh regarding the sixth horoscopic house; (c) the opinion of "the author," that is, Abraham Bar Ḥiyya, regarding Saturn when it is in opposition to the Sun; (d) the opinion of "the *Book of interrogations*," that is, Ibn Ezra's third version of *Sefer ha-She'elot*, which Bate also assigns here to Abraham Bar Ḥiyya, regarding a planet when it is in opposition to the Sun.[535]

(5) The fifth gloss (already mentioned in the last section), which stretches to approximately 2,700 words and deals with the "aspects of the directions," is divided into two parts.[536] The first presents the opinion of an anonymous Hebrew "glossator" about the last section on the aspects in *Mishpeṭei ha-Mazzalot*. The Hebrew "glossator" says that he prefers Abū Ma'shar's opinion in this regard, explains the latter's view, and grounds his criticism of the last section of *Mishpeṭei ha-Mazzalot* on Abū Ma'shar.[537] The second part offers Bate's own commentary on the gloss by the anonymous Hebrew scholar and on the last section of *Iudicia*.

---

[533] See *Iudicia*, gloss at § 10:7.
[534] See *Iudicia*, gloss at § 22:1.
[535] See *Iudicia*, gloss at § 50:3.
[536] See above, p. 49.
[537] See *Iudicia*, gloss at § 76:4 → 1–29.

4. Bate's Trajectory as a Translator of Ibn Ezra's Astrological Writings

We can now summarize Bate's trajectory as a translator of Ibn Ezra's astrological writings in a chronological chart (Table 8).

TABLE 8

Translations	Words/ passages	Date and place of completion	Days/years elapsed since the completion of the previous translation
Hagin le Juif's Hebrew into French translations	*Reshit Ḥokhmah*, *Moladot*, *Mivḥarim* II, *She'elot* II	1273, Mechelen	
Translation of *'Olam* III	3,700 words	around 1278	5 years
Nativitas	140 passages from 12 works	1280	2 years
De diebus creticis	7 passages from 4 works	around 1280	2 years
De mundo	9,800 words	October 20, 1281, started in Liège, completed in Mechelen	3 years
De luminaribus	5,500 words	June 4, 1292, Orvieto	11 years
Intoductorius	34,900 words	August 22, 1292, Orvieto	80 days, or 2 months and 19 days
Rationes I	16,100	September 15, 1292, Orvieto	24 days
Rationes II	14,100 words	September 23, 1292, Orvieto	8 days
Iudicia	16,300 words	October 29, 1292, Orvieto	36 days

We see, then, that of the 20 items in Ibn Ezra's astrological corpus known to us today, Henry Bate knew of and translated from 13: *Reshit Ḥokhmah*, *Ṭe'amim* I, *Ṭe'amim* II, *Mishpeṭei ha-Mazzalot*, *Moladot*, *Moladot* II, *De nativitatibus*, *Mivḥarim* II, *Mivḥarim* III, *She'elot* II, *Me'orot*, *'Olam* I, and *'Olam* III. This makes him the most prolific translator of Ibn Ezra of all the Latin schol-

ars who, starting in the last decades of the thirteenth century, produced various collections of Ibn Ezra's astrological writings. By comparison, Pietro d'Abano produced six complete translations of treatises by Ibn Ezra,[538] and Arnoul de Quincampoix two.[539] Pierre de Limoges had a hand in the Latin translation of only one complete work and of sections of two other works by Ibn Ezra.[540]

Ibn Ezra's astrological texts known to Bate belong to all the branches of Greco-Arabic astrology, but a closer look at those he selected for a complete (or incomplete) translation reveals Bate's predilections. Four of them— *Introductorius*, *Iudicia*, *Rationes* I, and *Rationes* II—are introductions to astrology. This indicates that Bate turned to Ibn Ezra principally in order to learn about the basic elements of the worldview that underlies astrology and about the technical concepts of its various branches. There is also one translation related to the critical days and medical astrology: *De luminaribus*. That this topic was high on Bate's agenda is shown by the fact that he himself composed *De diebus creticis*.

However, Bate's two earliest translations, the incomplete version of *'Olam* III and the complete translation of *'Olam* I, address world astrology. A clue to Bate's early propensity for this branch of astrology may be found in *Nativitas*, his astrological autobiography, written shortly after the translation of *'Olam* III, carried out around 1278, and almost simultaneously with *De mundo*, carried out in 1281. Bate writes in *Nativitas* that he was born twenty years after a Saturn-Jupiter conjunction (the main tool for world predictions or historical analysis),[541] that Libra was the sign of the present Saturn-Jupiter conjunction,[542] that in his natal horoscope Saturn and Jupiter were placed in Libra, which is the tenth sign after the ascendant of this natal horoscope (Sagittarius),[543] that a Saturn-Jupiter conjunction in the tenth house indicates the appearance of a king or a prophet, and that Libra is a sign of justice and indicates prophets, princes, and men obedient to divine matters.[544] Bate also quotes a passage by Abū Ma'shar on the signification of Libra, to explain his special affinity for religious

---

[538] Sela, Sela 2019 (d), 1–82.
[539] They are preserved in a single fifteenth-century manuscript, Ghent, MS Univ. 5 (416), fols. 85r–103r.
[540] See Sela, Sela 2019 (b), 9–57.
[541] *Nativitas*, ed. Steel et al. (2018), 968–971.
[542] *Nativitas*, ed. Steel et al. (2018), 982–983.
[543] *Nativitas*, ed. Steel et al. (2018), 957–959.
[544] *Nativitas*, ed. Steel et al. (2018), 957–969.

matters, public speech, trade, mathematics, and music.[545] All this seems to explain Bate's motivation to augment his knowledge of world astrology by means of translations of Ibn Ezra's books on this topic, not only to decode his natal horoscope but also to have foreknowledge of his political career.

That eight years elapsed between 1273, when Bate commissioned Hagin to produce his four French translations, and 1281, when he completed *De mundo*, and that three of Hagin's four French translations have no counterpart among Bate's complete Latin translations, demonstrate that he did not employ Hagin so that he could put the latter's French translations to immediate use as the basis for Latin translations of Ibn Ezra's astrological writings. At this stage, Bate needed Hagin's French translations so that he could take a first look at Ibn Ezra's astrological work and lay the astrological substratum for his own treatises.

As seen above, the nearly 140 references to twelve astrological treatises by Ibn Ezra that Bate incorporated into *Nativitas* in 1280, and into *De diebus creticis* soon after, use Ibn Ezra's texts in different ways. (i) Most of the references are paraphrases or loose paraphrases of identifiable passages from treatises written by or attributed to Abraham Ibn Ezra. (ii) In *Nativitas* and in *De diebus creticis* Bate incorporated identical translations of two passages from two treatises by Ibn Ezra, one right after the other.[546] (iii) Some of these references are precise translations of identifiable passages from treatises written by or attributed to Abraham Ibn Ezra.[547] (iv) Nine of the references are not translations or paraphrases from a Hebrew text by Ibn Ezra but verbatim quotations from one of the four versions transmitted in *De nativitatibus*, a Latin text attributed to Ibn Ezra that has no surviving Hebrew counterpart.[548]

It is highly implausible that relevant passages from certain texts can be selected and a translation or paraphrase can then be incorporated into another text, unless the author has access to full versions of the texts in question. It is also highly implausible that an author can do this when translating *à quatre mains*, because in order to select 150 relevant passages from a text he needs to have a complete picture of all the relevant passages in it. Therefore, the fact that *Nativitas* and *De diebus creticis* contain 150 translations or paraphrases from passages of identifiable treatises by Ibn

---

[545] *Nativitas*, ed. Steel et al. (2018), 971–981.
[546] See above, p. 19.
[547] See above, pp. 13, 19.
[548] See above, p. 2.

Ezra demonstrates that in 1280, seven years after commissioning Hagin, Bate owned virtually complete translations, probably in French, of twelve relevant Hebrew treatises by Ibn Ezra.

As we have seen, in all cases where translations in *Nativitas* and *De diebus creticis* have a counterpart in passages from the six complete translations carried out by Bate in 1281 and in 1292, *Nativitas* and *De diebus creticis*, on the one hand, and the six complete translations, on the other, differ considerably from each other. This indicates that in 1292 he did not use a Latin translation he might have produced in 1280 or earlier. The most plausible scenario is that when he incorporated translations or paraphrases into *Nativitas* and *De diebus creticis*, and later when he produced his six complete translations, Bate was translating from French intermediaries produced before 1280.

A look at the explicits of the five complete translations Bate produced in Orvieto in 1292 strongly suggests that he produced a draft which he then went back and revised and retouched until satisfied with his work. Take for example *Rationes* II: it was completed on September 23, 1292, in Orvieto, only eight days after he finished work on *Rationes* I, on September 15. But it is all but impossible that he translated *Rationes* II, which runs to 15,300 words, in only eight days. Similar considerations apply to the numbers in the last column of Table 8 with regard to *Rationes* I, *Iudicia*, and *Introductorius*.

The logical conclusion is that the dates given in the explicits are when Bate "completed" the translation, but cannot be taken as an indication of when he started work on the next translation. There is no reason to assume that he worked on only one treatise by Ibn Ezra at a time and produced each translation in one go. It is more likely that he improved and polished them over time after he had a first draft ready, and that the completion date is when he was willing to pronounce a particular job done, while continuing to work on other texts.

That Bate produced his translations gradually and that parts of them were executed months or years before the completion date in the explicit is borne out by two passages already mentioned above. The first is found in *Nativitas*, composed in 1280, where Bate refers to a passage in the middle of *Rationes* I, completed in 1292, as follows:

> *Nativitas*, ed. Steel et al. (2018): quemadmodum a nobis latius est expositum super *Libro rationum* Avenezre.[549]

---

[549] The significance of this passage was discovered by Carlos Steel. See Steel, "Editorial Principles," in *The Astrological Biography of a Medieval Philosopher*, p. 29.

As I have explained at length in a commentary on the *Book of reasons* by Ibn Ezra.

Rationes I, completed in Orvieto on September 15, 1292, does in fact incorporate a long gloss of approximately 890 words.[550] But the reference to a "commentary on the *Book of reasons* by Ibn Ezra" uses the past tense and appears in *Nativitas*, composed in 1280. This means that Bate had produced a draft of this "commentary on the *Book of reasons* by Ibn Ezra" before 1280, which surfaced in *Rationes* I at least twelve years later. This also strongly suggests that Bate had a complete version of his translation of *Ṭeʿamim* I well before 1280.

The second testimony is found in a passage extracted from the gloss that Bate appended to *Rationes* I:

> gloss at the end of *Rationes* I, → 2–3: secundum quod notum est ac satis declaratum in glossa quadam super *Introductorium Abrahe Ducis*, capitulo de aspectibus. Quapropter ad huiusmodi defectus ad implendos erroresque vitandos et aspectus ipsos artificiosius equandos, ac regularius ibidem regulare, quoddam et artificiosum ac breve tradidimus documentum.
>
> As has been noted and sufficiently explained in a certain gloss on *the Introduction by Abraham, the Prince*, in the chapter on the aspects. Therefore, to overcome defects of this kind, to avoid errors, to equate [correct] these aspects more skillfully, and more in accordance with the rules, we have transmitted a document that is skillful and brief.

The broad context of this passage has been already explained.[551] Here it is sufficient to point out the following points: (a) "*Introductorium Abrahe Ducis*" (= "the Introduction by Abraham, the Prince") refers ultimately to *Iudicia*, whose Hebrew source text, *Mishpeṭei ha-Mazzalot*, according to Bate, was composed by Abraham Bar Ḥiyya, the Prince. (b) "Glossa quadam super *Introductorium Abrahe Ducis*, capitulo de aspectibus" (= "certain gloss on *the Introduction by Abraham, the Prince*, in the chapter on the aspects") refers to the first part of the gloss at the end of *Iudicia*, translated by Bate but written by an anonymous Hebrew scholar.[552] (c) "quoddam et artificiosum ac breve tradidimus documentum" (= "a document that is skillful and brief") refers to the gloss reflecting Bate's own opinion at the end of *Iudicia*,

---

[550] See above, p. 106.
[551] See above, p. 52.
[552] See gloss at the end of *Iudicia*, → 1–29.

which follows the gloss translated by Bate but written by an anonymous Hebrew scholar.[553]

It is significant that all three references are in the past tense. Regarding the first two, Bate writes "secundum quod notum est ac satis declaratum" = "as has been noted and sufficiently explained"; regarding the third, he writes "tradidimus documentum" = "we have transmitted a document." Note that whereas Bate finished *Rationes* I on September 15, 1292, in Orvieto, he did not complete *Iudicia* until October 29. This means that at some point before Bate finished *Rationes* I, he already had a draft version of *Iudicia*, which he continued to revise and polish until it was deemed complete more than six weeks later.

Aims, Methodology and Editorial Principles

The methodology employed for the critical editions of each of Bate's Latin translations, as put forward above, is the same as that used in other editions. The objective of this volume, however, is not merely to publish critical editions of Bate's complete translations, but in particular to display Bate's modus operandi as a translator of Ibn Ezra and extract his attitude towards Ibn Ezra's texts. This task required a thorough collation of Bate's translations with their source texts (henceforth, "the collation"). The present section surveys the various components of the collation, introduces the typographical symbols and sigla that were chosen for identifying the various components of the collation, and explains why the methodology employed here it is the most appropriate to the context of this volume.

1. *The English Translations*

At the start of the work on this volume, and given that the critical editions of Ibn Ezra's Hebrew astrological writings were accompanied by English translations, the possibility was considered that it would be superfluous to toil on English versions of Bate's Latin translations. This idea was rejected because a preliminary scrutiny showed that, when read against the critical editions of Ibn Ezra's Hebrew astrological writings, Bate's Latin translations are full of divergent and alternative readings, omissions, glosses, stylistic alterations, and additions derived from lost Hebrew manuscripts. Moreover, to make readers aware of the special flavor, peculiarities, and minutiae of

---

[553] See gloss at the end of *Iudicia*, → 30–56.

Bate's work, which are essential for a proper collation of the Latin translations against their source texts, the English translations are meant to stick as close as possible to Bate's Latin.

Hence it was decided (a) to offer literal English translations of virtually every word in Bate's Latin translations, including, of course, the glosses, the numerous stylistic alterations, and the additions derived from lost Hebrew manuscripts; (b) to consistently translate Bate's doublets and triplets by means of different English words;[554] (c) to translate Latin technical terms literally, while giving their meaning in square brackets at their first occurrence, without undermining the integrity of the English language.

It was also decided that the English versions of Bate's Latin translations, as well as their critical editions, should be divided into the same chapters, sections, and sentences, and, as far as possible, employ the same punctuation, as the critical editions of Ibn Ezra's Hebrew texts. This allows readers to compare the English versions of Bate's Latin and their critical editions with the English translations and the critical edition of Ibn Ezra's Hebrew texts as found in the earlier volumes of this series.

2. Notes Explaining Technical Terms, Glossaries and Lists of Authorities and Sources

Because the editions of Ibn Ezra's Hebrew astrological writings were equipped with extensive notes explaining astrological or astronomical concepts and terms, locating Ibn Ezra's views in the wider context of medieval astrological lore, identifying sources, and establishing links within Ibn Ezra's astrological and scientific corpus, it was considered superfluous to repeat these notes regarding Bate's Latin translations. Hence as a matter of principle notes of this type are not found in the present volume. Nevertheless, it does include brief explanations of the most important astrological or astronomical concepts and terms, particularly in the introduction.

Bate's Latin translations are based on Hebrew and French source texts and exhibit idiosyncratic Latin technical vocabularies. To highlight this feature, the present volume includes, for *Commencement*, an English-Latin-French-Hebrew glossary of technical terms; and for Bate's other Latin trans-

---

[554] This refers, for example, to the following doublets involving close synonyms: (i) "distantia seu longitudo," denoting מרחק = "distance," was translated as "distance or longitude", or separately as "distance," on the one hand, and "longitude," on the other; (ii) "virtus seu fortitudo," denoting כח = "power," was translated as "power or strength," or separately as "power," on the one hand, and "strength," on the other.

lations, five English-Latin-Hebrew glossaries.[555] The same comparative approach is applied to the list of authorities and sources of Bate's Latin translations.[556]

3. *The Collation*

In this volume, "collating Bate's Latin translations against their source texts" means four main things:

(i) Identifying divergent readings, alternative readings, omissions, glosses, stylistic alterations, and additions derived from lost Hebrew manuscripts, in Bate's Latin translations as compared to the Hebrew and French (in the case of *Introductorius*) source texts.

(ii) Identifying the various types of divergent readings, alternative readings, and omissions (particularly in *Introductorius*), and four special categories of translations found only in *Introductorius*. These types of divergent readings, alternative readings, omissions, and the special cases of translations, are defined below.

(iii) Making clear to the reader and marking adequately the divergent readings, alternative readings, omissions, glosses, stylistic alterations and additions derived from lost Hebrew manuscripts, as well as the various types of divergent readings and omissions, and special cases of translations. These terms will be defined below.

(iv) Providing adequate documentation to demonstrate the nature of the diverse divergent readings, alternative readings, omissions, glosses, stylistic alterations and additions derived from lost Hebrew manuscripts, as well as special cases of translations.

In principle the collation has seven components: (1) divergent translations; (2) alternative readings; (3) omissions; (4) glosses; (5) stylistic alterations; (6) additions from lost Hebrew manuscripts; (7) special categories of translation. These components occur in the Latin critical editions and the corresponding English translations. Some of these components, in their turn, may be divided into subtypes, as will be shown below. A study of these components is of huge importance for understanding Bate's modus operandi as a translator and for grasping the special linguistic features of his Latin translations.

---

[555] See Appendices 4, 6, 8, 10, 12, 14.
[556] See Appendices 5, 7, 9, 11, 13, 15.

We turn now to describe the various components of the collation, the subtypes into which they are divided, and the typographical symbols and sigla used to mark them.

4. *Divergent Readings*

The term "divergent readings" refers to words or phrases whose meaning in Bate's Latin deviates from the parallel word or phrase in the source texts. For the three-tiered *Introductorius* these are noted vis-à-vis both the Hebrew and French source texts; for the other five Latin translations, vis-à-vis the Hebrew source texts alone. The existence and nature of these subtypes of divergent readings are not immediately evident and are made visible only by adequate documentation, which involves a comparison between the divergent readings, on the one hand, and their counterparts in the source texts, on the other.

To make things simple, it was decided to set the divergent readings in Bate's six Latin translations in bold, distinguishing the subtypes by means of superscript Greek letters. Let us turn now to the subtypes of divergent readings and the sigla assigned to them:

4.1. *Introductorius* Follows *Commencement* and Diverges from *Reshit Ḥokhmah*

This subtype is unique to *Introductorius* (the only text in three languages) and includes cases in which the meaning of words or phrases in *Introductorius* diverges from that of the corresponding words or phrases in *Reshit Ḥokhmah*, as found in the print edition of this work, but follows the meaning of the corresponding words or phrases in *Commencement* as found in the two extant manuscripts (**P** and **P¹**). The divergence occurs either because *Reshit Ḥokhmah* offers a variant reading in the relevant locus or because the word or phrase does not appear in *Reshit Ḥokhmah*. Divergent readings of this subtype reflect Bate's strong reliance on Hagin's *Commencement*, and suggest that Hagin employed a different Hebrew manuscript than those used for the print edition of *Reshit Ḥokhmah*, or that Hagin misunderstood the Hebrew, or that the person who wrote down Hagin's oral French translation misheard or miswrote. Words or phrases in this category, in both the Latin edition of *Introductorius* and in its English translation, are printed in bold and followed by a superscript α. In the English translation of *Introductorius*, the superscript α is accompanied by a note that documents this particular divergent reading, at least on its first appearance.

4.2. Bate's Six Latin Translations Diverge from All their Source Texts

This subtype includes cases where the meaning of words or phrases in Bate's Latin translations diverge from that of the corresponding words or phrases in all the corresponding source texts (that is, from both *Commencement* and *Reshit Ḥokhmah* in the case of *Introductorius*, and from the corresponding Hebrew text for the other five translations).

In the Latin editions these are printed in bold (because they are divergent readings), followed by a superscript γ (because they belong to this subtype). In the English translations, the superscript γ is accompanied by a note that documents this particular divergent reading, at least at its first appearance.

5. *Doublets and Triplets*

This category includes double or triple translations for a single word or locution, that is, alternative readings reflecting Bate's uncertainty about what Latin term best represents the Hebrew or French source. Alternative readings of this category occur in all six of Bate's Latin translations. Words or phrases in this category, in both the critical editions and the English translations of Bate's Latin translations, are printed in bold and are followed by a superscript β. Although Bate's doublets and triplets are (usually) obvious, documenting them by means of collation against the source texts can shed light on Bate's motivation for providing multiple Latin options for some word or expression in Ibn Ezra's Hebrew astrological writings. Therefore, in the English translation, the Greek letter is accompanied by a note that documents this particular double or triple translation, at least at its first appearance.

6. *Omissions*

"Omissions" are words or phrases that are not found in Bate's Latin translations but occur in their Hebrew source texts. Omissions are a powerful tool for gauging the extent of Bate's reliance on his source texts. Omissions occur in all six Latin translations, but the case of *Introductorius*, with two source texts, must be distinguished from that of the other five translation: regarding *Introductorius*, sometimes the French text features the same omission, and sometimes not.

6.1. Omissions in the Two-tiered Translations

Omissions in *Rationes* I, *Rationes* II, *Iudicia*, *De mundo*, and *De luminaribus* are collated against their corresponding Hebrew source texts as they appear in the print editions. There is only one subtype in this category; in the

Latin texts they are printed as an ellipsis enclosed in double angle brackets, i.e., ⟨⟨...⟩⟩. In the corresponding English translations the missing text is provided in double angle brackets, i.e., ⟨⟨the Woman⟩⟩. Since detection of this subtype depends on a collation against the corresponding Hebrew source text only, and because the missing words are provided in the English translation, they do not require any further documents. Hence the double angle brackets are not followed by a siglum or note.

6.2. *Introductorius* and *Commencement* Omit Words Found in *Reshit Ḥokhmah*

Omissions in *Introductorius* are collated against both *Reshit Ḥokhmah* and *Commencement*, so there are two subtypes. The first involves places where both *Introductorius* and *Commencement* omit the same word or phrase found in *Reshit Ḥokhmah*. Omissions of this type indicate that Bate was following *Commencement* rather slavishly and did not check the Latin translation against *Reshit Ḥokhmah* (at least as this text appears in the modern print edition).

We know that Pietro d'Abano, too, used *Commencement* as the basis for his Latin translation of *Reshit Ḥokhmah*.[557] So it is not surprising that Pietro shows the same omissions of this subtype as those in Bate's *Introductorius*.[558]

These omissions are printed in the Latin edition of *Introductorius* as an ellipsis enclosed in double angle brackets, followed by a superscript μ, i.e., ⟨⟨...⟩⟩^μ. In the corresponding English translation of *Introductorius*, the double angle brackets enclose the text supplied from *Reshit Ḥokmah*. The double angle brackets are followed by a superscript μ as well as by a note that documents the omission, i.e., ⟨⟨their mixture⟩⟩^μ,559

6.3. Omissions in *Introductorius* but not in *Commencement*

As noted above, omissions in *Introductorius* are collated against both *Reshit Ḥokhmah* and *Commencement*, and are thus of two subtypes. The second subtype involves cases where *Introductorius* omits words found in *Reshit Ḥokhmah*, even though they are found in *Commencement*. Here Bate was offering a translation independent of both *Commencement* and *Reshit Ḥokhmah*.

---

[557] See Sela 2021, 62–66.
[558] See, inter alia, § 1.1:1, note 3; § 2.2:24, note 31; § 2.3:3, note 1; § 2.3:20 note 15; § 2.3:48 note 62; § 2.3:52 note 63; § 2.4:49 note 54; § 2.5:34 note 60.
[559] mixture] P: om.; H: וממסכם = their mixtures.

Omissions of this subtype are printed in the Latin edition of *Introductorius* as an ellipsis enclosed in double angle brackets, followed by a superscript v, i.e., ⟨⟨...⟩⟩ᵛ. In the corresponding English translation of *Introductorius*, the double angle brackets enclose the text of the corresponding omission, rather than an ellipsis. The brackets are followed a superscript v and a note that documents this omission, i.e., ⟨⟨the Woman⟩⟩ᵛ.[560]

7. *Glosses*

Bate's Latin translations are replete with glosses. These glosses may be divided into three groups, by length:

(i) Short glosses, consisting sometimes of a single word but most often of several, explaining terms and names, clarifying the sense of the Hebrew source text, or completing what Bate took to be a fragmentary phrase by Ibn Ezra. Bate does not mark these short glosses, of course. Hence the overwhelming majority of them are not readily identifiable and can be detected only by collation with the Hebrew source text. Short glosses may be confused with some component of the doublets or triplets. However, short glosses can be distinguished from doublets or triplets because they usually begin with or involve expressions such as "hoc est = this is," "et est" = "and this is," "id est" = "that is," "scilicet" = "namely," etc., and also because they usually do not involve conjunctions such as "sive" or "seu," which distinguish the doublets or triplets.

(ii) Glosses of medium length—a few lines, a complete sentence, or even several sentences. In some of these Bate identifies himself as the glossator or the translator. Elswhere their nature as glosses can be detected by means of the collation with the Hebrew source text.

(iii) Long glosses consisting of multiple paragraphs and even pages, in which Bate provides his opinion about a burning issue stimulated by Ibn Ezra's text. These long glosses are easy to detect because Bate always identifies himself as the glossator or the author.

All the glosses—either short, medium size or long—are printed in italics in both the Latin critical edition and corresponding English translations of all six texts.

---

[560] the Woman] P, 2va: la fame; H: האשה = the woman.

8. Stylistic Alterations

These are Bate's creative interpretations of Ibn Ezra's repetitive conjunctive *waws*, like the biblical conjunctive *waw* that joins two parts of a sentence (as distinct from the conversive *waw*,) as well as other conjunctions and adverbs used by Ibn Ezra, such as והנה, etc. In many cases, however, Bate's conjunctions and adverbs are his additions. In both the critical edition and the corresponding English translation of all six Latin treatises, such stylistic alterations (vero, autem, etiam, igitur, ergo, ideo, quoque, porro, iterum, tamen, nam, itaque, etc.) are enclosed in single curly braces = { }.

9. Additions from Lost Hebrew Manuscripts

Some additions are not Bate's glosses but his translations of passages he found in other (now-lost) Hebrew manuscripts. These could be identified because they appear in Bate's Latin translations but not in the Hebrew source texts, but are also found in the Latin versions produced by other translators. The counterparts of the numerous additions of this type in *Iudicia* are in an anonymous translation of *Mishpeṭei ha-Mazzalot* found in Erfurt, Universitäts- und Forschungsbibliothek, Amplon. O.89, fols. 5r–19v; the counterparts of the additions of this type in *De luminaribus* are in Pietro d'Abano's *Liber de luminaribus* and in Pierre de Limoges' *Liber Abraham de terminatione morborum*; the counterparts of the additions of this type in *Rationes* II are in Pietro d'Abano's *Liber de rationibus*.

In both the critical edition and the corresponding English translation, additions of this type are enclosed in double curly braces = {{ }}. In the English translations, notes attached to these brackets present the Latin counterparts in the alternative Latin versions, accompanied by an English translation.

10. Special Categories of Translation in Introductorius

Four special catetories that are of great importance for assessing Bate's modus operandi as a translator, can be detected in *Introductorius* when we compare it to the French and Hebrew source texts. (One category, that of calques, can be found in the other translations as well.)

10.1. Translations of Names that Hagin Transliterates

This category includes the Hebrew names of stars, animals, plants, countries, diseases, stones, etc., which Hagin does not translate but transliterates into French. Bate understands or presumes to understand their meaning and uses their Latin counterpart in *Introductorius*. As a rule, this category coincides with the γ-type of divergence (see above, 4.2), because it is a

Latin translation that varies from the text offered by *Commencement* and *Reshit Ḥokhmah*. The triple collation of *Introductorius, Commencement,* and *Reshit Ḥokhmah* identified 26 cases of this. Given that Bate had little or no Hebrew, we must infer that Bate, besides using the written French translation of *Introductorius*, was assisted by a Hebrew scholar, in all likelihood Hagin le Juif. In both the Latin edition of *Introductorius* and its English translation, words or phrases in this category are printed in bold and followed by a superscript δ. In the English translation of *Introductorius*, the δ is accompanied by a note that documents the case, at least at its first appearance.

10.2. Calques of Hebrew Idioms

This category (which can be found in all the translations, and not just *Introductorius*) covers places where Bate offers literal Latin translations of Hebrew idioms. In *Introductorius*, it coincides with the α-type of divergence (see above, 4.1), because the Latin translation follows the French translation in *Commencement*. As far as possible, the corresponding English translations offered in this volume attempt to calque the Hebrew idioms, followed by their meaning in square parenthesis, i.e., בני אדם → sons of men [i.e., human beings]. But when the literal rendering would be incomprehensible, the English translation offers the meaning of the Hebrew idiom, and the literal translation is relegated to square brackets, i.e., הדין עמו → he is right [*lit.* he has the law]. In both the Latin editions and their English translations, words or phrases in this category are printed in bold and marked with a superscript θ. In the English translations, the θ is accompanied by a note that documents the special case, at least at its first appearance.

10.3. Transliterations of Hebrew Words in *Introductorius*

This category includes places where Hagin does not translate but transliterates the Hebrew text of *Reshit Ḥokhmah* into French, and Bate follows suit and transliterates the French text of *Commencement* into Latin. This category coincides with the α-type of divergence (see above, 4.1), because it is a Latin translation that relies on *Commencement*. In both the Latin edition of *Introductorius* and its English translation, words or phrases in this category are printed in bold and marked by a superscript ε. In the English translation of *Introductorius*, the Greek letter ε is accompanied by a note that documents the special case, at least at its first appearance.

10.4. Reliance on a Lost Manuscript of *Commencement*

This category includes two special cases from which it may be inferred that Bate employed a manuscript of *Commencement* that was earlier than and different from the two extant manuscripts of Hagin's French. (i) The first case includes places where Bate's Latin *Introductorius* agrees with the corresponding French translation found in P¹ but not with that in P. Since P¹ is later than P, this implies that Bate used a lost earlier manuscript of *Commencement* on which both P and P¹ were based. (ii) The second case includes instances in which Bate follows *Reshit Ḥokhmah*, but the French of P and P¹ omits this reading or, in a few cases, offers a divergent reading. This again implies that Bate relied on a manuscript of *Commencement* that was different from and earlier than P and P¹. In both the Latin edition of *Introductorius* and its English translation, words or phrases in this category are printed in bold and marked with a superscript π. In the English translation of *Introductorius*, the siglum is accompanied by a note that documents the special case, at least at its first appearance.

11. *Notes*

All the elements of the collation are accompanied by notes, except for additions, stylistic alterations, and omissions in the five Hebrew-Latin translations. In *Introductorius*, the omissions are accompanied by notes to distinguish those where Bate is following *Commencement* from those where Bate diverged from Hagin's translation.

The notes consist of three parts: (a) the incipit, which repeats the English translation of the Latin text; (b) in the five Hebrew-Latin translations, the Hebrew words underlying the incipit accompanied by a literal English translation; in *Introductorius*, also the underlying French of the incipit as found in P and the locus of the reading there; (c) additional remarks, introduced by an arrow: →.

Example of a note in *Introductorius*:

planets] P, 1rb: planetes; H: משרתים = servants. → Meaning, planets.

Example of a note in the other translations:

masters of judgments] H: בעלי הדינין = lords of judgments. → Meaning, experts in astrological judgments.

Summary of the typographical symbols and sigla in the Latin texts, their translations, and the apparatus to the critical editions

Divergent readings
Bold, followed by a superscript α   Divergent readings following *Commencement* and diverging from *Reshit Ḥokhmah* (in *Introductorius*)
Bold, followed by a superscript γ   Divergent readings from the source texts (in all the translations)

Alternative readings
Bold, followed by a superscript β   Doublets and triplets (in all the translations)

Omissions
⟨⟨...⟩⟩   Omissions in *Rationes* I, *Rationes* II, *Iudicia*, *De mundo*, and *De luminaribus*
⟨⟨...⟩⟩^μ   Both *Introductorius* and *Commencement* omit words found in *Reshit Ḥokhmah*
⟨⟨...⟩⟩^ν   Omissions in *Introductorius* but not in *Commencement*

Glosses
italics   In all the translations and their English translations

Stylistic alterations
{...}   In all the translations and their English translations

Additions from lost Hebrew manuscripts
{{...}}   In *Iudicia*, *De luminaribus*, *Rationes* I, *Rationes* II

Special cases of translation in *Introductorius*
Bold, followed by a superscript δ   Bate translates names which Hagin transliterates
Bold, followed by a superscript θ   *Introductorius* calques Hebrew idioms
Bold, followed by a superscript ε   *Introductorius* transliterates Hebrew words
Bold, followed by a superscript π   Bate had recourse to a lost manuscript of *Commencement*

Apparatus
< In the apparatus: for a given lemma, the word(s) following the siglum are added in the indicated manuscript after the lemma
\> In the apparatus: for a given lemma, the word(s) following the siglum are added in the indicated manuscript before the lemma

Miscellaneous sigla in the Latin texts and their translations
italics and underlined   Transliterations in the Latin texts and their translations of foreign words
[...]   Explanations of terms
⟨...⟩   Additions to clarify the meaning

PART ONE

*LIBER ABRAHE AVENERRE
INTRODUCTORIUS AD ASTRONOMIAM*

LATIN TEXT AND ENGLISH TRANSLATION

2ra   Incipit Liber Abrahe Avenerre Introductorius ad Astronomiam.¹

1 (1) Initium sapientie timor Domini, ⟨⟨...⟩⟩,ᵛ *huius autem verbi seu dicti² sensus hic est*, quod dum homo neque post oculos suos neque post cor suum **ire studet seu evagari**ᵝ ad concupiscentias suas perficiendas tunc in ipso quiescit intellectus. (2) Adhuc timor Dei preservat ipsum **a consuetis celorum,**ᵅ **legibus seu ordinationibus,**ᵝ **et fatis³ eorum,**ᵅ cunctis diebus vite sue, et, cum a corpore separata fuerit anima, faciat eam inhabitare vitam seculorum. (3) Incipiam {igitur} narrare **consuetudines celorum ac ordinationes seu leges**ᵝ secundum viam iudiciorum quam experti sunt Antiqui in generationibus post generationes. (4) **Postquam** {autem} **hunc librum compilavero, adiungam**ᵅ **librum explanationis rationum et causarum.**ᵝ (5) Ad hoc perficiendum Deus auxilium michi prestet.ᵅ Amen.

2 (1) Liber iste in .10. dividitur partes. (2) Prima quidem est **de figuratione spere**ᵅ *celestis* et partibus eius, de signis quidem et ymaginibus, necnon de .7. **planetis,**ᵞ et de ascensionibus eorum et virtutibus, adhuc et de motibus ipsorum **et dignitatibus.**ᵞ (3) Secunda est de virtutibus signorum et ascensionibus, ⟨⟨...⟩⟩,ᵛ de complexione stellarum **ac earum dispositione.**ᵞ (4) Tertia est de aspectibus graduum, et de virtute coniunctionis ac **diversitatis eorum,**ᵞ de **amicitia quidem et inimicitia**ᵞ illorum, et de partibus quartarum **celi,**ᵞ ac de .12. domibus. (5) Quarta de complexionibus .7. **planetarum**ᵅ et eorum virtutibus, ac de omnibus que significant in rebus creatis que sunt super terram. (6) Quinta de **dispositione planetarum**ᵅ secundum quod augmentantur virtutes eorum vel diminuuntur. (7) Sexta de **effectibus planetarum**ᵅ in se ipsis secundum quod sunt ante Solem aut **post eum seu retro.**ᵝ (8) Septima de aspectibus **planetarum,**ᵅ et coniunctionibus eorum ⟨⟨...⟩⟩ᵘ ac separationibus eorum, et universaliter de **habitudinibus et dispositionibus**ᵝ eorum⁴ qualiter commiscentur invicem eorum virtutes in omnibus que significant. (9) Octava **de quibusdam regulis ac iudiciis**ᵝ **planetarum**ᵅ **in nativitatibus, revolutionibus ac interrogationibus.** (10) Nona de **sortibus seu partibus**ᵝ **planetarum**ᵅ et domorum, ac de ⟨⟨...⟩⟩ᵘ aliis **partibus**ᵅ quas commemoraverunt **astrorum sapientes.**ᵞ (11) Decima de **proiectionibus radiorum planetarum,**ᵞ et de modo eorum et **permutationes**ᵅ secundum gradus spere, ac de omnibus dispositionibus illorum.

---

¹Incipit liber Abrahe Avenerre introductorius ad astronomiam] L; V Liber Abrahe ducis et Avenesre; W om.   ²seu dicti] V om.   ³fatis] V factis.   ⁴eorum] WV; L om.

HERE BEGINS THE INTRODUCTORY BOOK
TO ASTROLOGY BY ABRAHAM IBN EZRA

1 (1) The beginning of wisdom is the fear of the Lord (Psalms 111:10), ⟨⟨for it is the foundation⟩⟩,[v,1] *but this is the meaning of this word or saying*, that when man does not **strive to go or wander**[β,2] after his eyes and heart to satisfy his desires, then wisdom comes to rest inside him. (2) Furthermore, the fear of the Lord will protect him from the **customs of heavens,**[α,3] **laws and decrees,**[β,4] **and their destiny,**[α,5] all the days of his life; and, when the soul is separated from the body, He will make it [the soul] dwell in eternal life. (3) {Then,} I now begin to tell the **customs of heavens, and also decrees and laws,**[β] according to the method of the ⟨astrological⟩ judgments, which was verified experimentally by the ANCIENTS, generation after generation. (4) {However,} **after I compile** [meaning compose] THIS BOOK, I **will add**[α,6] [meaning compose] a BOOK OF EXPLANTION OF THE REASONS AND CAUSES.[β,7,8] (5) May **God furnish me assistance to accomplish this.**[α,9] Amen.

2 (1) THIS BOOK is divided into ten chapters. (2) The first is on the **configuration of the** *celestial* **sphere**[α,1] and its parts, its signs and images [constellations]; and also the seven **planets,**[γ,2] their ascensions and powers, also their motions, and **dignities.**[γ,3] (3) The second is on the powers of the signs and on the ascensions, ⟨⟨their effect⟩⟩,[v,4] and on the mixture of the ⟨fixed⟩ stars and **their condition.**[γ,5] (4) The third chapter is on the aspects of the degrees, and on the power of their conjunction and **diversity,**[γ,6] their **friendship and enmity,**[γ,7] the quadrants of **the heavens,**[γ,8] and the twelve ⟨horoscopic⟩ houses. (5) The fourth is on the mixture of the seven **planets**[α,9] and their powers, and everything they indicate for all creatures on Earth. (6) The fifth is on the **condition of the planets**[α,10] according to whether their powers are increased or diminished. (7) The sixth is on the **effects of the planets**[α,11] themselves, according to whether they are before the Sun or after or behind it.[β,12] (8) The seventh chapter is on the aspects of the **planets,**[α] their conjunctions, ⟨⟨their mixture⟩⟩[μ,13] and separations, and in general on **their conditions and dispositions**[β,14] related to how their powers are mixed in everything they indicate. (9) The eighth is on **certain** RULES AND JUDGMENTS[β,15] OF THE PLANETS[α] IN NATIVITIES, REVOLUTIONS AND INTERROGATIONS. (10) The ninth is on the **lots or parts**[β,16] of the planets[α] and the houses, and ⟨⟨all⟩⟩[μ,17] the other **parts**[α,18] [lots] which the SCHOLARS OF THE STARS[γ,19] put on record. (11) The tenth is on **the projections of the rays of the planets,**[γ,20] on their manner of being and **alterations**[α,21] according to the degrees of the sphere, and on all their conditions.

3 (1) Quicumque sapiens hanc scientiam indagare **voluerit,**[α] **considerare debet**[α] in motionibus .7. **planetarum, qualiter in motu suo transmutantur et cursu revolvi festinant**[γ] circa gradus **spere superioris**[α] ⟨⟨...⟩⟩,[μ] **et considerare**[1] **eos cum erunt**[α] in directo *stellarum fixarum*[γ] que sunt in circulo signorum, et omnes motus {huiusmodi} qui sunt circa **centrum,**[α] quod est terra, que tanquam punctus est in medio circuli. (2) **Experietur quod planete predicti,**[γ] cum eo quod motus | eorum equales sunt et recti, diversificantur cum eorum operationes secundum **regiones.**[α] (3) Hec {autem} res scita est per ⟨⟨...⟩⟩[μ] gradus spere, et per eius ymagines meridionales et septentrionales, adhuc et per cognitiones **planetarum**[α] septem et naturam suarum, **tam communium quam particularium,**[α] et omnium suarum operationum.

2rb

§1

1 (1) **Capitulum primum seu pars prima.**[β,2] **Spera**[α] {igitur} divisa est in .360. partes equales ⟨⟨...⟩⟩.[μ] (2) Et in hoc concors est omnium sapientia tam ANTIQUORUM quam POSTERIORUM,[γ] eo quod in hoc numero sunt omnium fractionum *species*, que sunt ⟨⟨...⟩⟩[μ] usque ad decimas, preterquam septime. (3) Similiter divisa est in .12. partes, que appellantur signa, et quodlibet signum .30. **gradus** continet **rectos seu equales,**[β] in quolibet {autem} gradu .60. **minuta prima,**[α] et in quolibet primo .60. secunda, et similiter usque ad decima **vel ultra.**[α]

2 (1) Signa {autem} sunt hec: Aries, Taurus, Gemini, Cancer, Leo, Virgo, Scorpius, Sagittarius, Capricornus, Aquarius, Pisces. (2) Et hec sunt in spera superiori, que est octava, cum ymaginibus septentrionalibus et meridionalibus. (3) Et sunt in universo ymagines .48., numerus autem stellarum suarum est .1022., secundum sententiam ANTIQUORUM ac etiam PTOLOMEI.[3]

3 (1) ⟨⟨...⟩⟩.[γ] (2) Et prime quidem ymaginis, que est Aries, stelle sunt .13., et inter eas sunt cornua, et venter tanquam de numero illarum. (3) In signo {autem} Tauri sunt .33. stelle, et **Pleiades**[γδ] sunt in dorso. (4) In signo

---

[1]considerare] W; LV considerans. [2]Capitulum primum seu pars prima] L; WV om.
[3]Ptolomei] LV; W > Sed hoc est de illis quas visus noster comprehendere potest. This appears in *Rationes* I, §1.2:4.

3   (1) Any scholar who **wishes**[α,1] to investigate this science **must observe,**[2] in the motions of the seven **planets, how they change in their motion and ⟨how⟩ they hasten in ⟨their⟩ running to revolve**[γ,3] around the degrees of **the upper sphere**[α,4] ⟨⟨and their motions in their spheres⟩⟩,[μ,5] **and ⟨must⟩ observe them when they are**[α,6] opposite the *fixed stars*[γ,7] in the circle of the signs, and ⟨must observe⟩ all the motions {of this sort} which are around the **center,**[α,8] which is the Earth, which is like a point in the middle of the circle. (2) ⟨Then⟩ **it will be proven that the aforementioned planets,**[γ,9] even though their motions are equal and straight, vary their effects according to **the regions.**[α,10] (3) This thing is known {however} by ⟨⟨the number⟩⟩[μ,11] of the degrees of the ⟨upper⟩ sphere, its **southern and northern**[α,12] images [constellations], also by the knowledge of the seven **planets**[α] and their natures, **those related to collectives as well as to individuals,**[α,13] and all their [the planets'] effects.

§1

1   (1) **First chapter or first part.**[β,1] The **sphere,**[α,2] {then,} is divided into 360 equal parts, ⟨⟨which are called degrees⟩⟩.[μ,3] (2) On this the wisdom of all the ANCIENTS and the LATER[γ,4] ⟨SCHOLARS⟩ is in agreement, because in this number are *the types of* all the fractions, which are ⟨⟨from one-half⟩⟩[μ,5] to one-tenth, except one-seventh. (3) Similarly, it [the sphere] is divided into 12 parts, which are called "signs," and each sign contains 30 **straight or equal degrees,**[β,6] and in each degree ⟨there are⟩ {however} 60 **first smaller parts**[α,7] [minutes], and in each first ⟨smaller part⟩ ⟨there are⟩ 60 seconds, and similarly down to the tenth ⟨smaller parts⟩, **or beyond.**[α,8]

2   (1) {So,} these are the signs: Aries, Taurus, Gemini, Cancer, Leo, Virgo, Libra, Scorpio, Sagittarius, Capricorn, Aquarius, and Pisces. (2) They are in the upper sphere, which is the eighth, together with the northern and southern images [constellations]. (3) In all there are 48 images [constellations], and the number of their stars is 1,022, according to the opinion of all the ANCIENTS, and also PTOLEMY.[1]

3   (1) ⟨⟨There are 346 stars in the images [constellations] ⟨corresponding to the⟩ signs⟩⟩.[ν,1] (2) There are 13 stars of the first image [constellation], which is Aries, and between them are the horns, and the abdomen as well is in their number. (3) {But} there are 33 stars in the sign of Taurus, and the **Pleiades**[γδ,2] are in the back. (4) There are 18 stars in the sign of Gemini; 9

Geminorum sunt stelle .18.; in Cancro .9.; in Leone .27.; ⟨⟨...⟩⟩;ᵘ in Libra .8.; in Scorpione .22.; et in Sagittario .13.; in Capricornio .28.; in Aquario .42.; in Piscibus .34.

4 (1) Ymagines meridionales .15.¹ et stelle earum .316. (2) Prima quidem est Leo Maris, quem quidam vocant Ursus, *et est Cetus*, stelle autem eius sunt .22. (3) Ymago secunda est Canis Fortis *et est Orion*,² stelle eius sunt .38. (4) Tertia est Flumen, et stelle eius .34. (5) Quarta Lepus, et stelle eius .13. (6) Quinta Canis Maior, et stelle eius .18. (7) Sexta Canis Minor, et sunt stelle eius due. (8) Septima Navis, et stelle eius .45. (9) Octava Bestia, *et est Ydra*, et stelle eius .25. (10) Nona Crater, et stelle eius septem. (11) Decima Corvus et stelle eius .7. (12) Undecima Portans Leonem, *et est Centaurus*, cuius media pars est in forma hominis et alia medietas in similitudine equi, stelle eius sunt .36. (13) Duodecima Leopardus, *et est Bestia Centauri*, et stelle eius .5. (14) .13ma. est Turibulum, eius stelle .7. (15) .14ma. Corona *Meridionalis*, et stelle eius .13. (16) .15ma. Piscis Meridionalis, et stelle eius .11.

5 (1) Ymagines {quoque} septentrionales sunt .21. et earum stelle .360. (2) Una³ est **Ursa Minor**ᵞᵟ cum Fetibus Suis, et stelle eius sunt septem. (3) Secunda est Ursus Maior, et stelle eius sunt .17. (4) Tertia Draco, et stelle eius sunt .31. (5) Quarta Domina Flamme, *alibi vocatur Flaminatus vel Cepheus*,⁴ et stelle eius sunt .11. (6) Quinta Canis Latrans, *alibi notatur Ululans, cuius 2va intentio est | vociferans, vel Boetes*, et stelle eius sunt .22. (7) Sexta **Corona Septentrionalis**,ᵞᵟ et stelle eius sunt .8. (8) Septima **Vadens Super Genus Sua seu Genuflexens**,ᵝ et stelle eius sunt .28. (9) Octava Aquila Cadens, et stelle eius .10. (10) Nona Gallina, et stelle eius .17.⁵ (11) Decima **Sedens super Sedem**,ᵅ et stelle eius .13. (12) Undecima Portans Caput Dyaboli, *et est Perseus*, stelle eius .26.⁶ (13) .12a. Pastor *seu Agitator*, in cuius Manu Frenum, et stelle eius .14. (14) .13a. Retinens Bestiam, *et est Serpentarius*, stelle eius .24. (15) .14. est Bestia *sive Serpens*, et stelle eius sunt .18. (16) .15. **Nocumentivus**ᵅ *et est Sagitta*, stelle eius quinque. (17) .16. Aquila Volans et stelle eius .9. (18). 17. Piscis Marinus, *et est Delphin*, stelle eius .10. (19) .18. Caput Equi *Posterioris*, stelle eius .4. (20) .19. Equus Alatus, stelle eius .20. (21) .20. ⟨⟨...⟩⟩ᵛ Qui non Habuit Maritum, stelle eius .23. (22) .21. est Triangulus, stelle eius sunt. .4. (23) Completus {igitur} nunc est numerus stellarum predictarum, qui sunt .1022.

---

¹.15.] WV; L om.   ²Orion] WV; L Orison.   ³Una] LW; V prima.   ⁴Cepheus] WV; L Zepheus.
⁵.17.] WV; L om.   ⁶.26.] WV; L 20.

in Cancer; 27 in Leo, ⟨⟨26 in Virgo⟩⟩;^µ,3 eight in Libra; 22 in Scorpio; 13 in Sagittarius, 28 in Capricorn; 42 in Aquarius; 34 in Pisces.

4 (1) There are 15 southern images [constellations], and their stars are 316. (2) The first is the Sea-Lion, which some call the Bear, *which is Cetus*,[1] with 22 stars. (3) The second image is the Mighty Dog, *and it is Orion*,[2] with 38 stars. (4) The third is the River, with 34 stars. (5) The fourth is the Hare, with 13 stars. (6) The fifth is the Greater Dog, with 18 stars. (7) The sixth is the Lesser Dog, with 2 stars. (8) The seventh is the Ship, with 45 stars. (9) The eighth is the Beast[3] *and it is Hydra*,[4] with 25 stars. (10) The ninth is the Cup, with 7 stars. (11) The tenth is the Crow, with 7 stars. (12) The eleventh is the Lion Carrier, *and it is Centaurus*,[5] half of which has the form of a man and the other half bearing the resemblance of a horse, with 36 stars. (13) The twelfth is the Leopard, *and it is the Beast of Centaurus*,[6] with 5 stars. (14) The thirteenth is the Incense-pan, with 7 stars. (15) The fourteenth is the *Southern* Crown, with 13 stars. (16) The fifteenth is the Southern Fish, with 11 stars.

5 (1) There are {also} 21 northern images [constellations], and their stars are 360. (2) One is the **Lesser Bear**^γδ,1 with Her Sons[2] (Job 38:32), with seven stars. (3) The second is the Greater Bear, with 17 stars. (4) The third is the Dragon, with 31 stars. (5) The fourth is the Lady of the Blazing Fire, *it is called elsewhere Flaminatus or Cepheus*,[3] with 11 stars. (6) The fifth is the Barking Dog, *elsewhere called Howling, whose meaning is shouting, or Boetes*,[4] with 22 stars. (7) The sixth is the **Northern Crown**,^γδ,5 with 8 stars. (8) The seventh is the **One Crawling on his Knees or Genuflecting**,^β,6 with 28 stars. (9) The eighth is the Falling Eagle, with 10 stars (10) The ninth is the Hen, with 17 stars. (11) The tenth is the **One Sitting on a Chair**,^α,7 with 13 stars. (12) The eleventh is the Carrier of the Devil's Head, *and it is Perseus*,[8] with 26 stars. (13) The twelfth is the Shepherd *or Agitator*,[9] with the Reins in his Hand, with 14 stars. (14) The thirteenth is the One who Holds the Beast[10] [meaning snake] *and it is Serpentarius*,[11] with 24 stars. (15) The fourteenth is the Beast [meaning snake[12]] *or Serpens*,[13] with 18 stars. (16) The fifteenth is **the Harmful**,^α,14 *and it is Sagitta*,[15] with 5 stars. (17) The sixteenth is the Flying Eagle, with 9 stars. (18) The seventeenth is the Sea Fish, *and it is Dolphin*,[16] with 10 stars. (19) The eighteenth is the Head of the Hindmost[17] Horse, with 4 stars. (20) The nineteenth is the Winged Horse, with 20 stars. (21) The twentieth is ⟨⟨the Woman⟩⟩^ν,18 who has no Husband, with 23 stars. (22) The twenty-first is the Triangle, with 4 stars. (23) This, {then,} completes the number of the aforementioned stars, which are 1,022.

6 (1) ANTIQUI {igitur} partiti sunt eas secundum .6. gradus; omnem enim stellam, cuius lumen **magnus est seu maximus**,^β appellant honoris primi, illam {vero} que est minor in **claritate seu lumine**^β secundi honoris dicitur esse, et sic gradatim diminuendo procedunt usque ad .6. gradum, quo inferior non est. (2) Et stelle que primi honoris sunt .15., et secundi honoris .48., tertii {vero} .208., .4ti. .474., quinti .217., sexti .49. Tres sunt stelle obscure que assimilatur nubeculis.

7 (1) **Planete**^α {autem} sunt septem: Saturnus, Iupiter, Mars, Sol, Venus, Mercurius, Luna. (2) Et supremus omnium est Saturnus, ipse enim est in spera septima a terra. (3) Et post eum Iupiter, et sic descendendo usque ad Lunam, que est in prima spera, que propinquior est terre.[1]

8 (1) Signa divisa sunt in .4. partes, secundum .4. naturas *elementares*. (2) Tria signa sunt secundum unam naturam *elementarem* et sunt Aries, Leo, Sagittarius, sunt calida et sicca sicut natura ignis; Taurus, Virgo, Capricornus sunt frigida et sicca ut natura terre; Gemini, Libra et Aquarius sunt calida et humida ut[2] natura aeris; Cancer, Scorpius et Pisces frigida et humida, ut natura aque.

9 (1) Saturnus quidem[3] est frigidus et siccus, Iupiter {vero} calidus et humidus, Mars, calidus et siccus adurens,[4] Sol calidus et siccus,[5] Venus frigida et humida, Mercurius, mutabilis est, natura eius est sicut natura stelle **cui adiungitur**,^γ et Luna frigida et humida. (2) Horum {autem} sunt quinque quorum hii quidem masculini sunt hii {vero} feminini, et quidam diurni et quidam nocturni, similiter **quidam sunt boni et quidam sunt mali, seu benefici et malefici**,^β (3) scilicet, duo luminaria, et duo boni, et duo mali, **et unus permutabilis, scilicet ad naturam cuiusque aliorum**.^γ (4) Unius autem luminarium videlicet Solis est virtus diurna et masculina, alterius vero scilicet Lune feminina et nocturna.^γ (5) Et bonorum quidem unus est | masculinus de stellis diurnis, et est Iupiter, alius {vero} femininus de stellis nocturnis, et est Venus. (6) {Similiter} de malis unus est masculinus, **diurnus**,^γ et est Saturnus, alius est femininus, **nocturnus**,^γ et est Mars. (7) *Reliquus quidem, scilicet* Mercurius, mixtus est et mutabilis, ita quod interdum masculinus et interdum femininus, et quandoque **diurnus**^γ quandoque **nocturnus**,^γ et quandoque bonus quandoque malus, secundum

---

[1]que propinquior est terre] W; L est enim propinquior est terre. [2]ut] W; L et. [3]quidem] W; L om. [4]adurens] W; L om. [5]Sol calidus et siccus] W; L om.

6   (1) The ANCIENTS, {then,} divided them [the stars] into six degrees; any star whose light is **great or the greatest**,[β,1] they call "of the first honor[2]" [i.e., of the first magnitude], {but} one which is less in **brightness or light**[β,3] is said to be of the second honor, and likewise they proceed gradually reducing ⟨the magnitude⟩ until the sixth degree, than which none is smaller. (2) There are 15 ⟨stars⟩ of the first honor, 48 of the second honor, {indeed} 208 of the third ⟨magnitude,⟩ 474 of the fourth ⟨magnitude,⟩ 217 of the fifth ⟨magnitude,⟩ 49 of the sixth ⟨magnitude,⟩. There are three dark stars, resembling little clouds.

7   (1) {But} there are seven **planets:**[α] Saturn, Jupiter, Mars, Sun, Venus, Mercury, Moon. (2) The highest of all is Saturn, for it is in the seventh sphere from the Earth. (3) Next to it is Jupiter, and so going down until the Moon, which is in the first sphere, which is the closest to the Earth.

8   (1) The signs are divided into four parts, according to the four *elementary* natures. (2) There are three signs corresponding to one *elementary* nature, and they are Aries, Leo and Sagittarius; they are hot and dry, like the nature of fire; Taurus, Virgo and Capricorn are cold and dry, like the nature of earth; Gemini, Libra and Aquarius are hot and moist, like the nature of air; Cancer, Scorpio and Pisces ⟨are⟩ cold and moist, like the nature of water.

9   (1) Saturn is cold and dry, {but} Jupiter is hot and moist, Mars is hot and dry burning, the Sun hot and dry, Venus cold and moist, and Mercury is mutable, its nature is like the nature of the star **to which it is conjoined**,[γ,1] and the Moon is cold and moist. (2) {And} some of the five ⟨planets⟩ are masculine {but} others are feminine, some are diurnal and some are nocturnal; similarly, **some are good and some are bad, or benefic and malefic**,[β,2] (3) namely, two luminaries, two good ⟨planets⟩, two bad ⟨planets⟩, **and one that is changeable, namely ⟨adapting itself⟩ to the nature of each of the others.**[γ,3] (4) **Now the power of one the luminaries, i.e., of the Sun, is diurnal and masculine, but ⟨the power⟩ of the other, namely, of the Moon, is feminine and nocturnal.**[γ,4] (5) Of the good ⟨planets⟩, one is masculine and of the diurnal stars, and it is Jupiter, {but} the other ⟨of the good planets⟩ is feminine and of the nocturnal stars, and it is Venus. (6) {Similarly,} of the bad ⟨planets⟩, one is masculine, **diurnal**,[γ,5] and it is Saturn, the other is feminine, **nocturnal**,[γ,6] and it is Mars. (7) *The remaining one, namely*, Mercury, is mixed and mutable, so that ⟨it is⟩ sometimes masculine and sometimes feminine, and at times **diurnal**[γ] and at times **nocturnal**,[γ]

naturam stelle cui **applicatur**,ᵞ aut per coniunctionem aut per aspectum, prout **inferus explanabitur**ᵅ in locus convenienti.

10 (1) Natura {quoque} stellarum quinque, necnon ipsius Lune, mutatur secundum **distantiam seu elongationem**ᵝ a Sole, prout etiam explanabo. (2) Item habent et aliam mutationem **secundum ascensum vel descensum**,ᵞ quandoque enim propinquiores terre sunt quandoque remotiores ab ea, item quandoque **sinistri scilicet septentrionales**ᵝ quandoque **dexteri seu meridionales.**ᵝ (3) Et cum erit **planeta**ᵞ in **auge circuli ecentrici**,ᵞ **tunc erit in maxima sua elongatione a terra**,ᵖ et econtrario cum erit **in opposito augis.**ᵞ (4) Draco {vero} seu *genzaai*ᵝ est locus coniunctionis circuli **planete**ᵅᵞ circulo signorum similis et circuli eius declivis. (5) Et caput draconis est **principium septentrionale**,ᵞ cauda {vero} **principium meridionale**,ᵞ et quando **planeta**ᵞ vel Luna cum capite vel cum cauda fuerit, tunc erit in **cingulo ymaginationis circuli signorum**,ᵅ in aliis {vero} locis **latitudinem habebit septentrionalem vel meridionalem**ᵞ secundum eius distantia a duobus punctis, *capitis scilicet et caude*.

11 (1) {Rursus} sunt **planetis**ᵅ **dignitates in zodiaco**,ᵞ **dignitas scilicet**ᵞ domus, et **dignitas**ᵞ **exaltationis seu honoris**ᵝ et **dignitas**ᵞ triplicitatis et **dignitas**ᵞ **termini**ᵅ et dignitas faciei. (2) Et **dignitas**ᵞ domus quinque habet fortitudines, **exaltationis**ᵞ .4., triplicitatis tres, **termini**ᵅ duas, et faciei dignitas unam. (3) Et cum fuerit **planeta**ᵞ in ⟨⟨...⟩⟩ᵛ domo sua, in toto signo **dignitatem**ᵞ habet, similiter et in signo ⟨⟨...⟩⟩ᵛ **honoris et exaltationis**ᵝ nisi quod in gradu **exaltationis**ᵞ plus habet fortitudines quam in aliis signi gradibus.

12 (1) Et ego quidem in ʜᴏᴄ ʟɪʙʀᴏ commemorabo ⟨⟨...⟩⟩ᵘ omnia in quibus concordate est Aɴᴛɪǫᴜᴏʀᴜᴍ sapientia—Bᴀʙʏʟᴏɴɪᴏʀᴜᴍ et ⟨⟨...⟩⟩ᵛ Pᴇʀsᴀʀᴜᴍ,ᵞ Iɴᴅᴏʀᴜᴍ et Gʀᴇᴄᴏʀᴜᴍ, quorum caput est Pᴛᴏʟᴏᴍᴇᴜs. (2) Et loquar de novenariis, et duodenariis, et de gradibus lucidis et obscuris, de vacuis, de

sometimes good and sometimes bad, according to the nature of the star **which it is approaching**,γ,7 either by conjunction or by aspect, **as will be explained below**α,8 in the appropriate place.9

10 (1) {Also} the nature of five stars, and of the Moon, too, changes as a function of **the distance or elongation**β,1 from the Sun, as I shall also explain. (2) {Likewise,} they also have another change **with respect to ascension or descension**,γ,2 for sometimes they are closer to the Earth and sometimes they move away from it, sometimes they are **on the left side ⟨of the ecliptic⟩, that is, northern**,β,3 and sometimes they are **on the right side ⟨of the ecliptic⟩ or southern**.β,4 (3) Now when the **planet**γ,5 is at the **apogee of the eccentric circle**,γ,6 **then it is in its greatest elongation with respect to the Earth**,π,7 and the opposite when it is **opposite its apogee**γ,8 [perigee]. (4) {Moreover} **the Dragon or *jawzahar*** β,9 is the place of the intersection of the circle **of the planet**αγ,10 which is similar to the circle of the signs and its inclined circle. (5) The Head of the Dragon is the **northern beginning**γ,11 {but} the Tail ⟨of the Dragon⟩ is the **southern beginning**,γ,12 and when the **planet**γ,13 or the Moon is with the Head or with the Tail, then it will be **in the girdle of the imagination of the circle of the signs**α,14 [the ecliptic], {but} in the other places ⟨on its course⟩ **it will have northern or southern ⟨ecliptical⟩ latitude**γ,15 according to its distance from the two points, *that is, from the Head and the Tail*.

11 (1) {In addition,} the **planets**α,1 ⟨are assigned⟩ **dignities in the zodiac**,γ,2 that is, the **dignity**γ,3 of the house, **the dignity**γ of the **exaltation or honor**,β,4 **the dignity**γ of the triplicity, **the dignity**γ of the **term**,α,5 and **the dignity**γ of the face⁶ [decan]. (2) **The dignity**γ of the ⟨planetary⟩ house has five powers, ⟨the dignity⟩ of the **exaltation**γ,7 ⟨has⟩ four ⟨powers⟩, ⟨the dignity⟩ of the triplicity ⟨has⟩ three, ⟨the dignity⟩ of the **term**α ⟨has⟩ two, ⟨the dignity⟩ of the face ⟨has⟩ one power. (3) Now when the **planet**γ is in ⟨⟨in the sign that is⟩⟩ν,8 its house, it has **dignity**γ over the whole sign, and similarly in the sign ⟨⟨that is the house of its⟩⟩ν,9 **honor or exaltation**,β but in the degree of the **exaltation**γ,10 itself it has more powers than in the other degrees of the sign.

12 (1) In THIS BOOK, then, I will put on record ⟨⟨for you⟩⟩μ,1 everything agreed upon by the wisdom of the ANCIENTS—the BABYLONIANS, and ⟨⟨the wise men of⟩⟩ν,2 the PERSIANS,γ,3 INDIANS and GREEKS, whose head is PTOLEMY. (2) I will speak about the *novenariae*⁴ [ninth-parts], the *duodenarie*⁵ [twelfths], the bright and dark degrees, the empty ones, the

masculinis, de femininis, de gradibus ⟨⟨...⟩⟩ᵛ **putealibus**,ᵞ et de gradibus **fortunam**ᵞ augmentantibus et honorem, necnon et de locis plures habentibus stellas **aggregatas**ᵅ que sunt in circulo signorum, et de longitudine earum et latitudine ad hoc, et *de coniunctionibus earum magnis*,ᵞ donec **perfectus**[1] sit ISTE LIBER MEUS et[2] **integer**,ᵝ nec indigens ALIO LIBRO secum ad initium sapientie istius.

§2

1 (1) **.2a. pars LIBRI.**ᵞ De signis et ascensionibus eorum et operationibus, 3ra et de complexionibus *stellarum fixarum*ᵞ que sunt in eis.[3] (2) | Scito quod signa sunt .12., quorum .6. sunt **septentrionalia**ᵞ ab **equali linea**,ᵞ scilicet a principio Arietis usque in finem Virginis, **et .6.**ᵅ meridionalia, a principio Libre usque in finem Piscium. (3) Est {autem} Aries signum igneum, masculinum, diurnum ⟨⟨...⟩⟩,ᵛ orientale. (4) De tempore caliditatis, et est **mobile seu tropicale**ᵝ in ipso enim mutantur tempora; et in eius principio sunt dies equales noctibus, incipiuntque dies augmentari et noctes diminui. (5) Hore ipsius maiores sunt **horis equalibus**,ᵞ et **ascensiones**ᵅ,[4] eius diminute, in omni loco minores sunt **eius ascensiones**ᵞ eis que sub **equalitatis**[5] **linea**ᵞ ⟨⟨...⟩⟩;ᵛ est {etiam} **signum obliquum**.ᵞ (6) **Et universaliter**ᵞ naturam ⟨⟨...⟩⟩ᵛ caliditatis significat que **augmentari debet**,ᵅ in ipso quidem *principium* est motus creaturarum. (7) Et est de signis bonis deliciosis, et significat super tonitrua et fulgura. (8) Principium eius **pluviosus** est **et ventosus**,ᵞ medium mixtum, et finis eius calidus cum **turbine**.ᵅ (9) **Pars eius septentrionalis** caliditatem **multiplicat**ᵞ cum humiditatem, **meridionalis**ᵞ {vero} infrigidat. (10) Est in figura quadrupedum, **soleas seu ungulas habentium**,ᵝ et eius membra secta sunt etenim in circulo **oblique**ᵞ transeunt. (11) **Et est**ᵞ bicolor[6] in apparentia, **et duarum figurarum seu bicorpor vel duas habens figuras**,ᵝ vocem habet dimidiam. (12) Et eius est cor orientis ⟨⟨...⟩⟩.ᵛ (13) De ⟨⟨...⟩⟩ᵛ **elementis**ᵅ pars eius est ignis; et caliditas eius est temperata; **de humoribus**ᵅ eius est sanguis. (14) De saporibus omne dulce; de coloribus rufus et omne croceum. (15) De bestiis, quidem pecudes, *id est greges minorum animalium*, et omnes bestie soleas habentes. (16) De metallis, aurum, argentum, ferrum, et cuprum. (17) {Item} in eius parte est **clima**ᵅ tertium, et terra Babylonie

---

[1]perfectus] W; L perficiens. [2]et] W; L om. [3]2a. pars libri, de signis et ascensionibus eorum et operationibus et de complexionibus stellarum fixarum que sunt in eis] V; LWG om. [4]ascensiones] V; LW ascendentes; G om. [5]equalitatis] LV; W equinoxiali; W om. [6]bicolor] WVG; L bicorpor.

masculine ⟨degrees⟩, the feminine ⟨degrees⟩, the degrees ⟨⟨of the stars⟩⟩^ν,6 **pertaining to a pit**,^γ,7 the degrees that increase **fortune**^γ,8 and honor, the position of the many **assembled**^α,9 stars that are in the circle of the signs, their longitude and latitude with respect to ⟨the circle of the signs⟩, and *their great conjunctions*,^γ,10 until MY BOOK is **complete and entire**^β,11 and there is no need for ANOTHER BOOK with it for the beginning of this wisdom.

§2

1   (1) **Second part of THE BOOK.**^γ,1 On the signs, their ascensions and effects, and on the mixtures of the *fixed stars*^γ,2 located in them. (2) Know that there are twelve signs, six of them **north**^γ,3 of the **equal line**^γ,4 [the equator], namely, from the beginning of Aries to the end of Virgo, **and six**^α,5 southern ⟨with respect to the equator⟩, from the beginning of Libra to the end of Pisces. (3) {So,} Aries is a fiery sign, masculine, diurnal ⟨⟨by nature⟩⟩,^ν,6 eastern. (4) Of the season of heat [the spring season], and it is **changeable or tropical**^β,7 because the seasons change in it; at its beginning days and nights are equal, but ⟨then⟩ the days begin to grow longer and the nights shorter. (5) Its hours are longer than the **equal hours**;^γ,8 its **ascensions**^α,9 are decreased, ⟨because⟩ in every location **its ascensions**^γ,10 are less than ⟨the ascensions⟩ at the **line of equality**^γ,11 [the equator] ⟨⟨on the Earth⟩⟩;^ν,12 and it is {also} an **oblique sign.**^γ,13 (6) **As a rule**,^γ,14 it indicates the nature of ⟨⟨temperate⟩⟩^ν,15 heat that **must increase**,^α,16 and in it is *the beginning* of the creatures' motion. (7) It is of the good, delightful signs, and indicates thunder and lightning. (8) In its beginning it is **rainy and windy**,^γ,17 in the middle it is mixed, and in its end it is hot with **whirlwind**.^α,18 (9) **Its northern part multiplies**^γ,19 heat with moistness, {but} ⟨its⟩ southern ⟨part⟩^γ,20 makes cold. (10) It has the form of four-footed ⟨animals⟩, **which have soles or hooves**,^β,21 and its limbs are cut off because they move **obliquely**^γ,22 along the circle. (11) **It is**^γ,23 bicolored in appearance, ⟨it is⟩ **of two forms or double-bodied or having two forms**,^β,24 and has half a voice. (12) The heart of the east belongs to it, ⟨⟨and the east wind⟩⟩.^ν,25 (13) Fire is its portion of the ⟨⟨four⟩⟩^ν **elements**;^α,26 its heat is tempered; **of the humors**^α,27 blood belongs to it. (14) Of the tastes, anything sweet; and of colors, red and anything that is saffron. (15) Of the animals, sheep, *that is, herds of small animals*, and any animal having soles. (16) Of the metals, gold, silver, iron, and copper. (17) {Likewise,} the third **climate**^α,28 is in its portion, and the land

⟨⟨...⟩⟩,ᵘ et Ardiam, ac Philistiam. (18) Loca {vero} terre, *sua sunt* campi, et pascualia **ovium seu gregum**,ᵝ et loca ignis, et **predonum** mansiones **seu latroni**,ᵝ et omnis domus foraminata; iuxta sapientiam {vero} PTOLOMEI, in parte sua sunt domus orationum, et loca iudiciorum. (19) ANTIQUI aut dixerunt quod de litteris *HEBREORUM* habet <u>aleph</u> et <u>num</u>. (20) Anni {quoque} ipsius sunt .15., et menses .15., dies {vero} .37. cum dimidio, et hore eius .4.

(21) Ascendit {autem} in prima facie eius ymago mulieris, **id est**,ᵅ lucens, et cauda piscis marini in similitudine serpentis, et caput trianguli, et figura bovis. (22) Dicunt {autem} INDIʸ quod ibidem est **caput secundum figuram canis**,ᵅ in cuius manu sinistra est candela et in manu dextra clavis. (23) Ait {quoque} **BENAKA**,ᵅ QUI EST EORUM SAPIENS, quod in hac prima facie ascendit Etyops, cuius oculi nigri et supercilia erecta, et est de gigantibus, in se ipso se iactans, et est involutus in albo mantello grandi, super se habens cingulum de corda, iracundus, et est stans super pedes suos. (24) Secundum sententiam {vero} PTOLOMEI ascendit in hac facie dorsum | Mulieris Super Sedem Sedentis, et genua eius ac manus sinistra, adhuc medietas dorsi Mulieris que Maritum Non Habet, una **cum partibus pudendorum eius**ᵅ ⟨⟨...⟩⟩,ᵛ {item} et Piscis secundus et una pars Fili Linei.

3rb

(25) Cum facie secunda ascendit **piscis marinus**,ᵅ et medietatem trianguli cum medietate bestie, et mulier tenens pectinem in capite, et lorica eream, et caput dyaboli. (26) Dicunt {autem} INDI quod ibi ascendit ymago mulieris in **pannos suos**ᵅ se involventis et **in sclavina vel sago sive cilicio quodam**,ᵝ et habet unum pedem, eius {autem} figura est sicut **equi**ᵅ figura. (27) Secundum sententiam {vero} PTOLOMEI ascendit illa que Sedet Super Sedem cum illo qui Portat Caput Dyaboli, et palma eius dextra, adhuc **locus pudendarum**ʸ Mulieris que Maritum Non Habet, similiter et pedes eius cum Triangulo et capite Arietis cum cornibus suis, et residuum Filorum Lineorum.

(28) In tertia {vero} facie, ascendit iuvenis quidem sedens super sedem, coopertorium qui habens super se, in cuius manu <u>terafim</u>ᵅᵉ *id est artificia magica*; {item} homo, caput suum inclinatus inferius, **Deum orans petendo veniam**;ʸ item ascendit ibidem venter piscis et caput eius cum fine trian-

of Babylonia ⟨⟨and Persia⟩⟩,^μ,29 Azerbaijan, and Palestine. (18) {Moreover} of places on earth, fields and pastureland for **sheep or flocks**^β,30 *belong to it*, the places of fire, the abode of **robbers or thieves**,^β,31 and any house roofed with beams; {but} according to PTOLEMY, houses of prayer and the place of the judges are in its portion. (19) The ANCIENTS said that of the *HEBREWS'* letters it has *aleph* and *nun*. (20) {Besides,} its years are 15, its months 15, the days {indeed} are 37½, and the hours 4.

(21) {However} in its first face [decan] the image of a woman, **that is**,^α,32 the shining one, rises, ⟨along with⟩ the tail of a sea fish with the resemblance of a snake, the head of the triangle, and the form of a bull. (22) {But} the **INDIANS**^γ,33 say that in the same place there is **a head following the form of a dog**,^α,34 holding a candle in its left paw and a key in its right paw. (23) {Besides,} **BENAKA**,^α,35 THEIR [the Indians'] WISE MAN, said that an Ethiopian rises in the first face, with black eyes and straight eyebrows; he is one of the giants, boasts about himself, is wrapped in a large white cloak, wears a belt made of rope, is irascible, and stands on his legs. (24) {But} according to PTOLEMY's opinion, the back of the Woman Sitting on a Chair [Cassiopeia] rises in it [the first face], and her knees and left hand, and half of the back of the Woman who has no Husband [Andromeda], **with parts of her pudenda**^α,36 ⟨⟨and the hem ⟨of her robe⟩⟩⟩;^γ,37 and {likewise} the second Fish and a bit of the Flaxen Thread.

(25) With its second face, **the sea fish**^α,38 rises, and the middle of the triangle with one-half of the beast, a woman with a comb on her head, copper armor, and the head of a devil. (26) {But} the INDIANS say that the image of a woman wrapped in **her clothes**^α,39 and in **certain *sclavina* or *sagum* or *cilicium*^β,40 [three types of cloaks] rises there; she has one leg, her form, {however,} is the form of a **horse**.^α,41 (27) {But} according to PTOLEMY's opinion, the ⟨Woman⟩ Sitting on a Chair [Cassiopeia] rises ⟨in it⟩, together with the Carrier of the Devil [Perseus], and his right hand, the **place of the pudenda**^γ,42 of the Woman who has no Husband [Andromeda]; and similarly her legs with the Triangle [Triangulum], the head of ⟨the constellation⟩ Aries and its horns, and the rest of the Flaxen Thread.

(28) {Moreover} in the third face, there rises a young man sitting in a chair, with a cover over him and, with ***terafim***,^αε,43 *that is, magical devices* in his hand; {likewise} ⟨along with⟩ a man whose head is lowered, **praying to God seeking pardon**;^γ,44 likewise the fish's belly and its head rise in the same

guli et secunda medietate bestie.¹ (29) Dicunt {autem} INDI^γ quod ibidem ascendit **homo rufus**^α cum pilis rufis; et ipse iracundus et **pertinax et discolus;**^β **in manu eius seu brachio**^β annuli lignei et virga, vestes eius rubee, et ipse faber ferrarius, et desiderium eius est bonum facere sed non potest. (30) In hac {autem} facie secundum sententiam PTOLOMEI, ascendit iste qui Portat Caput Dyaboli, et corpus Arietis.

(31) Qui {autem} natus fuerit *in hoc signo* temperatum erit corpus eius, facies eius longa, et oculi grandes, versus terram **respiciens seu respectivus;**^β,2 collum eius spissum et aures molles, pilosus satis et capilli eius crispi, tybie quidem eius graciles; et sermo placidus sed **extra modum vel nimis loquax**,^β satis comedendi appetitivus, iracundus, iustitiam amans, et vox eius non erit fortis. (32) {Quod} si in hoc signo Luna fuit, aut sors eius {similiter} cum aliqua **stellarum seu planetarum**^β malorum, hoc significat super **scabiem malam**,^α et super lepram, et surditatem, et allopitiam, et calvitium. (33) Ille qui nascitur in prima facie **rufus**^α erit, venter eius strictus **modice vel parve carnositatis;**^β et super pedem eius sinistrum habebit signum et in cubito manus sinistre,³ sufficientes quidem habebit amicos, et ipse malum odiet. (34) Qui {autem} in secunda facies natus, nigritudo in illo erit, similiter cum pulchritudine faciei, corpus eius **temperatum in complexione**,^γ

3va sed **festinans est sive paratus**^β,4 ad irascendi, | **circumspectus quidem non erit in motu ire**,^α **alti cordis est seu magnanimus**^β {similiter} cum sapientia perfecta et disciplina, et inimici eius plures erunt. (35) {Sed} ille qui natus fuerit in tertia facie **rufus erit ac** {etiam} **croceus**,^α **solitarius ab hominibus.**^α

(36) Humani {vero} corporis partes, ad hoc signum spectantes, sunt caput et facies cum pupilla oculi, et auribus. (37) Egritudines {quoque} sunt *epylencia*,^γ et dolores aurium, narum,⁵ dentium, et oculorum **aut morphea cum maculis faciei.**^γ (38) Et **secundum sapientiam**^γ quidem SAPIENTIUM EGYPTIORUM,⁶ **egritudo**^α **quam dat**^α Saturnus *in hoc signo* est in pectore, et Iupiter in corde, Mars in capite, et Sol **in genitalibus**,^α Venus in pedibus, Mercurius in tybiis, et Luna in genibus. (39) In parte {autem} huius signi, de hominibus, sunt reges, qui **principes**^γ sunt iustitie, et liberales, et bellicose, et ignis cum interfectione et sanguine, et **illi**⁷ **qui peregrinantur**^γ

---

¹bestie] WVG; L bestia. ²seu respectivus] L; WVG om. ³et in cubito manus sinistre] G om. ⁴sive paratus] G om. ⁵narum] WG; LV om. ⁶sapientiam quidem sapientium Egyptiorum] G Egiptios. ⁷illi] WVG; L illis.

place, with the end of the triangle, and the second half of the beast. (29) {But} the **INDIANS**[γ,45] say that a **reddish man**[α,46] with reddish hair rises there; he is irascible and **obstinate and of a bad temper;**[β,47] **on his hand or arm**[β,48] are wooden bracelets and ⟨he carries⟩ a scepter, his clothes are red, and he is a blacksmith, and wishes to do good but cannot. (30) {But} according to PTOLEMY's opinion, the Carrier of the Devil's Head [Perseus] and the body of Aries rise ⟨in it⟩.

(31) {But} a person born *in this sign* [one who has Aries as the ascendant of his nativity] will have a temperate body, a long face and large eyes; he **tends to look or looks**[β,49] towards the ground; his neck ⟨will be⟩ thick and his ears flaccid; he will have abundant curly hair, his shanks will be thin; his speech ⟨will be⟩ pleasant but he will be **talkative beyond measure or excessively;**[β,50] ⟨he will be⟩ very much desirous of eating, irascible, a lover of justice, and his voice will not be strong. (32) {But} if the Moon was in this sign ⟨at the nativity⟩, or if {similarly} its [the Moon's] lot was with any of the bad **stars or planets,**[β,51] it indicates a **bad roughness of the skin,**[α,52] leprosy, deafness, alopecia, and baldness. (33) One who is born in the first face ⟨of Aries⟩ [a person who has the first face of Aries as the ascendant of his nativity] will be **reddish,**[α,53] his belly tight **with slight or little flesh;**[β,54] he will have a mole on his left leg as well as in the armpit of his left hand; he will have many friends; and he will hate evil. (34) {But} one who is born in the second face, he will have blackness in him, similarly with beauty of the face, his body will be **temperate in its mixture,**[γ,55] he will be **quick or ready**[β,56] to anger, **but prudent not to be in a commotion,**[α,57] **high-minded or magnanimous**[β,58] {as well as} with total wisdom and discipline, and will have many enemies. (35) {But} one born in the third face [decan] will be bright **red and** {also} **saffron,**[α,59] **and isolated from human beings.**[α,60]

(36) {But} the parts of the human body belonging to this sign are the head, the face with the pupil of the eye, and the ears. (37) {Besides,} of diseases, *epilepsy,*[γ,61] and pain in the ears, nostrils, teeth, and eyes **or morphea with spots of the face.**[γ,62] (38) **According to the wisdom**[γ,63] of the EGYPTIAN SCHOLARS, the **disease**[α,64] that Saturn **gives**[α,65] [causes] *in this sign* is in the chest; Jupiter in the heart; Mars in the head; the Sun in the **genitals;**[α,66] Venus in the feet; Mercury in the shanks; the Moon in the knees. (39) {But} of human beings, in the portion of this signs are kings, who are **princes**[γ,67] of justice, the generous ones, those engaged in war, in fire with killing and blood, and **those who travel to foreign places.**[γ,68] (40) {But} *his sign* is

(40) Est {autem} *hoc*[1] *signum* domus Martis, et **honor** Solis **seu exaltatio**[β] in .19. gradu, ⟨⟨...⟩⟩,[v] et odium Veneris, **depressio seu humiliatio**[β] Mercurii in .25. gradu ad hoc tempus[2] **quod est a creatione Ade anno .4908.**,[α] *secundum* HEBRAYCAM VERITATEM, *quod est ab incarnatione domini nostri Ihesu Christi anno .1147.* (41) Et dominus triplicitatis in die est Sol et post eum Iupiter, de nocte {vero} Iupiter post eum Sol, particeps ipsorum in die et nocte est Saturnus. (42) Facies {autem} prima iuxta SAPIENTES EGYPTIORUM ac **aliarum**[γ] GENTIUM SAPIENTIORUM Martis[3] est, secunda est Solis, tertia Veneris;[4] secundum INDORUM {vero} SAPIENTES prima est Martis, secunda Solis, sed tertia **Veneris**.[α] (43) Et ecce **terminos**[α] secundum EGYPTIORUM **sapientiam et** BABYLONIORUM:[α] Iovis quidem .6. gradus, et Veneris .6. gradus, Mercurii .8., Martis .5., et Saturni .5. ⟨⟨...⟩⟩.[v] (44) **Prima**[α] {autem} huius novenaria Martis est, secunda Veneris, tertia Mercurii, quarta Lune, quinta Solis, sexta Mercurii, septima Veneris, octava Martis et nona Iovis; et est quidem novenaria signi tres gradus cum tertia gradus et unius, et totum novenaria est sicut natura signi et domini signi. (45) Prime {vero} duodenarie virtus est Martis, secunde Veneris, tertie Mercurii, quarte Lune, quinte Solis, sexte Mercurii, septime Veneris, octave Martis, none Iovis, decime et undecime Saturni, et duodecime Iovis. (46) **Deinde**[γ,5] ENOCH, QUI EST HERMES,[β α] ac ANTIQUI virtutem duodenariarum secundum aliam viam dicunt esse; aiunt enim gradum primum esse secundum naturam ipsius signi, secundum {vero} gradum secundum naturam signi **sequentis sive secundi**,[β] et tunc revertitur .13us. gradus et .25. super naturam ipsiusmet signi.

(47) Dicunt {autem} INDORUM SAPIENTES quod a principio signi usque ad .3. gradus sunt mediocres, neque lucidi neque obscuri, deinde quinque gradus tenebrosi,[6] post eos .8. mediocres, deinde | .4. lucidi, deinde .4. obscuri, deinde .5. lucidi, et **demum**[α] unus obscurus. (48) Septem {vero} primi gradus masculini, et post illos duo feminini, post ea .6. masculini, deinde .7. feminini, et **demum**[α] .8. masculini. (49) **Gradus** {autem} **puteales stella-**

---

[1]hoc] WVG; L huius. [2]tempus] L; WVG tempore. [3]Martis] WVG; L veritas. [4]Veneris] WVG; L > Iovis. [5]Deinde] WVG; L verum. [6]tenebrosi] G (in margin); WV lucidi; L om (lacuna).

the house of Mars, and **the honor or exaltation**$^\beta$ of the Sun at ⟨Aries⟩ 19°, ⟨⟨the dejection [the opposite of the exaltation] of Saturn at ⟨Aries⟩ 21°⟩⟩,$^{\nu,69}$ the hate^{70} [detriment or opposite of the house] of Venus, the **depression or humiliation**$^{\beta,71}$ [perigee] of Mercury at ⟨Aries⟩ 25° in the present time, **which is the year 4908 from the creation of Adam,**$^{\alpha,72}$ *according to the Hebrew truth, which is in the year 1147 from the Incarnation of our Lord Jesus Christ.* (41) The lords of the triplicity by day are the Sun and then Jupiter, {but} by night Jupiter and then the Sun; Saturn is their partner by day and by night. (42) {But} the first face [decan], according to the EGYPTIAN SCHOLARS and **others of**$^{\gamma,73}$ the GENTILE SCHOLARS, ⟨is assigned⟩ to Mars, the second to the Sun, and the third to Venus; {but} according to the INDIAN SCHOLARS, the first face ⟨is assigned⟩ to Mars, the second to the Sun, and the third to **Venus.**$^{\alpha,74}$ (43) These are the **terms**$^{\alpha,75}$ **according to the wisdom of the EGYPTIANS and BABYLONIANS:**$^{\alpha,76}$ Jupiter 6°, Venus 6°, Mercury 8°, Mars 5°, Saturn 5°; ⟨⟨and in Ptolemy's opinion: first, Jupiter 6°, second, Venus 8°, third, Mercury 7°, fourth, Mars 5°, fifth, Saturn 4°⟩⟩.$^{\nu,77}$ (44) {But} **the first**$^{\alpha,78}$ of its [Aries'] *novenariae* [ninth-parts] is ⟨assigned⟩ to Mars, the second to Venus, the third to Mercury, the fourth to the Moon, the fifth to the Sun, the sixth to Mercury, the seventh to Venus, the eighth to Mars, and the ninth to Jupiter; the *novenaria* [ninth-parts] of the sign covers three and one-half degrees, and each *novenaria* [ninth-part] has the nature of the sign and of the lord of the sign. (45) {Moreover,} the power of the first *duodenaria*^{79} [twefth] is ⟨assigned⟩ to Mars, {but} the second to Venus, the third to Mercury, the fourth to the Moon, the fifth to the Sun, the sixth to Mercury, the seventh to Venus, the eighth to Mars, the ninth to Jupiter, the tenth and the eleventh to Saturn, and the twelfth to Jupiter. (46) **Then**$^{\gamma,80}$ **ENOCH, WHO IS HERMES,**$^{\beta\alpha,81}$ and the ANCIENTS say that the power of the *duodenariae* [twelfths] is ⟨divided⟩ according to another method, for they say that the first degree ⟨of the sign is assigned⟩ according to the nature of the sign itself, the second degree according to the nature of the **subsequent or second**$^{\beta,82}$ sign, and then the 13th degree and the 25th degree are again ⟨assigned⟩ to the nature of the sign itself.

(47) {But} the INDIAN SCHOLARS say that from the beginning of the sign to three degrees ⟨of it⟩ the ⟨degrees⟩ are intermediate, neither bright nor dark; then ⟨there are⟩ five dark degrees, then eight intermediate degrees, then four bright ⟨degrees⟩, then four dark degrees, then five bright degrees, and **finally**$^{\alpha,83}$ one dark ⟨degree⟩. (48) {But} the first seven degrees ⟨of Aries⟩ are masculine, after them two feminine degrees, after them six masculine degrees, then seven feminine degrees, and **finally**$^{\alpha}$ eight masculine degrees.

146   PART ONE

rumʸ sunt hii: .6us. et .11. et .17us. et .23us. (50) Gradus {vero} augmentantes **fortunam**ʸ et honorem est .19us.

(51) Et est quidem in hoc signo, de stellis **maioribus**ʸ qui sunt primi honoris stella, que Finis appellatur Fluvii, et {autem} in hoc tempore est in .16. gradu signi Arietis, et latitudo eius meridiana est .13. gradus cum dimidio, et natura eius est de complexione Iovis et Veneris.

2 (1) Tauri signum de natura terre,[1] est femininum, nocturnum. (2) De tempore caliditatis, **fixum**.ʸ (3) Hore eius maiores sunt **horis equalibus**,ʸ et **ascensiones**ᵅ **minores seu diminute**,^(β,2) **obliquum**.ʸ (4) Est de **bonis seu benevolis**^β signis, est ac deliciosis, et significat **fertilitatem et habundantiam**.^(αθ,3) (5) Mixtum est ex calido et frigido, et humiditas eius maior est siccitate ipsius. (6) Principium eius super ventos significat et tenebrositatem, medium eius frigidum et humidum, et finis eius super **tempestates**ᵅ significat et ignes et fulmina et faces.[4] (7) Id {autem} quod eius **est septentrionale**ʸ mixtum est, **meridionale**ʸ {vero} adurens. (8) Est secundum figuram quadrupedis **soleas habentis seu ungulas**;^β et membra eius deficiunt et prescisa sunt; dimidiam habet vocem. (9) Et in parte eius est meridionalis pars dexter, et ventus meridionalis. (10) **Natura eius seu complexio**^(β,5) frigida est et sicca, temperata aliquantulum, et[6] eius est cholera nigra que aliquantulum temperata est, et de complexionibus **rectior seu convenientior**.^β (11) De saporibus, dulcedo cum ponticitate et restrictione;[7] de colorum apparentia, viridis et album.[8] (12) De animalibus, omnes quadrupedes **scissam** habentes **ungulam**;ᵅ et **de terre nascentibus seu de vegetabilibus**,^β ⟨⟨...⟩⟩^ν arbores, et omnis arbor fructum faciens, et omnis arbor aquam non indigens nisi modica, et omnis in montibus existens in cuius fructu **valor est et utilitas**,^β ac omnis arbor plantata cuius sapor et odor boni sunt. (13) Et de **climatibus**ᵅ {autem} est in parte eius quintum, et terra Etyopie, et terra Melian, et Ameden, et Haberach, et Africa et de Haknaen usque ad Arravalon, et Alcupa et Alhota, *credo quod est patria circa Damatia*,[9] Soem, Egyptus.^(γδ) (14) De campis {vero}, omnis terra arabilis que per armenta **colitur seu aratur**^β et per elephantes,[10] item eius sunt pomeria et viridaria, et

---

[1]Tauri signum de natura terre] L; V Tauri signum est de natura terre; V Taurus est nature terre; G Taurus est signum de natura terre.   [2]minores seu diminute] LWV; G minores.   [3]habundantiam] LVG; W > quia domus Veneris est.   [4]faces] W; LG facies; V om.   [5]seu complexio] G om.   [6]et] W > humor.   [7]restrictione] VG; L destructione; V om.   [8]album] L; WVG albus.   [9]credo quod est patria circa Damatia] L; WVG om.   [10]omnis terra arabilis que per armenta colitur seu aratur et per elephantes] WVG; L omnem terram arabilem super que aratus per iumenta.

(49) {But} these are the **degrees of the stars pertaining to a pit:**^γ,84 the 6th, 11th, 17th, and 23rd ⟨degree⟩. (50) {But} the degrees that add **fortune**^γ,85 and honor: the 19⟨th degree⟩.

(51) In this sign, of the **largest**^γ,86 stars of the first honor [first magnitude], there is one called the End of the River, {but} at the present time ⟨at longitude⟩ Aries 16°, its latitude is southern 13½°, its nature is a mixture of Jupiter and Venus.

2 (1) The sign of Taurus is of an earthy nature, feminine, nocturnal. (2) Of the season of heat [spring], **fixed.**^γ,1 (3) Its hours are longer than the **equal hours;**^γ its **ascensions**^α are **smaller or diminished,**^β,2 ⟨it is an⟩ **oblique**^γ,3⟨sign⟩. (4) It is one of the **good or benevolent**^β,4 signs, and it is of the delightful ⟨signs⟩, it indicates **fertility and abundance.**^αθ,5 (5) It is mixed of heat and cold, and its moistness is greater than its dryness. (6) Its beginning indicates winds and darkness, its middle ⟨indicates⟩ cold and moisture, and its end indicates **storms,**^α,6 fires, thunderbolts and torches. (7) {However,} what is in its portion and **is northern**^γ,7 is mixed, {but} ⟨what is in its portion and is⟩ **southern**^γ,8 is burning ⟨hot⟩. (8) It has the form of a four-footed ⟨animal⟩, **which has soles or hooves;**^β its limbs are missing and separated ⟨from it⟩, it has half a voice. (9) The right ⟨side⟩ of the south is in its portion, and the south wind. (10) Its **nature or mixture**^β,9 is cold and dry, somewhat tempered; black bile that is somewhat tempered belongs to it, and of the mixtures, **the straighter or more well-disposed**^β,10 [balanced]. (11) Of the flavors, the sweet that is accompanied by bitterness and restraint; of the appearance of the colors, green and white. (12) Of the animals, any that is four-footed and **has split hooves;**^α,11 and **of ⟨those⟩ born of the earth or of plants,**^β,12 ⟨⟨tall⟩⟩^ν,13 trees, and any tree making fruit, any tree that needs only a little water, and any ⟨tree⟩ in the mountains in whose fruit **there is value or use,**^β,14 and any planted tree whose flavor and smell are good. (13) {But} of the **climates,**^α,15 the fifth is in its portion, and Ethiopia, Māhin, Hamadhān, 'Akhraṭ, Africa, ⟨the region⟩ from Kairouan to Tripoli, al-Kufa, and al-Basra, *and I believe that it is the country around Damatia,*^16 Tanis, ⟨and⟩ **Egypt.**^γδ,17 (14) {Moreover} of plains, any arable land that is **cultivated or plowed**^β,18 by cattle and elephants; {likewise} orchards and plantations

loca omnium **fructificandum**ᵞ odoriferarum, et omnis locus cui commixtum est **cementum**ᵅ calidum ⟨⟨...⟩⟩.ᵘ (15) De litteris {quoque} *HEBRAYCIS* sunt in eius parte <u>daleth</u> et et littera <u>samech</u>. (16) Anni {vero} eius sunt .8, et mensium numerus similiter, dies .20., et hore .16.

4ra (17) Ascendit in eius prima facie, **fortis**ᵅ quidem **lanceam**ᵞ habens in sinistra manu, in dextra baculum, super humeros suos candelas | duas; et adhuc ascendit navis magna super quam leo et ibidem homo nudus sedens; et sub nave medietas corporis mulieris mortue, et itidem ascendit ibi ymago viri. (18) Et dicunt INDI quod est[1] mulier pilosa, filium habens, qui vestes induit in parte combustas. (19) Secundum PTOLOMEUM {vero}, ascendit medietas illius qui Caput Tenet Dyaboli, et **cauda**ᵅ Arietis, et effusorium aque quod est in fine Fluminis.

(20) Et in secunda facie ascendit navis, et ibidem homo nudus,[2] clavem portans in manu sua; item ascendit ibi secunda medietas mulieris mortue. (21) Et dicunt INDORUM SAPIENTES quod ascendit ibi vir, cuius facies et corpus assimilatur arieti; uxorem habens **tauro seu bovi**ᵝ similitudinem; et digiti eius caprorum ungulis assimilantur; {vero autem} ille valde calidus est et multum **comedens seu gulosus vel glutto**,ᵝ,[3] non dans anime sue requiem; **colet terras**,ᵅ et trahit boves ad arandum et seminandum; item ascendit ymago pulchra, in cuius manu dextra est virga, et manum sinistram elevat. (22) Iuxta sententiam PTOLOMEI, ascendunt genua Portantis[4] Caput Dyaboli, et tybie eius cum pedibus, et dorsum Tauri cum cornibus et manibus et ventre, ⟨⟨...⟩⟩,ᵘ et caput Fluminis cum eius medio.

(23) In tertia {autem} facie ascendit ultimum corpus, cuius caput assimilatur ⟨⟨...⟩⟩ᵛ cani, et homo stans, in cuius manu bestia, et habet currus duos, super quos vir sedens, et duo equi currum trahunt, et in manu viri **aries**.ᵞ (24) Sed INDORUM SAPIENTES dicunt quod ibi ascendit homo, cuius pedes albi, et dentes similiter, qui longa sunt ita quod apparent ultra labia sua, color oculorum eius rubeus est, et similiter pili, corpus eius corpori elephantis assimilatur et leonis, ⟨⟨...⟩⟩,ᵘ et ipse sedens super **pannum**;ᵞ item ascendit ibi equus et parvus canis ⟨⟨...⟩⟩.ᵘ (25) **Secundum**ᵞ PTOLOMEUS ibi ascendit

---

[1]est] WVG; L sit.   [2]nudus] W (above the line); LVG om.   [3]vel gluto] LW; VG om.   [4]Portantis] WG; L portanti; V portnates.

of trees, the place of any **tree bearing fruit**[γ,19] with a pleasant scent, and any place where hot **mortar**[α,20] is mixed ⟨⟨in which plants can grow⟩⟩.[μ,21] (15) {Besides,} of the HEBREW letters, _dalet_ and _samekh_ are in its portion. (16) {Moreover} its years are 8, and the same its months, the days 20, and the hours 16.

(17) In its first face [decan], there rises **a mighty one**[α,22] with a **spear**[γ,23] in his left hand, a club in his right hand, and two candles on his shoulders; there also rises a large ship, with a lion above it, and a naked man sitting there; beneath the ship there is half of a dead woman's body; the image of a man also rises ⟨there⟩. (18) The INDIANS say that she is a woman with hair, and has a son, and she wears clothes that are partly burned. (19) {But} according to PTOLEMY, half of the Carrier of the Devil's Head [Perseus] rises ⟨there⟩, and the **tail**[α,24] of ⟨the constellation⟩ Aries, and the stream of water which is at the end of the River [Eridanus].

(20) In its second face a ship rises; a naked man is there, holding a key in his hand; likewise, the second half of the dead woman rises there. (21) The INDIAN SCHOLARS say that a man, whose face and body resemble a ram, rises there; he has a wife resembling **a bull or an ox**;[β,25] and his fingers are similar to the hooves of goats; {however,} he is very hot and **he eats a lot, or is gluttonous or a glutton**,[β,26] and never allows his soul to rest; **he cultivates lands**[α,27] and leads the oxen out to plow and sow; likewise, a beautiful image with a scepter in her right hand rises ⟨there⟩, and she is holding up her left hand. (22) According to PTOLEMY's opinion, the knees of the Carrier of the Devil's Head [Perseus] rise ⟨there⟩, and its lower legs and feet, the back of ⟨the constellation⟩ Taurus, and its horns, front leg, abdomen ⟨⟨and right hind leg⟩⟩,[μ,28] and the beginning and middle of the River [Eridanus].

(23) {But} in the third face, the end of the body that resembles ⟨⟨the head of⟩⟩[ν,29] a dog rises, and a standing man, with a beast [meaning a snake] in his hand, and he has two carts, a man is sitting on them, and two horses pull the carts, and the man holds a **ram**[γ,30] in his hand. (24) But the INDIAN SCHOLARS say that a man rises there, whose feet are white, as are his teeth, which are so long that they stick out past his lips, and his eyes are red, and so too his hair, and his body resembles the body of an elephant and a lion, ⟨⟨and his mind is not at ease and all his thoughts are evil⟩⟩,[μ,31] and he sits on a **piece of cloth**;[γ,32] a horse, a dog, ⟨⟨and a little calf⟩⟩[μ,33] also rise there. (25) **According to**[γ,34] PTOLEMY, the right leg of the Carrier of the Devil's Head

pes dexter Portanti Caput Dyaboli, et humerus in manu Frenum Tenentis, et caput et genua ac manus eius sinister ⟨⟨...⟩⟩,^μ et finis Tauri et principium Fluminis.

(26) Qui {autem} natus fuerit in eo recta erit eius statura, facies longa, oculi grandes, collum eius spissum et breve, frons larga, nares acute, capilli crispi, sermo eius **intermixtus sive diffusus aut inconexus**^β et similiter sensus eius, pili eius nigri, et membra eius deficientia, desiderium eius vehemens, gulosus ac discolus. (27) Et ille[1] qui natus fuerit in aliquo[2] de gradibus **Pleiadum**,^γδ,3 qui sunt a .13o. gradus usque ad .15., egritudinem habebit in oculis. (28) Ac {vero} qui natus fuerit in prima facie erit statura brevis, oculi eius grandes, et labia spissa; signum {quoque} habebit in collo et aliud **in virga virili seu pudendo**;^β,4 **placens et liberalis corde**,^β amici eius satis multi, et {pluribus} deliciarum modis delectabitur. (29) Et ille qui natus 4rb fuerit in facie | secunda, faciem habebit rotundam, venter eius amplius, oculi eius pulchri, et anima liberalis, prudens; pilosus in humeris; et signum habens super lumbos, et quidam ex illis qui nascuntur in hac facie dolorem habebunt in **venis seu nervis**.^β (30) Qui {vero} natus fuerit in .3a. facie, pulcher erit corpore et facie, signum habens in oculo sinistro; laboriosus erit, et male fortunatus in mulieribus. (31) Et qui natus fuerit in fine signi huius, **eunuchus erit sine ferro sed naturaliter**^α aut hermafroditus.

(32) **De partibus corporis**,^γ in eius parte est collum, et guttur, et omnes egritudines que in illis locis eveniunt, sicut **apostemata, et spasmi**^γ colli et gutturis. (33) **Et secundum Egyptiorum sapientiam**,^γ **egritudo**^α Saturni in hoc signo est in corde, Iovis in ventre, Martis in collo, Solis in genibus, Veneris in capite, Mercurii in pedibus, et Lune in tybiis, et est de signis infirmitatum sicut Aries. (34) Et in parte eius ex hominibus sunt ⟨⟨...⟩⟩,^ν **luxuriosi et coitum desiderantes**,^β comestionum appetitivi et potationum, {similiter} et **coreas** amantes **sive saltationes**,^β et esse in gaudio. (35) Est {autem} domus Veneris, et **honor** Lune **seu exaltatio**^β in gradu .3., caput Draconis Martis est **in gradu tertio**,^α et est **odium eiusdem**.^γ (36) Domini {vero} triplicitatis in die Venus est et post eam Luna, de nocte Luna prima post eam Venus, et particeps in die et nocte Mars. (37) Facies prima secundum Egyptiorum sapientes et Persarum est **Veneris**,^α secunda Lune,

---

[1]ille] WVG; L om. [2]in aliquo] W om. [3]de gradibus Pleiadum] LW; VG graduum Pleiadum. [4]pudendo] LG; WV pudendis.

[Perseus] rises there, and the shoulder of the One Holding the Reins in his Hand [Auriga], and his head, knees, left hand ⟨⟨and his horn⟩⟩^μ,35 and the end of ⟨the constellation⟩ Taurus and the beginning of the River [Eridanus].

(26) {But} one who is born in it [one who has Taurus as the ascendant of his nativity] will be of erect stature; ⟨of⟩ long face, large eyes, his neck short and thick, a broad forehead, narrow nostrils, curly hair; **his speech muddled, vague or disconnected,**^β,36 and likewise his mind; his hair black, his limbs missing, his appetite intense, a glutton and of bad temper. (27) One who is born in the degrees of the **Pleiades**,^γ,δ,37 which are from 13° to 15° ⟨of Taurus⟩, will have a disease in the eyes. (28) {Moreover} one born in the first face [decan] ⟨of Taurus⟩ [a person who has the first decan of Taurus as the ascendant of his nativity] will be of short stature, his eyes large, thick lips; {besides,} he will have a mole on the neck and another **on the penis or the shameful ⟨member⟩;**^β,38 **pleasing and generous,**^β,39 with many friends, and will enjoy {many} sorts of pleasures. (29) One who is born in the second face will have a round face, a broad belly, beautiful eyes, a generous soul, prudent; with hair on his shoulders; he has a mole on the hips; and some of those born in this face will suffer pain in the **veins or nerves.**^β,40 (30) {Moreover} one who is born in the third face will have a handsome body and face, a mole on the left eye; he will be hardworking and will not have luck with women. (31) One born at the end of the degrees of the sign will be **a eunuch, without a knife but by nature**^α,41 [without surgical intervention] or a hermaphrodite.

(32) **Of the parts of the body**,^γ,42 the neck is in its portion, and the throat, and all the diseases affecting these places, such as **abscesses, and spasms**^γ,43 of the neck and throat. (33) **And according to the wisdom of the EGYPTIANS,**^γ,44 the **disease**^α,45 of Saturn in this sign is in the heart; of Jupiter in the abdomen; of Mars in the neck; of the Sun in the knees; of Venus in the head; of Mercury in the feet; of the Moon in the shanks; and it is one of the signs of disease, like Aries. (34) Of human beings, ⟨⟨middle-class people⟩⟩^ν,46 are in its portion, **those who are immoderate and lust for sexual intercourse,**^β,47 desirous of eating and drinking, and similarly lovers of **dancing and leaping,**^β,48 and rejoicing. (35) {But} it is Venus's house; the Moon's **honor or exaltation**^β is at ⟨Taurus⟩ 3°, and Mars's Head of the Dragon **at ⟨Taurus⟩ 3°,**^α,49 and this is **its** [Mars's] **hate**^γ,50 [detriment]. (36) {Moreover} the lords of the triplicity are Venus and then the Moon by day, and the Moon and then Venus by night; and Mars is their partner by day and by night. (37) The first face [decan], according to the EGYPTIAN and PERSIAN SCHOLARS, ⟨is

tertia Saturni; secundum **INDOS**ʸ {vero} prima est Veneris, secunda Mercurii, tertia Saturni.[1] (38) Et ecce **termini**ᵅ **secundum EGYPTIOS et SAPIENTES ASTRORUM:**ʸ Veneris quidem usque ad .8. gradus, Mercurii .6., postmodum Iovis .8., deinde Saturni .5., et deinde Martis .3.; secundum opinionem PTOLOMEI: Veneris .8., Mercurii .7., Iovis .7., **deinde Saturni .6., demum Martis duo.**ᵖ (39) Virtus novenarie prime et secunde est Saturni, tertie Iovis, quarte Martis, quinte Veneris, sexte Mercurii, septime Lune, octave Solis, et none Mercurii. (40) {Item} prime duodenarie virtus est Veneris, secunde Mercurii, tertie Lune, quarte Solis, quinte Mercurii, sexte Veneris, septime Martis, octave Iovis, none Saturni et decime Saturni, .11. Iovis, .12. Martis.

(41) A principio signi usque in finem tertium gradus sunt mixti, et postea .2. lucidi, et post duo vacui, deinde .8. lucidi, postmodum .5. vacui, deinde **.6. lucidi,**ᵅ demum .2. mixti (42) {Item} a principio signi usque .7. gradus sunt masculini, post .8. feminini, {demum} .15. masculini. (43) Putei {vero} stellarum sunt gradus quintus, .12us., et .18us., .24us., .25us., .26us. (44) Gradus **fortunam**ʸ augmentantes et honorem sunt .3us., .15us., .27.,[2] et .30us.

(45) {Rursus} in hoc signo sunt de *stellis fixis*ʸ Dorsum scilicet[3] Leprosi, *qui est Perseus*, et est in gradu .14. et latitudo eius septentrionalis, .22.20 minuta, et est honoris secundi, de complexione quidem Veneris.[4] (46) {Item} Caput Dyaboli, et est in .15. gradu, latitudo eius **septentrionale**ʸ .23. gradus et .3. 4va minuta, et est honoris secundi,[5] | de complexione quidem Iovis et Saturni. (47) {Et item} est ibi stella lucida vocata Oculus Tauri Sinister, et est in .28. gradus, latitudo eius meridionalis .5. gradus cum dimidio, et est primi honoris, de complexione quidem Martis et Veneris; est {autem} de stellis interficientibus cum ad ipsam pervenit *significator vite*.ʸ (48) {Denique} est ibi de stellis obscuris stella in .10. gradu, latitudo septentrionalis .20. gradus et .40. minuta. (49) {Item} est alia obscura similis in gradus .12., cuius latitudo septentrionalis **.70. gradus cum dimidio,**ᵅ et ipsa est de interficientibus.

---

[1]secundum Indos vero prima est Veneris, secunda Mercurii, tertia Saturni] WGV; L om. [2].27.] WVG + HJ; L .29. [3]scilicet] LV; WV om. [4]de complexione quidem Veneris] WVG; L om. [5]Item caput dyaboli et est in .15. gradu, latitudo eius septentrionale 23 gradus et 3 minuta, et est honoris secundi] WVG; L om.

LIBER ABRAHE AVENERRE INTRODUCTORIUS AD ASTRONOMIAM   153

assigned⟩ to **Venus**,^α,51 the second to the Moon, and the third to Saturn; {but} according to the **INDIANS**,^γ,52 the first face ⟨is assigned⟩ to Venus, the second to Mercury, and the third to Saturn. (38) These are the **terms**^α,53 **according to the EGYPTIANS and the SCHOLARS OF THE STARS:**^γ,54 Venus ⟨from the first degree of Taurus⟩ up to 8°, Mercury 6°, afterwards Jupiter 8°, then Saturn 5°, then Mars 3°; and in PTOLEMY's opinion: Venus 8°; Mercury 7°; Jupiter 7°; **then Saturn 6°; finally Mars 2°.**^π,55 (39) The power of the first and the second _novenaria_ [ninth-part] ⟨is assigned⟩ to Saturn, the third to Jupiter, the fourth to Mars, the fifth to Venus, the sixth to Mercury, the seventh to the Moon, the eighth to the Sun, and the ninth to Mercury. (40) {Likewise,} the power of the first _duodenaria_ [twelfth] ⟨is assigned⟩ to Venus, the second to Mercury, the third to the Moon, the fourth to the Sun, the fifth to Mercury, the sixth to Venus, the seventh to Mars, the eighth to Jupiter, the ninth and the tenth to Saturn, the eleventh to Jupiter, and the twelfth to Mars.

(41) From the beginning of the sign to the end of the third degree ⟨the degrees are⟩ mixed; then two bright degrees, then two empty ⟨degrees⟩, then eight bright ⟨degrees⟩, then five empty ⟨degrees⟩, **then six bright ⟨degrees⟩**,^α,56 and then two mixed ⟨degrees⟩. (42) {Likewise,} from the beginning of the sign to seven degrees, ⟨the degrees are⟩ masculine, then eight feminine ⟨degrees⟩, {finally} 15 masculine ⟨degrees⟩. (43) {Moreover} the pits of the stars are the 5th, 12th, 18th, 24th, 25th, and 26th degrees. (44) The degrees adding **fortune**^γ and honor are the 3rd, 15th, 27th, and 30th.

(45) {Besides,} in this sign, of the _fixed stars_^γ,57 ⟨we find⟩ the Back of the Leper, _which is Perseus_,[58] it is ⟨at longitude Taurus⟩ 14°, its northern ⟨ecliptical⟩ latitude 22° 20′, it is of the second honor [second magnitude], of the mixture of Venus. (46) {Likewise,} the Head of the Devil, it is at ⟨longitude Taurus⟩ 15°, its latitude is **northern**^γ,59 23° 3′, it is of the second honor, of the mixture of Venus and Saturn.(47) {Likewise} there is a bright star there, called the Left Eye of the Bull, it is at ⟨longitude Taurus⟩ 28°, its latitude is southern 5½°, of the first honor, of the mixture of Mars and Venus; {but} it is one of the lethal stars when the _significator of life_^γ,60 reaches it. (48) {Next,} of the dark stars, there is there a star at ⟨longitude Taurus⟩ 10°, ⟨its⟩ latitude northern 20° 40′. (49) {Likewise,} there is another dark star, similar ⟨to the previous one⟩, at ⟨longitude Taurus⟩ 12°, whose latitude is northern **70½°**;^α,61 it is one of the lethal ⟨stars⟩.

3 (1) *Geminorum signum est de natura aeris, masculinus, diurnus, occidentale.* (2) De tempore caliditatis, et est duorum corporum. (3) Hore eius maiores horis rectis, et in fine eius sunt dies longissimi de toto anno ⟨⟨...⟩⟩.^μ (4) Significat super **naturam equalem**,^γ que facit augere et que **augetur in numero**,^α et que perficit totum quidquid valet *viventibus*, seu animalibus et vegetalibus, universaliter **complexio eius mixta est**.^γ (5) Principium eius humidus est, medium temperatum, finis {vero} mobilis. (6) Et illud quod eius **septentrionale**^γ est, **tempestates facit**^α et ventus nasci, illud quod est meridionali **turbines**^α nasci facit. (7) Est {autem} figura hominis, et membra integra, sed est sterile. (8) Et in parte eius dextra pars occidentis et ventus occidentalis. (9) **Principium eius**^α calidum est et humidum, et sanguis est de parte eius. (10) Sapor eius dulcissimus, et apparentia coloris eius color ille qui multos colores **continet seu representat**.^γ,1 (11) De animalibus, in parte eius est homo, et simia, et aves bene cantantes. (12) De vegetalibus, arbores alte, et universaliter super omnis res altas, scilicet celos, aerem et ventos. (13) De **climatibus**^α {vero} in parte eius sunt **clima**^α sextum, et terra Gerien, et Armenia, et **India Maior**,^α Gillean, Brian, Bacaens, et Helnech, Barca, et terra Israel, et Egyptus, Estehen et Carmen. (14) {Item} in parte eius montes altissimi ⟨⟨...⟩⟩^μ et **loca** {vero} **capiuntur aves**,^α et loca similiter ubi ad aleas luditur et ad organa. (15) Littere eius sunt *gymel* et *ayn*. (16) Et anni .20., et similiter menses, dies .50., et hore .4.

(17) Ascendit {autem} in prima eius facie cauda ymaginis, cuius caput capiti canis simile est, et homo in cuius manu virga; {item} ascendit in ea versus meridiem currus duo in quibus trahunt duo equi, super quos sedens homo ducens eos; et item ascendit ibi caput bestie cornute. (18) Dicunt {vero} SAPIENTES INDORUM quod ibi ascendit mulier formosa stans in aere, et ipsa bene scit² consuere. (19) Et **secundum**^γ PTOLOMEUS ascendit ibi caput manu Tenentis Frenum, et pes eius dexter, et cornu Tauri, et humerus Canis *id est Orionis*, cum pede eius sinister, et caput Leporis cum manibus eius *et cum tybiis anterioribus.*

4vb (20) Et ascendit | in secunda facie homo tenens instrumenta cantus aurea organizans in illis; et ascendit ibi bestia stans ⟨⟨...⟩⟩,^μ et lupus signum habens in manu sua. (21) **Secundum INDOS**^γ ascendit ibi **Etyops sive Maurus**,^αβ

---

[1] seu representat] G om.   [2] bene scit] VG; L bene; W scit.

3 (1) The sign of Gemini is of airy nature, masculine, diurnal, western. (2) Of the season of heat [spring] and of two bodies. (3) Its hours are longer than the straight ⟨hours⟩, at its end come the longest days of all the year, ⟨⟨and in all climates its ascensions are crooked⟩⟩[μ,1] (4) It indicates an **equal nature**[γ,2] [balanced nature], which causes growth, **is increased in number**[α,3] and completes everything that is beneficial to *living creatures*, whether animals or plants; as a rule, **its complexion is mixed.**[γ,4] (5) Its beginning is moist, its middle is tempered, and its end {indeed} mutable. (6) What is in its portion and **northern**[γ] produces storms[α,5] and winds; what is southern produces **whirlwinds.**[α,6] (7) {But} it has the form of a human being, and healthy limbs, but it is sterile. (8) The right ⟨side⟩ of the west is in its portion, and the west wind. (9) **Its beginning** [α,7] is hot and moist, and blood is in its portion. (10) Its flavor is very sweet, and the appearance of its color is the color that **contains or represents**[γ,8] many colors. (11) Of animals, man is in its portion, and the monkey, and songbirds. (12) Of the plants, tall trees, and in general everything high, such as the heavens, the air, and the winds. (13) {Moreover} of the **climates,**[α] the sixth **climate,**[α] and the land of Gurgān, Armenia and **Greater India,**[α,9] Gilān, Barqān, **Bacaens**, Ḥalon, Barq'a, the land of Israel, Egypt,[10] Isfahān and Kirmān. (14) {Likewise,} every high ⟨⟨and steep⟩⟩[μ,11] mountain is in its portion, and {moreover} **places where birds are hunted,**[α,12] and so too places for playing with dice and musical instruments. (15) Its letters are *gimel* and *'ayin*. (16) Its years are 20, and so too its months, the days are 50, and the hours 4.

(17) {But} in its first face [decan], there rises the tail of the image whose head resembles the head of a dog, and a man holding a scepter in his hand; {likewise,} on the southern side ⟨of the horizon⟩ two carts pulled by two horses, with a man sitting on them [the carts] and directing them [the horses], rise in it [in the first decan]; likewise, the head of a horned beast rises there. (18) {But} the INDIAN SCHOLARS say that a beautiful woman standing in the air rises there, and she knows how to sew. (19) **According to**[γ,13] PTOLEMY, the head of the One Holding the Reins in ⟨his⟩ Hand [Auriga] rises ⟨there⟩, along with his right foot, the horn of ⟨the constellation⟩ Taurus, the shoulder of the Dog, *that is, Orion,*[14] with its left foot, and the head and paws of the Hare [Lepus], *and with the front shanks*.

(20) In the second face, there rises a man holding a golden musical instrument on which he is playing; a beast standing ⟨⟨on a tree⟩⟩[μ,15] rises there, ⟨too⟩, and a wolf with a mark on its paw. (21) **According to the INDIANS,**[γ,16] an **Ethiopian or Moor**[αβ,17] rises there, whose head is bound in lead; he holds

cuius caput ligatus est plumbo, in manus eius **arma seu instrumenta bellica**,^{β} et capillus ferreus in capite suo, et super capillum corona de serico, et in manu eius arcus et sagitte, diligens iocos et derisiones, et vadit in pomerium **ubi sunt arbores et plante insite**;^{γ} {item} in manu sua **statera seu lances**,^{β} in quibus manibus suis percussiens organizans, ⟨⟨...⟩⟩.^{μ} (22) **Iuxta Ptolomeum**^{γ} ibi ascendit palma Tenenetis Habenas, et unus de pedibus Tauri posterior videlicet, et manus **Fortis**^{α} *scilicet Orionis*, et caput eius cum humero et ventre et cingulo et genu ac pede ad hoc, et venter Leporis cum **cauda**.^{α}

(23) In tertia {vero} facie ascendit ymago hominis stupefactus, in cuius capite mitra conis, et in manu eius instrumentum cantus habens cordas aureas; {item} ascendit ibi canis latrans, et piscis vocatus delphinus, et ymago symie, et linea sartoris, et medietas prima ursi parvi, et cauda bestie cornute cum se involvit super radicem **puelle seu virginis**.^{β} (24) Dicunt {autem} Indorum sapientes quod ibi ascendit homo querens arma, et cum eo arcus et pharetra,[1] in cuius manus sagitte et panni et **peramenta aurea vel argentea**,^{β} et vult canere et ludere et iocari omnibus iocorum modis. (25) Secundum sententiam {vero} Ptolomeus ascendit ibi humerus Gemini posterioris cum manu eius et pede dextero[2] ac **pudendo**,^{α} et **cauda**^{α} Leporis, et os Canis cum manu et pede eius dextero, adhuc et primus remus ⟨⟨...⟩⟩^{ν} et parte remi secundi.

(26) Et {vero} qui natus fuerit in eo de **filiis hominum**^{αθ} erit stature recte,[3] et ventris ampli, **factura**^{α} corporis eius pulcher et similiter figura eius, ⟨⟨...⟩⟩,^{μ} vocem habebit fortem; et erit **acceptatus**;^{γ} humeri eius ampli, et oculi pulchri, capilli eius crispi, et erit **ioculator**^{γ} vel artificiosus in operibus suis omnibus, et erunt aliqui ex natis huius scriptores[4] et arismetici^{γ,5} et astrologi^γ et sapientes excellentes, et qui natus fuerit erit homo verax et mediocris in timore Dei. (27) {Igitur} qui in prima facie natus fuerit, erit corpus eius **formosum et placens**,^{β} similiter et oculi et crines eius; signum {autem} habebit in capite vel maxillis eius, acutus; sed non est iracundus, et est laboriosus, et non fortunatus in mulieribus. (28) Qui {autem} natus fuerit in secunda facie statura brevis erit et niger, sub cubito signum habebit nigrum, sermo eius acceptabilis et ipse homo **prudens et disciplinatus**,^{αβ} pulcher in figura, **placidus**,^{γ} inmiscens | se regibus.

5ra

---

[1]pharetra] WVG; L feretra.   [2]dextero] W; sinistro LGV.   [3]recte] WVG; L om.   [4]scriptores] LVW; G conscriptores.   [5]arismetici] V < geometrici.

a weapon or military device[β,18] in his hand, there is an iron helmet on his head, and a crown of silk on the helmet, he holds a bow and arrows in his hand, he loves laughter and mockery, he walks in a garden **where trees and plants are planted;**[γ,19] {likewise} he holds **a balance or the pans of a balance**[β,20] in his hand, striking them with his hand and making music, ⟨⟨and he picks flowers from the garden⟩⟩.[μ,21] (22) **According to PTOLEMY,**[γ,22] the right hand of the ⟨Shepherd⟩ Holding the Reins [Auriga] rises ⟨there⟩, and one of the hind feet of ⟨the constellation⟩ Taurus, the hand of **the Mighty One,**[α,23] *that is Orion,*[24] and his head with the shoulder, abdomen, hips, knees, and feet, and the belly and **tail**[α,25] of the Hare [Lepus].

(23) {Moreover} in the third face, the figure of a stunned man, with a conical turban on his head, holding a musical instrument with golden strings in his hand; {likewise,} a barking dog rises there, and the fish called dolphin, the image of a monkey, the tailor's cord, the first half of the lesser bear, and the tail of the horned beast that is wrapped around the lower part of **a girl or a virgin.**[β,26] (24) {But} the INDIAN SCHOLARS say that a man looking for a weapon rises there, along with a bow and a quiver, with an arrow in his hand, and clothes and a **pendant of gold or silver,**[β,27] and he wishes to sing and play [music], laugh, and jest in every kind of jesting. (25) {But} in PTOLEMY's opinion, the shoulder of the second Twin rises there, with his hand, right foot, and **genitals,**[α,28] the **tail**[α,29] of the Hare [Lepus], the mouth, forelegs, and right hind leg of the Dog [Canis Major], and the first oar ⟨⟨of the Ship [Argo Navis]⟩⟩[ν,30] and part of the second oar.

(26) {Moreover} a person born in it [one who has Gemini as the ascendant of his nativity], of the **sons of men**[αθ,31] [i.e., human beings] will be of erect stature; he will have a broad belly, the **shape**[α,32] of his body is handsome and so too his form, ⟨⟨pleasant speech⟩⟩, [μ,33] he will have a strong voice; he will be ⟨**socially**⟩ **acceptable;**[γ,34] broad shoulders, beautiful eyes, his hair curly, and he will be a **jester**[γ,35] or skilled in all his undertakings; some of its natives [the natives in Gemini] will be scribes, **ARITHMETICIANS,**[γ,36] **ASTROLOGERS,**[γ,37] GREAT SCHOLARS; one born ⟨in it⟩ will be truthful, and moderate in the fear of God [his religious belief]. (27) One who is born in the first face [decan] ⟨of Gemini⟩, {then,} will have a **handsome and pleasing**[β,38] body, and so too his eyes and hair; {but} he will have a mole on his head or cheeks, and will be eagle-eyed; but he is not irascible, and he is hardworking, and does not have luck with women. (28) {But} one who is born in the second face will be short and swarthy, with a black mole in his armpit, of pleasant speech, **prudent and learned,**[αβ,39] with handsome

(29) Qui {vero} natus fuerit in facie tertia, faciem habebit parvam, et oculos parvos; {similiter} **homo erit suspiriosus,**^{α} **adulter seu fornicator,**^{β} **loquens sermones frivolos,**^{γ} et mendax. (30) Et ille qui natus fuerit in fine signi **oculos habebit integros.**^{α}

(31) De partibus {autem} humani corporis, in parte sua habet humeros et brachia cum manibus ⟨⟨...⟩⟩.^{ν} (32) Et egritudines eius sunt omnis ex sanguine, et omnis egritudo in membris **enervens**^{γ} memoratis. (33) **Et iuxta**^{α} SAPIENTES EGYPTIOS **egritudo**^{α} Saturni est in ventre, Iovis **in lumbis et inferioribus ventribus,**^{β} Martis in humeris, Solis in tybiis, Veneris in collo, Mercurii in capite, et Lune in pedibus. (34) **De filiis** {autem} **homini,**^{αθ} in parte eius sunt **magnates et strenui, et sortilegii ac artifices magici;**^{γδ} **et omnia artificia ingeniosa,**^{γ} et omnis res iocosa, et cantus, et opera manualia, et universaliter omne artificium subtile. (35) Domus quidem est Mercurii, et **honor seu exaltatio**^{β} Capitis Draconis in tertio gradus, {videlicet} Iovis quidem est domus odii, et **locus augis** Solis et Veneris in .27. gradu ad hoc tempus, **depressio** {vero} **seu appositum augis**^{β} Saturni in .12. gradu. (36) Triplicitatis {autem} domini in die, Saturnus est et post eum Mercurius, nocte {vero} Mercurius et post eum Saturnus, particeps die et nocte est Iupiter. (37) Et facies prima **secundum**^{γ} EGYPTIOS quidem[1] et BABYLONIOS Iovis est, secunda Martis, tertia Solis; **secundum**^{γ} INDOS {autem} prima Mercurii est, secunda Veneris, tertia Saturni. (38) **Secundum**^{γ} EGYPTIOS quidem et ASTRORUM SAPIENTES^γ ecce **termini:**^{α} .6. gradus Mercurii, Iovis .6., Veneris .5., Martis .7., et Saturni .6.; secundum opinionem {vero} PTOLEMEI, Mercurii .7., Iovis .6., Veneris .7., Martis .6., et Saturni .4. (39) Initium {autem} **virtutis novenariarum**^{γ} Veneris est, secunda Martis, tertia Iovis, quarta Saturni, quinta eiusdem,[2] .6ta. Iovis, .7a. Martis, .8a. Veneris,[3] et .9a. Mercurii. (40) Duodenariarum {vero} prima Mercurii est, secunda Lune, tertia Solis, quarta Mercurii, quinta Veneris, sexta Martis, septima Iovis, octava et nona Saturni, .10a. Iovis, undecima Martis et duodecima Veneris.

---

[1]quidem] WVG; L > et astrorum sapientes.   [2]eiusdem] WVG; L eius.   [3]Veneris] WVG; L om.

form; **pleasing**,ʸ,⁴⁰ and mingling with kings. (29) {Moreover} one who is born in the third face will have a thin face and small eyes; {so too} **a man breathing with difficulty**,ᵅ,⁴¹ an **adulterer or fornicator**,ᵝ,⁴² **saying frivolous statements**,ʸ,⁴³ and a liar. (30) One born in the end of the sign **will have healthy eyes**.ᵅ,⁴⁴

(31) {But} of the parts of the human body, the shoulders are in its portion, and the arms and hands, ⟨⟨and shoulders⟩⟩.ᵛ,⁴⁵ (32) Its diseases are any disease of the blood and any disease **weakening**ʸ,⁴⁶ the aforementioned limbs. (33) **According to**ᵅ,⁴⁷ the EGYPTIAN SCHOLARS, the **disease**ᵅ,⁴⁸ of Saturn ⟨in Gemini⟩ is in the abdomen; of Jupiter **in the hips or lower abdomen**;ᵝ,⁴⁹ of Mars in the shoulders; of the Sun in the shanks; of Venus in the neck; of Mercury in the head; of the Moon in the feet. (34) {But} **among the sons of man**ᵅᵝ,⁵⁰ [i.e., human beings], in its portion are **noblemen and vigorous people, sorcerers and those skilled in magic;**ʸᵟ,⁵¹ **any ingenious craftsmanship,**ʸ,⁵² any humorous thing, music, and handiworks, and as a rule any delicate craft. (35) It is the house of Mercury, and the **honor or exaltation**ᵝ,⁵³ of the Head of the Dragon at the third degree ⟨of Gemini⟩, {namely} it is the house of the hate [detriment or opposite of the planetary house] of Jupiter, the **place of the apogee**ᵅ,⁵⁴ of the Sun and Venus at ⟨Gemini⟩ 27° in this time, {moreover} the **depression** [perigee] **or opposite of the apogee**ᵝ,⁵⁵ of Saturn at ⟨Gemini⟩ 12°. (36) {However,} the lords of the triplicity are Saturn and then Mercury by day, {but} Mercury and then Saturn by night; and Jupiter is the partner by day and by night. (37) **According to**ʸ the EGYPTIANS and BABYLONIANS, the first face [decan] ⟨is assigned⟩ to Jupiter, the second to Mars, and the third to the Sun; {but} **according to**ʸ the INDIANS, the first ⟨face is assigned⟩ to Mercury, the second to Venus, and the third to Saturn. (38) These are the **terms,**ᵅ,⁵⁶ in the opinion of the EGYPTIAN SCHOLARS and the **SCHOLARS OF THE STARS:**ʸ Mercury 6°, Jupiter 6°, Venus 5°, Mars 7°, and Saturn 6°; {but} in PTOLEMY's opinion: Mercury 7°, Jupiter 6°, Venus 7°, Mars 6°, and Saturn 4°. (39) {But} the beginning of the **power of the *novenariae*** ʸ,⁵⁷ ⟨is assigned⟩ to Venus, the second to Mars, the third to Jupiter, the fourth and fifth to Saturn, the sixth to Jupiter, the seventh to Mars, the eighth to Venus, and the ninth to Mercury. (40) {Moreover} the first of the ***duodenariae***ʸ,⁵⁸ ⟨is assigned⟩ to Mercury, the second to the Moon, the third to the Sun, the fourth to Mercury, the fifth to Venus, the sixth to Mars, the seventh to Jupiter, the eighth and ninth to Saturn, the tenth to Jupiter, the eleventh to Mars, and the twelfth to Venus.

160   PART ONE

(41) ⟨⟨...⟩⟩.ᵘ (42) Et a principio quidem signi usque ad finem .6. graduum feminini, deinde .11. masculini, post ea .6. feminini, deinde .4. masculini, et demum¹ .3. feminini. (43) **Gradus** {autem} **puteales stellarum**ᵞ sunt .2us., .12us., .17us., .26. et .30us. (44) Gradus **fortunam**ᵞ augmentantes et honorem est undecimus.

(45) Et est in *hoc signo* stella super sinistrum pedem Geminorum **in .15. gradu**,ᵅ cuius latitudo meridionalis .31. gradus .40 minuta, est {autem} honoris prima, de complexione Martis et Veneris. (46) Et est ibi stella super sinistrum humerum in .5. gradu, cuius latitudo meridionalis .17. gradus cum dimidio, et est honoris secundi, de complexione Martis et Mercurii. (47) {Item} est ibi stella illius | Manu Frenum Tenet, et est in gradu decimo, et latitudo eius septentrionalis .16. gradus, honoris primi est, de complexione Saturni et Iovis. (48) ⟨⟨...⟩⟩.ᵘ (49) {Similiter} est ibi medium cinguli, et est in .15. gradu, latitudo eius meridionalis .24. gradus .45. minuta; honoris secundi est, et de complexione Iovis et Saturni. (50) {Iterum} est ibi humerus Gemini in .16. gradu, latitudo eius meridionalis .17., et est honoris primi, de complexione Martis et Mercurii. (51) {Rursus} est ibi pes Gemini dexter in .24. gradu, latidudo eius meridionalis .11. gradus cum dimidio, et est honoris primi, de conplexione ⟨Martis⟩² et Veneris (52) ⟨⟨...⟩⟩.ᵘ (53) {Demum} est ibi de stellis obscuris, stella obscura qui est super caput **Fortis**,ᵅ *id est Orionis* in .12. gradu, cuius latitudo meridionalis .13. gradus .50 minuta, est ipsa est de interficientibus.

5rb

4 (1) Cancri **signum, de natura aque**,ᵞ femininus, **nocturnus, septentrionale**. (2) **De signis terre**,ᵅ et est mobile in ipso namque mutatur tempus; in eius principio incipit dies minuere, nox augere. (3) Hore eius longiores **equalibus**ᵞ et **ascensiones**ᵅ eius recte et incipientes augeri. (4) Universaliter significat super frigiditatem et humiditatem temperatas, **que multiplicabuntur et augescent**,ᵅᶿ,³ in ipso namque gradus sunt caliditatis et humiditatis. (5) Et principium quidem eius siccum est corruptivum, medium in complexione propria, et finis eius humidus. (6) **Quod** {autem} **eius est**⁴

---

¹demum] WVG; L ulterior.   ²Martis] lacuna in LGWV and HJ.   ³augescent] G augentur.
⁴Quod autem eius est] LW; G illud autem quod est eius; V pars eius.

(41) ⟨⟨From the beginning of the sign to the end of seven degrees, ⟨the degrees are⟩ bright; then ⟨come⟩ three mixed ⟨degrees⟩, then five empty ⟨degrees⟩, then six bright ⟨degrees⟩, then six mixed ⟨⟨degrees⟩⟩.^μ,59 (42) From the beginning of the sign to the end of six degrees, ⟨the degrees are⟩ feminine, then ⟨come⟩ eleven masculine ⟨degrees⟩, then six feminine ⟨degrees⟩, then four masculine ⟨degrees⟩, and then three feminine ⟨degrees⟩. (43) {But} these are the **degrees of the stars pertaining to a pit:**^γ,60 the 2nd, 12th, 17th, 26th, and 30th degrees. (44) The degree adding **fortune**^γ and honor is the 11th.

(45) *In this sign*, there is a star on the left leg of ⟨the constellation⟩ Gemini, at ⟨**longitude**⟩ 15°,^α,61 whose latitude is southern 31° 40'; {but} it is of the first honor [first magnitude], of the mixture of Mars and Venus. (46) A star is there on the left shoulder ⟨of the constellation Gemini⟩ at ⟨longitude⟩ 5° ⟨of Gemini⟩, whose latitude is southern 17½°, of the second honor, of the mixture of Mars and Mercury. (47) {Likewise,} the star ⟨in the Shepherd⟩ with the Reins in his Hand [Auriga] is there at ⟨longitude Gemini⟩ 10°, its latitude is northern 16°; it is of the first honor, of the mixture of Saturn and Jupiter. (48) ⟨⟨The big star ⟨called⟩ *al-ʿayyūq* is at ⟨longitude Gemini⟩ 11°, northern ⟨ecliptical⟩ latitude 22½°; it is of the first honor and a mixture of Saturn and Jupiter⟩⟩^μ,62 (49) {Similarly,} ⟨a star⟩ is there at the middle of the girdle at ⟨longitude Gemini⟩ 15°, its latitude is southern 24° 45'; it is of the second honor, and of the mixture of Jupiter and Saturn. (50) {In addition,} the right shoulder of Gemini is there at ⟨longitude Gemini⟩ 16°, its latitude is southern 17°; it is of the first honor, of the mixture of Mars and Mercury. (51) {Also,} the right leg of Gemini is there at ⟨longitude Gemini⟩ 24°, its latitude is southern 11½°; it is of the first honor, of the mixture of Mars and Venus. (52) ⟨⟨The dog called *al-shiʿrā al-ʿabūr* is there⟩⟩.^μ,63 (53) {Finally,} of the dark stars, a dark star is at the head of **the Mighty One**,^α,64 *that is Orion*,^65 at ⟨longitude Gemini⟩ 12°, whose latitude is southern 13° 50'; it is one of the lethal ⟨stars⟩.

4 (1) **The sign** of Cancer **is of watery nature**,^γ,1 feminine, **nocturnal, northern**. (2) **One of the earthy signs**,^α,2 changeable because the season changes in it; at its beginning the day begins to grow shorter and the night longer. (3) Its hours are longer than the **equal**^γ,3 ⟨hours⟩, and its **ascensions**^α are straight and increasing. (4) As a rule, it indicates tempered cold and moistness, which **will be multiplied and will grow**,^αθ,4 for there are degrees of heat and moistness in it. (5) Its beginning is dry and corrupting, ⟨its⟩ middle is of its own mixture, its end is moist. (6) {However,} **what is in its**

septentrionale[γ] calefacit et adurit ; **quod**[γ] {vero} meridionale humidum est. (7) Et est in figura animalium aquatilium. (8) Et in pars eius est cor **anguli**[α] septentrionalis, et ventus septentrionalis. (9) Natura quidem eius est frigida et humida; et significat super flegma in hominibus, et super omnem comple-xionen frigidam et humidam **in equalitate aliquantula seu temperamento quodam**[β] existentem. (10) Sapor eius acetosus est et salsus, **coloris aspectus**[αθ] albus et color **cinericius seu pulvereus,**[β] quem ad color fumosus et hoc quod eis assimilatur. (11) De animalibus quidem, in parte[1] eius sunt omnia aquatilia et reptilia et parvi pisciculi;[2] et de bestiis terre, scorpiones cum reptilibus. (12) Et universaliter significat super aquas magnos habentes motus, et super omnia vegetabilia aque propinqua, et[3] super aquas pluviarum, et omnes aquas dulces.[4] (13) De **climatibus**[α] quidem habet septimum, et terram **Armenie**,[α] et illud quod est post Marsaam et Edarul et Oriens Corastam et Sin et partem terra Africe et **Baldac seu Ballac**.[β] (14) {Item} in parte eius sunt **paludes**,[γ] et ripe maris, ac omnis ripa fluvis; necnon et arbores mediocre altitudinis.[5] (15) De litteris {vero} littera _daleth_ et littera _pe_. (16) Et anni[6] eius .25. sunt, et tot menses, dies .5., et hore totidem.

5va (17) Ascendit {autem} in prima eius facie medietas ursi magni | posterioris, et una ymago integra que se in pannis involvit, et est propinqua ymagini **cantanti seu organizanti**;[β] {item} ascendit ibi porcus ferreus, cuius caput ereum, et puella quedam[7] virgo. (18) Item dicunt INDORUM SAPIENTES quod ibi ascendit iuvenis quidam formosus, pannis vestitus, **et cum ipso ornamenta aurea vel argentea**,[α] in cuius facie ac digitis contractio aliquantula, et corpus eius corpori equi et elephantis assimilatur, pedes eius albi, et super corpus eius suspense sunt quidam deliciositates in similitudine arborum, et ipse sedet in pomerio ubi **rami** crescunt **pigmentorum**.[α] (19) **Secundum**[γ] PTOLOMEUM {vero} ibi ascendit **ymago**[γ] Ursi Maioris, et caput Geminorum prioris scilicet et posterioris; {item} **cauda**[α] Gemini prioris cum manibus eius, item Canis Minor, et reliquum Maioris Canis quod remanserat ascendunt adhuc et venter Navis.

(20) In facie {autem} secunda ascendit **iuvencula**[γ] que nubi similis est; item ascendit ibi medietas canis, et medietas auricularum asini sinister. (21) Et dicunt INDI[γ] quod ibi ascendit **iuvencula seu puella**[β] sermone pulchra, in

---

[1]in parte] WVG; L om.   [2]pisciculi] LV; WG pisces.   [3]et] LV; WG item.   [4]dulces] WVG; L om.   [5]arbores mediocre altitudinis] WVG; L arboris mediocre altitudine.   [6]Et anni] W anni quoque.   [7]quedam] LG; WV om.

portion and is northern[γ,5] heats and burns; {but} **what is**[γ,6] ⟨in its portion and is⟩ southern is moist. (7) It has the form of aquatic animals. (8) The heart of the northern **angle**[α,7] is in its portion, and the north wind. (9) Its nature is cold and moist; it indicates the phlegm in human beings, and any mixture of cold and moist that appears **equal to a slight extent or somewhat balanced.**[β,8] (10) Its taste is sour and salty; the **appearance of the color**[αθ,9] white and the color **of ashes or dust,**[β,10] which resembles a smoky color and what is like it. (11) Of living creatures, all aquatic animals are in its portion, and reptiles and small fish; of terrestrial animals, scorpions with reptiles. (12) As a rule it indicates swiftly flowing water, all plants that are close to water, rainwater, and all fresh water. (13) Of the **climates,**[α] it has the seventh, the land of **Armenia**[α,11] and what is beyond Mūqān, Azerbaijan, Eastern Khurāsān, and China, and parts of Africa, and **Balkh or Ballac.**[β,12] (14) {Likewise} **swamps**[γ,13] are in its portion, and sea shores and every river bank; and trees of medium height. (15) {Moreover} of the letters, the letters *dalet* and *peh*. (16) Its years are 25, and so are its months; the days are five and so are the hours.

(17) {But} in its first face [decan], half of the rear part of the Greater Bear rises, and a complete image which wraps itself in clothes and is close to the image that is **singing or playing music;**[β,14] {likewise,} an iron pig rises there, whose head is of brass, and a girl who is a virgin. (18) Likewise, the INDIAN SCHOLARS say that certain handsome young man rises there; he wears clothes and **with him ornaments of gold or silver;**[α,15] in his face and fingers a slight cramp, his body resembles the body of a horse and elephant, his legs are white, and certain delicacies hang on his body, as if from trees; he sits in an orchard where **branches of aromatic plants**[α,16] grow. (19) {But} **according to**[γ] PTOLEMY, **the image**[γ,17] of the Greater Bear [Ursa Major] rises in it [Cancer's first decan], along with the head of the first and second twins; {likewise,} **the tail**[α,18] of the first twin and his hands, the Lesser Dog [Canis Minor], the rest of the Greater Dog [Canis Major], and the hull of the Ship [Argo Navis].

(20) {But} in its second face, **a young girl**[γ,19] resembling a cloud rises; likewise, half of the dog and half of the left donkey's ears rise there. (21) The INDIANS[γ,20] say that a **young girl or maiden**[β,21] with beautiful speech

cuius capite corona de **mirto**ᵞᵟ et in manu eius baculus ligneus et querit vinum et cantus. (22) **Secundum**ᵞ PTOLOMEUM ascendit caput Ursi Maioris et latus Cancri et venter Navis.

(23) In tertia {vero} facie ascendit puella quedam virgo, que aliquando versus oriens vadit aliquando versus occidens; item ascendit ibi **Geminorum posterior**ᵅ et secunda medietas auricularum asini sinister, adhuc et secundus asinus meridionalis. (24) Et dicunt INDIᵞ quod ascendit ibi homo, cuius pedes bestie pedibus similes sunt; et super corpus eius bestia, et desiderium eius est intrare navem et ire per mare ad apportandum aurum et argentum ut ex eis fiant **annuli seu ornamenta vel redimicula**ᵝ **ad opus mulierum.**ᵞ (25) **Secundum**ᵞ PTOLOMEUS {vero} ascendit ibi collum Ursi Maioris cum manu dextera et cornua Cancri; {item} caput Fortis[1] Bellicosi, *id est Ydre*, adhuc et navis pars extrema.

(26) Ac {vero} qui natus fuerit de hominibus in hoc signo, erunt membra eius grossa, et frons magna, dentes eius separati, et est mutus et surdus, **diligens creaturas vel diligens esse cum hominibus**;ᵝ et ipse honoratus; et nativitas femellarum non est bona **super res duras.**ᵅ (27) Qui {autem} natus fuerit in prima facie placens erit in corpore et in capillis, supercilia[2] oculorum eius[3] coniuncta, nasus longus, et ampli humeri; signum habebit sub[4] cubito vel sub brachio dextro; **animus eius seu intellectus**ᵝ bonus; amici eius plures; et ipse **prudens vel ingeniosus.**ᵝ,[5] (28) Et qui in secunda 5vb facie natus rubeus erit, et stature brevis, | ac **imberbis;**ᵅ,[6] signum habebit nigrum[7] in oculis, et ipse dilectus ab **hominibus seu creaturis.**ᵝ (29) Qui {vero} natus fuerit in tertia facie pinguis erit, ac brevis stature, pilosus satis in superciliis, venter eius amplus et grandis, et ipse robustus erit; sed interdum dolorem patietur circa cor, et multum fatigatus erit sui ipsius. (30) Qui {autem} natus fuerit in fine huius signi eufortunium non habebit.

(31) De partibus quidem humani corporis, eius est pectus cum mamillis, et venter superior cum costis, et splene ac pulmone. (32) Et in parte sua ex egritudinibus, omnis egritudo que in hiis membris accidit;[8] item **impedimenta**ᵞ habet oculorum; gradus .**xxii.**ᵖ stelle nebulose egritudines

---

[1] cum manu dextera et cornua Cancri, item caput Fortis] WVG; L om.   [2] supercilia] WVG; L superciliis.   [3] eius] LV; WG om.   [4] sub] W super.   [5] ingeniosus] WVG; L religiosus.   [6] imberbis] W; LV inbarbis.   [7] nigrum] LVG; W magnum.   [8] accidit] LVG; W accidet.

rises there, with a crown of **myrtle**[γ,δ,22] on her head and a wooden stick in her hand, and she seeks wine and music. (22) **According to**[γ] PTOLEMY, the head of the Greater Bear [Ursa Major] rises in it [in Cancer's second decan], ⟨along with⟩ the side of ⟨the constellation⟩ Cancer, and the hull of the Ship [Argo Navis].

(23) {Moreover} in the third face, certain girl who is a virgin rises, who sometimes goes to the east and sometimes to the west; likewise, **the second twin**[α,23] rises there, and the second half of the left donkey's ears, and also the second southern donkey. (24) The **INDIANS**[γ] say that a man whose legs resembles an animal's leg rises there; an animal is on his body; he intends to board a ship and go to sea to bring gold and silver, and make them into **rings, ornaments and necklaces**[β,24] **for women.**[γ,25] (25) {But} **according**[γ] to PTOLEMY, the neck of the Greater Bear [Ursa Major] rises there, and its right paw, the horns of ⟨the constellation⟩ Cancer; {likewise} the head of the Fighting Warrior, *that is, Hydra*,[26] and the stern of the Ship [Argo Navis].

(26) {Moreover} a human being born in it [who has Cancer as the ascendant of his nativity], the parts of his body will be thick, his forehead big; he will be gap-toothed, dumb and deaf, **loving creatures or loving to be with human beings;**[β,27] he is respected; the nativity of women is not good **concerning harsh matters.**[α,28] (27) {But} one who is born in the first face [decan] ⟨of Cancer⟩ [a person who has the first decan of Cancer as the ascendant of his nativity] will have a pleasing body and hair, his eyebrows will be joined, his nose long, and his shoulders broad; he will have a mole in his armpit or on his right arm; his **mind or intellect**[β,29] ⟨will be⟩ good; his friends ⟨will be⟩ numerous; he ⟨will be⟩ **prudent or clever.**[β,30] (28) One who is born in the second face will be ruddy, of short stature, and **beardless;**[α,31] he will have a black mole on his eyes, and he will be beloved by **human beings or creatures.**[β,32] (29) {Moreover} one who is born in the third face will be fat, of short stature, with shaggy eyebrows; his belly will be broad and big; he will be powerful; but sometimes he will suffer pains in his chest, and will exhaust himself very much. (30) {But} one who is born in the end of the sign will not have good fortune.

(31) Of the parts of the human body, in its portion are the chest and the breasts, the upper abdomen with the ribs, the spleen, and the lungs. (32) Of diseases, in its portion is any disease that affects the aforementioned parts of the body; likewise **defects in the eyes;**[γ,33] the **22nd**[π,34] degree

significat oculorum et **impedimenta**ᵞ illic evenientia; et universaliter, hoc signum significat[1] super scabiem impetiginem serpiginem et lepram ac **maculas faciei seu letigines**;ᵝ {item} super calvitium ac barbe parvitatem. (33) Ex hominibus {autem}, in parte eius sunt homines despecti, **et rurales vel rustici**,ᵝ ⟨⟨...⟩⟩,ᵘ et peregrinantes. (34) Et **secundum** HERMETIS **sapientiam**,ᵞ hoc signum est **signum seculi sive mundi**.ᵝ (35) Secundum EGYPTIOSᵞ {autem}, **egritudo**ᵅ Saturni *in hoc signum* circa lumbos est, Iovis in pudentis, Martis in superiori ventre, Solis in pedibus, Veneris in manibus, Mercurii in collo, et Lune in capite. (36) Est quidem domus Lune, **honor** Iovis **seu exaltatio**ᵝ in .15. gradu, **casus** Martis **seu dedecus**ᵝ in .28. gradu, Saturni domus odii, Caput Draconis Iovis in .9. gradu, et Caput Draconis Saturni in .19. (37) Triplicitatis {autem} domini domini in die Venus et deinde Mars, in nocte Mars primus et postea Venus, particeps eorum in die et nocte Luna. (38) Facies quidem prima, **secundum**ᵞ EGYPTIOS et BABYLONIOS, Veneris est, secunda Mercurii, et tertia Lune; **secundum** INDOS,ᵞ prima Lune est, secunda Martis, et tertia Iovis. (39) **Termini**ᵅ {autem} **secundum** EGYPTIOSᵞ et SAPIENTES ASTRORUMᵞ sunt hii: Martis .7., Veneris .6., Mercurii .6., Iovis .7., et Saturni .4.; **secundum** PTOLOMEUM:[2] **Martis .3., Iovis .7., Mercurii .7., Saturni .6., Veneris .7.**ᵖ,[3] (40) Et novenaria quidem prima Lune est, secunda Solis, tertia Mercurii, quarta Veneris, quinta Martis, sexta Iovis, septima et octava Saturni, et nona Iovis. (41) Duodenariarum virtus prima[4] Lune, secunda Solis, tertia Mercurii, quarta Veneris, quinta Martis, sexta Iovis, septima et octava Saturni, nona Iovis, decima Martis, .11a. Veneris, .12a. Mercurii.

(42) A principio {quoque} signi usque ad finem .7. gradus sunt mixti, deinde .5. lucidi, et post .2. mixti, deinde .4. lucidi, postea .2. **obscuri vel tenebrosi**,ᵝ **postmodum .4. lucidi, et demum .2. tenebrosi**.ᵖ (43) {Item} a principio signi usque in finem .2.[5] gradus masculini, **deinde .6. feminini, post ea .2. masculini**,ᵅ deinde duo feminini, postea .11. masculini, denique .4. feminini, et ultimo .3. masculini. (44) Putei {vero} stellarum sunt in .12. gradu, et .17.,

---

[1]significat] W; LVG habet significationem.　[2]secundum Ptolomeum] LG; W secundum vero opinionem Ptolomei.　[3]Martis .3., Iovis .7., Mercurii .7., Saturni .6., Veneris .7.] LW; G Martis .6., Iovis .7., Mercurii .7., Saturni .3., Veneris .7.　[4]prima] WG; L primus.　[5].2.] W .7.

⟨at longitude Cancer⟩ of a nebulous star indicates diseases of the eyes and defects^γ,35 occurring there; as a rule, this sign indicates roughness of the skin, eczema, measles, leprosy, and **marks or spots on the face;**^β,36 {likewise} baldness and a thin beard. (33) {But} of human beings, in its portion are contemptible persons, **peasants or rustics,**^β37 ⟨⟨**sailors,**⟩⟩^μ,38 and travelers. (34) **According to the wisdom of HERMES,**^γ,39 this sign is the **sign of the age or of the world.**^β,40 (35) {But} according to the **EGYPTIANS,**^γ,41 the **disease**^α,42 of Saturn *in this sign* is in the hips; of Jupiter, in the pudenda; of Mars, in the upper abdomen; of the Sun, in the legs; of Venus, in the hands; of Mercury the neck; and of the Moon, in the head. (36) It is the house of the Moon; the **honor or exaltation**^β of Jupiter is at ⟨Cancer⟩ 15°, the **fall or shame**^β,43 [the dejection, the opposite of the exaltation] of Mars is at ⟨Cancer⟩ 28°, the house of hate [detriment] of Saturn, Jupiter's Head of the Dragon is at ⟨Cancer⟩ 9°, and Saturn's Head of the Dragon is at ⟨Cancer⟩ 19°. (37) {But} the lords of the triplicity are Venus and then Mars by day, and Mars and then Venus by night; the Moon is their partner by day and by night. (38) The first face [decan], **according to**^γ the EGYPTIANS and BABYLONIANS, ⟨is assigned⟩ to Venus, the second to Mercury, and the third to the Moon; **according to the INDIANS,**^γ,44 the first ⟨face is assigned⟩ to the Moon, the second to Mars, and the third to Jupiter. (39) {But} these are the **terms**^α,45 **according to the EGYPTIANS**^γ,46 and the **SCHOLARS OF THE STARS:**^γ Mars 7°, Venus 6°, Mercury 6°, Jupiter 7°, and Saturn 4°; **according to PTOLEMY: Mars 3°, Jupiter 7°, Mercury 7°, Saturn 6°, Venus 7°.**^π,47 (40) The first *novenaria* [ninth-part] ⟨is assigned⟩ to the Moon, the second to the Sun, the third to Mercury, the fourth to Venus, the fifth to Mars, the sixth to Jupiter, the seventh and eighth to Saturn, and the ninth to Jupiter. (41) The first power of the *duodenariae* [twelfths] ⟨is assigned⟩ to the Moon, the second to the Sun, the third to Mercury, the fourth to Venus, the fifth to Mars, the sixth to Jupiter, the seventh and eighth to Saturn, the ninth to Jupiter, the tenth to Mars, the eleventh to Venus, and the twelfth to Mercury.

(42) {Also,} from the beginning of the sign to the end of seven degrees ⟨the degrees are⟩ mixed, then ⟨come⟩ five bright ⟨degrees⟩, then two mixed ⟨degrees⟩, then four bright ⟨degrees⟩, then two **dark or tenebrous,**^β,48 **then four bright ⟨degrees⟩, and finally two dark ⟨degrees⟩.**^π,49 (43) {Likewise,} from the beginning of the sign to the end of two degrees, ⟨the degrees are⟩ masculine, **then ⟨come⟩ .6. feminine, next .2. masculine,**^α,50 then two feminine ⟨degrees⟩, then eleven masculine ⟨degrees⟩, then four feminine ⟨degrees⟩, and finally three masculine ⟨degrees⟩. (44) {Moreover} the pits of

168 PART ONE

et in .23., en in .26., et in .30. (45) Gradus {quoque} **fortunam**ᵞ augmentantes et honorem sunt primus, secundus et tertius, et .14. et .15.

6ra (46) De stellis ⟨⟨...⟩⟩ᵛ {autem} sunt ibi Canis scilicet | vocatus *Alsaheri Alahabor*, et est in hoc tempore in tertio gradu, latitudo eius meridionalis .39. gradus et .10 minuta, honoris primi est, et de complexione Iovis et Martis. (47) Item est ibi caput prioris Geminorum in .8. gradu ⟨⟨...⟩⟩ᵛ, latitudo eius septentrionalis .9. gradus et .40. minuta; est {autem} honoris secundi, de complexione quidem Iovis et Mercurii. (48) {Item} est ibi caput posterioris Geminorum, in .12. gradu ⟨⟨...⟩⟩,ᵛ latitudo eius septentrionalis .6. gradus .15. minuta, et est honoris secundi, **de natura Martis per se.**ᵅ (49) ⟨⟨...⟩⟩.ᵘ (50) Adhuc est ibi Canis vocatus *Alfaheri Alnemissia*, in .15. gradu ⟨⟨...⟩⟩,ᵛ latitudo eius meridionalis .16. gradus .10 minuta, et est honoris primi, de complexione Martis et Mercurii. (51) {Item} sunt ibi ⟨⟨...⟩⟩ᵘ stelle .4., que **valde propinqua**ᵅ sunt Urso Maiori: una est .12. gradus ⟨⟨...⟩⟩ᵛ et latitudo eius septentrionalis .22. gradus .50. minuta; secunda in .16. ⟨⟨...⟩⟩,ᵛ et latitudo eius septentrionalis **.22. gradus .2. minuta;**ᵅ tertia in .27. gradu ⟨⟨...⟩⟩,ᵛ et latitudo eius septentrionalis .22. gradus et .45. minuta; et quarta est in fine signi, et latitudo eius septentrionalis .20. gradus. (52) **Demum** adhuc est ibi una stella super ventrem eius, in .26. gradu, et latitudo eius septentrionalis .26. minuta.

5 (1) Leo, de signis est igneis, masculinus, **diurnus,**ᵞ,¹ orientale. (2) De signis estatis, fixum in ipso enim tempus figitur in eadem dispositione. (3) Hore eius longiores **equalibus,**ᵞ in **ascensionibus**ᵅ rectus, et ascensiones eius longe sunt. (4) Natura eius calida adurens et dissipans; principium eius calidus est aliquantulum; medium **corruptivum satis et dissipativum,**ᵝ egritudines faciens generari, et finis eius ventos generare facit. (5) **Quod**ᵞ eius est septentrionale, calidum et² adustivum, meridionale, {vero} humidum est. (6) Est {autem} in figura quadrupedum ungulas habentes, gambosum, *scilicet de gressibilibus*, membra eius secta sunt, dimidiam habet vocem. (7) Et in parte eius est **septentrionalis**ᵞ pars orientis, ac ventus orientalis. (8) Natura eius calida est et sicca; et **de humoribus eius**ᵅ est cholera rubens; de saporibus, amarus et acutus; et de coloribus croceus et **rubicundus.**ᵅ (9) De bestiis, eius sunt leones, leopardi, ⟨⟨...⟩⟩,ᵘ ursi et lupi. (10) Et de metallis, aurum et argentum, et lapides preciosi, ac lapis alios perforans lapides ⟨⟨...⟩⟩ᵛ qui vocatur **adamas,**ᵞᵟ et lapis attrahens paleas et allbuadi, et

---

¹diurnus] WV; L diuturnus; G om.   ²et] corrected; LWGV est.

the stars are at 12°, 17°, 23°, 26°, and 30°. (45) {Besides,} the degrees adding **fortune**^γ and honor: the 1st, 2nd, 3rd, 14th, and 15th degrees.

(46) {But} there [in the degrees of Cancer], of the ⟨⟨upper⟩⟩^v,51 stars, ⟨we find⟩ the Dog called *al-shi'rā al-'abūr*, ⟨at longitude Cancer⟩ 3° at the present time, its latitude is southern 39° 10', of the first honor [magnitude], of the mixture of Jupiter and Mars. (47) Likewise, the head of the first of the twins is there, too, at ⟨longitude Cancer⟩ 8° ⟨⟨at this time⟩⟩,^v,52 its latitude is northern 9° 40'; {but} of the second honor, of the mixture of Jupiter and Mercury. (48) {Likewise,} the head of the second Twin is there, too, at ⟨longitude Cancer⟩ 12° ⟨⟨at the present time⟩⟩,^v its latitude is northern 6° 15', of the second honor, **of the nature of Mars only**.^α,53 (49) ⟨⟨The end of head of the ⟨second⟩ Twin is there, too, with the nature of Mars only⟩⟩.^μ,54 (50) The Dog called *al-shi'rā al-ghumaysā'* is there, too, at ⟨longitude Cancer⟩ 15° ⟨⟨at the present time⟩⟩,^v its latitude is southern 16° 10', of the first honor, of the mixture of Mars and Mercury. (51) {Likewise,} four ⟨⟨dark⟩⟩^μ,55 stars are there, too, which are **very close**^α,56 to the Greater Bear [Ursa Major]: one is at ⟨longitude Cancer⟩ 12° ⟨⟨at the present time⟩⟩,^v its latitude is northern 22° 50'; the second at ⟨longitude Cancer⟩ 16° ⟨⟨at the present time⟩⟩,^v its latitude is northern **22° 2'**;^α,57 the third, ⟨at longitude Cancer⟩ 27° ⟨⟨at the present time⟩⟩,^v its latitude is northern 22° 45'; the fourth at the end of the sign [Cancer], its latitude northern 20°. (52) Finally a star is there, too, on its [Cancer's] belly, at ⟨longitude Cancer⟩ 26°, and its latitude northern **26'**.^γ,58

5 (1) Leo is of the fiery signs, masculine, **diurnal**,^γ,1 eastern. (2) It is of the signs of summer, fixed in itself because the season is fixed in the same condition. (3) Its hours are longer than the **equal**^γ ⟨hours⟩, it is straight in the ascensions, and its **ascensions**^α are long. (4) Its nature is burning hot and destructive; its beginning is somewhat hot, ⟨its⟩ middle is **very corrupting and destructive**;^β,2 it produces diseases, and its end produces winds. (5) **What is**^γ,3 in its portion and is northern is burning hot, {but} ⟨what is in its portion and is⟩ southern is moist. (6) {But} in ⟨its⟩ form it is four-footed with hooves, trampling under foot, *namely, of those able to walk*, its limbs are cut off, and it has half a voice. (7) The **northern**^γ ⟨side⟩ of the east is in its portion, and the east wind. (8) Its nature is hot and dry; **of the humors**,^α,4 the red bile is in its portion; of the tastes, the bitter and pungent, of the colors, saffron and **red**.^α,5 (9) Of the animals, lions are in its portion, ⟨and⟩ leopards, ⟨⟨hyenas⟩⟩^μ,6 bears, and wolves. (10) Of the metals, gold and silver; precious stones, the stone that pierces *other* ⟨⟨precious⟩⟩^v,7 stones called **adamas**,^γ,δ,8 the stone that attracts straw ⟨called⟩ *al-bazāri*, and any craft

omne opus igneum. (11) **De regionibus**,^{α} in parte eius sunt **clima**^{α} quartum, et Bagnezaze, *et terra circa Baldac*, et terra Persidis, et terra Turcorum usque ad finem **habitabilis**,^{α} et Niscebut et Tiressus. (12) Et omnis locus difficilis ad ascendendum, ac omnis terra frangens, et **domus seu palatia**^{β,1} regum, et munitiones fortes, ac omnis mons altus, ac locus omnis **expositus aeri et cuius aer apertus est**.^{β} (13) Et de litteris eius sunt littere <u>he</u> et littera <u>caf</u>.

6rb (14) Anni {vero} eius | .19., et menses totidem, dies .47. cum demidio, et hore eius .23.

(15) Ascendit {autem} in prima eius facie ⟨⟨...⟩⟩^{μ} canis super cuius dorsum arcus, et dimidia navis ibique sunt **remiges**;^{α} {item} caput bestie nigre et caput equi acque caput asini. (16) Et dicunt INDI^γ quod ibi ascendit arbor magna, super cuius ramos canis et avis vocata ***raihena***,^{αε} et homo **vestes indutus desideratas**^{α} sed **maculate sunt sive sordite**;^{β2} et desiderium suum est percutere patrem suum; item ascendit ibi dominus equi qui versus sinistram respicit. (17) Iuxta^γ PTOLOMEUM {vero} ascendit collum Ursi Maioris et manus eius sinister, et **caput**^{α} Leonis, acque collum **Fortis**,^{α} *id est, Ydre*, necnon et medietas Navis.

(18) In secunda facie ascendit ymago, cuius manus in altum elevate, clamans voce magna, et organizat et psaltat; item ascendit ⟨⟨...⟩⟩^{ν} vasa vini, et ciphus vitreus cum instrumentis cantus de cervi cornibus; {item} medietas secunda navis, et oculus bestie, ac medium equi cum medio asini. (19) Et dicunt INDI^γ quod ascendit ibi homo, cuius **nares subtiles sive nasus subtilis**,^{β} super cuius caput sicut similitudo corone de mirto albo, et in manu eius arcus, et ipse iracundus *nam autem eius* similis leoni, **et ipse coopertus est coopertorio**^{π} in apparentia tamquam de colore leonis. (20) Iuxta^γ PTOLOMEUM ascendit ibi humerus Ursi Maioris et pes eius dexter, et collus Leonis, ac medium **Fortis**^{α} *id est, Ydre*, et caput Navis.

(21) In tertia {autem} facie ascendit ymago viri, cuius officium est bestias ducere, in manu sua ⟨⟨...⟩⟩^{μ} et ipse trahit currum in quo sedet homo. et parvus puer[3] cum ipso,[4] in cuius manu sinistra pannus; item ascendit ibi corvus, et medietas bestie nigre, et finis equi, ac {etiam} finis asini. (22) Et dicunt INDI^γ quod ascendit ibi **Maurus seu Etyops niger**^{β} turpis et laborio-

---

[1]palatia] WVG; L palea. [2]sordite] WG; LV sorditate. [3]puer] WVG; L om. [4]ipso] WVG; L ipsa.

LIBER ABRAHE AVENERRE INTRODUCTORIUS AD ASTRONOMIAM 171

based on fire. (11) **Of the regions,**[α,9] the fourth **climate**[α] is in its portion, Baghdad, *and the land around Baghdad*, the land of Persia, the land of the Turks to the end of **the habitable**[α,10] ⟨part of the Earth⟩ [the ecumene], and Nisbor [Nishapur] and Tarsus. (12) And every place that is difficult to climb ⟨is in its portion⟩, and any land that is broken, the **houses or palaces**[β,11] of kings, strong fortresses, every high mountain, and every place **exposed to the air and whose air is open.**[β,12] (13) Of the letters, <u>heh</u> and <u>kaf</u> are in its portion. (14) {Moreover} its years are 19, as are its months, the days are 47½ and the hours 23.

(15) {But} in its first face [decan] there rises ⟨⟨a bear⟩⟩,[μ,13] a dog with a bow on its back, half of a ship and ⟨its⟩ **oarsmen**[α,14] are there; {likewise} the head of a black beast and the head of a horse and the head of a donkey. (16) The **INDIANS**[γ] say that a large tree rises there, with a dog and the bird called <u>*raihena*</u>[αε,15] [the bustard] on its branches, a man wearing **desirable clothes,**[α,16] but they are **marked with spots and unclean;**[β,17] his desire is to strike his fat; likewise, the owner of the horse that looks towards the left rises there. (17) {But}**according to**[γ] PTOLEMY, the neck of the Greater Bear [Ursa Major] rises there, and its left paw, **the head**[α,18] of ⟨the constellation⟩ Leo, the neck of the **Mighty One,**[α,19] *that is, Hydra,*[20] and half of the Ship [Argo Navis].

(18) In its second face, an image rises, its hands raised, calling out in a loud voice, playing an instrument and singing; likewise, ⟨⟨two⟩⟩[ν,21] wine vessels rise there, and a glass cup, a musical instrument made of the horns of deer; {likewise} the second half of the ship, the eye of the beast, the middle of the horse, and the middle of the donkey. (19) The **INDIANS**[γ] say that a man rises there, **his nostrils are thin or his nose is thin,**[β,22] with something like a crown made of white myrtle on his head, and a bow in his hand; he is irascible *because in this* he resembles a lion, **and he covers himself in a covering**[π,23] of leonine appearance and color. (20) **According to**[γ] PTOLEMY, the shoulder of the Greater Bear [Ursa Major] rises there, and its right leg, the neck of ⟨the constellation⟩ Leo, the middle of the **Mighty One,**[α,24] *that is, Hydra,*[25] and the prow of the Ship [Argo Navis].

(21) {But} in the third face, the figure of a young man rises; his occupation is driving animals, in his hand ⟨⟨a whip⟩⟩,[μ,26] and he draws a cart in which a man sits along with a little boy; in his left hand a garment; {likewise} a crow rises there, and the middle of the black beast, the end of the horse, and {also} the end of the donkey. (22) The **INDIANS**[γ] say that an ugly and hard-

sis, et ipse **prudens**;ᵞ in ore ipsius deliciositas et carnes in manibus suis. (23) **Secundum**ᵞ PTOLOMEUM ascendit ibi ymago Ursi Maioris, et medium Leonis, ac una pars **Fortis Bellicosi**,ᵅ *id est Ydre*.

(24) Ac {vero} qui natus fuerit in eo ex hominibus, erit corpus eius pulchrum et **rubicundum**,ᵅ et oculi eius sicut oculi cati, et ipse fortis et iracundus, visus eius **acutus, incisivus seu penetrativus**,ᵝ tybie **minute seu graciles**;ᵝ et ipse {vero} **disciplinatus seu prudens**,ᵅᵝ ingeniosus, ac diligens coitui, **acceptabilis seu placidus**,ᵝ ⟨⟨...⟩⟩,ᵘ in sermone stabilis, **in lamentis magnus seu lamentativus**,ᵝ se ipsum ducens in pericula, **discolus seu pertinax**,ᵝ et natura eius sicut natura **canis feri**,ᵞᵟ comestor magnus,¹ et appetens

6va totum comedere; | in nativitate femellarum significat **simplicitatem sive religiositatem**.ᵝ (25) Qui {autem} in prima facie natus fuerit pulcher erit corpore et facie, **color aspectus eius**ᵅᶿ rubicundus, oculi eius mixti, et pectus rectum et similiter tybie eius, **egritudinem**ᵅ habebit **in stomacho**,ᵞ notus erit inter homines, simplex, et **principibus**ᵞ se immiscens. (26) Et natus in secunda facie pulcher erit corpore, pectus eius **latum seu amplum**,ᵝ genitalia eius **minuta**ᵅ similiter et tybie, et ipse calvus, dolorem patietur in **dyafragmate**,ᵅ honoratus erit inter gentes, et ipse magnanimus. (27) Qui {vero} natus fuerit in facie tertia curtus erit aliquantulum in statura, **albas habens maculas et rubicundas**,ᵞ et vox eius fortis, mulierum amativus erit, et multos habebit amicos et inimicos similiter, ac egritudines multas. (28) Et qui in fine signi natus fuerit turpis erit, ac **plenus orbitationibus seu occasionibus defectivus**.ᵝ

(29) De partibus {autem} humani corporis, eius sunt pectus, et cor, **stomachus, et dyafragma, coste, spina dorsi**;ᵞ ⟨⟨...⟩⟩ᵘ ac fundus **stomachi**.ᵞ (30) De egritudines eius sunt ille que eveniunt in membris memoratis. (31) De hominibus, in parte eius sunt reges, **domini, principes**;ᵅ ac divitie operis auri et argenti et lapidum preciosorum ac omnis artificii preciosi.ᵅ (32) *Signum quidem hoc*² domus Solis est, et **odium seu domus dedecoris**³ **Saturni**,ᵝ et non est ibi **exaltationem**ᵞ aut **casus**ᵞ **planete**ᵅ alicuius, sed est in ipso **aux**ᵅ Martis in gradu .12. ad hoc tempus. (33) Domini {autem} triplicitatis in die quidem sunt primo Sol deinde Iupiter, **de nocte econtrario**,ᵞ particeps in die et nocte est Saturnus. (34) Facies prima **secundum**ᵞ

---

¹comestor magnus] G om.   ²hoc] WVG; L huius.   ³domus dedecoris] LGV; W dedecus domus.

LIBER ABRAHE AVENERRE INTRODUCTORIUS AD ASTRONOMIAM 173

working **Moor or black Ethiopian**[β,27] rises there; he is **prudent**;[γ,28] a delicacy is in his mouth and meat in his hand. (23) **According to**[γ] PTOLEMY, the image of the Greater Bear [Ursa Major] rises there, the middle of ⟨the constellation⟩ Leo, and a part of the **Fighting Mighty One**,[α,29]*that is, Hydra*.[30]

(24) {Moreover} one born in it [who has Leo as the ascendant of his nativity] of the human beings, his body will be beautiful and **red**,[α,31] his eyes like the eyes of a cat, he will be mighty and irascible, his vision **sharp, incisive and penetrating**,[β,32] his shanks **small and thin**;[β,33] {moreover} he will be **learned or prudent**,[αβ,34] ingenious, lustful, **acceptable and pleasant**,[β,35] ⟨⟨barren⟩⟩,[μ,36] true to his word, **great in weeping or given to weeping**,[β,37] putting himself in danger, **of bad temper and obstinate**,[β] his nature will be like the nature of **a wild dog**,[γδ,38] a glutton who loves every food; in the nativity of women it indicates **modesty and piety**.[β,39] (25) {But} one who is born in the first face [decan] ⟨of Leo⟩ will have a beautiful body and face, **the color of his appearance**[θ,40] is red, his eyes will be of mixed ⟨colors⟩, his chest will be straight and so too his shanks, he will have **a disease**[α,41] **in the stomach**,[γ,42] he will be famous among people, modest, and will mingle with **princes**.[γ,43] (26) One who is born in the second face will have a beautiful body, his chest **broad or wide**,[β,44] his genitals **small**[α,45] and also his shanks; he ⟨will be⟩ bald, suffer pain in the **diaphragm**;[α,46] he will be honored by his people and haughty. (27) {Moreover} one who is born in the third face will be somewhat short, **he has white and red spots**;[γ,47] his voice is strong, he loves women, he will have many friends and also many enemies, and many ailments. (28) One who is born in the end of the sign will be ugly, and **full of blemishes or weak on account of injuries**.[β,48]

(29) {But} of the parts of the human body, in its portion are the chest, the heart, **the stomach, the diaphragm, the ribs, the dorsal spine**;[γ,49] ⟨⟨it also indicates the color of the eyes⟩⟩[μ,50] and the bottom of **the stomach**.[γ,51] (30) Of the diseases, those affecting the aforementioned parts of the body are in its portion. (31) Of human beings, in its portion are kings, **lords, princes**;[α,52] **and riches from the craft of gold, silver, precious stones, and of any costly product of crafts**.[α,53] (32) *This sign* is the house of the Sun, and **the hate**[γ,54] [the detriment or opposite of the house] **or the house of shame of Saturn**[β,55] [Saturn's dejection, the opposite of its exaltation], no **planet**[α] has its **exaltation**[γ,56] or **fall**[γ,57] [dejection] there [in Leo]; but the **apogee**[α,58] of Mars is in it [Leo] at 12° at this time. (33) {But} the lords of the triplicity are the Sun and then Jupiter by day, **by night the contrary**,[γ,59] Saturn is their partner by day and by night. (34) **According to**[γ] the EGYPTIANS and

EGYPTIOS et BABYLONIOS Saturni est, secunda Iovis, tertia Martis; ⟨⟨...⟩⟩^μ. (35) **Termini**^α {autem} **secundum**^γ EGYPTIOS et **ASTRORUM SAPIENTES**^γ sunt Iovis quidem .6. gradus, Veneris .6., Mercurii .6., Saturni .7., et Martis .6.,[1] secundum opinionem PTOLOMEI, Saturni .6., Mercurii .7., Veneris .6. Martis .6., et Iovis .5. (36) Novenariarum {quidem autem,} prima Martis, secunda Veneris, tertia Mercurii, .4a. Lune, .5e. Solis, .6a. Mercurii, .7a. Veneris, .8a. Martis, .9a. Iovis. (37) Duodenariaum {vero} prima Solis, secunda Mercurii, tertia Veneris, .4a. Martis, quinta Iovis, .6a. et. .7a. Saturni, .8a. Iovis, nona Martis, .10a. Veneris, .11a. Mercurii, .12a. Lune.

(38) Et a principio quidem signi usque ad .7m. gradum sunt lucidi, postea .3. mixti, deinde .6. tenebrosi, et postea .5. vacui, demum .9. lucidi. (39) {Item,} a principio signi usque ad finem .5. gradus sunt masculini, deinde feminini .2., postmodum .6. masculini, deinde feminini .10., demum .7. masculini.

6vb (40) **Putealitas**[2] {vero} | **stellarum**^γ in .6. gradu est, et in .13o., in .15o., in .22o., in .23o., et in .28o. (41) Gradus **fortunam**^γ augmentantes et honorem sunt secundus, quintus, septimus et .17us.

(42) Et ibi, de *stellis fixis*,^γ Collum Bellicosi, *id est Ydre*, in gradu .16. ad hoc tempus, cuius latitudo meridionalis est .20. gradus cum dimidio, et est honoris secundi, de complexione Saturni et Veneris. (43) {Item} est ibi Cor Leonis in gradu .18. ad hoc tempus, cuius latitudo septentrionalis est .10. minutorum; est {autem} honoris primi, de complexione Martis et Iovis; et est de interficientibus. (44) {Item} est ibi stella vocata Dorsum Leonis, et est in fine signi ⟨⟨...⟩⟩,^ν latitudo eius septentrionalis est .13a. gradus .40. minuta, et est honoris secundi, de complexione Saturni et Veneris.

6 (1) Virgo est signum terreum, femininum, **nocturnum**,^γ meridionale. (2) De signis estatis, duorum corporum est. (3) Hore eius longiores **equalibus**,^γ et in finis eius equantur dies noctibus in omni **climate**,^α directum est in **ascensionibus**,^α et **ascensiones**^α sue longe sunt. (4) Natura eius est

---

[1] .6.] WVG; L quinque.   [2] Putealitas] WVG; G putei.

BABYLONIANS, the first face [decan] ⟨is assigned⟩ to Saturn, the second to Jupiter, and the third to Mars; ⟨⟨according to the Indian scholars, the first ⟨face is assigned⟩ to the Sun, the second to Jupiter, and the third to Mars⟩⟩^{μ,60} (35) {But} these are the **terms**^{α,61} **according to**^{γ} the EGYPTIANS and the **SCHOLARS OF THE STARS:**^{γ} Jupiter 6°, Venus 6°, Mercury 6°, Saturn 7°, and Mars 6°; and according to the opinion of PTOLEMY: Saturn 6°, Mercury 7°, Venus 6°, Mars 6°, and Jupiter 5°. (36) {But certainly} of the _novenariae_ [ninth-parts], **the first**^{γ} ⟨is assigned⟩ to Mars, the second to Venus, the third to Mercury, the fourth to the Moon, the fifth to the Sun, the sixth to Mercury, the seventh to Venus, the eighth to Mars, and the ninth to Jupiter. (37) {Moreover} of the _duodenariae_ [twelfths], the first ⟨is assigned⟩ to the Sun, the second to Mercury, the third to Venus, the fourth to Mars, the fifth to Jupiter, the sixth and the seventh to Saturn, the eighth to Jupiter, the ninth to Mars, the tenth to Venus, the eleventh to Mercury, and the twelfth to the Moon.

(38) From the beginning of the sign to the end of seven degrees, ⟨the degrees are⟩ bright, then ⟨come⟩ three mixed ⟨degrees⟩, then six dark ⟨degrees⟩, then five empty ⟨degrees⟩, and then nine bright ⟨degrees⟩. (39) {Likewise,} from the beginning of the sign to the end of five degrees, ⟨the degrees are⟩ masculine, then ⟨come⟩ two feminine ⟨degrees⟩, then six masculine ⟨degrees⟩, then ten feminine ⟨degrees⟩, and finally seven masculine ⟨degrees⟩. (40) {Moreover} **what pertains to the pits of the stars**^{γ,62} is at the 6th, 13th, 15th, 22nd, 23rd, and 28th degrees. (41) The degrees adding **fortune**^{γ} and honor are at the 2nd, 5th, 7th, and 17th degrees.

(42) There [in the degrees of Leo], of the _fixed stars_^{γ,63} ⟨we find⟩ the Neck of the Warrior, *that is, Hydra*,^{64} ⟨at longitude Leo⟩ 16° at the present time, its latitude is southern 20½°, of the second honor [second magnitude], of the mixture of Saturn and Venus. (43) {Likewise,} the Heart of the Lion is there at ⟨longitude Leo⟩ 18° at the present time, its latitude is northern 10'; {but} it is of the first honor, of the mixture of Mars and Jupiter; it is one of the lethal ⟨stars⟩. (44) {Likewise,} the star called the Back of the Lion is there at the end of the sign [Leo] ⟨⟨at the present time⟩⟩,^{ν} its latitude is northern 13° 40', of the second honor, of the mixture of Saturn and Venus.

6 (1) Virgo is an earthy sign, feminine, **nocturnal**,^{γ} southern. (2) One of the signs of summer, and of two bodies. (3) Its hours are longer than the **equal**^{γ} ⟨hours⟩, at its end days and nights are equal in every **climate;**^{α} it is direct in the **ascensions**^{α} and its **ascensions**^{α} are long. (4) Its nature indicates

significare super corruptionem propter excessum siccitatis sue, in principio tamen eius est humiditas et ipse est **mobile**,ᵞ et medium eius mixtum est, sed finis siccus. (5) **Et quod**ᵞ eius septentrionale est ventus generat, meridionale {vero} mixtum est. (6) Et est in figura hominis et volucris, vocem habet fortem. (7) Et de parte eius est dextra pars meridiei, ac ventus meridionalis. (8) Natura quidem eius frigida est et sicca, choleram nigram generans. (9) Sapores eius sunt ponticus et stipticus; colores {vero} albus et purpureus ac **pulvereus sive cinericius**.ᵝ (10) De animalibus, in parte sue sunt homines et volucres; de vegetabilibus, omne vegetabile parvus non habens **tubiam seu truncum ligneum**,ᵝ ut frumentum ordeum fabe et legumina, et omnes species seminum. (11) De **climatibus**,ᵅ habet secundum, et de regionibus in parte sua est Germech, et flumen Eufrates, et Baltesar et terra GRECORUM. (12) De **agris quidem seu locis**,ᵝ **terre culte sive seminate**ᵝ ac domus mulierum et viridaria. (13) De litteris _vaf_ et _zam_. (14) Anni eius sunt .20., et menses totidem, dies .7., et hore .4.

(15) Ascendit {autem} in prima facie eius virgo pulchra, cuius capillis prolixi, et in manu eius spice due; sedet super sedem, et nutrit infantem parvum, lactat eum et facit ipsum comedere; item ascendit ibi vir sedens super eandem sedem; et item ascendit ibi stella vocata Spica posterior bestie, et caput corvi cum capite leonis. (16) Et dicunt INDIᵞ quod ascendit ibi virgo se involvens in **sclavina vel sago**,ᵝ et vestes induit veteres,[1] in manu eius vas, et ipsa stat intra mirtos, volens ire ad domum patris sui. (17) **Iuxta**ᵞ PTO-
7ra LOMEUM[2] {vero} ascendit pars una Caude Draconis, et posterior pars Ursi | cum pedibus et cauda; {item} Ciphus qui est prope caput Bellicosi, et pars una Belligerantis ipsius.

(18) Et ascendit in secunda facie ymago palmas percutiens et cantans; item ascendit ibi vir dimidiam habens figuram, cuius caput est sicut caput tauri; in manu {vero} eius dimidius homo nudus; item ascendit ibi dimidia trabs, **in cuius capite seu extremitate crepatura seu fissura**,ᵝ³ et ipse cum illa terra arat; item[4] ascendit ibi cauda bestie nigre et leonis medium. (19) Et dicunt INDIᵞ quod ascendit ibi Etyops, totus pilosus super quem vestimenta tria, unum de corio, secundum de serito, et tertium de **sclavina rubea vel**[5] **sago rubeo**;ᵝ in manu eius **tabula**ᵅ,⁶ **ad computandum sive pro computo faciendo**.ᵝ (20) **Iuxta**ᵞ PTOLOMEUS ascendit ibi pars caude Draconis, et

---

[1]veteres] WVG; L vestes. [2]Iuxta Ptolomeum] G dicit Ptolomeus. [3]fissura] WV; L fixura; G om. [4]item] LW; GV om. [5]sclavina rubea vel] G om. [6]tabula] W tabella.

LIBER ABRAHE AVENERRE INTRODUCTORIUS AD ASTRONOMIAM 177

corruption because of its excess of dryness, yet in its beginning there is moistness and it is **changeable;**^γ,1 its middle is mixed, but the end is dry. (5) **What is**^γ in its portion and is northern produces winds, {but} ⟨what is in its portion and is⟩ southern is mixed. (6) It has the form of a human being and of a bird, and has a strong voice. (7) In its portion is the right ⟨side⟩ of the south, and the south wind. (8) Its nature is cold and dry, and it produces the black bile. (9) Its tastes are bitter and astringent; {moreover} ⟨its⟩ colors are white, purple, and ⟨the color⟩ similar to **dust and ashes**.^β (10) Of living creatures, human beings and birds are in its portion; of plants, every small plant without **a woody stem or trunk,**^β,2 such as wheat, barley, beans, and every type of grain. (11) Of the **climates,**^α the second is in its portion; of the regions, Jarāmaqa is in its portion, and the river Euphrates, Baltesar, and the land of the GREEKS. (12) **Of the arable lands or places,**^β,3 **cultivated or sown lands,**^β,4 gynaecea, and gardens. (13) Of the letters, _waw_ and _zayin_. (14) Its years are 20, and so are its months; its days are seven, and its hours four.

(15) {But} in its first face [decan] a beautiful virgin rises; she has long hair and two ears of grain in her hand; she sits on a chair, nourishing a little boy, and suckles and feeds him; likewise, a man sitting on the same chair rises there; likewise, the star called the Ear of Grain [Spica] that is in the rear part of the beast rises there, and the head of the crow and the head of the lion. (16) **The INDIANS**^γ say that a virgin wrapped in a _sclavina_ or _sagum_^β [two types of Latin cloaks] rises there; she wears old clothes and holds a jug in her hand; she stands among myrtle trees and wants to go to her father's house. (17) {But} **according to**^γ PTOLEMY, part of the Tail of the Dragon and the rear part of the Bear [Ursa Major] rise there with ⟨its⟩ legs and tail; {likewise} the Goblet [Crater] that is on the Warrior's [Hydra] head, and one part of the Warrior himself.

(18) In its second face, an image clapping its hands and playing music rises; likewise, a man who has half a shape rises there; his head is like the head of a bull; {moreover} in his hand there is half of a naked man; likewise, half of a plow beam, **in whose head or extremity there is a crack or fissure,**^β,5 with which he plows the earth, rises there; likewise the tail of the black beast and the middle of the lion rise there. (19) The **INDIANS**^γ say that an Ethiopian rises there; he is completely covered with hair and wears three garments, one of leather, the second of silk, the third of **red** _sclavina_ or red _sagum_^β [two types of Latin cloaks]; in his hand **a table**^α,6 [an abacus] **to calculate or to perform calculations.**^β,7 (20) **According to**^γ PTOLEMY, part of the Dragon's [Draco] tail rises there, and the **tail**^α of the Greater Bear

cauda^α Ursi Maioris, et caput Virginis cum humeris, acque caput corvi cum rostro et alis suis.

(21) In tertia {vero} facie ascendit medietas reliqua **figure sue ymaginis**^{β} dimidie¹, ac secunda medietas viri nudi, necnon et secunda trabis medietas,² et cauda leonis, ac duo boves, cum medietate hominis pastoris. (22) Et dicunt **INDI**^{γ} quod ascendit ibi mulier alba que se iactat in seipsam, indutam habens **sclavinam tinctam seu cilicium tinctum**,^{β} et manus eius leprose sunt, et ipsa orat Deum. (23) Et **secundum**^{γ} Ptolomeum ascendit ibi pars caude Draconis, et extremitas caude Ursi Maioris, ac humerus Symie meridionalis cum parte ventris sui, et venter Corvi et pes Bestie.

(24) Natus {autem} *in hoc signo* de **filiis hominum**,^{αθ} **stature convenientis** erit **et placide**,^{β} corpus eius rectum et pulchrum, et **sapiens et prudens**,^{γ} capilli eius non crispi, et erit amans iustitiam, vox sua fortis, et ipse **sterilis non generans**,^{β} animus eius bonus, et facies pulchra, et erit scriba et **sapiens in numeris**.^{α} (25) Qui {autem} natus fuerit in facie secunda, pulcher erit aspectu, sed oculi eius parvi, **nares eius pulchri sive nasus pulcher**,^{β} et ipse **homo disciplinatus**,^{α} et simplex, ac liberalis cordi, laudari desiderans. (26) Qui natus fuerit in tertia facie pulcher erit aspectu et **homo disciplinatus seu prudens, intentione sive sensu verax**,^{β} simplex ac sapiens.

(27) In parte {autem} eius de partibus³ humani corporis est venter cum intestinis et dyafragmate. (28) {Similiter} egritudines eius sunt in dictis membris, ac omnis egritudo cuius radix est melancolia. (29) De hominibus {quoque} in parte eius sunt homines⁴ mediocres, scribe, et sapientes, arismetrici cum geometricis, mulieres, et eunuchi, ac **hystriones**.^{γ} (30) Et {autem} {hoc signum} domus Mercurii, ac etiam **exaltatio sive honor**^{β} eius in .15. gradu; **casus**^{γ} {vero} **Veneris in .27. gradu**,^{π} et domus odii Iovis, atque **aux eiusque**^{γ} ibi est in .23. gradu ⟨⟨...⟩⟩.^{μ} (31) Triplicitatis quidem domini Venus in die | et post ipsam Luna, et de nocte **econtrario**,^{γ} particeps {vero} in die et nocte Mars est. (32) Facies {autem} prima, **secundum**^{γ} EGYP-

---

¹dimidie] W dimidia. ²ac secunda medietas viri nudi necnon et secunda trabis medietas] WVG; L om. ³de partibus] VG; L in parte; W de parte. ⁴homines] WVG; L om.

[Ursa Major], the head and shoulder of ⟨the constellation⟩ Virgo, and the head, beak, and wings of the Crow [Corvus].

(21) {Moreover} in the third face, the remaining half of **the form or image**[β,8] ⟨of a man⟩ rises, and the second half of the naked man, as well as the second half of the plow beam, and the tail of the lion, and two bulls with half of the shepherd. (22) The **INDIANS**[γ] say that a white woman praising herself rises there; she wears a **dyed *sclavina* or dyed *cilicium***[β] [two types of Latin cloaks], her hands are leprous, and she is praying to God. (23) **According to**[γ] PTOLEMY, part of the Dragon's [Draco] tail rises there, and the end of the Greater Bear's [Ursa Major] tail, the shoulder of the southern Monkey [? Virgo] with part of its belly, the belly of the Crow [Corvus], and the foot of the Beast [Centaurus].

(24) {But} one of the **sons of men**[αθ,9] [i.e., human beings] born *in this sign* [i.e., one who has Virgo as the ascendant of his nativity] will be of **appropriate and pleasing stature**[β,10] with an erect and handsome body, **wise and prudent,**[γ,11] his hair will not be curly, he will love justice, his voice will be strong, he will be **sterile and will not produce ⟨sons⟩**,[β,12] his character ⟨will be⟩ good, his face will be handsome, he will be a scribe and **learned in numbers.**[α,13] (25) {But} one who is born in the second face [a person who has the second face of Virgo as the ascendant of his nativity] will be handsome in ⟨his⟩ appearance, but his eyes ⟨will be⟩ small, and **his nostrils beautiful or his nose beautiful;**[β,14] he will be **a learned person,**[α,15] modest, generous in ⟨his⟩ heart, and eager to be praised. (26) One who is born in the third face will be handsome in appearance, **a learned or prudent person, truthful in intention or mind,**[β,16] modest and wise.

(27) {But} its portion of the human body is the stomach, the intestines, and the diaphragm. (28) {Similarly,} the diseases affecting the aforementioned parts of the body are in its portion, and every disease whose cause is black bile. (29) {Also,} of human beings, middle-class people are in its portion, and scribes, scholars, arithmeticians and geometricians, women, eunuchs, and **actors.**[γ,17] (30) {But} *this sign* ⟨is⟩ the house of Mercury, and also its **exaltation or honor**[β,18] is there [in Virgo] at 15°; {moreover} **Venus's fall**[γ,19] [dejection] ⟨is⟩ **at 27°;**[π,20] ⟨it is⟩ Jupiter's house of hate and the place of **its** [Jupiter's] **apogee**[γ,21] is there [in Virgo], at 23° ⟨⟨at the present time⟩⟩.[μ,22] (31) The lords of the triplicity are Venus and then the Moon by day, and by night **the opposite;**[γ,23] {moreover} Mars is the partner by day and by night. (32) {But} the first face [decan], **according to**[γ] the EGYPTIANS and

TIOS et BABYLONIOS, Solis est, secunda Veneris, tertia Mercurii ; **secundum INDOS**,[γ] prima Mercurii, secunda Saturni, .3a.[1] ⟨⟨...⟩⟩.[νπ] (33) **Termini**[α] sunt hii **secundum**[γ] EGYPTIOS et **SAPIENTES ASTRORUM:**[γ] Mercurii .7. Veneris .10., Iovis .4., Martis .7., Saturni .2.; secundum opinionem PTOLOMEI: **Solis .7., et Veneris .6.**[α,2] (34) Et novenariarum prima Saturni est et secunda, tertia Iovis, .4a. Martis, .5a. Veneris, sexta Mercurii, .7a. Lune, .8a. Solis, et .9a. Mercurii. (35) Duodenariarum prima est Mercurii, secunda Veneris, tertia Martis, .4a. Iovis, .5a. et .6a. Saturni, .7a. Iovis, .8a. Martis, nona Veneris, .10a. Mercurii, undecima Lune, .12a. Solis.

(36) {Rursus} ab initio signi usque ad finem .5. gradus sunt gradus mixti, deinde .4. lucidi, et post .2. vacui, deinde .9. lucidi et demum .10. mixti.[3] (37) {Rursus}[4] ab initio signi usque ad finem .7. gradus feminini, deinde quinque masculini, sunt postea .8. feminini, deinde .10. masculini. (38) **Putealitas** {autem} **stellarum**[γ] in .80. gradus est et .13., .16., .21., et .25. (39) Gradus **fortunam**[γ] augmentantes et honorem, .2us, quintus, .17. et .20.

(40) De *stellis fixis*[γ] est ibi Cauda Leonis in .10 gradu ⟨⟨...⟩⟩,[ν] cuius latitudo septentrionalis .11. gradus, et est honoris primi, de complexione Saturni et Veneris. (41) Item est ibi alia stella in eodem gradu *longitudinis*, sed latitudo eius septentrionalis .25. gradus, et est honoris primi, de complexione {similiter} Saturni et Veneris. (42) {Postea} sunt ibi stelle **nebulose sive obscure**[β] inter Ursum et Leonem, una est in gradu undecimo ⟨⟨...⟩⟩,[ν] et latitudo eius septentrionalis .20. graduum et .40 minuta, ⟨⟨...⟩⟩[μ]

7 (1) Libra signum est aereum, masculinum, **diurnum**,[γ] occidentale. (2) De signis hyemis, mobile, et in eius principio equatur dies nocti, et **incipiunt abbreviari dies et noctes prolongari.**[γ] (3) Hore eius breviores sunt **equalibus**, in **ascensionibus**[α] quidem rectus est, et longe sunt eius **ascensiones.**[α] (4) Natura eius calida est et humida, sed non bene temperata.

---

[1]3a.] WVG; L om.   [2]G margin: Iovis 5, Saturni .6., Martis .6.   [3]Rursus ab initio signi usque ad finem .5. gradus sunt gradus mixti, deinde .4. lucidi, et post .2. vacui, deinde .9. lucidi et demum 10 mixti] GV; W Rursus ab initio signi usque ad finem .5. gradus sunt gradus mixti, deinde .4. lucidi, et demum 10 mixti; L om.   [4]Rursus] L; WVG item.

BABYLONIANS, ⟨is assigned⟩ to the Sun, the second to Venus, and the third to Mercury; **according to the INDIANS,**[γ] the first ⟨face is assigned⟩ to Mercury, the second to Saturn, and the third to ⟨⟨Venus⟩⟩[νπ,24] (33) These are the **terms**[α] **according to**[γ] the EGYPTIANS and the **SCHOLARS OF THE STARS:**[γ] Mercury 7°, Venus 10°, Jupiter 4°, Mars 7°, and Saturn 2°; and according to the opinion of PTOLEMY: **the Sun 7°, Venus 6°.**[α,25] (34) The first _novenaria_ [ninth-part] ⟨is assigned⟩ to Saturn and also the second, the third to Jupiter, the fourth to Mars, the fifth to Venus, the sixth to Mercury, the seventh to the Moon, the eighth to the Sun, and the ninth to Mercury. (35) The first of the _duodenariae_ [twelfths] ⟨is assigned⟩ to Mercury, the second to Venus, the third to Mars, the fourth to Jupiter, the fifth and the sixth to Saturn, the seventh to Jupiter, the eighth to Mars, the ninth to Venus, the tenth to Mercury, the eleventh to the Moon, and the twelfth to the Sun.

(36) {Besides,} from the beginning of the sign to the end of five degrees ⟨the degrees are⟩ mixed, then ⟨come⟩ four bright ⟨degrees⟩, then two empty ⟨degrees⟩, then nine bright ⟨degrees⟩, and finally ten mixed ⟨degrees⟩. (37) {Besides,} from the beginning of the sign to the end of seven degrees, ⟨the degrees are⟩ feminine, then ⟨come⟩ five masculine ⟨degrees⟩, then eight feminine ⟨degrees⟩, then ten masculine ⟨degrees⟩. (38) {But} **what belongs to the pits of the stars**[γ] is at the 8th, 13th, 16th, 21st, and 25th degrees. (39) The degrees adding **fortune**[γ] and honor: the 2nd, 5th, 17th, and 20th degrees.

(40) There [in the degrees of Virgo], of the _fixed stars_[γ,26] ⟨we find⟩ the Tail of the Lion at ⟨longitude Virgo⟩ 10° ⟨⟨at the present time⟩⟩,[ν] northern ⟨ecliptical⟩ latitude 11°, of the first honor [first magnitude], of the mixture of Saturn and Venus. (41) Likewise, there is another star at the same degree _of longitude_, but its latitude is northern 25°, of the second honor, {similarly} of the mixture of Saturn and Venus. (42) {After that} there are there two **nebulous or dark**[β,27] stars between the Bear [Ursa Major] and ⟨the constellation⟩ Leo: the first ⟨at longitude Virgo⟩ 11° ⟨⟨at the present time⟩⟩,[ν] northern ⟨ecliptical⟩ latitude 20° 40'; ⟨⟨the other at the same degree ⟨of longitude⟩, but northern ⟨ecliptical⟩ latitude 25½°⟩⟩.[μ,28]

7 (1) Libra is an airy sign, masculine, **diurnal,**[γ] western. (2) One of the signs of winter, changeable; at its beginning day and night are equal, but then **the days begin to grow shorter and the nights longer.**[γ,1] (3) Its hours are shorter than the **equal**[γ] ⟨hours⟩, it is straight in its **ascensions,**[α] its **ascensions**[α] are long. (4) Its nature is hot and moist, but it is not properly tempered.

182   PART ONE

(5) Et significat super omnem aerem spissum et mixtum ventis et **vaporibus** ascendentibus **seu nubibus**[β] animalia corrumpentibus. (6) Et universaliter *natura eius* mutabilis est sed principium eius et medium meliora sunt fine. (7) **Et pars eius septentrionalis**[γ] ventos generat, {vero} meridionalis {autem} humiditates.[1] (8) Et est in forma humana secundum se. (9) Et in eius parte est cor occidentis, ac ventus meridionalis. (10) ⟨⟨...⟩⟩,[ν] *de humoribus quidem* eius[2] est sanguis. (11) **De saporibus**,[γ] dulcis; et **de coloribus**[γ] viridis ac **cinericius seu**[3] **pulvereus**.[β] (12) De animalibus, in parte eius est homo et **omnis avis magna;**[α] de vegetalibus {quoque} arbores alte. (13) **De climatibus**[α] **et regionibus, clima**[α] quintum, et terra Edom *sive* CHRISTIANORUM,[4] de Roma quidem usque in Affrica, et pars terre Etyopie; {item} mare Barka, et Sisten et Cabul seu Evastaen, et Ballac et Hamedin. (14) {Iterum} in parte eius est quidquid seminatus est in extremitate montium, et

7va   omnis terra non fortis, et omnis | locus altus; {similiter} et loca **nundinarum seu mercata**,[β] ac mercimoniorum loca *dicta*. (15) Littere {vero} eius sunt littera <u>hees</u>[5] et <u>sin</u>. (16) Anni octo, et menses totidem, dies viginti, et hore .16.

(17) Ascendit {autem} in prima facie eius ymago hominis iracundi, in cuius manu sinistra **statera seu trutina**,[β] in dextra **liber scripturarum**;[γδ] {demum} ascendit vir equitans super equum ⟨⟨...⟩⟩;[μ] {item} ascendit ibi caput draconis et principium maris aurei; et PERSARUM SAPIENTES ipsum vocant ursum magnum, et ascendit ibi pars navis. (18) Et **secundum** INDOS[γ] ascendit ibi homo in tabernaculo stans in mercato, in cuius manu statera et vult emere ac vendere. (19) **Secundum**[γ] PTOLOMEUM ascendit ibi medium ⟨⟨...⟩⟩[μ] Ursi Magni, et medietas corporis Virginis cum palma sinister in qua est Spica; {item} cauda Corvi, et pars caude Bellicosi, *id est Ydre*, et **pars**[α] caude Equi cum posterioribus suis.

(20) Et in secunda facie, ascendit homo ducens **currum sive bigam**,[β] super quam homo, in cuius manu **virga**,[α] et cum ipso vir induens vestimenta de serico, et sedet super lectum; item ascendit ibi puer parvus, ac medium navis, et **medium ursi magni, item medium draconis**,[α] item fons aque. (21) Et dicunt INDI[γ] quod ascendit ibi homo in similitudine aquile, qui nudus et sitibundus, in desiderio est volandi in aere. (22) **Secundum**[γ]

---

[1]humiditates] W < pluvias.   [2]eius] G suis.   [3]cinericius seu] WVG; L om.   [4]Edom sive christianorum] WVG; L christianorum.   [5]*hees*] LVG; W heez.

(5) It indicates thick air [fog] mixed with winds, and with ascending **vapors or clouds**[β,2] that corrupt living creatures. (6) As a rule, *its nature* is changeable, but its beginning and middle are better than its end. (7) **Its northern part**[γ,3] generates winds; {but} ⟨its⟩ southern ⟨part⟩ {however} generates⟩ moisture. (8) It has the shape of a solitary man. (9) The heart of the west is in its portion, and the south wind. (10) ⟨⟨Its nature is hot and moist,⟩⟩[ν,4] *and of the humors* the blood belongs to it. (11) **Of the tastes,**[γ,5] sweet; **of the colors,**[γ,6] green and the color of **ashes or dust.**[β] (12) Of living creatures, human beings and **every large bird**[α,7] are in its portion;[8] {besides,} of plants, the tall trees. (13) **Of the climates and regions,**[β,9] the fifth **climate,**[α] and the land of Edom *or of the Christians*, from Rome to Africa, and part of the land of Ethiopia; {likewise} the sea of Barqa [Cyrenaica], Sīstān, Kābul, Tabaristan, Balkh, and Hamadhān. (14) {In addition,} everything that may be sown on mountaintops is in its portion, and any land that is not strong, any high place; {similarly,} the places of **fairs and markets,**[β,10] and *the aforementioned* places of merchandises. (15) {Moreover} its letters are *het* and *shin*. (16) Its years are eight, and so too its months; the days are 20, and the hours 16.

(17) {But} in its first face [decan], the image of an irascible man rises; he holds a **balance pan or scales**[β,11] in his left hand, in ⟨his⟩ right ⟨hand⟩ **a book of written items;**[γδ,12] {finally} a man riding on a horse ⟨⟨and playing music⟩⟩[μ,13] rises there; {likewise,} the head of the dragon and the beginning of the golden sea, which the PERSIAN SCHOLARS call the Greater Bear, rise there; part of the ship rises there ⟨too⟩. (18) **According to the INDIANS**[γ] a man in a market stall, with a balance in his hand, rises there, and he wants to buy and sell. (19) **According to**[γ] PTOLEMY, the middle of the ⟨⟨tail⟩⟩[μ,14] of the Greater Bear [Ursa Major] rises there, ⟨along with⟩ the middle of the body of ⟨the constellation⟩ Virgo with the left hand in which is the Ear of Grain [Spica]; {likewise,} the tail of the Crow [Corvus], part of the tail of the Warrior, *that is, Hydra*,[15] and **part**[α,16] of the tail of the Horse [Pegasus/Centaurus?] with its rear parts.

(20) In its second face, a man driving a **chariot or a cart**[β,17] rises; a man with a **stick**[α,18] in his hand is in it, and with him a man wearing silk clothes, who is sitting on a bed; likewise, a little boy rises there, and the middle of the ship, and **the middle of the Greater Bear and the middle of the Dragon;**[α,19] likewise, a spring of water. (21) The **INDIANS**[γ] say that a man resembling an eagle rises there; he is naked and thirsty, and wants to fly through the

184 PART ONE

Ptolomeum, ascendit ibi cauda Draconis, et **pars**^α caude Ursi Maioris, ac **sumen**^γ Virginis.

(23) In facie {autem} tertia ascendit finis navis, et **finis seu extremitas**^β maris aurei, et **caput**^α hominis nudi cuius manus super caput eius; et ibi corona super capita duorum hominum in quorum utriusque capite cornua duo. (24) Et ascendit ibi **secundum Indos**^γ homo cuius facies faciei similis est equi, et in manu eius arcus et sagitte. (25) Et rursus **secundum**^γ Ptolomeum ascendit ibi **pars**^α caude Draconis cum manibus eius et brachiis, ac genu dexter; item et **pars**^α **pudibundorum**^γ Virginis cum pedibus suus.

(26) Universaliter {autem} qui natus fuerit in hoc signo de hominibus erit eius membra recta, sermo eius placidus; et ipse **prudens et disciplinatus**,^α mulieres amans et ipse paratus ad faciendum quodlibet artificiosum de instrumentis sicut cantum ac invenire cantiones, **venationes diliget seu venari**,^β perfectus corde est, **liberalis ac placens**,^β et corpus eius mundius est et pulcherius facie; *de hominibus* enim aliquis est niger. (27) Et qui natus fuerit in prima facie **formosus**^γ erit, in capite eius plaga, et super manum eius seu pedum cauterium, ipseque laboriosus, simplex, et **disciplinatus**.^α (28) Qui in secunda facie natus fuerit, pulcher erit facie et corpore ac statura, impedimentum {autem} habebit in oculis et in **yliis**;^α et ipse liberalis corde ac socialis. (29) {Sed} qui in tertia facie natus fuerit pulcher etiam est

7vb corpore, | et in vultu formosus cum impedimento in oculis, et ipse notus erit in gente sua et honoratus. (30) Qui {vero} in fine signi natus fuerit, neuter sexus, et vel **utriusque**^γδ **seu hermafroditus**.^γδ

(31) Ac {vero} in parte[1] eius de partibus humani corporis est venter inferior **et inguina**.^γ (32) Egritudines {quoque} ipsius sunt sicut **retentio** urine aut[2] **egestionem**,^β, ac sanguis per inferiorem distendens, et visus tenebrositas. (33) De hominibus, in parte eius sunt **mercatores**,^γ iudices, et arismetici ac **omnes instrumentis cantantes**,^α ⟨⟨...⟩⟩^ν et comestoribus et potationibus se immiscentes. (34) Et est domus Veneris, **honor** {vero} **seu exaltatio**^β Saturni in .21. gradu, **casus**^γ Solis in .19., **odium**^γ Martis; {item} et **aux**^α **Mercurii**^π in .25. gradu ad hoc tempus. (35) **Secundum Egyptios**^γ quidem

---

[1]in parte] GW; L de partibus; V om.   [2]aut] WV; LG ac.

air. (22) **According to**[Y] PTOLEMY, the tail of the Dragon [Draco] rises there, and **part**[α,20] of the Greater Bear's [Ursa Major] tail, and the **breast**[Y,21] of ⟨the constellation⟩ Virgo.

(23) {But} in the third face, the end of the ship rises, and the **end or the extremity**[β,22] of the golden sea, the **head**[α,23] of the naked man with his hand on his head; and there is a crown on the head of two persons, and each of them has two horns on his head. (24) **According to the INDIANS,**[Y] a man whose face resembles a horse's face rises there; he has a bow and arrows in his hand. (25) Also **according to**[Y] PTOLEMY, **part**[α,24] of Dragon's [Draco] tail rises there too, with his hands, arms, and his right knee; {likewise,} **part**[α25] of the **genitals**[Y,26] of ⟨the constellation⟩ Virgo with her feet.

(26) {But} in general, one born in this sign [one who has Libra as the ascendant of his nativity] of the human beings will have straight limbs and pleasant speech; he ⟨will be⟩ **prudent and learned,**[α,27] a lover of women, ready to engage in any art involving instruments, like instrumental music and composing songs, **loving the hunt or going hunting,**[β,28] pure of heart, **generous and pleasing,**[β,29] his body will be clearer and more beautiful than ⟨his⟩ face; *of human beings*, some of them are swarthy. (27) One who is born in the first face [a person who has the first decan of Libra as the ascendant of his nativity] **will be handsome,**[Y,30] in his head a wound, and a burn on his hand or foot; he will be hardworking, modest, and **learned.**[α] (28) One who is born in the second face will be handsome of body, face, and stature, {but} with a defect in his eyes and **flanks;**[α,31] he ⟨will be⟩ generous and sociable. (29) {But} one who is born in the third face will also have a handsome body, beautiful in ⟨his⟩ face with a defect in the eyes; he will be famous and honored among his people. (30) {Moreover} one who is born in the end of the sign will be neither of one sex nor of the other, or **of one as well as of the other**[Yδ,32] or rather a **hermaphrodite.**[Yδ,33]

(31) {Moreover} its portion of the human body is the lower abdomen and **the groin.**[Y,34] (32) {Besides,} its diseases are **retention or voiding**[β,35] of urine, hemorrhoids, and clouded vision. (33) Of human beings, in its portion are **merchants,**[Y,36] judges, arithmeticians, **all players on musical instruments,**[α,37] ⟨⟨traders⟩⟩[v,38] and those dealing with food and drink. (34) It [Libra] is the house of Venus, {moreover} the **honor or exaltation**[β,39] of Saturn at ⟨Libra⟩ 21°, the **fall**[Y,40] [dejection] of the Sun at ⟨Libra⟩ 19°, the **hate**[Y,41] of Mars; {likewise} the **apogee**[α,42] of **Mercury**[π,43] at ⟨Libra⟩ 25° at the present time. (35) **According to the EGYPTIANS,**[Y] *in this sign* the

in *hoc signo*, **egritudo**ᵅ Saturni est in genibus; Iovis in tybiis; Martis in ventre inferiori; Solis in manibus; Veneris in lumbis; Mercurii in corde *et circiter*, Lune in pectore. (36) Domini triplicitatis in die Saturnus et post ipsum Mercurius, de nocte **econtrario**,ᵞ et particeps earum die et nocte Iupiter. (37) Facies {autem} prima secundum EGYPTIOS et BABYLONIOS Lune est, secunda Saturni, tertia {vero} Iovis; **secundum INDOS**ᵞ prima Veneris est, secunda Saturni, et tertia Mercurii. (38) **Termini**ᵅ {vero} **secundum**ᵞ EGYPTIOS et **ASTRORUM SAPIENTES**ᵞ hii sunt: Saturni quidem .6. gradus, Mercurii .8., Iovis .7., Veneris .7., et Martis .2.;[1] **termini**ᵅ {vero} **secundum**ᵞ PTOLOMEUM: Saturni .6., Veneris .5., Iovis .8., Mercurii .5., et Martis .6. (39) Novenariarum {quoque} prima Veneris est, secunda Martis, tertia Iovis, quarta et quinta Saturni, sexta Iovis, septima Martis, .8a. Veneris, et nona Mercurii. (40) Duodenariarum {vero} prima est Veneris, secunda Martis, tertia Iovis, quarta et quinta Saturni, sexta Iovis, septima Martis, .8a. Veneris, nona Mercurii, decima Lune, undecima Solis et duodecima Mercurii.

(41) {Rursus} a principio signi usque in finem .5. gradus sunt lucidi, deinde .5. mixti, postea .8. lucidi, postmodum .3. mixti, deinde .7. lucidi, demum duo vacui. (42) {Similiter,} a principio signi usque in finem .5. gradus masculini, deinde .5. feminini, postea .11. masculini, deinde .7. feminini, et demum .2. masculini. (43) **Putealitas** {autem} **stellarum**ᵞ primus gradus est, et .7us. et **.23us.**ᵅ (44) Gradus **fortunam**ᵞ augmentantes et honorem sunt .3us, et .5us., et .2lus.

(45) {Insuper,} de *stellis fixis*,ᵞ est ibi Suppodiatus[2] Inhermis, qui vocatur <u>Samach Alaazel</u>, et est in gradu .12. ⟨⟨...⟩⟩,ᵛ latitudo quidem est meridionalis .2. gradus, et est primi honoris, de complexione Veneris et Mercurii. (46) {Item} est ibi Lancea, qui vocatur <u>Sanch Alremach</u>, et est in gradu .13. ⟨⟨...⟩⟩,ᵛ latitudo eius septentrionalis .31. gradus cum dimidio, et est honoris primi, de complexione quidem ⟨⟨...⟩⟩ᵘ Martis. (47) {Amplius} est ibi stella lucida in fine | signi, cuius latitudo septentrionalis .44. gradus cum dimidio, et est honoris secundi, de complexione quidem Veneris et Mercurii.

---

[1]Termini vero secundum Egyptios et astrorum sapientes hii sunt: Saturni quidem .6. gradus, Martis .8., Iovis .7., Veneris .7., et Martis .2.] WVG; L (after the terms according to Ptolemy) secundum Egyptios Saturni quidem .6. gradus, Mercurii .8., Iovis .7., Veneris .7., et Martis .2.
[2]suppodiatus] W subpedatus.

disease[α,44] of Saturn is in the knees; of Jupiter in the shanks; of Mars in the lower abdomen; of the Sun in the hands; of Venus in the hips; of Mercury in the heart *and around it*; of the Moon in the chest. (36) The lords of the triplicity are Saturn and then Mercury by day, and by night **the opposite**;[γ,45] and Jupiter is their partner by day and by night. (37) {But} the first face [decan], according to the EGYPTIANS and BABYLONIANS, ⟨is assigned⟩ to the Moon, the second to Saturn, and the third {indeed} to Jupiter; **according to the INDIANS**,[γ] the first ⟨face is assigned⟩ to Venus, the second to Saturn, and the third to Mercury. (38) {Moreover} these are the **terms**[α,46] **according to**[γ] the EGYPTIANS and the **SCHOLARS OF THE STARS**:[γ] Saturn 6°, Mercury 8°, Jupiter 7°, Venus 7°, and Mars 2°; {but} **these are the terms**[α] **according to** PTOLEMY: Saturn 6°, Venus 5°, Jupiter 8°, Mercury 5°, and Mars 6°. (39) {Besides,} the first of the *novenariae* [ninth-parts] ⟨is assigned⟩ to Venus, the second to Mars, the third to Jupiter, the fourth and the fifth to Saturn, the sixth to Jupiter, the seventh to Mars, the eighth to Venus, and the ninth to Mercury. (40) {Moreover} the first of the *duodenariae* [twelfths] ⟨is assigned⟩ to Venus, the second to Mars, the third to Jupiter, the fourth and the fifth to Saturn, the sixth to Jupiter, the seventh to Mars, the eighth to Venus, the ninth to Mercury, the tenth to the Moon, the eleventh to the Sun, and the twelfth to Mercury.

(41) {In addition,} from the beginning of the sign to the end of five degrees, ⟨the degrees are⟩ bright, then ⟨come⟩ five mixed ⟨degrees⟩, then eight bright ⟨degrees⟩, then three mixed ⟨degrees⟩, then seven bright ⟨degrees⟩, finally two empty ⟨degrees⟩. (42) {Similarly,} from the beginning of the sign to the end of five degrees, ⟨the degrees are⟩ masculine, then ⟨come⟩ five feminine ⟨degrees⟩, then eleven masculine ⟨degrees⟩, then seven feminine ⟨degrees⟩, finally two masculine ⟨degrees⟩. (43) {But} **what belongs to the pits of the stars**[γ] is at the 1st, 7th, 20th, and **23th**[α,47] degrees. (44) The degrees adding **fortune**[γ] and honor: the 3rd, 5th, and 21st degrees.

(45) {In addition,} of the *fixed stars*[γ,48] ⟨we find⟩ there the Unarmed One who is Leaning ⟨on a spear⟩, which is called ⟨*as-simāk al-ʾaʿzal*⟩, ⟨at longitude Libra⟩ 12° ⟨⟨at the present time⟩⟩,[ν] southern ⟨ecliptical⟩ latitude 2°, of the first honor [first magnitude], of the mixture of Venus and Mercury. (46) {Likewise,} the Spear, which is called ⟨*as-simāk al-rāmiḥ*⟩ [Arcturus], is there; it is at ⟨longitude Libra⟩ 13° ⟨⟨at the present time⟩⟩,[ν] its latitude is northern 31½°, of the first honor, of the of ⟨⟨Jupiter⟩⟩[μ,49] ⟨and⟩ Mars. (47) {Besides,} a bright star is there at the end of the sign [Libra], its latitude is northern 44½°, of the second honor, of the mixture of Venus and Mercury.

8 (1) Scorpio signum est aqueum, femininum, **nocturnum**,ᵞ **septentrionale**.ᵞ (2) **Hyemale**,ᵞ **fixum sive non mutabile**.ᵝ (3) Hore eius breviores sunt **equalibus**,ᵞ et ipsum in **ascensionibus**ᵅ rectum, **ascensiones**;ᵅ,[1] {quoque} ipsius longe sunt. (4) Et significat super ⟨⟨...⟩⟩ᵘ humiditatem **intemperatam**ᵞ et habet in se **saporem seu commutationem saporis**ᵝ qui animalibus non valet nisi modicum. (5) Et eius totalitas tonitrua generat et fulmina; principium {autem} eius humidus et mutabile, medium quidem mixtum, et finis **tempestuosus**.ᵅ (6) **Septentrionale**ᵞ {vero} *ipsius* humidum, et **meridionale**ᵞ frigidum. (7) Et est in figura scorpionis. (8) **De parte** {autem} **eius est pars septentrionalis**,ᵞ ac ventus septentrionalis. (9) *Et de humoribus* eius est flegma **habundans**ᵞ in homine; sapor eius omne salsum et insipidum; de coloribus {vero} rubeus et viridis et color pulvereus. (10) De animalibus, in parte eius sunt scorpiones, et bestie, et reptilia terre cum bestiolis aque; {similiter} et omnis aqua currentes, et aqua maris; {item} omne vegetabile quod est in aqua sicut corallus; et de vegetalibus arbores in altitudine mediocres. (11) De **climatibus** {vero} **et regionibus**,ᵝ in parte eius est **clima**ᵅ tertium, et terra Scena, et Arabia, et Tania, et Cabros. (12) {Item} partem habet in vineis ac **in ortis oleorum**,ᵞ **acque**ᵅ in omnibus locis fetidis, ac {etiam} in desertis. (13) Littere eius sunt *tes* et *syn*. (14) Anni {vero} .15, menses totidem, dies .37. cum dimidio, et hore .4.

(15) Ascendit in eius prima facie **pes equi posterior**,ᵞ {similiter} et posteriora bovis, et homo niger, in cuius manu baculus. (16) Et dicunt **Indi**ᵞ quod ibi ascendit ymago mulieris pulchre, cuius corpus rubeum et ipsa manducat. (17) **Secundum**ᵞ Ptolomeum {vero} ascendit ibi manus **Ursi Maioris**,ᵅ et caput Canis cum brachio dextro, et medietas **Statere sive Libre**.ᵝ

(18) Et in secunda facie ascendit homo nudus, et medium equi, et medium bovis. (19) Sed dicunt **Indi**ᵞ quod ibi ascendit mulier que domum sua **exivit seu exit**ᵝ nuda, et ipsa nichil habet, et intrat in mare. (20) **Secundum**ᵞ Ptolomeum {vero} ascendit ibi extremitas manus Ursi Minoris, et **pars**ᵅ caude Draconis, et Corona Septentrionalis, ac **pudenda**[2] **seu lances Libre**,ᵝ cum pedibus suis, acque corona Scorpionis.

(21) In tertia {autem} facie ascendit **caput**ᵅ equi, et ille qui portat leporem, ac {etiam} **caput**ᵅ bovis. (22) Sed dicunt **Indi**ᵞ quod ascendit ibi canis, et

---

[1]ascensiones] WVG; L om.   [2]pudenda] WGV; L pudentia.

8 (1) Scorpio is a watery sign, feminine, **nocturnal**,γ,1 **northern**.γ (2) **Wintry**,γ,2 **fixed or not changeable**.β,3 (3) Its hours are shorter than the **equal**γ ⟨hours⟩, it is straight in the **ascensions**;α {also} its **ascensions**α are long. (4) It indicates ⟨⟨every⟩⟩μ,4 **intemperate**γ,5 moistness, which has in it **a taste or an alteration of taste**β,6 that is of little benefit to living creatures. (5) All of it generates thunder and lightning; {but} its beginning is moist and variable, its middle is mixed, and ⟨its⟩ end is **stormy**.α,7 (6) {Indeed} what is **northern**γ,8 *and is in its portion*, is moist, **and what is southern**γ,9 is cold. (7) It is in the form of a scorpion. (8) {But} **the northern part is in its portion**,γ,10 and the north wind. (9) *Of the humors*, the phlegm that **abounds**γ,11 in human beings is in its portion); its taste is everything salty and ⟨everything⟩ insipid; {moreover} of colors, red, green, and similar to dust. (10) Of living creatures, scorpions are in its portion, and the animals that creep on the earth with the aquatic animals; {similarly,} any flowing water, the waters of the sea; {likewise,} all aquatic plants like coral; of plants, trees of medium height. (11) {Moreover} of the **climates and regions**,β the third **climate**α is in its portion, and the land of Sheba, Arabia, Tania, and Cabros. (12) {Likewise,} it has a portion in vineyards and **olive groves**,γ,12 **and**α,13 in any place that is fetid and {also} in deserts. (13) Its letters are *tet* and *śin*. (14) {Moreover} its years are 15, and so are its months; the days are 35½, and the hours 4.

(15) In the first face [decan], the **rear foot**γ,14 of a horse rises, and {similarly} the rear part of a bull, and a black man with a stick in his hand. (16) The **INDIANS**γ say that the image of a beautiful woman rises there, her body is red and she is eating. (17) {But} **according to**γ PTOLEMY, the paw of the **Greater Bear**α,15 [Ursa Major], the head of the Dog [Boötes] and its right foreleg, and the middle of **the Balance or Pair of Scales**β,16 [the constellation Libra] rise there.

(18) In the second face, a naked man rises, and the middle of the horse and the middle of the bull. (19) The **INDIANS**γ say that a naked woman who **has left or is leaving**β,17 her house rises there; she has nothing and she is entering the sea. (20) {But} **according to**γ PTOLEMY, the end of the Lesser Bear's [Ursa Minor] paw rises there, and **part**α,18 of the Dragon's [Draco] tail, the Northern Crown [Corona Borealis], **the genitals or the scales of Libra**β,19 with its feet, and the crown of ⟨the constellation⟩ Scorpio.

(21) {But} in the third face, the **head**α,20 of the horse rises, and the carrier of the hare, and the {also} **head**α,21 of the bull. (22) The **INDIANS**γ say that a dog rises there, and two pigs, a large tiger with white fur, and various

duo porci, ac leopardus magnus cuius pili albi, et species venationis. (23) **Secundum**ᵞ PTOLOMEUM {vero} ascendit ibi ymago Ursi Parvi, et pes Euntis Super Genua Sua, et humeri eius cum brachio dextro, et venter Scorpionis, | acque **caput seu extremitas**ᵝ Turibuli.

8rb

(24) Ac {vero} qui natus fuerit in *hoc signo*, ex hominibus, niger erit aliquantulum, acque pilosus, et de hiis aliqui erunt rubicundi secundum aspectum astrorum in nativitate; oculi {vero} eius recti sed parvi, tybie eius longe, et pedes magni, et ipse currens, et **agilis seu levis in eundo**,ᵝ facies eius magna, et frons stricta, **humeri ampli seu lati**,ᵝ et ipse **deformis**,ᵞ **non habens parllorem**[1] **placentem**,ᵅ filios habebit sufficientes, dissipator erit, **fallax**,ᵅ iracundus, mendax, et **accusator seu detractor**,ᵝ lamentativus, liberalis, **astutus et plenus calliditate homines circumveniendi**.ᵞ (25) Qui {autem} natus fuerit in prima facie aliquantulum pulcher erit, et signum habebit in capite, oculi eius sicut oculi cati, pectus latum, et aliquis horum est qui signum[2] habet super pedem eius sinistrum aut super manum dextra, et ipse **homo prudens**,ᵞ **plenus sensu bono**,ᵅ {sed} festinus in loquendo. (26) Et qui in secunda facie natus fuerit caput eius erit grande, et habebit formam aliquantulam pulchram, signum habebit **super ventrem**ᵞ ac super dorsum, et ipse homo **prudens**,ᵞ sed loquax. (27) Qui {vero} in tertia facie natus fuerit, erit statura brevis, oculi eius obliqui, diligens comestiones, et mulierum amator, ac **lamentativus multum**.ᵞ (28) Et qui natus fuerit in fine signi, ille filius est illegitimus aut **neutrus sexus**.ᵞᵟ

(29) De partibus {autem} humani corporis eius sunt ⟨⟨...⟩⟩,ᵛ *loca ani*,ᵞ et pudibundarum masculi et femelle. (30) Est {etiam} de signis **impedimentorum, orbationum seu mutilationum**,ᵝ que significant **impedimenta**ᵞ in oculis, et tineam, et **fistulas**ᵞᵟ et scabiem ac lepram, necnon et maculas faciei, necnon calvitium. (31) Nativitas {quoque} mulierum in hoc signo bona non est; a .21. gradu usque ad .24. super **impedimenta**ᵞ significat oculorum. (32) De hominibus quidem eius in parte sunt **sevi**[3] **seu feroces**ᵝ et abiecti. (33) Et est domus Martis, Lune {vero} **casus**ᵞ in gradu .3., et domus odii Veneris. (34) Domini triplicitatis in die {vero} Venus *primo*, postea Mars, in nocte **econtrario**,ᵞ et particeps die et nocte Luna. (35) **Secundum**

---

[1]parllorem] corrected according to P 20vb: parlure; LGWV: pallorem. [2]signum] WVG; L om. [3]sevi] G < homines.

game animals. (23) {But} **according to**ʸ PTOLEMY, the image of the Lesser Bear [Ursa Minor] rises there, the leg of the One Crawling on his Knees [Hercules], his right shoulder and arm, the abdomen of ⟨the constellation⟩ Scorpio, and the **head or extremity**^β,22 of the Firepan [Ara].

(24) {Moreover} one born in *this sign*, of human beings, [a person who has Scorpio as the ascendant of his nativity] will be somewhat swarthy, and hairy, ⟨although⟩ some of them [the natives in Scorpio] will be ruddy according to the power of the aspects of the stars in the nativity; {moreover} his eyes ⟨will be⟩ straight but small, his shanks long, his feet large; he runs, **and ⟨is⟩ agile or quick in ⟨his⟩ walking;**^β,23 his face ⟨will be⟩ large, his forehead narrow, ⟨his⟩ **shoulders broad or wide;**^β,24 he will be **deformed,**^γ,25 he does not have a pleasant speech;^α,26 he will have many sons, will be destructive, **deceitful,**^α,27 irascible, a liar, **an accuser or defamer,**^β,28 wailing, **generous, shrewd, and full of craftiness to plot against people.**^γ,29 (25) {But} one who is born in the first face [a person who has the first decan of Scorpio as the ascendant of his nativity] will be somewhat handsome, will have a mole on his head; his eyes will be like a cat's eyes; he will have a broad chest; some of them [natives in the first decan of Scorpio] will have a mole on the left foot or on the right hand; he will be **a prudent person,**^γ,30 **full of good sense,**^α,31 {but} quick to speak. (26) One who is born in the second face will have a large head, will have a somewhat handsome form, will have a mole **on the abdomen**^γ,32 and on the back, he ⟨will be⟩ a **prudent person**^γ but garrulous. (27) {Moreover} one who is born in the third face will be short of stature, cross-eyed, a lover of food and lover of women, and **frequently weeping.**^γ,33 (28) One who is born in the end of the sign will be illegitimate or **of neither one sex or the other.**^γδ,34

(29) {But} of the parts of the human body, ⟨⟨the pudenda⟩⟩,^v,35 *the place of the anus,*^γ,36 and the male and female genitals are in its portion. (30) It is {also} one of the signs of **defects, maimings or mutilations,**^β,37 which indicate **defects**^γ,38 in the eyes, dandruff, **fistulas,**^γδ,39 roughness of the skin, leprosy, freckles on the face as well as baldness. (31) {Besides,} a nativity in this sign [Scorpio] is not good for women; from ⟨Scorpio⟩ 21° to 24° indicates **defects**^γ in the eyes. (32) Of human beings, **cruel or fierce tempered**^β,40 [persons] and abject [persons] are in its portion. (33) It [Scorpio] is the house of Mars, {moreover} the **fall**^γ,41 [dejection] of the Moon at 3°, and Venus's house of hate [detriment]. (34) {Moreover} the lords of the triplicity are *first* Venus and then Mars by day, and by night **the opposite;**^γ,42 the Moon ⟨is their⟩ partner by day and by night. (35) **According to the**

EGYPTIOSᵞ in hoc signo est **egritudo**ᵅ Saturni in tybiis, Iovis in pedibus, Martis in pudendis, Solis in corde, Veneris in intestinis, Mercurii in ventre, Lune {vero}[1] in **ventre superiori seu stomacho**.ᵝ (36) Facies {autem} prima **secundum** EGYPTIOS **et** BABYLONIOSᵞ Martis est, secunda Solis, tertia Veneris; ⟨⟨...⟩⟩.ᵘ (37) Et **termini**ᵅ ⟨⟨...⟩⟩ᵘ {vero} sunt hii: Martis .7., Veneris .4., Mercurii .8., Iovis .5., et Saturni .6.; **secundum**ᵞ PTOLOMEUM: Martis .6., Mercurii .6., Iovis .7., Veneris .6., Saturni .5. (38) {Item} novenariarum, prima Lune est, secunda Solis, | tertia Mercurii, quarta Veneris, quinta Martis, sexta Iovis, septima et octava Saturni, nona Iovis. (39) Duodenariarum, prima Martis est, secunda Iovis, tertia et quarta Saturni, quinta Iovis, sexta Martis, septima Veneris, octava Mercurii, nona Lune, decima Solis, undecima Mercurii, .12a. Veneris.

8va

(40) {Item} a principio signi usque in finem .3. gradus mixti sunt, postea .5. lucidi, .6. vacui, postmodum .6. lucidi, deinde .2. tenebrosi sunt, et demum .3. mixti. (41) {Adhuc} a principio signi usque ad .4. sunt masculini, postea .6. feminini, deindi .4. masculini[2], postea .5. feminini, deinde .8. masculini, postea .3. feminini. (42) Putei {autem} stellarum sunt gradus nonus, .10us., .17us., ⟨⟨...⟩⟩,ᵛ .23us., et .27us. (43) Gradus **fortunam**ᵞ augmentantes et honorem, .7us., .12us., et .20.

(44) {Postmodum,} de *stellis fixis*,ᵞ est ibi Cornu Scorpionis in .7. gradu ⟨⟨...⟩⟩,ᵛ cuius latitudo septentrionalis .8. graduum cum dimidio, et est honoris secundi, de complexione Iovis et Veneris. (45) {Item} est ibi stella que vocatur Pes Bestie, et est in gradus .16. ad hoc tempus, latitudo eius meridionlis .41. gradus .10 minuta, et est honori primi, de complexione Iovis et Martis. (46) {Insuper} est ibi Cor Scorpionis in gradu .28. ⟨⟨...⟩⟩,ᵛ latitudo eius meridionalis .3. gradus, et est honoris secundi, de complexione Martis et Iovis.

---

[1] in ventre, Lune vero] WVG; L om.   [2] postea .6. feminini, deindi .4. masculini] WG; L om.

EGYPTIANS,ᵞ the **disease**^(α,43) of Saturn ⟨in Scorpio⟩ is in the shanks; of Jupiter in the legs; of Mars in the pudenda; of the Sun in the heart; of Venus in the intestines; of Mercury in the abdomen; of the Moon {indeed} in **the upper abdomen or stomach**.^(β,44) (36) {But} the first face [decan], **according to the EGYPTIANS and the BABYLONIANS**,ᵞ ⟨is assigned⟩ to Mars, the second to the Sun, and the third to Venus; ⟨⟨according to the INDIAN SCHOLARS, the first ⟨face is assigned⟩ to Mars, the second to Jupiter, and the third to the Moon⟩⟩.^(μ,45) (37) {Moreover} these are the **terms**^(α,46) ⟨⟨of the Egyptians and the scholars of the signs⟩⟩:^(μ,47) Mars 7°, Venus 4°, Mercury 8°, Jupiter 5°, and Saturn 6°; **according to**ᵞ PTOLEMY: Mars 6°, Mercury 6°, Jupiter 7°, Venus 6°, and Saturn 5°. (38) {Likewise,} of the *novenariae*, [ninth-parts], the first ⟨is assigned⟩ to the Moon, the second to the Sun, the third to Mercury, the fourth to Venus, the fifth to Mars, the sixth to Jupiter, the seventh and the eighth to Saturn, and the ninth to Jupiter. (39) Of the *duodenariae* [twelfths], the first ⟨is assigned⟩ to Mars, the second to Jupiter, the third and the fourth to Saturn, the fifth to Jupiter, the sixth to Mars, the seventh to Venus, the eighth to Mercury, the ninth to the Moon, the tenth to the Sun, the eleventh to Mercury, and the twelfth to Venus.

(40) {Likewise,} from the beginning of the sign to the end of three degrees ⟨the degrees are⟩ mixed, then ⟨come⟩ five bright ⟨degrees⟩, then six empty ⟨degrees⟩, then six bright ⟨degrees⟩, then two dark ⟨degrees⟩, then five bright ⟨degrees⟩, and finally three mixed ⟨degrees⟩. (41) {Also} from the beginning of the sign to the end of four degrees, ⟨the degrees are⟩ masculine, then ⟨come⟩ six feminine ⟨degrees⟩, then four masculine ⟨degrees⟩, then five feminine ⟨degrees⟩, then eight masculine ⟨degrees⟩, and then three feminine ⟨degrees⟩. (42) {But} the pits of the stars are the 9th, 10th, 17th, ⟨⟨22nd⟩⟩,ᵛ 23rd, and 27th degrees. (43) The degrees adding **fortune**ᵞ and honor: the 7th, 12th, and 20th degrees.

(44) {Afterwards,} of the *fixed stars*^(γ,48) [in the degrees of Scorpio], there is the Horn of the Scorpion at ⟨longitude Scorpio⟩ 7° ⟨⟨at the present time⟩⟩,ᵛ northern latitude 8½°, of the second honor [magnitude], of the mixture of Jupiter and Venus. (45) {Likewise,} there is a star called the Leg of the Beast, it is ⟨at longitude Scorpio⟩ 16° at the present time, southern latitude 41° 10′, of the first honor, of the mixture of Mars and Jupiter. (46) {Besides,} ⟨we find⟩ there the Heart of the Scorpion, ⟨at longitude Scorpio⟩ 28° ⟨⟨at the present time⟩⟩,ᵛ southern latitude 3°, of the second honor, of the mixture of Mars and Jupiter.

9 (1) Sagittarius signum est igneum, masculinum, **diurnum**,ʸ orientale. (2) De signis hyemis, **duorum corporum sive bicorpor.**ᵝ (3) Hore eius breviores sunt **equalibus**, et in fine eius mutatur tempus et augmentantur hore diei, et hore noctis minuuntur, **in omni regione**.ᵅ (4) In **ascensionibus**ᵅ rectus est, ac **ascensiones**ᵅ eius longe sunt. (5) Natura eius calida et sicca, corruptiva animalium ac vegetabilium. (6) Et eius totalitas ventosa est; sed principium eius humidum est et frigidum ac nivosum, medium eius mixtum, et finis calidus sicut ignis. (7) **In septentrione**ʸ {vero} natura eius sicca est, et in meridie humida. (8) Duas quidem habet figuras, et est una medietas in figura hominis, et reliqua {vero} in figura equi. (9) In parte eius sunt dextra *pars* orientis et **ventus orientale**.ʸᵟ (10) ⟨⟨...⟩⟩ᵘ (11) De animalibus {vero} in parte eius sunt homines, equi, et aves, ac bestie cum reptilibus terre. (12) De **metallis seu mineralibus**,ᵝ plumbum; et de lapidibus, ille qui vocatur *smaragdus*, ac omnis lapis suavis. (13) De **climatibus seu regionibus**,ᵝ **clima**ᵅ secundum, et **terra Medorum**,ᵅ et *Asperni* sive *Persarum*; et mons omnis. (14) {Item} partem habet in viridariis, et in omnibus **locis paludosis**,ʸ ac locis equorum et bovi ⟨⟨...⟩⟩.ᵛ (15) Littere eius sunt littera *ioze* et *taf*. (16) Et annni eius sunt .12., et menses totidem, dies .30., et hore .12.

(17) Ascendit in prima eius facie ymago hominis nudi, **perversi, caput habentis deorsum et pedes sursum**,ᵅ et super caput eius corvus; item 8vb ascendit ibi corpus canicule, et caput capre. (18) **Sed** dicunt **Indi**ʸ quod | ibi ascendit homo nudus, a capite usque ad umbilicum figuram[1] habens hominis; ab umbilico {vero} inferius figuram habens equi, in cuius manu arcus et sagitta et ipse clamat. (19) **Secundum**ʸ Ptolomeum {vero} ascendit ibi collum **Ursi Parvi seu Minoris**,ᵝ et **pars**ᵅ caude Draconis atque **femora**ᵅ Euntis Super Genua, et **dorsum**ᵅ eius et caput; {item} extremitas Scorpionis cum **ligaminibus seu nodis**ᵝ que sunt in cauda, acque corpus Turibuli.

(20) Et in secunda facie ascendit ymago dextra manu tenens cornua capre; item ascendit ibi **caput canis feri seu lupi**ᵝʸᵟ et **medietas leporis**,ᵖⁱ cum medietate navis, et prima medietate piscis vocati *delfin*, ac dimidia **aranea**.ᵅ (21) {Sed} **Indi**ʸ dicunt quod ibi ascendit ymago mulieris pulchre, pilose, vestes induentis ac anulos in auribus habentis, et coram ipsam scrinium apertum in quo **ornamenta preparatoria**.ᵅ (22) **Iuxta**ʸ Ptolomeum {vero}

---

[1]figuram] WVG; L om.

LIBER ABRAHE AVENERRE INTRODUCTORIUS AD ASTRONOMIAM 195

9 (1) Sagittarius is a fiery sign, masculine, **diurnal**,ʸ eastern. (2) ⟨It is⟩ of the signs of winter, **of two bodies or bicorporal**.ᵝ,¹ (3) Its hours are shorter than the **equal**ʸ ⟨hours⟩, and at its end the season changes and the day⟨time⟩ hours increase and the night⟨time⟩ hours decrease, **in every region**.ᵅ,² (4) It is straight in ⟨its⟩ **ascensions**ᵅ and its **ascensions**ᵅ are long. (5) Its nature is hot and dry and it corrupts animals and plants. (6) All of it is windy; but its beginning is moist and cold and full of snow, its middle is mixed, and its end hot as fire. (7) **In the north**ʸ,³ {indeed} its nature is dry, and in the south moist. (8) It has two forms; one half is in the form of a human being, {but} the remaining ⟨half⟩ is in the form of a horse. (9) In its portion are the right *part* of the east and **the east wind**.ʸᵟ,⁴ (10) ⟨⟨Its taste is bitter and pungent; it generates the yellow bile; its color is any yellow, reddish, and ochre⟩⟩.ᵘ,⁵ (11) {Moreover} of living creatures, human beings are in its portion, and horses, birds, beasts, and animals that creep on the earth. (12) Of the **metals or minerals**,ᵝ,⁶ lead; of the ⟨precious⟩ stones, the one called *smaragdus*⁷ [emerald], *and any smooth stone*. (13) Of the **climates or regions**,ᵝ the second **climate**,ᵅ and **the land of the Medes**,ᵅ,⁸ and *Asperin*ᵅ,⁹ or ⟨*the land*⟩ *of the* PERSIANS, and every mountain. (14) {Likewise,} it has a part in gardens, and every **marshy place**,ʸ,¹⁰ and the places of horses and bulls ⟨⟨and every pebble⟩⟩.ᵛ,¹¹ (15) Its letters are *yod* and *taw*. (16) Its years are 12, as are its months, the days are 30, and the hours 12.

(17) In the first face [decan], the image of a naked man rises, **turned the wrong way, having his head downwards and his feet upwards**,ᵅ,¹² there is a crow on his head; likewise the body of a female dog and the head of a goat rise there. (18) But the **INDIANS**ʸ say that a naked man rises there, from his head to his navel he has the form of a man; {moreover} from his navel down he has the form of a horse; he is holding a bow and arrows in his hand and shouting. (19) {But} **according to**ʸ PTOLEMY, the neck of **the Little or Lesser Bear**ᵝ,¹³ [Ursa Minor] rises there, and **a part**ᵅ,¹⁴ of the Dragon's [Draco] tail, the **thighs**ᵅ,¹⁵ of the One Crawling on his Knees [Hercules], his **back**ᵅ,¹⁶ and head; {likewise} the end of ⟨the constellation⟩ Scorpio with the **bands or joints**ᵝ,¹⁷ in its tail, and the body of the Firepan [Ara].

(20) In the second face, an image rises holding the horns of the goat in its right hand; likewise the head of **a wild dog or wolf**ᵝʸᵟ,¹⁸ rises there, and **half of a hare**ᵖ,¹⁹ with half of the ship, the first half of the fish called *delfin*, and half of a **spider**.ᵅ,²⁰ (21) {But} **the Indians**ʸ say that the image of a beautiful woman rises there, hairy, wearing clothes, and having rings in ⟨her⟩ ears; in front of her is an open box containing **preparatory ornaments**.ᵅ,²¹

ascendit venter Ursi Minoris, et **pars**ᵅ corporis Draconis cum **parte**ᵅ capitis eius, et genua Euntis Super Genua, *qui est Hercules*, et pes eiusdem cum ⟨⟨...⟩⟩ᵘ brachio, ac una parsᵅ ⟨⟨...⟩⟩ᵛ Bestie, et sagitta ac pharetra; {similiter} **pars**ᵅ Corone Meridionalis.

(23) In tertia autem facie ascendit ymago canis, et extremitas corporis **canis**[1] **feri**,ᵞᵟ ac corpus leporis, atque residuum corporis leonis; {item} alia medietas navis, ac residuum piscis vocati *delfin*, et cauda **aranee**,ᵅ atque medietas ursi maioris. (24) {Sed} dicunt INDIᵞ quod ibi ascendit homo, cuius **aspectus seu visio**ᵝ est sicut color auri, in cuius manu tamquam similitudo anulorum aureorum ligneorum, ⟨⟨...⟩⟩.ᵛ (25) **Iuxta**ᵞ PTOLOMEUM ascendit medium corporis Ursi Minoris, et **pars**ᵅ corporis Draconis cum **capite suo**,ᵅ atque **pars**ᵅ corporis Aquile Cadentis, et caput Sagittarii cum humeris et pede ⟨⟨...⟩⟩.ᵘ

(26) Ac {vero} qui natus fuerit ex hominibus *in hoc signo* erit statura rectus, et ipse **splendidus**,ᵅ **veretrum eius et testiculi**ᵅ longi, tybie eius grosse, et ipse homo gaudiosus, et **fortis seu robustus**,ᵝ et **placidus**,ᵞ frons eius acuta, et similiter barba eius, et capilli minuti, venter eius magnus, et ipse agilis erit ad saliendum, equos amabit, et sapiens erit in mensuris, atque cavillosus, {sed} **una via non se tenebit**,ᵅᶿ et **vox eius humilis seu gravis**,ᵅᵝ et filii eius pauci. (27) Qui {autem} natus fuerit in prima facie, figura pulcher erit et **aspectu seu colore**,ᵝ statura rectus, et bonum diligens, regibus ac {etiam} maioribus adiungetur. (28) Et qui secunda facie natus fuerit, erit corpus eius placidus, sed facies eius crocea, supercilia | eius coniuncta, et signum habebit super pectus. (29) Natus {vero} in tertia facie longus erit, et facies eius pulchrum, oculi eius sicut oculorum cati, pectus eius latum, et ipse **fortis seu robustus**,ᵝ signum habebit in tybiis sinistris, **et simplex seu religiosus**,ᵅᵝ **consiliator bonus, et homo disciplinatus sive prudens**.ᵅᵝ (30) Et qui natus fuerit in fine signum fornicator erit; universaliter {autem} significat signum hoc super hominem iustus.

---

[1]canis] WVG; L om.

(22) {But} **according to**ʸ PTOLEMY, the belly of the Lesser Bear [Ursa Minor] rises there, **part**^(α,22) of the Dragon's [Draco] body with **part**^(α,23) of its head, the knee of the One Crawling on his Knees, *who is Hercules*, his leg and ⟨⟨left⟩⟩^(μ,24) arm, **part**^α of the ⟨⟨body of the⟩⟩^(ν,25) Beast [Serpens], the arrow and the quiver ⟨of Sagittarius⟩; similarly **part**^α of the Southern Crown [Corona Australis].

(23) {But} in the third face, the image of a dog rises, and the end of the body of the **wild dog**,^(γδ,26) the body of the hare, the remainder of the lion's body; {likewise} the other half of the ship, the remainder of the fish called *delfin*, the tail of the **spider**,^(α27) and half of the greater bear. (24) {But} the **INDIANS**ʸ say that a man, whose **appearance or look**^(β,28) is like the color of gold, rises there; in his hand is something resembling gold and wooden rings, ⟨⟨and he is wrapped in a mantle of bark⟩⟩.^(ν,29) (25) **According to**ʸ PTOLEMY, the middle of the Lesser Bear's [Ursa Minor] body rises there, **part**^(α,30) of the body of Dragon [Draco] with **its head**,^(α,31) part of the body of the Falling Eagle [Lyra], the head of ⟨the constellation⟩ Sagittarius and its shoulder and leg, ⟨⟨and the Southern Crown⟩⟩^(μ,32) [Corona Australis].

(26) {Moreover} one born *in this sign* [who has Sagittarius as the ascendant of his nativity], of human beings, will be of erect stature, **brilliant**,^(α,33) **his penis and testicles**^(α,34) long, ⟨his⟩ shanks thick; he is a joyful man; **strong or powerful**,^(β,35) **pleasing**,^(γ,36) his forehead pointed and similarly his beard; ⟨of⟩ thin hair, large abdomen; he will be agile in jumping; he will love horses, learned in geometry, full of tricks, {but} **he will not hold to one way**^(αβ,37) [i.e., he will be fickle], **his voice low and deep**,^(αβ,38) and he will not have many children. (27) {But} one born in the first face [a person who has the first decan of Sagittarius as the ascendant of his nativity] will be handsome in ⟨his⟩ form, and **in appearance and color**;^(β,39) ⟨of⟩ straight stature; he will love goodness, and {also} mingle with kings and grandees. (28) One who is born in the second face will have a pleasant body but his face will be saffron, his eyebrows will be joined, and he will have a mole on his chest. (29) {Moreover} one who is born in the third face will be tall, his face beautiful; his eyes like a cat's eyes, his chest will be broad, **strong or powerful**,^(β,40) he will have a mole on his left shank, **modest and pious**,^(αβ,41) **a good counselor**,^(γ,42) **a learned or prudent man**.^(αβ,43) (30) One who is born in the end of the sign will be a fornicator; {but} as a rule the sign indicates that he will be a just man.

(31) De partibus quidem corporis humani eius sunt *coxe et partes circumiacentes,*ᵞ ⟨⟨...⟩⟩,ᵛ ac omne **membrum superfluum seu pars super existens**ᵝ sicut digitus superfluus et consimilia.¹ (32) Egritudines {quoque} ipsius sunt amissio visus, et febris; atque casus ab alto; item et **egritudines occasione malarum bestiarum accidentes,**ᵅ et per membrorum incisiones; et a gradu .15. usque ad .18. super **impedimenta**ᵞ significat oculorum. (33) De hominibus {autem} in parte eius sunt iudices, et illi qui Deo servant, **et pii**ᵞ atque misericordes; {item} somniorum interpretes, et sagittarii et mercatores. (34) Est {quoque} domus Iovis, et **exaltatio seu honor**ᵝ Caude Draconis in tertio gradu, sed est **odium**ᵞ Mercurii et ⟨⟨...⟩⟩ᵛ **aux**ᵅ Saturni in .12. gradu ad hoc tempore; item est ⟨⟨...⟩⟩ᵛ **oppositum augis**ᵞ Solis atque Veneris in .27. gradu. (35) **Secundum** Egyptiosᵞ {autem} **egritudo**ᵅ Saturni in hoc signo est in pedibus; Iovis in capite; Martis **in pudibundis;**ᵞ Solis in corde; Veneris in **coxis;**ᵞ Mercurii in intestinis; et Lune in ventre. (36) Domini triplicitatis huius signi de die Sol est et post ipse Iupiter, in nocte **econtrario,**ᵞ et particeps in die et nocte Saturnus. (37) Facies {autem} prima secundum Egyptios et Babylonios Mercurii est, secunda Lune, tertia Saturni; secundum Indos prima Iovis, secunda Martis, tertia Solis. (38) **Termini**ᵅ secundum Egyptiosᵞ et astrorum sapientesᵞ sunt hii: Iovis .12. gradus, Veneris .5., Mercurii .4., Saturni .5. et Martis .4.; **secundum** Ptolomeum, Iovis .8., Veneris .6., Mercurii .5. Saturni .6., et Martis .5. (39) {Praterea} novenariarum prima Martis est, secunda Veneris, .3a. Mercurii, .4a. Lune, quinta Solis, .6a. Mercurii, .7a. Veneris, octava Martis, nona Iovis. (40) {Rursus} duodenariarum prima Iovis est, secunda et tertia Saturni, .4a. Iovis, quinta Martis, sexta Veneris, septima Mercurii, .8a. Lune, nona Solis, decima Mercurii, undecima Veneris, et .12a. Martis.

(41) {Item} a principio signi usque ad finem .9. gradus lucidi, denique .3. mixti, postea .7. lucidi, denique .4. **obscuri seu tenebrosi**ᵝ et deinde .7. vacui. (42) {Item} a principio signi usque ad finem .2. gradus sunt masculini, deinde .3. feminini, postea .7. masculini, et deinde .12. feminini, et demum

---

¹consimilia] WVG; L similia.

(31) Of the parts of the human body, in its portion are *the hips and the parts around them*,ᵞ,⁴⁴ ⟨⟨marks⟩⟩,ᵛ,⁴⁵ and every **superfluous limb or extra part**,β,⁴⁶ such as a superfluous digit and the like. (32) {Besides,} its diseases are the loss of sight, and fever; also falling from a high place; {likewise} **the diseases produced by harmful beasts**,α,⁴⁷ and by the amputation of limbs; ⟨a nativity whose ascendant is in Sagittarius⟩ from 15° to 18° indicates **defects**ᵞ,⁴⁸ of the eyes. (33) {But} of human beings, in its portion are judges, worshipers of God, **pious**ᵞ,⁴⁹ and merciful people; {likewise} dream interpreters, archers, and traders. (34) It [Sagittarius] is {also} the house of Jupiter, the **exaltation or honor**β,⁵⁰ of the Tail of the Dragon at ⟨Sagittarius⟩ 3°, the **hate**ᵞ,⁵¹ [detriment] of Mercury, the ⟨⟨place of⟩⟩ᵛ,⁵² **apogee**α,⁵³ of Saturn's at ⟨Sagittarius⟩ 12° at the present time; likewise the ⟨⟨place of⟩⟩ᵛ **opposite of the apogee**ᵞ,⁵⁴ [perigee] of the Sun and Venus at ⟨Sagittarius⟩ 27° at the present time. (35) {But} **according to the** EGYPTIANS,ᵞ the **disease**α,⁵⁵ of Saturn in this sign is in the legs; of Jupiter in the head; of Mars **in the genitals**;ᵞ of the Sun in the heart; of Venus in **the hips**;ᵞ,⁵⁶ of Mercury in the intestines; of the Moon in the abdomen. (36) The lords of the triplicity are the Sun and then Jupiter by day, and **by night the opposite**;ᵞ,⁵⁷ and Saturn is their partner by day and by night. (37) {But} the first face [decan], according to the EGYPTIANS and BABYLONIANS, ⟨is assigned⟩ to Mercury, the second to the Moon, and the third to Saturn; according to the INDIANS, the first ⟨face is assigned⟩ to Jupiter, the second to Mars, and the third to the Sun. (38) These are the **terms**α,⁵⁸ according to the EGYPTIANSᵞ and the SCHOLARS OF THE STARS:ᵞ Jupiter 12°, Venus 5°, Mercury 4°, Saturn 5°, Mars 4°; and **according to** PTOLEMY: Jupiter 8°, Venus 6°, Mercury 5°, Saturn 6°, Mars 5°. (39) {Besides,} of the *novenariae* [ninth-parts], the first ⟨is assigned⟩ to Mars, the second to Venus, the third to Mercury, the fourth to the Moon, the fifth to the Sun, the sixth to Mercury, the seventh to Venus, the eighth to Mars, and the ninth to Jupiter. (40) {In addition,} of the *duodenariae* [twelfths], the first ⟨is assigned⟩ to Jupiter, the second and the third to Saturn, the fourth to Jupiter, the fifth to Mars, the sixth to Venus, the seventh to Mercury, the eighth to the Moon, the ninth to the Sun, the tenth to Mercury, the eleventh to Venus, and the twelfth to Mars.

(41) {Likewise,} from the beginning of the sign to the end of nine degrees, ⟨the degrees are⟩ bright, then ⟨come⟩ three mixed ⟨degrees⟩, then seven bright ⟨degrees⟩, then four **dark or tenebrous**β ⟨degrees⟩, and then seven empty ⟨degrees⟩. (42) {Likewise,} from the beginning of the sign to the end of two degrees, ⟨the degrees are⟩ masculine, then ⟨come⟩ three feminine ⟨degrees⟩, then seven masculine ⟨degrees⟩, then twelve feminine ⟨degrees⟩,

.6. masculini. (43) **Putealitas**[1] {vero} **stellarum**[Y] est in .7o. gradu, et .12o., .15., .24., .27., et .30. (44) Gradus **fortunam**[Y] augmentantes et honorem | .13us. et .20us.

9rb

(45) {Amplius,} de *stellis fixis*,[Y] sunt ibi stelle caliginose: stella que est post caudam scorpionis in .18. gradu hiis diebus, latitudo eius meridionalis est .13. gradus .15. minuta. (46) {Item} stella que vocatur Sagitta in gradu .18. ⟨⟨...⟩⟩,[v] et latitudo eius meridionalis .6. gradus .20. minuta. (47) {Insuper} est ibi stella vocata Oculus Sagittarii, et est in finem signi hiis diebus, latitudo eius septentrionalis .45. minuta.

10 (1) Capricornus est signum terreum, femininum, **nocturnum**,[Y] meridionale. (2) *De signis hyemis*,[Y] mobile, in ipso crescere incipiunt hore diei et noctis minuere. (3) {Sed} hore ipsius breviores sunt horis **equalibus**.[Y] (4) Natura eius frigida est et sicca; corruptiva; et primum eius est in similitudine calidi et humidi, medium ipsius mixtum, et finis pluviosus, sive quidem **in parte septentrionali**[Y] sive **in parte meridionali**.[Y] (5) Est **signum obliquum**,[Y] et **ascensiones**[α] eius breves, et est defectivum in **rebus suis seu effectibus**.[β] (6) Et **duarum figurarum est seu biforme**,[β] et duplicis nature, prima namque medietas in figura est bestie terrestris habentis ungulas, et secunda medietas in figura[2] bestie aquatice. (7) *De humoribus* quidem in parte eius sunt melancolia; de saporibus, amarus et ponticus; et de coloribus, nigredo et color pulvereus. (8) De animalibus {autem}, omnem quadrupes ungulas habens, et similiter pars una bestiarum aque; {item} in parte eius sunt vermes et pulices et musce; de vegetalibus, olive, et nuces, et *orobe*,[αε] et galle ac omnis arbor spinosa, adhuc **plante paludestres**[Y] ut canne et **calami seu arundines**.[β] (9) {Item} in eius parte est **clima**[α] primum, et terra Etyopie, et Nabreen, Haemen, et Feene, et Hallenas, *id est India*, et Halthoase, et extremitas **climatis**[α] terre Edom, *id est Christianorum*. (10) {Item} in parte eius sunt pomeria et omnis **arbor paludosa**,[Y] et fontes ac flumina, necnon et **maria seu piscium servatoria**,[β] adhuc et loca canum seu vulpium, ac domus **captivorum seu incarceratorum**,[β] et **servientium seu servorum**,[β] et loca accrescionis ignis post extractionem eius; {item} loca pascualia **ovium seu gregum**,[β] et **loca cementaria**[α] in quibus nichil germinat. (11) Et littere eius sunt *caph* et *theis*. (12) Anni suis .27., et menses totidem, dies .307, cum dimidio, et hore **.4**.[α]

---

[1]putealitas] WVG; L < Item a principio signi usque ad finem.   [2]medietas in figura] WVG; L figura medietate.

and finally six masculine ⟨degrees⟩. (43) {Moreover} **what pertains to the pits of the stars**ʸ is at the 7th, 12th, 15th, 24th, 27th, and 30th degrees. (44) The degrees adding **fortune**ʸ and honor: the 13th and 20th degrees.

(45) {Besides,} of the *fixed stars*ʸ,⁵⁹ there are dark stars there: the star that follows the Tail of the Scorpion ⟨at longitude Sagittarius⟩ 16° in these days, its latitude is southern 13° 15′. (46) {Likewise} the a star called the Arrow ⟨at longitude Sagittarius⟩ 18° ⟨⟨at the present time⟩⟩,ʸ its latitude is southern latitude 6° 20′. (47) {In addition,} there is there a star called the Eye of the Archer; it is at the end of the sign in these days, its latitude is northern 45′.

10 (1) Capricorn is an earthy signs, feminine, **nocturnal**,ʸ southern. (2) ⟨It is⟩ of the *signs of winter*,ʸ,¹ changeable, in it the daytime hours begin to increase and the nighttime hours to decrease. (3) {But} its hours are shorter than the **equal**ʸ ⟨hours⟩. (4) Its nature is cold and dry; corrupting; its beginning bears the resemblance of hot and moist, its middle is mixed, and its end brings rains, whether ⟨it is⟩ **in the northern part**ʸ,² or **in the southern part.**ʸ,³ (5) It is an **oblique sign**,ʸ its **ascensions**ᵅ are short, and it is defective in its **conditions or effects.**β,⁴ (6) It has **two shapes or two forms,**β,⁵ and two natures; the first half is of the form of a terrestrial beast with hooves, and the second half of the form of an aquatic animal. (7) *Of the humors*, the black bile is in its portion; of the tastes, pungent and bitter; of the colors, black and ⟨the color⟩ of dust. (8) {But} of living creatures, all four-footed that have hooves, and similarly part of the aquatic animals; {likewise} worms, fleas, and flies are in its portion; of plants, olives, nuts, *orobe*,ᵅᵉ,⁶ and gall-nuts, every thorn tree, also **plants growing around marshes,**ʸ,⁷ like canes, **reeds or *arundines*.**β,⁸ (9) {Likewise,} in its portion is the first **climate,**ᵅ and the land of Ethiopia, Makrān, Oman, Sind, Alhind, *that is the land of India*, al-Ahwāz, and the extremity of the **climate**ᵅ of the land of Edom, *that is, ⟨the land⟩ of the Christians*. (10) {Likewise,} in its portion are orchards, and every **tree growing in a marsh,**ʸ,⁹ fountains and rivers as well as **seas or fishponds,**β,¹⁰ also places of dogs or foxes, the houses of **captives or prisoners**β,¹¹ and of **servants or slaves,**β,¹² fireplaces after the fire has been extinguished; {likewise} pastureland for **sheep or flocks,**β,¹³ and **quarries**ᵅ,¹⁴ in which nothing grows. (11) Its letters are *kaf* and *het*. (12) Its years are 27, and so are its months; the days are 307½, and the hours **4**.ᵅ,¹⁵

(13) Ascendit {autem} in eius prima facie secunda medietas ursi magni, et **ymago organizans**,[α] et caput piscis magni, atque fons aque male; {item} corpus symie, et caput eius atque caput canis. (14) {Sed} dicunt INDI[γ] quod ascendit ibi **Maurus**[α] iracundus, cuius corpus sicut **corpus pinguis**,[γ] hirsutus, dentes eius acuti et longi sicut longitudo trabis, et habet secum | aculeum armentorum, et venatur pisces. (15) **Iuxta**[γ] PTOLOMEUM {vero} ascendit medium Ursi Minoris et collum eius, atque extremitas corporis Aquile Cadentis.

9va

(16) In secunda quidem facie ascendit mulier sedens super lectum, et cum ipsa vinea, ac piscis magnus, atque biga dimidia. (17) {Sed} dicunt INDI[γ] quod ascendit ibi mulier nigra se involvens in **sclavina sive sago sive cilicio**,[β] et ipsa equum habet. (18) **Secundum**[γ] PTOLOMEUM {vero} ascendit finis Ursi Parvi, et **pars**[α] corporis Draconis, et dexter Galline ala cum collo et capite eius, et corpus Aquile Volantis, et cornua Capricorni cum **capite suo**,[α] et **femora**[γ] Sagittarii.

(19) In tertia {autem} facie ascendit cauda piscis, et extremitas **ligni aculei**;[α] {item} extremitas symie, et secunda medietas **bige sive curus**,[β] ac dimidia ymago sine capite, in manu eius est caput suum. (20) {Sed} dicunt INDI[γ] quod ibi ascendit mulier pulchra nisi quod nigra est, **parata quidem facere**[α] omnia opera sua de serito operari. (21) **Iuxta**[γ] PTOLOMEUM {vero} ascendit ibi **pars**[α] Draconis, et finis corporis Galline cum pede dextro et ala sinistra, et Piscis vocatur _Delphin_, et medium corporis Capricorni, atque cauda Piscis.

(22) Ac {vero} qui natus fuerit _in hoc signo_ erit corpus eius placidus, et statura recta, sed erit siccus, et caput eius parvum, maxile eius spisse, et barba acuta, piles non habebit in pectore, vox[1] eius subtilis, et ipse iracundus et dissipator, **callidus, ingeniosus**,[β] et lamentativus, amans **concubitus seu coitum**,[β] fornicarius, et multos generabit filios, gemini nascentur[2] ei, et operationes eius prave, fortitudo eius parva, et divitias habebit ex parte regum, et pericula patietur gravia per mulieres. (23) Et qui natus fuerit in prima facie corpus eius placidus, et pectus latum, sub cubito signum habebit nigrum, et erit homo sciens, simplex, prudens et **acceptabilis**.[γ] (24) Qui

---

[1]vox] WVG; L uxor.   [2]nascentur] WVG; L nascuntur.

(13) {But} in the first face [decan], the second half of the greater bear rises, and **the image playing a musical instrument**,[α,16] the head of a great fish, a fountain with polluted water; {likewise} the body of a monkey, whose head is the head of a dog. (14) {But} the **INDIANS**[γ] say that an irascible **Moor**[α,17] rises there; his body is like a **fat body**,[γ,18] hairy, his teeth are sharp and as long as the length of a beam, and he has a cattle prod, and catches fish. (15) {But} **according**[γ] to PTOLEMY, the middle of the Lesser Bear's [Ursa Minor] body and its neck rise there, and the end of the body of the Falling Eagle [Lyra].

(16) In the second face, a woman sitting on a bed rises, along with a vine, a large fish, and half a cart. (17) {But} the **INDIANS**[γ] say that a black woman wrapped in a *sclavina, sagum,* **and** *cilicium*[β,19] [three types of Latin cloaks] rises there, and she has a horse. (18) {But} **according to**[γ] PTOLEMY, the end of the Lesser Bear [Ursa Minor] rises there, **part**[α,20] of the Dragon's [Draco] body, the Hen's right wing with its neck and head, the body of the Falling Eagle [Lyra], the horns of ⟨the constellation⟩ Capricorn with **its head**,[α,21] and the **thighs**[γ,22] of ⟨the constellation⟩ Sagittarius.

(19) {But} in the third face the tail of a fish rises, and the end of **the wooden sting**,[α,23] {likewise} the end of the monkey, the second half of the **chariot or cart**,[β,24] and half of the figure without a head, its head is in its hand. (20) {But} the **INDIANS**[γ] say that a woman rises there who is beautiful although black, and she is **prepared to do**[α,25] every craft of working with silk. (21) {But} **according to**[γ] PTOLEMY, **part**[α,26] of the Dragon [Draco] rises there, the end of the Hen's [Cygnus] body with its right leg and its right wing, the fish called dolphin, the middle of the body of ⟨the constellation⟩ Capricorn, and the tail of the ⟨Southern⟩ Fish.

(22) {Moreover} one born *in this sign* [who has Capricorn as the ascendant of his nativity] will have a pleasant body, of erect stature; but he will be dry, with a small head, thick cheeks, a pointed beard, no hair on his chest, his voice will be thin, he will be irascible and a wastrel, **shrewd and clever**,[β,27] wailing, a lover of **lying together or sexual intercourse**,[β,28] a fornicator, and will produce many sons. Twins will be born to him, he will do evil, will have little strength, will have riches from kings, and will face serious dangers because of women. (23) One who is born in the first face [a person who has the first decan of Capricorn as the ascendant of his nativity] will have a pleasant body, a broad chest, a black mole in his armpit; he will be knowledgeable, modest, prudent, and **acceptable**.[γ,29] (24) One who is born

204 PART ONE

natus fuerit in secunda facie pulcher erit cum **naso longo**ʸ et pulchris oculis, sed desiderium eius pravum, et erit iracundus ac **sciens**.ᵅ¹ (25) Qui {vero} in tertia facie natus fuerit similiter erit pulcher corpore, facies eius crocea, signum habebit super brachium eius sinistrum² ac super **ventrem**,ʸ cito irascitivus,³ despicies malum, et amans mulieres, prudens, et **socialis seu consortia diligens**.ᵝ (26) Et qui in fine signi natus fuerit, *filius erit incantationum*.ʸ (27) Et universaliter hoc signum non est bonum in nativitate mulierum.

(28) De partibus corporis humani sunt genua, et omnes egritudines hiis accedentes. (29) De egritudinibus quidem ipsius scabies, et fricatio, et lepra, **et amissio loquele seu mutitas**,ᵝ et surditas, et **febres**,ᵅ et caligo oculorum, ac sanguis per inferiora descendens, et a .22.⁴ gradu usque ad .25 super

9vb **impedimenta**ʸ | significat oculorum. (30) De hominibus quidem in parte eius sunt agricole, et naute, et mediocres, ac pastores gregum. (31) {Item} est domus Saturni, et **exaltatio**ʸ Martis in .28. gradu, et **casus**ʸ Iovis in⁵ .15. gradu, et domus odii Lune, et est ibi Caput Draconis Mercurii in .26. gradu. (32) Domini triplicitatis in die Veneris et post eam Luna, de nocte **econtrario**,ʸ et particeps eorum die ac nocte Mars. (33) **Secundum** Egyptios **egritudo**ᵅ Saturni *in hoc signo* est in capite, Iovis in collo, Martis in genibus, Solis in ventre, Veneris in genitalibus, Mercurii *in femoribus*,ʸ et Lune in intestinis. (34) Prima facie eius secundum Egyptios et Babylonos Iovis est, secunda Martis, tertia Solis; secundum Indos prima Saturni, secunda Veneris, .3a. Mercurii. (35) Et **termini**ᵅ secundum Egyptios et **astrorum sapientes**ʸ sunt hii: Mercurii .7.,⁶ Iovis .7., Veneris .8., Saturni .4., Martis .4.; **secundum**ʸ Ptolomeum Veneris .6., Mercurii .6., **Martis .5., Iovis .8., Saturni .5**. (36) Novenariarum prima et secunda Saturni, tertia Iovis est, .4a. Martis, quinta Veneris, .6a. Mercurii, .7a. Lune, .8a. Solis, et nona Mercurii. (37) Rursus duodenariarum, prima et secunda Saturni, et tertia Iovis, quarta Martis, quinta Veneris, .6a. Mercurii, septima Lune, octava Solis, nona Mercurii, .10a Veneris, undecima Martis, .12a. Iovis.

---

[1]et erit iracundus ac sciens] LWV; G om.   [2]brachium eius sinistrum] WVG; L brachia eius sinistra.   [3]irascitivus] G irascens.   [4]et a .22.] WVG; L et inter secundo.   [5]in] WVG; L om.   [6].7.] WVG; L 6.

LIBER ABRAHE AVENERRE INTRODUCTORIUS AD ASTRONOMIAM 205

in the second face will have a handsome body, **long nose**,[γ,30] beautiful eyes, but his desires ⟨will be⟩ evil, will be irascible and **knowledgeable**.[α,31] (25) {Moreover} one who is born in the third face [decan] will similarly have a handsome body, his face will be saffron; he will have a mole on his left arm and on his **abdomen**,[γ,32] he will be quick to anger, despise evil, a lover of women, prudent, and **sociable or loving company**.[β,33] (26) One who is born in the end of the sign will be the *son of a spell*.[γ,34] (27) In general, this sign is not good in the nativity of women.

(28) Of the parts of the human body, ⟨in its portion⟩ are the knees and any disease affecting them. (29) Of diseases, roughness of the skin is in its portion, and pruritus, leprosy, **loss of speech or dumbness**,[β,35] deafness, **fever**,[α,36] dimness of the eyes, and rectal hemorrhage; and from 22° to 25°, it indicates **defects**[γ] to the eyes. (30) Of human beings, in its portion are farmers, sailors, middle-class people, and shepherds of flocks. (31) {Likewise,} it [Capricorn] is the house of Saturn, the **exaltation**[γ,37] of Mars is at ⟨Capricorn⟩ 28°, the **fall**[γ,38] [dejection] of Jupiter at ⟨Capricorn⟩ 15°, the Moon's house of hate [detriment], and there [in Capricorn] is Mercury's Head of the Dragon at ⟨Capricorn⟩ 26°. (32) The lords of the triplicity are Venus and then the Moon by day, and by night **the opposite**;[γ,39] Mars is their partner by day and by night. (33) **According to the EGYPTIANS**,[γ] the **disease**[α,40] of Saturn *in this sign* [Capricorn] is in the head; of Jupiter, in the neck; of Mars, in the knees; of the Sun, in the abdomen; of Venus, in the genitals; of Mercury, in the *thighs*;[γ,41] of the Moon, in the intestines. (34) The first face [decan], according to the EGYPTIANS and BABYLONIANS, ⟨is assigned⟩ to Jupiter, the second to Mars, and the third to the Sun; according to the INDIANS, the first ⟨face is assigned⟩ to Saturn, the second to Venus, and the third to Mercury. (35) These are the **terms**[α,42] **according to**[γ] the EGYPTIANS and the **SCHOLARS OF THE STARS**:[γ] Mercury 7°, Jupiter 7°, Venus 8°, Saturn 4°, and Mars 4°; **according to**[γ] PTOLEMY: Venus 6°, Mercury 6°, **Mars 5°, Jupiter 8°**, Saturn 5°.[γ,43] (36) Of the *novenariae* [ninth-parts], the first and the second ⟨are assigned⟩ to Saturn, the third to Jupiter, the fourth to Mars, the fifth to Venus, the sixth to Mercury, the seventh to the Moon, the eighth to the Sun, and the ninth to Mercury. (37) In addition, of the *duodenariae* [twelfths], the first and the second ⟨are assigned⟩ to Saturn, the third to Jupiter, the fourth to Mars, the fifth to Venus, the sixth to Mercury, the seventh to the Moon, the eighth to the Sun, the ninth to Mercury, the tenth to Venus, the eleventh to Mars, and the twelfth to Jupiter.

(38) {Item} a principio signi usque in finem .7. gradus sunt mixti, deinde tres lucidi, postea .5. **tenebrosi seu caliginosi**,[β,1] deinde .4. lucidi, postea .2. mixti, postea .4.[2] vacui, et demum .5. lucidi. (39) {Item} a principio signi usque ad finem .11. gradus masculini, deinde .8. feminini, et postea .11. masculini. (40) Putei {vero} stellarum sunt gradus .2us, .17., .22us. .24us, .28. (41) Et gradus **fortunam**[γ] augentes et honorem .13. et .14us. et .20us.

(42) {Insuper,} de *stellis fixis*,[γ] est ibi Aquila Cadens in gradu .3., et latitudo septentrionalis .62. gradus ⟨⟨...⟩⟩,[μ] et est primi honoris, de complexione Veneris et Mercurii. (43) {Item,} est ibi **Aquila Volans**[π] in .19. gradu, cuius latitudo septentrionalis .29. gradus .10. minuta ⟨⟨...⟩⟩,[ν] et est honoris secundi, de natura Iovis. (44) {Item} sunt ibi **de stellis caliginosis**[γ] a .7. gradu usque ad .13.

11 (1) Aquarius signum est aereum, masculinum, **diurnum**,[γ] ⟨⟨...⟩⟩.[μ] (2) ⟨⟨...⟩⟩.[μ] (3) ⟨⟨...⟩⟩.[μ] (4) Et natura eius est calida et humida, corrumpens, et significat super omnem aerem animalia corrumpentem, et super omnem ventum destruentem et constringentem. (5) Principium eius satis humidum est, et medium mixtum, et finis eius ventos generat. (6) Et quando septentrionale est generat nives, et quando meridionale generat nubes.[3] (7) In figura est hominis **simplus seu per se**.[β] (8) Et in parte eius est **sinistra sive septentrionalis**[β] pars occidentis, similiter ventus de mari veniens, (9) {Item} in parte ipsius est sanguis; et sapor eius dulcis est; {similiter} et color viridis et croceus ac pulvereus. (10) {Item} in parte eius est homo et

10ra **principes excellentes scilicet**[4] **in | scientia, seu duces populi**,[αβ] et omnis homo **turpis seu deformis**.[β] (11) De **climatibus**,[α] in parte sua secundum, et terra Etyopum et Alcupa et Alhaiaue et Alkeno. (12) {Item} **aque currentes seu flumina**,[β] et maria in parte eius sunt, adhuc et loca vitrorum, ad bibendum ac loca in quibus vinum venditur, et loca terre que in montibus, et **loca paludosa**,[γ] necnon **lenonum seu scortorum**[β] habitacula, {item} in parte sua sunt **urne seu vasa** omnia quibus aqua trahitur. (13) Et littere eius sunt *lames* et *dales*. (14) Anni eius .30., et menses totidem, dies .75., et hore .6.

---

[1]seu caliginosi] WV; LG om.   [2]postea .2. mixti, postea .4.] WVG; L om.   [3]et quando meridionale generat nubes] WVG; L om.   [4]scilicet] LWV; G om.

(38) {Likewise,} from the beginning of the sign to the end of seven degrees, ⟨the degrees are⟩ mixed, then ⟨come⟩ three bright ⟨degrees⟩, then five **tenebrous or dark**^β ⟨degrees⟩, then four bright ⟨degrees⟩, then two mixed ⟨degrees⟩, then four empty ⟨degrees⟩, and finally five bright ⟨degrees⟩. (39) {Likewise,} from the beginning of the sign to the end of eleven degrees ⟨the degrees are⟩ masculine, then ⟨come⟩ eight feminine ⟨degrees⟩, and then eleven masculine ⟨degrees⟩. (40) {Moreover} the pits of the stars are the 2nd, 17th, 22nd, 24th, and 28th degrees. (41) The degrees adding **fortune**^γ and honor: the 13th, 14th, and 20th degrees.

(42) {Besides,} of the *fixed stars*^{γ,44} the Falling Eagle is there at ⟨longitude Capricorn⟩ 3° ⟨⟨at the present time⟩⟩,^{μ,45} northern latitude 62°, of the first honor [magnitude], of the mixture of Venus and Mercury. (43) {Likewise,} the **Flying Eagle**,^{π,46} at ⟨longitude Capricorn⟩ 19° ⟨⟨at the present time⟩⟩,^ν its latitude is northern 29° 10′, of the second honor, of the nature of Jupiter. (44) {Likewise,} there are **dark stars**^{γ,47} there from 7° to 13°.

11 (1) Aquarius is an airy sign, masculine, **diurnal**,^γ ⟨⟨western⟩⟩.^{μ,1} (2) ⟨⟨[It is] one of the signs of winter, and it remains in the same pattern.⟩⟩.^{μ,2} (3) ⟨⟨Its hours are shorter than the straight ⟨hours⟩ and its ascensions are crooked and short⟩⟩.^{μ,3} (4) Its nature is hot, moist and corrupting, it indicates any air that destroys life and any wind that destroys and constrains. (5) Its beginning is very moist, its middle mixed, and in its end it generates winds. (6) When northern it generates snow and when southern it generates clouds. (7) It [Aquarius] has the form of a human being **alone or by himself**.^{β,4} (8) The **left or northern**^{β,5} side of the west is in its portion, similarly the wind coming from the sea. (9) {Likewise} the blood is in its portion; its taste is sweet; {similarly} ⟨its⟩ color is green, saffron and ⟨the color⟩ of dust. (10) {Likewise,} human beings are in its portion, and **outstanding princes, namely in knowledge, or leaders of the people**,^{αβ,6} and any **ugly or deformed**^{β,7} person. (11) Of the **climates**,^α the second is in its portion, and Ethiopia, al-Kūfa, the Hejaz and the land of the Copts. (12) {Likewise,} **flowing waters or rivers**^{β,8} and the seas are in its portion, in addition the places of glasses, places for drinking or places where wine is sold, mountainous places on Earth, **marshy places**,^{γ,9} and the abodes of **bawds or prostitutes**;^{β,10} {likewise,} any **urn or vessel**^{β,11} for drawing water is in its portion. (13) Its letters are *lamed* and *dalet*. (14) Its years are 30, and so are its months; the days are 75, and the hours six.

(15) Ascendit {autem} in prima facie eius caput illius qui in manu tenet equum, et avis nigrum habens caput que pisces venatur. (16) Sed **Indi**ᵞ aiunt quod ascendit ibi **Maurus**ᵅ qui artifex est in ere *seu ioculator*. (17) Iuxtaᵞ Ptolomeum ascendit extremitas caude Ursi Maioris, et pes Galline, et caput Equi Prioris, ac posteriora Capricorni cum **cauda**ᵅ eius.

(18) Et in secunda facie ascendit corpus equi, et ala illius avis que pisces capit. (19) {Sed} **Indi**ᵞ aiunt quod ibi ascendit **Maurus**ᵅ valde niger, cuius barba prolixa, et in manu eius arcus et sagitte ac **pannus,**ᵅ in quo lapide preciosi et aurum. (20) Secundumᵞ Ptolomeum ascendit ibi cauda Ursi Maioris, et corpus Equi Secundi cum capite suo; {item} principium Urne, et medium ventris Piscis Meridiani.

(21) In tertia facie ascendit gallina, et posteriora eius qui equum in manu tenet, et extremitas **mergi seu avis**ᵝ pisces capientis.¹ (22) {Sed} dicunt **Indi**ᵞ quod ascendit ibi **Maurus,**ᵅ iracundus, **fallax seu deceptor,**ᵝ pilosus in auribus, et super ipsum corona de foliis arborum, et **mutat seu vertit se**ᵝ de loco ad locum. (23) Iuxtaᵞ Ptolomeum ascendit ibi cauda Ursi Minoris, corpus Equi, et extremitas **Situle seu Urne,**ᵝ,² atque caput Piscis Meridiani.

(24) Qui {igitur} natus fuerit ex hominibus *in hoc signo*, erit stature brevis cum magno capite, et una eius tybia grossior altera, liberalis corde, et pulcher in figura, ac iactans in se ipso, totus appetitus eius est congregare divitias, et ipse sterilis erit aut pauca habebit prolem. (25) {Sed}³ qui in prima facie natus fuerit, pulcher erit corpore et facie, signum habebit in pectore aut in pede sinistro, et ipse **vir disciplinatus,**ᵅ societatem diligens. (26) Qui natus fuerit in secunda facie, longus erit, et facies eius rubicunda, signum habebit super dorsum et sub cubito, et omnibus diebus suis **tristis erit seu in lamentis.**ᵝ (27) Qui {vero} natus fuerit in tertia facie, brevis erit stature, pulcher corpore et facie, rubicundus, signum | habebit sub cubitis, et mulieres amabit. (28) {Sed} qui in fine signum natus fuerit, extraneus erit in figura et in omnibus factis suis.

---

¹pisces capientis] G qui pisces capit. ²seu urne] G om. ³sed] LG; WV om.

(15) {But} in the first face [decan], the head of one holding a horse in his hand rises, a bird with a black head that catches fish. (16) The **INDIANS**[γ] say that a **Moor**[α,12] who is a coppersmith *or a jester* rises there. (17) **According to**[γ] PTOLEMY, the end of the Lesser Bear's [Ursa Minor] tail rises there, the Hen's [Cygnus] foot, the head of the First Horse [Equuleus], and the backside of ⟨the constellation⟩ Capricorn and its **tail**.[α]

(18) In the second face, the body of the horse rises, and the wing of the bird that catches fish. (19) {But} the **INDIANS**[γ] say that a very black **Moor**,[α] rises there; his beard is long; in his hand he holds a bow, arrows, and a **piece of cloth**,[α,13] containing precious stones and gold. (20) **According to**[γ] PTOLEMY, the tail of the Lesser Bear [Ursa Minor] rises there, the body and head of the Second Horse [Pegasus]; likewise the beginning of the Urn [Aquarius], and the middle of the belly of the Southern Fish [Piscis Austrinus].

(21) In the third face, the hen rises, and the backside ⟨of the man⟩ who holds a horse in his hand, and the end of **the diver [water-bird] or bird**[β,14] that catches fish. (22) {But} the **INDIANS**[γ] say that a **Moor**[α] rises there, irascible, **a liar or deceiver**;[β,15] he has hair in his ears, wears a crown of tree leaves, and **moves or turns himself**[β,16] from place to place. (23) **According to**[γ] PTOLEMY, the tail of the Lesser Bear [Ursa Minor] rises there, the body of the Horse [Aquarius], the end of **the Bucket or the Urn**[β,17] [Aquarius], and the head of the Southern Fish [Piscis Austrinus].

(24) A person born *in this sign* [who has Aquarius as the ascendant of his nativity], {then,} will be short of stature with a large head, one of his shanks will be thicker than the other, generous, handsome in ⟨his⟩ form, he praises himself, his only desire is to accumulate riches, and he will be barren or will have few children. (25) {But} one who is born in the first face [a person who has the first decan of Aquarius as the ascendant of his nativity] will have a handsome body and face and a mole on his chest and left foot; he ⟨will be⟩ **learned**,[α] companionable. (26) One who is born in the second face will be tall, ruddy-faced, with a mole on his back and in his armpit, and will always be **sad or mourning**.[β,18] (27) {Moreover} one who is born in the third face will be short, with a handsome body and face, ruddy, with a mole in his armpit, and will love women. (28) {But} one who is born in the end of the sign will be strange in his form and in all his undertakings.

210   PART ONE

(29) In parte eius sunt, ex hominibus, despecti, et **tristes seu lamentabiles**;[^β] {item} naute, et **cerdones preparatores coriorum**.[^β] (30) De partibus {autem} humani corporis[1] eius sunt tybie et omnes egritudines eis accedentes; {item} melancolia nigra, et ictericia nigra, ac venarum incisio, et a viginta gradibus usque ad .25. significat super oculorum **impedimenta**.[^γ] (31) Domus {autem} est Saturni, Solis *quoque* domus odii, sed in eo non est **exaltatio seu honor**[^β] nec **casus**[^γ] **planete**[^α] alicuius, {nisi quod} **oppositum augis**[^γ] Martis ibi est in .12. gradu ad hoc tempus. (32) **Secundum**[^γ] EGYPTIOS, in ipso est **egritudo**[^α] Saturni in collo, Iovis in manibus, Martis in tybiis, Solis in intestinis, Veneris in genibus, Mercurii in femoribus, et Lune **in genitalibus seu pudendis**.[^β] (33) Triplicitatis {autem} domini in die Saturnus primo deinde Mercurius, et nocte **econtrario**,[^γ] particeps in die et nocte Iupiter. (34) Facies prima **secundum**[^γ] EGYPTIOS et BABYLONIOS Veneris, et secunda Mercurii, tertia Lune; **secundum INDOS**[^γ] prima Saturni, secunda Mercurii, tertia Veneris. (35) Itaque **termini**[^α] **secundum**[^γ] EGYPTIOS et **SAPIENTES ASTRORUM**:[^γ] Mercurii .7. gradus, Veneris .6., Iovis .7., Martis .5., Saturni .5.; **secundum**[^γ] PTOLOMEUM: Saturni .6., Mercurii .6., Veneris .8., Iovis .5., Martis .5. (36) Novenariarum {autem} prima Veneris est, .2a. Martis, .3a. Iovis, .4a. et .5a. Saturni, sexta Iovis, .7a. Martis, .8a. Veneris, et nona Mercurii. (37) Duodenariarum Saturni prima est, .2a. Iovis, .3a. Martis, quarta Veneris, quinta Mercurii, sexta Lune, .7a. Solis, .8a. Mercurii, nona Veneris, decima Martis, undecima Iovis, .12. Saturni.

(38) Et a principio signi usque ad finem .4. gradus sunt obscuri, deinde .5. lucidi, postea .4. mixta, ⟨⟨...⟩⟩,[^μ] deinde .4. vacui, demum .5. lucidi. (39) {Item} a principio signi usque ad finem .5. sunt gradus masculini, deinde .7. feminini, postea .6. masculini, deinde .7. feminini, demum .5. masculini. (40) **Putealitas** {autem} **stellarum**[^γ] est in primo gradu et .12. et[2] .17., .22., .29. (41) Gradus **fortunam**[^γ] augmentantes .7us. est, et .16us, .17., et .20.

---

[1]corporis] WVG; L om.   [2]Putealitas autem stellarum est in primo gradu et .12. et] WGV; L Putei stellarum sunt .lus. gradus.

(29) In its portion, of human beings, contemptible persons, **sad people of full of sorrow**;[β,19] {likewise,} sailors, and **leatherworkers or those who prepare skins of animals.**[β,20,21] (30) {But} of the parts of the human body, in its portion are the shanks, and all the diseases affecting them; {likewise,} the black bile, black jaundice, and the cutting of veins; and ⟨in a nativity whose ascendant is Aquarius⟩ from 20° to 25°, it indicates **defects**[γ] to the eyes.[22] (31) {But} it [Aquarius] is the house of Saturn, *also* the Sun's house of hate [detriment]; no **planet**[α,23] has its **exaltation or honor**[β,24] or **fall**[γ,25] [dejection] in it [Aquarius]; {but} **the opposite of the apogee**[γ,26] [perigee] of Mars is at ⟨Aquarius⟩ 12° at the present time. (32) **According to**[γ] the EGYPTIANS, the **disease**[α,27] of Saturn ⟨in Aquarius⟩ is in the neck; of Jupiter, in the hands; of Mars, in the shanks; of the Sun, in the intestines; of Venus, in the knees; of Mercury, in the thighs; of the Moon, in **the genitals or the pudenda.**[β,28] (33) {But} the lords of the triplicity are Saturn and then Mercury by day, and by night **the opposite**;[γ,29] Jupiter is their partner by day and by night. (34) The first face [decan], **according to**[γ] the EGYPTIANS and BABYLONIANS, ⟨is assigned⟩ to Venus, the second to Mercury, and the third to the Moon; and **according to the INDIANS,**[γ] the first ⟨face is assigned⟩ to Saturn, the second to Mercury, and the third to Venus. (35) These are the **terms**[α,30] **according to**[γ] the EGYPTIANS and the **SCHOLARS OF THE STARS:**[γ] Mercury 7°, Venus 6°, Jupiter 7°, Mars 5°, and Saturn 5°; and **according to**[γ] PTOLEMY: Saturn 6°, Mercury 6°, Venus 8°, Jupiter 5°, and Mars 5°. (36) {But,} of the *novenariae* [ninth-parts], the first ⟨is assigned⟩ to Venus, the second to Mars, the third to Jupiter, the fourth and the fifth to Saturn, the sixth to Jupiter, the seventh to Mars, the eighth to Venus, and the ninth to Mercury. (37) Of the *duodenariae* [twelfths], the first ⟨is assigned⟩ to Saturn, the second to Jupiter, the third to Mars, the fourth to Venus, the fifth to Mercury, the sixth to the Moon, the seventh to the Sun, the eighth to Mercury, the ninth to Venus, the tenth to Mars, the eleventh to Jupiter, and the twelfth to Saturn.

(38) From the beginning of the sign to the end of four degrees ⟨the degrees are⟩ dark, then ⟨come⟩ five bright ⟨degrees⟩, then four mixed ⟨degrees⟩, ⟨⟨then eight bright degrees⟩⟩,[μ,31] then four empty ⟨degrees⟩, and finally five bright ⟨degrees⟩. (39) {Likewise,} from the beginning of the sign to the end of five degrees, ⟨the degrees are⟩ masculine, then ⟨come⟩ seven feminine ⟨degrees⟩, then six masculine ⟨degrees⟩, then seven feminine ⟨degrees⟩, and finally five masculine ⟨degrees⟩. (40) {But} **what pertains to the pits of the stars**[γ] is at the 1st, 12th, 17th, 22nd, and 29th degrees. (41) The degrees adding **fortune**[γ] and honor: the 7th, 16th, 17th, and 20th degrees.

212   PART ONE

(42) De *stellis fixis*⁷ est ibi Os Piscis Meridiani in .23. gradu ⟨⟨...⟩⟩,ᵛ et eius latitudo meridiana in .23. gradu est; {autem} honoris primi, de complexione Veneris et Mercurii. (43) {Item} est ibi alia stella vocata <u>Alradif</u>, in **cauda**ᵅ scilicet Galline, et est in .25. gradu ⟨⟨...⟩⟩,ᵛ latitudinis quidem septentrionalis .60. gradus, et est honoris secundi, de complexione Veneris et Mercurii. (44) {Insuper} sunt ibi .4. stelle caliginose in capite equi, et sunt inter .12. gradus ⟨⟨...⟩⟩.ᵘ

12 (1) Pisces signum aqueum, femininum, **nocturnum**,⁷ **septentrionale**.⁷ (2) De signis frigiditatis, duum corporum, et in fine eius equatur dies et nox. (3) Et hore eius breviores **equalibus**,⁷ et ipsum **obliquum**⁷ est in ascensioni-
10va **bus**ᵅ suis, que et | breves sunt. (4) Membra eius secta; et generat frigiditatem et humiditatem animalia corrumpentes ac vegetabilia; significat {autem} omnem aquam fetidam. (5) Et universaliter ventos **generat**,⁷ {sed} principium eius mixtum est, medium frigidum, **finis** {vero} **extremum**ᵝ calidum aliquantulum. (6) **Quod**⁷ ipsius septentrionale est ventos generat, **quod**⁷ {vero} meridionale aquas (7) Est in figura piscium. (8) Et in parte eius dextra pars **septentrionalis**,ᵅ ac ventus septentrionalis, qui inter **sinistram seu inter septentrionem**ᵝ et orienem est.[1] (9) Natura eius frigida et humida, generans malum flegma in corpore humano. (10) Sapor eius salsus et insipidus; color {vero} viridis et albus, atque color extraneus. (11) De animalibus eius sunt aquatilia, et omne vegetabile *aquatile*, et crystallus, et corallus, et lapides onychini. [onyx stones] (12) De **regionibus quidem et climatibus**,ᵝ,[2] **clima**ᵅ secundum, et terra Steva et Tabustaan, ac terra que **a sinistris est seu versus septentrionem**ᵝ e terra Gaan; {item} particeps est in terra Edom ac in terra Alexandrie. (13) {Item} in parte ipsius sunt **domus orationum et synagoge**ᵝ et ripe fluminum omnium, ac paludes. (14) Et littere eius sunt <u>mem</u> et <u>fazi</u>. (15) Anni eius .12., et menses totidem, dies .30., et hore .12. (16) Signum quidem est mutuum et multe proles generativum.

(17) Ascendit {autem} in prima eius facie dimidius equus habens alas duas, item principium fluminis, et cauda piscis vocati <u>altamesaich</u>. (18) {Sed} dicunt Indi⁷ quod ibi ascendit homo indutus vestibus cupiditis, in cuius manu instrumentum ferreum, et ipse domum sua ingreditur. (19) **Secundum**⁷ Ptolomeum ascendit ibi **pars**ᵅ caude Ursi Minoris, ⟨⟨...⟩⟩ᵘ ac **prima pars** Piscis Prioris.

---

[1] qui inter sinistram seu inter septentrionem et orienem est] WVG; L qui inter sinistram seu inter septentrionem est oriens.   [2] quidem et climatibus] W; LGV om.

LIBER ABRAHE AVENERRE INTRODUCTORIUS AD ASTRONOMIAM   213

(42) Of the *fixed stars*^γ,32 the Mouth of the Southern Fish is there at ⟨longitude Aquarius⟩ 23° ⟨⟨at the present time⟩⟩,^ν southern ⟨ecliptical⟩ latitude 20° 20'; {but} of the first honor [magnitude], of the mixture of Venus and Mercury. (43) {Likewise,} another star there is called *al-ridf*, in the **tail**^α of the Hen, at ⟨longitude Aquarius⟩ 25° ⟨⟨at the present time⟩⟩,^ν northern latitude 60°, of the second honor, of the mixture of Venus and Mercury. (44) {In addition,} four dark stars are there, in the Horse's Head, from 12° ⟨⟨to 14°⟩⟩.^μ

12 (1) Pisces is a watery sign, feminine, **nocturnal,**^γ **northern.**^γ (2) ⟨It is⟩ of the cold signs, of two bodies; at its end day and night are equal. (3) Its hours are shorter than the **equal**^γ ⟨hours⟩, and it is **oblique**^γ in its **ascensions,**^α which are short. (4) Its limbs are cut off; and it generates cold and moistness that corrupt living creatures and plants; {and} indicates any fetid water. (5) As a rule **it generates**^γ,1 winds; but its beginning is mixed, its middle cold, **its end or final part**^β,2 is {indeed} somewhat warm. (6) **What is**^γ in its portion and is northern generates winds, {but} **what is**^γ ⟨in its portion and is⟩ southern, ⟨generates⟩ water. (7) It has the form of a fish. (8) The right part **of the north**^α,3 is in its portion, and the north wind, which is between **the left or the north**^β,4 and the east. (9) Its nature is cold and moist, and it generates the bad phlegm in the human body. (10) Its taste is salty and insipid; {moreover} ⟨its⟩ color green and white, and a strange color. (11) Of the animals, aquatic animals are in its portion, and every *aquatic* plant, and crystal, corals, and onyx stones. (12) Of the **regions and climates,**^β5 the second **climate,**^α and the land of Sheba, Ṭabaristān, the country that is **to the left or to the north**^β of the land of Ğurğān; {likewise,} it has a share in the land of Edom and in the land of Alexandria. (13) {Likewise,} **houses of prayer or synagogues**^β,6 are in its portion, the banks of all rivers, and marshes. (14) Its letters are *mem* and *sadi*. (15) Its years are 12, and so are its months; the days are 30, and the hours 12. (16) It is a mute sign and generative of many children.

(17) {But} in the first face [decan], half of a horse with two wings rises, the beginning of the river, and the tail of the fish called *altamesaich* [crocodile]. (18) {But} the **INDIANS**^γ say that in the first face, a man wearing fine clothes rises, with an iron tool in his hand, and he is going home. (19) **According to**^γ PTOLEMY, **part**^α,7 of the Lesser Bear's [Ursa Minor] tail rises there, ⟨⟨the belly of the Second Horse⟩⟩^μ,8 [Pegasus], and **the first part**^γ,9 of the first Fish.

(20) Et in secunda facie ascendit medietas fluminis, et secunda medietas illius qui super genua sua vadet. (21) {Sed} dicunt INDI[γ] quod ibi ascendit mulier alba ⟨⟨...⟩⟩[μ] in navi sedens in mari, et vult exire in siccum. (22) Iuxta[γ] PTOLOMEUM ascendit ibi cauda Ursi Minoris, et manus super Sedem Sedentis, ac humerus Mulieris que Numquam Maritum Habuit, et caput equo se adiungentis, ac posteriora Piscis Primi.

(23) In facie {autem} tertia ascendit extremitas fluminis, atque extremitas vocatis <u>altamessaih</u>, et residuum euntis super genua. (24) {Sed} dicunt INDI[γ] quod ibi ascendit homo nudus, pedem ponens super ventrem suum, in manu eius lancea, et ipse **vociferans seu clamans**[β,1] pro timore **spoliatorum seu latronum**,[β] et ignis. (25) **Secundum**[γ] PTOLOMEUM {vero} ascendit ibi;[2] {vero} extremitas caude Ursi Minoris, et medium dorsi super Sedem Sedentis, ac pectus Mulieris qui Numquam Maritum Habuit, et pars Fili Linei, ac posteriora Serpentis.

10vb (26) {Igitur} qui natus fuerit *in hoc signo*, erit corpus eius **rectum et temperatum**,[β] **color eius albus ac etiam**[3] **facies**,[α] pectus latum, barba pulchra, | frons candida, oculi eius magis nigri quam albi; de hiis {autem} erit aliquis cui deficit membrum, somnum[4] amat et gulositatem et ebrietatem, ⟨⟨...⟩⟩[μ] (27) ⟨⟨...⟩⟩[μ] et habebit signum sub cubito vel in pede. (28) Qui {autem} natus fuerit in facie secunda brevis erit stature, pulcher **aspectu sive colore**,[β] barba nigra, et ipse pilosus, signum habebit sub cubito, et discolus erit cum omnibus. (29) Qui {vero} natus fuerit in tertia facie, **candidus erit sive nitidus**,[αβ] oculi eius pulchri, et erit morbidus. (30) Et qui natus fuerit in fine signi, **sui ipsius occisor erit vel seipsum occidet**.[β]

(31) De partibus {autem} humani corporis pedes sunt eius et articuli pedum, et omnes egritudines eius accidentes. (32) Facit {quoque} nasci egritudines paralysis, scabiei et lepre, et universaliter signum morbosum est. (33) De hominibus in parte eius sunt **viles seu despecti**[β] et piscatores.

---

[1]seu clamans] G om. [2]ascendit ibi] WVG; L om. [3]ac etiam] WGV; L et. [4]somnum] WVG; L < aliquo.

(20) In the second face, half of the river rises, and the second half of the one crawling on his knees. (21) {But} the **INDIANS**[γ] say that a ⟨⟨beautiful⟩⟩[μ,10] white woman rises there; she is sitting in a ship at sea, and wants to disembark on land. (22) **According to**[γ] PTOLEMY, the tail of the Lesser Bear [Ursa Minor] rises there, the hand of the ⟨Woman⟩ Sitting on a Chair [Cassiopeia], the shoulder of the Woman who never had a Husband [Andromeda], the head ⟨of the woman⟩ who is together with the Horse [Pegasus], and the backside of the First Fish.

(23) {But} in the third face, the end of the river rises, the end of the fish called *altamessaih* [crocodile], and the reminder of the one crawling on his knees. (24) {But} the **INDIANS**[γ] say that a naked man rises there, he puts his leg on his abdomen, he holds a lance in his hand, he is **shouting or crying**[β,11] aloud because he is afraid of **robbers or thieves**,[β,12] and of fire. (25) {But} **according to**[γ] PTOLEMY, the end of the tail of the Lesser Bear [Ursa Minor] rises there; {moreover} the middle of the back of the ⟨Woman⟩ Sitting on a Chair [Cassiopeia], the breast of the Woman who never had a Husband [Andromeda], a part of the Flaxen Thread [the cord that binds the two fishes of Pisces], and the rear of the Serpent [Cetus].

(26) One born *in this sign* [who has Pisces as the ascendant of his nativity], {then,} his body will be **straight and temperate**,[β,13] **his color white as well as ⟨his⟩ face**,[α,14] ⟨his⟩ chest broad; ⟨his⟩ beard will be handsome, ⟨his⟩ forehead shining; his eyes more black than white; {but} some of them [natives in Pisces] will be missing a limb; he loves sleeping, gluttony and drunkenness; ⟨⟨his mind will not be at ease, he will be irascible, moral and deceitful, and his voice will be thin⟩⟩.[μ,15] (27) ⟨⟨One who is born in the first face will have a handsome body and face, his chest will be broad⟩⟩[μ,16] he will have a mole in his armpit or on his foot. (28) {But} one who is born in the second face will be short of stature, handsome **in appearance or color**,[β,17] with a black beard and hairy; he will have a mole in his armpit, and be irritable with everyone. (29) {Moreover} one who is born in the third face will be **shining or radiant**,[αβ,18] his eyes beautiful, and suffer many diseases. (30) One who is born in the end of the sign will be **the killer of himself or will kill himself**.[β,19]

(31) {But} of the parts of the human body, in its portion are the feet and toes, and all the diseases affecting them. (32) It [Pisces] {also} causes the diseases of paralysis, roughness of the skin, and leprosy; and, in general, it is one of the signs of disease. (33) Of human beings, **base and contemptible**

(34) **Secundum**ʸ Egyptios quidem in ipso est **egritudo**ᵅ Saturni in manibus, Iovis in ventre superiori, Martis in pedibus, Solis in pudendis, Veneris in tybiis, Mercurii in genibus, Lune in **intestinis**.ʸ (35) Et est domus Iovis et[1] **exaltatio**ʸ Veneris in .27. gradu, **dedecus**[2] **sive casus**ᵝ Mercurii in .15. gradu, **odii eiusdem**,ʸ et **humiliatio**ʸ Iovis in .23. gradu in hoc tempore, **Caput Draconis seu *genzaar*ᵝ Veneris in .26. gradu**ᵖ ad hoc tempus. (36) Triplicitatis domini de die Venus et post ipsam Mars, sed nocte econverso, particeps die et nocte Luna. (37) Facies prima, **secundum**ʸ Egyptios et Babylonios, Saturni est, secunda Iovis, tertia Martis; {sed} **secundum Indos**ʸ prima Iovis, **secunda similiter**ʸ,[3] et tertia Martis. (38) **Termini**ᵅ secundum Egyptios et **sapientes in astris**ʸ sunt hii: Veneris .12., Iovis .4., Mercurii .3., Martis .9., Saturni .2.; **secundum**ʸ Ptolomeum, Veneris .8., Iovis .6., Mercurii sex, Martis .5., et Saturni .5. (39) Novenariarum prima Lune, secunda Solis, tertia Mercurii, quarta Veneris, quinta Martis, sexta Iovis, septima et .8a. Saturni, .9a. Iovis. (40) Duodenariarum prima Iovis, secunda Martis, .3a. Veneris, .4a. Mercurii, .5a. Lune, .6a. Solis, .7a. Mercurii, .8a. Veneris, .9a. Martis, .10a. Iovis, undecima et .12a Saturni.

(41) A principio signi usque ad finem .6. gradus sunt lucidi, deinde .6. mixti, postea .4. lucidi, denique .3. vacui, ⟨⟨...⟩⟩ᵘ demum .2. mixti. (42) {Item} a principio usque ad finem .10. gradus sunt masculini, deinde .10 feminini, postea .3. masculini, deinde .3. feminini, et demum .2.[4] masculini. (43) **Putealitas stellarum**ʸ in .4. gradu, .9.,[5] .24., .27. et .28. (44) Gradus **fortunam**ʸ augmentantes et honorem[6] sunt .18us. et .20us.

(45) Et ibi de *stellis fixis*ʸ Humerus Equi in gradu .18. ad hoc tempus, latitudo eius septentrionalis .31.gradus, et est honoris secundi, de complexione Martis et Mercurii.

---

[1]et] G; W om.; L seu.   [2]dedecus] G om.   [3]similiter] G Saturni.   [4].2.] GV; LW .4.   [5].9.] WVG; L om.   [6]et honorem] WVG; L om.

people[β,20] and fishermen are in its portion.(34) **According to the**[γ] EGYPTIANS, the **disease**[α,21] of Saturn in it [Pisces] is in the hands; of Jupiter, in the upper abdomen; of Mars, in the legs; of the Sun, in the pudenda; of Venus, in the shanks; of Mercury, in the knees; of the Moon, in the **intestines.**[γ,22] (35) It [Pisces] is the house of Jupiter, and the **exaltation**[γ,23] of Venus at ⟨Pisces⟩ 27°, **the shame or fall**[β,24] [the dejection, the opposite of the exaltation] of Mercury at ⟨Pisces⟩ 15°, and **its hate**[γ,25] [Mercury's detriment], and Jupiter's **humiliation**[γ,26] [perigee] at ⟨Pisces⟩ 23° at this time, **and Venus's Head of the Dragon or** *jawzahar*[β,27] **at** ⟨**Pisces**⟩ **26°**[π,28] at the present time. (36) The lords of the triplicity are Venus and then Mars, and the opposite by night; the Moon is their partner by day and by night. (37) The first face [decan], **according to**[γ] the EGYPTIANS and BABYLONIANS, ⟨is assigned⟩ to Saturn, the second to Jupiter, and the third to Mars; {but} **according to**[γ] the INDIANS, the first ⟨face is assigned⟩ to Jupiter, **similarly the second,**[γ,29] and the third to Mars. (38) These are the **terms**[α,30] of the EGYPTIANS and the **SCHOLARS IN RELATION TO THE STARS:**[γ,31] Venus 12°, Jupiter 4°, Mercury 3°, Mars 9°, and Saturn 2°; and **according to**[γ] PTOLEMY: Venus 8°, Jupiter 6°, Mercury six, Mars 5°, and Saturn 5°. (39) Of the *novenariae* [ninth-parts], the first ⟨is assigned⟩ to the Moon, the second to the Sun, the third to Mercury, the fourth to Venus, the fifth to Mars, the sixth to Jupiter, the seventh and the eighth to Saturn, and the ninth to Jupiter. (40) Of the *duodenariae* [twelfths], the first ⟨is assigned⟩ to Jupiter, the second to Mars, the third to Venus, the fourth to Mercury, the fifth to the Moon, the sixth to the Sun, the seventh to Mercury, the eighth to Venus, the ninth to Mars, the tenth to Jupiter, the eleventh and the twelfth to Saturn.

(41) From the beginning of the sign to the end of six degrees ⟨the degrees are⟩ bright, then ⟨come⟩ six mixed ⟨degrees⟩, then four bright ⟨degrees⟩, then three empty ⟨degrees⟩, ⟨⟨then three bright ⟨degrees⟩,⟩⟩[μ] and finally two mixed ⟨degrees⟩. (42) {Likewise,} from the beginning of the sign to the end of ten degrees ⟨the degrees are⟩ masculine, then ⟨come⟩ ten feminine ⟨degrees⟩, then three masculine ⟨degrees⟩, then three feminine ⟨degrees⟩, and finally two masculine ⟨degrees⟩. (43) **What pertains to the pits of the stars**[γ,32] is at the 4th, 9th, 24th, 27th, and 28th degrees. (44) The degrees adding **fortune**[γ] and honor: the 18th and 20th degrees.

(45) There [in the degrees of Pisces], of the *fixed stars*[γ,33] ⟨we find⟩ the Shoulder of the Horse at ⟨longitude Pisces⟩ 18° at the present time, its latitude is northern 31°, of the second honor [magnitude], of the mixture of Mars and Mercury.

13 (1) *De stellis fixis.*π,1 Hee quidem² stelle fixe memorate,ᵞ si fuerint in nativitate hominis in gradu ascendente, aut in gradu medii celi, qui est principium decime domus, aut in eodem gradu cum Sole de die, aut cum Luna de | nocte, aut cum gradu sortis Lune, que vocatur *pars fortune*,ᵞ tunc erit nato exaltatio magna qualis non fuit patribus suis **nec in corde hominis ascendit.**αθ (2) Omnium tamen Antiquorum concors in hoc est sententia quod malus erit finis eius, et hoc quidem certius si fuerit significator huius rei stella aliqua que sit in malorum commixtio stellarum.

11ra

14 (1) Nunc {autem} loquar de complexione stellarum que sunt in **cingulo orbis signorum**ᵞ ac in figuris **septentrionalibus**ᵞ et meridionalibus. (2) Dixerunt {autem} aliqui Antiqui quod stelle que sunt super os Arietis de natura sunt Mercurii et aliquantulum de natura Saturni; et stella que est super pedem eius est de natura Martis; illa que est super *femora*ᵞ de natura Veneris est; stelle que sunt super locum precisionis Tauri de natura sunt Veneris et aliquantulum de natura Iovis. (3) **Pleiades**ᵞᵟ {vero} sunt de complexione Martis et Lune.³ (4) Et stelle que sunt super caput Tauri sunt de natura Saturni et aliquantulum de natura Mercurii; inter illas {autem} est stella magna, scilicet Oculus Tauri, que vocatur <u>Aldebaran</u>, et est de natura Martis per se; {similiter} ille que sunt super cornua Tauri, de natura eius sunt. (5) Ille qui sunt super pedem Geminorum, de natura sunt Mercurii et aliquantulum de natura Veneris; et que *circa* pudenda⁴ Geminorum sunt de natura Saturni; duarum {vero} lucidarum que sunt in capite, prior **de natura Mercuri est, et secunda**π de natura Martis. (6) Stelle que sunt super pedem Cancri sunt de natura Mercuri et aliquantulum de natura Martis; que super caudam sunt de complexione Saturni et Mercuri; ille {vero} que super ventrem sunt **caliginose**ᵞ sunt ⟨⟨...⟩⟩.μ (7) Que⁵ super caput Leonis sunt, de natura Saturni sunt et aliquantulum de natura Martis; et ille que sunt super collum eius, sunt de natura Saturni et aliquantulum de natura Mercurii; ⟨⟨...⟩⟩.μ (8) Et que sunt super caput Virginis, super finem **dexteri lateris seu** <u>gironis</u>,α,6 sunt de natura Mercurii et aliquantulum de natura Martis; et que

---

¹De stellis fixis] GV; LG om. ²quidem] WVG; L > sunt. ³et Lune] WVG; L om. ⁴pudenda] LVG; W pudibunda. ⁵Que] LVG; W < stelle vero. ⁶gironis] LVW; G girationis.

13 (1) ***On the fixed stars.***π,1 The aforementioned fixed stars,γ,2 if they are in the ascendant degree of a man's nativity, or if ⟨they are⟩ in the degree of the midheaven, which is the beginning of the tenth house, or if ⟨they are⟩ in the same degree with the Sun by day, or with the Moon by night, or if ⟨they are⟩ in the degree of the lot of the Moon, which is called the ***part of fortune***,γ,3 then the native will attain high rank, one that his ancestors did not attain and **does not ascend in the heart of a man**αθ,4 [no one ever imagined]. (2) Yet all the ANCIENTS agreed that his end will be bad, particularly if the significator of this thing is one of the stars with the mixture of the bad stars.

14 (1) {But} now I will discuss the mixture of the stars that are in the **girdle of the circle of the signs**γ,1 and in the **northern**γ and southern foms. (2) {But} the ANCIENTS said that stars in the mouth of ⟨the constellation⟩ Aries are of the nature of Mercury with somewhat of the nature of Saturn; the star in its leg is of the nature of Mars; ⟨the star⟩ in ***its thighs***γ,2 is of the nature of Venus; the stars in the place cut off with ⟨the constellation⟩ Taurus are of the nature of Venus and somewhat of Jupiter. (3) {Moreover} the **Pleiades**γδ,3 are a mixture of Mars and the Moon. (4) The stars in the head of ⟨the constellation⟩ Taurus are of the nature of Saturn and somewhat of the nature of Mercury; {but} among them a large star, namely, the eye of the bull, which is called *al-dabarān*, and it is of the nature of Mars alone; {similarly,} the ⟨stars⟩ in the horns of ⟨the constellation⟩ Taurus, they are of its [Mars's] nature. (5) Those in the leg of ⟨the constellation⟩ Gemini are of the nature of Mercury and somewhat of Venus; those *around* the pudenda of ⟨the constellation⟩ Gemini are of the nature of Saturn; {moreover} the two bright ⟨stars⟩ in the head ⟨of the constellation Gemini⟩, the first **is of the nature of Mercury, and the second**π,4 of the nature of Mars. (6) The stars in the legs of ⟨the constellation⟩ Cancer are of the nature of Mercury and somewhat of Mars; the ⟨stars⟩ in its [Cancer's] tail are a mixture of Saturn and Mercury; those which are in the belly are {indeed} **dark**γ,5 ⟨stars⟩ ⟨⟨of the mixture of Mars and the Moon; ⟨the stars⟩ that are close to its [Cancer's] back, which are called mighty, are of the nature of Mars and the Sun⟩⟩.μ,6 (7) ⟨The stars⟩ which are in the head of ⟨the constellation⟩ Leo are of the nature of Saturn and somewhat of Mars; and those which are in its [Leo's] neck are of the nature of Saturn and somewhat of Mercury; ⟨⟨the bright star called the heart of the lion is a mixture of Mars and Saturn; the ⟨nature of the star⟩ on its [Leo's] waist is like the nature of Venus; ⟨the stars⟩ in its [Leo's] thighs are of the nature of Venus and somewhat of Mercury⟩⟩.μ,7 (8) Those ⟨stars⟩ that are in the head of ⟨the constellation⟩ Virgo, at the end of its [Virgo's] **right side or *giro*,**αβ,8 are of the nature of Mercury and

220   PART ONE

supra lumbos sunt de natura Veneris; que {vero} sunt super ***gironem***ᵞ sinistrum de complexione Saturni sunt et Mercurii; et stella qui vocatur ***Simach Alazel*** de natura Veneris est et aliquantulum de natura Mercurii; et stelle que sunt super pedes eius, de natura sunt Mercurii et aliquantulum natura Martis. (9) Stelle due que sunt super **palmas**ᵅ Libre de complexione sunt Iovis et Mercurii. (10) Stella que est super cornua Scorpionis, de natura Saturni est et aliquantulum de Mercurio et de Marte; stelle lucide que sunt super **collum**ᵞ Scorpionis, sunt de natura Martis et aliquantulum de natura Saturni; et cor eius est de natura Martis et aliquantulum de natura Iovis; et illud quod est in cauda eius,[1] de natura Saturni est et aliquantulum de Veneris; et stelle **caliginose seu tenebrose**,^(βᵞ) de complexione Martis sunt et Lune.

11rb (11) **Stelle | caliginose**ᵞ que sunt in Arcu, de complexione Mercurii sunt et Lune; ille que super dorsum sunt **Sagittarii seu trahentis arcum**,^β sunt de natura Iovis et aliquantulum de Mercurii; et pedes equi, de complexione Iovis sunt et Saturni; et stelle qui sunt cauda, de natura sunt Veneris et aliquantulum de natura[2] Saturni. (12) Stelle que sunt super os Capricorni, sunt de natura Martis et aliquantulum de Veneris; ille que sunt super ventrem, de complexione Martis sunt et Mercurii; que sunt supra cauda *Capricorni*, de complexione Saturni et Mercurii.[3] (13) Ille qui sunt super humerum Aquarii et super manum sinistram, de complexione Saturni sunt et Mercurii; et que super nares, de natura Mercurii et aliquantulum de Saturno; et que sunt super Effusione Aque, de natura Saturni et aliquantulum de Iove. (14) Stelle {vero} que sunt super caput Piscis, sunt de natura Mercurii et aliquantulum de Saturno; que super ventrem eius, de complexione Iovis et Mercurii; et super caudam, de natura Saturni et aliquantulum de Mercurio; et ille que super ventrem sunt versus sinistram, de natura Iovis sunt et aliquantulum de natura Veneris; et que in fine sunt Piscis, de natura Martis et aliquantulum de natura Mercurii.

15   (1) Et hee quidem stelle que in parte **septentrionali**ᵞ sunt **ab orbe signorum**.ᵞ (2) Lucide que sunt in Urso Minori, de complexione Saturni sunt et aliquantulum de Venere. (3) Ille que in Urso Maiori sunt ⟨⟨...⟩⟩ᵛ

---

[1]et illud quod est in cauda eius] W que sunt in cauda eius.   [2]natura] W; LGV om   [3]que sunt supra cauda Capricornii de complexione Saturni et Mercurii] WV (also in H); LG om.

somewhat of Mars; the ⟨stars⟩ in the hips ⟨of Virgo⟩ are of the nature of Venus; {moreover} the ⟨stars⟩ in the left *giro*[γ,9] ⟨of Virgo⟩ are of the mixture of Saturn and Mercury; the star called ⟨*al*⟩-*simāk al-ʾaʿzal* is of the nature of Venus and somewhat of Mercury; and the stars in its [Virgo's] legs ⟨are⟩ of the nature of Mercury and somewhat of Mars. (9) The two stars on the **palms**[α,10] of ⟨the constellation⟩ Libra are of the mixture of Jupiter and Mercury. (10) The star which is in the horns of ⟨the constellation⟩ Scorpio ⟨is⟩ of the nature of Saturn and somewhat of the nature of Mercury and Mars; the bright stars in the **neck**[γ,11] of ⟨the constellation⟩ Scorpio are of the nature of Mars and somewhat of Saturn; its [Scorpio's] heart is of the nature of Mars and somewhat of Jupiter; what is in its [Scorpio's] tail is of the nature of Saturn and somewhat of Venus; and the **dark or tenebrous**[βγ,12] stars are of the mixture of Mars and the Moon. (11) The **dark stars**[γ,13] which are in the Bow [in Sagittarius], of the mixture of Mercury and the Moon; those ⟨stars⟩ which are in the back of **Sagittarius or the One who draws the Bow,**[β,14] are of the nature of Jupiter and somewhat of Mercury; ⟨the stars in⟩ the legs of the horse ⟨of the constellation Sagittarius⟩, of the nature of Jupiter and Saturn; and the stars which are in the tail ⟨of the horse of the constellation Sagittarius⟩, of the nature of Venus and somewhat of the nature of Saturn. (12) The stars in the mouth of ⟨the constellation⟩ Capricorn are of the nature of Mars and somewhat of Venus; the ⟨stars⟩ in its [Capricorn's] belly are a mixture of Mars and of Mercury; ⟨the stars⟩ which are in the tail *of Capricorn*, of the mixture of Saturn and of Mercury. (13) The ⟨stars⟩ in the shoulder of ⟨the constellation⟩ Aquarius and his left arm, of the mixture of Saturn and Mercury; and ⟨the stars⟩ in his nostrils, of the nature of Mercury and somewhat of Saturn; and the ⟨stars⟩ in the Stream of Water, of the nature of Saturn and somewhat of Jupiter. (14) {Moreover} the stars in the head of ⟨the constellation⟩ Pisces are of the nature of Mercury and somewhat of Saturn; those ⟨stars⟩ in its belly, of the mixture of Jupiter and somewhat of Mercury; ⟨the stars⟩ in the tail ⟨of the constellation Pisces⟩, of the nature of Saturn and somewhat of Mercury; the ⟨stars⟩ in the belly ⟨of the constellation Pisces⟩ facing the left [north], of the nature of Jupiter and somewhat of the nature of Venus; and ⟨the stars⟩ which are at the end of ⟨the constellation of⟩ Pisces, of the nature of Mars and somewhat of the nature of Mercury.

15 (1) These are the stars which are in the **northern**[γ] side with respect to the **circle of the signs.**[γ,1] (2) The bright ⟨stars⟩ in the Lesser Bear [Ursa Minor], of the mixture of Saturn and somewhat of Venus. (3) The ⟨stars⟩ in the Greater Bear [Ursa Major] ⟨⟨which are ⟨called⟩ *ʿayish*⟩⟩[ν,2] with its child,

cum fetu suo, de complexione sunt Lune et Veneris. (4) Lucide que sunt in Dracone, de complexione Saturni et Martis. (5) Stelle Inflammate *vel Cephei*, de complexione sunt Iovis et Saturni. (6) Ille que sunt **in Armato**[γ] *seu Boete*, de complexione Saturni sunt et Mercurii. (7) Lucida que est in Corona **Septentrionali**,[γ] de complexione Veneris et Mercurii. (8) *Stelle Illius qui* Super Genua Vadit, de natura Mercurii. (9) Lucida que est Aquila[1] Cadens, de complexione Veneris et Mercurii. (10) Lucida que vocatur Gallina. (11) Et ille que sunt cum ea que Sedet Super Sedem, de complexione Veneris et Saturni. (12) Ille que sunt cum **Milite**[γ] Caput Dyaboli Portante, de complexione Saturni et Iovis, et ille que sunt super gladium eius, de complexione Martis et Mercurii. (13) Lucida que[2] vocatur *Alahaiac*, de complexione Martis et Mercurii. (14) ⟨⟨...⟩⟩.[μ] (15) ⟨⟨...⟩⟩.[μ] (16) Stelle piscis que vocatur *Delphin*, de complexione Saturni sunt et Martis. (17) Et lucide que sunt in Arcu, de complexione Martis sunt et Mercurii. (18) Stelle que sunt in Muliere que **Numquam Maritum Habuit**,[α] sunt de natura Veneris. (19) Et ille que sunt in Triangulo, sunt de natura Mercurii.

16 (1) Stelle {vero} meridionales a **cingulo orbis signorum**[γ] sunt hec. (2) Lucida que est in ore Piscis Meridionali, de complexione Veneris et Mercurii. (3) Illa que est **in Ceto**,[γ] de natura Saturni. (4) Que super humerum **Fortis**[α] est | *seu Orionis*, de complexione Martis est et Mercurii; alie {vero} luminose, de complexione Saturni sunt et Iovis. (5) ⟨⟨...⟩⟩.[ν] (6) Stelle Leporis, de complexione Saturni et Martis. (7) Stelle que sunt circa Canem Posteriorem, de complexione sunt Veneris et Mercurii. (8) Et ille que sunt super os Canis *Alsaeri Algemania*, de natura Iovis et aliquantulum de natura Martis. (9) Stelle **Bellicosi vel Magnanimi**[β] *seu Ydri* sunt de natura Saturni ⟨⟨...⟩⟩.[μ] (10) Ille que sunt in Navi, de natura Saturni sunt et Martis; lucida *que est in pede Orionis, in hebrayco* **vocata est** *kesil*,[αε] *id est ignis vel lucida vel fortuna*, de natura Iovis et Saturni; et due **obscure seu caliginose**,[β] de complexione Veneris sunt et Mercurii. (11) Que super ymaginem Equi sunt, de comple-

11va

---

[1]Aquila] WVG; L < in.   [2]que] WVG; L > est.

of the mixture of the Moon and Venus. (4) The bright ⟨stars⟩ in the Dragon [Draco], of the mixture of Saturn and Mars. (5) The stars set on fire³ *or of Cepheus*, of the mixture of Jupiter and Saturn.(6) The ⟨stars⟩ **in the Armed ⟨Warrior⟩**$^{\gamma,4}$ *or Boötes*,⁵ of the mixture of Saturn and Mercury. (7) The bright ⟨star⟩ in the **Northern**$^\gamma$ Crown [Corona Borealis], of the mixture of Venus and Mercury. (8) *The stars of* the One Crawling on his Knees [Hercules], of the nature of Mercury. (9) The bright ⟨star⟩ which is the Falling Eagle [Lyra], of the mixture of Venus and Mercury. (10) The bright ⟨star⟩ called the Hen [Cygnus]. (11) The ⟨stars⟩ which are with the ⟨Woman⟩ Sitting on a Chair [Cassiopeia], of the mixture of Venus and Saturn. (12) The ⟨stars⟩ which are with the **Soldier**$^{\gamma,6}$ Carrying the Devil's Head [Perseus], of the mixture of Saturn and Jupiter; and the ⟨stars⟩ which are in his sword, of the mixture of Mars and Mercury. (13) The bright ⟨star⟩ called *al-ʿayyūq* [in Auriga], of the mixture of Mars and Mercury. (14) ⟨⟨The ⟨stars⟩ in the Carrier of the Snake [Ophiuchus] are of the nature of Saturn and somewhat of Venus; the ⟨stars⟩ in his back are a mixture of Saturn and Mars⟩⟩.$^{\mu,7}$ (15) ⟨⟨The flying eagle [Aquila] is a mixture of Jupiter and Mars⟩⟩.$^{\mu,8}$ (16) The stars in the fish called Dolphin [Delphinus], of the mixture of Saturn and Mars. (17) The bright ⟨stars⟩ in the bow, of the mixture of Mars and Mercury. (18) The stars in the Woman who **Never had a Husband**$^{\alpha,9}$ [Andromeda], are of the nature of Venus. (19) The ⟨stars⟩ in the Triangle [Triangulum] are of the nature of Mercury.

16 (1) {Moreover} these are the stars that are south of the **girdle of the circle of the signs.**$^{\gamma,1}$ (2) The bright ⟨star⟩ in the mouth of the Southern Fish [Piscis Austrinus], of the mixture of Venus and Mercury. (3) The ⟨star⟩ in **Cetus**,$^{\gamma,2}$ of the nature of Saturn. (4) The ⟨star⟩ which is in the shoulder of **the Mighty One**$^{\alpha,3}$ *or Orion*,⁴ of the mixture of Mars and Mercury; {moreover} the other bright ⟨stars⟩, of the mixture of Saturn and Jupiter. (5) ⟨⟨The stars of the River [Eridanus], of the mixture of Saturn and Jupiter⟩⟩.$^{\nu,5}$ (6) The stars of the Hare [Lepus], of the mixture of Saturn and Mars. (7) The stars around the rear part of the Dog [Canis Major] are a mixture of Venus and Mercury. (8) The ⟨stars⟩ in the mouth of the Dog [Canis Minor] *al-shiʿrā al-ghumaysāʾ*, are of the nature of Jupiter and somewhat of Ma. (9) The stars of **the Warlike or the Valiant**$^{\beta,6}$ *or Ydra*⁷ [Hydra] are of the nature of Saturn ⟨⟨and Venus⟩⟩.$^{\mu,8}$ (10) The ⟨stars⟩ in the Ship [Argo Navis], of the nature of Saturn and Mars; the bright ⟨star⟩ *in the leg of Orion*,⁹ **called** *in Hebrew* **Kesil**,$^{\alpha\epsilon,10}$ *that is, fire, or bright, or fortune*,¹¹ of the nature of Jupiter and Saturn, and the two **dark or obscure**$^{\beta,12}$ ⟨stars⟩, of the mixture of Venus and Mercury. (11) The ⟨stars⟩ in the image of the Horse [Centaurus] are a mix-

xione sunt Veneris et Iovis; lucide que sunt super gutturem, de natura sunt Veneris et aliquantulum de natura Martis. (12) Ille qui sunt in Corona Meridionali, de natura sunt Mercurii. (13) Stelle **Lupi vel Bestie**^{βγδ} sunt de complexione Saturni et Mercurii. (14) Stelle qui sunt in Turibulo, de natura sunt Iovis et aliquantulum de natura Mercurii. (15) Hee sunt stelle quas experimentati sunt Antiqui.

(16) Explicit secunda pars huius libri.[1]

§ 3

1 (1) .3a. pars.^{γ} De aspectibus graduum circuli, et **amicitia et inimicitia**^{γ} eorum, atque de omnibus conditionibus quartarum et super qualibet significationes hora.[2] (2) Aspectus secundum .4or. modus sunt, et sunt hii aspectus sextilis, aspectus .4us., aspectus trinus et aspectus oppositus. (3) Signa {quoque} aspectuum sunt .7.,: .3m. scilicet et .4m., .5m., .7m., .9m. .10m., et .11m. (4) Aspectus qui est ad .3m. et ad .11m. est sextilis; aspectus ad .4m. et ad .10m. aspectus .4us. est; aspectus {vero} ad .5us. et .9us. trinus est aspectus; {sed} aspectus qui est ad .7m. est *ille qui* oppositus *vocatus est*; {item} aspectus qui est ad .3m. et ad .4m. et .5m. sinister est; aspectus {vero} qui ad .9m. et .10m. et .11m. est dexter. (5) Aspectus {autem} sextilis sexta pars est circuli, scilicet .60. gradus; et aspectus .4us. quarta pars est, que est .90. gradus; aspectus {vero} trinus tertia pars est circuli, que .120. gradus; {sed} oppositus medietas est circuli, scilicet .180. gradus. (6) Et huius exemplum est quod sit ascendens Arietis initium; tunc enim erit aspectus sextilis sinister in principio Geminorum; et aspectus sextilis dexter in principio Aquarii; et quartus dexter in principio Capricorno; quartus {vero} sinister in principio Cancri; et trinus sinister in principio Leonis; dexter {vero} trinus in principio Sagittarii; {sed} aspectus oppositus in principio Libre est. (7) Fortissimus {autem} aspectuum est oppositus, et post ipse quartus, deinde trinus, sed debilissimus omnium est sextilis. (8) Aspectus quidem oppositus perfecta est inimicitia, quartus vero dimidia inimicitia;[3] {sed} trinus perfecta **amicitia**^{γ} est et sextilis dimidia **amicitia.**^{γ} (9) Signa {vero} inter que non est aspectus seu commixtio sunt .4or.: .2m., videlicet .6m., .8m. et .12m. ⟨⟨...⟩⟩.^{μ}

---

[1]Explicit secunda pars huius libri] LG; WV om.   [2].3a. pars. De aspectibus graduum circuli, et amicitia et inimicitia eorum atque de omnibus conditionibus quartarum et super qualibet significationes hora] V; LWG om.   [3]quartus vero dimidia inimicita] WVG; L in margin.

ture of Venus and Jupiter; and the bright ⟨stars⟩ in the throat ⟨of the Horse⟩ are of the nature of Venus and somewhat of the nature of Mars. (12) The ⟨stars⟩ in the Southern Crown [Corona Australis] are of the nature of Mercury. (13) The stars in **the Wolf or Beast**^{βγδ,13} are of the mixture of Saturn and Mercury. (14) The stars of the Firepan [Ara] are of the nature of Jupiter and somewhat of Mercury. (15) These are the stars that have been tested by the ANCIENTS.

(16) Here ends the second part of THIS BOOK.

§3

1 (1) **Third part.**^{γ,1} On the aspects of the degrees of the circle, on their **friendship and enmity**,^{γ,2} and on all the conditions of the quadrants and significations at every moment. (2) The aspects are according to four modes, and they are sextile aspect, quartile aspect, trine aspect, and opposition aspect. (3) {Besides,} the signs of the aspects are seven, namely the third, fourth, fifth, seventh, ninth, tenth, and eleventh. (4) The aspect ⟨of the first sign⟩ to the third and eleventh ⟨signs⟩ is sextile; the aspect to the fourth and tenth ⟨signs⟩ is quartile; the aspect to the fifth and ninth ⟨signs⟩ is trine; {moreover} the aspect to the seventh ⟨sign⟩ *is the one called* opposition; {likewise,} the aspect to the third, fourth, and fifth ⟨signs⟩ is left; {moreover} the one to the ninth, tenth, and eleventh ⟨signs⟩ is right. (5) {But} the sextile aspect spans one-sixth of the circle [the zodiac], namely 60 degrees; the quartile aspect ⟨spans⟩ one-fourth ⟨of the circle⟩, which is 90 degrees; {moreover} the trine aspect ⟨spans⟩ one-third of the circle, which ⟨is⟩ 120 degrees; {but} opposition spans half of the circle, namely 180 degrees. (6) An example of this is that the ascendant is in the beginning of Aries; then the left sextile aspect will be at the beginning of Gemini; and the right sextile aspect at the beginning of Aquarius; and the right quartile at the beginning of Capricorn; {moreover} the left quartile at the beginning of Cancer; and the left trine at the beginning of Leo; and the right trine at the beginning of Sagittarius; {moreover} the opposition aspect at the beginning of Libra. (7) {But} the strongest of the aspects is opposition, after it [the next strongest] quartile, next trine, but the weakest of all is sextile. (8) The opposition aspect is complete enmity, quartile {though} ⟨is⟩ half enmity; {but} trine is complete **friendship**^{γ,3} and sextile half **friendship**.^{γ} (9) {Moreover} the signs with which there is neither aspect nor mixture are four, namely the second, sixth, eighth, and twelfth; ⟨⟨the weakest of these are the sixth and twelfth⟩⟩.^{μ,4}

2 (1) Signorum {autem} quedam sunt que **inimica**ʸ sunt aspectu et **amica**ʸ alio modo, eo quod sunt **convenientia in numero**ʸ **ascensionum**ᵅ aut in fortitudine aut in **cingulo | orbis signorum.**ʸ (2) Et illa quorum **ascensiones**ᵅ sunt equales sunt sicut Aries et Piscis, Virgo et Libra, Taurus et Aquarius, Leo et Scorpio, Geminus et Capricornus, Cancer et Sagittarius. (3) Illa {vero} que in una sunt fortitudine sunt ea quorum hore torte sunt equales, ut Cancer cum Geminis, Taurus cum Leone, Aries cum Virgine, Pisces cum Libra, Aquarius cum Scorpione, et Capricornus cum Sagittario. (4) Et **stella seu planeta**ᵝ qui fuerit in aliquo signorum rectorum vocatur **dominus seu principans,**ᵝ et ille qui in opposito gradu fuerit in aliquo **signorum obliquorum,**ʸ **servus** erit **seu subiectus.**ᵝ (5) Signa {vero} que sunt in **cingulo orbis signorum,**ʸ **convenientia**ʸ sunt omni duo signa que domus sunt eiusdem **planete,**ʸ sicut Aries et Scorpio Marti, Taurus et Libra Veneris, Gemini et Virgo Mercurii, Sagittarius et Piscis Iovis, Capricornus et Aquarius Saturni; et quamquam Lune sit domus una solum et Soli similiter, ambobus cum **principantibus,**ʸ domus eorum reputantur tamquam unius essent **principantis.**ʸ (6) Aries {autem} et Libra, Capricornus {quoque} et Cancer, Virgo et Pisces ⟨⟨...⟩⟩,ᵘ quamvis *convenientia sunt in virtutibus activis,*ʸ inimicitia tunc est inter ipsa propter aspectum oppositum.

11vb

3 (1) Dividitur quidem orbis quolibet hore momento in partes .4or. (2) Nam **.4a.,**ʸ que est a ⟨⟨...⟩⟩ᵘ medio celi usque ad gradum ascendentem orientalis est; et masculina, procedens; et quod ei assimilatur ex ⟨⟨...⟩⟩ᵛ **elementis**ᵅ est aer; et de corpore humano, sanguis; de temporibus anni, **ver;**ᵅ de partibus quartarum diei et nocti, prima; **de etatibus hominis,**ᵅ **infantiam;**ʸ et de coloribus, album. (3) *Secunda* quarta, que est a ⟨⟨...⟩⟩ᵘ medio celi usque ad gradum occidentem, meridionalis est; et debilis sicut femella; operatio eius est reversiva; et quod ei assimilatur de **elementis**ᵅ quatuor, ignis est; de temporibus anni, estas; de quartis diei et noctis, secunda pars; *de partibus* humani corporis, cholera rubea; **de etatibus,**ʸ adolescentia; et de coloribus, rubeus. (4) *Tertia* quarta, que quidem est a gradu occidente usque **ad gradum anguli terre,**ᵅ occidentalis est; masculine virtute, et est precedens; assimilatur enim ei de **elementis,**ᵅ terra; de temporibus anni, **antumpnus;**ᵅ de quartis diei et noctis, tertia; in humano corpore, ⟨habet⟩ melancoliam; **de etatibus**ʸ *senectus sive* quando prope .50. annos est; et de coloribus, nigritudo. (5) Quarta {vero} que est ab **angulo terre**ʸ usque ad gradum ascenden-

2 (1) {But} some of the signs are **unfriendly**$^{\gamma,1}$ in aspect and **friendly**$^{\gamma,2}$ in some other respect, because they **agree in the number**$^{\gamma,3}$ of the ascensions,$^{\alpha}$ in the power, or in the **girdle of the circle of the signs.**$^{\gamma,4}$ (2) Those whose **ascensions**$^{\alpha}$ are equal are Aries and Pisces, Virgo and Libra, Taurus and Aquarius, Leo and Scorpio, Gemini and Capricorn, Cancer and Sagittarius. (3) {Moreover} those which are in one power are those whose crooked hours [seasonal hours] are equal, such as Cancer and Gemini, Taurus and Leo, Aries and Virgo, Pisces and Libra, Aquarius and Scorpio, and Capricorn and Sagittarius. (4) A **star or planet**$^{\beta,5}$ which is in any of the straight signs is designated a **lord or ruler,**$^{\beta,6}$ and the one which is opposite its degree in any of the **oblique signs,**$^{\gamma}$ will be **a slave or subject.**$^{\beta,7}$ (5) {Moreover} ⟨regarding⟩ the signs which are in the **girdle of the circle of the signs,**$^{\gamma}$ **agreeing**$^{\gamma,8}$ ⟨with each other⟩ are every pair of signs which are the houses of one **planet,**$^{\gamma}$ such as Aries and Scorpio of Mars, Taurus and Libra of Venus, Gemini and Virgo of Mercury, Sagittarius and Pisces of Jupiter, and Capricorn and Aquarius of Saturn; although the Moon has only one house and similarly the Sun, because both are **rulers,**$^{\gamma,9}$ their houses are considered to be of one **ruler.**$^{\gamma}$ (6) {But} Aries and Libra, {also} Capricorn and Cancer, Virgo and Pisces, ⟨⟨and the others⟩⟩,$^{\mu,10}$ although they *agree in the active powers,*$^{\gamma,11}$ there is unfriendliness between them because of the opposition aspect.

3 (1) The circle [the zodiac] is divided at any moment of the hour into four parts. (2) For the **quadrant**$^{\gamma,1}$ which is from ⟨⟨the line of⟩⟩$^{\mu,2}$ midheaven to the ascendant degree is eastern; and masculine, advancing; and what resembles it of the ⟨⟨four⟩⟩$^{\nu,3}$ **elements**$^{\alpha,4}$ is the air; of the human body, blood; of the seasons of the year, **spring;**$^{\alpha,5}$ of the quarters of the day and night, the first; **of the ages of man,**$^{\alpha,6}$ **childhood;**$^{\gamma,7}$ of the colors, white. (3) The *second* quadrant, which is from ⟨⟨the line of⟩⟩$^{\mu,8}$ midheaven to the descendant degree, is southern; weak like a female; and its effect retreating; and what resembles it of the four **elements**$^{\alpha,9}$ is fire; of the seasons of the year, summer; of the quarters of the day and night, the second part; *of the parts* of the human body, red bile; **of** ⟨human⟩ **ages,**$^{\gamma,10}$ *youth;* of the colors, red. (4) The *third* quadrant, which is from the descendant degree **to the degree of the angle of the Earth,**$^{\alpha,11}$ is western; with masculine power, and it is advancing; and what resembles it of the **elements**$^{\alpha}$ is earth; of the seasons of the year, autumn;$^{\alpha,12}$ of the quarters of the day and night, the third; in the human body, black bile; **of** ⟨human⟩ **ages,**$^{\gamma,13}$ *old age or when one approaches fifty years;* and of colors, black. (5) {Moreover} the quadrant which is from the **angle of the Earth**$^{\gamma,14}$ to the ascendant degree

tem sinister est; in similitudine femelle; retrocedens; et quod ei assimilatur de **elementis**^{α} est aqua; de temporibus anni, **hiems**;^{α} de quartis diei et noctis, ultima; in humano corpore *flegma*;^{γ} **de etatibus**^{γ} **senium sive decrepita etas**;^{β} et de coloribus viridis. (6) Vocatur {autem} dextrum quidquid **orbis est spere**^{γ} supra terram,[1] et est a gradu ascendente usque ad gradum occidentem; et sinistrum, quidquid est sub terra. (7) Item vocantur due quarte masculine, dextre; et due feminine, sinistre. (8) {Iterum}, due quarte, que sunt **ab angulo terre usque ad gradum ascendentem, et a gradu ascendente usque ad medium celi**,^{γ} medietas vocatur **spere**^{α} ascendens; **relique** {vero} **due quarte, que** {scilicet} **a medio celi usque ad gradum occidentem sunt et ab hinc usque ad angulum terre**,^{γ,2} vocatur medietas **spere**^{α} descendens.

12ra **4** (1) {Rursus,} dividitur **spera**,^{α} momento quolibet, in partes .12., secundum **numerum .12. signorum**^{γ}, que vocantur domus. (2) Harum {autem} | quatuor, videlicet prima, quarta et septima et decima, uno quidem nomine nominatur, **anguli** {scilicet} **vel cardines**^{βγ} **propter similitudinem quandam**.^{γ} (3) Domus {vero} secunda et quinta et octava et undecima, uno nomine similiter vocantur, succedentes scilicet **angulorum**.^{γ} (4) {Sed} domus .3a. et .6a. et .9a. ac duodecima uno nomine **debiles** vocantur **seu cadentes**.^{αβ} (5) **Anguli** {autem} **seu cardines**^{βγ} fortiores sunt succedentibus, et succedentes **cadentibus**.^{γ} (6) Inter **angulos**,^{γ} fortes[3] sunt domus prima et decima; et de succedentibus, quinta et undecima; **cadentium**^{γ} {vero} fortis[4] est tertia et nona. (7) {Item} quolibet *hore* momento sunt **domus**^{γ} ipse in similitudine quatuor **elementorum**;^{γ} et huius exemplum patet in **anguli**,^{γ} ut sit ascendens signum Aries, qui est nature ignee, erit mediani celi linea Capricornus, qui est nature terrestris, et signum occidentis erit Libra, que est nature aeris; **linea** {vero} **anguli terre**^{γ} Cancer erit {quoque} aque nature; consimiliter de succedentibus est de succedentibus domibus ac **cadentibus**.^{γ} (8) Et hee domus .12. **radices**^{α} sunt in nativitatibus hominum et electionibus et interrogationibus, ac etiam in iudiciis mundi, que sunt universaliora.

---

[1]est spere supra terram] L; W spere super terram; G est spere supra; V om.   [2]que scilicet a medio celi usque ad gradum occidentem sunt et ab hinc usque ad angulum terre] G que sunt a medio celi usque ad angulum terre.   [3]fortes] G fortiores.   [4]fortis] G fortior.

is left [northern]; it bears the resemblance of a small woman; retreating; and what resembles it of the **elements**^{α} is water; of the seasons of the year, **winter**;^{α,15} of the quarters of the day and night, the last one; in the human body, ***phlegm***;^{γ,16} **of** ⟨human⟩ **ages**,^{γ} **senility or very old age**;^{β,17} of the colors, green. (6) {But} whatever belongs to the **circle of the sphere**^{γ,18} that is above the Earth, and is from the ascendant degree to the descendant degree is called "right"; and whatever is below the Earth ⟨is called⟩ "left." (7) Likewise, the two masculine quadrants are called "right"; and the two feminine quadrants, "left." (8) {In addition}, the two quadrants, which are **from the angle of the Earth to the ascendant degree, and from the ascendant degree to midheaven**,^{γ,19} are called "the ascending half of the **sphere**";^{α,20} {but} **the remaining two quadrants, which** {namely} **are from midheaven to the descendant degree, and from there to the angle of the Earth**,^{γ,21} are called "the descending half of the **sphere**".^{α}

4 (1) {Besides,} at any moment, the **sphere**^{α} [zodiac] is divided into twelve parts, according to **the number of the twelve signs**,^{γ,1} which are called houses. (2) {But} four of them, namely the first, fourth, seventh, and tenth, are called by the same name, {namely} **angles or cardines**,^{βγ,2} **because of a certain similarity.**^{γ,3} (3) {Moreover} the second, fifth, eighth, and eleventh are similarly called by the same name, namely succedent to the **angles**.^{γ,4} (4) {But} the third, sixth, ninth, and twelfth ⟨are called⟩ by the same name, **weak or cadent.**^{αβ,5}(5) {But} the **angles or cardines**^{βγ} are stronger than the succedent ⟨houses⟩, and the succedent ⟨houses⟩ are stronger than the **cadent**^{γ,6} ⟨houses⟩. (6) Among the **angles**,^{γ} the first and tenth ⟨houses⟩ are strong; of the succedent, the fifth and eleventh ⟨houses are strong⟩; of the **cadent**,^{γ} the sixth and ninth ⟨house⟩ is {indeed} strong. (7) {Likewise,} at any moment *of the hour* the **houses**^{γ,7} resemble the four **elements**;^{γ} here is an example for the **angles**:^{γ} when the ascendant sign is Aries, which is of fiery nature, Capricorn, which is of earthy nature, will be at the line of midheaven and the sign of the descendant will be Libra, which is of airy nature; Cancer, {also} of watery nature, will be {indeed} at the **line of the angle of the Earth**^{γ,8} [i.e., line of lower midheaven]; and so too regarding the succedent houses and the **cadent**^{γ} ⟨houses⟩. (8) These twelve places are the **roots**^{α,9} in the nativities of human beings, and in interrogations, elections, and also in the judgments of the world, which are related to collectives.

5 (1) Prima domus est illa que ascendit in linea orientali; et significat super vitam, et super corpus, et super loquelam et **sensum seu scientiam,**[β] et crementum, et principium omnium operationum, et quidquid in cogitatione hominis est; et de etatibus hominis significat super principium. (2) *Dominus {autem} triplicitatis primus*[γ] significat super vitam nati, et naturam eius ac interrogatoris similiter, et super eius desideria, et quidquid ei acta, de bono vel de malo, in principio vite. (3) Et *dominus triplicitatis secundus*[γ] significat super corpus, et virtute *eius*, ac super medium annorum hominis. (4) Dominus {vero} triplicitatis tertius, qui particeps est et commiscens se cum participantibus, quidquid significat super[1] **finem est vite vel etatis hominis.**[β]

6 (1) Secunda domus significat super possessiones, et acquisitiones, et **mutua ac dona;**[αθ] {item} super comestiones, et adiutores, ac paratos ad precepta, adhuc et super testimonia, et claves ac thesauros. (2) *Dominus {autem} triplicitatis primus*[γ] super possessiones significat in principio etate hominis. (3) Et *dominus secundus*[γ] super medietatem annorum; **tertius**[γ] {vero} super finem.

7 (1) Domus {vero} .3a. significat super fratres, et sorores, et propinques, ac generos, super **sensum et intellectum,**[αβ] ⟨⟨...⟩⟩[ν] **ac super religionem;**[π] {item} super cartas et rumores ⟨⟨...⟩⟩.[μ] (2) *Dominus {autem} triplicitatis primus*[γ] significat super fratres maiores; secundus super medios; et tertius super minores.

8 (1) Quarta domus significat super patrem, et super terras, domos, campos et agros, et patriam, ac edificia et reposita, atque super res occultas. (2) *Domus triplicitatis primus*[γ] super patres significat; secundus super terras; et tertius super finem omnium rerum.

9 (1) Quinta domus significat super filios, et delectationes, et exenia, et nuntios, et bladum, ac thesauros patris. (2) *Dominus {autem} triplicitatis primus*[γ] super filios significat; secundus super delectabilia; et tertius super nuntios.

---

[1]super] W om.

5 (1) The first house is the one which rises at the eastern line; it indicates life, the body, speech, **understanding or knowledge**,^{β,1} growth, and the beginning of every action, and whatever is in man's mind; of human ages, it indicates the beginning. (2) {But} the *first lord of the triplicity*^{γ,2} indicates the native's life and his nature and similarly that of the querent ⟨in an interrogational horoscope⟩, and his desires, and whatever occurs to him, good or bad, at the beginning of life. (3) And the *second lord of the triplicity*^{γ,3} indicates the body, *its* power, and the middle of man's years. (4) {Moreover} the third lord of the triplicity, which is the partner and commingles with ⟨its⟩ partners [the first and second lord of the triplicity], indicates whatever is about the **end of life or of the human lifetime**.^{β,4}

6 (1) The second house indicates possessions, acquisitions, and **loans and gifts**^{αθ,1}[negotiations]; {likewise,} meals, helpers, those who are ready to receive orders, also testimonies, keys, and treasures. (2) {But} the *first lord of the triplicity*^{γ,2} indicates possessions in the beginning of human lifetime; (3) The *second lord* ⟨of the triplicity⟩^{γ,3} indicates ⟨possessions⟩ in the middle of the years, and the **third**^{γ} ⟨lord of the triplicity indicates⟩ {indeed} ⟨possessions⟩ in the end ⟨of the human lifetime⟩.

7 (1) {Moreover} the third house indicates brothers, sisters, kin, in-laws, **understanding and comprehension**,^{αβ,1} ⟨⟨humility, counsel⟩⟩^{ν,2} **belief**;^{π,3} {likewise,} letters and rumors ⟨⟨journeys⟩⟩.^{μ,4} (2) {But} the *first lord of the triplicity*^{γ,5} indicates the older brothers, the second ⟨lord of the triplicity indicates⟩ the middle brothers, and the third ⟨indicates⟩ the younger ⟨brothers⟩.

8 (1) The fourth place indicates the father, landed property, houses, fields and estates, the city, buildings, buried treasures, and hidden things. (2) The *first lord of the triplicity*^{γ,1} indicates fathers, the second ⟨lord of the triplicity indicates⟩ landed property, and the third ⟨indicates⟩ the end of everything.

9 (1) The fifth house indicates sons, pleasures, gifts, messengers, grain, and the father's treasures. (2) {But} the *first lord of the triplicity*^{γ,1} indicates sons, the second ⟨lord of the triplicity indicates⟩ pleasures, and the third ⟨indicates⟩ messengers.

232   PART ONE

10 (1) Domus sexta significat omnem egritudinem **durabilem seu diuturnam**,ᵝ | et *infortunia*,ᵞ et super servos et ancillas, ac pecudum minutum, super domos captivitatum, et mendacia, et **accusationes**.ᵞ (2) *Dominus {autem} triplicitatis primus*ᵞ super egritudines significat et orbationes; secundus super servos; et tertius si valebunt ac nocebunt.

12rb

11 (1) Septima domus super mulieres significat, et super concubitus, et bella, et super **adversitates seu rixas**,ᵝ super litigia, et predones, super consortia, et mercaturas. (2) *Dominus {autem} triplicitatis primus*ᵞ super mulieres significat; secundus super bella; et tertius super consortes.

12 (1) Octava domus super mortem significat, et super hereditates, super **testamenta**,ᵞ et separationes, **terrores**,ᵞ tristitias et amissiones. (2) *Dominus {autem} triplicitatis primus*ᵞ significat super mortem; secundus super omnes res antiquas; et tertius super hereditates.

13 (1) Nona domus significat super **itinera et peregrinationes**,ᵞ super omnem hominem de gradu suo se mutantem, super sapientiam, et fidem, et servitium divinum, et nuntios, et rumores, et somnia, et iuramenta, et iudicia et significat mirabilia. (2) *Dominus {autem} triplicitatis primus*ᵞ super itinera significat; **secundus super gradum; tertius super fidem eius**.ᵅ

14 (1) Decima domus super **reges** significat, et **opera, sublimationes, ac exaltationes, regna, et famositates, et auctoritatem; item super magisteria, et matres, et gloriam, et laudem, et res furatas aut sublatas, adhuc super iudices, et principes, et prelatos, et significat super medium annorum vite**.ᵅ (2) **Dominus autem triplicitatis primus super omnia opera significat, et exaltationes, et mansiones altissimas; secundus super auctoritatem et audaciam in ea; et tertius stabilitatem et durabilitatem**.ᵅ

15 (1) Undecima domus super honorem significat, et **gratiam seu bonam fortunam**,ᵝᵞ et bonum nomen, super spem, et amicos, et **socios**,ᵞ et regum satrapas et thesaurarios eorum ⟨⟨...⟩⟩.ᵛ (2) *Dominus {autem} triplicitatis primus*ᵞ significat super spem **cognationum seu desideriorum**;ᵝ secundus super **socios**;ᵞ et tertius si boni sunt ei vel mali.

16 (1) Duodecima domus super tristitias significat, et pauperitates, super invidiam, et odium, et **terrorem**,ᵞ super astutias, ⟨⟨...⟩⟩ᵛ et omne dedecoro-

10 (1) The sixth place indicates every disease that is **lasting and of long duration**,[β,1] and *misfortunes*,[γ,2] male and female slaves, small cattle, prisons, false statements, and **accusations**.[γ,3] (2) {But} the *first lord of the triplicity*[γ,4] indicates diseases and maimings, the second ⟨lord of the triplicity indicates⟩ slaves, and the third ⟨indicates⟩ whether they will be beneficial to him or cause harm.

11 (1) The seventh house indicates women, sexual intercourse, wars, **enmities and squabbles**,[β,1] litigation, thieves, partnership, and merchandise. (2) {But} *the first lord of the triplicity*[γ,2] indicates women, the second ⟨lord of the triplicity indicates⟩ wars, and the third ⟨indicates⟩ partners.

12 (1) The eighth place indicates death, inheritances, **last wills**,[γ,1] divorces, **great fears**,[γ,2] sorrows, and losses. (2) {But} the *first lord of the triplicity*[γ,3] indicates death, the second ⟨lord of the triplicity indicates⟩ all ancient things, and the third ⟨indicates⟩ inheritances.

13 (1) The ninth house indicates ⟨long⟩ **travels and journeys to foreign places**,[γ,1] every person changing his rank, wisdom, faith, divine service, messengers, rumors, dreams, oaths, judgments and portents. (2) {But} the *first lord of the triplicity*[γ,2] indicates travels, **the second ⟨indicates⟩ rank, and the third ⟨indicates⟩ his faith**.[α,3]

14 (1) The tenth house indicates **kings, works, being raised to a higher rank, and promotion, kingdoms, fame and authority; likewise, crafts, mothers, glory, praise, something taken away or stolen, as well as judges, princes, prelates, and it indicates half of the years of life**.[α,1] (2) But the first lord of the triplicity indicates every work, promotions, and very high mansions; the second ⟨indicates⟩ authority, and boldness in it; the third ⟨lord of the triplicity indicates⟩ **stability and longevity**.[α,2]

15 (1) The eleventh place indicates honor, **favor or good fortune**,[βγ,1] a good name, hope, friends, **partners**,[γ,2] and the king's ministers and his treasurers, ⟨⟨**and masters of the wardrobe**⟩⟩.[ν,3] (2) {But} the *first lord of the triplicity*[γ,4] indicates hope of the **thoughts or desires**,[β,5] the second ⟨indicates⟩ **partners**,[γ] and the third ⟨indicates⟩ whether they are good or bad for him [the native].

16 (1) The twelfth place indicates sadness, poverty, jealousy, hate, **great fear**,[γ] shrewdness, ⟨⟨grudges, prisons and captivity,⟩⟩[ν,1] every disgraceful

sum, super lesuras, et **bestias hominibus equitabiles seu ad vecturas hominium valentes.**β (2) **Dominus** {autem} **triplicitatis primus**ᵞ super tristitiam significat; secundus super domos carcerum; et tertius super inimicos.

(3) Explicit .3a. pars HUIUS LIBRI.

§4

1 (1) **Quarta pars LIBRI.**ᵞ ⟨De⟩ complexionibus **planetarum,**ᵅ et virtutibus, et quidquid per eos significatum.¹ (2) Incipiam {autem} a Saturno, eo quod superior est omnibus, in spera enim septima est a terra.

(3) Saturnus: frigidus est et siccus, ⟨⟨...⟩⟩,ᵛ nocivus, super corruptionem significat et dissipationem, et mortem, **et fletum, et tristitias et lamentationes, et planctus, et clamores**ᵞ et super res antiquas.

(4) In parte eius est de humana anima, virtus cogitativa.

(5) Et eius est **clima**ᵅ primum, quod est terra Indie.

(6) De gentibus quidem, in parte eius sunt **Mauri seu Etyopes**ᵅᵝ, et Iudei, et Albarbarim *forte sunt Barbarici.*

12va (7) Et universaliter, | omnes seniores, et **laboratores terre seu agricole,**β edificatores, et cerdones coriorum, et cloacarum mundatores, servi, et viles homines, raptores, et fossores puteorum ⟨⟨...⟩⟩,ᵛ et ***spoliatores sepulchrorum.***ᵞ

(8) **De mineralibus,**ᵞ in parte eius est plumbum nigrum, et ferrum rubiginosum, lapides nigri, et **omne marmor nigrum;**ᵅ {item} lapis magnes, et omnis lapis ponderosus et niger.

(9) {Item} in parte eius *de locis* terre, sunt cripte, et **putei,**ᵅ et carceres, et omnis locus obscurus et non inhabitatus, adhuc et loca cemetariorum.

---

¹Quarta pars libri complexionibus planetarum et virtutibus et quicquid per eos significatum] V; LWG om.

thing, blows, and the **animals that men ride on or that are strong for the carriages of human beings.**β,2 (2) {But} the *first lord of the triplicity*γ,3 indicates sadness, the second ⟨indicates⟩ prisons, and the third ⟨indicates⟩ enemies.

(3) Here ends the third part of THIS BOOK.

§4

1 (1) **Fourth part of THE BOOK.**γ,1 ⟨On⟩ the mixtures of the **planets,**α,2 and powers, and whatever is indicated by them. (2) {But} I will begin with Saturn, because it is the highest of all ⟨the planets⟩, since it is in the seventh sphere from the Earth.

(3) Saturn. Cold and dry, ⟨⟨its nature is bad,⟩⟩v,3 harmful; it indicates corruption and ruin, death, **weeping, sadness and lamentation, and wailing, and cries**γ,4 and ancient things.

(4) Of the human soul, the power concerned with thought is in its portion.

(5) In its portion is the first **climate,**α which is the land of India.

(6) Of the nations, in its portion are the **Moors or Ethiopians,**αβ,5 the Jews, and the Albarbarim, ⟨who⟩ *perhaps are the Barbarici* [Berbers].

(7) In general, all of the elderly ⟨are in its portion⟩, and **cultivators of the land or farmers,**β,6 masons, tanners, privy-cleaners, slaves, base people, robbers, diggers of wells ⟨⟨**and graves,**⟩⟩v,7 and *plunderers of tombs.*γ,8

(8) **Of the minerals,**γ,9 in its portion are black lead and rusty iron, black stones, **every black marble;**α,10 {likewise} the loadstone, and any heavy and black stone.

(9) {Likewise,} *of the places* of the Earth, in its portion are caves, and **wells,**α,11 prisons, every dark and uninhabited place, and cemeteries.

(10) De bestiis {autem}, in parte eius sunt elephantes, et cameli, et omnis bestia grandis et deformis ut porci, et **ursi**,[α] et symie, et canes nigri et cati nigri.

(11) De avibus {quoque,} in parte eius ille que magnum habent corpus et collum longum, ut strucio, et aquila et *__rachem__*,[αε] ac omnis avis cuius vox horribilis est; {item} corvus, et cornicula, et omnis avis cuius color niger est.

(12) De reptilibus {vero} terre *et minutis vermibus*, sunt pulices, et cinifes, et musce, et sorices, ac omnis vermis devastans et fetidus qui est intra terra.

(13) De plantis {autem}, in parte eius est omnis arbor gallarum, et *__harobe__*,[αε] et aromatica qui vocatur *__balot__*,[αε] et cucurbite et cucumeres, ac omnis arbor spinam habens nocivam sine fructum, et lentes, et consiligines.

(14) De specibus {vero} medicinalibus, altabar quod vocatum est *__aloe__*, *__el alhahleg__*, et *__almaleg__*, que sunt in similitudine **pinorum**[γ] de India venientum, ac omnis planta in qua est potio mortifera, et omnis res amara ut absinthium. (15) Et universaliter, omne vegetale nigrum *cuius complexio*[γ] frigida est et sicca, et sapor **ponticus seu stipticus**[β] linguam stringens, et illud cuius sapor suavis non est, et odor fetidus.

(16) De specibus {quoque} aromaticis, *__alcassar__* id est *__quida__*, et *__cassur alhose__*, et sunt cortices ligni cuiusdam, et *__asseliqa__*, et *__almia__*, qui est *__nataf__*.[αε]

(17) De indumentis {autem}, eius sunt **cilicia sive saga**,[β] ac panni de lana, et tapeta, ac omnis pannus grossus.

(18) De humana natura, in parte eius est cogitatio, et pauca locutio, calliditas, et **mors**,[α1] ab hominibus esse solitarium, **ac extraneum eis**,[α] et conari ad se preferendum aliis,[2] et ad superandum, et ad **tollendum seu auferendum**[β] et **ad provocandum ad iram seu contristandum**,[β] in sermone constantem, in cogitationibus prolixum, **scire consilia seu secreta**,[β] ac servitium divinum, **homines afficere tedio et fatigare**,[βγ] esse discolum sive onerosum,[3] **esse timidum et dubitativum**,[β] **in nemine quidem considentem**;[γ] et uni-

---

[1]mors] W amans.   [2]aliis] G eis.   [3]onerosum] WVG; L honerosum.

(10) {But} of the beasts, in its portion are elephants, camels, and any animal that is big and ugly, such as pigs, **bears**,[α,12] monkeys, black dogs and black cats.

(11) {Also} of the birds, in its portion are those which have a big body and a long neck, such as the ostrich, the eagle, the *__rachem__*[αε,13] [the bustard], and any bird with a terrifying voice; {likewise,} the raven, **the crow**,[14] and any bird whose color is black.

(12) {Moreover} of the animals that creep on the earth *and tiny worms*, fleas, gnats, flies, shrew-mice, and every destructive and foul-smelling worms that dwell in the ground.

(13) {But} of the plants, in its portion is every gall-oak, and the *__harobe__*[αε,15] [the carob], and the aromatic called *__balot__*,[αε,16] and gourds and cucumbers, and every tree with harmful thorns without fruit, and lentils, and lung-worts.

(14) {Moreover} of the medicinal species, *__altabar__*, which is called *__aloe__*; *__alhahleg__*, and *__almaleg__*, which resemble the **pines**[γ,17] that come from India, and every tree that contains a deadly poison, and anything bitter, like wormwood. (15) In general, ⟨in its portion is⟩ every plant that is black, *whose mixture*[γ,18] is cold and dry, ⟨whose⟩ taste is **bitter or astringent**[β,19] paralyzing the tongue, and that whose taste is not agreeable and ⟨whose⟩ smell is foul.

(16) {Besides,} of the aromatic species, *__alcassar__*, that is *__quida__* [cassia: Ex. 30:24], and *__cassur alhose__*, which are tree barks, and *__asseliqa__*, and *__almia__*, which is *__nataf__*[αε,20]

(17) {But} of garments, in its portion are *__cilicium__* or *__sagum__*[β,21] [two types of cloaks], and woolen fabrics, silk fabric, and every thick fabric.

(18) Of human nature [human traits], thought is in its portion, and taciturnity, and craftiness, **death**,[α,22] to be isolated from other people, **strange to them**,[α,23] attempting to place himself before others, being victorious, **making away with or stealing**,[β,24] **provoking anger or causing sadness**,[β,25] keeping one's word, of lengthy thoughts, **knowledge of intentions and hidden things**,[β,26] divine service, **to make people tired and fatigue ⟨them⟩**,[βγ,27] **to be of bad temper or burdensome**,[β,28] **to be timid and hesitant**,[β,29] to

versaliter **fallacem esse quoquo modo**,[α1] **valor eius et utilitas**[β] in paucis est, **in multis** {vero} **seu multipliciter**[β,2] est **inutilis et non valens.**[β]

(19) **Colere terra et laborare**,[β] edificare, mineras extrahere, abscondita quaerere, fodere et adquirere in re mortuorum, ac in omni re durante multis annis. (20) Artificium eius omne laboriosum est et parum valens, ac omne opus despectum ut lapides incidere et puteos mundare | ac omne officium **sordidum seu labefactivum.**[β]

12vb

(21) Et significat super patres, et patrum patres, super mortuos, et super fletum, et **paralisim, et timorem**,[γ] et paupertatem, et abiectionem, et longa itinera periculosa, et non est ei **profectus** {etiam} **seu proficium**[β] in omnibus rebus.

(22) Et si in hominis nativitate principans fuerit super ipse, dabit ei de natura sua quidquid boni habuerit, si in bono loco fuerit ex parte Solis et **ex parte orbis signorum**,[γ] adhuc **ex parte hore seu horarum**,[β] secundum quod explanabo; {quod} si fuerit econtrario, dabit omne[3] despectum. (23) Cum {autem} fuerit **in sua dignitate**,[γ] si fuerit in eius complexione **stella benevola**,[γ] tunc omnes res suas convertit in bonum si quidam **stella benevola**[γ] **in dignitate sua**[γ] fuerit, si {autem} **humiliata**[γ] fuerit parvis erit valor eius. (24) Si {vero} **stella malivola**[γ] in eius complexione fuerit et ambe in fortitudine sua, tunc significabit hoc super **actionem et obtentum**,[β] ac **spoliationem et ablationem**[β] maximam; et si **stella malivola**[γ] in fortitudine sua non fuerit, tunc dabit omnem rem despectam et abiectam cum **vituperio, opprobrio et improperio**,[γ] secundum quod hoc totum in LIBRO NATIVITATUM explanabo.

(25) Et si {vero} fuerit Saturnus **solus super**[α] figuram hominis, tunc erit natus statura recta, color mediocris, inter album et nigrum; et erit **simplex seu religiosus**,[αβ] amabilis et fortis, capilli eius nigri et crispi, et pilosus in pectore, oculi eius mediocres, habundantes in frigiditate et humiditate. (26) Totum {autem} hoc erit si fuerit Saturnus orientalis a Sole, secundum quod explanabo; si {autem} occidentalis fuerit, erit ille macer, capilli non crispi, *complexio eius*[γ] frigida et sicca. (27) Et universaliter **deformitatem magnam** significat **in figuram et colore**,[γ] et pilositatem in corpore eius, **nasum spissum seu grossum**,[βγ] et similiter labia, et **dentes fetidi.**[γ]

---

[1]modo] WVG; L om.   [2]vero seu multipliciter] LW; GV om.   [3]omne] LWV; G ei.

agree with nobody;ᵞ,³⁰ in general, to be deceitful in the same way,ᵅ,³¹ of little worth or utility,ᵝ,³² many times {indeed} or in many waysᵝ,³³ useless and worthless.ᵝ,³⁴

(19) ⟨In its portion is⟩ tilling and cultivating the soil,ᵝ,³⁵ building, mining metals, searching for hidden things, digging and acquiring things related to the dead, and anything that lasts many years. (20) In its portion is every craft that is laborious and of little worth, any lowly occupation such as hewing stone, cleaning wells, and every filthy or debilitatingᵝ,³⁶ craft.

(21) It indicates fathers, grandfathers, the deceased, weeping, paralysis, fear,ᵞ,³⁷ poverty, dejection, long and dangerous journeys, and one who has no success or {also} profitᵝ,³⁸ in all his undertakings.

(22) In a man's nativity, if it [Saturn] is his [the native's] ruler, it will give him from its nature whatever good it has, if it [Saturn] is in a good place with respect to the Sun, and with respect to the orb of the signs,ᵞ,³⁹ also with respect to the hour or the hours,ᵝ,⁴⁰ as I shall explain;⁴¹ {but} in the opposite case it will give everything contemptible. (23) {But} when it [Saturn] is in its dignity,ᵞ,⁴² if a benevolent starᵞ,⁴³ is in its [Saturn's] mixture, then all his [the native's] affairs will turn ⟨from misfortune⟩ to good ⟨fortune⟩, if some benevolent planetᵞ is in its dignity;ᵞ,⁴⁴ {but} if it is humiliatedᵞ,⁴⁵ [in its perigee] it will be of little avail. (24) {Moreover} if a malevolent starᵞ,⁴⁶ is in its [Saturn's] mixture and both ⟨are⟩ in their strength, then this will indicate action and winning,ᵝ,⁴⁷ and the greatest plundering and taking away;ᵝ,⁴⁸ but if the malevolent starᵞ is not in its strength, then it will give him [the native] every contemptable and abject thing with dishonor, disgrace and reproach,ᵞ,⁴⁹ as I shall explain all this in the BOOK OF NATIVITIES.⁵⁰

(25) {Moreover} if Saturn is alone in chargeᵅ,⁵¹ of a man's form, then the native's stature will be erect, ⟨his⟩ color intermediate, between white and black; he will be modest and pious,ᵅᵝ,⁵² lovable and strong, his hair black and curly, with hair on the chest, eyes of medium size, with abounding in cold and moistness. (26) {But} all this will be if Saturn is oriental with respect to the Sun, as I shall explain; {but} if it is occidental ⟨of the Sun⟩ he [the native] will be lean, ⟨his⟩ hair will not be curly, and *his mixture*ᵞ,⁵³ will be cold and dry. (27) In general, it indicates a great deformity in shape and color,ᵞ,⁵⁴ hairiness in his body, a thick or large nose,ᵝᵞ,⁵⁵ and similarly ⟨regarding⟩ the lips, and foul-smelling teeth.ᵞ,⁵⁶

(28) In eius {autem} parte de corpore hominis sunt ossa, et splen, et auris dexter, **et anus, atque cholera nigra.**ᵞ

(29) Egritudines {quoque} ipsius sunt **furiositas**,ᵞ et desipientia, **tremor**,ᵅ et paralysis, **ablatio loquele**,ᵅ lepra, et podagra, et omnis **egritudo cronica seu diuturna**,^(βγ) ac omnis {etiam} morbus frigidus et siccus de frigiditate quidem accidens et siccitate.

(30) De etatibus {vero} hominis, in parte eius est **senium seu decrepita etas**^β ac ultimum vite.

(31) **De partibus mundi**,ᵞ habet oriens.

(32) De coloribus nigrum et **colorem pulvereum seu cinericium**.^β

(33) De diebus, diem **sabbati**,^π et de noctibus **illam que precedit diem Mercurii**;ᵅ et de horis primam et octavam.

(34) De litteris {vero} *pe* et *aya* et *syn*, ⟨⟨...⟩⟩;^μ de figuris {autem} hanc ⰉⰄ°.

(35) Et anni eius maximi sunt .256., magni .57., medii .43. cum dimidio, et minores .30. (36) Anni {vero} partis qui vocatur *firdaria* undecima. (37) Et **virtus radiorum corporis eius**,ᵞ .9. gradus ante retro totidem.

2 (1) Iupiter est sub Saturno ipse, enim est in spera .6a. respectu terra. (2) Et est calidus et humidus, in complexione **temperatus**,ᵞ et est inter **planetis**ᵞ melior. (3) Significat vitam et omnem boni multiplicationem, **fructificationem et crementum**,^(αθ) | sermones iustitie et equitatis.

13ra

(4) In parte eius est anima vegetativa.

(5) De **climatibus**,ᵅ secundum, quod est **terra Sceva, que vocatur Algeman**,ᵅ et terra Alehigese, que est terra Assur et Messa, *id est Assurorum et Medorum terra forte*.

(6) De gentibus quidem, in parte eius sunt BABYLONII et PERSE.

(28) {But} of the human body, the bones are in its portion, and the spleen, the right ear, **the anus, and the black bile.**[γ,57]

(29) {Besides,} the infirmities in its portion are **fury,**[γ,58] idiocy, **trembling,**[α,59] paralysis, **loss of speech,**[α,60] leprosy, podagra, every **chronic or protracted disease,**[βγ,61] and {also} every disease that is cold and dry and comes from cold and dryness.

(30) {Moreover} of the ages of man, **senility or extreme old age**[β,62] and the end of life are in its portion.

(31) **Of the parts of the world,**[γ,63] it has the east.

(32) Of colors, **the color of dust or ashes.**[β]

(33) Of the days ⟨of the week⟩, the day⟨time⟩ of the **Sabbath**[π,64] [from sunrise to sundown on Saturday]; of the nights, **the one that precedes the day of Mercury**[α,65] [Tuesday night]; of the hours, the first and **eighth.**

(34) {Moreover} of letters, _peh_, _'ayin_ and _shin_, ⟨⟨and some say also nun⟩⟩;[μ,66] {but} of the shapes, these two ⟨symbols⟩.

(35) Its greatest years are 256, the great ⟨years⟩ 57, the middle ⟨years⟩ 43½, the least ⟨years⟩ 30. (36) {Moreover} the years of the part called _al-fardār_ are 11. (37) The **power of the rays of its body**[γ,67] is nine degrees, ahead of or behind it.

2 (1) Jupiter is below Saturn, for it is in the sixth sphere with respect to the Earth. (2) It is hot and moist, **temperate**[γ,1] in its mixture, and it is the best of the **planets.**[γ] (3) It indicates life and every increase in good fortune, **fruitfulness and growth,**[αθ,2] and statements of justice and equity.

(4) The vegetative soul is in its portion.

(5) Of the **climates,**[α] the second, which is **the land of Sheba, which is called Algeman,**[α,3] and the land of Alehigese, which is of Assur et Messa, _that is, perhaps the land of the Assyrians and of the Medes._

(6) Of the nations, the BABYLONIANS and the PERSIANS are in its portion.

(7) Et de hominibus, iudices, et sapientes, ac Deo servantes, religiosi, **acceptabiles**ʸ et iusti.

(8) **De metallis**,ʸ stagnum, et illud quod vocatur *tutia*, et lapis vocatur *iacinctus* albus et citrinus, saphirus, onyx, et onyca atque cristallus, et omnis lapis albus lucidus in quo est **valor et utilitas**.ᵝ

(9) {Item} in parte eius sunt domus orationum, et loca servitiorum divinorum, et loca munda.

(10) De bestiis {autem}, eius est omnis illa que fissam habet ungulam, sicut oves et cervi, et omnis bestia pulchri aspectui, que nociva non est nisi modicum.

(11) De avibus, pavones et **altilia seu galline**,ᵝ et columbe; et universaliter omnis avis granum comedens, que utilis est hominibus.

(12) **De reptilibus terre seu vermibus**,ᵝ in parte eius est omnis vermis utilis et non nocivus, sicut **bombix qui facit sericum**.ᵅ

(13) **De plantis**,ʸ nuces, et amigdali, et fructus vocatus *pestet*, *id est pistatie*, et *benzar*, item *zedaar* vel *sacuar*ᵝ que est *saba* quedam; et universaliter, omnis fructus cuius cortex exterior sive resta[1] removetur et nucleus istius comeditur.

(14) {Item} in parte eius est frumentum, et ordeum, ⟨⟨...⟩⟩ᵛ ac **milium**.ᵅ

(15) **Et de fructibus**,ʸ ille qui vocatur *albahar*, et *algetemin*, et *almaruegos*, et quod hiis simile est.

(16) De specibus {vero} medicinalibus, omne illud cuius complexio temperata est et odor bonus, ac sapor {etiam} que vocatur aromatica, sicut muscus et *alhafor*, quod est canphora, et *succarum*, et *albasse*, *basse* et *semiebar*, et que hiis assimilantur.

(17) De indumentis, quidem pulchri sicut illa de **bombace**,ʸ et omnis pannum subtilis.

---

[1] sive resta] LW; GV om.

(7) Of human beings, judges ⟨are in its portion⟩, and scholars, worshipers of God, those who are pious, **acceptable**ᵞ,4 and righteous.

(8) **Of the metals**,ᵞ,5 tin, and what is called *tuti'a*, and the stone called white and yellow *iacinctus*, sapphire, onyx, and onycha and crystal, and any white and brilliant stone that **is valuable and useful**.β,6

(9) {Likewise,} in its portion are houses of prayer, places of divine service, and places that are pure.

(10) {But} of the animals, in its portion is any of those with a cloven hoof, like sheep and deer, and every animal of handsome appearance which is only slightly harmful.

(11) Of the birds, peacocks, and **altilia or hens**,β,7 and doves; and generally every bird that eats grain, which is useful to human beings.

(12) **Of the animals that creep on the earth or vermin**,β,8 in its portion is any vermin that is useful and does not cause harm, like the **worm that makes silk**.α,9

(13) **Of the plants**,ᵞ,10 nuts, almonds, the fruit called *pestet, that is, pistachio*, and *benzar*; likewise, *zedaar* **or** *sacuar*,β,11 which is a certain *saba*; in general, every fruit that is peeled and its inside is eaten.

(14) {Likewise,} in its portion is wheat, barley, ⟨⟨peas⟩⟩ᵛ,12 and **millet**.α,13

(15) And **of the fruits**,ᵞ,14 the one called *albahar*, and *algetemin*, and *almaruegos*, and those resembling them.

(16) {Moreover} of the medicinal species, everything whose mixture is tempered, and is good smelling, and {also} of taste called aromatic, such as moss and *alhafor*, which is camphor, and *succarum*, *albasse*, *basse* and *semiebar*, and those resembling them.

(17) Of garments, those that are beautiful, such as those made of **silk**,ᵞ,15 and every sheer fabric.

(18) {Item} *de moribus hominum*,ʸ est in eius parte **amabilitas seu amicabilitas**,ᵝ iustitia, pax, fides, et **conversatio pia sive religiosa**,ᵝʸ et bona fama *scilicet boni nominis*, et **pietas**,ʸ ac animi libertas in sermonibus veritatis,[1] atque constantia; facies {quoque} ipsius ridens est; et ipse bonum diligens, de malum odiens. (19) Et universaliter, omnem habet rem odio que secundum consuetudinem non est neque secundum iustitiam; amat {autem} loqui satis; **et desiderat iustum a filiis hominibus et doceri**;ᵅᶿ,ʸ et plurimum cogitationum eius est divitias acquirere et congregare, ac in omni re superare dum cum secundum rectam sit iustitie viam; scire vult leges et iudicia, ac explanationes somnorum, et servire in **synagogis et domibus orationum**.ᵝ (20) Item significat super filios, et filiorum filios; et universaliter significat super **felicitatem et eufortunium**ᵅ ac honorem.

(21) Si {autem} solus prefuerit nativitati hominis, de natura sua dabit ei omne quod honorabilem est, et econtrario si non fuerit in fortitudine sua. (22) Addunt {quoque} et diminuunt **planete**ᵅ **cum ei applicantur**,ʸ aut per coniunctionem aut per aspectum; {quod} si stelle **malivole**ʸ fuerint, diminuerint de bono eius, et **benevole**,ʸ bonum | super bonum augmentabunt. (23) De forma quidem hominis significat, si fuerit orientalis, super staturam **convenientem seu placidam**,ᵝ colorem album cum rubedine, **pili eius seu capilli**ᵝ pauci, oculi eius pulchri, et ipse homo amabilis in omnibus operibus suis, et *eius complexio*ʸ calida est et humida. (24) Si {vero} fuerit occidentalis, erit corpus eius rectum sed eius albedo non est pura, capilli eius crispis contrarii, et ipse calvus; habundabit {quoque} in ipso humiditas. (25) Et universaliter significat super hominem boni animi ac **bone voluntatis**,ʸ pulcros habentem oculos, cuius barba pulcra atque capilli subtiles.

(26) De corpore {autem} hominis, in eius parte est epar, et auris sinister, et coste. et totus etiam sanguis.

(27) Et egritudines eius ac {etiam} omnis egritudo **acuta seu velox, et levis est et que festinat**.ᵅᵝ

(28) De etatibus quidem hominis, **eius est senectus que scilicet inter iuventutem est et senium sive decrepitatem**.ᵝʸ

---

[1] veritatis] G veritas.

(18) {Likewise,} *of the customs of human beings*,[γ,16] in its portion is **loveliness or friendliness**,[β,17] justice, peace, faith, **pious or religious manner of life**,[βγ,18] a good reputation, *meaning a good name*, **piety**,[γ,19] freedom of the soul in statements of truthfulness, and constancy; {besides,} his face is smiling; he ⟨will be⟩ a lover of goodness and a hater of evil. (19) In general: he [the native] abhors everything that is not in accordance with custom and in accordance with justice; {but} he loves to speak a lot; **he desires to be taught what is just by sons of men**[αθ,20,γ,21] [i.e., human beings]; his thought is mainly to obtain and accumulate riches, and to prevail in everything, but only according to the straight path of justice; he wishes to know laws and judgments and interpretations of dreams, and to worship in **synagogues or in houses of prayer**.[β,22] (20) Likewise, [Jupiter] indicates sons and grandsons; and in general it indicates **happiness, good fortune**,[α,23] and honor.

(21) {But} if it [Jupiter] is in charge alone over a person's nativity, it [Jupiter] will give him [the native] everything that is honorable, and the opposite applies if it [Jupiter] is not in its strength. (22) {Besides,} the **planets**[α,24] increase and diminish ⟨these indications⟩ **when they approach it**,[γ,25] either by conjunction or by aspect; {but} if the stars are **malevolent**,[γ] they will diminish its [Jupiter's] good, and ⟨if⟩ **benevolent**,[γ] they will add good to good. (23) Of the human form, if it [Jupiter] is oriental ⟨of the Sun⟩, it indicates a **fine and pleasant**[β,26] stature, a color that is white with ruddiness, **his hair or the hair**[β,27] of the head sparse, his eyes beautiful, and he is a lovable person in all his actions, and *his mixture*[γ,28] is hot and moist. (24) {But} if it ⟨Jupiter⟩ is occidental ⟨of the Sun⟩, his body will be straight but his whiteness is not pure, his hair will the opposite of curly, he ⟨will be⟩ bald; {besides,} moisture will also be abundant in him. (25) In general: it indicates a man with a good soul, **good will**,[γ,29] having beautiful eyes, his beard is beautiful and the hair on his head is thin.

(26) {But} of the human body, the liver is in its portion, and the left ear, the ribs, and also all the blood.

(27) Of its infirmities, {also} every disease that is **acute or swift, and is light, and hurries up**[αβ,30] [passes quickly].

(28) Of the ages of man, **old age is in its portion, which is between youth and senility or extreme old age**.[βγ,31]

(29) De coloribus {vero} albus et viridis ac **citreus seu croceus**,^{β} ac omnis lucidus et radiosus.

(30) **De angulis**^{α} {quoque}, **septentrionalis.**^{γ}

(31) De diebus, *dies Iovis*,^{γ} et de noctibus, **illa que sequitur dies Lune**,^{α} et de horis earum, prima et octava.

(32) De litteris sunt *heez* et *lamech* et *beth* vel *bez*, et hec figura ⌇.

(33) Anni {vero} eius maximi sunt .427., magni .79., mediocres .45. et dimidius, et **parvi seu minimi**^{β} .12.

(34) Anni {vero} partis *firdaria* vocatur .12.[1]

(35) Et virtus corporis eius est .9. gradus ante se et totidem post se.

3   (1) Mars, calidus est, et siccus, adurens. (2) Nocivus et corrumpens; significat super devastationes, et **caristiam**,^{α} ac **combustiones ex igne**,^{γ} rebelliones, sanguinis effusiones, et occisiones, bella, rixas, et **tonitrua**^{γ} et **coruscationes seu fulgura.**^{βγ} (3) ⟨⟨...⟩⟩^{μ}

(4) ⟨⟨...⟩⟩^{μ}

(5) De **climatibus**^{α} quidem, in parte eius tertium, ut **Egyptus**^{γδ} et Alexandria.

(6) De gentibus {etiam}, eius sunt Alemangos, et Anglicai, et **illi qui colunt ignem seu igni servant**^{β} *ut Cumani vel Selani quidam.*

(7) De hominibus {autem} universaliter in parte eius sunt omnes viri bellici, et qui presunt eis, raptores, et **artifices armorum**^{γ} ac fabri; {item} artifices lancearum et gladiorum, et **viri sanguinum**,^{γ} et **bestiis servientes seu custodientes eas**^{β} *ut qui vocantur garciones*, et illi qui eis assimilantur.

(8) **De metallis** {vero} **seu mineralibus terre**,^{β} ferrum, et **cuprum**,^{γ} sulphur, et napta; {item} vasa vitrea, et instrumenta armorum, et omnis lapis rubicundus.

---

[1] Anni vero partis *firdaria* vocatur .12.] W; LGV om.

(29) {Moreover} of colors, white, green, and **citron or saffron**,[β,32] and any that is shining and radiant.

(30) {Besides,} **of the angles**,[α,33] **the northern**.[γ,34]

(31) Of the days, *the day of Jupiter*,[γ,35] of the nights, **the one which follows the day of the Moon**,[α,36] of their hours, the first and eighth.

(32) Of letters, *het*, *samekh*, and *bet* or *bez*, and this shape ≢.

(33) {Moreover} its greatest years are 427, the great ⟨years⟩ 79, the middle ⟨years⟩ 45½, **the small or least**[β,37] ⟨years⟩ 12.

(34) {Moreover} the years of the part called *al-fardār*, 12.

(35) The power of its body is nine degrees, ahead of or behind it.

3   (1) Mars. Hot, dry, burning. (2) Harmful and corrupting; it indicates destruction, **high price**,[α,1] **destruction by fire**,[γ,2] rebellions, bloodshed, killing, wars, quarrels, and **thunder**[γ,3] and **lightning flash or lightning**.[βγ,4] (3) ⟨⟨In general: everything that is not according to its ⟨own⟩ disposition and character⟩⟩.[μ,5]

(4) ⟨⟨Of human nature, the power of anger is in its portion⟩⟩.[μ,6]

(5) Of the **climates**,[α] the third is in its portion, such as **Egypt** [γδ,7] and Alexandria.

(6) {Also} of the nations, in its portion are Alemangos, and the English, and **those who worship or tend the fire**,[β,8] *like certain Cumans or Selans*.

(7) {But} of human beings, in general all soldiers, and those who command them, are in its portion, and robbers, **craftsmen of weapons**[γ,9] and smiths; {likewise,} craftsmen of spears and swords, **men of bloods**[γ,10] [bloodletters], **those who take care of animals or keep them safe**,[β,11] *who are called "garciones,"* and those who resemble them.

(8) {Moreover} **of the metals or the minerals of the Earth**,[β,12] iron and **copper**,[γ,13] sulfur, naphtha; {likewise,} glass vessels, weapons, and any red stone.

(9) Sunt {etiam} in parte eius **fortalicia seu munitiones**,^β et turres, **furni ac fornaces.**^β

(10) Et de bestiis, **lupi**^γδ et canes ac leopardi.

(11) De avibus, *albusia*, id est[1] **accipiter.**^α

(12) Et de vermibus terre, omnis nocivus ut serpens et scorpio et omnis venenosus mortiferus sue interficiens.

(13) **De plantis**,^γ spine, ⟨⟨...⟩⟩,^ν et illa qui vocatur *albacas* qui est lignum
13va quidam de quo tingitur ut bersilium et similiter | *alassor* et *aspiuma* et omni **planta seu arbor**^β spinosa; {item} piper, et synapium et tyminum, raphanus, porarum et allia et *hasse daabe* id est *tode*.

(14) De specibus medicinalibus, *estaberos*, et *tarebase*, et *tarebimage*, et *meserou*, et *parabion*, et stamonea, et ***perassion*** **vel prassum,**^β et *casebat*, et omnis **species**^γ nociens confestim, et omnis illa cuius sapor calidus est et acutus et non suavis.

(15) Et de aromaticis, *altendaal* et *zaferam*, id est, croceus.

(16) De indumentis, pellitia leporina et *alsanius*, ac vestes **scarlatice seu in grana**^βγδ tincte.

(17) De humana {vero} natura, in parte eius est **procacitas**,^γ et **violentia**,^γ et **victoria sive superatio rixe,**^β et contentiones, acritas et iracundia, obprobriorum multiplicatio et maledictionum, mendacia, accusationes et adulantia, faciei austeritas, animi inconstantia, falsitatis incrementum, temptatio hominis contra omnem prohibitum in lege, latrocinia, et omne opus malum, et crudelitas, et labor manus, et itinerari de loco ad locum, aggredi pericula, gentes afligere, percutere, incarcerare, captivare, et res accipere, parietes suffodere, et ostia aperire discooperire res quilibet absconditas; et universaliter: ipsius est omne malum, et non est in ipso bonum.

(18) Significat super fratres, et rixosos, conscisionem[2] infantis in utero matris, et facere mulieres abortare; et significat omnem malum subito accidens, et omnem devastationem et destructionem.

---

[1]id est] G om.   [2]conscisionem] WV; L consicionem; G concilionem.

(9) {Also} in its portion are **fortresses or strongholds**,[β,14] towers, and **ovens or furnaces.**[β,15]

(10) Of the animals, **wolves**,[γδ,16] dogs and leopards.

(11) Of the birds, *albusia*, which is the **hawk**.[α,17]

(12) Of the vermin of the earth, all that are harmful, like the serpent and the scorpion, and every ⟨animal⟩ that has a deadly or lethal poison.

(13) **Of the plants**,[γ,18] thorns, ⟨⟨pears⟩⟩,[ν,19] the one called *albacas*, which is a certain wood used for dyeing, like bersilium, and so too *alassor* and *aspiuma*, and any **plant or tree**[β,20] that has thorns; {likewise,} pepper, synapium [mustard], tyminus [cumin], raphanus [radish], porarum [leeks], garlic, and *hasse daabe* which is *tode*.

(14) Of the medicinal species, *estaberos*, *tarebase*, *tarebimage*, *meserou*, *parabion*, and *stamonea* [thorn-apple], and ***perassion* or prassum**[β,21] [leek], and *casebat*, and every **species**[γ,22] that harms immediately, and every one whose taste is hot, sharp, and unpleasant.

(15) Of the aromatics, *altendaal* and *zaferam*, which is saffron.

(16) Of clothes, rabbit and weasel skin and clothes dyed **scarlet or in the grain.**[βγδ,23]

(17) {Moreover} of human nature [i.e., human traits], **impudence**[γ,24] is in its portion, and **violence**,[γ,25] **victory or overcoming quarrels**,[β,26] disputes, irritability and proneness to anger, many reproaches and insults, falsehood, accusations and flattery, severity of the face, inconstancy of the soul, increase of treachery, temptation of man in relation to everything that is prohibited by law, robberies, and every evil action, cruelty, manual labor, moving from place to place, putting oneself in danger, distressing people, beating, putting in prison, capturing, stealing money, digging in walls, and opening doors to discover hidden things; in general: in its portion is any evil, and there is no good in it.

(18) It indicates brothers, quarrelsome people, tearing a child in pieces in the mother's womb, causing women to miscarry; and indicates every evil that happens suddenly, and every devastation and destruction.

(19) Si *ergo* solus *prefuerit* nativitati hominis, dabit ei de natura sua quidquid boni habuerit, si fuerit in fortitudine sua, et aspexerint eum **stelle benevole**,ᵞ econtrario {vero} si non fuerit in fortitudine sua, et commisceantur ei **stelle malivole**.ᵞ (20) {Quod} si fuerit orientalis a Sole, erit natus **procerus** *stature* **sive longus**,ᵝ et color eius albus declinans ad rubedinem, et pilosus in corpore; si {vero} fuerit occidentalis, erit stature brevis, et color eius rufus, facies eius rotunda, oculi parvi, et capilli rusi non crispi, et *complexio*ᵞ corporis eius sicca. (21) Et universaliter super illum significat cuius color rubeus est, et oculi eius *varii* sicut catorum oculorum, in **colore suo**ᵞ est aliquid turpe, signa habet et lentigines in facie; operationes {quoque} ipsi cum festinatione fuerint et discolia ac furore.

(22) De corpore quidem humano in parte eius est ⟨⟨...⟩⟩ᵛ naris dexter, et nervi, et renes, et **genitalia seu pudendum**.ᵝᵞ

(23) {Item} cholera rubea et sanguis adustus.

(24) Et egritudines eius sunt febres acute, et **supercalefactio**,ᵞ et **apostemata rubicunda seu carbunculi**,ᵝᵞ et cauteria, et timor alienationis, *et furiositas, et tediositas seu discolia*.

(25) De etatibus {autem} hominis, **iuventatis finem et principium senectutis**.ᵅ

(26) Et color eius **rubicundus**.ᵞ

(27) **De angulis**ᵅ quidem, eius est occidentalis.

(28) Et de diebus, ***die Martis***,ᵞ et de noctibus **illa que precedit diem sabbati**;ᵖ,ᵅ et de horis eius prima et octava.

(29) De litteris {autem} eius est *sazit* et *coph* et *ioze*, et de figuris ☿ et

13vb   quidam | dicunt quod ista ☤.

(30) Anni {vero} eius maximi sunt .284., mangni .66., medii .40. et dimidius, et minimi .15.

(31) Anni veri pars *firdarii* vocate sunt, .7.

(19) *Consequently,* If it [Mars] is *in charge* alone of the nativity in charge, it [Mars] will give him [the native] of its nature any good fortune it has, if it is in its strength, and **benevolent stars**ʸ aspect it; {but} the opposite applies if it is not in its strength, and if **malevolent stars**ʸ are mixed with it. (20) {But} if it [Mars] is oriental of the Sun, the native will be **tall or long**[β,27] *of stature,* his color white and tending to ruddiness, and hairy in ⟨his⟩ body; {moreover,} if it [Mars] is occidental ⟨of the Sun⟩, he [the native] will be short of stature, his color reddish, his face round, his eyes small, his hair red and not curly, and the *mixture*[γ,28] of his body dry. (21) In general: it indicates one whose color is red, whose eyes are *variegated* like cats' eyes, in **its color**[γ,29] he is something ugly, he has moles and freckles on his face; {besides,} ⟨his⟩ actions will be ⟨done⟩ with haste, perversity and madness.

(22) Of the human body, in its portion is ⟨⟨the gallbladder⟩⟩,[ν,30] the right nostril, the tendons, the kidneys, and the **genitals or the pudenda.**[βγ,31]

(23) {Likewise,} the red bile and burnt blood.

(24) Of its infirmities, acute fevers, **overheating,**[γ,32] **red abscesses or carbuncles,**[βγ,33] burns, fear of madness, *fury, fatigue or disaffection.*

(25) {But} of the ages of man, **the end of youth and the beginning of old age.**[α,34]

(26) Its color is **red.**[γ,35]

(27) **Of the angles,**[α,36] in its portion is the western.

(28) Of the days ⟨of the week⟩, the *day of Mars,*[γ,37] and of nights, **the one which precedes the Sabbath**;[π,38,α,39] of the hours, the first and eighth ⟨are⟩ in its portion.

(29) {But} of the letters, *sadi, qof,* and *yod,* and of the shapes this ♂ and some say this ♃.

(30) {Moreover} its greatest years are 284, the great ⟨years⟩ 66, the middle ⟨years⟩ 40½, the least ⟨years⟩ 15.

(31) The years of the period called *al-fardār,* seven.

(32) Fortitudo {autem} corporis eius est .8. gradus, ante se et totidem post.

4 (1) Sol calidus est et siccus **temperate**,ᵞ et vivat et nocet, et bonum facit et malum.

(2) Eius est lumen et animam sensitivam.

(3) In parte eius de **climatibus**ᵅ est quartum, sicut terra Babylonie et Alaerac et terra Israel.

(4) Et de gentibus, **Edom seu Ydoumei**ᵝ *id est Christiani*, et Thorach et Dilas.

(5) De hominibus {vero}, reges et **principes**ᵅ atque **consiliatores seu consules.**ᵝ

(6) Et **de metallis seu mineralibus**[1] **terre,**ᵝ aurum et lapides preciosi sicut **adamas**,ᵞᵟ et est in parte eius sal rubeum et *almaracasita*, que auro similis est, et *alsardabane* et omnis ladis lucens.

(7) **Sunt** {etiam} **in parte eius**ᵅ mansiones et domus regum.

(8) De animalibus {autem}, homines, et equi. et leones. et arietes magni qui vocatur *carim*,ᵅᵋ *transmarini scilicet*.

(9) De avibus {autem}, *alaeikenam*, id est, **strutio**,ᵞᵟ et *surame*.

(10) Et de vermibus terre, magni et interficientes.

(11) **Et de plantis**,ᵞ **lignum dactilorum seu palmarum**,ᵝ et vites, et olive, et pomi, et mori, *haneealmelont* id est cerafi, et ficus.

(12) {Item} in parte eiuis est rosa, et *allebia*, et sericum.

(13) De specibus quidem aromaticis, spica nardi, et *alarmese*, *olach*, et omnis illa cuius complexio calida est, et sapor fortis.

(14) Et est in parte eius omnis commixtio honorabilis.

---

[1]mineralibus] corrected; LWG mineris.

(32) {But} the power of its body is eight degrees, ahead of or behind it.

4 (1) The Sun is hot and dry **in a tempered way**,^(γ,1) it sustains life and is harmful, and makes good and bad.

(2) Light and the sensitive soul is in its portion.

(3) Of the **climates**,^α the fourth is in its portion, like the land of Babylonia, Iraq, and the land of Israel.

(4) Of the nations, **Edom or the Idumaeans**,^(β,2) *that is, the Christians*, and Thorach [the Turks] and Dilas [the Dailamites].

(5) {Moreover} of human beings, kings and **princes**^(α,3) and **counselors or consuls**.^(β,4)

(6) **Of the metals and the minerals of the Earth**,^β gold, precious stones like **adamas**,^(γδ,5); in its portion is also red salt and *almaracasita*, which resembles gold, and *alsardabane*, and every sparkling stone.

(7) {Also} **in its portion**^(α,6) are **mansions**^(α,7) and kings' houses.

(8) {But} of living creatures, human beings, horses, lions, and the large sheep that are called *carim*,^(αε,8) *that is, from across the sea*.

(9) {But} of birds, *alaeikenam*, that is, **the ostrich**,^(γδ,9) and *surame*.

(10) Of the vermin of the earth, those that are large and lethal.

(11) **Of the plants**,^γ **the date or palm tree**,^(β,10) grapevines, olives, apples, mulberries, *haneealmelont*, that is, *cerafi*, and the fig-tree.

(12) {Likewise,} in its portion is the rose, and *allebia*, and silk.

(13) Of the aromatic species, spikenard, and *alarmese*, *olach*, and everything whose nature is hot, and whose taste is pungent.

(14) In its portion is any noble mixture.

(15) De natura quidem hominis, sapientia vel intellectus, et prudentia, et pulchritudo, ac **fortitudo seu robur virium**,$^\beta$ exaltationis acquisitio, ⟨⟨...⟩⟩.$^\mu$

(16) ⟨⟨...⟩⟩.$^\mu$

(17) ⟨⟨...⟩⟩$^\mu$ ⟨⟨...⟩⟩$^\nu$ {item} patres et fratres medios, secundum {vero} fortitudinem ipsius dabit de natura eius.

(18) Et si prefuerit solus forme hominis, erit pinguis, et albus in colore, oculi eius mediocres, et pili eius **subtiles seu minuti**,$^\beta$ et **pulchram** habebit **faciem**.$^\alpha$

(19) De humano {autem} corpore, in parte eius cor, et oculus dexter de die, in nocte {vero} **sinister**,$^\gamma$ et cerebrum capitis, et **meatus**,$^\alpha$ ac medietas totis corporis dexter; significat etiam super choleram rubeam.

(20) Et de egritudinibus, eius sunt ille que accidunt in ore.

(21) Et de etatibus, **finis iuventutis**.$^\alpha$

(22) Color eius rubeus et similiter croceus, sapor eius fortis.

(23) **De angulis**$^\alpha$ quidem, eius est oriens.

(24) Et de litteris _aleph_ et _daleth_ et _lamech_, et de figuris, hoc ◢.

(25) Et de diebus, **dominica**,$^\alpha$ et de noctibus **illa que procedit diem Iovis**;$^\alpha$ et de horis earum prima et .8a.

(26) Anni {vero} ipsius maximi sunt .1461., magni .120., mediocres .39. et dimidius, et minimi .19. (27) Anni {quoque} _firadarie_ sunt .10.

(28) Et fortitudo corporis eius .15. gradus ante se et totidem post se.

5 (1) Venus frigida est et humida, bone commixtionis et **temperate**,$^\gamma$ est stella **benevola ac venusta**.$^\gamma$

(15) Of human nature [human traits], wisdom or intellect, prudence, beauty, **strength or effect of forces**,[β,11] the pursuit of high rank, ⟨⟨love of wealth, loquacity, quickness at responding, and passion⟩⟩.[μ,12]

(16) ⟨⟨Of the crafts, goldsmiths, silversmiths, and makers of crowns⟩⟩.[μ,13]

(17) ⟨⟨It [the Sun] also indicates ordinances and laws,⟩⟩[μ,14] ⟨⟨and joining the congregation⟩⟩[ν,15] {likewise,} fathers the middle brothers, and it will give {indeed} from its nature according to its power.

(18) If it [the Sun] alone is in charge of a person's form, he [the native] will be fat, white in color, his eyes of medium size, his hair **thin or short**,[β,16] and he will have **a beautiful face**.[α,17]

(19) {But} of the human body, the heart is in its portion, the right eye by day, {but} by night **the left**,[γ,18] the brain of the head, **a channel**[α,19] ⟨in the body⟩, and the whole right half of the body; it also indicates the red bile.

(20) Of the infirmities, in its portion are those affecting the mouth.

(21) Of the ages ⟨of man⟩, **the end of youth**.[α,20]

(22) Its color is red and so too saffron, of tastes, the pungent is in its portion.

(23) **Of the angles**,[α,21] the east is in its portion.

(24) Of the letters, _aleph_, _dalet_ and _lamed_, and of the shapes, this one ◢.

(25) Of the days, **the Lord's**[α,22] ⟨day⟩, of the nights **the one that precedes the day of Jupiter**,[α,23] of their hours, the first and eighth.

(26) {Moreover} its greatest years are 1461, the great ⟨years⟩ 120, the middle ⟨years⟩ 39½, the least ⟨years⟩ 19. (27) {Besides,} the years of _al-fardār_, ten.

(28) The power of its body is 15 degrees, ahead of or behind it.

5 (1) Venus is cold and moist, of good and **temperate**[γ,1] mixture, a **benevolent and pleasing**[γ,2] star.

(2) In parte eius est virtus anime concupiscibilis et **generatio seu fructificatio et crementum**.^{αθ}

(3) {Item} eius est **clima**^α quintum, in quo est Hyspania et pars terre Edom *id est Christianorum.*

14ra (4) {Item} de gentibus, Arabes, et ommes **in lege | Sarracenorum credentes**.^α

(5) De hominibus quidem, eius sunt iuvenes, et eunuchi, et mulieres, et ioculatores, et organiste, ac rithmizatores.

(6) Amplius, in parte eius est quod in ventre terre est scilicet estannum, *allazairas* et *abnaguenisia* et *alinaretach*, *eumisedadar* et *allonoge*, id est *atimetum* et *enetindar*.

(7) Et iocalia quelibet, et ornamenta, et annuli mulierum.

(8) {Item} ⟨⟨...⟩⟩^ν eius sunt viridaria et pomeria, et loca **mirtorum**^{γδ} ac **germinatorum**,^γ et loca mulierum et potacionum ac **cubitum seu lectorum**.^β

(9) De bestiis {autem}, eius sunt cervi et omnis bestia coloris pulchri.

(10) Et de avibus, *alhagal*, id est cuculus, et turtures et volucres.

(11) De vermibus terre, aranea ac formica ac etiam rane.

(12) **Et de plantis**,^γ pomi et malogranati (sic!) ac omnis fructus boni odoris, et in gustu delectabilis.

(13) {Item} eius est *albessan*, et quidquid **odorifer est**,^π et pingue.

(14) Et de indumentis, **omne opus de super contextum seu consutum acu**,^β ac omnis vestis pulcher.

(15) De natura {vero} hominis, **mundicia seu comptitudo**,^β et amorositas, ⟨⟨...⟩⟩^ν et gaudium, **saltatio seu plausus**,^β ⟨⟨...⟩⟩^μ et concubitus cum mulie-

LIBER ABRAHE AVENERRE INTRODUCTORIUS AD ASTRONOMIAM   257

(2) In its portion is the power of the appetitive soul, and **generation or fruitfulness and growth**,^{αθ,3}

(3) {Likewise,} the fifth **climate**^{α} is in its portion, which includes Spain, and part of the land of Edom, *that is, of the Christians.*

(4) {Likewise,} of the nations, the Arabs, and everyone **who believe in the law [religious system] of the Saracens.**^{α,4}

(5) Of human beings, youths, eunuchs, women, comedians, musicians, and poets.

(6) In addition, in its portion is what is in the belly of the Earth, namely, tin, *allazairas*, *abnaguenisia*, *alinaretach*, *eumisedadar*, and *allonoge*, that is, *atimetum* and *enetindar*.

(7) Any jewels, and ornaments, and women's rings.

(8) {Likewise,} ⟨⟨of the Earth⟩⟩,^{ν,5} in its portion are gardens, orchards, the place of **myrtles**^{γδ,6} and **plant nurseries**,^{γ,7} the places of women and drinking and **beds or couches.**^{β,8}

(9) {But} of the animals, deer, and every animal of beautiful color.

(10) Of the birds, *alhagal*, that is, the cuckoo, turtledoves and flying creatures.

(11) Of the vermin of the earth, spiders, ants, and also frogs.

(12) **Of the plants,**^{γ} apples, pomegranates, and all fruits with a pleasant scent and sweet flavor.

(13) {Likewise,} in its portion is *albessan* [balsam], and everything that **is flagrant**,^{π,9} and fat.

(14) Of clothes, **all embroidery or sewn with a needle**,^{β,10} and every beautiful garment.

(15) {Moreover} of human nature [i.e., human traits], **cleanliness or embellishment**,^{β,11} love, ⟨⟨mockery and laughter⟩⟩,^{ν,12} joy, **dancing or clapping the**

ribus, ac ludus alearum; {item} liberalitas, et nimietas concupiscendi rem quamcumque, et iurandi falsum, ac ebrietatem amandi, amare {quoque} superfluitatem coitus, sive secundum naturam sive non, ac infantes diligere, et mercata; universaliter: iustitiam amare ac domus servitiorum divinorum.

(16) De artificiis {autem}, eius est **opus tincturarum**ᵞ et **suturarum seu modorum consuendi.**ᵝ

(17) Et significat super omnem comestionem ac **potationem seu comessationes**,ᵝ et super matrem, et filias, et super sorores minores, et secundum eius fortitudinem in nativitatem apparebit de natura eius in homine.

(18) Si {ergo} sola prefuerit in nativitate hominis, et fuerit orientalis, erit ille pinguis, albi coloris, et formosus, oculi eius nigri, et ipse **procerus sive longus**;ᵝ si {vero} fuerit occidentalis, erit stature brevis, et albedo faciei eius pura non erit, neque capilli eius crispi, et erit calvus. (19) Et universaliter: significat super | omnem formositatem, cuius facies rotunda, et oculi nigri; et ipse **lusor.**ᵅ

14rb

(20) In parte {vero} eius de humano corpore, est caro, et pinguedo, et epar, ac **semen hominis sive genitura**;ᵝ {item} eius est omnis **humor seu humiditas.**ᵝ

(21) Et egritudines eius sunt quidquid accidit in **renibus seu lumbis**ᵝ ac in pudibundis.

(22) De etatibus, eius est adolescentia **post puericiam.**ᵞ

(23) De coloribus {quoque}, ipsius est albedo, aliquantulum declinans ad viriditatem.

(24) Et sapor eius dulcis et insipidus.

(25) **De angulis**ᵅ {autem}, eius est orientalis.

(26) Et de litteris, <u>*tes*</u> et <u>*dalem*</u>; de figuris {quoque} ista ♃.

(27) De diebus quidem, ***dies Veneris***;ᵞ et de noctibus, **illa qua dies Martis sequitur**;ᵅ de horis {vero}, ipsarum prima et octave.

hands,^(β,13) ⟨⟨elegant speech⟩⟩^(μ,14) lying with women, playing with dice; {likewise} generosity, extreme appetite for everything, perjury, a fondness for drunkenness, {also} a fondness for an excess of sexual intercourse, whether or not according to nature, loving children and marketplaces; in general: love of justice and houses of divine service.

(16) {But} of the crafts, in its portion is **the work of dyeing**,^(γ,15) and **stitching or sewing together patterns**.^(β,16)

(17) It indicates every food and **drink or feasts**,^(β,17) the mother, the daughters, and the younger sisters; what will be manifest in the nature of a person [the native] is according to its [Venus's] power in the nativity.

(18) {Therefore} if it [Venus] is in charge alone of a person's nativity, and is oriental ⟨of the Sun⟩, he [the native] will be fat, of a white color, handsome, his eyes black, and he ⟨will be⟩ **tall or long**;^(β,18) {but} if it is occidental ⟨of the Sun⟩, he will be of short stature, the whiteness of his face will not be pure, his hair will not be curly, and he will be bald. (19) In general: it [Venus] indicates everyone who is handsome, whose face is round, ⟨his⟩ eyes black; and he ⟨will be⟩ a **player**.^(α,19)

(20) {Moreover} of the human body, the flesh is in its portion, and the fat, the liver, and **the human sperm or seed of generation**;^(β,20) {likewise} any **humor or humidity**^(β,21) is in its portion.

(21) Of its infirmities, everything affecting **the kidneys or hips**,^(β,22) and the genitals.

(22) Of the ages ⟨of man⟩, youth **after childhood**^(γ,23) is in its portion.

(23) {Besides,} of colors, white, and tending slightly to green.

(24) Of tastes, the sweet and the insipid.

(25) {But} **of the angles**,^(α,24) in its portion is the eastern.

(26) Of letters, *tet* and *dalet*; {besides,} of the shapes, this one ♎.

(27) Of the days, the ***day of Venus***;^(γ,25) and of the nights, **the one which follows the day of Mars**;^(α,26) {moreover} of their hours, the first and eighth.

(28) Anni {vero} eius maximi sunt .1150.,ᵅ¹ magni .82., medii .45, et minuti .8. (29) Anni {vero} partis *firdarie*, .8.

(30) Et fortitudo corporis eius .7. gradus ante se et totidem retro.

6 (1) Mercurius mixtus est et permutabilis, ipse namque permutatur secundum **planetarum**ˠ naturam, ac etiam signorum; declinat {autem} aliquantulum *eius complexio*ˠ ad frigiditatem et siccitatem.

(2) In parte quidem eius est anima humana et virtus **prudentie seu intellectus.**ᵝ

(3) {Item} eius est **clima**ᵅ sextum, (4) ac gentes Gog et Magog, et **INDI**ˠᵟ **similiter.**ˠ

(5) De hominibus {autem}, philosophi, et sapientes, ac scribe, et medici, et arismetici, geometre, mercatores, et artifices omnis **edificationis et sculpture,**ᵝ **ac protractature seu picture.**ᵝ

(6) {Item} in parte eius ⟨⟨...⟩⟩ᵛ est argentum vivum, et omnis moneta, ac lapides insculpti.

(7) Sunt {etiam}² in eius parte mercata, et domus scolarum, similiter omnium artificiorum, fontes aquarum, et flumina, ⟨⟨...⟩⟩.ᵘ

(8) {Item} in parte eius homo, et **vulpes,**ˠ et onagri, ac omnis bestia agilis in saliendo.

(9) De avibus, quidem sturnelli, et apes, ac omnis avis agilis ad volandum.

(10) Et de reptilibus terre, vermes parvi.

(11) **De plantis**ˠ {autem}, arbor citri, et parte habet in granatis, et nucibus et **cannis seu** *casannis*,ᵝ et in bombace, ac lino.

(12) Est {etiam} in parte eius omnis species **gummi;**ᵅ similiter et *zinziber* et *genirdane ostar*, ac **dentes bestie**ᵅ qui in *Anglia*ˠᵟ invenitur, cuius quidem

---

¹.1150.] LWVG and also HJ; Hebrew = 1151.   ²Sunt etiam] WG; LV om.

(28) {Moreover} its greatest years are 1150,^{α,27} the great ⟨years⟩ 82, the middle ⟨years⟩ 45, the least ⟨years⟩ eight. (29) {Moreover} the years of the part *al-fardār*, eight.

(30) The power of its body is seven degrees, ahead of or behind it.

6 (1) Mercury is mixed and changeable, because it changes completely according to the nature of the **planets**,^{γ} and also of the signs; {but} *its mixture*^{γ,1} tends somewhat to coldness and dryness.

(2) In its portion is the human soul, and the power of **prudence or intellect**.^{β,2}

(3) {Likewise,} in its portion is the sixth **climate**,^{α} (4) and the nations of Gog and Magog, and **likewise**^{γ,3} **the INDIANS**.^{γδ,4}

(5) {But} of human beings, philosophers, scholars, scribes, physicians, arithmeticians, geometricians, traders, and craftsmen engaged in every sort of **building and engraving**,^{β,5} **drawing or painting**.^{β,6}

(6) {Likewise,} in its portion ⟨⟨of the metals⟩⟩^{ν,7} is quicksilver; and all coins and engraved stones.

(7) In its portion are {also} marketplaces, schoolhouses, and likewise ⟨buildings⟩ of every craft, springs of water, rivers ⟨⟨and fountains.⟩⟩^{μ,8}

(8) {Likewise,} in its portion ⟨is⟩ man, and **wolves**,^{γ,9} and wild asses, and every animal agile in jumping.

(9) Of birds, little starlings, bees, and every bird that is agile in flying.

(10) Of the animals that creep on the earth, the small vermin.

(11) {But} **of the plants**,^{γ} the lemon tree; it has a part in pomegranates, and nuts, and **canes or** *casanni*,^{β,10} cotton, and flax.

(12) {Also} every type of **gum**^{α,11} is in its portion; similarly *zinziber* [ginger] and *genirdane ostar*, **and the teeth of the animal**,^{α,12} which is found

262   PART ONE

cauda est in similitudine piscis, *id est*[1] *castoris*; {item} <u>acaar</u>, <u>careha</u>, et <u>bosague</u>, et <u>asserto</u>, <u>pochaich</u>, <u>aldelhar</u>, et <u>albine vaase</u>, et <u>alsiteregni</u>, et
14va <u>algaciana</u>, | et quidquid acetosi saporis est.

(13) De indumentis {quoque} vestimenta linea et quocumque desuper consuta.

(14) De humana {autem} natura, eius est **sermo hominis**,[α] et cogitatio *eius*, et prudentia, et intellectus, atque ASTRORUM SCIENTIA, et SORTILEGIA et omnis DIVINATIONIS species,[α] et **placida locutio et acceptabilis**,[β] ac IDIOMATUM INTERPRETATIO,[γ] velocitas in sermone, ORATIONUM SCIENTIA, et RITHMORUM INVENTIO, consiliorum notitia et secretorum, PROPHETICA, et pietas et caritas, et converti a malo, et organorum scientiam, res parvas amare, et **accomodare et recipere**,[αθ] et rixari verbis absque **manuum opere seu appositione**,[β] ac omnis ingeniositatis species et deceptionis, falsarum cartarum scriptio, et manuum habilitas ad omne genus artificiorum, desiderium magnum ad opus quodlibet, et divitias congregare et[2] dispergere; **naturam** quidem **eius**[α] est secundum cuiuslibet naturam hominis.

(15) Significat et fratres parvos, et **pueros parvos seu infantes**;[β] et secundum eius fortitudinem ⟨⟨...⟩⟩[μ] manifestabitur natura eius.

(16) Si {ergo} solus prefuerit humane forme, et fuerit orientalis, erit statura brevis, caput parvum, et oculi pulcri; si {vero} occidentalis, erit color eius medius, inter nigrum et album, et ipse macer, oculi eius parvi, et vincit in eo siccitas. (17) Universaliter {autem} significat hominem eius frons prominens est, et **nasus**[γ] longus, et ipse macilentus, **barba vacuus seu nudus**,[β] et digiti manuum eius longi; ipse {quoque} prudens et sapiens.

(18) De partibus {autem} humani corporis, eius est lingua, et os, ac nervi, et ipse partem habet in sanguine.

(19) Egritudines {vero} ipsius sunt egritudines anime, ut superfluitas cogitationum, et tristitia, ac omne suspiciosum.

(20) De etatibus {vero}, eius est infantia.

[1] id est] LV; G est; W om.   [2] et] WV; G ac; L ad.

in **England**,[γδ,13] whose tail resembles a fish, *that is, the beaver*; {likewise} *ʿāqar qarḥa, mādag, ʾasrun, faqāḥ al-ʾadaber, al-zarnabād, al-shiṭrag, al-ganiṭiʾabah*, and everything whose taste is sour.

(13) {Besides,} of clothes, linen garments and every ⟨garment⟩ that is embroidered.

(14) {But} of human nature [human traits], **a man's speech**[α,14] is in its portion, and *his* thought, prudence, intellect, and the SCIENCE OF THE STARS, and **SORCERY and every sort of DIVINATION**,[α,15] **pleasant and acceptable speech**,[β,16] INTERPRETATION OF LANGUAGES,[γ,17] rapidity in speaking, KNOWLEDGE OF RHETORIC, INVENTION OF VERSES, knowledge of intentions and hidden things, PROPHECY, piety and charity, turning away from evil, knowledge of musical instruments, loving small things, **borrowing and receiving**,[αθ,18] [negotiations] to quarrel by words and without the **work or laying on of hands**,[β,19] every sort of cunning and deceit, writing forged documents, the ability of the hands to engage in any sort of craft, a great desire to do anything, amassing riches and squandering ⟨them⟩, **its nature**[α,20] is according to the nature of any person.

(15) It indicates the younger brothers, and **little boys or infants**;[β,21] his nature will be manifest according to its power ⟨⟨in the nativity⟩⟩.[μ,22]

(16) {Therefore,} if it [Mercury] is in charge alone of the human form, and it is oriental ⟨of the Sun⟩, he [the native] will be of short stature, ⟨his⟩ head small, and ⟨his⟩ eyes beautiful; {but} if it is occidental ⟨of the Sun⟩, his color will be intermediate, ⟨that is,⟩ between black and white, and he ⟨will be⟩ thin, his eyes small, and dryness will predominate in him. (17) In general, {however,} it indicates a person with a protruding forehead, long **nose**,[γ,23] emaciated, **deprived of or devoid of a beard**,[β,24] his fingers long; {besides,} a prudent and wise person.

(18) {But} of the parts of the human body, the tongue is in its portion, and the mouth, the tendons, and it has a part in the blood.

(19) {Moreover} the diseases in its portion are diseases of the soul, such as excess of thoughts, melancholy, and every uncertainty.

(20) {Moreover} of the ages of man, childhood is in its portion.

(21) Et de coloribus, **persicus seu indus**,^αβ ac etiam omnis color in quo plures sunt commixti.

(22) **De saporibus** {quoque}, **eius est**^γ acetosus.

(23) {Item} **in angulis**,^α **septentrionalis**.^γ

(24) De litteris quidem *vauf* et *tauf* et *rees* et *men*, ac littere prolongationis; de figuris {vero}, hoc ☿.

(25) Et de diebus, *dies Mercurii*;^γ et de noctibus, **illa que diem dominicam precedit**;^α de horis {quoque} ipsarum prima et octava.

(26) Anni eius maximi sunt .480., magni .76., medii .48., et minimi .20. (27) Anni {vero} partis | *firdarie*, .13.

14vb

(28) Et fortitudo corporis eius .7. gradus, ante se et totidem retro.

7 (1) Luna frigida est et humida, estque in ea modicum caliditatis; et putrefacit corpora omnia, et facit muscida; et in opposito Solis est omnis fructus maturat.

(2) Et est in parte eius **virtus naturalis seu fortitudo nature**.^β

(3) De **climatibus**^α {autem} eius est septimum quod est finis **habitabilis**.^α

(4) De gentibus, *alcevaia*.

(5) Et de hominibus **marinarii sive naute**,^β et itinerantes, et nuncii, et servi.

(6) Et **de mineris**,^γ,[1] in parte eius est argentum, et cristallus, atque onix et calx.

(7) {Item} in parte eius sunt maria, et flumina, et **rivi**.^γ

(8) Et de bestiis, muli, et asini, et armenta, ac lepores, et pisces.

(9) De avibus {autem}, omnis avis alba.

[1]mineris] G > terre.

LIBER ABRAHE AVENERRE INTRODUCTORIUS AD ASTRONOMIAM

(21) Of the colors, **persicus or indigo**,[αβ,25] and also any color in which there are many mixed ⟨colors⟩.

(22) {Besides,} **of the tastes, in its portion is**[γ,26] sour.

(23) {Likewise,} **of the angles,**[α27] the **northern.**[γ]

(24) Of the letters, _waw_, _tav_, _resh_, and _mem_, and the letters of prolongation [_aleph_, _heh_, _waw_, and _yod_]; {moreover} of the shapes, this one ☿.

(25) Of the days ⟨of the week⟩, ***the day of Mercury***;[γ,28] of the nights, **the one which precedes the day of the Lord;**[α,29] {besides,} of their hours, the first and eighth.

(26) Its greatest years are 480, the great ⟨years⟩ 76, the middle ⟨years⟩ 48, the least ⟨years⟩ 20. (27) {Moreover} the years of the part _al-fardār_, 13.

(28) The power of its body is seven degrees, ahead of or behind it.

7 (1) The Moon is cold and moist, and there is a little heat in it; it putrefies all bodies and makes the mossy growth; and when it is opposite the Sun it ripens any fruit.

(2) In its portion is **the natural power or the strength of nature.**[β,1]

(3) {But} of the **climates,**[α] the seventh is in its portion, which is the far extremity of **the habitable**[α,2] ⟨part of the Earth⟩ [the ecumene].

(4) Of the nations, Alcevaia [the Sabaeans].

(5) Of human beings, **mariners or sailors,**[β,3] travelers, messengers, and servants.

(6) **Of the minerals,**[γ,4] silver, crystal, onyx, and lime is in its portion.

(7) {Likewise,} in its portion are the seas, rivers, and **streams.**[γ,5]

(8) Of the animals, mules, donkeys, cattle, rabbits, and fish.

(9) {But} of the birds, every white bird.

(10) Et de vermibus, similiter omnis albus.

(11) **De plantis**ʸ {vero}, salices de torrente, et persici, et omnis species oleris, et cucurbite, et melones, et cucumeres, et **citrulli**.ʸ

(12) {Item} in parte eius est <u>alcarpa</u>, id est cinamonum, et <u>daarpilpel</u>, et <u>daarcimi</u>, et omnis res ***cuius complexio***ʸ est frigida et humida, et cuius sapor salsus est, et color albus cum aliquantulum viriditatis.

(13) Et de specibus aromaticis, <u>alsaole</u>.

(14) *De vestimentis* {autem}, in parte eius sunt **mappe**.ʸ

(15) De natura {vero} humana, eius est plurimum cogitationis, et loquela anime cum defectu **sapientie vel sensis vel discretionis**,ᵝ et plurimum obliviationis, ac **timiditatis seu timoris multitudo**,ᵝ et **sine sollicitudine cordis**,ᵅ **consiliorum revelatio**,ᵅ et **diligere seu concupiscere gaudium**,ᵝ et **superationem seu prevalentiam**,ᵝ *scire hominum secreta*ʸ et historias, mendacia quidem, et accusatores et habundantiam comedendi; universaliter {autem} convertit se ad qualibet naturam.

(16) Significat super **annos lactationis seu nutritionis et infantie**,ᵝ et super matrem, et sorores, ac super **sorores magnas seu maiores**,ᵝ et super mulieres, ac super omnem mulierem impregnatam; secundum fortitudinem {autem} eius in nativitatem apparebit fortitudo nature eius.

(17) Si {ergo} sola prefuerit in nativitate hominis, erit statura eius recta, et color albus cum aliquantulum citruntatis, facies eius rotunda, et supercilia 15ra quasi coniuncta, et ipse festinus est in motibus suis et in ambulatione. |

(18) A principio {autem} mensis ad medium significat super albedinem, et a medio usque ad finem super aliquantulum nigritudinis.

(19) Et de partibus eius humani corporis, eius est oculus sinister de die, de nocte {vero} econverso *Soli*; {item} pulmo, et guttur, ac venter superior, et **pectus**,ᵅ atque latus sinistrum totius corporis.

(20) Egritudines {quoque} eius sunt omnis ille que ex habundantiam sunt flegmatis.

(10) Of the vermin, similarly all those that are white.

(11) {Moreover} **of the plants**,[γ,6] river willows, and peach trees, every type of green vegetable, gourds, melons, cucumbers, and **watermelons**.[γ,7]

(12) {Likewise,} in its portion is *alcarpa*, that is, cinnamon, *daarpilpel* [*dār* pepper], *daarcimi*, and everything *whose mixture*[γ,8] is cold and moist, whose taste is salty, and ⟨whose⟩ color is white with a little greenness.

(13) Of the aromatic species, *alsaole*.

(14) *Of garments*, {however,} in its portion are **underclothes**.[γ,9]

(15) {Moreover} of human nature, excessive thinking, utterance of the soul with an absence of **wisdom or thoughts or discretion**,[β,10] excessive forgetfulness and **timidity or fear of the multitude**[β,11] **without concern of the heart**,[α,12] revealing counsels,[α,13] loving or desiring joy,[β,14] conquering or prevailing,[β,15] *knowledge of human beings' hidden things*[γ,16] and stories, falsehood, accusers, and gluttony; in general, {however,} he [the native] turns himself to any nature.

(16) It indicates the **years of suckling or nourishment and infancy**,[β,17] the mother, the sisters, the **greater or older sisters**,[β,18] women, and every pregnant woman; the power of its nature, {however,} will be manifest according to its power in the nativity.

(17) {Therefore} if it [the Moon] is in charge alone of a person's nativity, ⟨the native⟩ will be of erect stature, white with a slight saffron color, his face round, his eyebrows as though joined, and he will be swift in his motions and walk.

(18) {But} from the beginning to the middle of the month, ⟨the Moon⟩ indicates whiteness; and from the middle to the end, blackness to a slight extent.

(19) Of the parts of the human body, in its portion is the left eye by day {but} the opposite *to the Sun* by night, {likewise,} the lung, the throat, the upper abdomen, **the breast**,[α,19] and the entire left side of the body.

(20) {Besides,} its infirmities are all those ⟨caused⟩ by an excess of phlegm.

(21) De etatibus {autem} hominis, eius est infantia scilicet **lactendi tempus.**ᵞ

(22) Et de coloribus, pulvereus et viridis.

(23) Et de saporibus, salsus.

(24) **De angulis**ᵅ {quoque}, dexter occidentis.

(25) Et de litteris, _zain_ et _ayn_, et de figuris ista ⊃.

(26) De diebus quidem, **dies Lune**,ᵞ et de noctibus, **illa que sequitur dies Veneris**;ᵅ de horisque earum, prima et octava.

(27) Anni {vero} eius magni sunt .520., magni .108., medii .39. cum dimidio, et minimi .25.

(28) Porro anni partis vocate _firdarie_ sunt novem.

(29) Et fortitudo corporis eius est .12. gradus ante se et totidem totidem.

(30) Explicit pars quarta.[1]

§5

1 (1) **Incipit pars quinta LIBRI.**[2] **De bonitate seu bono esse**ᵝ **planetarum**ᵅ et **malo seu malicia**,ᵝ,[3] ac de fortitudine eorum et debilitate. (2) Si fuerit **planeta**ᵅ in coniunctione cum **stella benivola**;ᵞ (3) aut in eius aspectu sexto vel quarto vel trino; (4) nec aspiciant ipsam **stelle malivole**ᵞ neque coniungitur **ibidem**; (5) aut **fuerit** _per separationem_ **recedens**ᵞ a **stella benevola**ᵞ et _per applicationem_ se coniungens **stelle benevole**;ᵞ (6) aut fuerit in medio ⟨⟨...⟩⟩ᵛ **stellarum benevolarum**;ᵞ (7) **aut in coniunctione corporali aut cum Sole**;ᵞ (8) aut in aspectu eius, trino vel sextili; (9) aut in aspectu Lune, et ipsa Luna in coniunctione **stellarum benevolarum**;ᵞ (10) aut fuerit stella

---

[1]Explicit pars quarta] LG; WV om. [2]Incipit pars quinta libri] L; WG Incipit quinta pars; V Quinta pars libri. [3]De bonitate seu bono esse planetarum et malo seu malicia] L; W de bono et malo seu bonitate et malitia planetarum; G de bonitate planetarum et malitia; V de bonitate seu bono esse et malo esse planetarum.

(21) Of the ages of man, {however,} in its portion is infancy, that is, **the time of suckling.**[γ,20]

(22) Of colors, ⟨the color⟩ of dust and green.

(23) Of the tastes, salty.

(24) {Besides,} **of the angles,**[α21] the right of the west.

(25) Of letters, *zayin* and ʿ*ayin*, and of the shapes this one ⊃.

(26) Of the days ⟨of the week⟩, ***the day of the Moon;***[γ,22] of the nights, **the one which follows the day of Venus;**[α,23] of their hours, the first and eighth.

(27) {Moreover} its greatest years are 520, the great ⟨years⟩ 108, the middle ⟨years⟩ 39½, the least ⟨years⟩ 25. (28) Moreover, the years of the part called *al-fardār* are 9.

(29) The power of its body is twelve degrees, ahead of or behind it.

(30) Here ends the fourth part.

§5

1 (1) **The fifth part of THE BOOK begins.**[γ,1] On the goodness or being good[β,2] of the **planets**[α] and on ⟨their⟩ evil or malice,[β,3] and on their power and weakness. (2) ⟨It is good fortune⟩ if **a planet**[α,4] is in conjunction with a **benevolent star;**[γ,5] (3) or in its sextile, quartile, or trine aspect; (4) ⟨or⟩ **malevolent stars**[γ,6] do not aspect it nor are they in conjunction **in the same place;**[γ,7] (5) or **it moves back**[γ,8] *by separation* from **a benevolent star,**[γ] and *by application* it conjoins **a benevolent star;**[γ] (6) or if it is in the middle of ⟨⟨two⟩⟩[ν,9] **benevolent stars;**[γ] (7) **or in a bodily conjunction or with the Sun;**[γ,10] (8) or in aspect with it [the Sun], either trine or sextile; (9) or in aspect with the Moon, and the Moon is with **benevolent stars;**[γ] (10) or ⟨if⟩

270 PART ONE

velox in cursu suo; (11) aut lumine aucta ac etiam aucta numero;[1] (12) aut sit in aliquo loco **dignitatum**[2] **suarum**,ʸ ut in domo sua, vel **exaltatio**,ʸ vel in domo triplicitatis, sue vel **termino**,ᵅ vel in facie vel in loco **augis**;ʸ (13) vel in gradu lucido; (14) aut sit receptus; (15) aut in similitudine sua. (16) Et duo luminaria, **cum fuerint in locis dignitatum stellarum benevolarum**,ʸ estimari debent tamquam **in propriis dignitatibus**ʸ existentes, et consimiliter **stelle benevole**,ʸ cum fuerint **in dignitatibus**ʸ **stellarum benevolarum**.ʸ (17) Quando {igitur} fuerit aliquis **planetarum**ᵅ super vias memoratas, fortificabitur natura eius et significabit super omne bonum alicuius nature; si {autem} fuerit econtrario cuilibet predictorum, debilitabitur natura illius.

15rb (18) Item si in bono congregantur due res vel tres aut plures, tunc plus | erit de bono quod significabitur secundum illud, et similiter **fortitudo maior**.ʸ

2 (1) Bonum {autem} **stellarum**ᵅ triplex est, unum bonum duplicatum, aliud bonum **integrum seu perfectum**,ᵝ et tercium bonum mediocre. (2) Bonum duplicatum est cum aggregantur stelle duo bona vel tria, ut[3] Mercurius cum fuerit in Virgine, tunc habebit duo bona, unum scilicet quia est in domo sua, et aliud quia est in **exaltatione**ʸ sua, {quod} si fuerit *ibidem* in **termino**ᵅ suo, tunc habebit tria bona. (3) Bonum **integrum seu perfectum**ᵝ est cum fuerit stella in domo sua in qua rectificatur natura sua, sicut Saturnus in Aquario, et Iupiter in Sagittatio, et Mars in Scorpione, et Venus in Tauro, et Mercurius in Virgine, et luminaria in domibus suis. (4) Bonum {vero} mediocre est ut sit stella in domo sua in qua non rectificatur natura sua, sicut Saturnus in Capricorno, et Iupiter in Piscibus, et Mars in Ariete, et Venus in Libra, et Mercurius in Geminis.

3 (1) Fortitudo {autem} stelle est cum[4] est ascendens **versus septentrionem**;ᵅ (2) aut ascendens **in circulo augis**,ʸ et **oppositi augis**,ʸ hoc est in **circulo ecentrico**;ʸ (3) aut ut sit in statione[5] sua secunda; (4) aut exiens de sub **radiis Solis**;ʸ (5) aut in aliquo **angulorum seu cardinum**ᵝʸ aut in succedentibus eorum; (6) aut ut fuerint tres superiores, Saturnus videlicet et Iupiter ad Mars, orientales a Sole, **et fuerint**ʸ cum ipso in aspectu sextili, {quia} tunc erit bonum eis; (7) aut ut sint in una quartarum masculinarum,

---

[1]numero] W in motu. [2]dignitatum] WVG; L dignitatem. [3]ut] WVG; L et. [4]cum] W; LVG cuius. [5]statione] WVG; L statura.

the star is swift in its course; (11) or ⟨the star is⟩ increasing in light and also increasing in number; (12) or if it is in any place of **its dignities**,^{γ,11} such as in its house, or ⟨its⟩ **exaltation**^{γ,12} or in the house of ⟨its⟩ triplicity, or in its **term**,^{α} or in ⟨its⟩ face [decan], or in the place of ⟨its⟩ **apogee**;^{γ,13} (13) or in a bright degree; (14) or if it is received ⟨by another planet⟩; (15) or if it is in its similitude. (16) The two luminaries, when they are in the places of **the dignities of benevolent stars**,^{γ,14} must be considered as if they are **in their own dignities**,^{γ,15} and similarly regarding **benevolent stars**,^{γ} when they are in the **dignities**^{γ} of **benevolent stars**.^{γ} (17) When one of the **planets**,^{α} {then,} is in one of the aforementioned ways, its nature will be strengthened and it will indicate every ⟨sort of⟩ good fortune, according to its nature; {but} if it [the planet] is in a condition contrary to any of the aforementioned ⟨conditions⟩, its nature will be weakened. (18) Likewise, if two, three, or more ⟨of the aforementioned conditions⟩ regarding goodness are together, there will be more of the goodness indicated by it, and similarly **greater power**.^{γ,16}

2 (1) The goodness of the **stars**,^{α,1} {however,} is of three types: one is double goodness, the other is **full or complete**^{β,2} goodness, and the third is intermediate goodness. (2) Double goodness is when two or three ⟨types of⟩ goodness are associated with the star, such as when Mercury is in Virgo, because then it [Mercury] has two ⟨types of⟩ goodness: one, because it is in its house, and the other because it is in its **exaltation**^{γ,3} {but} if it were *in this very place* in its **term**,^{α} it would have three ⟨types of⟩ goodness. (3) **Full or complete**^{β} goodness is when the star is in its house where its nature is rectified, as Saturn in Aquarius, Jupiter in Sagittarius, Mars in Scorpio, Venus in Taurus, Mercury in Virgo, or the luminaries in their houses. (4) {But} intermediate goodness is when the star is in its house where its nature is not rectified, as Saturn in Capricorn, Jupiter in Pisces, Mars in Aries, Venus in Libra, or Mercury in Gemini.

3 (1) The power of the star, {however,} is when it rises **towards the north**;^{α,1} (2) or when it ascends **in the circle of apogee**,^{γ,2} and **in that opposite to the apogee**^{γ,3} [the perigee], **that is, in the eccentric circle**;^{γ,4} (3) or when it is in the second station; (4) or when it moves away from ⟨being⟩ under **the rays of the Sun**;^{γ,5} (5) or when it is in one of the **angles or cardines**^{β,γ,6} or in their succedent ⟨houses⟩; (6) or when the three upper ⟨planets⟩, namely, Saturn, Jupiter and Mars, are oriental of the Sun, **and they are**^{γ,7} with it in sextile aspect, {because} then this will be good for them; (7) or when they are in one of the masculine quadrants, and in the masculine signs, and similarly

et in signis masculinis, et similiter de Sole nisi cum est in signo Libre. (8) Inferiorum {vero} virtus, scilicet Veneris et Mercurii atque Lune, *fortitudo est* ut sint occidentales a Sole aut in quartis femininis.

4 (1) **Debilitas**^α {autem} stelle est quando cursu tarda est; (2) aut cum est in statione prima; (3) aut retrograda, et gravior est retrogradatio **planetis**^γ inferioribus **quam superioribus,**^α et adhuc magis si combusti sunt a Sole; (4) aut cum est stella sub **radiis Solis**;^γ (5) aut in gradibus **obscuris seu tenebrosis**;^β (6) aut in contrario similitudinis eius; (7) aut in domo *casus sui*;^γ (8) aut descendens in meride aut meridionalis; (9) aut in aliqua domorum cadentium; (10) aut in via combustionis, qui est a .19. gradu Libre usque ad tertius gradus Scorpionis; (11) aut cum est in **domo exilii sui vel odii**;^β (12) aut ut sit coniuncta stelle retrograde, vel que fuerit **in casu suo,**^γ aut in domo cadente; (13) aut cum non est stella recepta; (14) aut **peregrina seu extranea**^β in loco suo, et magis grave est si non aspiciat eam stella; (15) aut cum fuerint tres superiores occidentales a Sole, aut in una quartarum | feminarum, ⟨⟨...⟩⟩;^μ
15va
(16) ⟨⟨...⟩⟩.^μ (17) ⟨⟨...⟩⟩.^μ

5 (1) {Rursus,} de inferiorum debilitate^α est **ut sunt applicantes malivolis,**^γ aut in eorum aspectu opposito vel quarto vel trino vel sextili; (2) et inter ipsam et **malivolam**^γ minus sit **termino**^α **planete**;^γ (3) aut in **termino**^α sit **malivole**^γ aut in domo eius; (4) aut aliqua **malivolarum**^γ elevata sit super ipsam, existens in domo decima vel undecima respectu loci stelle. (5) Et peius est **si stella non recipiat malivola,**^γ et sint malivole in coniunctione Solis, aut in aspectu quarto vel opposito; (6) aut sit stella cum Capite Draconis sui aut cum Cauda eius; (7) aut {etiam} cum Capite Draconis Lune aut cum cauda eius, et inter ea sit minus duodecim gradibus. (8) Est {autem} **impedimentum**^γ magnum Lune cum sic fuerit, et Soli quidem est **impedimentum**^γ est[1] a propinquitatio eius ad .4. gradus ante ipsa vel post.

---

[1]Lune cum sic fuerit, et Soli quidem est impedimentum est] WVG; L in margin.

for the Sun unless it [the Sun] is in the sign of Libra. (8) {But} the power of the lower ⟨planets⟩, namely, Venus, Mercury and the Moon, *it is power* when they are occidental of the Sun or in a feminine quadrant.

4 (1) The **weakness**[α,1] of a star takes, {however,} place when it is slow in its course; (2) or when it is in the first station; (3) or ⟨when it is⟩ retrograde; and being retrograde is worse for the two lower **planets**[γ] **than for the upper** ⟨**planets**⟩,[α,2] even more so if they are burnt by the Sun; (4) or when the star is under the **rays of the Sun**;[γ] (5) or in the **dark or tenebrous**[β] degrees; (6) or when opposite to its similitude; (7) or in the house of **its fall**[γ,3] [dejection]; (8) or descending in the south or southern; (9) or in one of the cadent houses; (10) or in the path of burning, which is from Libra 19° to Scorpio 3°; (11) or when it is in **the house of its banishment or hate**[β,4] [detriment]; (12) or when it conjoins a retrograde star, or one that is in **its fall**,[γ] or in a cadent house; (13) or when the star is not received ⟨by another planet⟩; (14) or ⟨when it is⟩ **peregrine or strange**[β,5] in its position, and it is worse if it is not aspected by a star; (15) or when the three upper ⟨planets⟩ are occidental of the Sun, or in one of the feminine quadrants, ⟨⟨or in the feminine signs.⟩⟩[μ,6] (16) ⟨⟨The same holds true for the Sun, unless it is in the ninth house, because that is the place of its joy⟩⟩.[μ,7] (17) ⟨⟨The lower planets are weak when they begin to be oriental of the Sun, or when they are in one of the masculine quadrants⟩⟩.[μ,8]

5 (1) {In addition,} **the weakness of the inferior** ⟨**planets**⟩[α,1] **is when they apply to malevolent**[γ,2] ⟨**planets**⟩, or they are in their opposition, or ⟨in their⟩ quartile or trine or sextile aspect; (2) or when there is less than ⟨the degrees of⟩ the **planet's**[γ] **term**[α] between it [the inferior planet] and the **malevolent**[γ] ⟨planet⟩; (3) or when it [the inferior planet] is in the **term**[α] of a **malevolent**[γ] ⟨planet⟩ or in its house; (4) or when one of the **malevolent**[γ] ⟨planets⟩ is raised above it [the inferior planet], when it [the malevolent planet] is in the tenth or eleventh house with respect to the position of the ⟨inferior⟩ star. (5) It is worse **if the** ⟨**inferior**⟩ **star does not receive the malevolent**[γ,3] ⟨**planet**⟩, and the **malevolent**[γ] ⟨planets⟩ are in conjunction with the Sun, or in quartile or opposition aspect ⟨with it⟩; (6) or if the star is with the Head or Tail of its [the planet's] Dragon; (7) or {also} with the Moon's Head or Tail of the Dragon, and there is less than 12° between them [between the Moon and the Head or the Tail of the Dragon]. (8) {But} there is a great **obstruction**[γ,4] to the Moon when it is in such a condition, and there is also an **obstruction**[γ] to the Sun when its nearness is 4° ahead of or behind it.

274					PART ONE

6   (1) Et dicunt Antiqui quod natura Capitis Draconis est augmentativa, et natura Caude diminutiva; cum ergo stelle benivole cum Capite fuerint, augmentabitur bonum earum, si {vero} **malivole**ʸ ibidem fuerint augmentabitur earum malum; et si benevole cum Cauda fuerint, diminuetur bonum earum, si {vero} **malivole**ʸ cum ipsa fuerint, diminuetur de malo earum. (2) Super hoc {igitur} ait quidam[1] Indorum sapiens quod Caput bonum est cum bonis et malum cum malis, et Cauda mala cum bonis et bona cum malis.

7   (1) {Ceterum,} de stellarum **debilitae**,ʸ est ut sit medie inter duas **malivolas**,ʸ ⟨⟨...⟩⟩ᵘ aut in aspectu, secundum quod adhuc explanabo.

8   (1) **Malicia** quidem **sive malum**ᵝ Lune secundum undecim species est. (2) Quarum una est que fuerit eclipsata. (3) Secunda cum est sub **radiis Solis**,ʸ et inter eos fuerint minus .12. gradibus, sive in accedendo ad eum sive recedendo ab eodem. (4) Tertia cum **secundum numerum horum graduum .10.**ᵅ Luna fuerit in opposito Solis, sive ante oppositionem sit sive post eam. (5) Quarta cum fuerit Luna in coniunctione cum **malivolis**ʸ vel in aspectu. (6) Quinta cum fuerit in fortitudine[2] duodenariorum Saturni aut Martis. (7) Sexta cum fuerit in Capite Draconis aut Cauda, et inter ea minus sit .12. gradibus. (8) Septima cum est meridionalis, vel descendens in meridie. (9) Octava cum fuerit in **via combusta**.ʸ (10) Nona cum est in fine signi, nam
15vb ibi sunt **termini**ᵅ **malivolarum**.ʸ (11) Decima cum fuerit tarda | cursu, et hoc scire poteris hoc enim est quando motus eius in die minor fuerit eius motu medio, qui scriptus est in tabulis. (12) Undecima {vero} est cum fuerit in domo nona, quia tunc est in oppositio domus gaudii.

(13) Explicit quinta pars libri huius.

---

[1]quidam] LVG; W unus.   [2]fortitudine] WVG; L > cum.

6   (1) The Ancients said that the nature of the Head of the Dragon is additive, and the nature of the Tail is reductive; therefore, when benevolent stars are with the Head ⟨of the Dragon⟩, their goodness will be increased, {but} if **malevolent**ʸ ⟨stars⟩ are there, their evil will be increased; and if benevolent ⟨stars⟩ are with the Tail, their goodness will be decreased, {but} if **malevolent**ʸ ⟨stars⟩ are with it [the Tail of the Dragon], their evil will be decreased. (2) Regarding this, {then,} a certain scholar of the Indians said that the Head is good with the good ones and bad with the bad ones, and the Tail is bad with the good ones and good with the bad ones.

7   (1) {Furthermore,} **as for the weakness**ʸ,¹ of the stars, this is when ⟨one⟩ is intermediate between two **malevolent**ʸ ⟨stars⟩, ⟨⟨in conjunction⟩⟩μ,² or in aspect, as I shall explain.

8   (1) The **malice or evil**ᵝ of the Moon is according to eleven types. (2) Of them, one is that it is eclipsed. (3) The second is when it is under **the rays of the Sun,**ʸ and between there are fewer than 12° between them, either moving towards it [the Sun] or separating from it. (4) The third is when, **according to their number of ten degrees,**ᵅ,¹ the Moon is in opposition to the Sun, either before or after opposition. (5) The fourth is when the Moon is in conjunction with the **malevolent**ʸ ⟨stars⟩ or in aspect ⟨to them⟩. (6) The fifth is that it [the Moon] is in the power of the *duodenariae* [twelfths] of Saturn or Mars. (7) The sixth is that it [the Moon] is in Head of the Dragon or the Tail, and there is less than 12° between them. (8) The seventh is when it [the Moon] is southern ⟨with respect to the ecliptic⟩ or descending in the south. (9) The eighth is that it is **in the burnt path.**ʸ,² (10) The ninth is when it is at the end of the sign, because that is where the **terms**ᵅ of the **malevolent**ʸ ⟨stars⟩ are. (11) The tenth is when it is slow in ⟨its⟩ course, and you may know this when in one day it moves less than its mean motion, which is written in the ⟨astronomical⟩ tables. (12) The eleventh is {indeed} when it is in the ninth house, because then it is opposite ⟨its⟩ house of joy.

(13) Here ends the fifth part of this book.

§6

1 (1) **Sexta pars.**^{γ} **De esse seu dispositione**^{βγ} **planetarum**^{α} in se ipsis est, et de esse eorum^γ ex parte Solis.[1] (2) {Item,} **de esse**^{γ} **planetarum**^{α} ⟨⟨...⟩⟩,^{ν} secundum **quasdam**[2] **alias**^{γ} vias.[3] (3) De hiis {autem} est ut sit **planeta**^{α} in medio circulo sui, et hoc est cum sunt inter ipsum et **augem suam**^{γ} .90. gradus, equaliter sive sit a dextris sive a sinistris; (4) aut ut sit ascendens in circulo **augis**^{γ} **vel descendens in eodem;**^{π} (5) **aut sit in principio augis sue;**^{π} (6) aut sit descendens a medio circuli sui ad **oppositum augis sue;**^{γ} (7) aut ascendens ab **opposito augis**^{γ} ad medium circuli sui; (8) aut ut sit **in puncto oppositi augis sue;**^{γ} (9) aut ut sit auctus cursu et similiter lumine ac fortitudine corporis; (10) aut diminutus in hiis tribus; (11) aut mediocris, sine augmento et diminutione; (12) aut sit in numero auctus aut diminutus; (13) **aut mediocris;**^{γ} (14) aut sit latitudo eius sinistre, ascendens vel descendens; (15) aut meridionalis ascendens vel descendens; (16) aut latitudo eius magna vel parva; (17) aut non habet latitudinem aliquam.

2 (1) ⟨⟨...⟩⟩.^{μ} (2) **Cum**^{γ} {ergo} distat **planeta**^{α} a principio **augis sue**^{α} minus .90. gradibus, et[4] est accendens ad eam **aut**^{α} ascendit,[5] **tunc est**^{γ} diminutus cursu et lumine et fortitudine corporis sui. (3) Et cum fuerit in loco **augis sue,**^{α} tunc est **diminutus seu deficiens**^{β} in omnibus. (4) Cum {ergo} descendit ab ⟨⟨...⟩⟩^{ν} auge sua ad medium circuli sui, tunc est auctus cursu et lumine et corporis fortitudine.[6] (5) Cum descendit a medio circuli sui **ad oppositum augis, tunc**^{α} est auctus ⟨⟨...⟩⟩.^{μ} (6) Cum {vero} est **opposito augis,** tunc est auctus omnibus. (7) Et quemadmodum dictus est de Luna, sic est de stellis superioribus, nam cum fuerit distans a Sole .12. gradibus, dicitur quod est aucta lumine donec sit in opposito Solis, et ab hinc donec iterum coniungatur Soli diminuitur lumen eius.

---

[1]Sexta pars. De esse seu dispositione planetarum in se ipsis est, et de esse eorum ex parte Solis] LV; G Incipit .6a. pars de dispositione planetarum in se ipsis et de esse eorum ex parte Solis; W om.   [2]quasdam] GV; LW om.   [3]Item de esse planetarum secundum quasdam alias vias] W om.   [4]et] G aut.   [5]ascendit] W descendit.   [6]fortitudine] WVG; L fortitudinem.

§6

1 (1) **Sixth part.**[γ,1] **On the existence or the condition**[βγ,2] **of the planets**[α] in themselves, **and their existence**[γ] with respect to the Sun. (2) {Likewise,} **on the existence**[γ] **of planets**[α] ⟨⟨in themselves⟩⟩[v,3] according to **certain other**[γ,4] ways. (3) {But} of them, ⟨one⟩ is that the **planet**[α] is in the middle of its circle, which is when there are 90° between it and **its apogee,**[γ,5] equally from the right or from the left; (4) or when it is ascending in the circle of the **apogee**[γ] **or descending in it;**[π,6] (5) **or when it is at the beginning of its apogee;**[π,7] (6) or when it is descending from the middle of the circle to **the opposite of its apogee**[γ,8] [perigee]; (7) or when it is ascending from **the opposite of its apogee**[γ] [perigee] to the middle of its circle. (8) Or when it is **in the point of the opposite of its apogee**[γ,9] [perigee]; (9) or when it is increasing in ⟨its⟩ course, and similarly light and power of ⟨its⟩ body; (10) or when it is decreasing in these three ⟨things⟩; (11) or when it is intermediate, without increase or decrease; (12) or when it is increasing or decreasing in number; (13) **or when it is intermediate;**[γ,10] (14) or when its ⟨ecliptical⟩ latitude is left, ascending or descending; (15) or southern, ascending or descending; (16) or when its ⟨ecliptical⟩ latitude is high or low; (17) or when it has no latitude ⟨at all⟩.

2 (1) ⟨⟨When a planet is 90° from the beginning of its apogee, it is direct in its motion, meaning ⟨it moves with its⟩ mean ⟨motion⟩, and the same holds true for its light and the power of its body⟩⟩.[μ,1] (2) {Therefore,} **when**[γ,2] a **planet**[α,3] is less than 90° distant from the beginning of **its apogee,**[α,4] and is moving towards it [the apogee], **or**[α,5] is ascending, **then it is**[γ,6] decreasing in motion, and the light and power of its body. (3) When it is in the place of **its apogee,**[α] then it is **decreasing or deficient**[β,7] in everything. (4) {Therefore,} when it descends from ⟨⟨the beginning of⟩⟩[v,8] its apogee to the middle of its circle, then it increases ⟨its⟩ course, light and the power of ⟨its⟩ body. (5) When it descends from the middle of its circle **to the opposite of the apogee**[γ,9] [perigee], **then**[α,10] it is increasing ⟨⟨in everything⟩⟩.[μ,11] (6) {Moreover} when it is in the place of the **opposite of the apogee**[γ,12] [perigee], then it is increasing in everything [its course, light, and power of its body]. (7) And what has been said about the Moon may be said about the upper stars, because when it is distant 12° from the Sun, it is said to be increasing in light until it is opposite the Sun, and from there its light decreases until it again conjoins the Sun.

278   PART ONE

3 (1) Si {autem} scire volueris quando stella aucta erit ⟨⟨...⟩⟩ᵛ numero, considera quando intraveris ⟨⟨...⟩⟩ᵛ lineas numeri **graduum equalium**:ᵞ si quidem fuerit in prima, erit aucta¹ numero, et si in secunda, diminuta² erit ⟨⟨...⟩⟩. (2) Et quando adderis numerum **equationis**ᵞ super medium locum in | fine **equationis**,ᵞ tunc appellatur auctus in numero; et si equatione diminutus, erit numero diminutus; {quod} si nec addas nec diminuas, tunc erit stella in **linea cinguli signorum**.ᵖ (3) Et in Venere quidem, cum subtraxeris **equationem eius**ᵞ a cursu medio nichilque remanserit aut si remanserit³ .180. gradus, tunc est ipsa cum Sole **in uno gradu**.ᵅ (4) **Planete**ᵞ {autem} superiores, cum fuerit motus eorum in die maior motu medio, tunc sunt veloces cursu,⁴ et si minor fuerit, tunc sunt tardi. (5) In Venere quidem et Mercurio, considera si fuerit motus⁵ eorum minor medio motu Solis, ipsi namque⁶ tunc sunt tardi cursu, et si maior fuerit, tunc sunt veloces; si {vero} motui Solis medio sit equalis, tunc **mediocris erit, necque tardus nec velox**.ᵞ

16ra

4 (1) Cum {autem} fuerit **latitudo**ᵖ **planete**ᵞ **septentrionalis**,ᵞ et hoc a Capite Draconis usque ad .90. gradus, tunc erit **septentrionalis**ᵞ ascendens, et ab hinc usque ad Caudam, **septentrionalis**ᵞ descendens. (2) A Cauda {vero} usque ad .90. gradus, meridionalis descendens; et **ab hic**ᵞ usque ad Caput, meridionalis ascendens. (3) Itaque cum est **in distantia**ᵖ .90. graduum a Capite Draconis vel a Cauda, ibi est in maxima latitudine, et quanto propinquior est Capiti vel Caude, tanto minor est. (4) Et cum est in Capite vel Cauda, tunc est in **linea cinguli signorum**.ᵞ

5 (1) **Dispositio** quidem **seu habitudo planetarum**ᵅ ex parte Solis multipharia est. (2) Nam **postquam**ᵞ superiores tres coniuncti fuerint Soli, **gradu per gradum**, quousque ad oppositionem perveniant Solis, dextri sunt **Soli**; ab hora {autem} oppositionis donec coniungantur *iterum* cum ipso, sinistri sunt eidem. (3) Mercurius {vero} et Venus, a tempore quo separati sunt a Sole, et retrogradi, donec directi sunt, et consequentes ipsum, attingant

---

¹aucta] W; LG auctus.   ²diminuta] W; LG diminutus.   ³aut si remanserit] WVG; L in margin.   ⁴cursu] WVG; L cursus.   ⁵motus] WVG; L om.   ⁶namque] LWV; G inquam.

3 (1) {But} if you want to know when the star will be increasing in ⟨⟨its⟩⟩ⱽ number, when you enter ⟨⟨in its number⟩⟩,ᵛ,¹ consider the lines of the number of **equal degrees:**ᵞ,² if it is in the first ⟨line⟩, it [the star] will be increasing in number; and if in the second ⟨line⟩, it will be decreasing ⟨in number⟩; ⟨⟨and if there is no number there, it is neither increasing nor decreasing⟩⟩.ᵛ,³ (2) When you add the number of the **equation**ᵞ,⁴ [correction] to the mean position at the end of the **equation**ᵞ [correction], then it is called increasing in number; and if it is decreasing in the equation, [if the correction is negative] it will be decreasing in number; {but} if you neither add nor subtract ⟨the equation⟩, the star is **in the line of the girdle of the signs**π,⁵ [the ecliptic]. (3) For Venus, when you subtract **its equation**ᵞ,⁶ [correction] from the mean motion and the remainder is zero, or the remainder is 180°, then it [Venus] is with the Sun **in one degree.**ʰ,⁷ (4) {But} the upper **planets,**ᵞ, when their motion in one day is greater than their mean motion, then they are swift in their course, and if it is less ⟨than their mean motion⟩, then they are slow ⟨in their course⟩. (5) For Venus and Mercury, consider whether their motion is less than the mean motion of the Sun, because then they are slow in ⟨their⟩ course; and if ⟨their motion is⟩ greater ⟨than the mean motion of the Sun⟩, then they are swift ⟨in their course⟩; {but} if ⟨their motion is⟩ equal to the mean motion of the Sun, **then** ⟨their motion⟩ **will be intermediate, neither slow nor swift.**ᵞ,⁸

4 (1) {But} when a **planet's**ᵞ **latitude**π,¹ is **northern,**ᵞ and it is from its Head of the Dragon to 90° ⟨after it⟩, then it will be **northern**ᵞ and ascending; and from there to the Tail ⟨of the Dragon⟩, it is **northern**ᵞ and descending. (2) {Moreover} from the Tail to 90°, southern and descending; and **from there**ᵞ,² to the Head of the Dragon, southern and ascending. (3) When it [a planet] is **at a distance**π,³ of 90° from the Head of the Dragon and from the Tail, there it is at its maximum latitude; the closer it is to the Head or to the Tail, the lower ⟨its latitude⟩. (4) When it is with the Head or with the Tail, it is at the **line of the girdle of the signs**ᵞ,⁴ [the ecliptic].

5 (1) The **disposition or condition**β,¹ of the **planets**α with respect to the Sun is manifold. (2) For **after**ᵞ,² the three upper ⟨planets⟩ [Saturn, Jupiter, Mars] are in conjunction with the Sun, **degree for degree,**ᵞ,³ until they reach opposition to the Sun, they are to the right **of the Sun;**ᵞ,⁴ {but} from the moment of opposition until they conjoin it [the Sun] *again*, they are to the left of it. (3) {Moreover} Venus and Mercury, from the moment of their separation from the Sun, and they are retrograde, until they become direct ⟨in their motion⟩, and they follow it [the Sun], and they catch up with it

et **corporaliter coniungantur**,ᵞ dextri sunt eidem; et ab hora qua separantur ab eo, et sunt directi tendentes **ad oriens**ᵞ **donec in stationem primam perveniant**,ᵞ et retrogradi a Sole attingantur, tunc quidem sunt sinistri. (4) Similiter et Luna, **postquam**ᵞ a Sole separatur usque ad oppositionem eius, sinistra est; et ab oppositione usque ad horam coniunctionis, ipsa est dexter.

6 (1) Et scito quod tribus **planetis**ᵞ superioribus .16. mutationes sunt a Sole. (2) Una quod **sint planete**ᵞ in uno gradu ⟨⟨...⟩⟩ᵛ cum Sole, et tunc vocatur planeta **coniunctus**,ᵅ dummodo non distat a Sole nisi minus .16. minutis, nam si plus distaret esset combustus; et quando **coniunctus**ᵅ est | significat omne bonum in rebus quibusque. (3) Et si ⟨⟨...⟩⟩ᵘ distat **planeta**ᵞ plus dictis minutis, usque ad distantiam .6., graduum, et est orientalis, tunc est combustus; et hoc quidem est in Saturno et Iove, sed Mars equidem combustus vocatur usque ad distantiam .10. gradus; **et hoc es secunda via.**ᵅ (4) Postquam {ergo} **distiterunt illi plus .6. gradibus**,ᵞ vel Mars plus .10., quousque sunt **in longitudine**ᵞ .15. graduum, dicuntur **sub radiis**,ᵞ et est via tertia. (5) Et quando **planeta**ᵞ combustus est nihil habet fortitudinis. (6) Cum {ergo} exivit de termino combustionis et fuerit **sub radiis**, tunc revertitur ad ipsum ⟨⟨...⟩⟩ᵘ **fortitudo sua seu virtus**,ᵝ et quanto plus distiterit tanto melius. (7) Dixerunt Antiqui **se expertos esse quod cum distat Mars .18. gradibus, tunc est sub radiis.**ᵞ (8) Et tunc est eis mediocritas fortitudinis in omnibus effectibus suis. (9) Et vocati sunt quidem orientales ⟨⟨...⟩⟩ᵛ quousque distent a Sole in aspectu sextili, et tunc est **planeta**ᵞ in sua magna fortitudine, et hoc est via quarta. (10) Deinde usque distet a Sole per aspectum quartum debilitabitur fortitudo **radiorum suorum**,ᵅ et hoc est via quinta. (11) Abhinc ergo usque ad stationem primam vadunt debilitando, et hoc est via sexta. (12) Et cum fuerit in statione prima, tunc quidem terminatur eorum fortitudo, et hoc est via septima. (13) **Cum** {vero} **retrogradatur**[1] **usque ad oppositionem Solis nihil habet fortitudinis, et hoc est via octava.**ᵖ (14) **Et quando sunt**ᵞ in opposito Solis est via nona, et significat **omnem**ᵅ conturbationem et spem aliquam **que in luce non exibit.**ᵅᶿ (15) Ab hora {vero} separationis eorum ab opposito Solis est via decima, et tunc apparebit aliquantulum fortitudinis eorum donec **sint**ᵅ in statione secunda. (16) ⟨⟨...⟩⟩ᵘ et hoc quidem

---

[1]retrogradatur] WVG; L retrogradantur.

and they **conjoin it bodily**,^{γ,5} they are to its right; and from the moment of their separation from it [the Sun], and they are direct ⟨in their motion⟩, moving towards **the east**,^{γ,6} and **until they reach their first station**,^{γ,7} and they turn retrograde, and the Sun catches up with them, then they are to its left. (4) Similarly, the Moon, **after**^{γ,8} its separation from the Sun until its opposition to it [the Sun], is to its left; and from opposition until the moment of conjunction, it is to the right.

6 (1) Know that there are 16 changes to the three upper **planets**^{γ} with respect to the Sun. (2) One is **that the planets are**^{γ,1} with the Sun in the same degree ⟨⟨and minute⟩⟩,^{ν,2} and then the **planet**^{γ} is called "**conjunct**,"^{α,3} as long as its distance from the Sun is less than 16′, but if its distance is more ⟨than 16′⟩ it is burnt; when ⟨the planet⟩ is **conjunct**^{α} it indicates every goodness in all matters. (3) If ⟨⟨the minutes are more than the aforementioned [16′]⟩⟩,^{μ,4} the distance between the **planet**^{γ} ⟨and the Sun⟩ is greater than the aforementioned minutes, up to 6°, and it is oriental ⟨of the Sun⟩, then it is burnt; this holds true for Saturn and Jupiter, but Mars is called burnt when it is up to 10° away ⟨from the Sun⟩; **and this is the second way.**^{α,5} (4) {Consequently,} after they have moved more than 6° **distant**,^{γ,6} or for Mars more than 10°, until they are 15° **in longitude**^{γ,7} [distance], they are called **under the rays,**^{γ,8} and this is the third way. (5) When a **planet**^{γ} is burnt it has no power. (6) {Consequently,} when it moved away from the boundary of burning and is **under the rays**,^{γ} it recovers ⟨⟨some of⟩⟩^{μ,9} its **strength or power**,^{β,10} and the farther away, the better ⟨its condition⟩. (7) The ANCIENTS said that **they have tested that when Mars is at a distance of 18° ⟨from the Sun⟩, then it is under the rays.**^{γ,11} (8) Then their [the planets'] power is intermediate for all their effects. (9) They are called eastern ⟨⟨and strong⟩⟩^{ν,12} until their distance from the Sun is the sextile aspect [60°], then the **planet**^{γ} is in its greatest strength, and this is the fourth way. (10) From that place until the distance from the Sun is quartile [90°], the power of **their rays**^{α,13} will grow weaker, and this is the fifth way. (11) From there until the first station, ⟨their power⟩ grows ⟨still⟩ weaker, and this is the sixth way. (12) When it is in its first station, its power is exhausted, and this is the seventh way. (13) {But} **when it is retrograde until ⟨it reaches⟩ opposition to the Sun it has no power, and this is the eighth way.**^{π,14} (14) **And when they are**^{γ,15} in opposition to the Sun is the ninth way, and it indicates **every**^{α,16} confusion and hope **that will not issue from the light**^{αθ,17} [will not be fulfilled]. (15) {But} from the moment of their separation from opposition to the Sun is the tenth way, and then a little of their power will be manifest until **they are**^{α,18} in the second station. (16) ⟨⟨When it is there⟩⟩^{μ,19} this is the eleventh

est via undecima, tunc quidem **ad ipsos revertitur** tota **eorum fortitudo**.ʸ (17) Deinde usque ad distantiam .90. graduum a Sole, *tunc* est occidentalis, tunc debilitatur ⟨⟨...⟩⟩ᵘ **virtus eorum**,ʸ et est via duodecima. (18) Et abhinc vadunt debilitando usque distent a Sole per **aspectum quartum**,ᵅ et hec esst via .13a., ⟨⟨...⟩⟩.ᵘ (19) **Magis** {autem} **debilitatur usque ad aspectum sextilem**,ᵅ et hoc est via .14., et tunc non remanet eis fortitudo. (20) Cum ergo fuerit **sub radiis**,ʸ tunc est via .15a. (21) Et in combustione est via decima sexta.

7 (1) Veneri autem et Mercurio sunt alie vie. (2) Cum enim sunt cum Sole **in uno gradu**,ᵅ seu minus predictis minutis, et sunt orientales, **computande sunt due vie**,ᵅ combusti namque sunt donec inter eos et Solem sit **longi-**

16va **tudo**ᵅ septem graduum. (3) **Et abhinc usque ad distantiam eorum**ᵅ | a Sole .12. gradibus, **sub radiis consistunt**.ʸ (4) Deinde crescit eorum fortitudo, et sunt orientales usque ad stationem primam, et hoc est via quinta. (5) Tunc ergo debilitatur eorum fortitudo quousque apropinquent Soli et sint inter ipsum et illos .12. gradus, **postmodum**ᵅ quidem erunt **sub radiis**.ʸ (6) **Et cum**ʸ distantia inter eos est .7. graduum, tunc erunt in termino combustionis, quousque sunt coniuncti prescise¹ Soli. (7) A tempore {vero} separationis eorum a Sole, que sunt occidentales, in termino sunt combustionis usque ad distantiam .7. graduum. (8) **Deinde**ʸ usque ad .12. gradus **sub radiis**.ʸ (9) Et cum exeunt **de sub radiis**,ʸ augmentabitur fortitudo eorum quamdiu directi fuerint **usque ad principium stationis ac retrogradationis**,ʸ tunc enim diminuetur fortitudo earum quousque sint prope Solem, minus .15. gradibus. (10) Deinde erunt **sub radiis**,ʸ et postmodum sub combustione.

8 (1) Luna {vero} ad Solem se habet secundum .16. vias. (2) Prima quando est coniuncta Soli, vel ante vel retro, minus .16. minutis. (3) Secunda via quando distat .6. gradibus et est occidentalis, tunc quidem incipit aliquantulum eius fortitudo. (4) Tertia via est cum distat .12. gradibus. (5) **Deinde, namque**ʸ augmentatur eius fortitudo quousque sit in longitudine .45. graduum, tunc erit quarta pars eius **luminosa seu illuminata**. (6) Et de hic usque .90. gradus augebitur eius fortitudo, et tunc erit medietas eius luminosa. (7) **Deinde**ʸ {vero} donec sint *inter Lunam* et Solem .135. gradus, et tunc erint tres quarte ipsius illuminate.² (8) Et ab hinc usque ad distan-

---

¹prescise] W; L presise; G precise. ²illuminate] WG; L lluminate.

way, then all **their power is restored to them**.$^{\gamma,20}$ (17) From that place until a distance of 90° from the Sun, *then* it is occidental ⟨of the Sun⟩, then **their power**$^{\gamma,21}$ grows ⟨⟨somewhat⟩⟩$^{\mu,22}$ weaker, and this is the twelfth way. (18) From there their ⟨power⟩ grows weaker until their distance from the Sun is **quartile aspect**,$^{\alpha,23}$ and this is the thirteenth way, ⟨⟨then less than a third of its power is left to it⟩⟩.$^{\mu,24}$ (19) {But} **it grows weaker still until the aspect of sextile**,$^{\alpha,25}$ and this is the fourteenth way, and no power is left to it. (20) When it is **under the rays**$^{\gamma}$ is the fifteenth way. (21) And in the burning is the sixteenth way.

7 (1) But Venus and Mercury have other ways ⟨with respect to the Sun⟩. (2) When they are with the Sun **in the same degree**,$^{\alpha,1}$ or less than the aforementioned minutes [16'], and they are oriental ⟨of the Sun⟩, **two ways must be counted**,$^{\alpha,2}$ for they are burnt until their **longitude**$^{\alpha,3}$ [distance] from the Sun is 7°. (3) **And from there until their distance**$^{\alpha,4}$ from the Sun is 12°, **they continue to be under the rays**.$^{\gamma,5}$ (4) From that place their power grows, and they are oriental ⟨of the Sun⟩ until the first station, and this is the fifth way. (5) Then their power grows weaker until they get closer to the Sun and there are 12° between it and them, **and afterwards**$^{\alpha,6}$ they are **under the rays**.$^{\gamma}$ (6) **And when**$^{\gamma,7}$ the distance between them is 7°, then they will be in the boundary of burning, until they are wholly conjunct with the Sun. (7) {but} from the time of their separation from the Sun, when they are occidental ⟨of the Sun⟩, they are in the boundary of burning until the distance is 7°. (8) **Next**$^{\gamma,8}$ until ⟨the distance is⟩ 12° they are **under the rays**.$^{\gamma}$ (9) When they move away from **under the rays**,$^{\gamma}$ their power will be increased long as they are direct ⟨in their motion⟩, **until the beginning of the station and of retrogradation**,$^{\gamma,9}$ for then their power will be diminished until they are close to the Sun, less than 15°. (10) From that place they will be **under the rays**,$^{\gamma}$ and later under the burning.

8 (1) {Moreover} the Moon has sixteen ways with respect to the Sun. (2) The first is when it [the Moon] is conjunct with it [the Sun], ahead or behind, less than 16'. (3) The second way is when it [the Moon] is at a distance of 6° and it is occidental ⟨of the Sun⟩, then its power begins a little. (4) The third way is when it is at a distance of 12°. (5) **Next, because**$^{\gamma,1}$ its power grows until ⟨its⟩ **longitude**$^{\alpha,2}$ [distance] is 45°, then a quarter of it **will shine or be illuminated**.$^{\beta,3}$ (6) From there until 90° its power will grow, and then half of it will shine. (7) {But} **next**,$^{\gamma,4}$ From that place until there are 135° *between the Moon* and the Sun, then three quarters of it will shine. (8) From there until the distance is 12° from opposition to the Sun, then

tiam .12. graduum ab oppositione eius cum Sole, tunc est in fortitudine sua, sed in hora oppositionis ipsa est in sua magna fortitudine. (9) In recessu {vero} eius ab oppositione Solis in distantiam quidem .12. graduum est via decima, quousque distet ab oppositione .45. gradus, quia tunc diminutum erit lumen eius in quarta parte. (10) Et deinde usque ad distantia eius ab oppositione .90. gradus remanebit in corpore eius medietas illuminata. (11) Ab hinc {vero} donec **longitudo**^{α} inter ipsa et Solem est .45. graduum remanebit *corporis eius* quarta pars illuminata. (12) **Deinde**^{γ} usque dum¹ **longitudo**^{α} sit .12. graduum **debilitabitur virtus eius**^{α} et tunc | intrabit **sub radiis Solis.**^{γ} (13) Et infra .6. gradus erit sub combustione, et scito quod cum subtraxeris scilicet **.2. vices**^{α,2} quibus est **sub radiis**^{γ} et **duas vices**^{α} quibus est sub combustione. (14) Remanebunt vie .12, et hec quidem vocate sunt .12. claves Lune, estque multum his opus in sciendis pluviarum rebus.

16vb

(15) Explicit sexta pars LIBER HUIUS.

§7

1 (1) **Septima quidem LIBRI pars.**^{γ} De **planetarum**^{α} habitudinibus, que sunt trintaginta, **et sunt hee:**^{α,3} **applicatio,**^{γ} coniunctio, commixtio, aspectus, separatio, **solitudo,**^{γ} **alienatio,**^{γ} translatio, collectio, reditus lucis, donum fortitudinis, donum potestatis, **donum nature,**^{π} donum duplicis nature, rectitudo, **obliquitas,**^{γ} inhibitio, reditio ad bonum, reditio ad malum, **refrenatio vel contradictio,**^{β} **impeditio vel accidens,**^{β} **frustratio,**^{γ} abscisio luminis, **compassio,**^{γ} remuneratio, receptio, benevolentia, similitudo, **obsessio,**^{γ} et **fortitudo.**^{γ}

2 (1) **Applicatio**^{γ} est quando sunt .2. **stelle seu planete**^{β} in uno signo, et sunt directi cursu, fueritque gradus **planete**^{γ} levioris pauciores gradibus **planete**^{γ} gravioris. (2) Et quamdiu gradus hii pauciores sunt vocantur **applicantes,**^{γ} et quando in eodem **gradu**^{α} est cum illo, tunc est perfecta **applicatio.**^{γ} (3) Principium {autem} **applicationis**^{γ} est cum fuerint inter eos minus **.13. gradibus,**^{α} et quanto pauciores gradus sunt tanto fortius est quidquid per eam signatur. (4) Secundum hanc itaque viam est {etiam} **applicatio in proiectionibus radiorum,**^{γ} qui sunt aspectus .7., secundum quod iam dictum est prius.

¹usque dum] L W quousque. ²vices] LWV; G vias. ³hee] W om.

it is in its strength, but at the moment of opposition ⟨to the Sun⟩ it is at its greatest strength. (9) {But} when it moves away from opposition with the Sun to a distance of 12° it is the tenth way, until it is at a distance of 45° from opposition with the Sun, because then one quarter of ⟨its⟩ light will disappear. (10) From that place until its distance from opposition is 90° half of its body will remain illuminated. (11) {But} from there until the **longitude**^{α} [distance] between it and the Sun is 45°, one-quarter *of its body* will remain illuminated. (12) **Next**,^{γ} until the **longitude**^{α} [distance] is 12° **its strength will grow weaker**,^{α,5} and then it will enter **under the rays of the Sun.**^{γ} (13) And when it is less than 6° it will be under the burning, and know that when you subtract ⟨these degrees⟩, **twice**^{α,6} it is **under the rays**^{γ} and **twice**^{α} under the burning. (14) Then 12 ways are left, and these are called the keys of the Moon, and they are very important for knowing about things related to rain.

(15) Here ends the sixth part of THIS BOOK.

§7

1 (1) **Seventh part of THE BOOK.**^{γ,1} On the conditions of the **planets**,^{α,2} which are thirty, **and are the following:**^{α,3} **application**,^{γ,4} conjunction, mixture, aspect, separation, **solitude**,^{γ,5} **alienation**,^{γ,6} translation, collection, reflecting the light, giving power, giving governance, **giving nature**,^{π,7} giving double nature, straightness, **obliquity**,^{γ,8} inhibition, returning to goodness, returning to evil, **restraint or contradiction**,^{β,9} **obstruction or accident**,^{β,10} **frustration**,^{γ,11} cutting the light, **compassion**,^{γ,12} recompense, reception, benevolence, similitude, **siege**,^{γ,13} and **strength**.^{γ,14}

2 (1) "**Application**"^{γ} is when two **stars or planets**^{β} are in the same sign, direct in ⟨their⟩ course, and the degrees of the lighter [swifter] **planet**^{γ} ⟨in the sign⟩ are less than the degrees of the heavier [slower] **planet**.^{γ} (2) As long as the degrees are less ⟨than the degrees of the heavier planet⟩ they are called "**in application**"^{γ,1} [approaching] and when it [the swifter planet] is with it [the slower planet] in the same **degree**,^{α,2} then the **application**^{γ} is complete. (3) {But} the beginning of the **application**^{γ} is when the distance between them [the two planets] is less than 13°,^{α,3} and the fewer degrees ⟨between them,⟩ the stronger is anything indicated by it. (4) According to the same way is {also} "**application in the projection of rays**,"^{γ,4} which are the seven aspects mentioned previously.

3 (1) Coniunctio est quando due **planete**ʸ sunt in uno signo, et in alterius fortitudine corporis fuerint uterque, tunc coniuncti vocantur. (2) Et cum in uno sunt **gradu**,ᵅ tunc est eorum virtus perfecta in omni eo quod significant. (3) Si {vero} unus eorum infra fortitudinem[1] alterius ⟨⟨...⟩⟩ᵛ fuerit, et alter non est fortitudine corporis illius, non est perfectus quidquid significat ex hoc preter quam usque ad medietatem fere. (4) Verbi gratia, si distantia inter Lunam et Saturnum esset .8. gradibus ante vel retro, tunc essent uterque in fortitudine corporis alterius, et si inter eos essent .10. gradus, tunc quidem esset Saturnus in fortitudine corporis Lune sed Luna in fortitudine corporis Saturni[2] non esset. (5) Quamdiu {autem} **planeta**ʸ levis ad coniunctionem vadit **gravioris seu ponderosioris**,^(β,3) plus habet fortitudinis | quam cum ab eo separatur, quamvis {etiam} sit in fortitudine corporis eius. (6) Si {vero} duo **planete**ʸ in duobus signis fuerint, et eorum quilibet in fortitudine corporis alterius, non est dicentum de illis quod sint coniuncti, eo quod sint in signis diversis. (7) Et hoc est sententia ANTIQUORUM, EGO {autem} ABRAHAM EVENERRE, **COMPILATOR**ᵅ HUIUS LIBRO, ab eis dissentio, secundum quod explanabo in LIBRO NATIVITATUM. (8) Item non commemoraverunt ANTIQUI stelle *fixis* superioribus que sunt in **orbe signorum**ᵅ quanta scilicet est **fortitudinis earum mensura**,ᵅ preter quam DORONIUS solus, qui ait quod est quarta signi. (9) Sententias {vero} precise considerantium in hac scientia est quod eadem cum est mensura fortitudinis corporum **planetarum**,ᵅ sive stella sit honoris primi sive secundi. (10) Et causa quidem coniunctionis est quando coniunguntur due stelle vel plures, *quia* spera unius inferior est spera alterius, et cum ambe sunt in directo ⟨⟨...⟩⟩ᵛ partis unius in **orbe signorum**ᵅ (11) Levior graviorem occultabit ne appareat visui, nam ingressus est sub eo. (12) Et hoc est si nulla est inter eas latitudo ⟨⟨...⟩⟩,ᵛ et **super hoc adhuc erit sermo.**ʸ

17ra

4 (1) Commixtio est quando coniungitur stella cum alia **planeta sive cum stella**,^(β,4) tunc ex natura earum nascetur natura alia. (2) Ut Saturnus et Mars, quorum uterque nocivus est, quando coniunguntur dixerunt ANTIQUI quod significat bonum. (3) Veritas {autem} est quod eorum uterque opus destruit alterius, et per hoc salvatur natus a nocumento, quapropter non significat bonum nisi ⟨⟨...⟩⟩ᵛ quod non nocet. (4) **Et Iovis quidem**

---

[1]fortitudinem] WVG; L virtutem fortitudinem. [2]Saturni] WVG; L om. [3]seu ponderosioris] LW; GV om. [4]sive cum stella] G; LW scilicet cum planeta; V vel planetarum planeta.

3 (1) "Conjunction" is when two **planets**ʸ are in the same sign, each of them within the power of the other's body, they are said to be "in conjunction." (2) When they are in one **degree**,ᵅ then their power is complete in everything they signify. (3) {But} if one of them is within the power of the other⟨⟨'s body⟩⟩,ᵛ,¹ and the latter is not within the power of the former's body, all their indications will not be complete except for approximately up to one half. (4) As an illustration, if the distance between the Moon and Saturn is 8°, ahead of or behind ⟨it⟩, then each of them is within the power of the other's body, but if there are 10° between them, then Saturn is within the power of the Moon's body but the Moon is not within the power of Saturn's body. (5) {But} during the time that the light [swift] **planet**ʸ moves towards conjunction with **the heavier or weightier**ᵝ,² [slower planet], it has more power than after it separates from it, even though it [the light planet] is {still} within the power of its [the heavy planet's] body. (6) {But} if two **planets**ʸ are in two signs, and each of them is within the power of the other's body, they are not said to be "in conjunction," because they are in different signs. (7) This is the opinion of the ANCIENTS; {but} I, ABRAHAM IBN EZRA,³ COMPILERᵅ,⁴ of THIS BOOK, disagree with them, as I shall explain in the BOOK OF NATIVITIES.⁵ (8) Likewise, the ANCIENTS, regarding the *fixed* upper stars that are in **the orb of the signs**,ᵅ,⁶ did not put on record how much is **the size of their power**,ᵅ,⁷ with the exception of DOROTHEUS alone, who said that it is one quarter of a sign [7½°]. (9) {But} the opinion of those who investigated this science closely is that it is the same as the size of the power of the bodies of the **planets**ᵅ ⟨that is in a mixture with the upper star⟩, whether the ⟨upper⟩ star is of the first or second honor [magnitude]. (10) The reason for conjunction is that two or more stars conjoin each other, *because* the orb of one of them is below the orb of the other, and that both are direct ⟨⟨in one degree and⟩⟩ᵛ,⁸ in one minute in the **orb of the signs**.ᵅ (11) The lighter ⟨planet⟩ will hide the heavier ⟨planet⟩ so that it does not appear to vision, because it [the lighter] has gone below it [the heavier]. (12) This happens if there is no latitude between them ⟨⟨in the girdle of the vest [the zodiac]⟩⟩,ᵛ,⁹ and **there will still be an explanation of this**.ʸ,¹⁰

4 (1) "Mixture" is when one star conjoins another **planet or star**,ᵝ and then another nature will be generated from their nature. (2) Such as Saturn and Mars, both of which are harmful, ⟨but⟩ the ANCIENTS said, they indicate goodness when they conjoin. (3) {But} the truth is that one cancels the action of the other, and by that means the native is saved from harm, and for that reason they do not indicate goodness but only ⟨⟨the goodness⟩⟩ᵛ,¹ that they do no harm. (4) **The conjunction of Jupiter with Saturn**ʸ,² is the great

coniunctio cum Saturnoᵞ est coniunctio magna, eo quod ipsi superiores sunt, et secundum alterius eorum fortitudine manifestabitur natura eius. (5) Martis {vero} coniunctio cum Venere temperata est sicut explanabo. (6) Coniunctio {autem} **planetarum**ᵅ cum Sole est eis nociva, et gravius est omnibus Veneri et Lune et rursus Saturnus et Mars, nocivi sunt Soli cum ei coniunguntur. (7) Iupiter {autem} et Venum benignantur et non malignantur. (8) Mercurius {vero}, propter multitudinem motuum suorum *et mobilitatem*, et quia *semper* propinquus est Soli, modicum ledi potest quando **sub radiis**ᵞ Solis est aut sub termino combustionis. (9) Cum {autem} precise ⟨⟨...⟩⟩ᵛ coniunctus est Soli, secundum Antiquorum sententiam, fortitudinem habet magnam, | intantum quod dixerunt: quando sic se habet Mercurius, duo Mercurii sunt **in celo**,ᵅ {sed} Ptolomeus ab eis dissentit, et ipse **ius habet.**ᵅᶿ (10) Coniuncto {vero} Lune cum Saturno et Marte nociva est; si {autem} coniuncta fuerit Saturno Lune diminuta hoc peius est, et si aucta lumine alleviabitur nocumentum, et econtrario cum **est coniuncta**ᵅ Marti. (11) {Quod} si in fortitudine sua fuerit Luna, diminuent illi de fortitudine ipsius et non nocebunt multum.

17rb

5 (1) ⟨⟨...⟩⟩.ᵘ **Aspectuum inicium quidem,**ᴨ sive sit aspectus sextilis sive quartus sive trinus aut oppositus, secundum quod explanavi in tertia parte **libri huius,**ᵅ est quando distantia est ab aspectu .12. gradus, et Ptolomeus dicit .6., **et tunc est in fortitudine aspectus.**ᵅ (2) Exemplum {autem} dabo tibi: si fuerit **planeta**ᵞ respectu alterius ad .54. gradus, erit in fortitudine aspectus sextilis; et cum est **longitudo**ᵅ inter eos .60. gradus, tunc est in aspectu perfecto, et significat perfectionem omnis rei quam significat, et sic est de ceteris aspectibus.

6 (1) Separatio est quando transit stella levior graviorem per unum gradum, sive in coniunctione sive in aspectu, et hoc est secundum duos **modus.**ᵞ (2) Nam si levior qui separatur **applicat**ᵞ alii stelle, aut secundum coniunctionem aut secundum aliquam aspectuum, tunc erit eius commixtio cum illa stella alia. (3) Si {autem} non **applicet seu non coniungatur alii stelle**ᵝ nec aspiciat eam, sitque inter ipsam et graviorem in coniunctione minus fortitudinis corporis eius, adhuc erit in eius commixtione; **sed si plus tunc separatur commixtio.**ᵅ

conjunction, because they are upper ⟨planets⟩, and its nature [the nature of one of them] will be manifest according to the power of the other of them. (5) {But} the conjunction of Mars and Venus is tempered, as I shall explain. (6) The conjunction of the **planets**^(α) with the Sun, {however,} is harmful to them, and the most severe of all is that of Venus and the Moon and also of Saturn and Mars, ⟨for⟩ they are harmful to the Sun when they conjoin it. (7) Jupiter and Venus do good and do not do evil. (8) {But} Mercury, because of its many motions *and rapidity of movement*, and because it is *always* near the Sun, is only slightly harmed when it is **under the rays**^(γ) of the Sun or in the boundary of burning. (9) When ⟨⟨the star⟩⟩,^(γ,3) {however,} is wholly conjoined with the Sun, according to the ANCIENTS, it has great power, so much that they said: when Mercury is in such a condition, there are two Mercuries **in the heavens;**^(α,4) {but} PTOLEMY disagrees with them, and **he is right**^(αθ,5) [lit. he has the law]. (10) {Moreover} the Moon's conjunction with Saturn and Mars is harmful; {but} it is worse when it [the Moon] is conjoined with Saturn and when the Moon is decreasing [is waning]; and the opposite holds when **it is conjoined**^(α,6) with Mars. (11) {But} if the Moon is in its strength, they will diminish its power and will not harm much.

5 (1) ⟨⟨"Aspect."⟩⟩^(μ,1) **The beginning of the aspects,**^(π,2) whether it is sextile aspect, or quartile, or trine, or opposition, as I explained in the third chapter **of THIS BOOK,**^(α,3) is when it [the planet] is 12° away from the aspect; but PTOLEMY says 6°, **and then it is in the power of the aspect.**^(α,4) (2) {But} I shall give you an example: if a **planet**^(γ) is up to 54° with respect to another **planet,**^(γ) it will be within the power of the sextile aspect; and when the **longitude**^(α,5) [the distance] between them is 60°, then is it in full aspect, and indicates the completion of everything indicated by it, and likewise regarding the other aspects.

6 (1) "Separation" is when a lighter [swift] ⟨planet⟩ passes 1° beyond a heavier [slow] ⟨planet⟩, whether in conjunction or in aspect, and this ⟨condition⟩ may have two **modes.**^(γ,1) (2) For if the lighter ⟨planet⟩ that is separating ⟨from the heavy planet⟩ **applies to**^(γ,2) [approaches] another star, either in conjunction or any of the aspects, then its [the lighter planet's] mixture is with the other star ⟨and not with the heavy planet⟩. (3) {But} if it [the lighter planet] does not **apply to** [approach] **the other star or conjoin it,**^(β,3) nor aspect it, and between it [the lighter planet] and the heavier ⟨planet⟩ there is less than ⟨the number of degrees⟩ of the power of its body in conjunction, it will still be in its mixture; **but if more then it separates from the mixture.**^(α,4)

7 (1) {Preterea} semper considerare debes ad gradus equalium **ascensionum**.ᵅ (2) Verbi gratia: **si**ᵞ unus **planeta**ᵞ est in decimo gradu Arietis et alius in .20. gradu Piscium, tunc enim eorum distantia equalis est ab **equinoctiali linea**,ᵞ et debent estimari tamquam coniuncti. (3) {Item} est in alius modus, videlicet ut si sunt in duobus gradibus quorum **partes horarum**ᵞ sunt equales, ut .16. gradus Leonis et .14. Tauri; ratio {autem} huius est quia eorum distantia a capite **Arietis vel Libre**ᵅ est equalis, **et ideo vocatur earum coniunctio equalis**.ᵅ (4) Illorum {vero} quorum **longitudo**ᵅ equalis est a punctis septentrionis et meridiei, que sunt caput Cancri et caput Capricornii, vocatur coniunctio contraria.

8 (1) **Solitudo**ᵞ est quando separatur **planeta**ᵞ ab **alio**,ᵞ aut in coniunctione per .15. | gradus, aut in aspectu per .6.; et non coniungitur alii **planete**ᵞ quamdiu est in illo signo, aut non aspicit eum **planeta**ᵞ quamdiu ibi est aspectu perfecto quocumque.

17va

9 (1) **Alienatio**ᵞ est quod sit **planeta**,ᵞ quamdiu ibi est[1] in signo aliquo et non aspiciat eum aliquis **planeta**,ᵞ quamdiu erit in eodem nec separetur {etiam} ab aliquo. (2) Et hoc quidem Lune {tamen} attingit propter velocitatem motus eius.

10 (1) Translatio est duobus **modis**.ᵞ (2) Unus cum separatur **planeta**ᵞ levior a graviori et coniungitur alii aut aspiciatur ab alio, tunc namque fortitudinem prioris transfert ad posteriorem. (3) Secundus {vero} **modus**ᵞ est si coniungatur **planeta**ᵞ levis alterius graviori et hic gravior adhuc alii[2] graviori se, tunc enim medius lumen levis[3] transfert ad **magis**ᵅ graviorem.

11 (1) Collectio est cum duo **planete**ᵞ vel plures coniunguntur unum, tunc enim totum colligit **planeta**ᵞ gravior inter eos.

12 (1) Reditio luminis est duobus **modis**.ᵞ (2) Primus est cum planeta alii **planete**ᵞ non coniungitur, nec alter alterum aspicit, sed hii duo coniunguntur alii aut aspiciunt illum, et hic aspiciat domum qua opus est, vel stellam que queritur; tunc enim redit lumen ad quesitam. (3) Secundus {vero}

[1] est] WVG; L > aspectu.   [2] alii] W om.   [3] levis] W; LGV gravioris.

7 (1) {Besides,} you must always consider the ⟨pairs of⟩ degrees that have the same **ascensions**.ᵅ (2) As an illustration: **if**ᵞ,¹ one **planet**ᵞ is at Aries 10° and another at Pisces 20°, then their distance from the **equinoctial line**ᵞ,² [the equator] is the same, and they must be considered as if there were in conjunction. (3) {Likewise,} there is another way, namely, if they were in two degrees whose **parts of the hours**ᵞ,³ are equal, such as Leo 16° and Taurus 14°, {but} the reason is because their distance from the head of **Aries or of Libra**ᵅ,⁴ is the same, **and for that reason their conjunction is called "equal."**ᵅ,⁵ (4) {But} regarding those whose **longitude**ᵅ,⁶ [the distance] is equal from the southern and northern points, which are the head of Cancer and the head of Capricorn, it is called "conjunction by opposition."

8 (1) **"Solitude"**ᵞ,¹ is when a **planet**ᵞ moves away from **another**,ᵞ,² either 15° from conjunction or 6° from ⟨some⟩ aspect; and it is not conjoined to other **planet**ᵞ as long as it is in the same sign, or no **planet**ᵞ aspects it as long as any complete aspect is there.

9 (1) **"Alienation"**ᵞ,¹ is ⟨about⟩ a **planet**,ᵞ as long as it is there in any sign and no **planet**ᵞ aspects it, as long as it is in the same ⟨sign⟩ and does not {also} separate from any ⟨planet⟩. (2) {Nevertheless,} this happens indeed to the Moon because of the quickness of its motion.

10 (1) "Translation" is in two **modes**.ᵞ (2) One is when a lighter **planet**ᵞ separates from a heavier ⟨planet⟩ and is conjoined to another ⟨planet⟩ or is aspected by the other ⟨planet⟩, then it transfers the power of the first ⟨planet⟩ to the latter ⟨planet⟩. (3) {But} the second **mode**ᵞ is if a light **planet**ᵞ is conjoined to another ⟨planet⟩ that is heavier than it is, and that heavier ⟨planet is conjoined⟩ to another ⟨planet that is⟩ heavier than it is, then the intermediate ⟨planet⟩ transfers the light of the light ⟨planet⟩ to the **even**ᵅ,¹ heavier ⟨planet⟩.

11 (1) "Collection" is when two or more **planets**ᵞ are conjoined to one ⟨planet⟩; then the heavier **planet**ᵞ among them collects everything.

12 (1) "Reflecting the light" is in two **modes**.ᵞ (2) The first is when a **planet**ᵞ is not conjoined to other ⟨planet⟩, nor do they aspect each other, but both ⟨planets⟩ conjoin or aspect another planet, and that ⟨planet⟩ aspects the ⟨horoscopic⟩ house that one needs, or the requested star; then it reflects the light onto the requested ⟨planet⟩. (3) {But} the second **mode**ᵞ is when

modusʸ est cum non coniungitur dominus ascendentis domino rei quesite, vel non aspiciat alter alterum, vel separatur alter ab altero; si lumen transferat inter eos **planeta**ʸ aliquis, reputatur etiam ac si esset coniunctio.

13 (1) Donum fortitudinis est ut sit **planeta**ʸ in domo sua, aut **exaltatione**,ʸ aut in domo triplicitatis sue, aut in **termino**,ᵅ vel facie, et coniungatur alii **planete**ʸ vel aspiciat illum, tunc enim dabit fortitudinem suam illi alii.

14 (1) **Donum virtutis**ᵅ est ut aspiciat **planeta**ʸ **planetam**ʸ *alium*, aut aspectu **amicitie**ʸ perfecte aut aspectu **amicitie**ʸ dimidie, tunc erit eorum commixtio **equalis seu temperata**.ᵝ

15 (1) Donum nature est **si**ʸ coniungatur **planeta**ʸ cum domino signi in quo est, aut domino **exaltationis**,ʸ vel **termini**,ᵅ vel triplicitatis, vel faciei, tunc enim dabit illi **planete**ʸ naturam suam.

16 (1) Donum duplicis nature est duobus **modis**;ʸ (2) Uno modo cum est **planeta**ʸ in signo in quo **dignitatem**ʸ habet, et coniungitur alii **planete**ʸ qui {etiam} habet **dignitatem**ʸ in eodem signo aut aspiciat illum, ut Venus | cum Iove in Piscibus. (3) Secundo **modo**ʸ cum **planeta**ʸ **planete**ʸ coniungitur que de eius¹ natura est, ut diurnus cum diurno, et nocturnus cum nocturno.

17vb

17 (1) Rectitudo **est cum** est **planeta**ʸ in magnitudine gradus sui, et hoc est in aliquo angulorum vel **succedentium angulis seu angulorum**.ᵝ,²

18 (1) **Obliquitas**ʸ est cum est **planeta**ʸ in aliquo cadentium.

19 (1) Prohibitio est duobus **modis**.ʸ (2) **Primus modus est**ᵅ ut sunt tres **planete**ʸ in uno signo, gradus {autem} eorum sunt diversi, gravisque sit in gradibus plus, medius prohibet leviorem qui in gradibus minus est ne coniugatur graviori donec transivit *medium*. (3) Ut Saturno in .20. gradu Arietis existente, Mercurioque in .15., Venus in undecima, Mercurius quidem prohibebit Veneri a coniunctione eius cum Saturno quousque transivit ipsum *Mercurius*, et postea coniungetur Venus *Saturno*. (4) Secundus **modus**ʸ est

¹eius] G sua. ²seu angulorum G om.

the lord of the ascendant does not conjoin the lord of the requested thing, or they do not aspect each other, or they are separating; if some **planet**ʸ transfers the light between them, this, too, is considered to be conjunction.

13 (1) "Giving power" is when a **planet**ʸ is in its house, or **exaltation**ʸ,¹ or in the house of its triplicity, or in the **term**,ᵅ or in the face [decan], and is conjoined to another **planet**ʸ or aspects it, then it will give its power to this other ⟨planet⟩.

14 (1) "**Giving power**"ᵅ,¹ is when one **planet**ʸ aspects *another* **planet**,ʸ in an aspect of complete **friendship**ʸ,² or of half **friendship**,ʸ then their mixture is **equal or tempered**.ᵝ,³

15 (1) "Giving nature" is **if**ʸ,¹ a **planet**ʸ is conjoined with the lord of the sign in which it is, or with the lord of the **exaltation**ʸ,² or ⟨the lord⟩ of the **term**,ᵅ or ⟨the lord⟩ of the triplicity, or ⟨the lord⟩ of the face [decan]; then it will give its nature to this **planet**.ʸ

16 (1) "Giving double nature" is in two **modes**.ʸ (2) One mode is when a **planet**ʸ is in a sign in which it has a **dignity**,ʸ,¹ and is conjoined with another **planet**ʸ that {also} has a **dignity**ʸ in this sign or aspects it, such as Venus with Jupiter in Pisces. (3) The second **mode**ʸ is when a **planet**ʸ is conjoined with another **planet**ʸ of the same nature, such as a diurnal ⟨planet⟩ with ⟨another⟩ diurnal ⟨planet⟩, and a nocturnal ⟨planet⟩ with ⟨another⟩ nocturnal ⟨planet⟩.

17 (1) "Straightness"¹ is when a **planet**ʸ is in its greatest degree, and this is when it is in one of the **angles**ʸ,² or the **succedent to the angles or of the angles**.ᵝ,³

18 (1) "**Obliquity**"ʸ,¹ is when a **planet**ʸ is in one of the cadent ⟨houses⟩.

19 (1) "Prohibition"¹ is in two **modes**.ʸ (2) **The first mode**ᵅ,² is when three **planets**ʸ are in one sign, {but} in different degrees, and the heavier has the most degrees, ⟨then⟩ the middle one prohibits the lighter, which has the fewest degrees, from conjoining the heavier until it passes *the middle one*. (3) Such as Saturn located at Aries 20°, Mercury at ⟨Aries⟩ 15°, Venus at ⟨Aries⟩ 11°, then Mercury will prohibit Venus from conjoining Saturn until it passes *Mercury*; after that Venus will conjoin *Saturn*. (4) The second **mode**ʸ

PART ONE

per aspectum, ut si sunt duo **planete**ᵞ in uno signo et levior **applicet graviori per coniunctionem**,ᵅ alius {vero} **planeta**ᵞ illum graviorem aspiciat aspectu quocumque, tunc **planeta qui coniungitur cum illo**ᵅ, prohibebit aspectante et dissipabit **eius habitudinem seu effectum**ᵞ dummodo gradus eorum sunt **equales in distantia**.ᵞ (5) Si {vero} gradus aspicientis propinquiores sunt **per aspectum quam coniungentis seu applicantis, non poterit aspicientem prohibere**.ᵞ

20 (1) **Reditio seu reditus¹ ad bonum.**^(β,2) ⟨⟨...⟩⟩ᵛ est³ quando coniungitur **planeta**ᵞ **planete**ᵞ **sub radiis Solis**ᵞ existenti ⟨⟨...⟩⟩,ᵘ **quia tunc**ᵞ non poterit **Sol**^(α,4) recipere lumen propter eius debilitatem et ideo **tunc redet seu redire faciet illud**.^β (2) Adhuc est alius **modus**ᵞ ut si coniungatur **planete**ᵞ retrogrado, quia {tunc} {etiam} **redire faciet seu redet**^β illi quidquid recepit. (3) Et sit autem **reditio seu reditus ad bonum**^β tribus **modis**.ᵞ (4) Primus est ut ille qui habet fortitudinem ad se reversam, sit recipiens **datorem seu reditorem**.^β (5) Secundus **modus**ᵞ est ut sit **planeta**ᵞ levis directus in cursu suo, gravis {vero} **combustus sub radiis Solis** vel retrogradus. (6) Et tertius **modus**ᵞ ut **planeta**ᵞ que **redire facit**ᵅ sit in una domorum cadentium, et **planeta**ᵞ ad quam reversum est lumen sit in uno angulorum vel succedentium.

21 (1) Reditus {autem} ad malum est econtrario hiis tribus modis iam dicitis.

22 (1) **Refrenatio seu contradictio**^β est ut si est **planeta**ᵞ in fortitudine corporis alterius **planete**,ᵞ et antequam ei coniungatur in uno gradu, retrogradus fiat.

18ra **23** (1) | **Accidens seu eventus accidentalis**^β est us sunt .3. **planete**ᵞ in uno signo, et unus levis existens sit plus in gradibus, et secundus existens gravior illo sit minus in gradibus, tertius {vero} levior primo coniungatur graviori, primus {autem} levis, cuius gradus plures sunt, per retrogradationem⁵ graviori coniungatur.

---

¹Reditio seu reditus] WG; LV Redditio sive redditus.   ²ad bonum] W; LGV om.   ³est] GV; LW om.   ⁴Sol] LG; VW om.   ⁵illo sit minus in gradibus, tertius vero levior primo coniungatur graviori, primus autem levis, cuius gradus plures sunt per retrogradationem] WVG; L in margin.

is by aspect, when two **planets**ʸ are in the same sign and the lighter **applies by conjunction to**^(α,3) the heavier, {but} another **planet**ʸ aspects the heavier in any aspect, then **the planet that was conjoined with it**^(α,4) prohibits the aspecting **planet**ʸ and destroys **its disposition or effect**,^(γ,5) on condition that their degrees are **at an equal distance.**^(γ,6) (5) {But} if the degrees of the aspecting ⟨planet⟩ are closer **in aspect than ⟨the degrees⟩ of the conjoining or applying ⟨planet⟩, it will not be able to prohibit the aspecting planet.**^(γ,7)

20 (1) "Returning or coming back to goodness".^(β,1) ⟨⟨Know that returning to goodness⟩⟩^(ν,2) is when one **planet**ʸ is conjoined to ⟨another⟩ **planet**ʸ **under the rays of the Sun**ʸ ⟨⟨or aspects it⟩⟩;^(μ,3) **because then**^(γ,4) the **Sun**^(α,5) cannot receive the light because of its weakness, **therefore it returns or causes it** [the light] **to return.**^(β,6) (2) In addition another **mode**ʸ is if ⟨a planet⟩ is conjoined with a retrograde **planet**,ʸ since {then} it {also} **returns or makes return to it**^(β,7) [the other planet] whatever it received. (3) "**Returning or coming back to goodness,**"^(β) {however,} is in three **modes.**ʸ (4) The first is when the one [planet] that holds the power that is returned to it receives **the giver** ⟨of the power⟩ **or the one that returns.**^(β,8) ⟨it⟩ (5) The second **mode** is when the light **planet**ʸ is direct in its course, {but} the heavy one is **burnt under the rays of the Sun** or retrograde. (6) The third **mode**ʸ is when the **planet**ʸ **that makes return**^(α,9) ⟨the power⟩ is in one of the cadent houses, and the **planet**ʸ to which the light is given back is in one of the angles or the succedent ⟨houses⟩.

21 (1) {But} "returning to evil" is the opposite of the three aforementioned modes.

22 (1) "**Restraint or contradiction**"^(β) is when a **planet**ʸ is within the power of the body of another **planet**,ʸ and becomes retrograde before it conjoins it in one degree.

23 (1) "**Accident or accidental event**"^(β,1) is when three **planets**ʸ are in the same sign, and one is light and has more degrees, the second is heavier than it and has fewer degrees, {but} the third is lighter than the first and is conjoined to the heavier one, then the first light ⟨planet⟩, {however,} that has more degrees, turns retrograde and is conjoined with the heavier one.

24 (1) **Frustratio seu evasio**$^\beta$ est ut sit **planeta**$^\gamma$ vadens ad se coniungendum alii **planete**$^\gamma$ in eodem signo, antequam a illi coniugatur, moveatur gravior signum, exeundo et coniugatur ei alius **planeta**.$^\gamma$

25 (1) **Abscissio luminis seu interceptio**$^\beta$ est tribus **modis**.$^\gamma$ (2) Unus est ut sit **planeta**$^\gamma$ levis **vadens seu applicans ad coniunctionem**$^\beta$ gravioris et sunt ambo in uno signo, sit {autem} **planeta**$^\gamma$ tertius $\langle\langle...\rangle\rangle^\mu$ in sequenti signo; {sed} antequam levis primus graviori coniungatur, **planeta**$^\gamma$ *tertius* in sequenti signo existens per retrogradationem ingrediatur signum in quo gravior est et coniungatur eidem; tunc enim abscindit lumen primi **planete**.$^\gamma$ (3) Secundus quidem **modus**$^\gamma$ est cum **planeta**$^\gamma$ levis vadit ad coniunctionem gravioris et sunt ambo in uno signo, sitque gravius iste vadens etiam ad coniunctionem alterius adhuc gravioris; et antequam primus perveniat ad secundum, coniungatur secundus tertio et pertranseat ipsum, tunc enim abscidet lumen primi. (4) Tertius {vero} **modus**$^\gamma$ est quando coniungit **planeta**$^\gamma$ alii planete quo non est opus.

26 (1) **Compassio seu largitio**$^\beta$ est ut sit **planeta**$^\gamma$ in **gradu puteali**,$^\gamma$ aut **in casu suo**,$^\gamma$ et coniungatur ei alius **planeta**,$^\gamma$ aut ipse alii qui sit ei amicus aut dominus domus, aut **dignitatem habens**$^\gamma$ in illo signo; tunc enim extrahet eum de puteo suo, aut de **casu**,$^\gamma$ et **compacietur ei**.$^\gamma$

27 (1) Remuneratio {autem} *est ut si* **planeta**$^\gamma$ ille qui priorem extraxit de puteo vel **de casu**,$^\gamma$ in puteum cadat aut **in casu**$^\gamma$ fuerit, et extractorem illum aspiciat prior extractus eundem a puteo vel casu, extrahat vice versa.

28 (1) Receptio est quando coniungitur **planeta**,$^\gamma$ sive **corporaliter**$^\gamma$ sive per aspectu, alii planete qui sit dominus domus, vel dominus **exaltationis**,$^\gamma$ vel triplicitatis, vel **termini**$^\alpha$ aut faciei, $\langle\langle...\rangle\rangle$.$^\nu$ (2) {Item} si$^\gamma$ **planeta**$^\gamma$ coniungatur alii **planete**$^\gamma$ existenti in domo qua dat fortitudinem, aut **in exaltatione sua**,$^\gamma$ est etiam receptio; sed si fuerit in triplicitate sua, aut in $\langle\langle...\rangle\rangle^\nu$ **termino**,$^\alpha$ aut in $\langle\langle...\rangle\rangle^\nu$ facie, non recipit ipsum receptione perfecta. (3) Si {vero} congregentur due **dignitates**,$^\gamma$ triplicitatis scilicet cum **termino**$^\alpha$ aut cum facie, et aspectu trino aut sextili, | tunc est etiam receptio. (4) Rursus si fuerint in gradibus signorum qui equales sint in **ascensionibus**.$^\alpha$ (5) Pla-

24 (1) "**Frustration or evasion**"^(β,1) is when a **planet**^γ moves towards conjunction with another **planet**^γ in the same sign, but before it conjoins it, the heavier one moves out of the sign, and another **planet**^γ conjoins with it when it is leaving ⟨the sign⟩.

25 (1) "**Cutting or intercepting the light**"^(β,1) is in three **modes**.^γ (2) One is when a light **planet**^γ **moves or applies to the conjunction**^(β,2) of a heavier one and both are in the same sign, and a third ⟨⟨light⟩⟩^(μ,3) **planet**,^γ {however,} is in the next sign; {but} before the first light **planet**^γ conjoins the heavier one, the *third* **planet**^γ that is in the next sign retrogresses and enters the sign where the heavier one is and conjoins it; then it cuts the its light of the first **planet**.^γ (3) The second **mode**^γ is when a light ⟨planet⟩ moves towards conjunction with a heavier one and both are in the same sign, and this heavier one moves towards conjunction with another **planet**^γ still heavier; but before the first reaches the second, the second conjoins the third and passes it; then it will cut the light of the first one. (4) {But} the third **mode**^γ is when a **planet**^γ conjoins another **planet**,^γ of which there is no use.

26 (1) "**Compassion or generosity**"^(β,1) is when a **planet**^γ is **in a degree pertaining to a pit**,^γ or in its **fall**^(γ,2) [dejection], and another **planet**^γ conjoins it, or it ⟨conjoins⟩ another which is friendly to it or is the lord of the house or **exerts some dignity**^(γ,3) over this sign; then it will pull it out of its pit, or its **fall**^(γ,4) [dejection], and **will have compassion for it**.^(γ,5)

27 (1) {But} "recompense" *is as if* the **planet**,^γ which pulled the first ⟨planet⟩ out of the pit or the **fall**^(γ,1)[dejection], falls into a pit or is in the **fall**,^γ and the first ⟨planet⟩, which was pulled out, aspects the one that pulled it out of the pit or fall, and pulls it out the other way around.

28 (1) "Reception" is when a **planet**,^γ whether **bodily**^(γ,1) or by aspect, conjoins another **planet**^γ that is the lord of the ⟨planetary⟩ house, or the lord of the **exaltation**^(γ,2) or of the triplicity, or of the **term**,^α or of the face [decan], ⟨⟨then it is received by this planet⟩⟩.^(γ,3) (2) {Likewise,} if^(γ,4) a **planet**^γ is conjoined to another **planet**^γ located in a house in which it gives power, or in its **exaltation**^(γ,5) this is also reception; but if it is in its triplicity, or in ⟨⟨its⟩⟩^γ **term**,^α or in ⟨⟨its⟩⟩^γ face [decan], it will not receive it in a complete reception. (3) {But} if two **dignities**,^γ namely of the triplicity with the **term**^α or with the face [decan], are combined, or ⟨if they are⟩ in trine or sextile, then this is also reception. (4) In addition, if they are in the degrees of signs whose **ascensions**^α are the same. (5) A **benevolent planet**^γ receives

neta benevolus⟨ʸ⟩ recipit benevolum eo quod natura ipsorum **equalis est seu temperata**,^β sed Mars et Saturnus recipit alter alterum dummodo sit ⟨⟨...⟩⟩^μ in aspectu sextili aut trino et non in aliis aspectibus.

29 (1) Est {autem} in receptione fortitudo, mediocritas et debilitas. (2) Receptio fortis est semper Lune a Sole, a quolibet enim signo **recipit eam**,⟨ʸ⟩ quia lumen eius *a Sole* pervenit, ab oppositione {tamen} erit in labore et tristitia; si {vero} fuerit in signo in quo **dignitate**⟨ʸ⟩ habeat aliqua, tunc erit duplex receptio. (3) Et consimiliter est quando Mercurius **planetam**⟨ʸ⟩ recipit in signo Virginis, eo quod domus eius est {etiam} **exaltatio**;⟨ʸ⟩ tunc erit receptio perfecta. (4) Et receptio {autem} a domo est mediocris. (5) Receptio {vero} a triplicitate ⟨⟨...⟩⟩^μ vel a facie debilis est.

30 (1) **Benevolentia sive liberalitas**^β est ut si fuerint duo **planete**⟨ʸ⟩ quorum alter sit in domo alterius, aut **in exaltatione**,⟨ʸ⟩ aut **in eius dignitatem**;⟨ʸ⟩ quamvis non coniunctus sit alter alteri nec alterum aspiciat, {nihilominus} inter eos erit receptio.[1]

31 (1) **Similitudo sive haiz sive esse in suo limite**^β est cum **planeta**⟨ʸ⟩ masculinus de die super terram est, et in signo masculino, ac in gradu masculino; et **planeta**⟨ʸ⟩ femininus de nocte super terram, et de die sub ea, et {etiam} in signo feminino et gradu feminino. (2) Si {autem} res econtrario fuerit, quidquid significavit **planeta**⟨ʸ⟩ non erit convenienter.

32 (1) **Obsessio**⟨ʸ⟩ est quando **planeta**⟨ʸ⟩ separatur a **planeta**⟨ʸ⟩ **malivolo**⟨ʸ⟩ et coniungitur **malivolo**,⟨ʸ⟩ sive per coniunctionem sive per aspectum; aut si est **planeta benevolus aut nocivus**⟨ʸ⟩ in signo quod ante ipsum est et alius **planeta**⟨ʸ⟩ in signo post ipsum. (2) Si {tamen} Sol aspexerit **planetam**⟨ʸ⟩ **obsessum**⟨ʸ⟩ inter illos duos nocivos, de nocumento satis alleviabit.

33 (1) **Fortitudo**˙ est ut si sint tres **planete**⟨ʸ⟩ superiores orientales a Sole, ab hora eam qua incipit apparere visui, sunt in **fortitudine** magna quousque inter eos et Solem sextilis sit aspectus. (2) Deinde usque ad aspectum quartum diminuitur gradus **fortitudinis**⟨ʸ⟩ eorum. (3) Et ab hic usque ad stationem secundam non est eis **fortitudo**.⟨ʸ⟩ (4) Si {autem} orientales a Sole sunt hii et occidentales a Luna, non est maior hac **fortitudo**⟨ʸ⟩ aliqua.

---

[1]receptio] WVG; L > benevolentie vel liberalitas scilicet.

a benevolent one because their nature is **equal or tempered**,[β,6] but Mars and Jupiter receive each other provided that they are ⟨⟨in conjunction⟩⟩[μ,7] ⟨or⟩ in a sextile aspect or in trine, but not in the other aspects.

29 (1) {But} in "reception" there is strength, moderation, and weakness. (2) Strong reception belongs always to the Moon from the Sun, because it [the Sun] **receives her**[γ,1] [the Moon] from all the signs, since its [the Moon's] light comes from *the Sun*, {yet} from opposition it will be with toil and sadness; {but} if it is in a sign in which it exerts some **dignity**,[γ] then the reception is double. (3) The same applies when Mercury receives a planet in the sign of Virgo, because it is its house, and {also} its **exaltation**[γ,2] then the reception will be complete. (4) {But} reception from the house is moderate. (5) {Moreover} reception from triplicity, ⟨⟨or term,⟩⟩[μ,3] or face [decan] is weak.

30 (1) "**Benevolence or generosity**"[β,1] is when each of two **planets**[γ] is in the other's house, or in the ⟨other's⟩ **exaltation**[γ,2] or in **its dignity**;[γ] even though they do not conjoin or aspect each other, {nevertheless} there will be reception between them.

31 (1) "**Similitude or *ḥayyz* or being in its domain**"[β,1] is when a masculine **planet**[γ] is above the earth by day, and in a masculine sign and in a masculine degree; and ⟨when⟩ a feminine **planet**[γ] is above the earth by night, and under the earth by night, {also} in a feminine sign, and in a feminine degree. (2) {But} in the opposite case, whatever the **planet**[γ] indicates will not be convenient.

32 (1) "**Siege**"[γ,1] is when a **planet**[γ] moves away from a **malevolent**[γ] **planet**[γ] and conjoins a **malevolent**[γ] ⟨planet⟩, whether in conjunction or in aspect; or if **a benevolent or harmful planet**[γ,2] is in the sign before it and another **planet**[γ] is in the sign after it. (2) {Nevertheless,} if the Sun aspects the **planet**[γ] that is **besieged**[γ,3] between the two harming ⟨planets⟩, it will mitigate much of the harm.

33 (1) "**Strength**"[γ,1] is when the three upper **planets**[γ] are oriental of the Sun, from the moment it [the Sun] begins to be visible to sight, they are in great **strength**[γ] until there is a sextile aspect between them and the Sun. (2) From there to the quartile aspect the degree of their **strength**[γ] is decreased. (3) From there to the second station they have no **strength**.[γ] (4) {But} if they are oriental of the Sun and occidental of the Moon, the **strength**[γ] is

(5) **Planetis**ʸ {vero} .3. inferioribus incipit **fortitudo**ʸ ab hora qua prima videtur in occidente post occasum Solis. (6) Et **fortitudo**ʸ Veneris ac Mercurii perseverat usque ad tempus retrogradationis eorum, si {autem} cum ipsi occidentales fuerint a Sole sint {etiam} orientales a Luna, nulla est hac eis maior **fortitudo**.ʸ (7) Lune quidem fortitudo est usque ad medietati mensis. (8) Dicit PTOLOMEUS {quod} si fuerit proportio signo in quo est aliquis **planeta**ʸ ad signum in quo est Sol vel Luna, sit proportio domorum suarum secundum quod distinguntur, tunc erit **planeta**ʸ **fortitudo**ʸ magna.

(9) Explicit septima pars LIBER HUIUS.

§8

1 (1) **Octava**[1] **pars HUIUS LIBRI.**ʸ Universalia quidem {igitur} **iudicia** quidem **sive regule**ᵝ sunt in nativitatibus, et revolutionibus, ac interrogationibus, et sunt .120.

2 (1) **Quarum una est**ᵅ quia Luna propinqua terre est, et velox in motu suo et **multiplicat commixtionem sive multotiens commiscetur**ᵝ cum **planetis**ʸ ipsa, namque dat eis virtutem et nullus **planeta**ʸ ille, et ipsa transfert lumen unius ad alium, et assimilatur {etiam} nato, quia lumine eius paulatim, et paulatim crescit donec sit perfectum, et postmodum paulatine diminuitur quousque nihil de ipso videatur et a mundo auferatur; idcirco dixerunt ANTIQUI quod Luna super omnem rem significat et super cogitationes et super[2] principia[3] omnium operationum. (2) Si {igitur} in fortitudine sua fuerit et eius dispositiones bone, perficietur res omnis qua incipiat homo in hora illa, et econtrario si **fuerit cum nocivis seu impedita**.ᵝ (3) Dixerunt {etiam} quod **querente seu interrogatore**ᵝ considerandum est ad signum ascendentis et ad eius dominum, **pro re** {vero} **quesita**ᵅ ad signum septimum et[4] dominum eius; semper ponenda est Luna particeps cum illo.

(4) .2m.[5] est si Luna est solivaga; hoc significat super omnem rem vacuam, et quod nichil esse potest de omni re de qua querit **querens seu interrogator**.ᵝ

---

[1]Octava] LW; GV < incipit.   [2]super] WVG; L om.   [3]principia] W principium.   [4]et] WVG; L om.   [5].2a.] WVG; L om; and so on regarding the numbers at the beginning of all the following aphorisms.

the greatest. (5) The **strength**ʸ of the three lower **planets**ʸ begins {indeed} from the moment they are first visible in the west after sunset. (6) The **strength**ʸ of dominion of Mercury and Venus lasts until the time of their retrogradation, {but} if when they are occidental of the Sun they are {also} oriental of the Moon, there is no greater **strength**ʸ than this. (7) The Moon's **strength** is until the middle of the month. (8) {But} PTOLEMY says that if the proportion between the sign where the **planet**ʸ is located and the sign where the Sun or the Moon is located is as the proportion between their [the planets'] houses according to their divisions, then the **planet**ʸ will have a great **strength**.ʸ

(9) Here ends the seventh part of THIS BOOK.

§8

1 (1) **Eighth part of THIS BOOK.**ʸ,¹ All the **judgments or rules,**β,² {then,} are related to nativities, revolutions, and interrogations, and they are 120.

2 (1) **One of which is**α,¹ because the Moon is close to the Earth and quick in its motion, and **multiplies the mixture or it is more mixed**β,² with the **planets,**ʸ since it [the Moon] gives power to them and no **planet**ʸ ⟨gives its power⟩ to it [the Moon], and it [the Moon] transfers light from one to another, and it {also} resembles the native in that its light increases gradually and gradually grows until it is complete and afterwards decreases gradually until it is invisible and departs from the world; consequently all the ANCIENTS said that the Moon indicates everything, and thoughts, and the beginnings of every action. (2) {Therefore} if it [the Moon] is in its strength and its conditions are good, everything that a person begins doing at this moment will succeed, but the opposite applies if **it is with harmful ⟨planets⟩ or it is hindered.**β,³ (3) They {also} said that **for the querent or interrogator**β,⁴ one must observe the ascendant sign and its lord, {but} **for the requested thing**α,⁵ ⟨one must observe⟩ the seventh sign ⟨counting from the ascendant sign⟩ and its lord; the Moon should be always made a partner with it.

(4) The second is if the Moon is wandering in solitude; this indicates every empty thing, and that nothing the **querent or interrogator**β asks can be.

(5) .3m. Coniunctio, qua Luna **planete**[γ] coniungitur aut aspicit eum, significat super omnem rem futuram et **quidquid sperat interrogator vel expectare debet**;[β] si quidem **planeta**[γ] bonus fuerit, bonum, si malus, malum.

(6) .4m. Separatio Lune super res significat preteritas; et si quidem separata fuerit a coniunctione aut ab aspectu **planete**[γ] boni, bonum fuerit, si {vero} mali, malum.[1]

(7) .5m. Si **planeta**[γ] cui Luna dat **virtutem vel fortitudinem**[β] fuerit in fortitudine sua, tunc fiet res convenienter, et econtrario si fuerit debilis.

(8) .6m. Consimiliter **planeta**[γ] quibuscum dat | alii fortitudinem suam, secundum receptionis fortitudinem erit res illa.

18vb

(9) .7m. In die qua Luna fuerit cum **malivolis**,[γ] quidquid quesiverit **quesitor vel homo**[β] non perficietur convenienter; et si **planeta**[γ] fuerit in ascendente et Luna similiter in aliquo **angulorum**,[γ] tunc est hoc peius, quia hoc significat in anima timorem et egritudinem in corpore; si {vero} fuerit in domibus cadentibus, hoc significat timorem et non egritudinem.

3 (1) .8m. **Stellarum seu planetarum**[β,2] quidem due sunt species, una bona alia {vero} mala, ubique ergo **planetam**[γ] bonum invenieris dic bonum, et econtrario dic ubi contrarium.

(2) .9m. **Planete**[γ] **benevoli**[γ] et temperati ipsi *semper* valent, sive recipiant sive non, si {tamen} receperint tanto melius est; **malivoli**[γ] {vero} dissipantes sunt secundum ipsorum naturam; si {tamen} ab eis receptus fuerit **planeta**[γ] alleviabitur eorum nocumentum; et consimiliter est de aspectu eorum ad illum sextili aut trino.

(3) .10m. Non vocatur **planeta**[γ] **impeditus**[γ] donec super ipsum **radii**[α] sint **planete malivoli**[γ] secundum fortitudinem corporis eius; et si minus fuerint quam ita, non significat nisi parvum nocumentum. (4) Postquam {autem} ab illo separatur fuerit ⟨⟨...⟩⟩,[μ] etiam per unum gradum et adhuc melius si plus, terrebit terrore qui ad opus non perveniet. (5) Consimilisque modus est in **planeta benevolo**[γ]; **planeta**[γ] {vero} signans omnem rem que ad

---

[1]malum] G > fuerit.   [2]seu planetarum] L; WGV om.

(5) 3rd. Conjunction, in which the Moon is conjoined to a **planet**ʸ or aspects it, indicates any future event[6] and **whatever the interrogator is hoping for or must expect;**[β,7] if the **planet**ʸ is good, goodness, if it is bad, evil

(6) 4th. Separation by the Moon indicates past events;[8] if it [the Moon] separates from conjunction or aspect with a good **planet**,ʸ ⟨this is⟩ goodness, {but} ⟨with a⟩ bad ⟨planet⟩, ⟨this is⟩ evil.

(7) 5th. If the **planet**ʸ to which the Moon gives its **power or strength**[β] is in its strength, then the event will be as it should be, and the opposite holds true if it is weak.

(8) 6th. The same holds true for any **planet**ʸ that gives its power to another ⟨planet⟩; the event will be according to the power of the receiver.

(9) 7th. On a day when the Moon is with **malevolent**ʸ ⟨planets⟩, whatever **the querent or the person**[β,9] asks about will not be completed appropriately; if the **planet**ʸ is in the ascendant and the Moon is similarly in one of the **angles**,[γ,10] then this is worse, because this indicates fear in the soul and disease in the body; {but} if it [the Moon] is in the cadent houses, it indicates fear but not disease.

3 (1) 8th. There are two sorts of **stars or planets**,[β] one is good {but} the other is bad, and in every place you find a good **planet**ʸ pronounce good, and in the opposite case pronounce the contrary.

(2) 9th. **Benevolent**ʸ and mixed **planets**ʸ are *always* beneficial in themselves, whether or not they receive ⟨another planet⟩, {nevertheless} it is better if they receive ⟨another planet⟩; {but} **malevolent**ʸ ⟨planets⟩ are destructive by their nature; {nevertheless,} if the **planet**ʸ is received by them, their harm is diminished; the same holds true regarding their sextile or trine aspect to it.

(3) 10th. A **planet**ʸ is not called **hindered**[γ,1] until the **rays**[α,2] of a **malevolent planet**ʸ reach it according to the power of its body; and if they [the rays] are less than that [the power of the body], it indicates only slight harm. (4) {But} after it [the planet] separates from ⟨⟨its aspect⟩⟩,[μ,3] even if only one degree and particularly if more ⟨degrees⟩, it will terrify with a great fear that will not come to pass. (5) The same applies to a **benevolent planet**;ʸ {but} ⟨regarding⟩ the **planet**ʸ that indicates everything **that will come into effect**

effectum veniet et erit,ᵅ nisi aspiciat signum ascendens **non exibit in lucem**ᵅᶿ spes querentis.

(6) .11m. **Planete benevoli**,ᵞ si **malivolos**ᵞ aspiciant, diminuetur eorum malicia.

(7) .12m. Boni **planete**ᵞ semper bonum significant, et **male**ᵞ **planete**ᵞ malum; si {tamen} **malus**ᵞ fuerit in fortitudine sua magna significabit bonum, sed per laborem veniet et per tristitiam.

(8) .13m. Si fuerint boni ⟨⟨...⟩⟩ᵘ in **domo casus sui aut in domo odii**ᵅ vel in domibus cadentibus et non sit aspectus inter eos et ascendens, non valebunt.

(9) .14m. Item si **mali**ᵞ hoc modo se habuerint, non **nocebunt nec dissipabunt**ᵝ nisi ad modicum.

(10) .15m. Si fuerit **planeta**ᵞ bonus in fortitudine sua et **solus prefuerit**ᵞ nato, tunc multiplicabitur bonum eius.

(11) .16m. Si aspexerit Iupiter **aspicientem**,ᵅ convertet naturam eius ad bonum; sed Venus auferre non potest **malum**ᵞ Saturni nisi cum auxilio Iovis; Iupiter {autem} **malum**ᵞ aufert Saturni, et Venus **malum**ᵞ aufert Martis melius quam Iupiter.

19ra (12) .17m. **Cum**ᵞ fuerint | **planete**ᵞ boni et mali in locis malis vel combusti, ⟨⟨...⟩⟩ᵘ necque bonum faciunt necque malum propter debilitatem.

(13) .18m. Si fuerit **malivolus**ᵞ orientalis a Sole, in fortitudine sua, in signo quo **dignitatem**ᵞ habet, et non aspexerit eum **malivolus**ᵞ alter, melior est **benivolo**ᵞ combusto vel retrogrado.

(14) .19m. Si malivoli fuerit domini rei quesite, et coniungatur eis dominus ascendentis, et Luna aspectu quarto vel opposito, et si quidem evenerit res quesita, finis {tamen} eius malus erit.

(15) .20m. Si fuerit **malivolus**ᵞ in ascendente, et habuerit in eo **dignitatem**ᵞ aliquam, alleviabitur eius malicia, sed si fuerit retrogradus, malum super malum addetur.

and will be,^{α,4} the hope of the querent **will not issue from the light**^{αθ,5} [will not come to pass] unless it does not aspect the ascendant sign.

(6) 11th. The **benevolent planets**,^Y if they aspect **malevolent**^Y ⟨planets⟩, their malice is diminished.

(7) 12th. Good **planets**^Y always indicate goodness, and **bad**^{Y,6} **planets**^Y ⟨indicate⟩ evil; {nevertheless,} if the **bad**^Y ⟨planet⟩ is in its great strength it will indicate goodness, but it will come with toil and sadness.

(8) 13th. If the good ⟨planets⟩ are ⟨⟨opposite their similitude⟩⟩^{μ,7} in their **house of fall or in the house of hate**,^{α,8} or in cadent houses and there is no aspect between them and the ascendant sign, they will not be beneficial.

(9) 14th. Likewise, if the **bad**^Y ⟨planets⟩ are also in the same condition, they will **harm or destroy**^{β,9} only a little.

(10) 15th. If the good **planet**^Y is in its strength and **alone is in charge**^{Y,10} of the native, then its goodness will be multiplied.

(11) 16th. If Jupiter aspects **an aspecting**^{α,11} ⟨planet⟩, it changes its nature for good; but Venus cannot remove Saturn's **evil**^{Y,12} without Jupiter's assistance; {But} Jupiter removes Saturn's **evil**^{Y,13} and Venus removes Mars's **evil**^{Y,14} better than Jupiter does.

(12) 17th. **When**^{Y,15} the good and bad **planets**^Y are in bad places or are burnt, ⟨⟨they indicate an ignoble thing⟩⟩,^{μ,16} and they do not cause goodness or evil because of ⟨their⟩ weakness.

(13) 18th. If a **malevolent**^Y ⟨planet⟩ is oriental of the Sun, in its strength, in a sign where it has **dignity**,^Y and is not aspected by another **malevolent**^Y ⟨planet⟩, it is better than a **benevolent**^Y ⟨planet⟩ that is burnt or retrograde.

(14) 19th. If malevolent ⟨planets⟩ are the lords of the requested event, the lord of the ascendant is conjoined to them, and the Moon is in quartile aspect or opposition ⟨to them⟩, if the requested event takes place, its outcome will be {nevertheless} bad.

(15) 20th. If the **malevolent**^Y ⟨planet⟩ is in the ascendant, and it has some **dignity**^Y there, its malice will be mitigated, but if it is retrograde, evil will be added to evil.

(16) .21m. **Si aspexerit malivolum aspectu quarto,**[α] diminuetur de bono eius.

(17) .22m. Si fuerit **malivolus**[γ] in loco **dignitatis**[γ] sue, in aliquo **angulorum**[γ] aut succedentium, computanda est eius fortitudo quemadmodum fortitudo **planete benevoli.**[γ]

(18) .23m. Si **malivolus**[γ] peregrinus fuerit in loco in quo est, tunc multiplicabitur eius malicia.

(19) .24m. Si fuerit **malivolus**[γ] in aliquo **angulorum,**[γ] **damnificetque**[γ] **planetam**[γ] aspectu quarto vel opposito, tunc perfecta erit eius malicia, et eo plus si fortior fuerit illo **planeta;**[γ] per aspectum aut trinum vel sextilem alleviabitur eius malicia.

(20) .25m. Si **malivolus**[γ] rei quesite dominus fuerit hoc, significat retardationem rei et quod non eveniet nisi cum tristitia et dolore.

(21) .26m. Si dederit **malivolus**[γ] **malivolo**[γ] fortitudinem suam, addetur malum super malum; et si bonus bono,[1] addetur bonum super bonum; et si malus bono, mutabitur res de malo in bonum; si {vero} econverso erit econverso.

4   (1) ⟨⟨...⟩⟩.[μ]

(2) ⟨⟨...⟩⟩.[μ]

(3) .29m.[2] Omni **planete**[γ] que fuerit in principio domus usque ad .15. gradus est[3] fortitudo magna.

(4) .30m.[4] Si fuerit **planeta**[γ] in aliquo **angulorum**[γ] **malivoli,**[γ] et separetur ab aspectu eius per unum gradum, apparebit timor que **non perveniet ad opus nec erit.**[α]

---

[1]addetur malum super malum, et si bonus bono] G om.   [2]29m.] G; WV .27.; L om.   [3]est] WVG; L om.   [4].30m.] WG; V .28.; L om.

(16) 21st. **If it aspects the malevolent in quartile aspect**,[α,17] its goodness will be diminished.

(17) 22nd. If a **malevolent**[γ] ⟨planet⟩ is in a place of its **dignity**,[γ] in one of the **angles**[γ] or succedent ⟨places⟩, its power is reckoned to be like the power of a **benevolent planet**.[γ]

(18) 23rd. If a **malevolent**[γ] ⟨planet⟩ is peregrine in its place, then its malice will be multiplied.

(19) 24th. If a **malevolent**[γ] ⟨planet⟩ is in one of the **angles**,[γ] **and it harms**[γ,18] a **planet**[γ] from quartile aspect or opposition, then its malice will be complete, particularly if it is stronger than this **planet**;[γ] but in trine or sextile its malice will be mitigated.

(20) 25th. If a **malevolent**[γ] ⟨planet⟩ is the lord of the requested event, it indicates the delay of the event, and then only with sadness and worry.

(21) 26th. If a **malevolent**[γ] ⟨planet⟩ gives its power to a **malevolent**[γ] ⟨planet⟩, evil will be added to evil; if a good ⟨planet gives power⟩ to a good ⟨planet⟩, goodness will be added to goodness; and if a bad ⟨planet gives power⟩ to a good ⟨planet⟩, the matter changes from evil to goodness; {but} in the opposite ⟨case⟩ it will be the opposite ⟨result⟩.

4 (1) ⟨⟨27th. Every planet, whether benefic or malefic, always indicates good fortune if it is in its house or in the house of its exaltation⟩⟩.[μ,1]

(2) ⟨⟨28th. Every planet at the cusp of a sign is considered to be weak until it is 5° past it [the cusp of the sign]. Likewise, if the planet is less than 5° from the ⟨cusp of a horoscopic⟩ place, it is considered to be within the power of the place; but if it more ⟨than 5°⟩ it escapes the power of the place⟩⟩.[μ,2]

(3) 29th. There is a great power to any **planet**[γ] is from the beginning of a house until 15°.

(4) 30th. If a **planet**[γ] is at one of the **angles**[γ] of a **malevolent**[γ] ⟨planet⟩ and it [the planet] separates from its aspect ⟨even⟩ by one degree, a fear that will **neither come into effect nor will be**[α,3] will appear.

(5) .31m. Si fuerit **planeta**ʸ **in casu suo**,ʸ hoc significat tristitiam et anxietates atque angustias.

(6) .32m. **Planeta**ʸ retrogradus rebellionem significat et dissipationem eorum que cogitata sunt.

(7) .33m. **Planeta**ʸ existens in statione prima est sicut homo nesciens quid faciet et eius finis ad malum est; in secunda {vero} existens statione est sicut 19rb homo sperat aliquantum | et **non frustrabitur spes eius.**ᵅ

(8) .34m. Si fuerit **planeta**ʸ tardus cursu, tardabit et **res**ʸ sive bona sive mala; et si fuerit Iupiter **aut**ᵅ Saturnus in signis mobilibus, festinabitur res.

(9) .35m. **Planeta existens**ʸ in fine signi, fortitudinem amisit signi precedentis et tota eius fortitudo in signo est in quod ingredietur; si {autem} fuerit **planeta**ʸ in .29. gradu signi, adhuc est eius fortitudo in signo illo in quo est; in tribus enim gradibus fortitudinem habet **planeta**:ʸ in gradu **in quo est planete virtus,**ʸ et in gradu que est ante ipsum, et in eo que post ipsum.

(10) .36m. Si fuerit **planeta**ʸ vadens ad coniunctionem alterius, et antequam coniungantur exeat alter ad signum sequens, primus {vero} sequitur hunc et attingat eum ibidem, et antequam ipsum consequitur non coniungatur ei alius **planeta**,ʸ perficietur utique res post desperationem.

(11) .37m. Si aspexerit **planeta**ʸ **planetam**ʸ alterum qui motus est de loco suo ante consecutionem **planete**ʸ levis, non nocebit aspectus enim coniunctionem non deficiet corporalem.

(12) .38m. Si fuerit **planeta**ʸ in signo simili nature sue, augetur eius fortitudo; si {vero} in contrario nature eius, debilitatur, ut Saturnus in domo frigida et sicca.

(13) .39m. **Planeta**ʸ receptus, si est benivolus augmentatur eius fortitudo, et si nocivus alleviabitur malum eius.

(14) .40m. **Planeta**ʸ non existens **in aliqua dignitatum suarum**,ʸ si fuerit in domo sexta vel duodecima, **hoc est bonum ei.**ʸ

(5) 31st. If the **planet**ʸ is in its **fall**ʸ,⁴ [dejection], this indicates sadness, anxieties, and affliction.

(6) 32nd. A retrograde **planet**ʸ indicates rebellion and destruction of everything that is planned.

(7) 33rd. A **planet**ʸ in its first station is like a man who does not know what to do and his end is unfortunate; {but} in the second station, it is like a man who hopes and **whose hope will not be frustrated**.ᵅ,⁵

(8) 34th. If a **planet**ʸ is slow in ⟨its⟩ course, the event, whether good or evil, will be delayed; but if Jupiter orᵅ,⁶ Saturn is in the changeable signs, the event will come sooner.

(9) 35th. **A planet located**ʸ,⁷ at the end of the sign loses the power of the preceding sign, and all its poer is in the sign it is entering; {but} if the **planet**ʸ is in the 29th degree of the sign, it still has the power of the sign where it is, because the **planet**ʸ has power in three degrees: in the degree **in which the power of the planet is,**ʸ,⁸ in the previous degree, and in the next degree.

(10) 36th. If a **planet**ʸ is moving towards the conjunction of another ⟨planet⟩, and the other ⟨planet⟩ enters the next sign before they reach conjunction, {but} the first planet pursues it and catches up with it there, and before it catches up with it no other **planet**ʸ is conjoined to it, **the** event will be completed in any case after despair.

(11) 37th. If a **planet**ʸ aspects another **planet,**ʸ which moved from its position before the light **planet**ʸ overtakes it, it will not hurt because an aspect does not cancel out the ⟨power of a⟩ bodily conjunction.

(12) 38th. If a **planet**ʸ is in a sign that resembles its nature, its power is increased; {but} if is in ⟨a sign⟩ opposed to its nature, it is weakened; such as Saturn in a sign that is cold and dry.

(13) 39th. A **planet**ʸ that is received ⟨by another planet⟩, if it is a benevolent one its power is increased, and if a harmful one, its evil will be mitigated.

(14) 40th. A **planet**ʸ that is not located **in one of its dignities,**ʸ,⁹ if it is in the sixth or twelfth house, **this is good for it.**ʸ,¹⁰

(15) .41m. **Planeta**ᵞ **sub radiis**ᵞ existens, si fuerit de superioribus, nihil habet fortitudinis; et consimiliter de inferioribus; sed si sunt retrogradi, nihil ita malum ut hoc est.[1]

(16) .42m. Si **planeta**ᵞ significator rei fuerit retrogradus et incipiat in cursu dirigi, tunc significat quod eveniet pars rei; et consimilis si fuerit **sub radiis**ᵞ Solis et exeat de sub illis.

(17) .43m. Si fuerit **planeta**ᵞ in puteo et fuerit **benevolus**,ᵞ diminuetur de bono eius; si {vero} **malivolus**,ᵞ addetur malum super malum.[2]

(18) .44m. Si fuerit **planeta benivolus**ᵞ in octava domus, nec bonum nec malum significat; si {vero} malivolus extiterit, malum significat perfectum.

(19) .45m.[3] ⟨⟨...⟩⟩.ᵏ

(20) .46m. Si fortitudo duodenarii **planete**ᵞ in bono loco fuerit, addetur bonum super bonum.

(21) .47m. **Cum est planeta**ᵞ in **signo fixo**,ᵞ significat omnem rem stabilem et firmam, et si in signo mobili, mutabitur et res; si {vero} in signo | bicorpore, significat quod pars rei firma erit aut iterabitur res duabus vicibus.

19va

(22) .48m. Si **planeta**ᵞ recipiens ⟨⟨...⟩⟩ᵛ in malo ⟨⟨...⟩⟩ᵛ fuerit, malum significat.

(23) .49m. Si dominus ⟨⟨...⟩⟩ᵛ ascendentis in domo fuerit odii sui, non habet voluntatem integram **in re quesita**.ᵅ

(24) .50m. Si coniungatur **planeta**ᵞ cum bonis et cum malis, manifestabitur natura fortioris eorum.

(25) .51m. Si dominus ⟨⟨...⟩⟩ᵛ ascendentis det fortitudinem domino domus rei quesite, **eveniet res ad omnem suam voluntatem**,ᵅ et si econverso, tunc erit absque labore.

---

[1] nihil ita malum ut hoc est] V hoc est peius.   [2] addetur malum super malum] WVG; L in margin.   [3] .45m.] LGV; W om;

(15) 41st. A **planet**ʸ located **under the rays**ʸ ⟨of the Sun⟩, if it is one of the upper ⟨planets⟩, has no power; the same holds true for the lower ⟨planets⟩; but if they are retrograde, nothing can be worse.

(16) 42nd. If the **planet**ʸ indicating the event is retrograde and begins to be direct in ⟨its⟩ course, then it indicates that ⟨only⟩ part of the event will occur; the same holds true if it is **under the rays**ʸ of the Sun and moves out of them [the rays].

(17) 43rd. If the **planet**ʸ is in a pit and it is a **benevolent**ʸ one, its goodness will be diminished; {but} if it is a **malevolent one**,ʸ evil will be added to evil.

(18) 44th. If a **benevolent**ʸ **planet**ʸ is in the eighth house, it indicates neither goodness nor evil; {but} if it is a malevolent one, it indicates complete evil.

(19) 45th. ⟨⟨A planet indicates that the requested ⟨event⟩ will not take place, difficulty and loss, if it begins to be retrograde, and it indicates good fortune, power, and moderation in the event [the object of the query], if it begins to be direct ⟨in its motion⟩⟩.^(μ,11)

(20) 46th. If the power of the *duodenaria* [twelfth] of a **planet**ʸ is in a good place, goodness will be added to goodness.

(21) 47th. **When a planet**^(γ,12) is in a **fixed sign**,^(γ,13) it indicates everything that is stable and enduring; and if in a changeable sign, the event will be changed; {but} if in a bicorporal sign, it indicates that part of the event will be enduring or that it will occur twice.

(22) 48th. If a **planet**ʸ that receives ⟨⟨power⟩⟩^(ν,14) is in a bad ⟨⟨place⟩⟩,^(ν,15) it indicates evil.

(23) 49th. If the lord of the ⟨⟨sign of the⟩⟩^(ν,16) ascendant sign is in the house of its hate, he does not wholly wish **the requested event**.^(α,17)

(24) 50th. If a **planet**ʸ is conjoined by good and bad ⟨planets⟩, the nature of the strongest of them will be manifest.

(25) 51st. If the lord of the ⟨⟨sign of the⟩⟩ᵛ ascendant gives power to the lord of the house of the requested event, **the event will happen according to all his wish**,^(α,18) and if the opposite ⟨case takes place⟩, then it will be without effort.

5 (1) .52m. Si fuerit **planeta**ʸ prohibens inter eos, hoc quidem significat super hominem qui separabit inter illum et rem quesitam.

(2) .53m. Si dominus **ascendentis** a domino rei quesite separetur, auferet desiderium illius.

(3) .54m. Si nullus **planetarum**ʸ Lunam aspexerit, hoc quidem pigritiam significat.

(4) .55m. Si **planete**ʸ plures Lunam aspexerint, erunt auxiliatores ad rem complendam plures.

(5) .56m. Si fuerit **planeta**ʸ transferens a domino ⟨⟨...⟩⟩ᵛ ascendentis ad dominum rei quesite, eveniet res per manum mediatoris.

(6) .57m. Si fuerit dominus ascendentis in domo triplicitatis sue et domini ⟨⟨...⟩⟩ᵛ triplicitatis aspexerint eum, **erunt auxiliatores plures.**ᵅ

6 (1) .58m. Si fuerit **planeta**ʸ **in dispositione**ʸ qua dicimus **reditionis vel reditum luminis,**ᵝ **hoc significat quod**ʸ res erit post desperationem.

(2) .59m. Si fuerit significator **in dispositione**ʸ dandi fortitudinem, hoc significat quod res perficietur ad voluntatem suam.

(3) .60m. Si fuerit signator **in dispositione**ʸ **donandi virtutis,**ʸ hoc significat quod res **manifestabitur seu revelabitur**ᵝ alii.

(4) .61m. Testimonium signatoris **existentis in dispositione**ʸ donandi naturam, significat gaudium magnum in **re quesita.**ʸ

(5) .62m. Testimonium signatoris **existentis in dispositione**ʸ donandi naturam duplicem, significat super gaudium querentis et illius ad quem spectat res quesita.

(6) .63m. Testimonium signatoris **existentis in dispositione**ʸ rectitudinis, significat super finem bonum in omni re quesita.

5 (1) 52nd. If a **planet**ʸ prohibits them, this indicates a person who separates him [the querent] from the requested thing.

(2) 53rd. If the lord of the **ascendant** is separated from the lord of the requested thing, it will take away his [the querent's] desire.

(3) 54th. If no **planet**ʸ aspects the Moon, it indicates laziness.

(4) 55th. If many **planets**ʸ aspect the Moon, there will be many helpers to realize the event.

(5) 56th. If a **planet**ʸ transfers ⟨power⟩ from the lord of the ⟨⟨sign of the⟩⟩ᵛ ascendant to the lord of the requested event, the thing [the object of the query] will come true through an intermediary.

(6) 57th. If the lord of the ascendant is in the house of its triplicity and the lords ⟨⟨of the signs⟩⟩ᵛ of the triplicity aspect it [the lord of the ascendant], **there will be many helpers.**^(α,1)

6 (1) 58th. If the **planet**ʸ is **in the condition**^(γ,1) which we call "**returning or reflecting the light,**"^(β,2) **this indicates that**^(γ,3) the event will take place after despair.

(2) 59th. If the significator is **in the condition**^(γ,4) of "giving power,"⁵ this indicates that the event will come to pass according to his wish.

(3) 60th. If the significator is **in the condition**^(γ,6) of **giving power,**^(γ,7) this indicates that the thing will be **made clear or revealed**^(β,8) to somebody else.

(4) 61st. The testimony of the significator **situated in the condition**^(γ,9) of "giving nature"¹⁰ indicates great joy at **the requested event.**^(γ,11)

(5) 62nd. The testimony of the significator **situated in the condition**^(γ,12) of "giving double nature"¹³ indicates joy for the querent and for the one from whom the requested thing is expected.

(6) 63rd. The testimony of the significator **situated in the condition**ʸ of "straightness"¹⁴ indicates a good outcome for any requested thing.

314   PART ONE

(7) .64m. Testimonium signatoris **existentis in dispositione**[γ] **obliquitatis**,[γ] significat quod rem dimittet.

(8) .65m. Testimonium signatoris **existentis in dispositione**[γ] prohibitionis, significat dissipationem rei postquam sperabatur.

19vb (9) .66m. Testimonium signatoris **existentis in dispositione**[γ] refrenationis | significat evenire res dissipantes rem quesitam.

(10) .67m. Testimonium signatoris **existentis in dispositione**[γ] reditus ad malum significat quod interrogator questione sue penitebit.[1]

(11) .68m. Testimonium signatoris **existentis in dispositione**[γ] accidentis **significat**[α] rem evenire quod abscidet questionem eius.

(12) 69m. Testimonium signatoris **existentis in dispositione**[γ] **frustrationis**[γ] **significat**[α] querentem aliud consilium quesiturum.

(13) 70m. Testimonium signatoris **existentis in dispositione**[γ] abscisionis luminis significat super hominem **questionem eius**[γ] dissipantem.

(14) .71m. Testimonium signatoris **existentis in dispositione**[γ] **compassionis**[γ] significat super hominem que benefacit illi.

(15) .72m. Testimonium signatoris **existentis in dispositione**[γ] remunerationis significat quod adhuc benefaciet aliis.

(16) .73m. Testimonium receptionis signatorum, unius scilicet ab altero, significat super causas preparatas rem que **super cor non ascendit**.[αθ]

(17) .74m. Testimonium signatoris **existentis in dispositione**[γ] benevolentie significat quod querens et quesitus se invicem amabunt, alter videlicet alterum.

(18) .75m. Testimonium signatoris **existentis in dispositione**[γ] similitudinis seu <u>*haiz*</u>[β] significat sententiam super omnem ⟨⟨...⟩⟩[ν] bonum.

---

[1]Testimonium signatoris existentis in dispositione reditus ad malum significat quod interrogator questione sue penitebit.] WVG; L in margin.

(7) 64th. The testimony of the significator **situated in the condition**$^\gamma$ of "**obliquity**"$^{\gamma,15}$ indicates that he [the querent] will give up the thing.

(8) 65th. The testimony of the significator **situated in the condition**$^\gamma$ of "prohibition"[16] indicates the destruction of the thing after it is expected.

(9) 66th. The testimony of the significator **situated in the condition**$^\gamma$ of "restraining"[17] indicates that events that undo the request thing will take place.[18]

(10) 67th. The testimony of the significator **situated in the condition**$^\gamma$ of "returning to evil"[19] indicates that the querent will regret his question.[20]

(11) 68th. The testimony of the significator **situated in the condition**$^\gamma$ of "accident"[21] **indicates**$^{\alpha,22}$ an event that will take place that will terminate his question.

(12) 69th. The testimony of the significator **situated in the condition**$^\gamma$ of "**frustration**"$^{\gamma,23}$ **indicates**$^{\alpha,24}$ that the querent will seek another opinion.

(13) 70th. The testimony of the significator **situated in the condition**$^\gamma$ of "cutting the light" indicates someone destroyng **his question.**$^{\gamma,25}$

(14) 71st. The testimony of the significator **situated in the condition**$^\gamma$ of "**compassion**"$^{\gamma,26}$ indicates someone who benefited him.

(15) 72nd. The testimony of the significator **situated in the condition**$^\gamma$ of "recompense"[27] indicates indicates that he will benefit others.

(16) 73rd. The testimony of "reception"[28] of the significators, one with respect to the other, indicates causes rectifying a thing which **did not rise in the heart** [i.e., no one imagined].$^{\alpha\theta,29}$

(17) 74th. The testimony of the significator **situated in the condition**$^\gamma$ of "benevolence"[30] indicates that the querent and the person asked about, each of them, will love each other.

(18) 75th. The testimony of the significator **situated in the condition**$^\gamma$ of "**similitude or _hayyz_**"$^{\beta,31}$ indicates a decision about every ⟨⟨possible⟩⟩$^{\nu,32}$ goodness.

(19) .76m. Testimonium signatoris **existentis in dispositione**[γ] **obsessionis**[π] significat **malum esse futurum**[γπ] ⟨⟨...⟩⟩.[μ]

(20) .77m. Testimonium signatoris in **fortitudine seu principatu**[β] **existentis**[γ] significat **exaltationem bonam et magnam seu excellentiam**.[α]

7   (1) .78m. De septem **planetis**[α] a locis suis **in zodiaco**[γ] reddentibus testimonia. Si fuerit **planeta**[γ] in domo sua, similitudo est hominis existentis in domo suum.

(2) .79m. **Planeta**[γ] in **exaltatione seu in domo honoris**[β] existens, est sicut homo in excellentia status sui.

(3) .80m. **Planeta**[γ] in **termino**[α] suo est sicut homo in sede sua.

(4) .81m. **Planeta**[γ] in domo triplicitatis sue est sicut homo inter consanguineos suos.

(5) .82m. **Planeta**[γ] in facie sua est sicut homo in ornamentis suis ac **vestimentis mutatoriis**.[γ]

(6) .83m. **Planeta**[γ] in **auge sua**[α] est sicut homo super equum suum.

(7) .84m. **Planeta**[γ] **existens** in similitudine sua est sicut homo in dispositione sibi convenienti.

(8) .85m. **Planeta**[γ] qui est in contrario similitudinis sue est sicut homo in dispositione non convenienti.

(9) .86m. **Planeta**[γ] in domo odii sui est sicut homo erga se ipsum contendens.

(10) .87m. **Planeta**[γ] in loco ubi **dignitatem** nullam habet est sicut homo qui in patria sua non est *scilicet ut peregrinus*.

(11) .88m. **Planeta**[γ] **in domo depressionis eius seu in opposito augis**[β] est 20ra   sicut homo a magnitudine famositatis sue descendens. |

(12) .89m. **Planeta**[γ] **sub radiis**[γ] Solis est sicut homo in domo carceris.

(19) 76th. The testimony of the significator **situated in the condition**^γ of "siege"^π,33 indicates **future evil**.^γπ,34 ⟨⟨and if in the matter ⟨of intermediacy of⟩ goodness, it indicates the highest goodness.⟩⟩^μ,35

(20) 77th. The testimony of the significator **situated**^γ in ⟨the condition of⟩ **"power or dominion"**^β,36 indicates **good and great exaltation or excellency**.^α,37

7 (1) 78th. On the seven **planets**^α rendering testimonies from their places **in the zodiac.**^γ,1 A **planet**^γ in its house resembles a man situated in his house.

(2) 79th. A **planet**^γ situated in its **exaltation or in the house of honor**^β,2 is like a man at the pinnacle of his rank.

(3) 80th. A **planet**^γ in its **term**^α is like a man on his seat.

(4) 81st. A **planet**^γ in the house of its triplicity is like a man with his kin.

(5) 82nd. A **planet**^γ in its face [decan] is like a man with his ornaments and **changes of clothing.**^γ,3

(6) 83rd. A **planet**^γ in **its apogee**^α is like a man on his horse.

(7) 84th. A **planet**^γ situated in its similitude is like a man in a situation that is appropriate to him.

(8) 85th. A **planet**^γ in the opposite of its similitude is like a man in a situation not appropriate to him.

(9) 86th. A **planet**^γ in the house of its hate [detriment] is like a man struggling against himself.

(10) 87th. A **planet**^γ in a place where it has no **dignity**^γ, is like a man who is not in his country, *that is, like a stranger.*

(11) 88th. A **planet**^γ **in the house of its depression or in the opposite of the apogee**^β,4 [perigee] is like a man descending from the greatness of fame.

(12) 89th. A **planet**^γ **under the rays**^γ of the Sun is like a man in prison.

(13) .90m. **Planeta**ʸ combustus est sicut declinans ad mortem.

(14) .91m. **Planeta**ʸ **stationarius**ʸ ad retrogradationem est sicut homo stupefaciens et metuens mala sibi super ventura.

(15) .92m. **Planeta**ʸ retrogradus est sicut homo adversans et rebellis.

(16) .93m. **Planeta**ʸ in statione secunda est sicut homo sperans bonum.

(17) .94m. **Planeta**ʸ tardus in cursu suo est sicut homo non potest ambulare.

(18) .95m. **Planeta**ʸ velox cursu est sicut homo iuvenis cursor.

(19) .96m. **Planeta**ʸ orientalis est sicut homo gaudens ad complendum eius desiderium.

(20) .97m. **Planeta**ʸ occidentalis est sicut homo piger.

(21) .98m. **Planeta**ʸ **precise coniunctus sive compressus**[1] **Soli**ᵝ *quod quidem vocatur* <u>zamin</u> *cum Sole* est sicut **homo seu vir sedens**ᵝ cum rege in una sede.

(22) .99m. **Planeta**ʸ aspiciens est sicut homo voluntatem suam querens.

(23) .100m. **Planeta**ʸ **separans sive recedens a coniunctione** est sicut homo penitetur super rem.

(24) .101m. **Planeta**ʸ **in angulo**ʸ est sicut homo stans in loco suo.

(25) .102m. **Planeta**ʸ in succedente **angulo**ʸ,[2] est sicut homo qui sperat.

(26) .103m. **Planeta**ʸ in domo cadente est sicut homo qui **movetur** de loco suo.

(27) .104m. **Planete**ʸ **coniuncti precise seu compressi**ᵝ *id est* <u>zamin</u> sunt sicut duo vires **associati**.ʸ

---

[1]coniunctus sive compressus] WG; L coniuncta sive compressa; V coniunctus quod vero vocatur zammim. [2]angulo] WVG; L angulum.

(13) 90th. A burnt **planet**ʸ is like someone declining to death.

(14) 91st. A **stationary**ʸ,⁵ **planet**ʸ that is about to be retrograde is like a stunned man who is afraid of misfortunes that may befall him.

(15) 92nd. A retrograde **planet**ʸ is like a hostile and rebellious man.

(16) 93rd. A **planet**ʸ in its second station is like a man who hopes for goodness.

(17) 94th. A **planet**ʸ that is slowing down in its course is like a person who cannot walk.

(18) 95th. A **planet**ʸ that is speeding up in ⟨its⟩ course is like a young man running.

(19) 96th. A **planet**ʸ oriental ⟨of the Sun⟩ is like man who enjoys satisfying his desire.

(20) 97th. A **planet**ʸ occidental ⟨of the Sun⟩ is like a lazy man.

(21) 98th. A **planet**ʸ **precisely joined with or embracing the Sun,**^(β,6) *which is called* zamim *with the Sun,* is like a **person or man**^(β,7) sharing a chair with the king.

(22) 99th. An aspecting **planet**ʸ is like a man who seeks to fulfill his wish.

(23) 100th. A **planet**ʸ that is **separating or retreating from conjunction**^(β,8) is like a man who repents of something.

(24) 101st. A **planet**ʸ in **an angle**ʸ is like a man standing in his place.

(25) 102nd. A **planet**ʸ in a succedent **angle**ʸ is like a man who hopes.

(26) 103rd. A **planet**ʸ in a cadent house is like a man who **is moved**^(α,9) from his place.

(27) 104th. ⟨Two⟩ **planets**ʸ precisely joined to or embracing^β ⟨the Sun⟩, *that is,* zamim,¹⁰ are like two **partners.**^(γ,11)

(28) .105m. **Planete**ᵞ aspicientes se aspectu sextili sunt sicut duo vires **amicitiam** querentes.

(29) .106m. **Planete**ᵞ in aspectu trino existentes sunt sicut duo vires quorum equalis est natura.

(30) .107m. **Planete**ᵞ in aspectu quarto sunt sicut duo vires quorum unusquisque sibi querit dominium.

(31) .108m. **Planete**ᵞ in aspectu opposito sunt sicut duo vires fortiter[1] invicem preliantes.

8 (1) .109m. *De planeta que est in ascendente, quod est prima domus, et aliis etiam domibus.*[2] **Planeta**ᵞ in ascendente est sicut natus exiens de ventre matris aut res que est **in operatione sua.**ᵞ

(2) .110m. **Planeta**ᵞ in domo secunda est sicut homo stans in domo auxiliatorum surorum.

(3) .111m. **Planeta**ᵞ in domo tertia est sicut homo visitans fratres suos.

(4) .112m. **Planeta**ᵞ in domo quarta est sicut homo in domo parentum aut in terra sua.

(5) .113m. **Planeta**ᵞ in domo quinta est sicut homo in mercaturis suis et in gaudio.

(6) .114m. **Planeta**ᵞ in domo sexta est sicut homo debilis fugitivus.

(7) .115m. **Planeta**ᵞ in domo septima est sicut homo paratus ad prelium.

(8) .116m. **Planeta**ᵞ in domo octava est sicut homo super quem irruit timor et suspicio.

20rb (9) .117m. **Planeta**ᵞ in domo nona est sicut | homo peregrinatus a loco sua aut depositus a magnitudine status sui.

---

[1]fortiter] G fortes. [2]de planeta que est in ascendente, quod est prima domus et aliis etiam domibus] L; G de planeta que est in ascendente, quod est prima domus de domibus; V de planeta in .12. domibus; W om.

(28) 105th. ⟨Two⟩ **planets**[Y] aspecting each other in sextile aspect are like two men seeking **friendship**.[Y,12]

(29) 106th. ⟨Two⟩ **planets**[Y] situated in trine aspect are like two men with the same nature.

(30) 107th. ⟨Two⟩ **planets**[Y] in quartile aspect are like two men each of whom seeks rulership over himself.

(31) 108th. ⟨Two⟩ **planets**[Y] in opposition aspect are like two men fiercely fighting one with each other.

8 (1) 109th. *On the planet that is in the ascendant, which is the first house, and in the other houses.* A **planet**[Y] in the ascendant sign is like a newborn emerging from its mother's womb or something that **is being made**.[Y,1]

(2) 110th. A **planet**[Y] in the second house is like a man who is in the house of his assistants.

(3) 111th. A **planet**[Y] in the third house is like a man visiting his brothers.

(4) 112th. A **planet**[Y] in the fourth house is like a man in the house of his parents or on his land.

(5) 113th. A **planet**[Y] in the fifth house is like a man with his merchandise and joy.

(6) 114th. A **planet**[Y] in the sixth house is like a man who is weak and runs away.

(7) 115th. A **planet**[Y] in the seventh house is like a man who is ready for battle.

(8) 116th. A **planet**[Y] in the eighth house is like a man upon whom fear and suspicion fell.

(9) 117th. A **planet**[Y] in the ninth house is like a man who has been exiled from his home or deposed from the greatness of his position.

(10) .118m. Planeta^γ in domo decima est sicut homo in **dignitate sua et potestate**,^β et in sublimitate sua, ac in **magisterio seu artificio**^β suo.

(11) .119m. Planeta^γ in domo undecima est sicut vir in domo amicorum suorum.

(12) .120m. Planeta^γ in domo duodecima est sicut homo in domo carceris.[1]

(13) Explicit pars octava.[2]

§9

1 (1) **Nona pars LIBER HUIUS.**^γ De sortibus **planetarum**^α,[3] ac domorum et sunt .97.^α **partes.**^γ,[4]

(2) Sors Lune *sic accipitur*: locum Solis in signo suo et **gradibus equalibus**^γ subtrahe a loco Lune in signo suo, et quod superfuerit[5] inter eos adde super gradum ascendentis, et ubi exeunt ibi erit sors, que {etiam} vocatur **sors bona sive sors fortune**.^β (3) Et sic quidem facere debes cum nativitas est diurna, si {vero} nocturna subtrahe locum Lune a loco Solis, et quod superexstiterit adde super gradum ascendentem, et ibi erit sors bona secundum mentem ANTIQUORUM. (4) PTOLOMEUS {autem} ab eis dissentit, nam ipse dicit quod semper subtrahendus est locus Solis a loco Lune, sive de die fuerit sive de nocte. (5) Et ipse **perfecto ius**^γ habet, sicut enim se habet proportio signi ascendentis ad Solem sic erit proportio sortis bone ad Lunam, unde et Lune ascendens appellatur. (6) **INDORUM itaque SAPIENTIUM UNUS, sicut**^α MESSEHALLHA IN SUO EXPERIMENTORUM LIBRO, dicit quod sors secretorum de nocte fortior est quam sors bona; et ipse quidem ad opinionem PTOLOMEI **declinavit**^γ sed non **admittit**. (7) **Sors** {autem} **ista bona sive pars fortune**^β super corpus significat, et super vitam, ac **possesiones sive substantiam**,^β et ac perfectum, atque super famam bonam, et principium omni operationi, ac super id quod in animo hominis est.

---

[1]carceris] W > et tenebrarum. [2]Explicit pars octava] L; G > huius libri; WV om. [3]planetarum] WVG; L > et. [4]Nona pars liber huius. De sortibus planetarum ac domorum et sunt .97. partes] L; G < incipit; W om. [5]superfuerit] WVG; L in margin.

(10) 118th. A planet^γ in the tenth house is like a man in **his dignity and governance**,^(β,2) and in his high position, and in his **art or craft**.^(β,3)

(11) 119th. A planet^γ in the eleventh house is like a man in the house of his friends.

(12) 120th. A planet^γ in the twelfth house is like a man in prison.

(13) Here ends the eighth part.

§ 9

1 (1) **Ninth part of this book.**^(γ,1) On the lots of the **planets**^α and the houses, and there are **97**^(α,2) **parts**^(γ,3) [lots].

(2) The lot of the Moon *is taken in this way*: subtract the position of the Sun in its sign, in **equal degrees**,^(γ,4) from the position of the Moon in its sign, and add the remainder to the ascendant degree; and where they come out there is the lot, which is {also} designated **the good lot or the lot of fortune**.^(β,5) (3) You must proceed in this way when the nativity is diurnal, {but} if it is nocturnal subtract the position of the Moon from the position of the Sun, and add what remains to the ascendant degree; and the good lot is there according to the opinion of the Ancients. (4) {But} Ptolemy disagrees with them, because he says that one must always subtract the position of the Sun from the position of the Moon, whether ⟨the nativity is⟩ by day or by night. (5) He is **completely right**,^(γ,6) because the proportion of the ascendant sign to the Sun will be as the proportion of the good lot to the Moon; consequently it [good lot] is called the ascendant of the Moon. (6) **One of scholars of the Indians, such as**^(α,7) Māshā'allāh, says in his Book of Experiments that at night the lot of the hidden things is stronger than the good lot; however he had **deviated**^(γ,8) to Ptolemy's opinion but does not **admit**^(γ,9) ⟨this⟩. (7) {But} **this good lot or part of fortune**^(β,10) indicates the body, life, **possessions or wealth**,^(β,11) success, reputation, the beginning of any action, and a man's thoughts.

2 (1) Sors {autem} Solis *hec est*: subtrahe locum Lune de die a loco Solis et superfluum adde super gradum ascendentis; et tunc inveneris locum sortis; vocatur {autem} **sors secretorum sive celati animi**.ᵝ (2) Si nativitate {vero} nocturna, subtrahe locum Solis a loco Lune et residuum adde super gradum ascendentis, et tunc invenies locum sortis. (3) Et hec est sententia Antiquorum, Ptolomeus {autem} | dicit quod de die et de nocte idem est et hoc est veritas. (4) Sors {autem} ista significat super animam, et super divinum servicium, et super omnem rem occultam et secretam.

3 (1) Sors Saturni: accipe **longitudinem**ᵅ que inter locum Saturni est et gradum sortis bone et adde super gradum ascendentis **si nativitas diurna fuerit**,ᵅ si {vero} nocturna fac econverso. (2) Et hoc quidem significat profunditatem cogitationum, et super **humectationem terre**,ᵞ super **furta**,ᵞ et latrocinia, et paupertatem, et captivitatem, ac mortem.

(3) Sors Iovis: accipe de die **longitudinem**ᵅ inter sortem secretorum et Iovem et adde super ascendens, et ibi est sors, de nocte {vero} econtrario. (4) Et hec sors significat super veritatem, et **misericordiam**,ᵅ et sapientiam, ⟨⟨...⟩⟩,ᵛ et bonam famam, atque **substantiam seu possessiones**.ᵝ

(5) Sors Martis: accipe de die **longitudinem**ᵅ que inter ipsam est et bonam sortem, et adde super gradum ascendentem, de nocte {vero} econtrario, et ibi est sors. (6) Significat {autem} hec sors super fortitudinem, et **strenuitatem**,ᵞ et iracundiam, impetuositatem, ingenuositatem atque caliditatem.

(7) Sors Veneris: accipe de die **longitudinem**ᵅ que fuerit[1] inter sortem bonam et sortem secretorum, de nocte {vero} econtrario, et adde super **gradum ascendentem**,ᵅ et ibi est sors. (8) Significat {autem} hec *sors* super amorem, et gaudium, et delicias, et comessationes, et desideria, et coitus.

(9) Sors Mercurii: accipe de die **longitudinem**ᵅ que fuerit[2] inter sortem secretorum et sortem bonam, de nocte {autem} econtrario, et adde super ascendens. (10) Significat {quoque} hec sors super pauperitatem, et odium, et rancorem, et super **mutuum causa recipiendi qua prestandi in mercationibus**,ᵅᶿ ⟨⟨...⟩⟩ᵘ ac super omnem **philosohiam**ᵞ et sapientiam.

---

[1]fuerit] LW; GV est.   [2]fuerit] LW; GV est.

2 (1) *This is* the lot of the Sun: subtract the position of the Moon by day from the position of the Sun, and add the remainder to the degree of the ascendant; then you will find the position of the lot; it is called, {however,} the "**lot of hidden things or of the hidden soul**".^{β,1} (2) {But} if the nativity is nocturnal, subtract the position of the Sun from the position of the Moon and add the remainder to the degree of the ascendant, and then you will find the place of the lot. (3) This is the opinion of the ANCIENTS; {but} PTOLEMY says that by day or by night it is the same, and this is true. (4) This lot, {however,} indicates the soul, divine service, and everything that is hidden and secret.

3 (1) The lot of Saturn: take the **longitude**^{α} [distance] between the position of Saturn and the degree of the good lot and add it to the ascendant degree **if the nativity is diurnal**,^{α,1} {but} if it is nocturnal do the opposite. (2) This indicates profundity of thoughts, **moistening of the earth**^{γ,2} [agriculture], **stolen things**,^{γ,3} theft, poverty, imprisonment, captivity, and death.

(3) The lot of Jupiter: take by day the **longitude**^{α} [distance] between the lot of hidden things and ⟨the position of⟩ Jupiter and add ⟨it⟩ to the ascendant, and the lot is there; {but} by night is the opposite. (4) This lot indicates truth, **compassion**,^{α,4} wisdom, ⟨⟨honor⟩⟩,^{ν,5} reputation, and **wealth or possessions**.^{β,}

(5) The lot of Mars: take by day the **longitude**^{α} [distance] between it [the position of Mars] and the good lot, and add it to the ascendant, {but} by night the opposite, and the lot is there. (6) This lot, {however,} indicates power, **vigor**,^{γ,6} anger, hastiness, deceit, and cunning.

(7) The lot of Venus: take by day the **longitude**^{α} [distance] between the good lot and the lot of the hidden things, {but} by night the opposite, and add it to the **ascendant degree**,^{α,7} and the lot is there. (8) This *lot*, {however,} indicates love, joy, delights, feasts, desires, and sexual intercourse.

(9) The lot of Mercury: take by day the **longitude**^{α} [distance] between the lot of hidden things and the good lot, {but} by night the opposite, and add it to the ascendant. (10) {Besides,} this lot indicates poverty, hatred, resentment, and **a loan for the sake of receiving and borrowing in business**,^{αθ,8} ⟨⟨mathematics⟩⟩^{μ,9} and any **philosophy**^{γ,10} and science.

4 (1) De sortibus domorum, **et sunt .12.**^(α,1) (2) Domus prima tres habet sortes.

(3) Prima est sors vite, et accipitur ⟨⟨...⟩⟩^μ a distantia que est inter Iovem et Saturnum, de nocte {autem} econtrario, et proiciatur ab ascendente.

(4) Secunda sors sustentationis et **pulchritudinis**,^α accipiatur de die a sorte bone ad sortem secretorum, de nocte {vero} econtrario, et proiciatur ab ascendente. ⟨⟨...⟩⟩.^μ

(5) Tertia rationis et **sensus**,^(π,2) ⟨⟨...⟩⟩^μ

20vb **5** (1) | Domus secunda tres habet sortes.

(2) Una sors substantie, accipiatur de die et de nocte a domino domus secunde usque ad principium domus secunde secundum terre latitudinem **equate**,^α et proiciatur ab ascendente.

(3) Secunda sors **fenerationis vel cambiendi**,^β accipiatur de die et de nocte a Saturno in Mercurium, et proiciatur ab ascendente.

(4) Tertia sors est inventionis, accipiatur de die a Mercurio in Venerem et de nocte econtrario, et proiciatur ab ascendente.

6 (1) Domus tertia tres habet sortes.

(2) Una est sors fratrum, accipiatur de die et de nocte **a Mercurio in Saturnum**,^α et proiciatur ab ascendente.

(3) Secunda sors numeri fratrum, accipiatur die et nocte a Mercurio in Saturnum, et proiciatur ab ascendente.

(4) Tertia sors mortis fratrum, accipiatur de die a Sole ad gradum linee medii celi **equatum**^α secundum terre **longitudinem**,^γ de nocte {vero} econverso, et proiciatur ab ascendente.

---

[1] De sortibus domorum et sunt .12.] L; V De sortibus .12. domorum; WG om.   [2] rationis et sensus] WVG; L om.

LIBER ABRAHE AVENERRE INTRODUCTORIUS AD ASTRONOMIAM   327

4 (1) On the lots of the houses, **and they are .12.**[α,1] (2) The first house has three lots.

(3) The first is the lot of life, and it is taken ⟨⟨by day⟩⟩[μ,2] from the distance between Jupiter and Saturn, {but} by night the opposite, and it is cast out from the ascendant.

(4) The second lot is the lot of support and **beauty**,[α,3] and it is taken by day from the good lot to the lot of hidden things, {but} by night the opposite, and it is cast out from the ascendant; ⟨⟨this lot is like the lot of Venus⟩⟩.[μ,4]

(5) The third ⟨lot is the lot⟩ of reason and **sense**,[π,5] ⟨⟨which is taken by day from Mercury to Mars, and the opposite by night; it is cast out from the ascendant.⟩⟩[μ,6]

5 (1) The second house has three lots.

(2) The first is the lot of wealth, it is taken by day and by night from the lord of the second house to the beginning of the second house, **equated**[α,1] [i.e., corrected] according to the latitude of the country, and it is cast out from the ascendant.

(3) The second is the lot of **usury and barter**,[β,2] it is taken by day and by night from Saturn to Mercury, and is cast out from the ascendant.

(4) The third is the lot of the discovery, it is taken by day from Mercury to Venus, and the opposite by night, and it is cast out from the ascendant.

6 (1) The third house has three lots.

(2) The first is the lot of brothers, it is taken by day and by night **from Mercury to Saturn**,[α,1] and it is cast out from the ascendant.

(3) The second is the lot of the number of brothers, it is taken by day and by night from Mercury to Saturn, and it is cast out from the ascendant.

(4) The third is the lot of the death of brothers, it is taken by day from the Sun to the degree of the line of midheaven, **equated**[α,2] [i.e., corrected] for the **longitude**[γ,3] of the country, {but} the opposite by night, and it is cast out from the ascendant.

7 (1) Domus quarta septem habet sortes.

(2) Prima est sors patris, que accipiatur de die a Sole ad Saturnum, de nocte {vero} econtrario, et proiciatur ab ascendente; et si Saturnus **sub radiis**ᵞ Solis fuerit, accipiatur de die a Sole in Iovem, de nocte {vero} econtrario, et proiciatur ab ascendente.

(3) Secunda sors mortis patris, accipiatur de die a Saturno in Iovem, de nocte {vero} econtrario, et proiciatur ab ascendente.

(4) Tertia sors patris patris *scilicet avi*, accipiatur de die a domino domus Solis in Saturnum, de nocte {vero} econverso, et proiciatur ab ascendente. (5) Si {autem} fuerit Sol in domo sua, aut in aliqua domorum Saturni, accipiatur de die a Sole in Saturnum,[1] de nocte econverso, et proiciatur ab ascendente; nec cures si fuerit **sub radiis**ᵞ Solis.

(6) Quarta sors **nobilitatis parentum**,^(α,) accipiatur de die a Saturno in Martem, de nocte {vero} econverso, et proiciatur ab ascendente.

(7) Quinta sors **terrarum**,^α accipiatur die et nocte a Saturno ad Lunam, et proiciatur ab ascendente.

(8) Sexta sors **humectationis seu adaquationis terre**,^β accipiatur die et nocte a Venere in Saturnum, et proiciatur ab ascendente.

(9) Septima sors **finis seu exitus**,^β accipiatur die et nocte a Saturno ad **domum**^(α,2) coniunctionis luminarium, si fuerit nativitas in prima mensis medietatis; et ad dominum domus oppositionis, si fuerit nativitas in medietate mensis posteriore, et proiciatur ab ascendente. |

8 (1) Domus quinta sortes habet .5.

(2) Prima sors **filiorum**,^ᵞ sumatur de die a Iove in Saturnum, de nocte {vero} econverso, et proiciatur ab ascendente.

---

[1]in Saturnum] WV; LG om.   [2]domum] LGV; W dominum domus.

7 (1) The fourth house has seven lots.

(2) The first is the lot of the father, it is taken by day from the Sun to Saturn, {but} the opposite by night, and it is cast out from the ascendant; but if Saturn is **under the rays**[γ] of the Sun, it is taken by day from the Sun to Jupiter, b the opposite by night, and it is cast out from the ascendant.

(3) The second is the lot of the death of the father, it is taken by day from Saturn to Jupiter, {but} the opposite by night, and it is cast out from the ascendant.

(4) The third is the lot of the father's father, *namely, the grandfather*, it is taken by day from the lord of the house of the Sun to Saturn, {but} the opposite by night, and it is cast out from the ascendant. (5) {But} if the Sun is in its house [Aries], or in one of Saturn's houses [Aquarius or Capricorn], it [the lot of the grandfather] is taken by day from the Sun to Saturn, and the opposite by night, and it is cast out from the ascendant; do not be concerned if it [Saturn] is **under the rays**[γ] of the Sun.

(6) The fourth is the lot of the **parents' noble origin**,[α,1] it is taken by day from Saturn to Mars, {but} the opposite by night, and it is cast out from the ascendant.

(7) The fifth is the lot of **landed properties**,[α,2] it is taken by day and by night from Saturn to the Moon, and it is cast out from the ascendant.

(8) The sixth is the lot of **moistening or watering of the earth**[β,3] [agriculture], it is taken by day and by night from Venus to Saturn, and it is cast out from the ascendant.

(9) The seventh is the lot of the **end or exit**,[β,4] it is taken by day and by night from Saturn to the **house**[α,5] of the luminaries' conjunction, if the native was born in the first half of the month; and to the lord of the house of the ⟨luminaries'⟩ opposition, if the nativity is in the second half of the month, and it is cast out from the ascendant.

8 (1) The fifth house has five lots.

(2) The first is the lot of **children**,[γ,1] it is taken by day from Jupiter to Saturn, {but} the opposite by night, and it is cast out from the ascendant.

(3) Secunda sors temporis quando scilicet nascetur ei filius, et utrum erit masculus vel femella; accipiatur die et nocte a Marte in Saturnum, et proiciatur ab ascendente.

(4) Tertia sors de filiis masculis,[1] scilicet accipiatur die et nocte a Luna ad Iovem, et proiciatur ab ascendente.

(5) Quarta sors filiarum, accipiatur die et nocte a Lune in Venerem, et proiciatur ab ascendente.

(6) Quinta sors interrogantis an sit masculus ⟨⟨...⟩⟩,^{μ} accipiatur de die a domino domus Solis ad Lunam, et proiciatur ab ascendente.

9 (1) Domus sexta .3.sortes habet.

(2) Prima sors infirmitatum et **impedimentorum seu *axemena*,**^{β} accipiatur de die a Saturno in Martem, de nocte {vero} econverso, et proiciatur ab ascendente.

(3) Secunda sors servorum, accipiatur die et nocte a Mercurio in Lunam, et proiciatur ab ascendente.

(4) Tertia sors carceris et captivitatis, accipiatur de die a domino domus Solis ad Solem, de nocte {vero} a domino dominus Lune ad Lunam, et proiciatur ab ascendente.

10 (1) Domus septima .13. habet sortes.

(2) Prima sors **concubitus** masculinorum cum femellis, *id est, carnalis copulatio maris et femelle*,[2] accipiatur die et nocte a Venere ad gradum occidentem, et proiciatur ab ascendente.

(3) Secunda sors coitus in nativitatibus masculinorum secundum HERMETEM,^{γ} accipiatur die et nocte a Saturno in Venerem, et proiciatur ab ascendente; secundum sententiam {vero} VELII, accipiatur de die a Sole in Lunam, et proiciatur ab ascendente.

---

[1]masculis] W; LWV om.   [2]id est, carnalis copulatio maris et femelle] L; WGV om.

(3) The second is the lot of the time when a child will be born to him and whether it will be a boy or a girl; it is taken by day and by night from Mars to Saturn, and it is cast out from the ascendant.

(4) The third is the lot of male children, it is taken by day and by night from the Moon to Jupiter, and it is cast out from the ascendant.

(5) The fourth is the lot of daughters, it is taken by day and by night from the Moon to Venus, and it is cast out from the ascendant.

(6) The fifth is the lot of asking whether ⟨the fetus⟩ is male ⟨⟨or female⟩⟩,[μ,2] it is taken by day and by night from the lord of the house of the Sun to the Moon, and it is cast out from the ascendant.

9 (1) The sixth house has three lots.

(2) The first is the lot of diseases, and of **defects or *axemena*,**[β,1] it is taken by day from Saturn to Mars, {but} the opposite by night, and it is cast out from the ascendant.

(3) The second is the lot of slaves, it is taken by day and by night from Mercury to the Moon, and it is cast out from the ascendant.

(4) The third is the lot of imprisonment and captivity, it is taken by day from the lord of the house of the Sun to the Sun, {but} by night from the lord of the house of the Moon to the Moon, and it is cast out from the ascendant.

10 (1) The seventh house has thirteen lots.

(2) The first is the lot of lying together of males with females, *that is, of carnal sexual union of a male and a female*, it is taken by day and by night from Venus to the descendant degree, and it is cast out from the ascendant.

(3) The second is the lot of sexual intercourse in the nativities of males, according the HERMES;[γ,1] it is taken by day and by night from Saturn to Venus; it is cast out from the ascendant; {but} in the opinion of VELIS[2] it is taken by day and by night from the Sun to Venus, and it is cast out from the ascendant.

(4) Tertia sors ⟨⟨...⟩⟩ᵛ

(5) Quarta sors de ingenio concubitus, accipiatur die et nocte a Sole ad Lunam, et proiciatur a Venere, ⟨⟨...⟩⟩.ᵘ

(6) Quinta pars est **simplicitas seu pietatis femelle**,ᵝ accipiatur die et nocte a Luna in Venerem, et proiciatur ab ascendente.

(7) Sexta sors luxuriositatis femellarum, accipiatur die et nocte a Venere in Saturnum, et proiciatur ab ascendente.

(8) Septima sors **ingenii seu fallacie virorum**,ᵝ accipiatur die et nocte a Sole in Venerem, et proiciatur ab ascendente.

(9) Octava sors fallacie mulierum, accipiatur | die et nocte a Luna in Martem, et proiciatur ab ascendente.

(10) Nona sors luxuriandi cum masculis, accipiatur die et nocte a Sole in Venerem, et proiciatur ab ascendente.

(11) Decima sors concubitus, accipiatur die et nocte a Luna ad Martem, et proiciatur ab ascendente.[1]

(12) Undecima sors **amoris**,ᵅ accipiatur die et nocte a Luna in Martem, et proiciatur ab ascendente.

(13) Duodecima sors contentionum, accipiatur die et nocte a Marte in Iovem, et proiciatur ab ascendente.

(14) Tria decima sors generorum, accipiatur die et nocte a Saturno in Venerem, et proiciatur ab ascendente.

11 (1) Domus octava .5. sortes habet.

---

[1]Decima sors concubitus accipiatur die et nocte a Luna ad Martem et proiciatur ab ascendente] WVG; L om.

LIBER ABRAHE AVENERRE INTRODUCTORIUS AD ASTRONOMIAM 333

(4) The third is the lot ⟨⟨of the time of sexual intercourse, it is taken by day and by night from the Sun to the Moon, and it is cast out from the ascendant⟩⟩.ᵛ,³

(5) The fourth is the lot of the cunning of sexual intercourse, it is taken by day and by night from the Sun to the Moon, and it is cast out from Venus, ⟨⟨and there is the lot⟩⟩.ᵘ,⁴

(6) The fifth is the lot of **the woman's modesty or piety**,ᵝ,⁵ it is taken by day and by night from the Moon to Venus, and it is cast out from the ascendant.

(7) The sixth is the lot of women's licentiousness, it is taken by day and by night from Venus to Saturn, and it is cast out from the ascendant.

(8) The seventh is the lot of **men's cunning or deceit**,ᵝ,⁶ it is taken by day and by night from the Sun to Venus, and it is cast out from the ascendant.

(9) The eighth is the lot of women's deceit, it is taken by day and by night from the Moon to Mars, and it is cast out from the ascendant.

(10) The ninth is the lot of licentiousness with males, it is taken by day and by night from the Sun to Venus, and it is cast out from the ascendant.

(11) The tenth is the lot of intercourse, it is taken by day from the Moon to Mars, and it is cast out from the ascendant.

(12) The eleventh is the lot of **love**,ᵅ,⁷ it is taken by day and by night from the Moon to Mars, and it is cast out from the ascendant.

(13) The twelfth is the lot of quarrels, it is taken by day and by night from Mars to Jupiter, and it is cast out from the ascendant.

(14) The thirteenth is the lot of sons-in-law, it is taken by day and by night from Saturn to Venus, and it is cast out from the ascendant.

11 (1) The eighth house has five lots.

(2) Prima sors mortis, accipiatur die et nocte a gradu Lune ad principium domus octave, **equate**^{α} secundum terre latitudinem, et proiciatur a loco Saturni, et ibi sors.

(3) Secunda sors stelle interficientis, accipiatur de die a domino gradus ascendentis ad Lunam, de nocte {vero} econverso, et proiciatur ab ascendente.

(4) Tertia sors anni periculosi, accipiatur de die et nocte a Saturno ad dominum[1] domus[2] coniunctionis luminarum si fuerit nativitas in medietate mensis prima; vel ad dominum domus oppositionis si fuerit nativitas in medietate mensis postrema; et proiciatur ab ascendente.

(5) Quarta sors **egritudinis**,^{α,3} accipiatur de die a Saturno in Martem, de nocte[4] {vero} econtrario, et proiciatur ab ascendente.

(6) Quinta sors angustie, accipiatur de die a Saturno in Mercurium, de nocte {vero} econtrario, et proiciatur ab ascendente.[5]

12 (1) Domus nona .7. sortes habet.

(2) Prima sors itinerandi, accipiatur die et nocte a domino domus none ad principium domus none ad terre latitudine **equate**,^{α} et proiciatur ab ascendente.

(3) Secunda sors **eundi per aquam sive navigandi**,^{β} accipiatur de die a Saturno ad .15. gradum Cancri, de nocte {vero} econtrario, et proiciatur ab ascendente; {quod} si fuerit Saturnus in gradu iam dicta, erit sors gradus ascendentis.

(4) Tertia sors **simplicitatis seu pietatis et religionis**,^{β} accipiatur de die a Luna in Mercurium, de nocte {vero} econtrario, et proiciatur ab ascendente.

---

[1] anni periculosi, accipiatur de die et nocte a Saturno ad dominum] WVG; L om. [2] domus] W; LGV om. [3] egritudinis] W > secundum Albumasar. [4] de nocte] WVG; L om. [5] Quinta sors angustie, accipiatur de die a Saturno in Mercurium, de nocte vero econtrario, et proiciatur ab ascendente] WVG; L om.

(2) The first is the lot of death, it is taken by day and by night from the degree of the Moon to the beginning of the eighth house, **equated**[α,1] [i.e., corrected] for the latitude of the country, and it is cast out from the position of Saturn, and the lot is there.

(3) The second is the lot of the lethal star, it is taken by day from the lord of the degree of the ascendant to the Moon, {but} the opposite by night, and it is cast out from the ascendant.

(4) The third is the lot of the dangerous year, it is taken by day and by night from Saturn to the lord of the house of the luminaries' conjunction, if the nativity is in the first half of the month; or to the lord of the house of the opposition, if the nativity is in the second half of the month; and it is cast out from the ascendant.

(5) The fourth is the lot of **disease**,[α,2] it is taken by day from Saturn to Mars, {but} the opposite by night, and it is cast out from Mercury, and the lot is there.

(6) The fifth is the lot of anxiety, it is taken by day from Saturn to Mercury, {but} the opposite by night, and it is cast out from the ascendant.

12   (1) The ninth house has seven lots.

(2) The first is the lot of traveling ⟨by land⟩, it is taken by day and by night from the lord of the ninth house to the beginning of the ninth house, **equated**[α,1] [i.e., corrected] for the latitude of the country, and it is cast out from the ascendant.

(3) The second is the lot of **going by water or traveling by ship**,[β,2] it is taken by day from Saturn to Cancer 15°, {but} the opposite by night; and it is cast out from the ascendant; {but} if Saturn is at this degree, the lot is in the ascendant.

(4) The third is the lot of **modesty or piety and religion**,[β,3] it is taken by day from the Moon to Mercury, {but} the opposite by night, and it is cast out from the ascendant.

(5) Quarta sors **intellectus**,ᵅ accipiatur de die a Saturno in Iovem, nocte {vero} econtrario, et proiciatur a loco Mercurii, ibique sors.

(6) Quinta sors **sapientie et scientie**,ᵝ accipiatur de die a Saturno in Iovem, nocte {vero} econtrario, et proiciatur ab ascendente.

21va (7) Sexta sors annuntiationum, accipatur de die a Sole | ad Iovem, nocte {vero} econtrario, et proiciatur ab ascendente.

(8) Septima sors si **rumor**ᵞ verus est an mendax, accipiatur die et nocte a Mercurio in Lunam, et proiciatur ab ascendente.

13 (1) Domus decima .11. habet sortes.

(2) Prima sors **regni seu regnandi**,ᵝ accipiatur de die a Marte ad Lunam, nocte {vero} econtrario, et proiciatur ad ascendente.

(3) Secunda sors **vincendi seu victorie**,ᵝ accipiatur de die a Sole in Saturnum, nocte {vero} econtrario, et proiciatur ab ascendente; ⟨⟨...⟩⟩.ᵘ

(4) Tertia sors consilii, accipiatur de die a Mercurio in Martem, et proiciatur ab ascendente.

(5) Quarta sors **benevolientie seu liberalitatis**,ᵝ accipiatur die et nocte a Mercurio in Solem, et proiciatur ab ascendente.

(6) Quinta sors **dignitatis**,ᵅ accipiatur de die a Saturno ad bonam sortem, {vero} nocte econtrario, et proiciatur ab ascendente.

(7) Sexta sors operationis, accipiatur die et nocte a Saturno in Lunam, et proiciatur ab ascendente.

(5) The fourth is the lot of **understanding**,[α,4] it is taken by day from Saturn to Jupiter, {but} the opposite by night, and it is cast out from the position of Mercury, and the lot is there.

(6) The fifth is the lot of **wisdom and knowledge**,[β,5] it is taken by day from Saturn to Jupiter, {but} the opposite by night, and it is cast out from the ascendant.

(7) The sixth is the lot of proclamations, it is taken by day from the Sun to Jupiter, {but} the opposite by night, and it is cast out from the ascendant.

(8) The seventh is the lot of whether a **rumor**[γ,6] is true or false, it is taken by day and by night from Mercury to the Moon, and it is cast out from the ascendant.

13 (1) The tenth house has eleven lots.

(2) The first is the lot of **kingship or reigning**,[β,1] it is taken by day from Mars to the Moon, {but} the opposite by night, and it is cast out from the ascendant.

(3) The second is the lot of **conquering or victory**,[β,2] it is taken by day from the Sun to Saturn, {but} the opposite by night, and it is cast out from the ascendant; ⟨⟨but if Saturn is under the rays of the Sun it is taken by day from the Sun to Jupiter, the opposite by night, and it is cast out from the ascendant⟩⟩.[μ,3]

(4) The third is the lot of counsel, it is taken by day from Mercury to Mars, the opposite by night, and is cast out from the ascendant.

(5) The fourth is the lot of **benevolence or generosity**,[β] it is taken by day and by night from Mercury to the Sun, and it is cast out from the ascendant.

(6) The fifth is the lot of **dignity**,[α,4] it is taken by day from Saturn to the good lot, {but} the opposite by night, and it is cast out from the ascendant.

(7) The sixth is the lot of performance of tasks, it is taken by day and by night from Saturn to the Moon, and it is cast out from the ascendant.

(8) Septima sors operis manualis, accipiatur de die a Mercurio in Venerem, nocte {vero} econtrario, et proiciatur ab ascendente.

(9) Octava sors operis quod debet fieri, accipiatur de die a Sole ad Iovem, nocte {vero} econtrario, et proiciatur ab ascendente.

(10) Nona sors mercationum, accipiatur de die a **sorte secretorum sive celati**[β] ad sortem bonam, nocte {vero} econtrario, proiciatur ab ascendente.

(11) Decima sors **exaltationis magne**,[γ] accipiatur de die a Solem in gradu **exaltationis**[γ] sue, nocte {vero} a Luna in gradu **exaltationis**[γ] sue, et si Sol de die in gradu honoris sui fuerit aut Luna de nocte in suo, erit sors in gradu ascendente.

(12) Undecima sors matris, accipiatur de die a Venere in Lunam, nocte {vero} econtrario, et proiciatur ab ascendente.

14 (1) Domus undecima .10. habet sortes.

(2) Prima est sors **anime**,[γ] accipiatur de die a bona sorte ad sortem secretorum, nocte {vero} econtrario, et proiciatur ab ascendente.

(3) Secunda sors **considerationis et prudentie hominis**,[β] accipiatur de die a bona sorte in Solem, nocte {vero} econtrario, et proiciatur ab ascendente.

(4) Tertia sors profectus, accipiatur de die a sorte bona ad Iovem, nocte {vero} econtrario, et proiciatur ab ascendente.

(5) Quarta sors spei, accipiatur de die a Saturno in Venerem, nocte {vero} econtrario, et proiciatur ab ascendente.

(6) Quinta sors boni multiplicandi, accipiatur die et nocte a Luna in Mercurium, et proiciatur | ab ascendente.

21vb

(8) The seventh is the lot of performance of manual tasks, it is taken by day from Mercury to Venus, {but} the opposite by night, and it is cast out from the ascendant.

(9) The eight is the lot of performance of a task that must done, it is taken by day from the Sun to Jupiter, {but} the opposite by night, and it is cast out from the ascendant.

(10) The ninth is the lot of merchandise, it is taken by day from the **lot of hidden things or of the hidden ⟨soul⟩**[β] to the good lot, {but} the opposite by night, and it is cast out from the ascendant.

(11) The tenth is the lot of the **great exaltation**,[γ,5] it is taken by day from the Sun to the degree of its **exaltation**[γ,6] {but} by night from the Moon to the degree of its **exaltation**[γ,7] if the Sun by day is in the degree of its honor or the Moon by night is in its ⟨degree of its exaltation⟩, the lot will be in the degree of the ascendant.

(12) The eleventh is the lot of the mother, it is taken by day from Venus to the Moon, {but} the opposite by night, and it is cast out from the ascendant.

14   (1) The eleventh house has ten lots.

(2) The first is the lot of the **soul**,[γ,1] it is taken by day from the good lot to the lot of hidden things, {but} the opposite by night, and it is cast out from the ascendant.

(3) The second is the lot of **a man's contemplation and prudence**,[β,2] it is taken by day from the good lot to the Sun, {but} the opposite by night, and it is cast out from the ascendant.

(4) The third is the lot of success, it is taken by day from the good lot to Jupiter, {but} the opposite by night, and it is cast out from the ascendant.

(5) The fourth is the lot of hope, it is taken by day from Saturn to Venus, {but} the opposite by night, and it is cast out from the ascendant.

(6) The fifth is the lot of increase of goodness, it is taken by day and by night from the Moon to Mercury, and it is cast out from the ascendant.

(7) Sexta sors **liberalitatis anime**,ᵞ accipiatur de die a Mercurio in Iovem, nocte {vero} econtrario, et proiciatur ab ascendente.

(8) Septima sors **laudis**,ᵞ accipiatur de die a Iove in Venerem, nocte {vero} econtrario, et proiciatur ab ascendente.

(9) Octava sors desiderii, accipiatur de die a bona sorte in sortem secretorum, nocte econtrario, et proiciatur ab ascendente.

(10) Nona sors **nobilitatis**,ᵞ accipiatur die et nocte a sorte secretorum ad Mercurium, et proiciatur ab ascendente.

(11) Decima sors **sodalium seu consortium**,ᵝ accipiatur die et nocte a Mercurio in Lunam, et proiciatur ab ascendente.

15 (1) Domus duodecima duas habet sortes.

(2) Una est sors inimicorum, accipiatur die et nocte a domino domus duodecime ad principium domus duodecime, ad terre latitudinem **equate**,ᵅ et proiciatur ab ascendente.

(3) Secunda sors accipiatur secundum sententiam HERMETISᵞ de die a Saturno in Marte, nocte {vero} econtrario, et proiciatur ab ascendente.

(4) In universali {igitur} sortes domorum iam dicte sunt .71.

16 (1) Sortes {autem} per se existentes sunt novem.

(2) Prima sors numeri annorum vite; considera itaque si fuerit nativitas in medietate mensis priori, et accipe **longitudinem**ᵅ gradus coniunctionis luminarium ad Lunam in hora nativitatis, et proice ad ascendente; si {vero} nativitas fuerit in medietate mensis posteriori, accipiatur a gradu oppositionis luminarium in Lunam, et proice ab ascendente.

(7) The sixth is the lot of the **generosity of the soul**,^(γ,3) it is taken by day from Mercury to Jupiter, {but} the opposite by night, and it is cast out from the ascendant.

(8) The seventh is the lot of **praise**,^(γ,4) it is taken by day from Jupiter to Venus, {but} the opposite by night, and it is cast out from the ascendant.

(9) The eighth is the lot of desire, it is taken by day from the good lot to the lot of hidden ⟨things,⟩ the opposite by night, and it is cast out from the ascendant.

(10) The ninth is the lot of **renown**,^(γ,5) it is taken by day and by night from the lot of the hidden ⟨things⟩ to Mercury, and it is cast out from the ascendant.

(11) The tenth is the lot of **companions or partners**,^(β,6) it is taken by day and by night from Mercury to the Moon, and it is cast out from the ascendant.

15 (1) The twelfth house has two lots.

(2) The first is the lot of enemies, it is taken by day and by night from the lord of the twelfth house to the beginning of the twelfth house, **equated**^(α,1) [i.e., corrected] for the latitude of the country, and it is cast out from the ascendant.

(3) The second ⟨is the lot of enemies⟩ according to **HERMES**;^γ it is taken by day from Saturn to Mars, {but} the opposite by night, and it is cast out from the ascendant.

(4) {Therefore} all the lots of the houses are seventy-one.

16 (1) {But} there are nine lots that exist by themselves.

(2) The first is the lot of the number of years of life; Observe: if the nativity is in the first half of the month, take the **longitude**^α [distance] of the degree of the conjunction of the luminaries to the Moon at the time of the nativity, and cast it out from the ascendant; {but} if the nativity is in the second half of the month, ⟨the longitude⟩ from the degree of the opposition of the luminaries to the Moon should be taken, and cast it out from the ascendant.

(3) Secunda sors **inpedimentum seu *azemena*,**[β] *id est defectus in corpore*, accipiatur de die a bona sorte in Martem, nocte {vero} econtrario, et proiciatur ab ascendente.

(4) Tertia sors dilationis,[1] accipiatur die et nocte a gradu Martis ad principium domus tertie, ad terre latitudinem **equate**,[α] et proiciatur ab ascendente; **HERMES**[γ] {vero} convenientius ait esse quod accipiatur a sorte amoris in Mercurium, et proiciatur a loco **Solis**,[α] et id est sors.

(5) Quarta sors calliditatis, accipiatur de die a Mercurio in sortem secretorum, nocte {vero} econtrario, et proiciatur ab ascendente.

(6) Quinta sors loci quesiti, accipiatur die et nocte a Saturno in Martem, et proiciatur a loco Mercurii.

(7) Sexta sors **retributionis vel insidiationis**,[β] accipiatur de die a Marte in Solem, nocte {vero} econtrario, et proiciatur ab ascendente.

(8) Septima sors veritatis, accipiatur de die a Mercurio in Martem, nocte {vero} econtrario, et proiciatur ab ascendente.

22ra (9) Octava sors **fortitudinis et audacie**,[β] accipiatur | de die a Saturno in Lunam, nocte {vero} econtrario, et proiciatur ab ascendente.

(10) Nona sors **feritatis vel occisionis**,[β] accipiatur de die a domino ascendentis in Lunam, nocte {vero} econtrario, et proiciatur ab ascendente.

17 (1) Hiis {autem} sortibus dicendis opus est in revolutione anni coniunctionis magne, ad sciendum **esse regum et res eorum**,[β] et quamdiu regnabunt.

(2) Harum {igitur} una vocata est sors regnandi, qua opus quidem est in annis mundi; accipiatur de die a Marte in Lunam, et proiciatur ab ascendente in revolutione anni **coniunctionis**[α] que significat **super transmuta-**

---

[1]dilationis] LVG dilectionis; W > secundum hermetis.

(3) The second is the lot of **defects or _axemena_**,[β,1] *that is, a defect in the body*, it is taken by day from the good lot to Mars, {but} the opposite by night, and it is cast out from the ascendant.

(4) The third is the lot of delay, it is taken by day and by night from the degree of Mars to the beginning of the third house, **equated**[α,2] [i.e., corrected] for the latitude of the country, and it is cast out from the ascendant; {but} **Hermes**[γ] said that it is more convenient to take it from the lot of love to Mercury, and cast out from the position of **the Sun**,[α,3] and the lot is there.

(5) The fourth is the lot of craftiness, it is taken by day from Mercury to the lot of hidden ⟨things⟩, {but} the opposite by night, and it is cast out from the ascendant.

(6) The fifth is the lot of the place inquired about, it is taken by day and by night from Saturn to Mars, and it is cast out from the position of Mercury.

(7) The sixth is the lot of **retribution or ambush**,[β,4] it is taken by day from Mars to the Sun, {but} the opposite by night, and it is cast out from the ascendant.

(8) The seventh is the lot of truth, it is taken by day from Mercury to Mars, {but} the opposite by night, and it is cast out from the ascendant.

(9) The eighth is the lot of **power and courage**,[β,5] it is taken by day from Saturn to the Moon, {but} the opposite by night, and it is cast out from the ascendant.

(10) The ninth is the lot of **brutality and killing**,[β,6] it is taken by day from the lord of the ascendant to the Moon, {but} the opposite by night, and it is cast out from the ascendant.

17   (1) {But} these are the lots needed at the revolution of the year of the great conjunction, to know **the condition of the kings and their affairs**,[β,1] and how long will they reign.

(2) One of them, {then,} is designated the lot of kingship, which is needed in the ⟨revolution of the⟩ world-years; it is taken by day from Mars to the Moon, and is cast out from the ascendant at the revolution of the year of the **conjunction**[α,2] which indicates **the relocation or transfer to another place**

tionem seu translationem gentis.^{β} (3) Quidam {autem} hanc sortem extrahunt secundum aliam viam, videlicet ut accipiatur a gradu ascendentis in revolutione anni coniunctionis usque in gradum coniunctionis, et proiciatur a gradu ascendentis in revolutione anni. (4) Adhuc et alii quidem secundum aliam viam ita quod accipiatur a gradu linee medi celi respectu Solis ad lineam medii celi respectu revolutionis anni et proiciatur a **gradu**^{γ} Iovis.

(5) Sors numeri dierum **regi vel regum**,^{β} accipiatur in anno sublimationis regis a[1] loco quidem Solis in .15. gradu Leonis, et proiciatur a loco Lune. (6) Item accipiatur a loco Lune in .15. gradu Cancri, et proiciatur a loco Solis. (7) Et scito quod hee ⟨⟨...⟩⟩^{μ} sortes semper exibunt in domibus unius *et eiusdem* **planete**,^{γ} nisi cum una in domo exeunt alterius luminarium, tunc enim altera in alterius exibit domo.

(8) Item sors alia in anno sublimationis regi, accipiatur de die a Iove in Saturnum, nocte {vero} econtrario, et proiciatur ab ascendente in revolutione anni. (9) Si {autem} fuerit Iupiter in signo duum corporum, et sit revolutio diurna, sitque Iupiter in domo cadente, accipiatur a Saturno in Iovem, cum additione super **longitudinem**^{α} .30. graduum, et proiciatur ab ascendente. (10) Et si Saturnus in opposito Iovis, et sint ambo in domibus cadentibus, accipiatur medietas **longitudinis**^{α} que sint inter eos, et proiciatur ab ascendente. (11) Si {vero} fuerit Iupiter in domo sui **honoris seu exaltationis**^{β} sua, et sit revolutio nocturna, accipiatur ab ipso in Saturnum, et proiciatur ab ascendente.

18 (1) Sortes magne due sunt.

(2) Una earum est quod tu consideras in anno **sublimationis seu elevationis regis**^{β} | quo pervenit illo anno locus coniunctionis triplicitatis qua fuerit ante sublimationem regis, et des singulis triginta gradibus annum unum, singulis {quoque} duobus gradibus et dimidio mensem unam; et cum scivis gradum ad quem pervenit numerus, ab illo quidem equabis sortem prima.

(3) Scito {igitur} revolutionem anni sublimationis regis, et considera Saturnum aut Iovem quis eorum, *inquam*, sit orientalis a Sole, et accipe

---

[1] a] WVG; L in.

of the nation.^{β,3} (3) {But} some calculate this lot in another way, namely, that it is taken from the degree of the ascendant at the revolution of the year of the conjunction to the degree of the conjunction, and it is cast out from the ascendant degree at the revolution of the year. (4) And others ⟨calculate this lot⟩ in another way, so that it is taken from the degree of the line of midheaven with respect to the Sun to the line of midheaven with respect to the revolution of the year, and it is cast out from the **degree**^{γ,4} of Jupiter.

(5) The lot of the number of days of **the king or of the kings**,^{β,5} in the year of the king's accession it is taken from the Sun to Leo 15°, and it is cast out from the position of the Moon. (6) Likewise, it can be taken from the position of the Moon to Cancer 15°, and cast out from the position of the Sun. (7) Know that these ⟨⟨two⟩⟩^{μ,6} lots will always come out in the houses of one *and the same* **planet**,^{γ} but when one ⟨lot⟩ comes out in the house of one of the luminaries, then the other ⟨lot⟩ comes out in the house of the other ⟨luminary⟩.

(8) Likewise, another lot in the year of the king's accession is taken by day from Jupiter to Saturn, {but} the opposite by night, and it is cast out from the ascendant at the revolution of the year. (9) If Jupiter, {however,} is in a sign of two bodies [bicorporal], the revolution is diurnal, and if Jupiter is in a cadent house, it is taken from Saturn to Jupiter, with the addition of 30° to this **longitude**^{α} [distance], and it is cast out from the ascendant. (10) If Saturn is in opposition to Jupiter, and both are in cadent houses, half the **longitude**^{α} [distance] between them is taken and is cast out from the ascendant. (11) {But} if Jupiter is in the house of its **honor or exaltation**,^{β,7} and the revolution is nocturnal, it is taken from it [Jupiter] to Saturn and cast out from the ascendant.

18 (1) There are two great lots.

(2) One of them is that you observe, in the year of **the king's accession or elevation**,^{β,1} the place reached by the position of the conjunction of the triplicity that took place before the king's accession, and assign one year to each ⟨interval of⟩ 30°, and {also} one month to each ⟨interval of⟩ 2½°, and when you know the degree reached by this reckoning, you will calculate the first lot from there, ⟨as follows⟩.

(3) {Therefore} determine the revolution of the year of the king's accession and observe Saturn and Jupiter, ⟨and find out⟩ which of them, *I say*, is

346　PART ONE

longitudinem seu distantiam^β que fuerit inter ipsum in principio revolutionis anni et inter gradum predictum; a quo videlicet sortem equare debebas, et **superfluum sive id quod inventum fuerit**^β proice ab ascendente in principio revolucionis anni, et ibi erit sors.

(4) Sors {vero} secunda est quod tu consideres Iovem aut Saturnum, quis eorum occidentalis fuerit a Sole in hora revolutiones anni, et accipe **superfluum sive longitudinem**^β qua fuerit inter ipsum et gradum predictum a quo quidem equavisti sortem primam,[1] et proice illud superfluum a gradu ascendente in revolutione anni.

19　(1) Sors pluvie, accipe de die a gradu coniunctionis luminarium ad gradum Lune, nocte {vero} a Luna ad gradum coniunctionis, et proice ab ascendente mane aut sero, et in quo loco terminabitur numerus, ibi erit sors. (2) {Quod} si aliquis **planetarum**^γ inferiorum fuerit cum hac sorte in aliquo **angulorum**,^γ scias quod cum pervenerit Luna ad locum illius **planete**,^γ tunc pluet; et hoc quidem est in omnibus **pagis et locis**^β in quibus signum dominatur in quo est Luna. (3) HERMES^γ {autem} ait quod accipiatur quolibet die a loco Solis ad locum Saturni, et illud quod erit proice in mane a loco Lune, et ibi sors; et hoc quidem expertum est. (4) {Quod} si exivit sors in una domorum Saturni, erit[2] frigus; et si una domorum Iovis erunt **venti fortes**;^α ⟨⟨...⟩⟩^μ et si in domo Lune, erunt nubes aut pluvia; si {vero} in domo Solis, **erit aer purus et serenus**.^β

(5) Sors rei future utrum scilicet eveniet aut non: accipe **longitudinem**^α que fuerit inter Solem et dominum hore, **secundum terre latitudinem equate, et multiplica ipsam per .10., collectum** {vero} **divide per .12.**^α et illud quod per divisionem exiverit adde super residuum totum, quod collectum insimul proice a loco domini hore, et ibi erit sors. |

22va

20　(1) Sortes in omni revolutione ad sciendum de re qualibus utrum cara erit an vilis;[3] debes {autem} sic facere. (2) Considera quidem locum sortis,

---

[1] qua fuerit inter ipsum et gradum predictum a quo quidem equavisti sortem primam] WVG; L et ibi est sors. Sors vero secunda est que sunt inter ipsum et gradum predictum a quo quidem equatum sortem primam.　[2] erit] WVG; L exit.　[3] vilis] WVG; L utilis.

oriental of the Sun, and take the **longitude or distance**[β,2] between it at the beginning of the revolution of the year and the aforementioned degree; you must calculate the lot from there, and cast out **the remainder or what has been found**[β,3] from the ascendant at the beginning of the revolution of the year, and the lot is there.

(4) {Indeed} the second lot is that you observe Jupiter or Saturn, ⟨and find out⟩ which of them is occidental of the Sun at the moment of the revolution of the year, and take the **remainder or longitude**[β,4] [distance] between it and the aforementioned degree with which you calculated the first lot, and cast out the remainder from the ascendant degree at the revolution of the year.

19 (1) The lot of rain, ⟨is that you⟩ take by day from the degree of the luminaries' conjunction to the degree of the Moon, {but} by night from the Moon to the degree of the conjunction, and cast it out from the ascendant sign in the morning or evening, and the lot is in the position where the reckoning is completed. (2) {But} if one of the lower **planets**[γ,] is with this lot in one of the **angles**,[γ] know that when the Moon reaches the position of this **planet**,[γ] it will rain then; and this is in every **country and place**[β,1] ruled by the sign where the Moon is located. (3) {But} HERMES[γ] says that it [the lot of rain] is taken on any day from the position of the Sun to the position of Saturn, and in the morning you should cast out the result from the position of the Moon, and the lot is there; and this has been tested. (4) {But} if the lot came out in one of Saturn's houses, it will be cold; if in one of Jupiter's houses, there will be **strong winds**,[α,2] ⟨⟨if in one of Mars's houses, it will be hot; if in one of Venus's houses, there will be rain or fog; if in one of Mercury's houses, there will be strong winds⟩⟩;[μ,3] if in the Moon's house, there will be clouds and rain; {but} if in the Sun's house, **the air** [sky] **will be clear and unclouded**.[β,4]

(5) The lot of a future event, whether it will come to pass or not: take the **longitude**[α] [distance] which is between the Sun and the lord of the hour, **equated according to the latitude of the country, multiply it by 10, divide** {indeed} **the result by 12**,[α,5] and add what results from the division to all the remainder, and cast out the final result from the position of the lord of the hour, and the lot is there.

20 (1) In every revolution there are lots to know whether something will be expensive or cheap; {but} you must proceed as follows. (2) Determine

quis, *inquam*, est dominus domus eiusdem, et vide si est retrogradus, aut combustus, aut in domo cadente ⟨⟨...⟩⟩^μ respectu gradus ascendentis in revolutione anni, quia tunc erit vile omne super quod significavit sors; si {autem} fuerit dominus domus fortis in sua fortitudine, et eo melius si fuerit in linea medii celi, tunc erit carus. (3) Et quando pervenerit dominus domus sortis ad **exaltationem suam sive ad domum honoris sui**,^β erit carius; si {vero} **ad domum casus sive dedecoris**,^β erit res econtrario. (4) {Quod} si aliquis **planetarum benivolorum**^γ aspexerit sortem, erit **habundantia vel sufficientia**^β rei super qua significat sors; si {vero} aspexerint **malivoli**,^γ modica erit et dissipabitur.

21 (1) Sors aqua, accipitur a Luna in Venerem.

(2) Sors tritici, a Sole ad Marte.

(3) Sors ordei, a Luna ad Iovem.

(4) Sors pisorum, a Venere in Solem.

(5) Sors lenticularum, a Marte in Saturnum.

(6) Sors fabarum, a Saturno in Martem.

(7) Sors **lactis vel pinguedinis**,^β a Sole in Venerem.

(8) Sors mellis, a Luna in Solem.

(9) Sors **milii**,^α a Iove in Saturnum.

(10) Sors olivarum, a Mercurio in Venerem.

(11) Sors uvarum, a Saturno in Venerem.

(12) Sors bombicis, a Mercurio in Venerem.

(13) Sors **cucurbitarum quarundam**,^γ a Mercurio ad Saturnum.

(14) Sors eorum que saporis sunt acetosi, a Saturno in Martem.

the place of the lot, ⟨and find out⟩, *I say*, which is the lord of its house, and observe whether it is retrograde, or burnt, or in a cadent house ⟨⟨from the cardines⟩⟩^(μ,1) with respect to the degree of the ascendant at the revolution of the year, because then everything indicated by the lot will be cheap; {but} if the lord of the house of the lot is powerfull in its power, particularly if it is at the line of midheaven, then it will be expensive. (3) When the lord of the house of the lot reaches its **exaltation or the house of its honor**,^(β,2) the price will rise even more; {but} ⟨when it reaches⟩ **the house of fall or shame**^(β,3) [dejection], the opposite will occur. (4) {But} if one of the **benevolent planets**^γ aspects the lot, there will be **abundance or sufficient supply**^(β,4) of the thing indicated by the lot; {but} if **malevolent**^γ ⟨planets⟩ aspect ⟨the lot⟩, ⟨the supply of the item indicated⟩ will be moderate, and will be wasted.

21 (1) The lot of water is taken from the Moon to Venus.

(2) The lot of wheat ⟨is taken⟩ from the Sun to Mars.

(3) The lot of barley ⟨is taken⟩ from the Moon to Jupiter.

(4) The lot of peas, from Venus to the Sun.

(5) The lot of lentils, from Mars to Saturn.

(6) The lot of beans, from Saturn to Mars.

(7) The lot of **milk or fat**,^(β,1) from the Sun to Venus.

(8) The lot of honey, from the Moon to the Sun.

(9) The lot of **millet**,^(α,2) from Jupiter to Saturn.

(10) The lot of olives, from Mercury to the Moon.

(11) The lot of grapes, from Saturn to Venus.

(12) The lot of cotton, from Mercury to Venus.

(13) The lot of **certain gourds**,^(γ,3) from Mercury to Saturn.

(14) The lot ⟨of foods⟩ whose taste is sour, from Saturn to Mars.

(15) Sors dulcium saporum, a Sole in Venerem.

(16) Sors fortis saporis,[1] a Marte in Saturnum.

(17) Sors amari saporis, a Mercurio in Saturnum.

(18) ⟨⟨...⟩⟩.$^\mu$

(19) Sors radicum medicinalium ⟨⟨...⟩⟩$^\mu$, a Marte in Lunam.

(20) Sors potionum mortiferarum, a Capite Draconis in Saturnum.

(21) Et omnis quidem sortes hee, a gradu proiciuntur ascendentis.

22 (1) Sortes {quidem autem} has quas commemoravimus extraxerunt SAPIENTES$^\gamma$ duabus de causis. (2) Una est quia **planetarum**$^\alpha$ commixtio alterius cum altero, in coniunctione et in aspectu, multimoda est, et ex eorum commixtione | perveniet bonum et malum in omni loco et omni hora. (3) Idcirco precipue demonstrabitur fortitudo sortis, qua quidem est res sumpta de duobus **planetis**$^\gamma$ super unam rem significantibus, puta a Saturno et Sole, qui ambo sunt patres significatores; opportet ergo nos **longitudinem**$^\alpha$ scire que est inter eos hora qualibet ad inquirendo **dispositionem seu esse**$^\beta$ patrum.

22vb

23 (1) Secunda causa est quia res omnis super qua planete significant duobus indiget[2] testimoniis aut tribus; potest ergo tunc esse testimonium suspectum; cum est alter **planetarum**$^\alpha$ **diurnus**$^\gamma$ et alter **nocturnus**,$^\gamma$ **quapropter**$^\alpha$ secundum fortius est quam primum, aut possibile est quod alter super principium rei significat et alter super finem; propter has ergo causas necesse nobis erat extrahere sortes.

24 (1) **Constituitur itaque sors super**$^\gamma$ tria, quorum duo stabilia sunt semper et fixa in seipsis, tertium {vero} mutabile. (2) Unum quidem stabilium est illud a que accipitur sors; secundum {vero} illud in quod accipitur; et tertium est illud ubi exit respectu gradus ascendentis, et hoc est mutabile, nam qualibet hora mutatur. (3) Oportet {autem} nos proicere sortes a gradu

---

[1]fortis saporis] WVG; L fortium saporum. [2]indiget] WVG; L indigent.

(15) The lot ⟨of foods⟩ of sweet tastes, from the Sun to Venus.

(16) The lot ⟨of foods⟩ of strong taste [pungent taste], from Mars to Saturn.

(17) The lot ⟨of foods⟩ of bitter taste, from Mercury to Saturn.

(18) ⟨⟨The lot of the essences of salty medicines from Mars to the Moon⟩⟩.^μ,4

(19) The lot of ⟨⟨...⟩⟩^μ,5 medicinal roots, from Mars to the Moon.

(20) The lot of deadly potions, from the Head of the Dragon to Saturn.

(21) All these lots should be cast out from the ascendant degree.

22 (1) {But certainly} the **SCHOLARS**^γ,1 calculated the lots we have mentioned for two reasons. (2) One is because the mixture of the **planets**^α with each other, by conjunction and aspect, is of many kinds, and ⟨because⟩ from their mixture, goodness and evil will take place in every place and at every time. (3) For that reason, the power of the lot will be especially shown when the matter is taken from two **planets**^γ that indicate the same thing, say from the Sun and Saturn, both of which are significators of fathers; therefore we need to know the **longitude**^α [distance] between them at any time to investigate the **situation or condition**^β,2 of fathers.

23 (1) The second reason is that everything indicated by the stars needs two or three witnesses, since it is possible that the testimony is doubtful; as when one of the **planets**^α is **diurnal**^γ and the other **nocturnal**,^γ **on account of which**^α,1 the latter is stronger than the former, or it is possible that one indicates the beginning of the matter and the other its end; for these reasons it is necessary for us to calculate the lots.

24 (1) **Accordingly the lot is composed of**^γ,1 three ⟨elements⟩, two of which are always fixed, {but} the third is variable. (2) One of the fixed ⟨elements⟩ is that from which the lot is taken; {but} the second is that to which ⟨the lot⟩ is taken; and the third is the one where it comes out with respect to the ascendant, and this one is variable because it changes every moment. (3) {But} we have to cast out these lots from the ascendant

ascendentis, eo quod ipse super principium significat omnis operis; hee proiciuntur etiam a principio domus qua super **rem** significat **et effectum eius.**ʸ

25 (1) {Rursus} extrahuntur sortes hee secundum gradus equales, eo quod perambulant **planete**ᵅ viam **orbis signorum,**ʸ cum enim dicitur[1] hic **planeta**ʸ est in hoc signo ac in tali gradu, similiter est[2] ascendens tale in tali signo, omnia sunt secundum gradus equales. (2) Et ideo extraxerunt sortes has in gradibus equalibus; gradus {vero} **ascensionum,**ᵅ quia sunt gradus spera supreme, que est super circulum signorum, eo quod movet circulum signorum super duos polos; idcirco computantur omnes aspectus secundum gradus equales respectu circuli signorum. (3) Et Antiqui experti sunt ita in nativitatibus, et in interrogationibus, atque in electionibus, quod cum dat Luna fortitudinem suam alicui planetarum secundum gradus equales in fortitudine aspectuum, viderunt iudicia eorum vera qualibet hora, tam in aspectu quarto quam trino et sextili. (4) Secundum hanc quoque viam experimentati sumus etiam **multis vicibus**ᵅ et ad punctus evenit nobis. Explicit

23ra nona pars HUIUS LIBRI. |

§10

1 (1) **Decima pars LIBRI HUIUS**ᵅ in aspectibus et directionibus.[3]

(2) Scito quod aspectus et directiones ⟨⟨...⟩⟩ʸ duobus sunt **modis.**ʸ (3) Uno **modo**ʸ est in aspectu **radiorum**ʸ secundum numerum **ascensionum**ᵅ signorum in **regione qualibet.**ᵅ (4) Secundus {vero} **modus**ʸ iuxta numerum graduum signorum, et sunt equales in **omni regione.**ᵅ (5) Et si fuerit **stella** in gradu ascendente, tu dirigere debes eum secundum **ascensiones**ᵅ signorum **que mutantur in quolibet loco;**ᵅ et si fuerit in principio domus septime, tu diriges eum econtrario gradui **planete,**ʸ hoc est per gradum suo gradui oppositum; si {vero} fuerit in principio linee medii celi aut in principio domus quarte, tu dirigere debes in **ascensionibus**ᵅ signorum **circuli recti,**ʸ et hoc est **HERMETIS**ʸ opinio. (6) Secundus {autem} **modus,**ʸ iuxta sententiam **SAPIENTIUM ASTRORUM,**ʸ dirigere debes **planetam**ʸ quemcumque aut

---

[1]dicitur] WVG; L om.   [2]est] WVG; L et.   [3]Decima pars libri huius in aspectibus et directionibus] L (in margin); W om; G Incipit .10. pars libri huius in aspectibus et directionibus; V Incipit .10. et ultima pars libri huius in aspectibus et directionibus

degree because it indicates the beginning of any action; these ⟨lots⟩ are also cast out from the beginning of the house that indicates **the matter and its accomplishment.**^γ,2

25 (1) {In addition,} these lots are calculated in equal degrees, because the **planets**^α move along the path of the **orb of the signs,**^γ,1 for when it is said that this **planet**^γ is in that sign and at certain degree, and similarly that a certain ascendant is in a certain sign, all these are in equal degrees. (2) For that reason the lots are calculated in equal degrees; {but} ⟨there are also⟩ degrees of the **ascensions,**^α since these are degrees of the highest sphere, which is above the circle of the signs, since it [the highest sphere] moves the circle of the signs around two poles; hence all the aspects are calculated in equal degrees with respect to the circle of the signs. (3) The ANCIENTS tested this in this way in nativities, interrogations, and elections, that when the Moon gives its power to one of the **planets**^α according to equal degrees in the power of the aspects, they realized that their judgments are true at every moment just as much for quartile, as for trine and sextile. (4) We also tested ⟨this⟩ according to this way **many times**^α,2 and proved that it is so. Here ends the ninth part of THIS BOOK.

§10

1 (1) **Tenth part of THIS BOOK,**^α,1 on the aspects and directions.

(2) Know that the aspects and the directions ⟨⟨to them⟩⟩^ν,2 are in two **modes.**^γ,3 (3) One **mode**^γ is by the aspect of the **rays**^γ,4 according to the reckoning of the **ascensions**^α of the signs in **any region.**^α,5 (4) {But} the second **mode**^γ is according to the number of degrees of the signs, which are the same in **every region.**^α (5) If the **star** is in the degree of the ascendant, you must direct it according to the **ascensions**^α of the signs, **which change in any ⟨terrestrial⟩ place;**^α,6 if it is in the beginning of the seventh house, direct it by inverting the degree of the **planet,**^γ that is, by the degree that is opposite its [the planet's] degree; {but} if it is at the beginning of the line of midheaven or in the beginning of the fourth house, you must direct it in **ascensions**^α of the signs at the **upright circle**^γ,7 [sphaera recta]; this is the opinion of HERMES.^γ (6) {But} the second **mode,**^γ according to the opinion of SCHOLARS OF THE STARS,^γ,8 is that you must direct whatever

sortem qualibet qua dirigere oportet, quoque loco circuli, secundum gradus equales respectu signorum circuli, non respectu **circuli recti**;[γ] et hanc rem sufficienter experti sunt sine fine, et eam veracem invenerunt. (7) *Secundum hunc* ergo *modum* semper erit aspectus oppositus .180. gradus, et aspectus trinus .120., et aspectus quartus .90., aspectus {vero} sextilis .60. gradus, et omnes gradus quidem equales. (8) Et hoc, *inquam*, verum est si non fuerit latitudo stelle a **cingulo zodiaci**, si {autem} latitudinem habuit parum nocebit. (9) Et sic operatus est ALBATEGNI IN LIBRO SUO, et ANTIQUI omnes, et POST EOS SEQUENTES.

2 (1) Harum {autem} directionum **causa et ratio et utilitas**[β] est quod cum direxeris stella aut gradum ad corpus stelle, aut ad aspectum **radiorum**[γ] eius, ad sciendum quot[1] sunt anni inter eos. (2) Per directiones quidem scietur totum et bonum et malum quod accidet regibus, et superationes regnorum a gente ad gentem alteram, adhuc et mutationes que in mundo initiantur in communi et in particulari de bono ad malum, sive de malo ad bonum.

(3) Directiones secundum quinque vias existunt.

(4) Una est ad sciendum **dispositiones et esse mundi**[β] **in comuni seu universaliter**,[β] ut sunt aque diluviorum ⟨⟨...⟩⟩[μ] que destruxerunt **seculum**,[α] vel dispositiones regionum per bella, et innovationes legum. (5) Et erit mundus in fortitudine signi .1000. annis, et pars anni in hac directione est .1. minutus, et .48. secunda.

23rb (6) Directio {autem} secunda est sub directione millenariorum, et significat super omne quod accidit genti ad gentem, et cuilibet **climati ad clima aliud**.[γ] (7) Et est **seculum sive mundus**[β] in fortitudine signi cuilibet .100. annis, et pars quidem anni unius in hac directione est .18. minuta.

(8) Tertia {quoque} est sub directione centenariorum, et significat super omnem quod renovatur in ⟨⟨...⟩⟩[ν] **regionibus et regionibus**,[γ] parentelis et parentelis. (9) Et erit mundus sub potestate cuiuslibet signi decem annis; et hoc {etiam} modo erit homo quilibet sub potestatem signi decem annis

---

[1] quot] WVG; L quod.

planet^γ or whatever lot it is necessary to direct, and at any location on the circle [the zodiac], in equal degrees with respect to the circle of the signs, not with respect to the **upright circle**^γ [sphaera recta]; this thing has been sufficiently tested innumerable times, and they found it to be correct. (7) Consequently, *according to this mode* the opposition aspect will be always 180°, the trine aspect 120°, the quartile aspect 90°, {but} the sextile aspect 60°, all in equal degrees. (8) This, *I say*, is true if the star has no latitude with respect to the **girdle of the zodiac**^γ,9 [the ecliptic], {but} if it has latitude, it will harm [affect] ⟨the calculation⟩ slightly. (9) AL-BATTĀNĪ IN HIS BOOK proceeded in this manner, and all the ANCIENTS, and THOSE WHO FOLLOWED THEM.

2 (1) {But} the **cause, reason and utility**^β,1 of these directions is that when you direct a star or degree to the body of a star, or to the aspect of its **rays,**^γ ⟨this is⟩ in order to know how many years there are between them. (2) All good and evil that will befall kings will be known by the directions, and the conquest of kingdoms from one nation to another, also the alterations that are initiated in the world affecting collectives and individuals, from evil to good and from good to evil.

(3) The directions occur in five ways.

(4) One is to know the **dispositions and conditions of the world**^β,2 **in general or universally,**^β,3 such as the waters of floods ⟨⟨and drought⟩⟩^μ,4 that devastate **the age,**^α,5 or the dispositions of the regions by wars, and the introduction of new religions. (5) ⟨In this direction⟩ the world will be under the power of one sign for a thousand years, and the part of one year in this direction is 1' 48".

(6) The second direction, {however,} is subordinate to the direction of the thousands, and indicates what happens to any nation and nation, and **to any climate and another climate.**^γ,6 (7) ⟨In this direction⟩ **the age or the world**^β,7 is under the power of each sign for 100 years, and the part of one year in this direction is 18'.

(8) {Besides,} the third ⟨way of direction⟩ is subordinate to the direction of the hundreds, and indicates everything new that happens ⟨⟨in any⟩⟩^μ,8 **region and region,**^γ,9 family and family. (9) ⟨In this direction⟩ the world is under the governance of one sign for 10 years; and in this way an individual

usque ad finem .10. annorum,ᵅ et pars unius anni in hac dirctione est .3. gradus.

(10) Quarta {vero} est directio vocata *alphardar*; dirigunt {autem} sic in rebus **seculi sive mundi,**ᵝ quod incipit a quoque **planeta**ᵞ cuius **exaltatio sive domus honoris**ᵝ prius fuerit respectu signi Arietis; sed in natis de die incipiunt ipsi a Sole, de nocte {vero} a Luna; et in universali numerus temporis *alphardar* est .75. anni.

(11) Quinta directio est unitatum in rebus **seculi,**ᵅ ad sciendum quod eveniet quolibet anno; {et similiter} natus erit anno quolibet in fortitudine unius signi, et vocatur **signum revolutionis**;ᵞ proficitur {autem} hoc directio in .12. annis, et pars anni unius est .30. graduum, qui sunt gradus unius signi.

3 (1) {Item} {autem} dirigere debes coniunctionem magnam quousque transmutentur Saturnus et Iupiter a triplicitate in triplicitate donec revertantur ad locum eorum pristinus, et hoc erit in .960. annis; pars {vero} unius anni est .22. minuta et .16. secunda et .5. tertia. (2) Debes etiam dirigere coniunctionem mediam, que est mutatio dictorum de triplicitate ad triplicitatem, et hoc erit in .240. annis; pars {vero} unius anni est gradus unius .29. minuta et .4. secunda. (3) Item dirigere debes coniunctionem minorem, in mutatione predictorum de signo in signum **triplicitatis**,ᵞ et hoc erit in quibuslibet .20. annis secundum propinquitate; et pars unius anni est .18. gradus fere. (4) {Postremo} est adhuc alia directio in nativitatibus hominum ac | revolutionibus annorum mundi, et est quod tu dirigere debes gradum ascendentem ad corpora stellarum, aut ad aspectus **radiorum**ᵞ aᵅ signo scito ac aᵅ gradu scito, quolibet anno .1. gradus. (5) Directio {vero} sortium secundum contrarium signorum, ita est ut commemorat Ptolomeus in Libro Fructus, *id est Centiloquii*.[1]

23va

Complete sunt .10. partes libri huius quem compilavit Magister Abraham Avenezre, quod interpretatur Magister Adiutorii; et Magister Hynricus de Malinis, dictus Bate, cantor Leodiensis transtulit, translationemque complevit in Urbe Veteri, anno Domini MCCXCII, in octava Assumptionis Beate

---

[1]Centiloquii] L; WGV om.

is {also} under the governance of the sign for 10 years, until the end of **10 years**,$^{\alpha,10}$ and the part of one year in this direction is 3°.

(10) {But} the fourth direction is called *alfardār*; {but} they direct it in this manner in things related to the **age or the world**,$^{\beta}$ it begins from any **planet**$^{\gamma}$ whose **exaltation or house of honor**$^{\beta}$ is the first with respect to Aries; but for those born by day they start from the Sun, by night {indeed} from the Moon; and in general the reckoning of the time of *alfardār* is 75 years.

(11) The fifth is the direction of single ⟨years⟩ with regard to the affairs of **the age**,$^{\alpha}$ to know what will take place each year; {similarly} in any year the native will be under the power of one sign, and this is called **"the sign of the revolution;"**$^{\gamma,11}$ {but} this direction is completed in 12 years, and the part of one year is 30°, which are the degrees of one sign.

3 (1) {But} you must {likewise} direct the great conjunction as long as Saturn and Jupiter move from triplicity to triplicity until they return to their initial position, and this will be in 960 years; the part of one year is {indeed} 22 minutes and 16 seconds and 5 third-parts. (2) You must also direct the middle conjunction, which is the movement of the aforementioned ⟨planets⟩ [Saturn and Jupiter] from triplicity to triplicity, and this will be in 240 years; the part of one year is {indeed} 1° 29 minutes and 4 seconds. (3) Likewise, you must direct the small conjunction, in the movement of the aforementioned ⟨planets⟩ [Saturn and Jupiter] from sign to sign **of the triplicity**,$^{\gamma,1}$ and this will be in any ⟨period of⟩ approximately 20 years; the part of one year is approximately 18°. (4) {Finally,} there is another direction in the nativities of human beings and in the revolutions of the world-years, and it is that you must direct the degree of the ascendant to the bodies of the stars, or to the aspects of the **rays**$^{\gamma}$ **from**$^{\alpha,2}$ a certain sign and **from**$^{\alpha}$ a certain degree, one degree to each year. (5) {But} the direction of the lots is the opposite of the ⟨direction⟩ of the signs, that is, as PTOLEMY mentions in the BOOK OF THE FRUIT, *that is, the* CENTILOQUIUM.

The ten chapters of THIS BOOK, which Master Abraham Ibn Ezra, ⟨a name⟩ whose translation is Master of Help, compiled, are completed; Master Henry of Malines, called Bate, cantor of Liège, executed the translation, which he completed in Orvieto, in the year of the Lord 1292, on the eighth day after

Marie Virginis Gloriose; laudationes illi Domini qui extendit aera sive celos et qui scientiam ampliavit. Amen.[1]

---

[1] Complete sunt .10. partes libri huius quem compilavit Magister Abraham Avenezre, quod interpretatur Magister Adiutorii; et Magister Hynricus de Malinis, dictus Bate, cantor Leodiensis transtulit, translationemque complevit in Urbe Veteri, anno Domini MCCXCII, in octava assumptionis Beate Marie Virginis Gloriose; laudationes illi Domini qui extendit aera sive celos et qui scientiam ampliavit. Amen] L; W Complete sunt modo decem partes huius libri, Deo gratias. Hunc librum edidit Abraham Avenezre, quod interpretartur Magister Adiutorii; translatus est a Magistro Henrico de Malynis, dicto Bate cantor Leodiensis; perfecta est hoc translation in Urbe Vetere in anno Domini .1292. in .8a. assumptinois Beate Virgine Gloriose; G Hunc librum edidit Habraham Aveneszre quod interpretatur Magister Adiutorii quod Argentem; V Hunc librum edidit Habraham Avenesre, quod interpretatur Magister Adiutorii; translatus est hic liber a Magistro Henrico de Malines, dicto Bate, cantor Leodiensis, et est hec translatio perfecta in Urbe Vetere, anno domini 1292o in octava assumptionis Beate Marie virginis gloriose. Deo gratias.

the Assumption of the Glorious Virgin Mary [i.e., August 22, the eighth day counting from the feast on August 15]; praised be the Lord who extended the Heavens and augmented wisdom. Amen.[3]

PART TWO

NOTES TO *LIBER ABRAHE AVENERRE INTRODUCTORIUS AD ASTRONOMIAM*

§1

[1]1: **For it is the foundation.** P, 1ra: et c'est li chasti; H: כי היא המוסד. → Although this phrase is missing in L, Bate begins his translation of *Ṭe'amim* I: "Fundamentum quidem volo ponere Libro Initii Sapientie."

[2]1: **Strive to go or wander.** P, 1ra: cerche aprés; H: יתור = explore.

[3]2: **Customs of heavens.** P, 1ra: des coustumes des cieus; H: חקות השמים = ordinances of heavens.

[4]2: **Laws and decrees.** P: om.; H: ומשטרם = and their dominion.

[5]2: **Their destiny.** P, 1ra: leur destine; H: ומשטרם: their dominion.

[6]4: **After I compile this book, I will add.** P, 1ra: et aprés je arai ajousté ce livre je ajousterai; H: ואחר שאשלים זה הספר, אחבר = After I complete the book, I will compose [*lit.* add]. → Here Bate, following Hagin, coined the verb adiungare, a mistranslation of לחבר, *lit.* add or combine, which means "compose," in the sense of write.

[7]4: **A Book of explantion of the reasons and causes.** P, 1ra: un livre des esplanemens des resons; H: ספר בפירוש הטעמים = Book of explantion of the reasons.

[8]4: **I will add a Book of explantion of the reasons and causes.** → This is a reference to *Ṭe'amim* I (= *Rationes* I), a close commentary on *Reshit Ḥokhmah* and full of quotations from *Reshit Ḥokhmah*, which are presented and commented on in the same order that they appear in *Reshit Ḥokhmah*.

[9]5: **God will furnish me assistance to accomplish this.** P, 1ra: et Dieus m'aït a parfaire; H: ואל השם אתחנן לעזרני = I implore God to assist me.

§2

[1]2: **Configuration of the sphere.** P, 1ra: la samblance de l'espere; H: דמות הגלגל = appearance of the circle.

[2]2: **Planets.** P, 1ra: estoiles errables; H: כוכבי לכת = walking stars. → Meaning, planets.

[3]2: **Dignities.** P, lrb: leur poeté; H: ממשלתם = their dominion.

[4]3: **Their effect.** P, lrb: leur ouvraigne; H: מפעלם = their effects.

[5]3: **Their condition.** P, lrb: leur faitures = their images; H: והצורות = and the images.

[6]4: **Their diversity.** P, lrb: leur changement = their alteration; H: תמורתם = their alterations.

[7]4: **Friendship and enmity.** P, lrb: leur amor et leur haine = their love and hate; H: אהבתם ושנאתם = their love and hate.

[8]4: **The heavens.** P, lrb: cercle = circle; H: הגלגל = the circle.

[9]5: **Planets.** P, lrb: planetes; H: משרתים = servants. → Meaning, planets. Ibn Ezra adopted the Hebrew משרתים, *mešaretim*, "servants," to denote the concept of plants. Ibn Ezra found the word in Psalms 103:21, where he glossed it as referring to the seven planets. This is the biblical neologism most frequently employed by Ibn Ezra in his oeuvre, scientific and nonscientific, both translations and in original works.

[10]6: **Condition of the planets.** P, lrb: l'afaire des planetes; H: דברי המשרתים = matters concerned with the servants. → Meaning, matters concerned with the planets. See above note on § 2:5, s.v., "planets".

[11]7: **Effects of the planets.** P, lrb: la force des planetes; H: כח המשרתים = power of the servants. → Meaning, power of the planets. See above note on § 2:5, s.v., "planets".

[12]7: **After or behind it.** P, lrb: ou derriers; H: לאחריה = after it.

[13]8: **Mixture.** P: om.; H: וממסכם = their mixtures.

[14]8: **Their conditions and dispositions.** P, lrb: leur afaire; H: דבריהם = their matters.

[15]9: **Certain rules and judgments.** P, lrb: le jugement; H: דיני = judgments.

[16]10: **Lots or parts.** P, lva: pars = parts; H: גורלות = lots.

[17]10: **All.** P: om.; H: כל.

[18]10: **Parts.** P, lva: pars; H: גורלות = lots.

[19]10: **Scholars of the stars.** P, lva: les sages des signes; H: חכמי המזלות = the scholars of the signs.

[20]11: **The projections of the rays of the planets.** P, lva: reflambissement de la clarté des .7. planetes; H: זריחת אור השבעה משרתים = the shining of the light of the seven servants. → See above note on § 2:5, s.v., "planets".

[21]11: **Alterations.** P, lva: remuement; H: העתקתם = their translation.

§ 3

[1]1: **Wishes.** P, lva: qui veut; H: om.

[2]1: **Must observe.** P, lva: se doit avertir; H: שיחקור = who will study.

[3]1: **How they change in their motion and ⟨how⟩ they hasten in ⟨their⟩ running to revolve.** P, lva: qui sont hatif en leur aler et en leur mouvement; H: שהם מהירים בהליכתם מתנועתם = which are quicker in their journey than their motion.

[4]1: **The upper sphere.** P, : l'espere haute = the upper sphere; H: הגלגל העליון = the upper circle.

[5]1: **And their motions in their spheres.** P: om.; H: ותנועתם בגלגליהם.

[6]1: **And ⟨must⟩ observe them when they are.** P, lva: et s'avertissent quant il seront; H: ותנועתם בגלגליהם = and their motions in their circles.

[7]1: **Fixed stars.** P, lva: les estoiles hautes; H: הכוכבים העליונים = the upper stars. → This divergent translation is in fact a gloss where Bate instantiates Ibn Ezra's vague term "upper stars".

[8]1: **Center.** P, lva: le centre; H: המוצק = *muṣaq*, lit. "solid, stable, or strong." → Meaning, "center." For this neologism, see Sela 2003, 113–116.

[9]2: **It will be proven that the aforementioned planets.** P, 1va: adonc s'esprouvera en son cuer que se les mouvemens les ramenteus; H: אז יתברר בליבו כי התנועות הנזכרות = then it will be made clear in his heart that the aforesaid motions.

[10]2: **The regions.** P, 1va: les regions; H: הגבולים = the territories, terms.

[11]3: **The number.** P: om.; H: במספר.

[12]3: **Southern and northern.** P, 1vb: les meridianes et les septentrionaus; H: השמאליות והדרומיות = left ones and southern. → Meaning, northern and southern.

[13]3: **Those related to collectives as well as to individuals.** P, 1vb: les communes et les particulieres; H: והכללים והפרטים = the collectives and the individuals.

§ 1.1

[1]1: **First chapter or first part.** P, 1vb: Chapitre de la devision de l'espere en 48. figures et en ses parties; H: השער הראשון = the first gate. → Meaning, first chapter.

[2]1: **Sphere.** P, 1vb: l'espere; H: הגלגל = the circle.

[3]1: **Which are called degrees.** P : om.; H: יקראו מעלות = which are called degrees. → Pietro d'Abano: om.

[4]2: **Later ⟨scholars⟩.** P, 1va: derreins; H: האחרונים = the last ones.

[5]2: **From one-half.** P : om.; H: מחצי = from one half.

[6]3: **Straight or equal degrees.** P, 1vb: grés drois; H: מעלות ישרות = straight degrees.

[7]3: **First smaller parts.** P, 1vb: menus premiers = first smaller parts; H: ראשונים = first ones.

[8]3: **Or beyond.** P, 1vb: ou plus; H: om.

§1.2

[1]3: **Ptolemy.** P, 2ra: Bertelmieu; H: בטלמיוס = Baṭalmiyūs. → This is "Ptolemy" with an Arabic accent.

§1.3

[1]1: **There are 346 stars in the images ⟨corresponding to the⟩ signs.** P, 2ra: et il i a d'eus es figures des signes .346. estoiles; H: והנה יש מהם בצורות המזלות שמ"ו כוכבים = There are 346 stars in the images ⟨corresponding to the⟩ signs.

[2]3: **Pleiades.** P, 2ra: *kima*; H: כימה = *kimah*.

[3]4: **26 in Virgo.** P : om.; H: בבתולה כ"ו = 26 in Virgo.

§1.4

[1]2: **Which is Cetus.** in margin of P, 2ra: Cetus; H: om.

[2]3: **And it is Orion.** in margin of P, 2ra: Orion; H: om.

[3]9: **Beast.** P, 2rb: la biche; H: החיה = the animal. → Ibn Ezra calls this constellation החיה, *ha-ḥayyah*, *lit.* "the animal," but which he uses to mean "snake." This is so because the Hebrew word is homophonous with Arabic الحية, *al-ḥayya*, "the snake."

[4]9: **And it is Hydra.** in margin of P, 2rb: Ydra; H: om.

[5]12: **And it is Centaurus.** in margin of P, 2rb: Centaurus; H: om.

[6]13: **And it is the Beast of Centaurus.** P: om.; H: om.

§1.5

[1]2: **Lesser Bear.** P, 2rb: עיש = *'ayish*, in Hebrew letters; H: עיש = *'ayish*.

[2]2: **With Her Sons.** P, 2rb: et ses enfans; H: ובניה = and her sons.

[3]5: **It is called elsewhere Flaminatus or Cepheus.** H: om.; in margin of P, 2rb: Flaminatus vel Cepheus.

[4]6: **Elsewhere called Howling, whose meaning is shouting, or Boetes.** H: om.; above the line and in margin of P, 2rb: Ululans, cuius intentio est vociferans, vel Boetes.

[5]7: **Northern Crown.** P, 2va: la corone senestre; H: הנזר השמאלי = the left crown. → Meaning, the northern crown.

[6]8: **One Crawling on his Knees or Genuflecting.** P, 2va: celi qui va sur ses genous; H: ההולך על ארכבותיו = the One Crawling on his Knees.

[7]11: **One Sitting on a Chair.** P, 2va: celi qui siet sur le siege. H: היושבת על הכסא = the ⟨Woman⟩ Sitting on a Chair.

[8]12: **And it is Perseus.** on margin of P, 2rb: Perseus; H: om. See below § 2.2:45.

[9]13: **Or Agitator.** H: om.; in margin of P, 2rb: Agitator. → Meaning, Charioteer. This is an obsolete Latin name for the constellation of Auriga.

[10]14: **Beast.** → See above note on § 1.4:9, s.v. "Beast".

[11]14: **And it is Serpentarius.** in margin of P, 2rb: Serpentarius; H: om.

[12]15: **Beast.** → See above note on § 1.4:9, s.v. "Beast".

[13]15: **Or Serpens.** H: om.; in margin of P, 2rb: Serpens.

[14]16: **The Harmful.** P, 2rb: nuiseur; H: השטן = Satan.

[15]16: **And it is Sagitta.** H: om.; in margin of P, 2rb: Sagitta.

[16]18: **And it is Delphin.** in margin of P, 2rb: Delphin; H: om.

[17]19: **Hindmost.** P: om.; H: om.

[18]21: **The Woman.** P, 2va: la fame; H: האשה = the woman.

§1.6

[1]1: **Great or the greatest.** P, 2vb: grande; H: גדול = great.

[2]1: **Honor.** P, 2rb: l'oneur; H: כבוד = honor. → Meaning, magnitude. To denote the concept of magnitude of fixed stars, Ibn Ezra employed כבוד, "honor," as a calque from the Arabic شرف. That word, in the sense of the magnitude of fixed stars, appears in Arabic texts such as the Arabic version of *Liber de stellis beibeniis* (Book of the fixed stars; Kunitzsch 2001, 56–81, esp. 60 lines 1,2 *et passim*), Abū Ma'shar's *Kitāb aḥkām al-mawālīd* (Book of the judgments of the nativities; *Kitāb aḥkām al-mawālīd* 2001, 84–99, esp. 84 lines 5, 7 *et passim*), and al-Bīrūnī's *Kitāb al-Tafhīm* (*Ta*, § 157, 68). The use of כבוד for the magnitude of fixed stars is sporadic in Ibn Ezra's oeuvre and found only in some parts addressing the fixed stars. It contrasts with his frequent use of כבוד, also as a calque of شرف, to denote the astrological concept of exaltation.

[3]1: **Brightness or light.** P, 2vb: clarté; H: אור = light.

§1.9

[1]1: **To which it is conjoined.** P, 3ra: qui est ensemble lui; H: שיהיה עמו = with which it is.

[2]2: **Some are good and some are bad, or benefic and malefic.** P, 3va: et si i a tes qui sont bons et mauvais; H: ויש טובים ורעים = some of them good and others bad.

[3]3: **And one that is changeable, namely ⟨adapting itself⟩ to the nature of each of the others.** P, 3rb: et .1. mellé, trestornant avec chascune nature; H: ואחד ממוסך, מתהפך עם כל תולדת = and one is mixed, adapting itself to every nature.

[4]4: **Now the power of one the luminaries, i.e., of the Sun, is diurnal and masculine, but ⟨the power⟩ of the other, namely, of the Moon, is feminine and nocturnal.** P, 3rb: Et l'une des lui sernes c'est le soleil, et sa force si est de jor et il est malles. Et le secont ele est femele, c'est la lune et sa force si est de nuit; H: והנה אחד מהמאורות הוא השמש, והוא זכר וכוחו ביום, והשני נקבה והיא הלבנה וכחה בלילה. = Now one of the luminaries, the Sun, is masculine

and its power is felt by day; and the other luminary, the Moon, is feminine and its power is felt by night.

[5]6: **Diurnal.** P, 3rb: des estoiles du jor; H: מכוכבי היום = of the stars of day.

[6]6: **Nocturnal.** P, 3rb: des estoiles de la nuit; H: מכוכבי הלילה = of the stars of night.

[7]7: **Which it is approaching.** P, 3rb: qui est ensemble li; H: שיהיה עמו = with which it is.

[8]7: **As will be explained below.** P, 3vb: com je esplanerai ça avant; H: כאשר אפרש = as I will explain.

[9]7: **As will be explained below, in the appropriate place.** → This is a reference to chapter 4 of *Reshit Ḥokhmah*, where the planets' properties are detailed in the separate sections on each of them.

§ 1.10

[1]1: **The distance or elongation.** P, 3va: l'alongement; H: המרחק = distance.

[2]2: **With respect to ascension or descension.** P, 3va: ou monter et ou descendre; H: לעלות ולרדת = to ascend or descend.

[3]2: **On the left side ⟨of the ecliptic⟩, that is, northern.** P, 3va: devers senestre; H: לצד שמאל = to the left side. → Meaning, to the northern side.

[4]2: **On the right side ⟨of the ecliptic⟩ or southern.** P, 3va: devers destre; H: לצד ימין = to the right side.

[5]3: **Planet.** P, 3va: l'estoile; H: הכוכב = the star.

[6]3: **At the apogee of the eccentric circle.** P, 3va: ou degré haut du cercle encentricle qui n'est mie fait au centre de la terre; H: במעלת גבה הגלגל המוצק שאינו במוצק הארץ = in the degree of the height of the circle of the center, whose center is not the Earth.

[7]3: **Then it is in its greatest elongation with respect to the Earth.** P: om.; H: אז יהיה במקום גבהותו מן הארץ = then it is in the place of its height with respect to the Earth.

[8]3: **Opposite its apogee.** P, 3va: ou lieu de sa baisseté; H: במקום שפלותו = in the place of its lowness.

[9]4: **Dragon or *jawzahar*.** P, 3va: dragon; H: התלי = *ha-teli*. → Talmudic term for Dragon.

[10]4: **Of the planet.** P, 3va: de l'estoile; H: om.

[11]5: **The northern beginning.** P, 3va: l'acommençal du senestre; H: התחלת השמאל = the beginning of the left → Meaning, the beginning of the north.

[12]5: **Southern beginning.** P, 3va: l'acomrnençal du destre; H: תחלת הימין = the beginning of the right.

[13]5: **Planet.** P, 3vb: l'estoile; H: הכוכב = the star.

[14]5: **In the girdle of the imagination of the circle of the signs.** P, 3va: ou pourceint de l'imaginacion du cercle des signes; H: בחשב אפודת גלגל המזלות = in the girdle of the vest of the circle of the signs. → To denote the concept of "ecliptic" Ibn Ezra uses חשב אפודת הגלגל *ḥešev 'afudat ha-galgal*, "the girdle of the vest of the circle," or shorter cognates such as חשב האפודה *ḥešev ha-'afudah*, "girdle of the vest." Both are derived from Exodus 28:8. Why Ibn Ezra thought fit to use this bizarre expression is answered in his two commentaries on Exodus 28:8, where he wrote that there is a deep astronomical and astrological secret behind the high priest's ceremonial dress and suggests that it included some sort of visual representation of the zodiac in general and of the ecliptic in particular. Note that in the first word of the expression חשב אפודת הגלגל, the root חשב means to think or to imagine. From here derives Hagin's "imaginacion," which is echoed by Bate's "ymaginatio."

[15]5: **It will have northern or southern latitude.** P, 3va: il ara largece a senestre ou a destre; H: יש לו מרחב לשמאל או לימין = it has latitude to the left and to the right. → Meaning, it has latitude to the north and to the south.

§ 1.11

[1]1: **Planets.** P, 3vb: planetes; H: משרתים = servants. → Meaning, planets. See above note on § 2:5, s.v., "planets".

[2]1: **Dignities in the zodiac.** P, 3vb: poesté ou cercle; H: ממשלת בגלגל = dominion in the circle.

[3]1: **That is, the dignity.** P, 3vb: il i a poesté; H: יש ממשלת = there is dominion.

[4]1: **Exaltation or honor.** P, 3vb: eneur; H: כבוד = honor. → Meaning, exaltation. To denote the concept of exaltation, here and elsewhere Ibn Ezra employed the Hebrew כבוד, *lit.* "honor," a calque from شرف. The Latin works that fall within the ambit of Ibn Ezra's astrological and astronomical work use the corresponding calque (honor) for exaltation.

[5]1: **Term.** P, 3vb: termine; H: גבול = term.

[6]1: **Face.** P, 3vb: faces; H: פנים = face.

[7]2: **Exaltation.** P, 3vb: eneur; H: כבוד = honor. → Here Bate offers the common Latin technical term for the concept of "exaltation".

[8]3: **In the sign that is.** P, 3vb: en signe qui est; H: במזל שהוא = in the sign which is.

[9]3: **That is the house of its.** P, 3vb: qui est la meson; H: שהוא בית = which is the house.

[10]3: **Exaltation.** P, 3vb: eneur; H: כבוד = honor.

§ 1.12

[1]1: **For you.** P: om.; H: לך = for you.

[2]1: **The wise men of.** P, 3vb: des sages; H: חכמי = the wise men of.

[3]1: **Persians.** P, 3vb: sages de Perse; H: חכמי פרס = scholars of Persia.

NOTES TO *LIBER ABRAHE AVENERRE INTRODUCTORIUS* 373

[4]2: **Novenariae.** P, 3vb: les noveines; H: תשיעיות = ninth-parts.

[5]2: *Duodenariae.* P, 3vb: les .12nes.; H: שנים העשר = the twelfths.

[6]2: **Of the stars.** P, 4ra: des estoiles; H: הכוכבים = of the stars.

[7]2: **Pertaining to a pit.** P, 4ra: de la puisete; H: בורות = pits.

[8]2: **Fortune.** P, 4ra: grace; H: חן = grace.

[9]2: **Assembled.** P, 4ra: poplés; H: om.

[10]2: **Their great conjunctions.** P, 4ra: le mellement des grans d'eus; H: ממסך הגדולים שבהם = the mixture of the largest among them. → This divergent translation glosses on Ibn Ezra's vague expression: "the mixture of the largest among them." Bate's gloss "their great conjunctions" refers to the Saturn-Jupiter conjunctions, usually called "the great conjunctions," when the "mixture" of Saturn and Jupiter, the two largest planets, takes place.

[11]2: **Complete and entire.** P, 4ra: enterin; H: שלם = complete.

§ 2.1

[1]1: **Second part of the book.** P, 4ra: Or commence le .2. chapitre; H: השער השני = the second gate. → Meaning, second chapter.

[2]1: **Fixed stars.** P, 1va: les estoiles hautes; H: הכוכבים העליונים = the upper stars. → Bate's divergent translation glosses on Ibn Ezra's vague expression "the upper stars". See above § 3:1, s.v., "fixed stars".

[3]2: **North.** P, 4ra: senestrains; H: שמאליים = left ones. → Meaning, northern ones.

[4]2: **Equal line.** P, 4ra: ligne droite; H: הקו הישר = straight line.

[5]2: **And six.** P, 4ra: et .6.; H: om.

[6]3: **By nature.** P, 4ra : de la nature du; H: מתולדת = of the nature.

[7]**4: Changeable or tropical.** P, 4ra: trestournans; H: מתהפך = reversing direction.

[8]**5: Equal hours.** P, 4rb: eures droites; H: שעות ישרות = straight hours.

[9]**5: Ascensions.** P, 48ra: ascensions; H: מצעדים = steps, processions. → Meaning, ascensions.

[10]**5: Its ascensions.** P, 4rb: il monte; H: הוא יעלה = it ascends.

[11]**5: Line of equality.** P, 4rb: la ligne ounie; H: הקו השוה = the equal line.

[12]**5: On the Earth.** P, 4rb: en la terre; H: בארץ = on the Earth.

[13]**5: Oblique sign.** P, 4ra: il est tort; H: מעוות = crooked.

[14]**6: As a rule.** P, 4rb: et il est tretous; H: וכולו = All of it.

[15]**6: Temperate.** P: om.; H: ממוסך = temperate.

[16]**6: Must increase.** P, 4rb: doit croistre; H: שיגדל וירבה = which grows and increases.

[17]**8: Rainy and windy.** P, 4rb: pluieus seigneur de vens; H: מגשים בעל רוחות = brings rains and lord of winds.

[18]**8: Whirlwind = turbine.** P, 4rb: estorbellion = whirlwind; H: קֶטֶב מרירי = deadly pestilence (Deut. 32:24).

[19]**9: Its northern part multiplies.** P, 4rb: et s'il est a senestre; H: ואם היה שמאלי = and if it is left. → Meaning, and if it is northern.

[20]**9: ⟨Its⟩ southern ⟨part⟩.** P, 4rb: et s'il est meridional; H: ואם דרומי = if it is southern.

[21]**10: Which have soles or hooves.** P, 4rb: qui a plante; H: שיש לה פרסה = with hooves.

[22]**10: Obliquely.** P, 4rb: tors; H: מעוותים = crooked.

[23]11: **It is.** P, 4va: et si enseigne; H: ויורה = it indicates.

[24]11: ⟨**It is**⟩ **of two forms or double-bodied or having two forms.** P, 4rb: 2 figures; H: שתי צורות = two forms.

[25]12: **And the east wind.** P, 4rb: et vent oriental; H: ורוח מזרחי = and the east wind.

[26]13: **Elements.** P, : elemens; H: שרשים = roots.

[27]13: **Of the humors.** P, 4rb: et des humeurs; H: om.

[28]17: **Climate.** P, 4va: climat; H: גבול = term, territory. → Ibn Ezra's neologism for climate. Medieval and modern Hebrew use אקלים *'aklim*, derived from the Arabic إقليم *'iqlim* to denote the concept of "climate," but Ibn Ezra never does. Ibn Ezra considered the biblical גבול *gevul* (Psalms 74:17) to be the original Hebrew term. In his commentary on Psalms 74:17 he explained the use of this biblical word to denote the concept of climate to be the original Hebrew term.

[29]17: **And Persia.** P: om.; H: ופרס = and Persia.

[30]18: **Sheep or flocks.** P, 4va: l'ouaille; H: הצאן = sheep.

[31]18: **Robbers or thieves.** P, 4va: robeurs; H: הליסטים = robbers.

[32]21: **That is.** P, 4va: c'est; H: היא = she.

[33]22: **Indians.** P, 4vb: les homes d'Inde; H: אנשי הודו = the people of India.

[34]22: **A head following the form of a dog.** P, 4vb: chief en faiture de chien; H: ראש צורת כלב = the head of the form of a dog.

[35]23: **Benaka.** P, 4vb: Beuneka; H: כנכה = Kanakah. → Pietro d'Abano: "Bemeka."

[36]24: **With parts of her pudenda.** P, 4vb: ensamble le cul et le con; H: עם פחדיה = with her thighs.

[37]**24: And the hem ⟨of her robe⟩.** P, : et ses orliaus; H: ושוליה = and the hem ⟨of her robe⟩.

[38]**25: The sea fish.** P, 4vb: le poisson de la mer; H: דגים = Pisces.

[39]**26: Her clothes.** P, 5ra: ses dras; H: בבגדים = in clothes.

[40]**26: Certain *sclavina* or *sagum* or *cilicium*.** P, : esclavine; H: אדרת = cloak.

[41]**26: Horse.** P, 5ra: jument; H: סוסיה = mare.

[42]**27: Place of the pudenda.** P, 5ra: les ourchons; H: שולי = the hem.

[43]**28: Terafim.** P, 5ra: terafim; H: תרפים = terafim.

[44]**28: Praying to God seeking pardon.** P, 5ra: et crie merci a Dieu; H: והוא צועק אל השם = and he is shouting at the Lord.

[45]**29: Indians.** P, 5ra: les homes d'Inde; H: חכמי הודו = the scholars of India.

[46]**29: Reddish man.** P, 5ra: home rous = reddish man; H: אדם צהוב = yellow man.

[47]**29: Obstinate and of a bad temper.** P, 5ra: alant en durece; H: הולך בקרי = defiant.

[48]**29: On his hand or arm.** P, 5ra: en sa mein; H: בידו = on his hand.

[49]**31: Tends to look or looks.** P, 5rb: il regardera; H: מביט = looks.

[50]**31: Talkative beyond measure or excessively.** P, 5rb: et parlere plus que droit; H: וידבר יותר מדי = he will be garrulous.

[51]**32: Stars or planets.** P, 5rb: estoiles; H: כוכבים = stars.

[52]**32: Bad roughness of the skin.** P, : rongne male; H: שחין רע = bad boils.

[53]**33: Reddish = rufus.** P, 5rb: rous = reddish; H: צהוב = yellow.

[54]33: **With slight or little flesh.** P, 5rb: petit de charneure; H: מעט בשר = little flesh.

[55]34: **Temperate in its mixture.** P, 5va: atrempé; H: ממוסך = tempered.

[56]34: **Quick or ready.** P, 5va: se hastera; H: ממהר = quick.

[57]34: **Prudent not to be in a commotion.** P, 5va: il ne sera mie gardant de maltalant; H: אינו נוטר = not vindictive.

[58]34: **High-minded or magnanimous.** P, 5va: haut de cuer; H: גבה לב = proud.

[59]35: **Red and saffron.** P, 5va: rous et jerres safrenas; in margin: id est, color croceus; H: צהוב מכורכם = bright yellow.

[60]35: **Isolated from human beings** = **solitarius ab hominibus.** P, 5va: seus d'enfans d'ome; in margin: id est solitarius; H: משתומם מבני אדם = wary of human beings.

[61]37: **Epilepsy.** P, 5ra: la maladie de quoi on chiet en desoute de quoi en ne se prent garde; H: החולי שנופל פתאום ולא ירגיש = the disease that strikes unexpectedly and without being felt. → This gloss explains by means of one word ("epilepsy") Ibn Ezra's long description of the disease ("the disease that strikes unexpectedly and without being felt").

[62]37: **Or morphea with spots of the face.** P, 5va: et les taches qui sont en semblance de plaies; H: והבהרות שהן כדמות פצעים = and bright spots that resemble sores.

[63]38: **According to the wisdom.** P, 5va: selonc le sens; H: על דעת = according to the opinion.

[64]38: **Disease** = **egritudo.** P, 5ra: maladie = disease; H: כאב = pain.

[65]38: **Gives.** P, 5va: done; H: om.

[66]38: **Genitals.** P, 5va: es menbres de generacion; H: הפחדים = the thighs.

[67]39: **Princes.** P, 5vb: reis; H: מלכי = kings.

[68]**39: Those who travel to foreign places.** P, 5vb: ceus qui vont par chemins; H: ההולכים בדרכים = those who walk in the roads.

[69]**40: The dejection of Saturn at ⟨Aries⟩ 21°.** P, 5b: et la honte de Saturne en 21 gres; H: וקלון שבתאי בכ״א מעלות = the shame of Saturn at ⟨Aries⟩ 21°. → This sentence is missing in all the Latin manuscripts.

[70]**40: Hate.** P, 5vb: la haine; H: שנאה = hate.

[71]**40: Depression or humiliation.** P, 5vb: la baisseté; H: שפלות = the baseness. → Pietro d'Abano: "oppositum augis" = "opposite the apogee". Cf. below § 2.3:35.

[72]**40: Which is the year 4908 from the creation of Adam.** P, 5vb: que c'est l'ennee de .4908. de creement d'Adam; H: שהוא שנת תת״קח = which is the year ⟨4⟩908. → Pietro d'Abano: "tempore moderno quod est a creatione Ade .4908. anni."

[73]**42: Others of.** P, 5vb: le plus; H: רובי = most of.

[74]**42: Venus.** P: 5rb: a Venus; H: לצדק = to Jupiter. → Pietro d'Abano: "Iovis." But MS Paris, BnF, héb. 1056 reads לנגה = to Venus.

[75]**43: The terms.** P, 5vb: les terms; H: הגבולים = the terms. → Meaning, astrological planetary terms.

[76]**43: According to the wisdom of the Egyptians and Babylonians.** P, 5vb: selonc le sens as Egypciens as Babiloniens; H: על דעת חכמי מצרים והבבליים = according to the opinion of the scholars of Egypt and the Babylonians.

[77]**43: And in Ptolemy's opinion: first, Jupiter 6°, second, Venus 8°, third, Mercury 7°, fourth, Mars 5°, fifth, Saturn 4°.** P, 6ra: Et selonc le sens Bertelmieu a Jupiter 6 a a l'acommensal, et le secont a venus 8, et le tiers a Mercurre 7 et le queart a Mars 5 et le quint a Saturne; H: ועל דעת בטלמיוס לצדק שש בתחלה, והשני לנוגה שמנה, והשלישי לכוכב חמה שבע, והרביעי למאדים חמש, והחמישי לשבתאי ארבע.

[78]**44: The first.** P, 6ra: la premiere; H: תחלת = the beginning.

[79]**45:** *Duodenaria.* P, 6ra: douzeines; H: שנים העשר = the twelfths.

[80]46: **Then.** P, 6ra: mes; H: רק = but.

[81]46: **Enoch, who is Hermes.** P, 6ra: Enoch; H: חנוך = Enoch.

[82]46: **Subsequent or second.** P, 6rb: secont,; H: שני = second.

[83]47: **Finally.** P, 6rb: et puis; H: om.

[84]49: **Degrees of the stars pertaining to a pit.** P, 6va: les puisetes des estoiles = the pits of the stars; H: בורות הכוכבים = the pits of the stars.

[85]50: **Fortune.** P, 4ra: grace; H: חן = grace.

[86]51: **Largest.** P, 6rb: grans; H: גדולים = large.

§ 2.2

[1]2: **Fixed.** P, 6br: il est sur une voie; H: והוא עומד על דרך אחת = it remains in the same pattern. → Pietro d'Abano: "fixus."

[2]3: **Smaller or diminished.** P, 6br: amermans; H: חסרים = lacking.

[3]3: **Oblique.** P, 4ra: il est tort; H: מעוות = crooked.

[4]4: **Good or benevolent.** P, 6va: bons; H: טובים = good.

[5]4: **Fertility and abundance.** P, 6va: fructisement et acroisement; H: פריה ורביה = fertilization and increase. → Hebrew idiom meaning procreation.

[6]6: **Storms.** P, 5va: tormente; H: רעם = thunder.

[7]7: **Is northern.** P, 6va: vers senestre; H: בפאת שמאלית = on the left side. → Meaning, on the northern side.

[8]7: **Southern.** P, 6va: devers destre; H: בפאה ימנית = on the right corner. → Meaning, on the southern side.

[9]10: **Nature or mixture.** P, 6va: nature; H: תולדת = nature.

[10]**10: The straighter or more well-disposed.** P, 6va: le plus droit; H: המיושר = straightened out.

[11]**12: Split hooves.** P, 6vb: il a l'ongle fendu; H: מפריס = has hooves.

[12]**12: Of ⟨those⟩ born of the earth or of plants.** P, 6vb: des choses qui germinent; H: ממיני הצמחים = of the plant species.

[13]**12: Tall.** P, 6vb: haus; H: גבוהים = tall.

[14]**12: There is value or use.** P, 6vb: il a vaillanche; H: יש תועלת = is useful.

[15]**13: Climates.** P, vb: des climas; H: גבולים = terms, territories. → Meaning, climates. See above, note on § 2.1:17, s.v., "climate".

[16]**13: And I believe that it is the country around Damatia.** P, 6vb, adds in margin: Je croi que se soit le païs Damiete.

[17]**13: Egypt.** P, 6vb: *Miseraim*; H: מצרים. → Transliterated as *Miṣerayim*, meaning Egypt.

[18]**14: Cultivated or plowed.** P, 6vb: que erent en li; H: שיחרשו בה = plowed.

[19]**14: Tree bearing fruit.** P, 6vb: bourjon; H: ציץ = flower.

[20]**14: Mortar.** P, 6vb: mortier; H: טיט = mud.

[21]**14: In which plants can grow.** P: om.; H: שיצמח בו צמח = in which plants can grow.

[22]**17: A mighty one.** P, 7ra: un fort; H: הגבור = the hero.

[23]**17: Spear.** P, 7ra: glaive; H: חרב = sword.

[24]**19: Tail.** P, 11va: la keue; H: אלית = the fat tail. → Meaning, the fat tail of the lamb.

[25]**21: A bull or an ox.** P, 7rb: buef; H: שור = bull.

NOTES TO LIBER ABRAHE AVENERRE INTRODUCTORIUS 381

[26]21: **He eats a lot, or is gluttonous or a glutton.** P, 7rb: mengierres; H: אכלן = a glutton.

[27]21: **He cultivates lands.** P, 7ra: il eige terres = he cultivates lands; H: בונה ארצות = he builds countries.

[28]22: **And right hind leg.** P: om.; H: ורגלו הימנית.

[29]23: **The head of.** P, 7rb: a teste; H: ראש = the head of.

[30]23: **Ram.** P, 7rb: un mouton; H: כבש = lamb.

[31]24: **And his mind is not at ease and all his thoughts are evil.** P: om.; H: ואין דעתו מיושבת עליו וכל מחשבותיו לרע. → Pietro d'Abano: om.

[32]24: **Piece of cloth.** P, 7va: le drap; H: סמיכה = a blanket.

[33]24: **And a little calf.** P: om.; H: ועגל קטן.

[34]25: **According to.** P, 7ra: selonc le sens; H: על דעת = according to the opinion.

[35]25: **And his horn.** P: om.; H: וקרנו.

[36]26: **His speech intermixed, vague or disconnected.** P, 7va: et il ara entremellemens en ses paroles; H: ויש בלבול בדבריו = there is confusion in his speech.

[37]27: **Pleiades.** P, 7va, *kima*; H: כימה = *kimah*.

[38]28: **The penis or the shameful ⟨member⟩.** P, 7vb: son mallin; H: על זכורו = on his penis.

[39]28: **Pleasing and generous.** P, 7vb: volentis de cuer; H: נדיב לב = generous.

[40]29: **Veins or nerves.** P, 7vb: ses vaines; H: בעורקיו = their blood vessels.

[41]31: **An eunuch, without a knife but by nature.** P, 7vb: escoulliés sans fer et naturelment; H: סריס חמה = a Talmudic term denoting a person born a eunuch.

[42]32: **Of the parts of the body.** P, 7vb: en sa partie du cors a l'ome; H: בחלקו מגוף האדם = in its portion of the body of a man.

[43]32: **Abscesses and spasms.** P, 8rb: la maladie des gourmons et le crampisement; H : חולי החזירים ועוות = mumps and a twist.

[44]33: **And according to the wisdom of the Egyptians.** P, 8ra: Et sur le sens as mestres d'Egypte; H: ועל דעת חכמי מצרים = and in the opinion of the scholars of Egypt.

[45]33: **Disease.** P, 8ra: la maladie = the disease; H: כאב = the pain.

[46]34: **Middle-class people.** P, 8ra: les moiens; H: האמצעיים. → Pietro d'Abano: "mediocres."

[47]34: **Those who are immoderate and lust for sexual intercourse.** P, 8ra: et tous les desirrans acouchement; H: וכל המתאוים למשגל = and all those who lust for sexual intercourse.

[48]34: **Dancing and leaping.** P, 8ra: a treper; H: לרקוד = dancing.

[49]35: **At ⟨Taurus⟩ 3°.** P, 8ra: ou gré tiers; H: במעלה העשירית ממנו = at its tenth degree.

[50]35: **Odium eiusdem.** P, 8ra: meson de la haine; H: בית שנאתו = house of its hate. → Pietro d'Abano: "et domus occasus illius."

[51]37: **Venus.** P, 8ra: Venus; H: כוכב חמה = Mercury.

[52]37: **Indians.** P, 8rb: sages d'Inde; H: חכמי הודו = scholars of India.

[53]38: **Terms.** → See above, note on § 2.1:43, s.v. "terms".

[54]38: **According to the Egyptians and the scholars of the stars.** P, 8rb: selonc le sens as sages d'Egypte et tous les sages des signes; H: על דעת חכמי מצרים וכל חכמי המזלות = in the opinion of the Egyptian scholars and all the scholars of the signs.

[55]38: **Then Saturn 6°; finally Mars 2°.** P, 84b: et a Saturne .6; H: ולמאדים שתים, ולשבתאי שש = Mars 2°; Saturn 6°.

[56]**41: Then six bright ⟨degrees⟩.** P, 8va: .6. clers; H: שלש מאירות = three bright ⟨degrees⟩.

[57]**45: Fixed stars.** P, 1va: les estoiles hautes; H: הכוכבים העליונים = the upper stars. → Bate's divergent translation glosses on Ibn Ezra's vague expression "the upper stars". See above § 3:1, s.v., "fixed stars".

[58]**45: Which is Perseus.** → See above note on § 1.5:12, s.v. "Perseus".

[59]**46: Northern.** P, 8va: senestre; H: שמאלי = left. → Meaning, northern.

[60]**47: Significator of life.** P, 8va: le seigneur de poesté de la vie = the lord of the dominion over live; H: בעל ממשלת החיים = the lord of the dominion over life. → Bate's divergent translation is in fact a gloss explaining the main function of what Ibn Ezra calls "the lord of the dominion over life".

[61]**49: 70½°.** P, 7ra: .70. grés et demi; H: ארבעים מעלות וחצי = 40½°.

§ 2.3

[1]**3: And in all climates its ascensions are crooked.** P: om.; H: ובכל הגבולים הוא מעוות במצעדיו. → Also Pietro d'Abano: om.

[2]**4: Equal nature.** P, 8vb: nature droite = straight nature; H: תולדת ישרה = straight nature. → Pietro d'Abano: "naturam erectam".

[3]**4: Increases in number.** P, 8vb: acroit en nombre = increases in number; H: המרבה = increases.

[4]**4: Its complexion is mixed.** P, 8vb: mellee; H: ממוסך = tempered.

[5]**6: Produces storms.** P, 8va: fait tormenter; H: מרעיש = makes noise. → See above, note on § 2.2:6, s.v. "storms".

[6]**6: Whirlwinds.** → See above, note on § 2.1:8, s.v. "whirlwind".

[7]**9: Its beginning.** P, 9ra: son commençal = its beginning; H: תולדתו = its nature. → Pietro d'Abano: "eius quippe initium".

[8]10: **Contains or represents.** P, 9ra: se tome a; H: מתהפך = turns into.

[9]13: **Greater India.** P, 9ra: Inde la Grant = Greater India; H: ואדרביגאן הגדולה = Greater Azerbaijan.

[10]13: **Egypt.** → Cf. above, § 2.2:13.

[11]14: **And steep.** P: om.; H: ותלול = and steep.

[12]14: **Places where birds are hunted.** P, 9ra: lieu la ou on prent les oisiaus = places where birds are hunted; H: מקומות ציידי העוף = places of hunters of birds.

[13]19: **According to.** P, 9rb: selonc le sens; H: על דעת = according to the opinion of.

[14]19: **That is, Orion.** in margin of P, 9rb: Orion; → see above, note on § 1.4:3, s.v. "Orion".

[15]20: **On a tree.** P: om.; H: על אילן = on a tree. → Pietro d'Abano: om.

[16]21: **According to the Indians.** P, 7ra: Et dient les sages d'Inde; H: ויאמרו חכמי הודו = and the scholars of India said.

[17]21: **Ethiopian or Moor.** P, 9rb: .l. Meur; H: כושי = Ethiopian. → Pietro d'Abano: "Maurus."

[18]21: **A weapon or military device.** P, 9va: armure; H: נשק = a weapon.

[19]21: **Where trees and plants are planted.** P, 9va: ou il a entes et arbres; H: שיש בו ציצים ואילנים = where there are flowers and trees.

[20]21: **A balance or the pans of a balance.** P, 9ra: balances; H: אבני מאזנים = balance weights.

[21]21: **And he picks flowers from the garden.** P: om.; H: ויקח הציצים מן הגן = and he picks flowers from the garden.

[22]22: **According to Ptolemy.** P, 9ra: selonc le sens Bertelmieu; H: על דעת בטלמיוס = according to the opinion of Ptolemy.

NOTES TO *LIBER ABRAHE AVENERRE INTRODUCTORIUS* 385

[23]22: **The Mighty One.** P, 9ra: fort; H: הגבור = the hero.

[24]22: **That is Orion.** in margin of P, 9va: Orion; → See above, note on § 1.4:3, s.v. "Orion".

[25]22: **Tail.** P, 11va: la keue; H: אלית = the fat tail. → Meaning, the fat tail of the lamb.

[26]23: **A girl or a virgin.** P, 9va: la pucele; H: בתולה = a virgin.

[27]24: **Pendant of gold or silver.** P, 9vb: paremens d'or; H: חֲלִי כֶתֶם = pendant of gold.

[28]25: **Genitals.** P, 9vb: mallin = penis; H: פחדיו = thighs.

[29]25: **Tail.** P, 11va: la keue; H: אלית = the fat tail. → Meaning, the fat tail of the lamb.

[30]25: **Of the Ship.** P, 9vb: la nef; H: הספינה = the ship.

[31]26: **Sons of men.** P, 9vb: d'enfans d'ome = of the sons of a man; H: מבני אדם = of the sons of a man. → Hebrew idiom for "human beings."

[32]26: **Shape.** P, 9vb: faiture = shape; H: תואר = appearance.

[33]26: **Pleasant speech.** P: om.; H: מדברו נאוה = pleasant speech.

[34]26: **Acceptable.** P, 9vb: volentif; H: נדיב הנפש = generous.

[35]26: **Jester.** P, 9vb: menestrel en son uraigne; H: מהיר במלאכתו = quick in his work.

[36]26: **Arithmeticians.** P, 9vb: seigneurs de comte; H: בעלי חשבון = experts in calculation.

[37]26: **Astrologers.** P, 9vb: astronomiens; H: בעלי מזלות = experts in the signs.

[38]27: **Handsome and pleasing.** P, 10ra: bel; H: נאה = handsome.

386　　　　　　　　　　　　PART TWO

[39]28: **Prudent and learned.** P, 10ra: home de chasti = a person of education; H: איש מוסר = a moral person.

[40]28: **Pleasing.** P, 7ra: volentis; H: נדיב = generous.

[41]29: **A person breathing with difficulty.** P, 10ra: home souspirant; H: איש מתנפח = a person who becomes swollen. → Meaning, a person who becomes haughty.

[42]29: **Adulterer or fornicator.** P, 10ra: houlier; H: זונה = promiscuous.

[43]29: **Saying frivolous statements.** P, 10ra: il parlera paroles qui ne seront mie rainables; H: ידבר דברים שלא כהוגן = speaks indecently.

[44]30: **Will have healthy eyes.** P, 10ra: seront ses ieus enterins = will have healthy eyes; H: לא יהיו עיניו שלמות = will not have healthy eyes.

[45]31: **And shoulders.** P, 10ra: et ses espaules; H: והכתפים = and shoulders.

[46]32: **Weakening.** P, 10ra: qui avient; H: שיקרה = which happens.

[47]33: **According to.** P, 10ra: selonc = according to; H: ועל דעת = according to the opinion.

[48]33: **Disease.** P, 10rb: la maladie = the disease; H: כאב = the pain.

[49]33: **In the hips or lower abdomen.** P, 10rb: es jambes; H: השוקים = the shanks.

[50]34: **Among the sons of man.** P, 10rb: d'enfans d'ome = of the sons of a man; H: מבני אדם = of the sons of a man. → Hebrew idiom for "human beings."

[51]34: **Those skilled in magic.** P, 10rb: les seigneurs de *terafim*; H: בעלי התרפים = masters of *terafim*.

[52]34: **Noblemen and vigorous people, sorcerers and those skilled in magic; any ingenious craftsmanship.** P, 10rb: les rois, les grans, et les fors, et les sorciers, et les seigneurs de terafim, et les figures et les cleufichemens; H: המלכים והגדולים, והגבורים, והבדים, והמכשפים, ובעלי התרפים והצורות

והפתוחים = kings and grandees are in its portion, and mighty heroes, fabulists, sorcerers, masters of terafim, images, engravings.

[53]35: **Honor or exaltation.** → See above, note on § 1.11:1, s.v. "honor or exaltation".

[54]35: **Place of the apogee.** P, 10rb: le lieu de l'auge; H: מקום גבהות = the place of height. → Meaning, apogee.

[55]35: **Depression or opposite of the apogee.** P, 10rb: le lieu de la basseté; H: מקום שפלות = place of lowness. → Meaning, perigee. Cf. above § 2.1:40

[56]38: **Terms.** → See above, note on § 2.1:43, s.v. "terms".

[57]39: **Power of the novenariae.** P, 10va: la force des 9mes; H התשיעית.

[58]40: *Duodenariae.* P, 10va: la force des 12mes; H הכח השנים עשר = the power of the twelfths.

[59]41: **From the beginning of the sign to the end of seven degrees, ⟨the degrees are⟩ bright; then ⟨come⟩ three mixed ⟨degrees⟩, then five empty ⟨degrees⟩, then six bright ⟨degrees⟩, then six mixed ⟨degrees⟩.** P: om.; H: מתחלת המזל עד סוף שבע מעלות, מאירות, ואחריהן שלש מתערבות, ואחריהן חמש אין בהם כלום, ואחריהן שש מאירות, ואחריהן שש מתערבות. → Pietro d'Abano: "Et ab initio signi usque ad ternium .7. gradus sunt lucidi, .3. mixti, .5. lucidi, .3. vacui, .6. lucidi et .6. mixti." The omission of this sentence demonstrates that while Bate followed Hagin, Pietro d'Abano followed an alternative Hebrew manuscript.

[60]43: **Degrees of the stars pertaining to a pit.** → See above, note on § 2.1:49, s.v., "degrees of the stars pertaining to a pit".

[61]45: **15°.** P, 10vb: 15. degrés; H: בחמש מעלות = at five degrees.

[62]48: **The big star ⟨called⟩** *al-'ayyūq* **is at ⟨longitude Gemini⟩ 11°, northern ⟨ecliptical⟩ latitude 22½°; it is of the first honor and a mixture of Saturn and Jupiter.** P: om.; H: ושם הכוכב הגדול הנקרא אל עיוק במעלת אחת עשרה, ורחבו שמאלי שתים ועשרים מעלות וחצי, והוא מהכבוד הראשון, ממסך שבתאי וצדק. → Pietro d'Abano: om.

[63]52: **The dog called *al-shiʿrā al-ʿabūr* is there.** P: om.; H: ושם הכלב הנקרא אלשער אלעבור. → Pietro d'Abano: om.

[64]53: **The Mighty One.** P, 9ra: fort; H: הגבור = the hero.

[65]53: **That is Orion.** → see above, note on §1.4:3, s.v. "Orion" et passim.

§2.4

[1]1: **The sign is of watery nature.** P, 11ra: des signes de l'iaue; H: ממזלות המים = of the signs of water.

[2]2: **One of the earthy signs.** P, 11ra: des signes de la terre; H: ממזלות הקיץ = one of the signs of summer. → Here Bate follows Hagin, and what they write contradicts the previous sentence, where it is stated that Cancer is of watery nature. However, Pietro d'Abano translates: "et est de signis estatis."

[3]3: **Equal.** P, 11ra: droites; H: ישרות = straight.

[4]4: **Will be multiplied and will grow.** P, 11ra: qui fructefieront et qui croistront; H: שירבו ויפרו = will be multiplied and will bear fruit. → Hebraism for procreation.

[5]6: **What is in its portion and is northern.** P, 11rb: et quant il est a senestre; H: ובהיותו שמאלי = when it is left. → Meaning, when it is northern.

[6]6: **What is.** P, 11rb: et quant is est; H: ובהיותו = and when it is.

[7]8: **Angle.** P, 11rb: l'angle; H: הפאה = the corner.

[8]9: **Equal to a slight extent or somewhat balanced.** P, 11rb: en un petit de droiture; H: במעט יושר = to a slight extent of straightness. → Meaning, somewhat balanced.

[9]10: **The appearance of the color.** P, 11rb: la vision des couleurs; H: מראה העינים = the appearance of the colors. → Hebraism meaning "color."

[10]10: **Of ashes or dust.** P, 11rb: de la poudre; H: עפר = dust.

[11]13: **Armenia.** P, 11rb: Ermenie; H: ארמיניא הקטנה = Lesser Armenia.

[12]13: **Balkh or Ballac.** P, 11va: Ballac; H: בלך = Balkh.

[13]14: **Swamps.** P, 11va: les mares; H: האגמים = the lakes.

[14]17: **Singing or playing music.** P, 11va: chante; H: מזמרת = sings.

[15]18: **With him adornments made of gold or silver.** P, 11va: et avec li parement d'or ou d'argent; H: ועמו חלי = with him a golden pendant.

[16]18: **Branches of aromatic plants.** P, 11vb: verges de pimens; H: קנה בשם = cane of perfume.

[17]19: **The image.** P, 11vb: les faces; H: פני = the face of.

[18]19: **Tail.** P, 11va: la keue; H: אלית = the fat tail. → Meaning, the fat tail of the lamb.

[19]20: **Young girl.** P, 11vb: jone pucele; H: נערה בתולה = young virgin.

[20]21: **Indians.** P, 5ra: les homes d'Inde; H: חכמי הודו = the scholars of India.

[21]21: **Young girl or maiden.** P, 11vb: meschine; H: נערה = maiden.

[22]21: **Myrtle.** P, 11vb: *hezasz*; H: הדס = myrtle. → In the French, *hezasz* is a transliteration of הדס, the Hebrew word for myrtle.

[23]23: **The second twin.** P, 12ra: le jumel le deerrein = the rear part of the twins; H: הכלב המאוחר = the rear part of the dog.

[24]24: **Rings, ornaments and necklaces.** P, 12ra: aniaus; H: טבעות = rings.

[25]24: **For women.** P, 12ra: a ses fames; H: לנשיו = for his women.

[26]25: **That is, Hydra.** → See above, note on § I.4:9, s.v. "Hydra".

[27]26: **Loving the creatures or loving being with human beings.** P, 12ra: amant les creatures; H: אוהב את הבריות = loving the creatures.

[28]26: **Concerning harsh matters.** P, 12ra: sur choses dures; H: כי יורה על דברים קשים = because it indicates harsh matters.

[29]27: **Mind or intellect.** P, 12rb: s'arme; H: נפשו = his soul.

[30]27: **Prudent or clever.** P, 12rb: sachans et sires d'engins; H: בעל מרמות = a schemer.

[31]28: **Beardless.** P, 12rb: vuit de barbe = beardless; H: זלדקן = with a thin beard (Sanhedrin 100b).

[32]28: **Human beings or creatures.** P, 12ra: creatures; H: בריות = creatures.

[33]32: **Defects in the eyes.** P, 12rb: pesantumes d'ieus; H: כבדות בעינים = heaviness in the eyes.

[34]32: **22nd.** P: om.; H: שתים ועשרים = 22.

[35]32: **Defects.** P, 12va: mehaing; H: מום = deformity.

[36]32: **Marks or spots on the face.** P, 12va: le pointelement des faces; H: נקודות בפנים = points in the face.

[37]33: **Peasants or rustics.** P, 12va: gens de la terre = people of the earth; H: עמי הארץ = people of the earth. → This is a Hebrew idiom for "commoners."

[38]33: **Sailors.** P: om.; H: המלחים = the sailors.

[39]34: **According to the wisdom of Hermes.** P, 12va: selonc le sens Enoch; H: על דעת חנוך = according to the opinion of Enoch.

[40]34: **Sign of the age or of the world.** P, 12va: le signe du siecle; H: מזל העולם = sign of the world. → The Hebrew עולם has two basic meanings: one, biblical, is temporal and means "eternity;" the other, post-biblical, is spatial, and means "world." From the present locus, we learn that Hagin le Juif, in his translation of this word, transferred only the biblical temporal meaning, "siecle", which Bate rendered as "seculum." But Bate knew that Ibn Ezra's עולם, in this and other loci, has predominantly a spatial meaning. Therefore, sensing that Hagin le Juif's translation is incomplete, Bate offered

[41]35: **According to the Egyptians.** P, 12va: selonc de sens des sages d'Egypte; H: על דעת חכמי מצרים = according to the opinion of the scholars of Egypt.

[42]35: **Disease = egritudo.** P, 12va: maladie = disease; H: כאב = pain.

[43]36: **Fall or shame.** P, 12va: la honte; H: קלון = shame. → Meaning, dejection, i.e., the opposite of the house of exaltation.

[44]38: **According to the Indians.** P, 12va: selonc le sens as sages d'Inde; H: על דעת חכמי הודו = according to the opinion of the scholars of India.

[45]39: **Terms.** → See above, note on § 2.1:43, s.v. "terms".

[46]39: **According to the Egyptians.** P, 12va: selonc le sens as Egypciens; H: לדעת חכמי המצריים = according to the opinion of the Egyptian scholars.

[47]39: **According to Ptolemy: Mars 3°, Jupiter 7°, Mercury 7°, Saturn 6°, Venus 7°.** P: om.; H: ועל דעת בטלמיוס למאדים שש, ולצדק שש, ולכוכב חמה ולנגה שבע, ולשבתאי ארבע. = and according to the opinion of Ptolemy: Mars 6°, Jupiter 6°, Mercury and Venus 7°, and Saturn 4°.

[48]42: **Dark or tenebrous.** P, 13ra: oscurs; H: חשוכות = dark.

[49]42: **Then four bright ⟨degrees⟩, and finally two dark ⟨degrees⟩.** P: om.; H: ואחר כן שמונה מאירות, ואחר כן שתים חשוכות = then eight bright ⟨degrees⟩, and finally two dark ⟨degrees⟩.

[50]43: **Then ⟨come⟩ .6. feminine, next .2. masculine.** P, 13ra: et aprés .6. femeles, et puis .2. malles; H: om.

[51]46: **Upper.** P, 13ra: souvreines; H: עליונים = upper.

[52]47: **At this time.** P, 13ra: ou tans d'orendroit; H: בזמן הזה = at this time.

[53]48: **Of the nature of Mars only.** P, 13rb: de la nature de Mars par li; H: ממסך צדק וכוכב חמה = a mixture of Jupiter and Mercury.

[54]49: **The end of head of the ⟨second⟩ Twin is there, too, with the nature of Mars alone.** P: om.; H: גם שם סוף ראש התאום בתולדת מאדים לבדו. → Pietro d'Abano: om.

[55]51: **Dark.** P: om.; H: חשוכים = dark.

[56]51: **Very close.** P, 13rb: bien pres; H: סמוכים = near.

[57]51: **22° 2′.** P, 13rb: .22. grés et .2. menus; H: שתים ועשרים מעלות ועשרים חלקים = 22° 20′.

[58]52: **26′.** P, 13rb: .6. menus; H: ששה הלקים = 6′.

§ 2.5

[1]1: **Diurnal.** P, 13rb: des signes du jor; H: ממזלות היום = of the signs of the day.

[2]4: **Very corrupting and destructive.** P, 13ra: desibant assés; H: משחית הרבה = very destructive.

[3]5: **What is.** P, 13va: et quant il est; H: בהיותו = when it is.

[4]8: **Of the humors.** P, 13va: et des humeurs; H: om.

[5]8: **Red.** P, 13va: le rous tournant a rouge; H: הצהוב = yellow. → Although צהוב is usually taken to be the color of gold, its meaning is sometimes imprecise.

[6]9: **Hyenas.** P: om.; H: הצבועים = hyenas.

[7]10: **Precious.** P, 13va: chieres; H: יקרות = precious.

[8]10: **Adamas.** P, 13vb: *alaas*; H: אלמאס = *al-mās* [diamond]. → Here H, and F are transliterating الماس, meaning diamond. But L translates "adamas," a native Latin word for diamond.

[9]11: **Of the regions.** P, 13vb: des regions; H: מן הגבולים = of the territories, terms.

NOTES TO *LIBER ABRAHE AVENERRE INTRODUCTORIUS*   393

[10]11: **The habitable.** P, 13vb: l'abitable; H: הישוב = the settlement. → Meaning, ecumene.

[11]12: **Houses or palaces.** P, 13vb: les manoirs; H: ארמוני = the palaces.

[12]12: **Exposed to the air and whose air is open.** P, 13vb: que son air est ouvert; H: שאוירו פתוח = whose air is open.

[13]15: **A bear.** P: om., H: דוב = a bear.

[14]15: **Oarsmen.** P, 13vb: remeurs; H: מלחיה = its sailors.

[15]16: *Raihena.* P, 13vb: raihema; H: רחמה = *raḥamah*.

[16]16: **Desired clothes.** P, 13vb: vestures convoitiés = desired clothes; H: מלבושים נחמדים = fine clothes.

[17]16: **Marked with spots and unclean.** P, 13vb: soulliés; H: מטונפים = soiled.

[18]17: **Head.** P, 14ra: la teste; H: קדקוד = top of the head.

[19]17: **The Mighty One.** P, 9ra: fort; H: הגבור = the hero.

[20]17: **That is, Hydra.** → See above, note on § 1.4:9, s.v. "Hydra".

[21]18: **Two.** P, 14ra: 2; H: שני = two.

[22]19: **His nostrils are thin or his nose is thin.** P, 14ra: ses narines deliees; H: נחיריו דקות = his nostrils are thin.

[23]19: **And he covers himself in a covering.** P: om.; H: והוא מתכסה באדרת = wraps himself in a cloak.

[24]20: **The Mighty One.** P, 9ra: fort; H: הגבור = the hero.

[25]20: **That is, Hydra.** → See above, note on § 1.4:9, s.v. "Hydra".

[26]21: **A whip.** P: om.; H: שוט = a whip.

[27]22: **Moor or black Ethiopian.** P, 14rb: .l. Meur; H: כושי = Ethiopian.

[28]22: **Prudent.** P, 14rb: avertissant; H: נבון = clever.

[29]23: **Fighting Mighty One.** P, 14rb: fort bataillant; H: הגבור הנלחם = the fighting hero.

[30]23: **That is, Hydra.** → See above, note on § 1.4:9, s.v. "Hydra".

[31]24: **Red.** P, 14ra: vermel; H: הצהוב = yellow.

[32]24: **Sharp, incisive and penetrating.** P, 14rb: trenchant; H: חד = sharp.

[33]24: **Small and thin.** P, 14rb: menues; H: דקות = thin.

[34]24: **Learned or prudent.** → See above, note on § 2.3:28, s.v. "prudent and learned."

[35]24: **Acceptable and pleasant.** P, 14va: volentis; H: נדיב = generous.

[36]24: **Barren.** P: om.; H: עקר = barren.

[37]24: **Great in weeping or given to weeping.** P, 14va: grant de dolousement; H: רב עצבון = full of grief.

[38]24: **A wild dog.** P, 14va: *sevohacim*; (here *sevohacim* is a transliteration of צבעים, the Hebrew word for hyenas); H: הצבעים = hyenas. → Cf. below § 2.9:20.

[39]24: **Modesty and piety.** P, 14va: simpleté; H: צניעות = modesty.

[40]25: **The color of his appearance.** P, 14va: la coulour de sa vision; H: עין מראהו = the color of his appearance. → Meaning, his color.

[41]25: **A disease.** P, 14va: maladie; H: כאב = pain.

[42]25: **In the stomach.** P, 14va: ou ventre souvrein; H: בקרב העליון = in the upper stomach.

[43]25: **Princes.** P, 14va: reis; H: מלכים = kings.

[44]26: **Broad or wide.** P, 14va: large; H: רחב = broad.

[45]**26: Small.** P, 14va: menues; H: דקות = thin.

[46]**26: Diaphragm.** P, 14va: diafragma; H: עורקיו = his arteries.

[47]**27: He has white and red spots.** P, 14vb: si ara blanchece et vermelesce; H: יש בו לובן ואדמדמות = he has witnness and redness.

[48]**28: Full of blemishes or weak on account of injuries.** P, 14vb: pleins de mehains; H: מלא מומין = full of blemishes.

[49]**29: The stomach, the diaphragm, the ribs, the dorsal spine.** P, 14vb: le ventre souvrein, et le diaframe, et le dos, et les longnes, et les costes, et l'eschine; H: והקרב העליון, והעורקים, והגב, והמתנים, והצלעות, והמפרקת = the upper abdomen, the arteries, the back, the hips, the ribs, and the nape of the neck.

[50]**29: It also indicates the color of the eyes.** P: om.; H: גם יורה על מראה העינים = it also indicates the color of the eyes.

[51]**29: The stomach.** P, 14vb: ventre souverein; H: הקרב העליון = upper intestine.

[52]**31: Lords, princes.** P, 14vb: les seigneurs et les princes; H: והשרים, והנדיבים = ministers, noblemen.

[53]**31: Riches from the craft of gold, silver, precious stones, and of any costly product of crafts.** P, 14vb: et le receche de l'oevre de l'or et de l'argent et des pierres precreuses et tout mestier vaillant; H: ועושי מלאכת הזהב והכסף והאבנים היקרות, וכל אומנות מעולה = goldsmiths, silversmiths, jewelers, and practitioners of every fine craft.

[54]**32: Hate.** P, 19rb: meson de la haine; H: בית שנאת = house of hate. → Meaning, house of detriment, i.e., the opposite of the planetary house or the seventh sign from the planetary house of each planet.

[55]**32: The hate or the house of dishonor of Saturn.** P, 14vb: la meson de la haine de saturne; H: בית שנאת שבתאי = the house of Saturn's detriment. → This doublet, which appears in all the available Latin manuscripts, includes an error: the "hate" or detriment is not equivalent to the "dishonor" or dejection, and the "dishonor" or dejection of Saturn is not in Leo but in Aries.

[56]**32: Exaltation.** P, 3vb: eneur; H: כבוד = honor.

[57]**32: Fall.** P, 14vb: honte; H: קלון = dishonor. → Meaning, dejection, i.e., the opposite of the house of exaltation.

[58]**32: Apogee.** P, 14vb: l'aus; H: מקום גבהות = place of height. → Meaning, apogee.

[59]**33: By night the contrary.** P, 15ra: et de nuis jupiter et après li le soleil; H: ובלילה צדק ואחריו שמש = and Jupiter and then the Sun by night.

[60]**34: According to the Indian scholars, the first ⟨face is assigned⟩ to the Sun, the second to Jupiter, and the third to Mars.** P: om.; H: ועל דעת חכמי הודו הראשונים לשמש, השניים לצדק, השלישיים למאדים. → Pietro d'Abano: om.

[61]**35: Terms.** → See above, note on § 2.1:43, s.v. "terms".

[62]**40: What pertains to the pits of the stars.** P, 15b: la puisete des estoiles; H: בורות הכוכבים = the pits of the stars.

[63]**42: Fixed stars.** P, 1va: les estoiles hautes; H: הכוכבים העליונים = the upper stars. → Bate's divergent translation glosses on Ibn Ezra's vague expression "the upper stars". See above §3:1, s.v., "fixed stars".

[64]**42: That is, Hydra.** → See above, note on § 1.4:9, s.v. "Hydra," et passim.

§ 2.6

[1]**4: Changeable.** P, 15va: tormentant; H: מרעיד = it causes thunder.

[2]**10: A woody stem or trunk.** P, 15vb: jambe; H: שוק = trunk.

[3]**12: Of the arable lands or places.** P, 15vb: des lieus; H: מן המקומות = of the places.

[4]**12: Cultivated or sown lands.** P, 15vb: toute terre semee; H: כל ארץ זרועה = any sown land.

[5]18: **In whose head or extremity there is a crack or fissure.** P, 15vb: en son chief crenure; H: בראשה חריץ = in whose head there is a crack.

[6]19: **Table.** P, 16ra: table; H: קסת = inkwell.

[7]19: **To calculate or to perform calculations.** P, 15vb: pour faire conte; H: לעשות חשבון = to perform calculations.

[8]21: **The form or image.** P, 16rb: figure; H: הצורה = the form.

[9]24: **The sons of men.** P, 17ra: des fieus d'ome = of the sons of a man; H: מבני אדם = of the sons of a man. → Hebrew idiom for "human beings."

[10]24: **Appropriate and pleasing stature.** P, 17ra:; H: קומתו נאה = fine stature.

[11]24: **Wise and prudent.** P, 17ra: il sachant et avertissant; H: הוא יודע ומבין = he knows and understands.

[12]24: **Sterile and will not produce ⟨sons⟩.** P, 17ra: brehaing; H: עקר = sterile.

[13]24: **Learned in numbers.** P, 17ra: sachant de nombre; H: יודע חשבון = versed in mathematics.

[14]25: **His nostrils beautiful or his nose beautiful.** P, 17rb: ses narines beles; H: נחיריו יפות = his nostrils beautiful.

[15]25: **A learned person.** P, 17ra: home de chasti = a person of education; H: איש מוסר = a moral man.

[16]26: **A learned or prudent person, truthful in intention or mind.** P, 17rb: home de chasti et de sens vrai; H: איש מוסר ודעת נכונה = moral and right-thinking.

[17]29: **Actors.** P, 17rb: les seigneurs de tretout ceus qui aiment agabois; H: ובעלי כל אומנות מביאה לידי שחוק = practitioners of any craft that promotes laughter.

[18]30: **Exaltation or honor.** → See above, note on § 1.11:1, s.v. "exaltation or honor".

[19]30: **Fall.** P, 14vb: honte; H: קלון = dishonor.

[20]30: **Venus's fall at 27°.** P: om.; P¹, 27rb: et la honte Venus en .27; H: וקלון נוגה בשבע ועשרים מעלות = and the shame of Venus at 27°. → It turns out, then, that L agrees with P¹ and H but not with P. Since P¹ is later than P, this demonstrates that Bate used a lost French manuscript on which both P and P¹ were based.

[21]30: **Its apogee.** P, 17rb: le lieu de sa hautece; H: מקום גבהותו = place of its height.

[22]30: **At the present time.** P: om.; H: בזמן הזה = at the present time.

[23]31: **The opposite.** P, 17rb: et de nuis la lune et aprés li venus; H: בלילה הלבנה ואחריו נגה = and the Moon and then Venus by night.

[24]32: **Venus.** P: om.; P¹, 27rb: Venus. H: נוגה = Venus.

[25]33: **The Sun 7°, Venus 6°.** P, 17va: au soleil .7. at a venus .6.; H: לכוכב חמה שבע, ולנגה שש, ולצדק י׳, ולמאדים ה׳, ולשבתאי ב׳ = Mercury 7°, Venus 6°, Jupiter 10°, Mars 5°, and Saturn 2°.

[26]40: **Fixed stars.** P, 1va: les estoiles hautes; H: הכוכבים העליונים = the upper stars. → Bate's divergent translation glosses on Ibn Ezra's vague expression "the upper stars". See above §3:1, s.v., "fixed stars".

[27]42: **Nebulous or dark.** P, 17vb: oscures; H: חשוכים = dark.

[28]42: **The other at the same degree, but northern latitude 25½°.** P: om.; H: והאחר במעלה הנזכרות, רק רחבו שמאלית חמש ועשרים מעלות וחצי = the other at the same degree, but northern latitude 25½°.

§2.7

[1]2: **The days begin to grow shorter and the nights longer.** P, 18ra: acommencera la nuit a alonger et acourcera le jor; H: יחל הלילה להאריך ויקצר היום = .

[2]5: **Vapors or clouds.** P, 18ra: nue; H: איד = vapor.

[3]7: **Its northern part.** P, 18ra: et quant il est a senestre; H: בהיותו שמאלי = when it is left. → Meaning, when it is northern.

[4]10: **Its nature is hot and moist.** P, 18ra: et sa nature est chaude et moiste; H: ותולדתו חמה ולחה = Its nature is hot and moist.

[5]11: **Of the tastes.** P, 18ra: sa saveur; H: מטעמו = its taste.

[6]11: **Of the colors.** P, 18ra: la vision de sa couleur; H: מראה עיניו = the appearance of its color.

[7]12: **Every large bird.** P, 18ra: tout oisel grant = every large bird; H: כל עוף שראשו גדול = every bird with a large head.

[8]12: **Every large bird.** P, 18ra: tout oisel grant; H: כל עוף שראשו גדול = every bird with a large head.

[9]13: **Of the climates and regions.** P, 18rb: des climas; H: מן הגבולים = of the territories, terms. → Meaning, climates. See above, note on § 2.1:17, s.v., "climate".

[10]14: **Fairs and markets.** P, 18rb: marchiés; H: שווקים = markets.

[11]17: **Balance pan or scales.** P, 18rb: balance; H: מאזנים = balance.

[12]17: **A book of written items.** P, 18rb: le livre de *kessuvim*; H: ספרים כתובים = *sefarim ketubim*. → In the French, *kessuvim* is the transliteration of כתובים, *ketubim*, meaning written items or books. In the Hebrew *sefarim ketubim* means written books.

[13]17: **And playing music.** P: om.; H: והוא מזמר = and playing music.

[14]19: **Of the tail.** P: om.; H: זנב = tail.

[15]19: **That is, Hydra.** → See above, note on § 1.4:9, s.v. "Hydra".

[16]19: **Part.** P, 18va: une partie; H: קצה = the end.

[17]20: **Chariot or a cart.** P, 18va: une charete; H: עגלה = a cart.

[18]**20: Stick.** P, 18va: verge; H: שוט = a whip.

[19]**20: The middle of the greater bear and the middle of the dragon.** P, 18va: et le milieu de l'ours grant et le milieu du dragon; H: אמצעית התנין, ואמצעית הדוב הגדול = the middle of the dragon, and the middle of the greater bear.

[20]**22: Part.** P, 18va: une partie; H: קצה = the end.

[21]**22: Breast.** P, 18va: les fons; H: שולי = the hem of.

[22]**23: End or the extremity.** P, 18vb: emploial; H: סוף = end.

[23]**23: Head.** P, 18vb: teste; H: קדקד = top of the head.

[24]**25: Part.** P, 18vb: une partie; H: קצה = the end.

[25]**25: Part.** P, 18vb: une partie; H: קצה = the end.

[26]**25: The genitals.** P, 18vb: des ourles; H: שולי = the hem of.

[27]**26: Prudent and learned.** P, 18vb: home de savoir et de chasti = knowledgeable and learned; H: איש דעת ומוסר = knowledgeable and moral.

[28]**26: Loving the hunt or going hunting.** P, 18vb: aime a vener; H: אוהב לצוד = loves hunting.

[29]**26: Generous and pleasing.** P, 18ra: volentis de cuer; H: נדיב לב = generous.

[30]**27: Handsome.** P, 19ra: sera de bele faiture; H: יהיה יפה צורה = will have a fine figure.

[31]**28: Flanks.** P, 19ra: ses flans; H: בעורקיו = in his arteries.

[32]**30: Of one as well as of the other.** P, 19ra: *tumtum*; H: טומטום = a person of uncertain sex. → In the French, *tumtum* is a transliteration of טומטום, i.e., a person of uncertain sex

[33]**30: Hermaphrodite.** P, 19ra: *endroginos*; H: אנדרוגינוס = androginos. → Meaning, an androgyne.

NOTES TO *LIBER ABRAHE AVENERRE INTRODUCTORIUS* 401

[34]**31: The groin.** P, 19ra: pres de la laidure; H: סמוך אל הערוה = near the pudenda.

[35]**32: Retention or voiding.** P, 19ra: retienement; H: עצור = retention.

[36]**33: Merchants.** P, 19rb: les homes du marchié; H: אנשי השוק = people of the market.

[37]**33: All players on musical instruments.** P, 19rb: et tous ceus qui chantent es estrumens; H: המנגנים = musicians.

[38]**33: Traders.** P, 19rb: marcheans; H: הסוחרים = traders.

[39]**34: Honor or exaltation.** → See above, note on § 1.11:1, s.v. "honor or exaltation".

[40]**34: Fall.** P, 14vb: honte; H: קלון = dishonor.

[41]**34: Hate.** P, 19rb: meson de la haine; H: בית שנאת = house of hate. → Meaning house of detriment.

[42]**34: The apogee.** P, 19rb: l'aus; H: גבהות = height.

[43]**34: Mercury.** P, 19rb: mars; P¹, 19va: mercure; H: כוכב חמה = Mercury.

[44]**35: Disease.** P, 19rb: maladie = disease; H: כאב = pain.

[45]**36: The opposite.** P, 19rb: et en la nuit mercure et aprés li saturne; H: בלילה כוכב חמה ואחריו שבתאי = and Mercury and then Saturn by night.

[46]**38: Terms.** → See above, note on § 2.1:43, s.v. "terms".

[47]**43: 23th.** P, 19vb: 23; H: שלשים = 30.

[48]**45: Fixed stars.** P, 1va: les estoiles hautes; H: הכוכבים העליונים = the upper stars. → Bate's divergent translation glosses on Ibn Ezra's vague expression "the upper stars". See above § 3:1, s.v., "fixed stars".

[49]**46: Jupiter.** P: om.; H: צדק = Jupiter.

§2.8

[1]1: **Nocturnal.** P, 20ra: des signes de la nuit; H: ממזלות הלילה = of the nocturnal signs.

[2]2: **Wintry.** P, 20ra: des signes de l'yver; H: ממזלות החורף = One of the signs of winter.

[3]2: **Fixed or not mutable.** P, 20ra: et il est sur une voie; H: והוא עומד על דרך אחד = and it remains in the same way.

[4]4: **Every.** P: om.; H: כל = every.

[5]4: **Intemperate.** P, 20ra: qui n'est mie droite; H: איננה מיושרת = which is not straight. → Meaning, unbalanced.

[6]4: **A taste or an alteration of taste.** P, 20ra: muement de saveur; H: שנוי טעם = a change of taste.

[7]5: **Tempestuous.** P, 20ra: tormentant; H: מרעיש = causing earthquakes.

[8]6: **What is northern.** P, 20ra: et quant il est senestres; H: ובהיותו שמאלי = when it is left.

[9]6: **And what is southern.** P, 20ra: quant il est meridional; H: בהיותו דרומי = when it is southern.

[10]8: **The northern part is in its portion.** P, 20ra: et en sa partie est la senestre de septentrional; H: ובחלקו שמאל הצפון = the left ⟨side⟩ of the north is in its portion.

[11]9: **That abounds.** P, 20ra: qui enforce; H: המתגברת = that overpowers.

[12]12: **Olive groves.** P, 20ra: vergiers de poree; H: בגנות = gardens.

[13]12: **And.** P, 20rb: et; H: רק = except for.

[14]15: **Rear foot.** P, 20rb: le cul; H: אחורי = the rear.

[15]17: **Greater Bear.** P, 20va: l'ours grant; H: הדוב הקטן = the Lesser Bear.

NOTES TO *LIBER ABRAHE AVENERRE INTRODUCTORIUS* 403

[16]17: **The Balance or Pair of Scales.** P, 20va: balances; H: מאזנים = balance.

[17]19: **Has left or is leaving.** P, 20va: est issue; H: יצאה = has left.

[18]20: **Part.** P, 20ra: une partie; H: קצה = the end.

[19]20: **The genitals or the scales of Libra.** P, 20va: les coullons des balances; H: פחדי המאזנים = the thighs of Libra.

[20]21: **Head.** P, 20va: le chief; H: ראשית = beginning.

[21]21: **Head.** P, 20va: le chief; H: ראשית = beginning.

[22]23: **Head or extremity.** P, 20vb: le chief; H: ראש = head.

[23]24: **And ⟨is⟩ agile or quick in ⟨his⟩ walking.** P, 20vb: legier en son aler; H: קל במהלכו = quick in his walking.

[24]24: **⟨His⟩ shoulders broad or wide.** P, 20ra: s'espaule large; H: שכמו רחב = his shoulders broad.

[25]24: **Deformed.** P, 20ra: lais; H: מכוער = ugly.

[26]24: **He does not have a pleasant speech.** P, 20vb: n'ara pas parlure avenant; H: אין לו קול ולא דבור נאה = he does not have a pleasant voice or speech.

[27]24: **Deceitful.** P, 20ra: boissans = deceitful; H: בוגד = a traitor.

[28]24: **Accuser or detractor.** P, 20vb: encuseur; H: רכיל = scandalmonger.

[29]24: **Shrewd, and full of craftiness to plot against people.** P, 20vb: sires de chasti et plains d'enginier les gens; H: בעל מוסר ומרמה וערמה = moral, deceitful, and shrewd.

[30]25: **A prudent person.** P, 21ra: home de chasti; H: איש מוסר = moral person.

[31]25: **Full of good sense.** P, 21ra: plain de bon sens; H: איש דעת = wise.

[32]26: **On the abdomen.** P, 21ra: sur son mallin = on his penis; H: על זכורו = on his penis.

[33]27: **Frequently weeping.** P, 21ra: grant de clolousement; H: רב עצבון = very gloomy.

[34]28: **Neither of one sex nor of the other.** P, 21ra: *tumtum*; H: טומטום = a person of uncertain sex. → In the French, *tumtum* is a transliteration of טומטום, i.e., a person of uncertain sex.

[35]29: **The pudenda.** P, 21ra: des li eus de honte; H: המבושים = the pudenda.

[36]29: **The place of the anus.** P, 21ra: le lieu cuté = the hidden place; H: המקום הנסתר = the hidden place. → Bate's divergent translation glosses on Ibn Ezra's expression "the hidden place".

[37]30: **Defects, maimings or mutilations.** P, 21ra: les mehaignans; H: המומין = defects.

[38]30: **Defects.** P, 21ra: mehaing; H: מום = mutilation.

[39]30: **Fistulas.** P, 21ra: et sur mehaing qui est apelé *sereten*; in margin: id est, cancre; H: ועל המום הנקרא סרטן = the abnormality called cancer. → In the French, *sereten* is a transliteration of סרטן "sartan", the Hebrew word for cancer.

[40]32: **Cruel or fierce tempered.** P, 21rb: home felon; H: איש בליעל = wicked person.

[41]33: **Fall.** P, 14vb: honte; H: קלון = dishonor.

[42]34: **The opposite.** P, 21rb: et en la nuit mars et aprés li venus; H: ובלילה מאדים ואחריו נגה = and Mars and then Venus by night.

[43]35: **Disease.** P, 21rb: la maladie; H: כאב = the pain.

[44]35: **The upper abdomen or stomach.** P, 21va: le ventre souverein; H: הקרב העליון = the upper abdomen.

NOTES TO *LIBER ABRAHE AVENERRE INTRODUCTORIUS* 405

[45]36: **According to the Indian scholars, the first ⟨face is assigned⟩ to Mars, the second to Jupiter, and the third to the Moon.** P: om.; H: ועל דעת חכמי הודו הראשונים למאדים, והשניים לצדק, והשלישיים ללבנה = according to the Indian scholars, the first ⟨face is assigned⟩ to Mars, the second to Jupiter, and the third to the Moon.

[46]37: **Terms.** → See above, note on § 2.1:43, s.v. "terms".

[47]37: **Of the Egyptians and the scholars of the signs.** P: om.; H: המצריים וחכמי המזלות = of the Egyptians and the scholars of the signs.

[48]44: **Fixed stars.** P, lva: les estoiles hautes; H: הכוכבים העליונים = the upper stars. → Bate's divergent translation glosses on Ibn Ezra's vague expression "the upper stars". See above § 3:1, s.v., "fixed stars".

§ 2.9

[1]2: **Of two bodies or bicorporal.** P, 21vb: a .2. cors; H: יש לו שני גופות = it has two bodies.

[2]3: **In every region.** P, 22r: en toutes les regions; H: בכל הגבולין = in all the territories, terms.

[3]7: **In the north.** P, 22ra: quant il est senestre; H: בהיותו בשמאל = when it is in the left. → Meaning when it is in the north.

[4]9: **The east wind.** P, 22ra: vent de *ruahih* (a transliteration of רוח, the Hebrew word for wind); H: רוח קדים = *ruaḥ qadim*. → In the French, *ruahih* is a transliteration of רוח, the Hebrew word for wind. In the Hebrew, *ruaḥ qadim* is "wind of *qadim*," meaning east wind.

[5]10: **Its taste is bitter and pungent; it generates the yellow bile; its color is any yellow, reddish, and ochre.** P: om.; H: וטעמו מר וחריף; והוא מוליד המרה האדומה; ומראה עיניו כל צהוב ואדמדם ועין העפר.

[6]12: **Metals or minerals.** P, 22ra: metaus; H: מתכות = metals.

[7]12: ***Smaragdus.*** P, 22ra: esmeraude; H: זמרד.

[8]13: **The land of the Medes.** P, 22ra: la terre de Mazai; H: וארץ בגדאד = the land of Baghdad.

[9]13: *Asperin.* P, 22ra: *Asperin*; H: אספהן = Iṣfahān.

[10]14: **Marshy place.** P, 22ra: lieu d'aboivrement; H: מקום משקה = well-watered place.

[11]14: **And every pebble.** P, 22rb: et toute pierre soueve; H: וכל אבן חלוקה = and every pebble

[12]17: **Turned the wrong way, having his head downwards and his feet upwards.** P, 22rb: tornes, (in margin) a le chief de sous et le pies desure; H: הפוך = upside down.

[13]19: **The Little or Lesser Bear.** P, 22rb: l'ours petit; H: הדוב הקטן = the Lesser Bear.

[14]19: **A part.** P, 22rb: une partie; H: קצה = the end.

[15]19: **Thighs.** P, 22ra: le burellion; H: אלית = the fat tail.

[16]19: **Back.** P, 22ra: eschinee = back; H: מפרקת = the nape of the neck.

[17]19: **Bands or joints.** P, 22rb: les loiens; H: הקישורים = joints.

[18]20: **A wild dog or wolf.** P, 22va: *scevoa*; in margin: canis ferus; H: צבוע = hyena. → In the French, *scevoa* is a transliteration of צבוע "hyena". Cf. above § 2.5:24.

[19]20: **Half of a hare.** P: om.; P¹, 22vb: la moitie du lievre; H: חצי ארנבת = half of a hare.

[20]20: **Spider.** P, 22va: iraigne; H: סממית = lizard.

[21]21: **Preparatory ornaments.** P, 22va: paremens d'adoubemens; H: חֲלִי כֶתֶם = pendant of gold.

[22]22: **A part.** P, 22rb: une partie; H: קצה = the end.

[23]**22: A part.** P, 22rb: une partie; H: קצה = the end.

[24]**22: Left.** P: om.; H: שמאלית = left.

[25]**22: Body of the.** P, 22va: cors; H: גוף = body.

[26]**23: Wild dog.** P, 22va: *scevoa*; H: צבוע = hyena. → In the French, *scevoa* is a transliteration of צבוע "hyena". Cf. above, § 2.9:20.

[27]**23: Spider.** → See above, note on § 2.9:20, s.v. "spider".

[28]**24: Appearance or look.** P, 22va: vision; H: עין מראהו = the color of his appearance. → Meaning, his color.

[29]**24: And he is wrapped in a mantle of bark.** P, 22vb: et il se cuvre en wis qui est fait d'escorce de buche; H: והוא מתכסה בטלית עשויה מקליפת עצים = and is wrapped in a mantle made of tree bark.

[30]**25: A part.** P, 22rb: une partie; H: קצה = the end.

[31]**25: Its head.** P, 22vb: sa teste; H: קדקדו = the top of its head.

[32]**25: And the Southern Crown.** P: om.; H: והנזר הדרומי = and the Southern Crown.

[33]**26: Brilliant.** P, 22vb: et il cler; H: והוא צהוב = he is yellow.

[34]**26: His penis and testicles.** P, 22va: sen vit et si coullion; H: ופחדיו = his thighs.

[35]**26: Strong or powerful.** P, 22vb: fort; H: גבור = a hero.

[36]**26: Pleasing.** P, 22vb: volentif; H: נדיב = generous.

[37]**26: He will not hold to one way.** P, 22vb: ne se tient mie sur une voie; H: אינו עומד על דרך אחת = he does not hold to one way. → Hebrew idiom meaning "he is not stable".

[38]**26: His voice low and deep.** P, 22va: sa vois basse; H: קולו דק = his voice thin.

[39]**27: In appearance and color.** P, 23ra: et bele vision; H: ויפה מראה = good-looking.

[40]**29: Strong or powerful.** P, 23ra: fort; H: גבור = a hero.

[41]**29: Modest and pious.** P, 23ra: simple; H: עניו = modest.

[42]**29: A good counselor.** P, 23ra: conseilleur; H: יועץ = a counselor.

[43]**29: A learned or prudent man.** → See above, note on § 2.3:28, s.v. "prudent and learned".

[44]**31: The hips and the parts around them.** P, 23ra: le vit et les coullions; H: הפחדים = the thighs. → Bate's divergent translation glosses on Ibn Ezra's expression "the thighs".

[45]**31: Marks.** P, 23ra: les enseignes; H: סימנים = marks.

[46]**31: Superfluous limb or extra part.** P, 23ra: menbre surcroissant; H: אבר נוסף = extra limb.

[47]**32: Diseases produced by harmful beasts.** P, 23rb: les maladies qui vienent de par les males biches; H: התחלואים הבאים מסם החיות ומאפעה = the diseases produced by the venom of animals and snakes.

[48]**32: Defects.** P, 23ra: mehaing; H: מום = mutilation.

[49]**33: Pious.** P, 23rb: les volentis; H: נדיבים = generous.

[50]**34: Exaltation or honor.** → See above, note on § 1.11:1, s.v. "exaltation or honor".

[51]**34: Hate.** P, 19rb: meson de la haine; H: בית שנאת = house of hate. → Meaning, house of detriment.

[52]**34: Place of.** P, 23ra: le lieu; H: מקום = place.

[53]**34: Apogee.** P, 23ra: l'aus; H: גבהות = height; → Meaning, apogee.

[54]34: **Opposite of the apogee.** P, 23ra: basseté; H: שפלות = lowness; → Meaning, perigee.

[55]35: **Disease.** P, 23rb: maladie = disease; H: כאב = pain.

[56]35: **The hips.** P, 23ra: la laidure = the genitals; H: הערוה = the pudenda.

[57]36: **By night the opposite.** P, 23va: et de nuis jupiter et aprés li le soleil; H: ובלילה צדק ואחריו השמש = and Jupiter and then the Sun by night.

[58]38: **Terms.** → See above, note on § 2.1:43, s.v. "terms".

[59]45: **Fixed stars.** P, 1va: les estoiles hautes; H: הכוכבים העליונים = the upper stars. → Bate's divergent translation glosses on Ibn Ezra's vague expression "the upper stars". See above § 3:1, s.v., "fixed stars".

§ 2.10

[1]2: **Of the signs of winter.** P, 24ra: des signes des jours du froit; H: ממזלות ימי הקור = of the signs of the days of cold. → Bate's divergent translation glosses on Ibn Ezra's expression "of the signs of the days of cold".

[2]4: **In the northern part.** P, 24ra: senestre; H: שמאלי = left, meaning northern.

[3]4: **In the southern part.** P, 24ra: meridional; H: דרומי = southern.

[4]5: **Conditions or effects.** P, 24ra: ses afaires; H: עניניו = its conditions.

[5]6: **Two shapes or two forms.** P, 24ra: .2. figures; H: שתי צורות = two forms.

[6]8: ***Orobe.*** P, 24rb: le *harobe*; H: החרוב = carob. → In the French, le *harobe* is a transliteration of החרוב = carob.

[7]8: **Plants growing around marshes.** P, 24rb: ce qui est environ les mares; H: ההווה סביבות האגמים = what is around the lakes.

[8]8: **Reeds or *arundines*.** P, 24rb: rosiaus; H: הסוף = rush. → *Arundines* or *harundines* are synonyms of calami, meaning reeds.

[9]10: **Tree growing in a marsh.** P, 24rb: terre d'aboivrement; H: מקום משקה = well-watered place.

[10]10: **Seas or fishponds.** P, 24rb: les sauvoirs; H: הכיורים = basins.

[11]10: **Captives or prisoners.** P, 24rb: prisonniers; H: האסירים = the prisoners.

[12]10: **Servants or slaves.** P, 24rb: serjans; H: העבדים = the slaves.

[13]10: **Sheep or flocks.** P, 24va: l'ouvaille; H: הצאן = sheep.

[14]10: **Quarries.** P, 24va: lieu de mortier; H: שיש = which is.

[15]12: **4.** P, 23va: 4; H: ארבע עשרה = 14.

[16]13: **The image playing a musical instrument.** P, 24va: faiture organant; H: צורת אשה מנגנת = the form of a woman playing a musical instrument.

[17]14: **Moor.** P, 24va: Meur; H: כושי = Ethiopian.

[18]14: **Fat body.** P, 24va: cors corn le porc le cras; H: גוף החזיר הבר = the body of a wild boar.

[19]17: ***Sclavina*, *sagum*, and *cilicium*.** → See above, note on § 2.1:26, s.v. "*sclavina* or *sagum* or *cilicium*".

[20]18: **Part.** P, 24vb: une partie; H: קצה = the end.

[21]18: **Its head.** P, 24vb: sa tests; H: וקדקדו = and the top of its head.

[22]18: **Thighs.** P, 24vb: les ourles; H: שולי = the hem of.

[23]19: **Wooden sting.** P, 24vb: fust de l'aguilon; H: העין המרע = the fountain with polluted water.

[24]19: **Chariot or cart.** → See above, note on § 2.7:20, s.v. "chariot or cart".

[25]20: **Prepared to do.** P, 24vb: appareillié a faire; H: וידיה נכונות לעשות = her hands are ready to do.

[26]**21: Part.** P, 24vb: une partie; H: קצה = the end.

[27]**22: Shrewd and clever.** P, 25ra: sires de chasti et d'engins; H: בעל מוסר ומרמות = moral and deceitful.

[28]**22: Lying together or sexual intercourse.** P, 25ra: le gisement; H: אוהב המשגל = sexual intercourse.

[29]**23: Acceptable.** P, 25ra: volentif; H: נדיב = generous.

[30]**24: Long nose.** P, 25ra: ses narines longues; H: נחיריו ארוכים = of long nostrils.

[31]**24: Knowledgeable.** P, 25ra: home de science = man of knowledge; H: איש רעים = sociable. → Here *Reshit Ḥokhmah* has איש רעים, *'iš reʿim*, a biblical expression (Prov. 40:22) meaning "sociable." But Hagin mistook the *reš* in the second word for a *dalet*, read איש דעים, *'iš deʿim*, and consequently translated the expression as "home de science" = "man of knowledge." Bate followed suit and translated "sciens" = "knowledgeable."

[32]**25: Abdomen.** P, 25rb: mallin = penis; H: פחדיו = his thighs.

[33]**25: Sociable or loving company.** P, 25rb: amant compaignons; H: אוהב רעים = companionable.

[34]**26: The son of a spell.** P, 25ra: fieus des charroiemens = son of fornications; H: בן זנונים = son of fornication. → Bate's divergent translation glosses on Ibn Ezra's expression "son of fornication".

[35]**29: Loss of speech or dumbness.** P, 25rb: l'amuïssement; H: אלמות = dumbness.

[36]**29: Fever.** P, 25rb: la fievre; H: קרחת = baldness. → Here Hagin mistook the *reš* in קרחת for a *dalet*, read קדחת, *qadaḥat*, and consequently translated the word as "la fievre" = "fever." Bate followed suit and translated "la fievre" = "febres."

[37]**31: Exaltation.** P, 3vb: eneur; H: כבוד = honor.

[38]**31: Fall.** P, 14vb: honte; H: קלון = dishonor.

[39]**32: The opposite.** P, 25va: et de nuis la lune et aprés li venus; H: ובלילה הלבנה ואחריו נגה = the Moon and then Venus by night.

[40]**33: Disease** = egritudo. P, 25va: maladie = disease; H: כאב = pain.

[41]**33: Thighs.** P, 25ra: la laidure; H: הערוה = the pudenda. → Bate's divergent translation glosses on Ibn Ezra's expression "the pudenda".

[42]**35: Terms.** → See above, note on § 2.1:43, s.v., "terms".

[43]**35: Mars 5°, Jupiter 8°, Saturn 5°.** P, 25vb: a saturne .6., et a mars .5. et a venus .5; H: לצדק שבע, ולשבתאי שש, ולמאדים חמש = Jupiter 7°, Saturn 6°, and Mars 5°.

[44]**42: Fixed stars.** P, 1va: les estoiles hautes; H: הכוכבים העליונים = the upper stars. → Bate's divergent translation glosses on Ibn Ezra's vague expression "the upper stars". See above § 3:1, s.v., "fixed stars".

[45]**42: At the present time.** P: om.; H: בזמן הזה = at the present time.

[46]**43: The Flying Eagle.** P, 26ra: laigle; P¹, 26rb: laigle volant; H: הנשר המעופף = the flying eagle.

[47]**44: Dark stars.** P, 26ra: estoiles ennuees; H: כוכבים מעוננים = nebulous stars.

§ 2.11

[1]**1: Western.** P: om.; H: מערבי = western.

[2]**2: One of the signs of winter, and it remains in the same pattern.** P: om.; H: ממזלות הקור, עומד על דרך אחד = One of the signs of cold, and it remains in the same pattern.

[3]**3: Its hours are shorter than the equal ⟨hours⟩, and its rising times are crooked and short.** P: om.; H: ושעותיו קצרות מן הישרות, ומעוות במצעדיו ומצעדיו קצרים = Its hours are shorter than the straight ⟨hours⟩, and its ascensions are crooked and short.

[4]7: **Alone or by himself.** P, 26rb: par li; H: לבדו = alone.

[5]8: **Left or northern.** P, 26rb: senestre; H: שמאל = left.

[6]10: **Outstanding princes, namely in knowledge, or leaders of the people.** P, 26rb: les princes; H: השדים = the demons. → Here Hagin misread a *dalet* as a *rešh*, השדים "demons" with השרים "princes," and Bate followed suit after Hagin.

[7]10: **Ugly or deformed.** P, 26rb: lait; H: מכוער = ugly.

[8]12: **Flowing waters or rivers.** P, 26rb: iaues courans; H: המים הרצים = flowing waters.

[9]12: **Marshy places.** P, 26rb: et tout aboivrement; H: וכל משקה = every well-watered place.

[10]12: **Bawds or prostitutes.** P, 26rb: bouliers; H: הנואפים = adulterers.

[11]12: **Urn or vessel.** P, 26rb: vaisiau; H: כלי = vessel.

[12]16: **Moor.** P, 26rb: Meur; H: כושי = Ethiopian.

[13]19: **Piece of cloth.** P, 26va: drap; H: חריטים = purses.

[14]21: **The diver or bird.** P, 26va: l'oisel; H: העוף = the bird.

[15]22: **A liar or deceiver.** P, 26rb: tricheur; H: רמאי = a swindler.

[16]22: **Moves or turns himself.** P, 26rb: se trestorne; H: מתהפך = turns himself.

[17]23: **The Bucket or the Urn.** P, 26rb: la seille; H: דלי = bucket.

[18]26: **Sad or mourning.** P, 26vb: en dolousement; H: בעצבון = sad.

[19]29: **Sad people of full of sorrow.** P, 27ra: sire de dolousement; H: בעל עצבון = sad person.

[20]29: **Leatherworkers or those who prepare skins of animals.** P, 27ra: les taneurs de cuir; H: מעבדי העורות = tanners.

[21]29: **In its portion, of human beings, contemptible person, sad people of full of sorrow, sailors, and leatherworkers or those who prepare skins of animals.** → This complete sentence corresponds to § 2.11:30 in the Hebrew and French source texts.

[22]30: **Of the parts of the human body, in its portion are the shanks, and all the diseases affecting them, also the black bile, black jaundice, and the cutting of veins; and ⟨in a nativity whose ascendant is Aquarius⟩ from 20° to 25°, it indicates defects of the eyes.** → This complete sentence corresponds to § 2.11:29 in the Hebrew and French source texts.

[23]31: **Planet.** P, 27ra: planetes; H: כוכבים = stars.

[24]31: **Exaltation or honor.** → See above, note on § 1.11:1, s.v., "exaltation or honor".

[25]31: **Fall.** P, 14vb: honte; H: קלון = dishonor.

[26]31: **The opposite of the apogee.** P, 27ra: le lieu de la basseté; H: מקום שפלות = the place of lowness.

[27]32: **Disease.** P, 27ra: la maladie = the disease; H: כאב = the pain.

[28]32: **The genitals or the pudenda.** P, 27ra: la laidure; H: הערוה = the pudenda.

[29]33: **The opposite.** P, 27rb: et de nuis mercure et aprés li saturne; H: ובלילה כוכב חמה ואחריו שבתאי = and Mercury and then Saturn by night.

[30]35: **Terms.** → See above, note on § 2.1:43, s.v., "terms".

[31]38: **Then eight bright ⟨degrees⟩.** P: om.; H: ואחריהן שמנה מאירות = then eight bright ⟨degrees⟩.

[32]42: **Fixed stars.** P, 1va: les estoiles hautes; H: הכוכבים העליונים = the upper stars. → Bate's divergent translation glosses on Ibn Ezra's vague expression "the upper stars". See above § 3:1, s.v., "fixed stars".

§ 2.12

[1]5: **It generates.** P, 28ra: fait acroistre; H: מרבה = increases.

[2]5: **Its end or final part.** P, 28ra: sa fin; H: סופו = its end.

[3]8: **Of the north.** P, 28ra: septentrion; H: השמאל = the left.

[4]8: **The left or the north.** P, 28ra: senestre; H: שמאל = the left.

[5]12: **Climates.** → See above, note on § 2.1:17, s.v., "climate."

[6]13: **Houses of prayer or synagogues.** P, 28ra: les mesons d'amassees; H: בתי כנסיות = synagogues.

[7]19: **Part.** P, 28rb: une partie; H: קצה = the end.

[8]19: **The belly of the Second Horse.** P: om.; H: ובטן הסוס השני = the belly of the Second Horse.

[9]19: **The first part.** P, 28rb: le commencement; H: תחלת = the beginning.

[10]21: **Beautiful.** P: om.; H: יפה = beautiful.

[11]24: **Shouting or crying.** P, 28va: crie; H: צועק = shouts.

[12]24: **Robbers or thieves.** P, 28va: robeurs; H: הלסטים = thieves.

[13]26: **Straight and temperate.** P, 28va: droit; H: ממוסך = mixed.

[14]26: **His color white as well as ⟨his⟩ face.** P, 28va: et sa vision blanche et ausinc ses faces; H: ומראהו לבן = his appearance white.

[15]26: **He will be irascible, moral and deceitful, and his voice will be thin.** P: om.; H: ואין דעתו מיושבת עליו, והוא כעסן, ובעל מוסר ומרמות, וקולו דק = he will be irascible, moral and deceitful, and his voice will be thin.

[16]27: **One who is born in the first face will have a handsome body and face, his chest will be broad.** P: om.; H: והנולד בפנים הראשונים יהיה גופו נאה, וככה פניו, וחזהו רחב = One who is born in the first face will have a handsome body and face, his chest will be broad.

416 PART TWO

[17]28: **In appearance or color.** P, 28vb: de vision; H: מראה = appearance.

[18]29: **Shining or radiant.** P, 28vb: clers; H: צהוב = yellow.

[19]30: **The killer of himself or will kill himself.** P, 28vb: sera ociant soi meesmes; H: יהרוג נפשו בעצמו = will commit suicide.

[20]33: **Base and contemptible people.** P, 28vb: les despis; H: הנבזים = base people.

[21]34: **Disease.** P, 28vb: la maladie = the disease; H: כאב = the pain.

[22]34: **Intestines.** P, 29ra: coullions = the testicles; H: הפחדים = the thighs.

[23]35: **Exaltation.** P, 3vb: eneur; H: כבוד = honor.

[24]35: **The shame or fall.** P, 29ra: la honte; H: קלון = shame.

[25]35: **Its hate.** P, 29ra: la meson de sa haine; H: בית שנאתו = the house of its hate.

[26]35: **Humiliation.** P, 29ra: la basseté; H: שפלות = lowness. → Meaning perigee. Cf. above, note on § 2.1:40, s.v., "depression or humiliation".

[27]35: **Dragon or** *jawzahar*. P: om.; H: התלי = *ha-teli*. → Talmudic term for Dragon.

[28]35: **And Venus's Head of the Dragon or** *jawzahar* **at ⟨Pisces⟩ 26°.** P: om.; H: וראש התלי של נגה במעלת שלש ועשרים = and Venus's Head of the Dragon at ⟨Pisces⟩ 23°.

[29]37: **Similarly the second.** P, 29ra: et les secons a mars; H: והשניים ללבנה = the second to the Moon.

[30]38: **Terms.** → See above, note on § 2.1:43, s.v., "terms".

[31]38: **Scholars in relation to the stars.** P, 29ra: les sages des signes; H: חכמי המזלות = scholars of the zodiacal signs.

[32]**43: What pertains to the pits of the stars.** P, 29rb: le puis des estoiles; H: בורות הכוכבים = the pits of the stars.

[33]**45: Fixed stars.** P, 1va: les estoiles hautes; H: הכוכבים העליונים = the upper stars. → Bate's divergent translation glosses on Ibn Ezra's vague expression "the upper stars". See above § 3:1, s.v., "fixed stars".

§ 2.13

[1]**1: On the fixed stars.** P: om.; H: הכוכבים הגבוהים = the upper stars. → Bate's divergent translation glosses on Ibn Ezra's vague expression "the upper stars". See above § 3:1, s.v., "fixed stars".

[2]**1: The aforementioned fixed stars.** P, 29va: les estoiles que j'ai ramenteues; H: אלה הכוכבים שהזכרתי = the stars I have mentioned.

[3]**1: Part of fortune.** P, 29va: le sort bon; H: גורל הטוב = the good lot. → Bate's divergent translation offers the common Latin technical term of Ibn Ezra's "the good lot".

[4]**1: Does not ascend in the heart of a man.** P, 29va: non montera sur cuer d'ome; H: לא עלתה על לב אדם = did not ascend in the heart of a man.

§ 2.14

[1]**1: Girdle of the circle of the signs.** P, 29vb: ceint de l'ymagination du circle; H: חשב אפודת הגלגל = girdle of the vest of the circle. → See above note on § 1.10:5, s.v., "in the girdle of the imagination of the circle of the signs".

[2]**2: Its thighs.** P, 29vb: le bureillon; H: על אליתו = on its fat tail. → Bate's divergent translation glosses on Ibn Ezra's expression "on its fat tail".

[3]**3: The Pleiades.** P, 24vb: *kima*; H: כימה = *kimah*. → See above note on § 1.3:3, s.v., "Pleiades".

[4]**5: Is of the nature of Mercury and the second.** P: om.; P¹, 30va: de la nature de Mercure et le second; H: הוא כתולדת כוכב המה והשני = is of the nature of Mercury and the second.

[5]6: **Dark.** P, 39ra: ennuees; H: מעוננים = nebulae.

[6]6: **Are of the mixture of Mars and the Moon; ⟨the stars⟩ that are close to its [Cancer's] back, which are called mighty, are of the nature of Mars and the Sun.** P: om.; H: ממסך מאדים והלבנה, ואשר הם סמוכים אל גבו ויקראו הגבורים הם כתולדת מאדים וחמה = are of the mixture of Mars and the Moon; ⟨the stars⟩ that are close to its [Cancer's] back, which are called mighty, are of the nature of Mars and the Sun.

[7]7: **The bright star called the heart of the lion is a mixture of Mars and Saturn; the ⟨nature of the star⟩ on its [Leo's] waist is like the nature of Venus; ⟨the stars⟩ in its [Leo's] thighs are of the nature of Venus and somewhat of Mercury.** P: om.; H: והכוכב המאיר הנקרא לב האריה ממסך מאדים ושבתאי; וההווה במתניו כתולדת נגה, והכככים שהם בפחדיו כתולדת נגה ומעט מתולדת כוכב חמה = and the bright star called the heart of the lion is a mixture of Mars and Saturn; the ⟨nature of the star⟩ on its [Leo's] waist is like the nature of Venus; ⟨the stars⟩ in its [Leo's] thighs are of the nature of Venus and somewhat of Mercury.

[8]8: **Right side or *giro*.** P, 30ra: de son giron la destre; H: כנפה הימנית = its [Virgo's] right wing.

[9]8: ***Giro*.** P, 30ra: l'ele; H: כנף = wing.

[10]9: **Palms.** P, 30rb: la paume; H: כף = the pan. → Note that the Hebrew term כף means both "palm of the hand" and "pan of a balance".

[11]10: **Neck.** P, 29vb: le dos; H: גב = the back.

[12]10: **Dark or tenebrous.** P, 30rb: ennuees; H: מעוננים = nebulous.

[13]11: **Dark stars.** P, 30rb: estoiles ennuees; H: מעוננים = nebulous.

[14]11: **Sagittarius or of the One who draws the Bow.** P, 30rb: traiant de l'arc; H: הקשת = the bowman.

§ 2.15

[1]1: **Circle of the signs.** P, 39vb: pourceint de l'ymagination; H: מחשב האפודה = girdle of the vest. → See above note on § 1.10:5, s.v., "in the girdle of the imagination of the circle of the signs".

[2]3: **Which are ⟨called⟩ 'ayish.** P, 30vb: que c'est *aeis*, (the transliteration of עיש = 'ayish); H: הם עיש = which are ⟨called⟩ 'ayish (Job 38:32). → See above, note on § 1.5:2, s.v., "Lesser Bear".

[3]5: **Set in fire or of Cepheus.** P, 30vb: Et les estoiles du flamboiant; H: המתלהב = blazing one. → See above, note on § 1.5:4, s.v., "it is called elsewhere Flaminatus or Cepheus".

[4]6: **Armed ⟨Warrior⟩.** P, 39vb: ou lit a l'armé; in margin boetes; H: במיטת הגבור המזויין = in the bed of the armed warrior.

[5]6: **Or Boötes.** → See above note on § 1.5:6, s.v., "elsewhere called Howling, whose meaning is shouting, or Boetes".

[6]12: **Soldier.** P, 31ra: le chevalier; H: הפרש = the horseman.

[7]14: **The ⟨stars⟩ in the Carrier of the Snake [Ophiuchus] are of the nature of Saturn and somewhat of Venus; the ⟨stars⟩ in his back are a mixture of Saturn and Mars.** P: om.; H: ואשר הם עם נושא החיה, תולדת שבתאי ומעט מנגה, ואשר הם על גבו, ממסך שבתאי ומאדים = The ⟨stars⟩ in the Carrier of the Snake [Ophiuchus] are of the nature of Saturn and somewhat of Venus; the ⟨stars⟩ in his back are a mixture of Saturn and Mars.

[8]15: **The flying eagle [Aquila] is a mixture of Jupiter and Mars.** P: om.; H: והנשר המעופף, ממסך צדק ומאדים = The flying eagle [Aquila] is a mixture of Jupiter and Mars.

[9]18: **Never had a Husband.** P, 31ra: ne fu onques a mari = never had a husband; H: שלא ראתה בעל = has not seen a husband.

§ 2.16

[1]1: **Girdle of the circle of the signs.** P, 31ra: ceint de l'ymagination du circle; H: חשב האפודה = girdle of the vest. → See above note on § 1.10:5, s.v., "in the girdle of the imagination of the circle of the signs".

[2]3: **Cetus.** P, 31rb: avec le soleil; in margin: in Ceto; H: עם החמה = with the Sun.

[3]4: **The Mighty One.** P, 31rb: fort; H: הגבור = the hero.

[4]4: **Or Orion.** P, 31rb: above the line: in Orione; H: om.

[5]5: **The stars of the River [Eridanus], of the mixture of Saturn and Jupiter.** P, 31rb: Et les estoiles du flun sont du mellement saturne et jupiter; H: וכוכבי הנהר, ממסך שבתאי וצדק = The stars of the River, of the mixture of Saturn and Jupiter.

[6]9: **The Warlike or the Valiant.** P, 31rb: du combatant; H: הנלחם = the warrior.

[7]9: **Or Ydra.** P, 31rb: in margin: Ydra, l'magnanimus; H: om, → See above, note on § 1.4:9, s.v., "and it is Hydra".

[8]9: **And Venus.** P: om.; H: ונגה = and Venus.

[9]10: **In the leg of Orion.** P, 31vb: in margin: Orion lucida; H: om.

[10]10: **Called** *kesil*. P, 31vb: qui est apeles kescil; H: הנקרא כסיל = called *kesil*.

[11]10: **That is, fire, or bright, or fortune.** P, 31vb: in margin: id est feu ou cler ou aventure; H: om.

[12]10: **Dark or obscure.** P, 31rb: oscures; H: חשוכים = dark.

[13]13: **The Wolf or Beast.** P, 31va: *scevoe* (transliteration of צבוע = *ṣavuaʿ*); above the line: lupus; in margin: id est, bestia; H: הצבע = the hyena.

§3.1

[1]1: **Third part.** P, 31vsra: Or commence li tiers capitle; H: השער השלישי = the third gate. → Meaning, third chapter.

[2]1: **Friendship and enmity.** P, 31va: leur amor et leur haine = their love and hate; H: אהבתם ושנאתם = their love and hate.

[3]8: **Friendship.** P, 33ra: amour; H: אהבה = love.

[4]9: **The weakest of these are the sixth and twelfth.** P: om.; H: והחלשים שבהם הששי והשנים עשר = the weakest of these are the sixth and twelfth.

§3.2

[1]1: **Unfriendly.** P, 32ra: enemis; H: אויבות = enemies.

[2]1: **Friendly.** P, 32ra: amans; H: אוהבות = loving.

[3]1: **Agree in the number.** P, 32ra: sur voie d'un conte; H: על דרך חשבון אחד = by the way of one number.

[4]1: **Girdle of the circle of the signs.** P, 32ra: ceint de l'ymagination du circle; H: חשב האפודה = girdle of the vest. → See above note on §1.10:5, s.v., "in the girdle of the imagination of the circle of the signs".

[5]4: **A star or planet.** P, 32rb: l'estoile; H: הכוכב = the star.

[6]4: **Lord or ruler.** P, 32rb: le seigneur; H: הנגיד = governor.

[7]4: **Slave or subject.** P, 32rb: le servant; H: העבד = the slave.

[8]5: **Agreeing.** P, 32ra: tous; H: נכונים = prepared.

[9]5: **Rulers.** P, 32va: poestans; H: מושלים = rulers.

[10]6: **And the others.** P: om.; H: והאחרים = and the others.

[11]6: **Agree in the active powers.** P, 32va: il sont de la nature qui oevre en voie ounie; H: הם מהתולדת הפועלת בדרך שווה = they are of the active nature in the same way. → Bate's divergent translation glosses on Ibn Ezra's expression "they are of the active nature in the same way".

§ 3.3

[1]2: **Quadrant.** P, 32va: le quart de l'orbe; H: רביעית הגלגל = quarter of the circle.

[2]2: **The line of.** P: om.; H: קו = the line of.

[3]2: **Four.** P, 32va: .4.; H: ארבעה = four.

[4]2: **Elements.** P, 32va: elemens; H: roots = שורשים.

[5]2: **Spring.** P, 32va: le prinstans; H: זמן החום = the time of heat.

[6]2: **Of the ages of man.** P, 32va: de l'aage de l'ome; H: משנות האדם = of the years of man.

[7]2: **Childhood.** P, 32va: le tans de l'enfance; H: זמן הילדות = the time of childhood.

[8]3: **The line of.** P: om.; H: קו = the line of.

[9]3: **Elements.** P, 32vb: elemens; H: roots = שורשים.

[10]3: **Of ⟨human⟩ ages.** P, 32vb: et ou terme de ses anees; H: מזמן שנותיו = of the time of its years.

[11]4: **The degree of the angle of the Earth.** P, 32vb: au gré d'abisme; H: עד מעלת התהום = to the degree of the abyss.

[12]4: **Autumn.** P, 32vb: wains = autumn; H: חורף = winter.

[13]4: **Of ⟨human⟩ ages.** P, 32vb: de ses anees; H: משנותיו = of its years.

[14]5: **Angle of the Earth.** P, 32vb: au ligne d'abisme; H: קו התהום = the line of the abyss.

[15]5: **Winter.** P, 33ra: l'yver = the winter; H: הקור = the cold.

[16]5: **Phlegm.** P, 33ra: le froit qui s'entremelle ensamble moisteur; H: הקור המתערב עם הלחה = cold mixed with humidity. → Bate's divergent translation summarizes in one word Ibn Ezra's expression "cold mixed with humidity".

[17]5: **Senility or very old age.** P, 33ra: vieleté; H: ימי הזקנה והשיבה = the days of old age.

[18]6: **Circle of the sphere.** P, 33ra: l'orbe; H: הגלגל = the circle.

[19]8: **From the angle of the Earth to the ascendant degree, and from the ascendant degree to midheaven.** P, 33ra: de la ligne de la moitié des cieus juques au gré l'ascendant et du gré l'escendant jusques a la ligne d'abisme; H: מקו חצי השמים עד המעלה הצומחת ומהמעלה הצומחת עד קו התהום = from the line of midheaven to the ascendant degree and from the ascendant degree to the line of abyss.

[20]8: **Sphere.** P, 33ra: l'orbe; H: הגלגל = the circle.

[21]8: **The remaining two quadrants, which namely are from midheaven to the descendant degree, and from there to the angle of the Earth.** P, 33rb: l'autre moitié, que c'est de la ligne d'abisme jusques au gré l'enclinant et du gré l'enclinant jusques a la moitié des cieus; H: והחצי האחר, שהוא מקו התהום עד המעלה השוקעת ומהמעלה השוקעת עד קו חצי השמים = the other half, from the line of lower midheaven to the descendant degree, and from the descendant degree to the line of midheaven.

§ 3.4

[1]1: **The number of the twelve signs.** P, 33rb: .12. parties ou nombre des signes; H: שנים עשר חלקים, כמספר המזלות = twelve parts, like the number of the signs.

[2]2: **Angles or cardines.** P, 33rb: chevillies = pegs; H: יתדות = pegs. → Meaning, cardines, i.e., the cusps of the first, fourth, seventh and tenth house of the horoscope.

[3]2: **Because of a certain similarity.** P, 33rb: car eles sont en samblance de poins; H: כי הם כדמות נקודות = because they resemble points.

[4]3: **Angles.** P, 33rb: chevilles = pegs; H: היתדות = the pegs. → Meaning, cardines of the horoscope.

[5]4: **Weak of falling.** P, 33rb: foibles ou cheans; H: חלשים = weak.

[6]5: **Cadent.** P, 33rb: foibles; H: החלשים = the weak.

[7]7: **Houses.** P, 33rb: les mesons de l'orbe; H: בתי הגלגל = the houses of the circle.

[8]7: **Line of the angle of the Earth.** P, 33va: la ligne d'abisme; H: קו התהום = in the line of the abyss.

[9]8: **Roots.** P, 33va: racines; H: עיקרים = roots.

§ 3.5

[1]1: **Understanding or knowledge.** P, 33va: le savoir; H: הדעת = knowledge.

[2]2: **First lord of the triplicity.** P, 3va: le sire de la triplicité premiere; H: בעל השלישות הראשונה = the lord of the first triplicity. → There is no "lord of the first triplicity" but "first lord of the triplicity." Bate's divergent translation corrects Ibn Ezra's incorrect expression.

[3]3: **Second lord of the triplicity.** P, 33vb: le sire de la triplicité seconde; H: בעל השלישות השנית = the lord of the second triplicity. → There is no "lord of the second triplicity" but "second lord of the triplicity." Bate's divergent translation corrects Ibn Ezra's incorrect expression.

[4]4: **End of life or of the human lifetime.** P, 33vb: la fin.; H: סוף שנות אדם = the end of the human years.

§ 3.6

[1]1: **Loans and gifts.** P, 33vb: le prest el le don; H: משא ומתן = carrying and giving. → This is the literal translation of a Hebrew idiom meaning negotiations, bargaining.

[2]2: **First lord of the triplicity.** P, 3va: le sire de la triplicité premiere; H: בעל השלישות הראשונה = the lord of the first triplicity. → See above, note on § 3.5:2, s.v. "first lord of the triplicity".

[3]3: **Second lord ⟨of the triplicity⟩.** P, 33vb: le sire de la triplicité seconde; H: בעל השלישות השנית = the lord of the second triplicity. → See above, note on § 3.5:3, s.v. "second lord of the triplicity".

§ 3.7

[1]1: **Understanding and comprehension.** P, 34ra: le sens; H: החכמה = wisdom.

[2]1: **Humility, counsel.** P, 34ra: la simpleté; H: והענוה והעצה = humility, counsel.

[3]1: **Belief.** P: om.; H: האמונה = faith.

[4]1: **Journeys.** P: om.; H: ההליכה = journeys.

[5]2: **The first lord of the triplicity.** P, 3va: le sire de la triplicité premiere; H: בעל השלישות הראשונה = the lord of the first triplicity. → See above, note on § 3.5:2, s.v. "first lord of the triplicity".

§ 3.8

[1]2: **First lord of the triplicity.** P, 3va: le sire de la triplicité premiere; H: בעל השלישות הראשונה = the lord of the first triplicity. → See above, note on § 3.5:2, s.v. "first lord of the triplicity".

§3.9

[1]2: **First lord of the triplicity.** P, 3va: le sire de la triplicité premiere; H: בעל השלישות הראשונה = the lord of the first triplicity. → See above, note on §3.5:2, s.v. "first lord of the triplicity".

§3.10

[1]1: **Lasting and of long duration.** P, 34rb: durable; H: עומד = stable.

[2]1: **Misfortunes.** P, 34rb: com aventure; H: כמו מקרה = like a contingency. → Bate's divergent translation explains Ibn Ezra's expression "like a contingency".

[3]1: **Accusations.** P, 34rb: l'encusement; H: רכילות = gossip.

[4]2: **First lord of the triplicity.** P, 3va: le sire de la triplicité premiere; H: בעל השלישות הראשונה = the lord of the first triplicity. → See above, note on §3.5:2, s.v. "first lord of the triplicity".

§3.11

[1]1: **Enmities and squabbles.** P, 34rb: le contraliement; H: quarrels = הקטטה.

[2]2: **First lord of the triplicity.** P, 3va: le sire de la triplicité premiere; H: בעל השלישות הראשונה = the lord of the first triplicity. → See above, note on §3.5:2, s.v. "first lord of the triplicity".

§3.12

[1]1: **Last wills.** P, 34rb: la commandise; H: הפקדון = deposits.

[2]1: **Great fears.** P, 34rb: la tremeur; H: היראה = feat.

[3]2: **First lord of the triplicity.** P, 3va: le sire de la triplicité premiere; H: בעל השלישות הראשונה = the lord of the first triplicity. → See above, note on §3.5:2, s.v. "first lord of the triplicity".

§ 3.13

[1]1: **Travels and journeys to foreign places.** P, 34va: sur l'aler, et sur les voies; H: ההליכה ועל הדרכים = journeys and highways.

[2]2: **The first lord of the triplicity.** P, 3va: le sire de la triplicité premiere; H: בעל השלישות הראשונה = the lord of the first triplicity. → See above, note on § 3.5:2, s.v. "first lord of the triplicity".

[3]2: **The second ⟨indicates⟩ position, and the third ⟨indicates⟩ his faith.** P, 34va: le secont sur son degré, et le tiers sur sa creance; H: השני על האמונה, והשלישי על החכמה = the second ⟨indicates⟩ faith and the third wisdom.

§ 3.14

[1]1: **Kings, works, being raised to a higher rank, and promotion, kingdoms, fame and authority; likewise, crafts, mothers, glory, praise, something taken away or stolen, as well as judges, princes, prelates, and it indicates half of the years of life.** P, 34va: rois et oevres, et hautece, et essaucement, et roiaume, et memoire, et vois .l. [sic] de commandement, et sur maistries, et sur les meres, et gloire, et loenge, et chose emblee ou ostee, et les juges, et les princes et les prelas, et enseigne sur la moitié des ans de la vie.; H: האם, ועל המלוכה, ועל השם, ועל כל אומנות. = the mother, kingship, reputation, and every craft. → Cf. Pietro d'Abano: "reges, opera, sublimitatem, exaltationem, regnum, memoriam id est nominationem, vocem imperii, magisteria, matres, gloriam et laudem, rem ablatam aut furatam aut iudices, principes, prelatos atque dimidium annorum vite."

[2]2: **But the first lord of the triplicity indicates every work, promotions, and very high mansions; the second ⟨indicates⟩ authority, and boldness in it; the third ⟨lord of the triplicity indicates⟩ stability and longevity.** P, 34va–vb: Et dit Alendezgoz que le sires de la triplicité premiere enseigne sur oevre et essachement, ch'est haute de siege et mansion tres haute; le secont enseigne sur vois de commandement et hardiece en cele; li tiers senefie l'estableté et la durableté; H: ובעל השלישות ראשונה יורה על האם, והשני על מעלתו, והשלישי על אומנותו = The first lord of the triplicity indicates the mother, the second ⟨indicates⟩ his [the native's] rank, and the third ⟨indicates⟩ his craft. → Cf. Pietro d'Abano: "Et inquit Alendechos dominum

triplicitatis primum denotare opus, exaltationem, id est, sedis altitudinem, et status sublimationem; secundum vocem imperii, et audaciam in illi; tertium vero stabilitatem et durabilitatem eiusdem."

§ 3.15

[1]1: **Favor or good fortune.** P, 34ra: la grace; H: החן = grace.

[2]1: **Partners.** P, 34vb: amis; H: והאוהבים = lovers.

[3]1: **Master of the wardrobe.** P, 34vb: les seigneurs du vestement; H: ובעלי והמלבוש = masters of the wardrobe.

[4]2: **The first lord of the triplicity.** P, 3va: le sire de la triplicité premiere; H: בעל השלישות הראשונה = the lord of the first triplicity. → See above, note on § 3.5:2, s.v. "first lord of the triplicity".

[5]2: **Thoughts or desires.** P, 34vb: la pensee; H: המחשבת = thoughts.

§ 3.16

[1]1: **Grudges, prisons and captivity.** P, 34vb: le garder, et sur mesons de prisons et d'eschaitivoisons; H: והנטירה, ועל בית האיסורים והשבי = grudges, prisons and captivity.

[2]1: **Animals that men ride on or that are strong for the carriages of human beings.** P, 34vb: les bestes qui sont a chevauchure <l'orne; H: הבהמות שהם למרכבת האדם = animals that men ride on.

[3]2: **The first lord of the triplicity.** P, 3va: le sire de la triplicité premiere; H: בעל השלישות הראשונה = the lord of the first triplicity. → See above, note on § 3.5:2, s.v. "first lord of the triplicity".

§ 4.1

[1]1: **Fourth part of the book.** P, 35ra: Or commence le quart capitle; H: השער הרביעי = the fourth gate. → Meaning, fourth chapter.

NOTES TO *LIBER ABRAHE AVENERRE INTRODUCTORIUS* 429

[2]1: **Planets.** P, 35ra: planetes; H: משרתים = servants (meaning planets). → See above note on § 2:5, s.v., "planets".

[3]3: **Its nature is bad.** P, 35ra: mal; H: ותולדתו רע = its nature is bad.

[4]3: **Weeping, sadness and lamentation, and wailing and cries.** P, 35ra: et pleur, et doulousement, et cri; H: ועצבון, ואבל, ובכי ואנקה = sadness, mourning, crying and wailing.

[5]6: **Moors or Ethiopians.** P, 35ra: les Mors; H: הכושים = the Ethiopians.

[6]7: **Cultivators of the land or farmers.** P, 35ra: les laboureurs de la terre; H: עובדי האדמה = farmers.

[7]7: **And graves.** P, 35ra: fosses; H: והקברים = and graves.

[8]7: **Plunderers of tombs.** P, 35ra: les preneurs les ensevelissemens a mors; H: לוקחי תכריכי המתים = those who take shrouds of the dead. → Bate's divergent translation glosses on Ibn Ezra's expression "those who take shrouds of the dead".

[9]8: **Minerals.** P, 35rb: metaus de la terre; H: מתכות הארץ = metals of the earth.

[10]8: **Every black marble.** P, 35rb: tout marbre noir; H: כל כחול שחור = everything that is blue and black.

[11]9: **Wells.** P, 35rb: les puis; H: והבארות והבורות = wells and pits.

[12]10: **Bears.** P, 35rb: ours; H: הזאבים = wolves.

[13]11: *Rachem.* P, 35rb: *raihem*; H: הרחם = bustard. → In the French, *raihem* is the transliteration of הרחם = bustard.

[14]11: **Crow.** P, 35rb: çuete = owl; H: העטלף = bat.

[15]13: *Harobe.* P, 35va: *harrobe*; H: החרוב = carob. → In the French, *harrobe* is the transliteration of החרוב = carob.

[16]**13: *Balot*.** P, 35va: *balot*; H: בלוט = acorn. → In the French, *balot* is the transliteration of בלוט = acorn.

[17]**14: Pines.** P, 35va: pronnes = prunes; H: פרונש = *prunas*.

[18]**15: Whose mixture.** P, 35va: sa nature; H: ותולדתו = whose nature. → Bate's divergent translation glosses on Ibn Ezra's concept of "nature".

[19]**15: Bitter or astringent.** P, 35va: galles; H: עפיץ = astringent.

[20]**16: *Nataf*.** P, 35va: *nathaf* = transliteration of נָטָף; H: נָטָף = storax. → In the French, *nathaf* is the transliteration of נָטָף = storax: Ex. 30:34.

[21]**17: *Cilicium* or *sagum*.** P, 35va: l'esclavine; H: האדרת = a mantle.

[22]**18: Death.** P, 35vb: mort; H: om.

[23]**18: Strange to them.** P, 35vb: et a estre estrangié d'aus; H: om.

[24]**18: Making away with or stealing.** P, 35vb: faire taute; H: לעשות חמס = to plunder.

[25]**18: Provoking anger or causing sadness.** P, 35vb: a courrecier; H: לכעוס = to get angry.

[26]**18: Knowledge of intentions and hidden things.** P, 35vb: savoir des consaus; H: דעת הסודות = knowledge of secrets.

[27]**18: To make people tired and fatigue ⟨them⟩.** P, 35vb: a fortraire enfans s'orne; H: לפתות בני אדם = seducing people.

[28]**18: To be of bad temper or burdensome.** P, 35vb: a aler en duresce; H: ללכת בקרי = to be defiant.

[29]**18: To be timid and hesitant.** P, 35vb: a espeurir; H: ולפחוד = to be afraid.

[30]**18: To agree with nobody.** P, 35vb: a douter; H: לדאוג = to be worried.

[31]**18: To be deceitful in the same way.** P, 35vb: a fauseté sur une voie; H: לשקוד על דרך אחד = persevering in a single path.

[32]18: **Worth or utility.** P, 35vb: vaillance; H: תועלת = benefit.

[33]18: **Many times or in many ways.** P, 35vb: grant; H: הרבה = a lot.

[34]18: **Useless and worthless.** P, 35vb: son desibement; H: השחתתו = its harm.

[35]19: **Tilling and cultivating the soil.** P, 35vb: laborer la terre; H: לעבוד האדמה = tilling the soil.

[36]20: **Filthy or debilitating.** P, 35vb: soulliant; H: מטונפת = filthy.

[37]21: **Paralysis, fear.** P, 36ra: le departement et le movement; H: הפירוד והנדידה = separation, wandering.

[38]21: **Success or also profit.** P, 36ra: pourfitement; H: הצלחה = success.

[39]22: **With respect to the orb of the signs.** P, 36ra: des parties de l'orbe; H: מחלקי הגלגל = with respect to the parts of the circle.

[40]22: **With respect to the hour or the hours.** P, 36ra: les parties de l'eure; H: חלקי הרגע = the parts of the minute.

[41]22: **As I shall explain.** → Here Ibn Ezra instructs readers to consult chapter 6 of *Reshit Ḥokhmah*, which is concerned with "the existence or the condition of the planets in themselves, and their existence with respect to the Sun" (see below § 6.1:1).

[42]23: **In its dignity.** P, 36ra: en degré; H: במעלה גדולה = in an high degree.

[43]23: **Benevolent star.** P, 36ra: bone estoile; H: כוכב טוב = good star.

[44]23: **In its dignity.** P, 36ra: en son haut degré; H: במעלתו הגבוהה = in its high degree.

[45]23: **Humiliated.** P, 36ra: ou basse; H: בשפלה = in the lowness. → See above, § 2.1:40

[46]24: **Malevolent star.** P, 36ra: estoile mauvaise; H: כוכב רע = bad star.

[47]24: **Action and winning.** P, 36ra: vainquement; H: נצוח = victory.

[48]24: **Plundering and taking away.** P, 36ra: taute; H: חמס = plundering.

[49]24: **Dishonor, disgrace and reproach.** P, 36ra: honte et ledengement; H: קלון וחרפה = dishonor and shame.

[50]24: **As I shall explain all this in the *Book of Nativities*.** → This is a general reference to the first version of *Sefer ha-Moladott*, which is concerned with the doctrine of nativities. In particular, the current locus may be a reference to *Moladot* (III ii 5, 1–5, 124–125), which focuses on how the native's health is affected by Saturn's changing position on its eccentric circle.

[51]25: **Alone in charge.** P, 36rb: seul sur; H: מתבודד על = rules alone over.

[52]25: **Modest and pious.** P, 36rb: simple; H: עניו = humble; see above, § 2.9:29.

[53]26: **His mixture.** P, 36rb: sa nature; H: תולדתו = his nature. → Bate's divergent translation glosses on Ibn Ezra's concept of "nature".

[54]27: **Great deformity in shape and color.** P, 36rb: lait forment en faiture et en vision; H: מכוער בתואר ומראה = ugly of face and feature.

[55]27: **A thick or large nose.** P, 36rb: ses narines espesses; H: נחיריו עבים = his nostrils thick.

[56]27: **And similarly the lips, and foul-smelling teeth.** P, 36rb: et ausinc ses levres et ses dens, et s'omeur puant.; H: וככה שפתיו ושיניו, וריחו נבאש = as well as thick lips and teeth, and foul-smelling.

[57]28: **The anus and the black bile.** P, 36rb: le lieu de l'escloi et la cole rouge; H: מקום השתן והמרה = the place of the urine and the bile.

[58]29: **Fury.** P, 36va: l'esragement; H: שגעון = madness.

[59]29: **Trembling.** P, 36va: le tramblement; H: ריעוש = palsy.

[60]29: **Loss of speech.** P, 36va: la maladie qui ataist l'orne; H: החולי שידמם האדם = the disease when a man is bleeding.

[61]**29: Chronic or protracted disease.** P, 36va: maladie qui dure jors assés,; H: כאב עומד ימים רבים = pain which stands many days.

[62]**30: Senility or extreme old age.** P, 36va: la senzretune; H: זקנה = old age.

[63]**31: Of the parts of the world.** P, 36va: des parties; H: מהפאות = of the sides.

[64]**33: Sabbath.** P, 36va: le samadi; H: שבת = Sabbath.

[65]**33: The one that precedes the day of Mercury.** P, 36va: cele dont le merquidi est aprés; H: ליל רביעי = the night of the fourth ⟨day⟩.

[66]**34: And some say also nun.** P: om.; H: ויש אומרים גם הנן = and some say also nun.

[67]**37: Power of the rays of its body.** P, 36va: la force de son cors; H: כח גופו = the power of its body. → Bate's divergent translation glosses on Ibn Ezra's expression "the power of its body".

§ 4.2

[1]**2: Temperate.** P, 36vb: droit; H: ישר = straight.

[2]**3: Fruitfulness and growth.** P, 36vb: fructissement, et croissement; H: פריה ורביה = fertilization and increase. → Hebrew idiom for procreation.

[3]**5: The land of Sheba, which is called Algeman.** P, 36ra: la tere de Sceva, et ele est apelee Algemen; H: ארץ אלימן, היא שבא = the land of Aliman, that is, Sheba.

[4]**7: Acceptable.** P, 36vb: volentis; H: נדיבים = generous.

[5]**8: Of the metals.** P, 36vb: du metal de la terre; H: ממתכות הארץ = of the metals of the Earth. → Cf. above note on § 4.1:8, s.v., "minerals".

[6]**8: Is valuable and useful.** P, 36vb: il a en li vaillance; H: יש בה תועלת = is useful.

[7]11: **Altilia or hens.** P, 37ra: gelines; H: תרנגולים = chickens.

[8]12: **Of the animals that creep on the earth or vermin.** P, 37ra: de la terre tout celi qui vaut; H: מרמש האדמה = of the animals that creep on the earth.

[9]12: **Worm that makes silk.** P, 37ra: le ver de la soie; H: תולעת שני = kermes louse.

[10]13: **Of the plants.** P, 37ra: des arbres; H: מהאילנים = of the trees.

[11]13: *Zedaar* or *sacuar*. P, 37ra: satuar; H: צנובר = pine nut.

[12]14: **Peas.** P, 37ra: joirres; H: אפונים = peas.

[13]14: **Millet.** P, 37ra: milg = millet; H: האורז = rice.

[14]15: **Of the fruits.** P, 37ra: des bourjons; H: מן הציצים = of the flowers.

[15]17: **Silk.** P, 37rb: coton; H: צמר גפן = cotton.

[16]18: **Of the customs of human beings.** P, 37rb: de la nature de l'orne; H: מתולדת האדם = of human nature. Bate's divergent translation glosses on Ibn Ezra's expression "of human nature".

[17]18: **Loveliness or friendliness.** P, 37ra: la chierté; H: היקר = dignity.

[18]18: **Pious or religious manner of life.** P, 37rb: le simplement aler; H: הצנע לכת = walk humbly. → Meaning, to behave modestly.

[19]18: **Piety.** P, 37rb: volunté du cuer; H: נדבת הלב = generosity of the heart. → Meaning, generosity.

[20]19: **Sons of men.** P, 37rb: enfans d'ome = sons of a man; H: בני אדם = sons of a man. → Hebrew idiom for "human beings."

[21]19: **He desires to be taught what is just by sons of men.** P, 37ra: et quiert que l'ensegnent enfans d'ome; H: מבקש שיודוהו בני אדם = wants sons of human beings to thank him.

[22]19: **Synagogues or in houses of prayer.** P, 37va: es mesons des amassees; H: בבתי כנסיות = in synagogues.

[23]20: **Happiness, good fortune.** P, 37va: eur bon et grace; H: מזל טוב, וחן = good fortune, grace.

[24]22: **Planets.** P, 37va: planetes; H: משרתים = servants. → Meaning planets. See above note on § 2:5, s.v., "planets".

[25]22: **When they approach it.** P, 37va: quant il s'ajoustent ensamble Ji; H: בהתערבם עמו = when they are mixed with it.

[26]23: **Fine and pleasant.** P, 37va: avenant; H: נאה = fine.

[27]23: **His hair or the hair.** P, 37va: son poil; H: שערו = his hair.

[28]23: **His mixture.** P, 37va: sa nature; H: תולדתו = his nature. → Bate's divergent translation glosses on Ibn Ezra's concept of "nature".

[29]25: **Good will.** P, 37vb: talent bon; H: יצר טוב = good impulses.

[30]27: **Acute or swift, and is light, and hurries up.** P, 37vb: legiere qui est hostee en haste; H: שיסור מהרה = that will pass quickly.

[31]28: **Old age is in its portion, which is between youth and senility or extreme old age.** P, 37vb: le terme qui est entre la bachelerie et la vielleté; H: הזמן שהוא בין הבחרות והזקנה = the time between youth and old age.

[32]29: **Citron or saffron.** P, 37vb: le safrenas; H: מכורכם = saffron.

[33]30: **Of the angles.** P, 37vb: des angles; H: מן הפאות = of the sides, or of the edges.

[34]30: **The northern.** P, 37vb: le senestre; H: השמאלית = the left. → Meaning, the northern.

[35]31: **The day of Jupiter.** P, 37vb: le joedi; H: יום חמישי = ⟨the daytime of⟩ the fifth ⟨day⟩. → Bate's divergent translation glosses on Ibn Ezra's expression "fifth day".

[36]31: **The one which follows the day of the Moon.** P, 37vb: la nuit dont li lundis est aprés; H: ליל שני = the night of the second ⟨day⟩.

[37]33: **The small or least.** P, 38ra: petites; H: הקטנות = the least.

§ 4.3

[1]2: **High price.** P, 38ra: chierté; H: בצורת = drought.

[2]2: **Destruction by fire.** P, 38ra: arson de feu; H: ומוקדי אש = hearths of fire.

[3]2: **Thunder.** P, 38ra: caus = blows; H: מכות = blows.

[4]2: **Lightning flash or lightning.** P, 38ra: le departement; H: הפירוד = separation.

[5]3: **In general: everything that is not according to its ⟨own⟩ disposition and character.** P: om.; H: והכלל: כל דבר שאיננו על מתכונתו ומשפטו = In general: everything that is not according to its ⟨own⟩ disposition and character.

[6]4: **Of human nature, the power of anger is in its portion.** P: om.; H: ובחלקו מתולדת האדם כח הכעס = of human nature, the power of anger is in its portion.

[7]5: **Egypt.** P, 6vb: *Miseraim*; H: מצרים. → Transliterated as *Miṣerayim*, meaning Egypt.

[8]6: **Those who worship or tend the fire.** P, 38ra: ceus qui servent le feu; H: עובדי האש = fire-worshipers.

[9]7: **Craftsmen of weapons.** P, 38ra: les menestreus de fer; H: אומני הברזל = ironworkers.

[10]7: **Men of bloods.** P, 38ra: les saigneurs de sans; H: מקיזי הדם = bloodletters.

[11]7: **Those who take care of animals or keep them safe.** P, 38ra: les serveurs de bestes; H: משרתי הבהמות = those who tend animals.

[12]8: **Of the metals or the minerals of the Earth.** P, 38rb: des metaus de la terre; H: ממתכות הארץ = of the metals of the earth.

[13]8: **Copper.** P, 38rb: le coivre rouge; H: הנחושת האדום = red copper.

[14]9: **Fortresses or strongholds.** P, 38rb: les fortereces; H: המבצרים = fortifications.

[15]9: **Ovens or furnaces.** P, 38rb: les forges; H: הפורני = furnaces.

[16]10: **Wolves.** P, 38rb: *scevoe* = transliteration of צבעים, meaning hyenas; H: הצבועים = hyenas.

[17]11: **Hawk.** P, 38ra: ostoir = Old French corresponding to the modern French autour, a kind of hawk; H: אסתור = astor.

[18]13: **Of the plants.** P, 38rb: des arbres; H: מן האילנים = of the trees.

[19]13: **Pears.** P, 38ra: les priers; H: אגסים = pears.

[20]13: **Plant or tree.** P, 38rb: arbre; H: איל = tree.

[21]14: *Perassion* **or prassum.** P, 38ra: perassion; H: פרסיון = *persion*.

[22]14: **Species.** P, 38va: arbre; H: איל = tree.

[23]16: **Scarlet or in the grain.** P, 38ra: en *alcarmeze*; H: באל כרמז = in *al-karmez*. → Meaning, with carmine. In the French, *en alcarmeze* is a transliteration of באל כרמז = in *al-karmez*, meaning, with carmine

[24]17: **Impudence.** P, 38va: la hativece; H: מהירות = speed.

[25]17: **Violence.** P, 38va: la force; H: הגבורה = courage.

[26]17: **Victory or overcoming quarrels.** P, 38va: le vainquement; H: הנצוח = victory.

[27]20: **Tall or long.** P, 38vb: lons; H: ארוך = tall.

[28]**20: Mixture.** P, 38vb: la nature; H: תולדת = nature. → Bate's divergent translation glosses on Ibn Ezra's concept of "nature".

[29]**21: Its color.** P, 39ra: sa vision; H: מראהו = its appearance.

[30]**22: The gallbladder.** P, 39ra: la cole; H: המרירה = the gallbladder.

[31]**22: Genitals or the pudenda.** P, 39ra: le menbre; H: האבר = the penis.

[32]**24: Overheating.** P, 39ra: l'eschaufoison; H: השחפת = tuberculosis.

[33]**24: Red abscesses or carbuncles.** P, 39ra: les buberues rouges qui issent ou cors de l'ome; H: האבעבועות האדומות שיצאו בגוף האדם = red pox that erupt on the human body.

[34]**25: The end of youth and the beginning of old age.** P, 39ra: la bachelerie duques en la fin de la bachelerie; H: ימי הבחרות = the days of youth.

[35]**26: Red.** P, 39ra: rouge forment; H: אדום הרבה = intense red.

[36]**27: Of the angles.** P, 39ra: des angles; H: מן הפאות = of the sides, or of the edges.

[37]**28: Day of Mars.** P, 39ra: le mardi; H: יום שלישי = ⟨the daytime of⟩ the third day. → Bate's divergent translation glosses on Ibn Ezra's expression "third day".

[38]**28: Sabbath.** P, 39ra: le samadi; H: שבת = Sabbath.

[39]**28: The one which precedes the Sabbath.** P, 39ra: avant le samedi; H: ליל שבת = the night of Sabbath.

§4.4

[1]**1: In a tempered way.** P, 39rb: en droiture = in straightness; H: ביושר = in straightness. → Meaning in a tempered manner.

[2]**4: Edom or the Idumaeans.** P, 39rb: Edom; H: אדום = 'Edom. → 'Edom = Idumea, in medieval Hebrew, is a code name for Rome.

NOTES TO *LIBER ABRAHE AVENERRE INTRODUCTORIUS* 439

[3]5: **Princes.** P, 39rb: les princes; H: שרים = rulers.

[4]5: **Counselors or consuls.** P, 39rb: conseillieurs; H: יועצים = counselors.

[5]6: **Adamas.** P, 39rb: *alemas*; H: אלמאס = *al-mās*. → Here the French and Hebrew transliterate الماس = *al-mās*, meaning diamond. See above, note on § 2.5:10, s.v., "adamas". But the Latin translates "adamas," a native Latin word for diamond.

[6]7: **In its portion.** P, 39rb: en sa partie; H: בחלקו מהארץ = in its portion of the Earth.

[7]7: **Mansions.** P, 39rb: manoirs; H: ארמונים = palaces.

[8]8: **Which are called *carim*.** P, 39va: les *carim* = a transliteration of כרים; H: הכרים = *ha-carim*. → Here the French "les *carim*" is a transliteration of הכרים = *ha-carim*, a biblical word for sheep.

[9]9: **The ostrich.** P, 39ba: *aozeniia* = transliteration of העזניה; H: העזניה = *ha-oʿzniah*. → Here, the French *aozeniia* is a transliteration of העזניה = *ha-oʿzniah*, meaning black vulture.

[10]11: **The date or palm tree.** P, 39va: des datiers; H: עצי התמרים = date palms.

[11]15: **Strength or effect of forces.** P, 39va: la force; H: הגבורה = courage.

[12]15: **Love of wealth, loquacity, quickness at responding, and passion.** P: om; H: ואהבת העושר, ודבר יותר מדאי, והמהירות בתשובה, ורוב התאוה = love of wealth, loquacity, quickness at responding, and passion.

[13]16: **Of the crafts, goldsmiths, silversmiths, and makers of crowns.** P: om.; H: ומהאומנות צורפי הזהב והכסף, ומעשה הנזר = of the crafts, goldsmiths, silversmiths, and makers of crowns.

[14]17: **It also indicates ordinances and laws.** P: om.; H: גם יורה על התורות והחוקים = It also indicates ordinances and laws.

[15]17: **And joining the congregation.** P, 39va: et ajoustement de la communité; H: וחיבור הקהל = and joining the congregation.

[16]18: **Thin or short.** P, 39va: menu; H: דק = thin.

[17]18: **A beautiful face.** P, 39va: biauté de faces; H: הדרת פנים = a majestic appearance.

[18]19: **The left.** P, 39vb: a rebours; H: הפוך = the opposite.

[19]19: **A channel.** P, 39vb: les conduis; H: העורקים = the arteries.

[20]21: **End of youth.** P, 39vb: le terme de la bachelerie; H: זמן הבחרות = the time of youth.

[21]23: **Of the angles.** → see above, note on § 4.2:30, s.v., "of the angles".

[22]25: **The Lord's.** P, 49vb: le dimenche; H: יום ראשון = the daytime of the first day.

[23]25: **The one that precedes the day of Jupiter.** P, 39vb: dont le joedi est aprés; H: ליל חמישי = the night of the fifth ⟨day⟩.

§ 4.5

[1]1: **Temperate.** P, 40ra: droiturier; H: ישר = straight. → Meaning, temperate.

[2]1: **Benevolent and pleasing.** P, 40ra: bone et afaitié; H: טוב מתקן = good and amending.

[3]2: **Generation or fruitfulness and growth.** P, 36vb: fructissement, et croissement; H: פריה ורביה = fertilization and increase. → Hebrew idiom for procreation.

[4]4: **Who believe in the law of the Saracens.** P, 40ra: qui corit in loi de Sarrazin; H: מי שהוא על תורת ישמעאל = who belongs to the law of Ishmael.

[5]8: **Of the Earth.** P, 40ra: de la terre; H: מהארץ = of the Earth.

[6]8: **Myrtles.** P, 40ra: *hezasim*; H: הדסים = myrtles. → Here, the French *hezasim* is a transliteration of הדסים, meaning myrtles

NOTES TO *LIBER ABRAHE AVENERRE INTRODUCTORIUS* 441

[7]8: **Plant nurseries.** P, 40ra: boutons; H: ציצים = flowers.

[8]8: **Beds or couches.** P, 40ra: lis; H: מיטות = beds.

[9]13: **Is flagrant.** P: om.; H: יש לו ריח טוב = with a pleasant scent.

[10]14: **All embroidery or sewn with a needle.** P, 40rb: toute oevre de broudis; H: כל מעשה רקמה = all embroidery.

[11]15: **Cleanliness or embellishment.** P, 40rb: la neteté; H: הנקיות = cleanness.

[12]15: **Mockery, laughter.** P, 40rb: le gaber; H: והלעג והשחוק = mockery and laughter.

[13]15: **Dancing or clapping the hands.** P, 40rb: le trepe; H: הרקוד = dancing.

[14]15: **Elegant speech.** P: om.; H: דבור יפה = elegant speech.

[15]16: **The work of dyeing.** P, 40va: toute chose de tainture; H: כל דבר צבוע = everything that is dyed.

[16]16: **Stitching or sewing together patterns.** P, 40va: coutur; H: התפירה = sewing.

[17]17: **Drink or feasts.** P, 40va: boivre; H: משקה = drink.

[18]18: **Tall or long.** P, 40va: lonc; H: ארוך = tall. → See above, note on § 4.3:20, s.v., "tall or long".

[19]19: **Player.** P, 40va: joueur; H: צחקן = a frequent smiler.

[20]20: **The human sperm or seed of generation.** P, 40va: la semence de l'ome; H: זרע האדם = the sperm of man.

[21]20: **Humor or humidity.** P, 40va: moiteur = humidity; H: הלחה = humidity.

[22]21: **The kidneys or hips.** P, 40va: regnons; H: כליות = kidneys.

[23]22: **After childhood.** P, 40va: c'est a dire cil qui est a passés .13. ans; H: והכלל: משיעבר שלש עשרה שנה = as a rule, after he is 13 years old.

[24]25: **Of the angles.** → See above, note on § 3.2:30, s.v., "of the angles".

[25]27: **Day of Venus.** P, 40vb: le vendredi; H: יום ששי = ⟨the daytime of⟩ the sixth day. → Bate's divergent translation glosses on Ibn Ezra's expression "sixth day".

[26]27: **The one which follows the day of Mars.** P, 40vb: cele ou le mardi est aprés; H: ליל שלישי = the night of the third day.

[27]28: **1150.** P, 49vb: 1150; H: אלף ומאה וחמישים ואחת = 1151.

§ 4.6

[1]1: **Its mixture.** P, 40vb: sa nature; H: תולדתו = its nature. → Bate's divergent translation glosses on Ibn Ezra's concept of "nature".

[2]2: **Prudence or intellect.** P, 40vb: l'avertissance; H: הבינה = understanding.

[3]4: **Likewise.** P: om; H: ומן האומות = of the nations.

[4]4: **The Indians.** P, 40vb–41ra: les homes de *Hodu* = the people of *Hodu*; H: אנשי הודו = the people of *Hodu*, meaning the people of India. → In the French, *Hodu* is a transliteration of הודו, meaning India.

[5]5: **Building and engraving.** P, 41ra: clofichement; H: פתוח = engraving.

[6]5: **Drawing or painting.** P, 41ra: pourtraiement; H: ציור = painting.

[7]6: **Of the metals.** P, 41ra: des metaus; H: מן המתכות = of the metals.

[8]7: **Fountains.** P: om.; H: גולות = fountains.

[9]8: **Wolves.** P, 41ra: groupis; H: שועלים = foxes.

[10]11: **Canes or *casanni*.** P, 41ra: tuiaus; H: קנים = cane.

NOTES TO *LIBER ABRAHE AVENERRE INTRODUCTORIUS*   443

[11]**12: Gum.** P, 41ra: gome; H: שרף = resin.

[12]**12: And the teeth of the animal.** P, 41rb: et des dens de la beste; H: הם אשכי הבהמה = which are the testicles of an animal.

[13]**12: England.** P, 41ra: *Engleterre*; H: אינגלאטירא = *Ingleterra* [= England]. → In the French, *Engleterre* is a transliteration of אינגלאטירא, meaning England.

[14]**14: A man's speech.** P, 41rb: la parole de l'orne; H: הדבור = speech.

[15]**14: Sorcery and any sort of divination.** P, 41rb: le sorticement et toute maniere de devinaille; H: הניחוש, וכל מיני קסם = divination and all sorts of magic.

[16]**14: Pleasant and acceptable speech.** P, 41rb: parler congrue; H: ודבר צחות = purity of language.

[17]**14: Interpretation of languages.** P, 41rb: pointoiement de language; H: דקדוק הלשון = precision of the language.

[18]**14: Borrowing and receiving.** P, 41rb: prester et recevoir; H: משא ומתן = carrying and giving. → This is the literal translation of a Hebrew idiom meaning negotiations, bargaining. See above, note on § 3.6:1, s.v., "loans and gifts".

[19]**14: Work or laying on of hands.** P, 41rb: oevre de main; H: מעשה יד = blow.

[20]**14: Its nature.** P, 41va: sa nature; H: השתנות תולדתו = the change of its nature.

[21]**15: Little boys or infants.** P, 41va: les enfans petis; H: הבנים הקטנים = younger sons.

[22]**15: In the nativity.** P: om.; H: במולד = in the nativity.

[23]**17: Nose.** P, 41va: ses narines; H: נחיריו = his nostrils.

[24]**17: Deprived of or devoid of a beard.** P, 41va: wit de barbe; H: וזלדקן = with a scraggly

[25]21: **Persicus or indigo.** P, r2va: perse; H: תכלת = azure.

[26]22: **Of the tastes, in its portion is.** P, 41vb: sa saveur est; H: טעמו = its taste.

[27]23: **Of the angles.** → See above, note on §3.2:30, sv. "of the angles".

[28]25: **The day of Mercury.** P, 41vb: merquedi.; H: יום רביעי = ⟨the day-time of⟩ the fourth day. → Bate's divergent translation glosses on Ibn Ezra's expression "fourth day".

[29]25: **The one which precedes the day of the Lord.** P, 41vb: la nuit dont le dimenche est aprés; H: ליל ראשון = the night of the first day.

§4.7

[1]2: **The natural power or the strength of nature.** P, 42ra: la force de la nature; H: כח התולדת = the power of nature.

[2]3: **The habitable.** P, 42ra: l'abitable; H: הישוב = the settlement. → Meaning, ecumene.

[3]5: **Mariners or sailors.** P, 41ra: les rimeurs; H: מלחים = sailors.

[4]6: **Of the minerals.** P, 42ra: des metaus; H: מהמתכות = of the metals.

[5]7: **Streams.** P, 42ra: viviers = ponds; H: בריכות = ponds.

[6]11: **Of the plants.** P, 42ra: des arbres; H: מהאילנים = of the trees.

[7]11: **Watermelons.** P, 42ra: coucombres; H: הקרא = pumpkins.

[8]12: **Whose mixture.** P, 42ra: que sa nature; H: שתולדתו = whose nature. → Bate's divergent translation glosses on Ibn Ezra's concept of "nature".

[9]14: **Underclothes.** P, 42ra: les napes; H: עור המלבוש והמפות = leather for clothes and table-coverings.

[10]15: **Wisdom or thoughts or discretion.** P, 42rb: savoir; H: הדעת = knowldege.

[11]15: **Timidity or fear of the multitude.** P, 42rb: plenté de peur; H: רוב פחד = extreme fear.

[12]15: **Without concern of the heart.** P, 42rb: non songnance de cuer; H: תמימות הלב = naiveté.

[13]15: **Revealing counsels.** P, 42rb: descouvremens de consel; H: גילוי הסוד = revealing the secret.

[14]15: **Loving or desiring joy.** P, 42rb: amer la joie; H: אהבת השמחה = love of joy.

[15]15: **Conquering or prevailing.** P, 42rb: le vainquement; H: הנצוח = subjugation.

[16]15: **Knowledge of human beings' hidden things.** P, 42rb: savoir le sorcellement; H: דעת הכישוף = knowledge of sorcery. → Bate's divergent translation glosses on Ibn Ezra's concept of "sorcery".

[17]16: **Years of suckling or nourishment and infancy.** P, 42rb: les ans de l'alaitement; H: שנות הגמול = the years of weaning.

[18]16: **Greater or older sisters.** P, 42rb: les sereurs grans; H: האחיות הגדולות = the older sisters.

[19]19: **The breast.** P, 42va: le pis; H: הרחם = the womb.

[20]21: **The time of suckling.** P, 42va: quant il est alaitant; H: כשהוא יונק = when he is a suckling.

[21]24: **Of the angles.** → See above, note on § 3.2:30, s.v., "of the angles".

[22]26: **The day of the Moon.** P, 42va: le lundi; H: יום שני = ⟨the daytime of⟩ the second day. → Bate's divergent translation glosses on Ibn Ezra's expression "second day".

[23]26: **The one which follows the day of Venus.** P, 42ra: la nuit dont le vendredi est a prés; H: ליל ששי = the night of the sixth ⟨day⟩.

§5.1

[1]1: **The fifth part of the book begins.** P, 42vb: Li chapitres .5e; H: שער חמישי = fifth gate. → Meaning, fifth chapter.

[2]1: **On the goodness or being good.** P, 42vb: en la bonté; H: בטובת = on the goodness.

[3]1: **Evil or malice.** P, 42vb: leur mauvaitié; H: רעתם = their evil.

[4]2: **A planet.** P, 42vb: une des planetes; H: אחד מן המשרתים = one of the servants. → Meaning, one of the planets. See above note on §2:5, s.v., "planets".

[5]2: **Benevolent star.** P, 42vb: bone estoile; H: כוכב טוב = good star.

[6]4: **Malevolent stars.** P, 42ra: les mauvaises estoiles; H: הכוכבים הרעים = the bad stars.

[7]4: **In the same place.** P, 42vb: ensamble lui; H: עמו = with it.

[8]5: **It moves back.** P, 42vb: departant; H: מתפרד = separates.

[9]6: **Two.** P, 42vb: .2.; H: שני = two.

[10]7: **Or in a bodily conjunction or with the Sun.** P, 42vb: ou en conjunction de l'empressement ou ensamble le soleil; H: או במחברת הדבק עם השמש = or in conjunction with the one joined to the Sun.

[11]12: **Its dignities.** P, 42vb: en .l. sa poesté; H: ממשלתו = in its dominion.

[12]12: **Exaltation.** P, 3vb: eneur; H: כבוד = honor.

[13]12: **Apogee.** P, 43ra: sa hautece; H: גבהותו = its height. → Meaning, its apogee.

[14]16: **The dignities of benevolent stars.** P, 43ra: la poesté des bones estoiles; H: ממשלת הכוכבים הטובים = the dominion of good stars.

[15]16: **In their own dignities.** P, 43ra: leur poesté; H: בממשלתם = in their dominion.

[16]18: **Greater power.** P, 43ra: plus fort; H: יותר תקיף = it [the planet] is strengthened.

§ 5.2

[1]1: **Stars.** P, 43ra: estoiles; H: הכוכב = the star.

[2]1: **Full or complete.** P, 43rb: enterin; H: שלמה = complete.

[3]2: **Exaltation.** P, 3vb: eneur; H: כבוד = honor.

§ 5.3

[1]1: **Towards the north.** P, 43rb: devers senestre = towards the left; H: בפאת שמאלית = in the left side, or in the left edge. → In the French, "devers senestre" means towards the north, and in the Hebrew בפאת שמאלית means in the northern side or edge.

[2]2: **In the circle of apogee.** P, 43va: cercle de sa hautece; H: בגלגל הגבהות = in the circle of the height.

[3]2: **In that opposite to the apogee.** P, 43va: de, sa basseté; H: והשפלות = of the lowness.

[4]2: **That is, in the eccentric circle.** P, 43va: c'est celi que son centre est loing du centre de la terre; H: שמוצקו רחוק ממוצק הארץ = whose center is far from the center of the Earth. → Here Ibn Ezra uses the neologism מוצק = center, meaning literally "solid". For this neologism, see Sela 2003, 113–116.

[5]4: **The rays of the Sun.** P, 43va: la clarté du soleil; H: אור השמש = the light of the Sun.

[6]5: **Angles or cardines.** P, 43va: chevillies = pegs; H: יתדות = pegs. → Meaning, cardines of the horoscope.

[7]6: **And they are.** P, 43va: et s'il sont; H: ואם היו = and if they were.

§5.4

[1]1: **Weakness.** P, 43va: foibleté; H: דלות = poorness, thinness.

[2]3: **Than for the upper ⟨planets⟩.** P, 43vb: que as souvreieines; H: om.

[3]7: **Its fall.** P, 43vb: sa honte; H: קלונו = its shame.

[4]11: **The house of its banishment or hate.** P, 43vb: en la rneson de sa haine; H: בית שנאתו = the house of its hate.

[5]14: **Peregrine or strange.** P, 43vb: estrange; H: גר = a stranger.

[6]15: **Or in the feminine signs.** P: om.; H: ובמזלות נקבות = or in the feminine signs.

[7]16: **The same holds true for the Sun, unless it is in the ninth house, because that is the place of its joy.** P: om.; H: וככה השמש, רק אם היתה בבית התשיעי כי היא בית שמחתה. = The same holds true for the Sun, unless it is in the ninth house, because that is the place of its joy.

[8]17: **The lower planets are weak when they begin to be oriental of the Sun, or when they are in one of the masculine quadrants.** P: om.; H: ומדלות הכוכבים השפלים שיהיו בתחלת היותם מזרחיים מהשמש, או שיהיו באחת הרביעיות הזכרים = The lower planets are weak when they begin to be oriental of the Sun, or when they are in one of the masculine quadrants.

§5.5

[1]1: **The weakness of the inferior ⟨planets⟩.** P, 43vb: la foiibleté des estoiles basses; H: רעת הכוכב = the evil of the star. → Cf. above, note on §5.4:1, s.v., "weakness".

NOTES TO *LIBER ABRAHE AVENERRE INTRODUCTORIUS* 449

[2]1: **When they apply to malevolent ⟨planets⟩.** P, 44ra: quant sont ou commencement de leur estre domachans; H: שיהיה במחברת עם כוכבים מזיקים = when it is in conjunction with malefic planets.

[3]5: **If the ⟨inferior⟩ star does not receive the malevolent ⟨planet⟩.** P, 43ra: se non est le damachant recevant l'estoile; H: אם לא יהיה המזיק מקבל הכוכב = if an harmful ⟨star⟩ does not receive the planet.

[4]8: **Obstruction.** P, 44ra: la durece; H: קושי = difficulty, hardness.

§ 5.7

[1]1: **As for the weakness.** P, 44rb: de la poverté; H: מדלות = as for the poorness, thinness.

[2]1: **In conjunction.** P: om.; H: במחברת = in conjunction.

§ 5.8

[1]4: **According to their number of ten degrees.** P, 43ra: il i a le nombre de ses degrés .10.; H: שיהיה כמספר אלו המעלות = is the same number of degrees.

[2]9: **Burnt path.** P, 44va: en la voie de l'arson; H: בדרך השריפה = in the path of burning.

§ 6.1

[1]1: **Sixth part.** P, 44va: li chapitres .6e.; H: השער הששי = the sixgth gate. → Meaning, sixth chapter.

[2]1: **On the existence or the condition.** P, 44va: l'afaire; H: בעניני = on the affairs.

[3]2: **In themselves.** P, 44vb: en eus meesmes; H: בעצמם = in themselves.

[4]2: **Certain other.** P, 44vb: assés; H: רבים = many.

[5]3: **Its apogee.** P, 44vb: sa hautece; H: גבהותו = its height.

[6]**4: Or descending in it.** P: om; P¹, 45va: ou descendant en lui; H: או יורד בו = or descending in it.

[7]**5: Or when it is at the beginning of its apogee.** P: om.; P¹, 45va: ou que il est ou commencement de haultesce; H: או שיהיה בתחלת הגבהות = Or when it is at the beginning of the height.

[8]**6: The opposite of its apogee.** P, 44vb: sa basseté; H: שפלותו = its lowness.

[9]**8: In the point of the opposite of its apogee.** P, 44vb: ou lieu de sa tresbasseté; H: במקום שפלותו = in the place of its lowness.

[10]**13: Or when it is intermediate.** P, 43ra: ou que soit son nombre acreu ou faillant ou moien; H: או חשבונו נוסף או חסר או אמצעי = or when its calculation is increasing, decreasing, or intermediate.

§6.2

[1]**1: When a planet is 90° from the beginning of its apogee, it is direct in its motion, meaning ⟨it moves with its⟩ mean ⟨motion⟩, and the same holds true for its light and the power of its body.** P: om.; H: ואם היה המשרת רחוק מתחלת גבהותו תשעים מעלות אז הוא ישר בהליכתו, והטעם אמצעי, וככה אורו ועוצם גופו. = When a servant (i.e., planet) is 90° from the beginning of its height, it is direct in its motion, meaning ⟨it moves with its⟩ mean ⟨motion⟩, and the same holds true for its light and the power of its body.

[2]**2: When.** P, 44vb: et; H: אם = if.

[3]**2: Planet.** P, 44vb: planete; H: משרת = servant. → Meaning, planet. See above note on §2:5, s.v., "planets".

[4]**2: Its apogee.** P, 45ra: son aus; H: גבהותו = its height.

[5]**2: Or.** P, 45ra: ou; H: אז = then.

[6]**2: Then it is.** P, 45ra: et il est; H: ויהיה = it is.

[7]**3: Decreasing or deficient.** P, 45ra: la faillance; H: חחסרון = the decrease.

NOTES TO *LIBER ABRAHE AVENERRE INTRODUCTORIUS*   451

[8]4: **The beginning of.** P, 45ra: l'acommençal; H: תחלת = the beginning of.

[9]5: **To the opposite of the apogee.** P, 45ra: a son lieu bas; H: אל מקום שפלותו = to the place of its lowness.

[10]5: **Then.** P, 45ra: adonc; H: גם הוא = it too.

[11]5: **In everything.** P: om.; H: בכל = in everything.

[12]6: **Opposite of the apogee.** P, 45ra: en son trebas; H: שפלותו = its lowness.

§6.3

[1]1: **In its number.** P, 45ra: en son conte; H: במספרו = in its number.

[2]1: **Equal degrees.** P, 45rb: degrés drois; H: המעלות הישרות = the straight degrees.

[3]1: **And if there is no number there, it is neither increasing nor decreasing.** P, 45ra: et s'il n'i a point de conte, il n'est ne creu ne amermé; H: ואם אין שם מספר, איננו נוסף ולא חסר = and if there is no number there, it is neither increasing nor decreasing.

[4]2: **Equation.** P, 45ra: l'appareillement; H: התיקון = the correction.

[5]2: **Line of the girdle of the signs.** P: om.; P[1], 46ra: ou pourceint de l'imaginacion du cercle; H: בחשב אפודת הגלגל = in the girdle of the vest of the circle of the signs. → See above note on §1.10:5, s.v., "in the girdle of the imagination of the circle of the signs".

[6]3: **Its equation.** P, 45rb: l'appareillement du soleil; H: תיקון השמש = the correction of the Sun.

[7]3: **In one degree.** P, 45rb: en un gré; H: בחלק אחד = in one minute.

[8]5: **Then ⟨their motion⟩ will be intermediate, neither slow nor swift.** P, 45va: adonc ne sont il ne tardif ne hatif; H: לא ממתינים ולא מהירים = they are neither slowing down nor speeding up.

§6.4

[1]1: **Latitude.** P, 45ra: la largece; H: רוחב = latitude.

[2]2: **From there.** P, 45ra: et de .90.; H: ומתשעים = and from 90°.

[3]3: **At a distance.** P, 45va: a la longeté; H: עד מרחק = at a distance.

[4]4: **Line of the girdle of the signs.** P, 45va: pourceint de l'ymaginacion du cercle; H: בחשב אפודת הגלגל = girdle of the vest of the circle. → See above note on §1.10:5, s.v., "in the girdle of the imagination of the circle of the signs".

§6.5

[1]1: **Disposition or condition.** P, 45va: la maniere; H: עניני = the affairs.

[2]2: **After.** P, 45va: des quant; H: ב = when.

[3]2: **Degree for degree.** P, 45va: parti encontre partie en .1. gré; H: חלק כנגד חלק במעלה אחת = minute for minute, in the same degree.

[4]2: **Of the Sun.** P, 45va: de li; H: ממנה = of it.

[5]3: **Conjoin it bodily.** P, 45vb: s'apresent ensamble li; H: וידבקו עמה = they are joined to it.

[6]3: **East.** P, 45vb: occident; H: מערב = west.

[7]3: **Until they reach their first station.** P, 45vb: qu'il sont en leur estage; H: עד היותם במעמדם = until they are in their station.

[8]4: **After.** P, 45vb: des le tans; H: מרגע = from the moment.

§6.6

[1]2: **That the planets are.** P, 45vb: que soient les estoiles; H: שיהיה הכוכב.

[2]2: **And minute.** P, 45vb: et en une partie; H: ובחלק אחד = and minute.

NOTES TO *LIBER ABRAHE AVENERRE INTRODUCTORIUS* 453

[3] 2: **Conjunct.** P, 45vb: empressee; H: מדובק = stuck.

[4] 3: **The minutes are more than the aforementioned [16′].** P: om.; H: חלקיו יותר מן הנזכרים = the minutes are more than the aforementioned.

[5] 3: **And this is the second way.** P, 46ra: et c'est la seconde voie; H: om.

[6] 4: **After they have moved more than 6° distant.** P, 46ra: et quant il sont plus de .6. grés; H: ובהיותם יותר משש מעלות = when they are more than 6°.

[7] 4: **In longitude.** P, 46ra: loing; H: רחוקים = distant.

[8] 4: **Under the rays.** P, 46ra: desous la clarté; H: תחת האור = under the light.

[9] 6: **Some of.** P: om.; H: מעט = some of.

[10] 6: **Strength or power.** P, 46ra: la force; H: הכח = the power.

[11] 7: **They have tested that when Mars is at a distance of 18°, then it is under the rays.** P, 46ra: qu'il ont veu que quant est loing mars .18. grés, adonc est il desous la clarté; H: ראוי שיהיה מאדים רחוק שמונה עשרה מעלות אז יצא מתחת האור. = it is appropriate that Mars should be 18° away, then it will no longer be under the light.

[12] 9: **And strong.** P, 46rb: fors; H: חזקים = strong.

[13] 10: **Their rays.** P, 46rb: de leur rais; H: זריחתם = their shining.

[14] 13: **When it is retrograde until ⟨it reaches⟩ opposition to the Sun it has no power, and this is the eighth way.** P and P¹ om; H: ובהיותו חוזר אחורנית עד נכח השמש, הדרך השמינית, ואין לו כח כלל.

[15] 14: **And when they are.** P, 46rb: Et quant il; H: ובהיותו = and when it is.

[16] 14: **Every.** P, 46rb: tout; H: om.

[17] 14: **Will not issue from the light.** P, 46rb: qui n'istra mie a clarté; H: שלא יצא לאור = that will not issue from the light. → This is the literal translation of a Hebrew idiom meaning will not be fulfilled.

[18]15: **They are.** P, 46rb: il soit; H: היותו = it is.

[19]16: **When it is there.** P: om.; H: ובהיותו שם = when it is there.

[20]16: **Their power is restored to them.** P, 46rb: retornera a li toute la force; H: ישוב כחו אליו = its power will be restored to it.

[21]17: **Their power.** P, 46va: sa forse; H: כחו = its power.

[22]17: **Somewhat.** P: om.; H: מעט = somewhat.

[23]18: **Quartile aspect.** P, 46va: regard quart; H: מבט ששית = sextile aspect.

[24]18: **Then less than a third of its power is left to it.** P: om.; H: אז לא נשאר לה רק פחות משלישית כחה = then less than a third of its power is left to it.

[25]19: **It grows weaker still until the aspect of sextile.** P, 46va: Et puis va afoiblisant duques il soit a regart .6°.; H: ובהיותה רחוקה מהשמש חמש עשרה מעלות = when its distance from the Sun is 15°.

§ 6.7

[1]2: **In the same degree.** P, 46va: en une partie; H: בחלק אחד = in the same part. → Meaning, in the same minute.

[2]2: **Two ways must be counted.** P, 46va: conte .2. voies; H: הנה שני דרכים = these are two ways.

[3]2: **Longitude.** P, 46va: l'alongnement; H: מרחק = distance.

[4]3: **And from there until their distance.** P, 46va: Et quant il sont loing; H: ובהיותם רחוקים = and when they are distant.

[5]3: **They continue to be under the rays.** P, 46va: eus sont desous la clarté; H: הם תחת האור = they are under the light.

[6]5: **And afterwards.** P, 46va: et puis; H: om.

[7]6: **And when.** P, 46va: et se; H: ואם = and if.

[8]8: **Next.** P, 46vb: et d'iluec; H: ומשם = and from there.

[9]9: **Until the beginning of the station and of retrogradation.** P, 46vb: jusques qu'il accomemcent a estre en leur estage et retornent arrieres; H: עד שיחלו להיותם במעמדם וישובו אחורנית = until they being to be in their station and turn retrograde.

§6.8

[1]5: **Next, because.** P, 44ra: et d'iluec; H: ומשם = and from there.

[2]5: **Longitude.** P, 47ra: l'alongnement; H: מרחק = distance.

[3]5: **Will shine or be illuminated.** P, 47ra: esclarcissant; H: מאירה = shines.

[4]7: **Next.** P, 47ra: et d'iluec; H: ומשם = and from there.

[5]12: **Its strength will grow weaker.** P, 47rb: afoiblira sa force,; H: om.

[6]13: **Twice.** P, 47rb: .2. fois; H: פעמים = sometimes. → But Hagin read פעמיים, meaning twice.

§7.1

[1]1: **Seventh part of the book.** P, 47rb: Le .7e. chapitre; H: שער השביעי = the seventh gate. → Meaning, seventh chapter.

[2]1: **Planets.** P, 47rb: planetes; H: המשרתים = the servants. → Meaning the planets. See above note on §2:5, s.v., "planets".

[3]1: **And are the following.** P, 47rb: et ves les ci; H: om.

[4]1: **Application.** P, 47rb: l'aprochement; H: הקירוב = getting close.

[5]1: **Solitude.** P, 47rb: L'aler seul; H: הילוך בדד = solitary motion.

[6]1: **Alienation.** P, 47rb: l'atissement; H: השומם = desolation.

[7]1: **Giving nature.** P: om.; H: תת התולדת = giving nature.

[8]1: **Obliquity.** P, 47rb: la tortece; H: העוות = distortion.

[9]1: **Restraint or contradiction.** P, 47rb: le destorbement; H: הביטול = cancellation.

[10]1: **Obstruction or accident.** P, 47rb: l'accident; H: המקרה = the accident.

[11]1: **Frustration.** P, 47rb: le deperdement; H: האבוד = the loss.

[12]1: **Compassion.** P, 47va: le souvantume; H: הנועם = the pleasantness.

[13]1: **Siege.** P, 47va: l'amoiement.; H: האמצעיות = intermediacy. → For the rationale behind the meaning of these terms, see below § 7.23:1–2.

[14]1: **Strength.** P, 47va: le prinçoiement; H: השררה = the dominion.

§ 7.2

[1]2: **In application.** P, 47va: aprochant; H: מתקרב = getting close.

[2]2: **Degree.** P, 47va: gré; H: חלק = minute.

[3]3: **13°.** P, 47va: .13. grés; H: חמש עשרה מעלות = 15°.

[4]4: **Application in the projection of rays.** P, 47va: l'aprochement es rais de la clarté; H: הקירוב בניצוצי האור = getting close in the sparks of light.

§ 7.3

[1]3: **⟨Other⟩'s body.** P, 47va: du cors; H: הגוף = the body.

[2]5: **The heavier or weightier.** P, 47vb: pesant; H: הכבד = the heavy one.

[3]7: **Abraham Ibn Ezra.** P, 47vb: Abraham Even Azre; H: אברהם ן׳ עזרא = Abraham Ibn Ezra.

[4]7: **Compiler.** P, 47vb: ajoustant = compiler; H: מעתיק = translator.

[5]7: **As I shall explain in the Book of Nativities.** → This is a reference to the first version of *Sefer ha-Moladot* (*Moladot*, III i 15, 1–4, 118–121), where Ibn Ezra takes issue with Māshā'allāh over the physical reality of the zodiacal signs therefore questioning the rationale behind the condition of conjunction as defined in the current passage.

[6]8: **The orb of the signs.** P, 48ra: orbe des signes; H: גלגל המזלות = circle of the signs.

[7]8: **The size of their power.** P, 48ra: la mesure de lur force; H: שיעור כח גופם = the size of the power of their body.

[8]10: **One degree.** P, 48ra: un gré; H: מעלה אחת = one degree.

[9]12: **In the girdle of the vest.** P, 48ra: du pourceint de l'ymaginacion; H: מחשב האפודה = from the girdle of the vest. → See above note on §1.10:5, s.v., "in the girdle of the imagination of the circle of the signs".

[10]12: **There will still be an explanation of this.** P, 48ra: et encore parlerai je sur ce; H: ועוד אדבר על זה = I shall still speak about this.

§ 7.4

[1]3: **Goodness.** P, 48ra: bien; H: טובה = goodness.

[2]4: **The conjunction of Jupiter with Saturn.** P, 48rb: jupiter avec saturne; H: צדק עם שבתאי = Jupiter with Saturn.

[3]9: **The star.** P, 48va: l'estoile; H: הכוכב = the star.

[4]9: **In the heavens.** P, 48ra: ou ciel = in the heavens; H: בגלגל = in the circle.

[5]9: **He is right.** P, 48va: et il a droit; H: הדין עמו = the law is on his side. → Meaning, he is right.

[6]10: **It is conjoined.** P, 48va: est conjointe; H: om.

§7.5

[1]1: **Aspect.** P: om.; H: מבט = aspect.

[2]1: **The beginning of the aspects.** P, 48va: le regards; H: תחלת המבטים = the beginning of the aspects.

[3]1: **Of this book.** P, 48vb: de ce livre; H: om.

[4]1: **And then it is in the power of the aspect.** P, 48vb: adonc est il en la force du regart; H: והוא האמת = and this is true.

[5]2: **Longitude.** P, 48va: l'alongnement; H: המרחק = the distance.

§7.6

[1]1: **Modes.** P, 48vb: voies; H: דרכים = ways.

[2]2: **Applies to.** P, 48vb: se conjoint; H: יתחבר = conjoins.

[3]3: **Apply to the other star or conjoin it.** P, 49ra: se conjoint a autre estoilr; H: יתחבר עם כוכב אחר = conjoin another star.

[4]3: **But if more then it separates from the mixture.** P, 49ra: et plus de ce se se depart le mellement; H: ואם באחד המבטים ירחק ממנו פחות משש מעלות, גם הוא בממסכו ויותר מזה יבטל הממסך = and if its distance from some aspect with it [the heavy planet] is less than 6°, in this case, too, it [the light planet] is mixed with ⟨the heavy planet⟩, but if the distance is greater the mixture is canceled.

§7.7

[1]2: **If.** P, 49ra: Et la sarnblance est; H: שיהיה = suppose that there is.

[2]2: **Equinoctial line.** P, 49ra: la lingne de la juste; H: קו הצדק = the line of justice.

[3]3: **Parts of the hours.** P, 49ra: eures tortes; H: שעותיה המעוותות = its crooked hours.

[4]3: **Aries or of Libra.** P, 49ra: l'engnel ou des balances; H: סרטן = Cancer.

[5]3: **And for that reason their conjunction is called "equal".** P, 59ra: Et eus sont apelees conjunction droite; H: וככה אם היה מרחקם מראש גדי. = and likewise if they were equidistant from the head of Capricorn.

[6]4: **Longitude.** P, 49ra: l'alongnement; H: המרחק = the distance.

§ 7.8

[1]1: **Solitude.** P, 49ra: L'aler seul; H: הילוך בדד = solitary motion.

[2]1: **Another.** P, 49rb: de son compaignon; H: מחבירו = from its compagnion.

§ 7.9

[1]1: **Alienation.** P, 49rb: l'atissement; H: השומם = desolation.

§ 7.10

[1]3: **Even.** P, 49rb: plus; H: האחרון = last.

§ 7.13

[1]1: **Exaltation.** P, 3vb: eneur; H: כבוד = honor.

§ 7.14

[1]1: **Giving power.** P, 49vb: doner la poesté; H: תת הממשלה = giving dominion. → See above § 7.1:1, where the same condition is called "giving governance" = "donum potestatis".

[2]1: **Friendship.** P, 48vb: amour; H: אהבה = love.

[3]1: **Equal or tempered.** P, 49vb: droit; H: ישר = straight. → Meaning, tempered.

§ 7.15

[1]1: **If.** P, 49rb: que; H: ש = that.

[2]1: **Exaltation.** P, 3vb: eneur; H: כבוד = honor.

§ 7.16

[1]2: **Dignity.** P, 49vb: prinçoiement; H: שררה = dominion.

§ 7.17

[1]1: **Straightness.** P, 50ra: la droiture; H: היושר = straightness.

[2]1: **Angles.** P, 50ra: chevilles = pegs; H: היתדות = the pegs. → Meaning, cardines of the horoscope.

[3]1: **Succedent to the angles or of the angles.** P, 50ra: des soupoies; H: סמוכים = succedent.

§ 7.18

[1]1: **Obliquity.** P, 50ra: Le torchonnoiernent; H: העיוות = distortion.

§ 7.19

[1]1: **Prohibition.** → See above § 7.1:1, where the same condition is called "inhibition" = inhibitio.

[2]2: **The first mode.** P, 50ra: L'une ausi; H: om.

[3]4: **Applies by conjunction.** P, 50rb: conjoingnant; H: מתחבר = conjoins.

[4]4: **The planet that was conjoined with it.** P, 50rb: l'estoile qui est ensamble li; H: הכוכב שהוא עמו = the star that is with it.

[5]4: **Its disposition or effect.** P, 50rb: son afaire; H: דברו = signification.

[6]4: **At an equal distance.** P, 50rb: leur grés onnis; H: מעלותיהן שוות = their degrees are the same.

[7]5: **In aspect than ⟨the degrees⟩ of the conjoining or applying ⟨planet⟩, it will not be able to prohibit the aspecting planet.** P, 50rb: du regart non porra le conjongnant a deveer le rgardant; H: אל המבט, לא יוכל המתחבר למנוע המביט. = to the aspect, the applying planet cannot prohibit the aspecting planet.

§7.20

[1]1: **Returning or coming back to goodness.** P, 50rb: le retornement a bien; H: ההשבה לטוב = Returning to goodness.

[2]1: **Know that returning to goodness.** P, 50rb: Saches que le returnement a bien; H: דע כי ההשבה לטוב = Know that the returning to goodness.

[3]1: **Or aspects it.** P: om.; H: או יביט אליו = or aspects it.

[4]1: **Because then.** P, 50rb: et donc; H: והנה = and so.

[5]1: **Sun.** P, 50rb: le soleil; H: הכוכב = the star.

[6]1: **Therefore it returns or causes it to return.** P, 50rb: et donc retornera il; H: והנה ישיבנו = and so it returns it.

[7]2: **Returns or makes return to it.** P, 50rb: retornera il a lui; H: ישיב עליו = it returns to it.

[8]4: **The giver or the one that returns.** P, 50rb: le donneur; H: הנותן = the giver.

[9]6: **That makes return.** P, 50va: qui fait retourner; H: המשיב = the one that returns.

§7.23

[1]1: **Accident or accidental event.** P, 50va: l'accident; H: המקרה = the accident. → See above §7.1:1, where the same condition is called obstruction or accident = "impeditio vel accidens".

§7.24

[1]1: **Frustration or evasion.** P, 50vb: la deperdicion; H: האבוד = loss.

§7.25

[1]1: **Cutting or intercepting the light.** P, 50vb: le taillement de la clarté; H: כריתות האור = Cutting the light. → See above §7.1:1, where this condition is called cutting the light = "abscisio luminis".

[2]2: **Moves or applies to the conjunction.** P, 50vb: est conjongnant; H: מתחבר = conjoins.

[3]2: **Light.** P: om.; H: קל = light.

§7.26

[1]1: **Compassion or generosity.** P, 51ra: la sovantume; H: הנועם = pleasantness. → See above §7.1:1, where this condition is called compassion = "compassio".

[2]1: **Fall.** P, 14vb: honte; H: קלון = dishonor.

[3]1: **Exerts some dignity.** P, 51ra: il a poeté; H: יש לו שום ממשלה = it has some dominion.

[4]1: **Fall.** P, 14vb: honte; H: קלון = dishonor.

[5]1: **Will have compassion for it.** P, 51ra: assouavera sur li; H: ינעים עליו = gives it pleasure.

§7.27

[1]1: **Fall.** P, 14vb: honte; H: קלון = dishonor.

§7.28

[1]1: **Bodily.** P, 51ra: en conjonction; H: במחברת = by conjunction.

[2]1: **Exaltation.** P, 3vb: eneur; H: כבוד = honor.

[3]1: **Then it is received by this planet.** P, 51ra: et il reçoit cele es toile; H: והנה יקבלנו אותו הכוכב = then it is received by this planet.

[4]2: **If.** P, 51ra: ou; H: או = or.

[5]2: **Exaltation.** P, 3vb: eneur; H: כבוד = honor.

[6]5: **Equal or tempered.** P, 51rb: droite; H: ישרה = straight. → See above, §7.14:1.

[7]5: **In conjunction.** P: om.; H: במחברת = in conjunction.

§7.29

[1]2: **It receives her.** P, 51rb: ele le reçoit; H: היא תקבלנו = she receives it.

[2]3: **Exaltation.** P, 3vb: eneur; H: כבוד = honor.

[3]5: **Or term.** P: om.; H: או הגבול = or term.

§7.30

[1]1: **Benevolence or generosity.** P, 51va: La volentiveté; H: נדיבות = generosity. → See §7.1:1, where the same condition is called "benevolence" = "benevolentia".

[2]1: **Exaltation.** P, 3vb: eneur; H: כבוד = honor.

§ 7.31

[1]1: **Similitude or** *ḥayyz* **or being in its domain.** P, 51va: la samblance; H: הדמיון = the similitude. → See § 7.1:1, where this condition is called "similitude" = "similitudo".

§ 7.32

[1]1: **Siege.** P, 51vb: la miloennetes; H: האמצעיות = intermediacy.

[2]1: **Benevolent or harmful planet.** P, 51vb: estoile bone ou mauvaise; H: כוכב טוב או רע = good or bad star.

[3]2: **Besieged.** P, 51vb: la miloennee; H: ממוצע = intermediate.

§ 7.33

[1]1: **Strength.** P, 51vb: le prinçoiement; H: השררה = the dominion.

§ 8.1

[1]1: **Eighth part of this book.** P, 52ra: Le .8e. chapitre; H: השער השמיני = the eighth gate. → Meaning, eighth chapter.

[2]1: **Judgments or rules.** P, 52ra: jugement; H: דינין = judgments.

§ 8.2

[1]1: **One of which is.** P, 52ra: l'un es; H: om.

[2]1: **Multiplies the mixture or it is more mixed.** P, 52ra: et acroit mellement; H: ויותר ממסך = it is more mixed.

[3]2: **It is with harmful ⟨planets⟩ or it is hindered.** P, 52rb: est ensamble les damachans.; H: היתה עם המזיקים = it is with the harmful ones.

[4]3: **For the querent or interrogator.** P, 52ra: pour le demandeur; H: לשואל = for the querent.

NOTES TO *LIBER ABRAHE AVENERRE INTRODUCTORIUS* 465

[5]3: **For the requested thing.** P, 52ra: pour la chose qui est demandee; H: לדבר שישאל בשבילו = for the thing he is posing a question about.

[6]5: **Any future event.** P, 52ra: toute chose atendant; H: כל דבר עתיד = any future thing. → The Latin "res" is polysemic, like Hebrew דבר, and can mean both "object" and "event". Authors in Hebrew and Latin can confound and alternate the two senses; it doesn't work in English.

[7]5: **Whatever the interrogator is hoping for or must expect.** P, 52va: tout quamque esperra li demandans; H: כל מה שיקוה השואל = anything the querent is hoping for.

[8]6: **Past events.** P, 52ra: les choses qui sont passe s; H: הדברים שעברו = past things.

[9]9: **The querent or the person.** P, 52va: home; H: האדם = the person.

[10]9: **Angles.** P, 53vb: chevilles; H: יתדות = pegs. → Meaning, cardines of the horoscope.

§ 8.3

[1]3: **Hindered.** P, 52vb: domagié; H: מוזק = harmed.

[2]3: **Rays.** P, 52vb: rais; H: ניצוץ = spark.

[3]4: **Its aspect.** P: om.; H: במבט = in aspect.

[4]5: **Will come into effect and will be.** P, 53ra: qui venra a oevre et qui sera; H: על הדבר שיהיה = what will be.

[5]5: **Will not issue from the light.** P, 53ra: non istra a clarté; H: לא תצא לאור = will not issue from the light. → This is the literal translation of a Hebrew idiom meaning will not come to pass; cf. above § 6.6:14.

[6]7: **Bad.** P, 53ra: les damachans; H: המזיקים = the harmful ones.

[7]8: **Opposite their similitude.** P: om.; H: בהפך דמיונם = opposite their similitude.

[8]8: **House of fall or in the house of hate.** P, 53ra: la meson de leur honte ou en la meson de leur haine; H: בבית קלונם, או בבית שנאתם = in the house of their shame or the house of their hate.

[9]9: **Harm or destroy.** P, 53rb: clesiberont; H: יזיקו = will harm.

[10]10: **Alone is in charge.** P, 53rb: est seul en la poesté; H: מתבודד בממשלת = secludes itself in the dominion.

[11]11: **An aspecting.** P, 53rb: regardant = an aspecting; H: המזיק = the harmful one.

[12]11: **Evil.** P, 53rb: le damache; H: תולדת = nature.

[13]11: **Evil.** P, 53rb: le damache; H: נזק = harm.

[14]11: **Evil.** P, 53rb: le damache; H: נזק = harm.

[15]12: **When.** P, 53rb: se; H: אם = if.

[16]12: **They indicate an ignoble thing.** P: om.; H: יורו על דבר נבזה = they indicate an ignoble thing.

[17]16: **If it aspects the malevolent in quartile aspect.** P, 53va: Se regarde le domachant en regart quart; H: אם יביט המזיק אל הטוב מבט רביעית או נכח = if the harming ⟨planet⟩ aspects the good ⟨planet⟩ in quartile or opposition.

[18]19: **And it harms.** P, 53va: ou damache; H: או יזיק = or it harms.

§8.4

[1]1: **27th. Every planet, whether benefic or malefic, always indicates good fortune if it is in its house or in the house of its exaltation.** P: om.; H: כ"ז. כל כוכב טוב או רע, אם היה בביתו או בבית כבודו, לעולם יורה על טוב = Every planet, whether benefic or malefic, always indicates good fortune if it is in its house or in the house of its exaltation.

[2]2: **28th. Every planet at the cusp of a sign is considered to be weak until it is 5° past it [the cusp of the sign]. Likewise, if the planet is less than 5°**

from the ⟨cusp of a horoscopic⟩ place, it is considered to be within the power of the place; but if it more ⟨than 5°⟩ it escapes the power of the place. P: om.; H: כ״ח. כל כוכב שיהיה בתחלת המזל, יחשב חלש עד היותו בחמש מעלות ממנו; וככה, אם היה הכוכב רחוק מאחד הבתים פחות מחמש מעלות, יחשב בכח הבית; ואם יותר הוא נופל מכח הבית. = 28th. Every planet at the cusp of a sign is considered to be weak until it is 5° past it [the cusp of the sign]. Likewise, if the planet is less than 5° from the ⟨cusp of a horoscopic⟩ place, it is considered to be within the power of the place; but if it more ⟨than 5°⟩ it escapes the power of the place.

[3]4: **Neither come into effect nor will be.** P, 53vb: non istra a oevre et non sera; H: לא יוציא לידי מעשה = will not come into effect.

[4]5: **Fall.** P, 14vb: honte; H: קלון = dishonor.

[5]7: **Whose hope will not be frustrated.** P, 54ra: non sera deperdue s'esperance; H: לא תאבד תקותו = his hope will not be lost.

[6]8: **Or.** P, 54ra: ou; H: ו = and.

[7]9: **A planet located.** P, 54ra: Se est l'estoile; H: אם היה הכוכב = if the star is.

[8]9: **In which the power of the planet is.** P, 54ra: la ou il est; H: שהוא שם = in which it is.

[9]14: **In one of its dignities.** P, 54va: en .l. des lieus de sa poesté; H: באחד ממקומות ממשלתו = in one of the places of its dominion.

[10]14: **This is good for it.** P, 54va: adonc bon a li; H: אין טוב בו = there is no good in it.

[11]19: **A planet indicates that the requested ⟨event⟩ will not take place, difficulty and loss, if it begins to be retrograde, and it indicates good fortune, power, and moderation in the event, if it begins to be direct ⟨in its motion⟩.** P: om.; H: מ״ה. אם היה הכוכב עומד לחזור, יורה על חסרון המבוקש והקושי וההפסד; ואם עומד על היושר, יורה על טוב הדבר וכחו ויושרו = A planet indicates that the requested ⟨event⟩ will not take place, difficulty and loss, if it begins to be retrograde, and it indicates good fortune, power, and moderation in the event, if it begins to be direct ⟨in its motion⟩.

[12]21: **When a planet.** P, 54vb: Se est l'estoile; H: אם היה הכוכב = if the star.

[13]21: **Fixed sign.** P, 54vb: signe estant; H: מזל עומד = stable sign.

[14]22: **Power.** P, 54vb: la force; H: הכח = the power.

[15]22: **Place.** P, 54vb: lieu; H: מקום = place.

[16]23: **Sign of the.** P, 54vb: signe; H: המזל = המזל.

[17]23: **The requested event.** P, 54vb: en la chose que est demandee; H: בדבר שישאל = the think about which he poses a question.

[18]25: **The thing will happen according to all his wish.** P, 54vb: sera quise la chose en toute sa volunté; H: יבקש הדבר בכל חפצו = he will pursue the thing with all his wish.

§8.5

[1]6: **There will be many helpers.** P, 55ra: seront ses aideurs pluseurs; H: יעזרוהו קרוביו = his kin will help him.

§8.6

[1]1: **In the condition.** P, 55ra: sur la voie; H: על דרך = in the way.

[2]1: **Returning or reflecting the light.** → See above, §7.12:1–3.

[3]1: **This indicates that.** P, 55ra: sera; H: יהיה = will be.

[4]2: **In the condition.** P, 55rb: en maniere; H: בענין = on the matter.

[5]2: **Giving power.** → See above, §7.13:1.

[6]3: **In the condition.** P, 55rb: sur la voie; H: על דרך = in the way.

[7]3: **Giving power.** P, 55rb: cloner la poeté; H: תת הממשלה = giving dominion. → See above, §7.14:1.

NOTES TO *LIBER ABRAHE AVENERRE INTRODUCTORIUS* 469

[8]3: **Made clear or revealed.** P, 55rb: descouverra; H: יגלה = will be revealed.

[9]4: **Situated in the condition.** P, 55ra: s'il est en manere; H: אם היה בעניין = if it is on the matter.

[10]4: **Giving nature.** → See above § 7.15:1.

[11]4: **The requested event.** P, 55rb: en la chose; H: בדבר = in the thing.

[12]5: **Situated in the condition.** P, 55ra: s'il est en manere; H: אם היה בעניין = if it is on the matter.

[13]5: **Giving double nature.** → See above § 7.16:1–3.

[14]6: **Straightness.** → See above § 7.17:1.

[15]7: **Obliquity.** P, 55vb: tortece; H: עוות = distortion. → See above § 7.18:1.

[16]8: **Prohibition.** → See above § 7.19:1.

[17]9: **Restraining.** → See above § 7.22.1.

[18]9: **66th. The testimony of the significator situated in the condition of "restraining" indicates that events that undo the request thing will take place.** → This judgment corresponds to the 67th. judgment in the Hebrew and French source texts.

[19]10: **Returning to misfortune.** → See above § 7.11:1.

[20]10: **The testimony of the significator situated in the condition of "returning to evil" indicates that the querent will regret his question.** → This judgment corresponds to the 66th. judgment in the Hebrew and French source texts.

[21]11: **Accident.** → See above § 7.32:1.

[22]11: **Indicates.** P, 56ra: ce ensegne; H: יקרבו = will bring closer.

[23]12: **Frustration.** P, 56ra: perdicion; H: אבוד = loss. → See above § 7.24:1.

[24]**12: Indicates.** P, 56ra: ce ensegne; H: om.

[25]**13: His question.** P, 56ra: sa requeste; H: בקשתו = his request.

[26]**14: Compassion.** P, 56ra: le souvantune; H: הנועם = the pleasantness.

[27]**15: Recompense.** → See above § 7.27:1

[28]**16: Reception.** → See above § 7.28:1–5.

[29]**16: Did not rise in the heart.** P, 56rb: n'est monté sur son cuer; H: לא עלה על לבו = did not ascend to his heart. → Hebrew idiom for "imagine" or "realize".

[30]**17: Benevolence.** → See above § 7.30:1.

[31]**18: Similitude or ḥayyz.** P, 56rb: miloennetes = mediation; H: דמיון = similitude. → See above § 7.31:1–2.

[32]**18: Possible.** P, 56rb: qui s'appareille a estre; H: שיתכן להיותו = possible.

[33]**19: Siege.** P: om.; H: אמצעיות הרעה = bad intermediacy. → See above § 7.32:1–2.

[34]**19: Future evil.** P: om.; H: האסורים ועל העינויים = prisoners and tortures.

[35]**19: And if in the matter ⟨of intermediacy of⟩ goodness, it indicates the highest goodness.** P: om.; H: אם הוא בענייני הטובה, יורה על כל טוב שאין למעלה ממנו = and if in the matter ⟨of intermediacy of⟩ goodness, it indicates the highest goodness.

[36]**20: Power or dominion.** P, 56rb: prinçoiement; H: שררה = dominion. → See above § 7.33:1–8.

[37]**20: Good and great exaltation or excellency.** P, 56rb: tout degré bon et grandece; H: כל מעלה גדולה = every great exaltation.

§8.7

[1]1: **In the zodiac.** P, 56va: de l'orbe; H: מן הגלגל = from the circle.

[2]2: **Exaltation or in the house of honor.** → See above, §1.11:1.

[3]5: **Changes of clothing.** P, 56va: ses vestures; H: מלבושו = his garments.

[4]11: **In the house of its depression or in the opposite of the apogee.** P, 56vb: en la meson de sa basseté; H: במקום שפלותו = in the place of its lowness. → See above §2.1:40.

[5]14: **Stationary.** P, 56vb: este por retorner arrieres; H: העומד לחזור אחורנית = is about to be retrograde.

[6]21: **Precisely joined with or embracing the Sun.** P, 57ra: empressee avec le soleil; H: הדבק עם השמש = joined to the Sun.

[7]21: **Person or man.** P, 57ra: un home; H: אדם = human being.

[8]23: **Separating or retreating from conjunction.** P, 57ra: se depart; H: המתפרד = separating.

[9]26: **Is moved.** P, 57rb: se muet; H: נוסע = travels.

[10]27: **That is, *zamim*.** → See above §8.7:21.

[11]27: **Partners.** P, 57rb: homes acompagnans; H: מתחברים = persons who meet.

[12]28: **Friendship.** P, 57rb: l'amour l'un a l'autre; H: אהבת זה את זה = mutual love.

§8.8

[1]1: **Is being made.** P, 57rb: qui est en sa eure; H: הדבר ההוה בשעתו = something that occurs at its proper hour.

[2]10: **His dignity and governance.** P, 57va: sa poeté; H: שלטונו = his governance.

[3]10: **Art or craft.** P, 57va: son mestier; H: אומנותו = his art.

§9.1

[1]1: **Ninth part of this book.** P, 57vb: Le .9e. chapitres de ce livre; H: השער התשיעי = the ninth gate. → Meaning, ninth chapter.

[2]1: **97.** P, 57vb: .97.; H: תשעה ושבעים = 79.

[3]1: **Parts.** P, 57vb: sors; H: גורל = lots.

[4]2: **Equal degrees.** P, 57vb: gré drois; H: מעלות ישרות = straight degrees.

[5]2: **The good lot or the lot of Fortune.** P, 57vb: le sort le bon; H: הגורל הטוב = the good lot.

[6]5: **Completely right.** P, 57vb: il a droit; H: הדין עמו = he is right.

[7]6: **One of scholars of the Indians, such as.** P, 58ra: uns sages d'Inde, qui fu ausinc com; H: חכם הודו שהיה שמו = An Indian scholar, whose name was.

[8]6: **Deviated.** P, 58ra: se returna; H: שב = returned.

[9]6: **Admit.** P, 58ra: aperçut; H: הרגיש = feel.

[10]7: **This good lot or part of fortune.** P, 58ra: ce sort le bon; H: הגורל הטוב = the good lot.

[11]7: **Possessions or wealth.** P, 58ra: l'avoir; H: הממון = wealth.

§9.2

[1]1: **Lot of hidden things or of the hidden soul.** P, 58ra: le sort du reçoilement; H: גורל התעלומה = lot of the hidden thing.

§9.3

[1]1: **If the nativity is diurnal.** P, 58rb: se est la nativité de jours; H: ושם הגורל אם הנולד ביום = the lot is there if the nativity is diurnal.

[2]2: **Moistening of the earth.** P, 58rb: le laborernent de la terre; H: עבודת האדמה = working of the earth, meaning agriculture.

[3]2: **Stolen things.** P, 58rb: la perte; H: האבידה = loss.

[4]4: **Compassion.** P, 58rb: la misericorde; H: החסד = benevolence.

[5]4: **Honor.** P, 58rb: l'onneur; H: הכבוד = honor.

[6]6: **Vigor.** P, 58va: le barnage; H: הגבורה = courage.

[7]7: **Ascendant degree.** P, 58va: le germinant degré; H: הצומחת = the ascendant.

[8]10: **A loan for the sake of receiving and borrowing in business.** P, 58va: prest et reçoit; H: משא ומתן = carrying and giving. → Literal translation of a Hebrew idiom meaning negotiations, bargaining. See above, note on §3.6:1, s.v., "loans and gifts".

[9]10: **Mathematics.** P: om.; H: חשבון = mathematics.

[10]10: **Philosophy.** P, 58va: clergie; H: ספרות = literature.

§9.4

[1]1: **And they are .12.** P, 58vb: de quoi il en i a .12; H: om.

[2]3: **By day.** P: om.; H: ביום = by day.

[3]4: **Beauty.** P, 58vb: la biauté; H: ההדר = splendor.

[4]4: **This lot is like the lot of Venus.** P: om.; H: וזה הגורל כגורל נגה = this lot is like the lot of Venus.

[5]5: **Sense.** P: om.; H: הדבור = speech.

[6]5: **Which is taken by day from Mercury to Mars, and the opposite by night; it is cast out from the ascendant..** P: om.; H: יוקח ביום מכוכב חמה אל מאדים, ובלילה הפוך, ויושלך מהצומחת = which is taken by day from Mercury to Mars, and the opposite by night; it is cast out from the ascendant.

§9.5

[1]2: **Equated.** P, 58vb: equié; H: מתוקן = corrected.

[2]3: **Usury and barter.** P, 58vb: prest; H: הלואה = loan.

§9.6

[1]2: **Mercury to Saturn.** P, 59ra: de mercure a saturne; H: משבתאי אל צדק = from Saturn to Jupiter.

[2]4: **Equated.** P, 59ra: equié; H: מתוקן = corrected.

[3]4: **Longitude.** P, 59ra: latitude; H: מרחב = latitude.

§9.7

[1]6: **Parents' noble origin.** P, 59rb: nobleté de parenté; H: היחס = lineage.

[2]7: **Landed properties.** P, 59rb: des terres; H: הקרקע = the soil.

[3]8: **Moistening or watering of the earth.** P, 59rb: labourement de la terre; H: עבודת האדמה = working of the earth.

[4]9: **End or exit.** P, 59rb: la fin; H: האחרית = the end.

[5]9: **House.** P, 59rb: meson; H: בעל בית = lord of the house.

§ 9.8

[1]2: **Children.** P, 59va: fil; H: הבן = the son.

[2]6: **Or female.** P: om.; H: אם נקבה = or female.

§ 9.9

[1]2: **Defects or *axemena*.** P, 59va: des mahains; H: המומין = mutilations. → Cf. below § 9.16:3, s.v., "defects or *axemena*".

§ 9.10

[1]3: **Hermes.** P, 59vb: Enoc; H: חנוך = Enoch.

[2]3: **Velis.** → This refers to Vettius Valens, a second century Helenistic astrologer, who is repeatedly mentioned in Abū Ma'shar' *Great Introduction*, one of Ibn Ezra's main sources for *Reshit Ḥokhmah*. The same astrologer is mentioned in *Ṭe'amim* I, § 4.6:13, 68–69 as ואליס = "Velis" or "Valis", and in *Rationes* I as "Baalim".

[3]4: **Of the time of sexual intercourse, it is taken by day and by night from the Sun to the Moon, and it is cast out from the ascendant.** P, 59vb: des femmes, soit prins de jour de saturne a venus, et de nuis a rebours, et soit getté du germinant; H: עת הבעילות, יוקח ביום ובלילה מהשמש אל הלבנה, ויושלך מהצומחת = of the time of sexual intercourse, it is taken by day and by night from the Sun to the Moon, and it is cast out from the ascendant.

[4]5: **And there is the lot.** P: om.; H: ושם הגורל = and there is the lot.

[5]6: **The woman's modesty or piety.** P, 60ra: la simpleté a la fame; H: צניעות האשה = the woman's chaste behavior.

[6]8: **Men's cunning or deceit.** P, 60ra: l'engin des malles; H: ערמת הזכרים = the cunning of men.

[7]12: **Love.** P, 60ra: l'amour; H: החשק = erotic desire.

§9.11

[1]2: **Equated.** P, 60rb: equié; H: מתוקן = corrected.

[2]5: **Disease.** P, 60va: maladie; H: מקום החולי = the place of the disease.

§9.12

[1]2: **Equated.** P, 60va: equié; H: מתוקן = corrected.

[2]3: **Going by water or traveling by ship.** P, 60va: l'aler par l'iaue; H: ההליכה במים = travel by water.

[3]4: **Modesty or piety and religion.** P, 60va: la simpleté; H: הענוה = humility.

[4]5: **Understanding.** P, 60vb: sens; H: החכמה = wisdom.

[5]6: **Wisdom and knowledge.** P, 60vb: savoir; H: הדעת = knowledge.

[6]8: **Rumor.** P, 60vb: la chose; H: הדבר = the thing.

§9.13

[1]2: **Kingship or reigning.** P, 60vb: la roiauté; H: המלוכה = kingship.

[2]3: **Conquering or victory.** P, 60vb: vainquement; H: הנצוח = subjugation.

[3]3: **But if Saturn is under the rays of the Sun it is taken by day from the Sun to Jupiter, the opposite by night, and it is cast out from the ascendant.** P: om.; H: ואם היה שבתאי תחת אור השמש יוקח ביום מהשמש אל צדק, ובלילה הפוך, ויושלך מהצומחת = but if Saturn is under the rays of the Sun it is taken by day from the Sun to Jupiter, the opposite by night, and it is cast out from the ascendant.

[4]6: **Dignity.** P, 61ra: prinçoiement; H: השתרר פתאום = prevailed suddenly.

[5]11: **Great exaltation.** P, 61rb: la grandece; H: הגדולה = high rank.

[6]11: **Exaltation.** P, 3vb: eneur; H: כבוד = honor.

[7]11: **Exaltation.** P, 3vb: eneur; H: כבוד = honor.

§9.14

[1]2: **Soul.** P, 61rb: l'amé; H: האהוב = being loved.

[2]3: **A man's contemplation and prudence.** P, 61rb: le seu avertissances de l'ome; H: הידוע בינות האדם = what is known among human beings.

[3]7: **Generosity of the soul.** P, 61va: la franchise de l'arme; H: חופש הנפש = liberty of the soul.

[4]8: **Praise.** P, 61va: los,; H: המהולל = the praised.

[5]10: **Renown.** P, 61va: trestornernent; H: התהפוכות = vicissitudes.

[6]11: **Companions or partners.** P, 61va: des compagnons; H: הרעים = the friends.

§9.15

[1]2: **Equated.** P, 61vb: equié; H: מתוקן = corrected.

§9.16

[1]3: **Defects or *axemena*.** P, 62ra: des mahains; H: המום בגוף = the mutilation in the body. → Cf. above note on §9.9:2, s.v., "defects or *axemena*".

[2]4: **Equated.** P, 62ra: equié; H: מתוקן = corrected.

[3]4: **The Sun.** P, 62rb: Soleil; H: כוכב חמה = Mercury.

[4]7: **Retribution or ambush.** P, 62rb: l'agait; H: הָעֵקֶב = reward (Ps. 19:12).

[5]9: **Power and courage.** P, 62rb: la force; H: הגבורה = courage.

[6]10: **Brutality and killing.** P, 62rb: l'ocision; H: ההריגה = the killing.

§ 9.17

[1]1: **The condition of the kings and their affairs.** P, 62va: les choses des rois; H: דברי המלכים = the affairs of kings.

[2]2: **Conjunction.** P, 62va: la conjonction; H: המחברת הגדולה לדעת דברי המלכים = the great conjunction in order to know the affairs of kings.

[3]2: **The relocation or transfer to another place of the nation.** P, 612va: la translacion de la gent; H: העתקת דברי האומה = the relocation of the affairs of the nation.

[4]4: **Degree.** P, 62va: lieu; H: מקום = place.

[5]5: **The king or of the kings.** P, 62va: rois; H: מלכים = kings.

[6]7: **Two.** P: om.; H: שני = two.

[7]11: **Honor or exaltation.** → See above, note on § 1.11:1, s.v., "honor or exaltation".

§ 9.18

[1]2: **The king's accession or elevation.** P, 63ra: lievement du roi; H: קימת המלך = the king's accession.

[2]3: **Longitude or distance.** P, 63ra:; H: המרחק = the distance.

[3]3: **The remainder or what has been found.** P, 63ra: le surcroissement; H: היתרון = the remainder.

[4]4: **Remainder or longitude.** P, 63rb: le surcroissement; H: המרחק = the distance.

§9.19

[1]2: **Country and place.** P, 63rb: païs; H: מדינה = city.

[2]4: **Strong winds.** P, 63va: vens fo rs; H: רוחות = winds.

[3]4: **If in one of Mars's houses, it will be hot; if in one of Venus's houses, there will be rain or fog; if in one of Mercury's houses, there will be strong winds.** P: om.; H: ואם באחד בתי מאדים יהיה חום, ואם באחד בתי נוגה יהיה גשם או ערפל, ואם באחד מבתי כוכב חמה יהיו רוחות חזקים, = if in one of Mars's houses, it will be hot; if in one of Venus's houses, there will be rain or fog; if in one of Mercury's houses, there will be strong winds.

[4]4: **The air will be clear and unclouded.** P, 63va: sera l'air net; H: יהיה האויר זך = the air will be pure.

[5]5: **Corrected according to the latitude of the country, multiply it by 10, divide the result by 12.** P, 63va: aver la latitude de la terre, et le monteploie sur .17., et l'ajousté part sur .12; H: ומה שיהיה תערכנו בשעות השלמות המעווֹתות שעברו מן היום או מן הלילה, והנחבר שמרהו, ואחר כן קח מצעדי המזל ששם בעל השעה כפי רוחב הארץ ותערכנו על שבעים, והנחבר חלקנו על שנים עשר = multiply the result by the whole crooked hours of day or night that have passed and save the result. Then take the rising time of the sign where the lord of the hour is located, according to the latitude of the country, multiply it by 70, divide the result by 12.

§9.20

[1]2: **From the cardines.** P: om.; H: מהיתדות = from the cardines.

[2]3: **Exaltation or the house of its honor.** P, 63vb: la meson de s'onneur; H: בית כבודו = the house of its honor.

[3]3: **The house of fall or shame.** P, 63vb: la meson de sa honte; H: בית קלונו = the house of its shame.

[4]4: **Abundance or sufficient supply.** P, 63vb: assés; H: הרבה = a lot.

§9.21

[1]7: **Milk or fat.** P, 64ra: la creme; H: החמאה = butter.

[2]9: **Millet.** P, 64ra: milg; H: אורז = rice.

[3]13: **Certain gourds.** P, 64ra: bousacles; H: האבטיחים = the melons.

[4]18: **The lot of the essences of salty medicines from Mars to the Moon.** P: om.; H: גורל עקרי הרפואות המלוחים ממאדים אל הלבנה = The lot of the essences of salty medicines from Mars to the Moon.

[5]19: **Salty.** P: om.; H: המלוחים = the salty.

§9.22

[1]1: **Scholars.** P, 64rb: les anciens; H: הקדמונים = the Ancients.

[2]3: **Situation or condition.** P, 64rb: l'afaire; H: ענין = matter.

§9.23

[1]1: **On account of which.** P, 64va: car donc; H: אז = then.

§9.24

[1]1: **Accordingly the lot is composed of.** P, 64va: Et le sort est sur; H: והנה הגורל = so the sort.

[2]3: **The matter and its accomplishment.** P, 6vra: l'afai re; H: הענין = the matter.

§9.25

[1]1: **Orb of the signs.** P, 64va: cercle des signes; H: גלגל המזלות = circle of the signs.

[2]4: **Many times.** P, 64vb: assés de fois; H: om.

§10.1

[1]1: **Tenth part of this book.** P, 64vb: La partie .10e. de ce livre; H: השער העשירי = the tenth gate. → Meaning, tenth chapter.

[2]2: **To them.** P, 64vb: a eus; H: אליהם = to them.

[3]2: **Modes.** P, 64vb: voies; H: דרכים = ways.

[4]3: **Rays.** P, 65ra: la clarté; H: האור = the light.

[5]3: **Any region.** P, 65ra: chascun païs; H: כל מדינה ומדינה = any city and city.

[6]5: **Which change in any place.** P, 65ra: qui est muable en chascun lieu; H: על המקום = in the place.

[7]5: **Upright circle.** P, 65ra: cercle de la droiture; H: בגלגל היושר = the circle of straightness.

[8]6: **Scholars of the stars.** P, 65ra: sages des signes; H: חכמי המזלות = scholars of the signs.

[9]8: **Girdle of the zodiac.** P, 65ra: pourceint de l'ymaginacion de l'orbe; H: חשב אפודת הגלגל = girdle of the vest of the circle. → See above note on §1.10:5, s.v., "in the girdle of the imagination of the circle of the signs".

§10.2

[1]1: **Cause, reason and utility.** P, 65rb: la reson; H: טעם = reason.

[2]4: **Dispositions and conditions of the world.** P, 65va: les afaires du siecle; H: עניני העולם = the affairs of the world.

[3]4: **In general or universally.** P, 65ra: en voie de communité; H: בדרך כלל = in a general way.

[4]4: **And drought.** P: om.; H: והבצורת = and drought.

[5]4: **Age.** P, 65ra: le siecle; H: העולם = the world.

[6]**6: To any climate and another climate.** P, 65va: a chascun angle et angle; H: וכל פאה ופאה = and any corner and corner.

[7]**7: The age or the world.** P, 65va: le siecle; H: העולם = the world.

[8]**8: Chascun.** P, 65va: chascun; H: בכל = in every.

[9]**8: Region and region.** P, 65va: païs et païs; H: מדינה ומדינה = city and city.

[10]**9: 10 years.** P, 65vb: .10. ans; H: מאה ועשרים שנה = 120 years.

[11]**11: The sign of the revolution.** P, 65vb: le signe qui retorne en carole; H: מזל החוזר חלילה = the sign that returns again.

§ 10.3

[1]**3: Of the triplicity.** P, 66ra: es mesons de la triplicité; H: בבתי השלישות = in the houses of the triplicity.

[2]**4: From.** P, 66ra: a; H: אל = to.

[3]**5: The ten chapters of this book, which Master Abraham Ibn Ezra, ⟨a name⟩ whose translation is Master of Help, compiled, are completed; Master Henry of Malines, called Bate, cantor of Liège, executed the translation, which he completed in Orvieto on the eighth day after the Assumption of the glorious Virgin Mary [i.e., August 22, the eighth day counting from the feast on August 15]; praised be the Lord who extended the Heavens and augmented wisdom. Amen..** P, 66rb: Ci define li livres du Commencement de Sapience que fist Abraham even Azre ou Aezera, qui est interpretés maistre de aide, que translata Hagins li Juis de ebrieu en romans, et Obers de Mondidier escrivoit le romans, et fu fait a Malines en la meson sire Henri Bate, et fu finés l'en de grace .1273. l'endemein de la Seint Thomas l'apostre; H: והנה נשלם העשרה שערים, ושבח ליוצר כל היצורים. והשלימו בחדש תמוז שנת ת׳ת׳ק׳ח״ תם תם תהלה לאל עולם. = The ten chapters are completed. Praise to the Creator of all the creatures. ⟨The author⟩ finished it in the month of Tammuz in the year ⟨4⟩908. ⟨The book⟩ is completed. Glory to the Everlasting God.

PART THREE

LIBER CAUSARUM SEU RATIONUM

LATIN TEXT AND ENGLISH TRANSLATION

60vb   INCIPIT LIBER CAUSARUM SEU RATIONUM SUPER HIIS QUE
         DICUNTUR IN INTRODUCTORIO ABRACHE AVI⟨NEZRA⟩,
         INCIPIT: ⟨INITIUM⟩ SAPIENTIE TIMOR DOMINI

§ 1

1   (1) Capitulum primum. {{Excelsus Dominus et metuendus, adaperiat et illuminet oculos nostros in LIBRO RATIONUM, et dirigat gressus nostros in viam veritatis}}. **Circulus .360. partes habet,**ᵞ eo quod non invenerunt numerum minorem ipso, **tot habente fractiones,**ᵞ ⟨⟨...⟩⟩. (2) Unde, si numerum hunc per septem multiplicaveris, invenies numerum omnes habentem fractiones, et est .2520. (3) Iterum, elegerunt numerum hunc, eo quod propinquus est numero dierum ⟨⟨...⟩⟩ anni. (4) Distraxerunt {etiam} gradus circuli per *signa* .12., eo quod non invenerunt numerum minorem ipso fractiones habentem quales habet ipse; rursus quia quilibet annus .12. etiam
61ra habet | **lunationes.**ᵞ (5) **Secundum divisionem autem exeunt cuilibet correspondentes signo gradus .30.,**ᵞ et hic quidem numerus plures habet fractiones quam duodenarius. (6) {Amplius,} quoniam *huic numero* non erat quarta hinc, oportebat eos multiplicare numerum, dividendo scilicet gradu qualibet in .60. *divisiones, que vocantur* **minuta prima,**ᵞ similiter et **minutum**ᵞ quodlibet in .60. secunda, et sic deinceps usque ad decima.

2   (1) Nomina {vero} signorum vocata sunt secundum ymaginum nomina, que sunt ymagines stellarum **cingulo signorum seu ecliptice linee.**ᵝ (2) Secundum veritatem {autem} omnes divisiones signorum equales sunt, quamvis ymaginum altera grandis est, ut est ymago Leonis, que a principio usque ad finem est fere .40. graduum, *altera {vero} minor, ut* ymago Arietis, que septem gradus continet et non plus. (3) IN FINE {autem} LIBRI, per Dei adiutorium, loquar de secreto mutationis locorum {et} signorum, dicit enim PTOLOMEUS quod temporibus suis erat cor Leonis **in longitudine**ᵞ .122. gradum a principio **linee equalitatis,**ᵞ et quod erat in secundo gradu Leonis; nunc {autem}, scilicet in anno ⟨⟨...⟩⟩ {ERE HEBREORUM,} est in .18. Leonis; **HERMES**ᵞ {vero} in **LIBRO LONGITUDINUM**ᵞ ait quod erat in .25. gradus Cancri. (4) Quod {autem} dixerunt, numerum stellarum esse .1022., hoc est de

HERE BEGINS THE BOOK OF CAUSES AND REASONS FOR WHAT IS SAID IN THE INTRODUCTION BY ABRAHAM IBN ⟨EZRA⟩, ⟨WHICH⟩ BEGINS: THE BEGINNING OF WISDOM IS THE FEAR OF THE LORD

§ 1

1 (1) First chapter. {{Exalted and fearsome Lord, open and enlighten our eyes in the BOOK OF REASONS, and direct our steps in the path of truth.}} **The circle has 360 parts**,[Y,1] because they did not find a smaller number which has **so many fractions**[Y,2] ⟨⟨except for one-seventh⟩⟩. (2) Therefore, if you have multiplied this number by 7, you will find the number that has all the fractions, and it is 2,520. (3) In addition, they chose this number [i.e., 360] because it is close to the number of days of the ⟨⟨solar⟩⟩ year. (4) They {also} divided the degrees of the circle into 12 *signs*, because they found no smaller number that has as many fractions as it does, and also because any ⟨solar⟩ year has 12 **lunations**.[Y,3] (5) **So according to the division come out 30 degrees which correspond to each degree**,[Y,4] and this number has more fractions than 12. (6) {Furthermore,} since *this number* does not have a quarter, it was necessary for them to multiply the number, {namely} dividing each degree into 60 *divisions, which were called* **first smaller parts**[Y,5] [i.e., minutes], and likewise ⟨they divided⟩ each **smaller part**[Y] [i.e., minute] into sixty seconds, and in this manner ⟨they divided⟩ next down to the tenths.

2 (1) {Moreover} the names of the signs are called according to the names of the images which are the images of the stars [constellations] **in the girdle of the signs or of the ecliptic line**[β,1] [the ecliptic]. (2) {However,} in accordance with the truth, all the divisions of the signs are equal, although one of the images is large, like the image of Leo, which from beginning to end occupies approximately 40 degrees, {but} ⟨there is⟩ *another image, like* the image of Aries, which occupies about 7 degrees and no more than that. (3) {However,} AT THE END OF THE BOOK, with God's help, I shall speak of to the secret of the change of the places {and} of the signs,[2] for, in his times, PTOLEMY says that Cor Leonis was at a **longitude**[Y,3] of 122° from the beginning of the **line of equality**[Y,4] [the equator], so that it was at Leo 2°; {but} today, namely, in the year ⟨⟨⟨5⟩908 [1147/8 C.E.]⟩⟩ {of the ERA OF THE HEBREWS,} it is at Leo 18°; {but} HERMES[Y,5] says in the BOOK OF LONGITUDES[Y,6] that it was at Cancer 25°. (4) {But} what they said, that the number of the stars is 1022, this refers to those that are visible

illis quas visus noster comprehendere potest. (5) Ymagines quoque septentrionales ac meridionales **sunt tamquam similitudines existentes signorum quorundam diversi formarum quidem secundum consideraciones diversas**,ᵞ ut puta Vultur Cadens, que vocat PTOLOMEUS **properante seu impetuosum**,ᵝ potest enim mutare nomina secundum quod visui suo apparebat figure, **eligens stellam a stella**,ᵞ eo quidem quod **spera**ᵞ est rotunda, **et non est res naturalem locum habens**ᵞ **certum aut scitum**,ᵝ (6) **inter ymagines quas commemorati sunt** ANTIQUI.ᵞ

61rb
3 (1) Sunt {autem} .48. ymagines in superiori existentes **spera**,ᵞ que vocatur **orbis**ᵞ signorum. (2) | Et sub ipsa septe sunt **spere**ᵞ septem stellarum, que **planete**ᵞ vocantur, eo quod sunt terre propinque; et accidunt eis accidentia que supremis non accidunt, videlicet in motibus eorum qui mutantur, **in elongationibus eorum et approximationibus ad terram**;ᵞ {item} coniungitur hic cum illo postquam separati fuerunt, et separantur coniuncti prius; et totum hoc accidit etiam rebus creatis que sunt super terram. (3) Amplius et horum cursus **planetarum**ᵞ propinquus est **cingulo signorum sive linee ecliptice**,ᵝ non sic {autem} ymagines septentrionales ac meridiane. (4) {Quia vero} **planetis**ᵞ inferior est Luna, ac terre propinquior omnibus, {ideo} super corpus significat humanum, ac super initium omnis operis atque cogitationis. (5) **Voluerunt**ᵞ {autem} ANTIQUE scire quis superior est **planetarum**ᵞ alter altero, per duas vias. (6) Quarum una est per coniunctionem duorum **planetarum**,ᵞ ⟨⟨...⟩⟩, **et per hac**ᵞ sciverunt quod Mercurius inferior est Venere. (7) Secunda via est per motum, motus {autem}ᵞ Saturni per circulum signorum est in .30. annis fere, Iovis quidem in .12., Martis in duobus, Solis in uno, et Lune in minori .28. diebus. (8) {Quia vero} motus equalis Veneris et Mercurii similis est cum equali motu Solis, item et quando coniungitur eorum quilibet cum Sole non videtur propter **lumen**ᵞ Solis, idcirco dissentes fuerunt inter SAPIENTES, nam quidam eorum dicunt quod Venus et Mercurius super Solem sunt et alii contrarium dicunt. (9) Alii quoque dicunt quod interdum superiores sunt et interdum inferiores, **ad** LIBRUM HUNC **non spectat super tales negotiari**ᵞ sermones, (10) nisi quod omnium ASTROLOGIE SAPIENTIUMᵞ DOMINORUMQUE IUDICIORUMᵞ concors est opinio quod ambo sunt sub **spera**ᵞ Solis, et quod est medius, ac tres superiores ipso. (11) Illi {autem} ab ipso **elongantur**ᵞ usque ad aspectum

to our eyes. (5) The northern as well as the southern images **are like the diverse likenesses of certain signs, actually of shapes according to diverse considerations,**[γ,7] as for example the Falling Eagle, which PTOLEMY calls **hastening or rushing,**[β,8] because he can change the names according to what appeared to his sight of the form, **when he picks out a star from ⟨another⟩ star,**[γ,9] because the **sphere**[γ,10] is round, **and it** [the image] **is not a thing that has a natural place,**[γ,11] **certain and known,**[β,12] (6) **among the images which have been mentioned by the ANCIENTS.**[γ,13]

3 (1) {But} the 48 images are located in the upper **sphere,**[γ,1] which is called the **orb**[γ,2] of the signs. (2) Underneath it are the seven **spheres**[γ] of the seven stars, which are called **planets,**[γ,3] because they are close to the Earth; events happen to them which do not occur to the upper ⟨stars⟩, namely, they undergo variations in their motions, **in their elongations and approximations to the Earth;**[γ,4] {likewise,} one conjoins with another after they were separated, and they move apart after having entered into conjunction previously; and all this also happens to the creatures on Earth. (3) Furthermore, the path of these **planets**[γ] is close to **the girdle of the signs or the ecliptic line**[β,5] [the ecliptic], {but} the northern and the southern images are not like that. (4) {Moreover, since} the Moon is lower than the ⟨other⟩ **planets,**[γ] and closer to the Earth than all ⟨the stars⟩, {consequently} it indicates the human body, and the beginning of any action and thought. (5) {But} the ANCIENTS **desired**[γ,6] to know which **planet**[γ] is higher than the other by two ways. (6) One of them is by the conjunction of two **planets,**[γ,7] ⟨⟨when the lower hides the upper⟩⟩, **and by this**[γ,8] they knew that Mercury is beneath Venus. (7) The second way is the motion, {however}[γ,9] Saturn's motion through the circle of the signs takes approximately thirty years, Jupiter's twelve, Mars' two years, the Sun's one year, and the Moon's less than twenty-eight days. (8) {Moreover, since} the equal motion [mean motion] of Venus and Mercury is similar to the equal motion of the Sun, also ⟨since⟩ when either of them is in conjunction with the Sun it cannot be seen because of **the light**[γ,10] of the Sun, consequently there was a disagreement among the SCHOLARS, for some of them said that Venus and Mercury are above the Sun and the others said the opposite. (9) Still others say that sometimes they are higher and sometimes lower, and **it does not belong to THIS BOOK** [the Book of Causes and Reasons] **to be busy with**[γ,11] these statements, (10) but the opinion of all the **SCHOLARS OF ASTROLOGY**[γ,12] and the **MASTERS OF JUDGMENTS**[γ,13] agrees that both [Venus and Mercury] are beneath the Sun's **sphere,**[γ] and that it [the Sun] is intermediate, and the three [Mars, Jupiter and Saturn] are higher than it [the Sun]. (11) {However,}

488   PART THREE

61va oppositum, {sed} Venus et Mercurius **non sic**,ᵞ finis enim | **elongationis**ᵞ Veneris est .48. gradus, **elongatio**ᵞ {vero} Mercurii .28., et hii ambo coniunguntur Soli. (12) Luna {autem}, que omnium planetarum est infima, nullum habet lumen nisi lumen Solis, et non ita cetere **stelle erratice**ᵞ neque supreme, hec enim **lucent sive luminose sunt**ᵝ a se ipsis.

4 (1) Quare {autem} Aries et Leo et Sagittarius sunt tamquam nature ignee, quidam dicunt quod hoc scitum est per experientiam. (2) Et ait IACOB ALKINDI: scitur quod calidum et frigidum sunt activa, et quia calidum est **activum**[1] **maius sive magis**,ᵝ a signo {autem} Arietis incipit tempus calefieri, idcirco dixerunt quod natura eius est natura ignis. (3) Dicit etiam quod signum Cancri est principium **mutationis**ᵞ temporis; et {ideo} quia **septentrionalis est sive sinistrum**,ᵝ dixerunt quod eius natura est sicut activum minoris. (4) Secundum meam {vero} opinionem **dixerunt**ᵞ Arietem esse calidum et siccum propter ymaginem stellarum que Arieti assimilatur; et hec est ratio de Leone ac etiam de[2] signo Sagittarii, **que sunt tamquam ymagines caliditatis seu calidorum**.ᵝ

Dicit TRANSLATOR: *si autem veritatem considerandum est, multo melius assignat* ALBUMASAR *huius racionem* IN SUO MAIORI INTRODUCTORIO, LIBRO SCILICET .2., CAPITULO .7.[3]

(5) De Tauri {quoque} signo dixerunt quod frigidum est et siccum propter ymaginem, et consimiliter de Capricorno. (6) Et quia signum Virginis eiusdem triplicitatis est cum ipsis, {ideo} **dixerunt**ᵞ de hoc signo etiam quod frigidum est et siccum; rationem {vero} triplicitatis in aspectibus explanabo. (7) Gemini {autem} et Libra et Aquarius, quia sunt secundum figuram hominis, qui calidus est et humidus temperate, {ideo} **dixerunt**ᵞ quod hec signa sunt **secundum naturam aeris**;ᵞ,[4] {rursus} quia Cancer et Scorpius ac
61vb Pisces sunt ymagines frigide et humide, secundum hoc **dixerunt**ᵞ hec | signa **talis esse nature**.ᵞ

Inquit TRANSLATOR *quod hic insufficientem dictum est, satis completum est per* ALBUMASAR.

---

[1]Here begins *Rationes* I in MS Limoges, BM, 9 (28), fol. 24r. [2]de] M; L in. [3]libro scilicet .2., capitulo .7.] M; L scilicet capitulo. [4]aeris] M; L Arietis.

they **elongate**^(γ,14) move away from it until they are in opposition ⟨to the Sun⟩, {but} Venus and Mercury **do not ⟨move⟩ in this way**,^(γ,15) because the end of the [i.e., the greatest] **elongation**^(γ,16) of Venus [i.e., from the Sun] is 48°, {but} the ⟨greatest⟩ **elongation**^(γ) of Mercury is 28°, so that these two are conjoined to the Sun. (12) {But} the Moon, the lowest of all the planets, has no light except for the Sun's light, but this does not apply to the rest of the **wandering stars**^(γ,17) or the upper ⟨stars⟩, for these **shine or are luminous**^(β,18) by themselves.

4 (1) {As for} why Aries, Leo, and Sagittarius are of a fiery nature, some say that this is known by experience. (2) Yaʿqūb al-Kindī says: it is known that heat and cold are active agents, and since heat is **the greater active ⟨agent⟩ or ⟨the active agent⟩ to a greater degree**,^(β,1) {and} the weather begins to get warmer from the sign of Aries, therefore they said that its nature is like the nature of fire. (3) He also says that Cancer is the beginning of the **change**^(γ,2) of the weather; and {since} it is **northern or on the left**,^(β,3) they said that its nature is like the smaller active agent. (4) {But} in my opinion they **said**^(γ,4) that Aries is hot and dry because the image of the stars resembles a ram; and this is the explanation for Leo and also for the sign of Sagittarius, **which are like images of heat or of hot things.**^(β,5)

THE TRANSLATOR *says: if the truth is to be taken into consideration,* ABŪ MAʿSHAR *gives a much better explanation in* HIS GREAT INTRODUCTION, *NAMELY THE SECOND BOOK, SEVENTH CHAPTER.*[6]

(5) Regarding Taurus, {too,} they said that it is cold and dry on account of the image ⟨of a bull⟩, and similarly regarding Capricorn. (6) Because the sign of Virgo is in the same triplicity with them, {therefore,} they **said**^(γ,7) that this sign is cold and dry; {moreover,} I shall explain the reason for the triplicity in ⟨the discussion of⟩ the aspects.[8] (7) {But} Gemini, Libra, and Aquarius, because they are according to the form of a human being, which is hot and moist in a mixed manner, {consequently} they **said**^(γ,9) that these signs are **according to the nature of air**;^(γ,10) {also} because Cancer, Scorpio, and Pisces are cold and moist images, according to that they **said**^(γ,11) that these signs have such a nature.^(γ,12)

THE TRANSLATOR *says that this has been insufficiently said, it has been better completed by* ABŪ MAʿSHAR.

5   (1) Ratio {quidem autem} nature **planetarum**γ difficilis est, invenietur etiam in LIBRO .4. PARTIUM, quod PTOLOMEUS Lunam ait esse frigidam et humidam propter **nubes seu vapores**β que a terra ad ipsam ascendunt, ac etiam quia Sole inferior est. (2) Idem quoque dicit de Venere et Mercurio nisi quia Mercurius propter velocitatem motuum suorum *et preparationem* ad se coniungendum Soli, et quia multis vicibus in anno termini ingreditur combustionis, {ideo} **mutatur**γ in natura sua, interdum namque calidus erit. (3) Item de Marte **dixit**γ quod est calidus ad ustivus, eo quod est prope Solem, **cuius lumen seu caliditas**β ad illum ascendit. (4) Saturnus etiam dixit esse frigidum, eo quod remotus est a Sole; quia {vero} Iupiter medius est inter Martem calidum et Saturnum frigidum, idcirco temperata est eius natura. (5) Et EGO, ABRACHAM[1] COMPILATOR, dico quod librum illum non compilavit PTOLOMEUS, quia in eo **multi sunt sermones otiosi**[2] **scientie**[3] **et experientie contra pensationem,**γ,[4] prout in LIBRIS explanabo IUDICIORUM.γ (6) Alii {vero} dicunt quod hee nature per viam experientie scita sunt et veritatis. (7) Nulla namque stella est, **neque superior neque inferior,**γ **qui sit frigida aut calida de natura,**γ et enim **quinte sunt essentie,**γ secundum quod declarat ARISTOTELES **bonis rationibus et perfectis.**β (8) Sed pro quanto corpus Solis magnus est, maius enim est corpore terre .166. vicibus, et non est etiam a terra remota, pro tanto virtutem {caliditatis} generat in aere per motum suum qui calefacit. (9) Et quia Luna, quamvis propinqua sit terre, corpus {tamen} eius illo minus est, {ideo} per motum in aere generat[5] humiditatem, natura namque rei omnis in terra existentis quando modicum calefacit[6] **ipsa retinet caliditatem.**γ (10) Et quia | magnus est calor Solis statim exsiccat, et ideo Luna virtutem humectationis generat in specibus vegetabilium et cerebellis, et hec res est experimentata. (11) Universaliter {igitur} nulla stella est nec tamen aliquod luminare frigiditatem generans,[7] sed caliditatem tantum, propter motum et naturam luminis ab ipsa exeuntis. (12) Non **dixerunt**γ {autem} de Luna quod sit frigida nisi quia caliditatem non generat humane complexionis temperamento **similem seu convenientem,**β secundum quod dixerunt medici, carnes bovinas frigidas esse, et scitum est quod omnis caro calida est, nisi quod respectu **temperamenti complexionis humane**γ ipsa frigida est et ei nociva. (13) Consimiliter

---

[1]Abracham] L; M Abraham.   [2]otiosi] L; M om.   [3]scientie] corrected; LM secundum scientie.   [4]Et ego, Abracham compilator, dico quod librum illum non compilavit Ptolomeus, quia in eo multi sunt sermones otiosi scientie et experientie contra pensationem] Cf. De mundo, prologue 12: Et ego Abraham compilator dico quod hunc librum non compilavit Ptholomeus, nam in eo sunt multi sermones frivoli secundum scientie contraponderationem et experientie.   [5]generat] M; L generant.   [6]calefacit] M; L calefecit.   [7]generans] M; L generant.

5 (1) {But certainly} the explanation of the natures of the **planets**ᵞ is difficult, it may be found in the BOOK OF FOUR PARTS, to the effect that PTOLEMY says that the Moon is cold and moist because of the **clouds or vapors**^(β,1) that ascends from the Earth to it, and also because it is below the Sun. (2) He also says the same about Venus and Mercury, but Mercury, on account of the swiftness of its motion *and its disposition* to conjoin itself to the Sun, and since it enters the boundary of burning many times a year, {consequently} it **changes**^(ᵞ,2) in its nature, because sometimes it will be hot. (3) Likewise, about Mars he **said**^(ᵞ,3) that it is hot and burning, because it is close to the Sun, whose [the Sun's] **light or heat**^(β,4) ascends to it [i.e., to Mars]. (4) Also Saturn, he said,^(ᵞ,5) is cold, because {indeed} it is far from the Sun; moreover Jupiter, because it is intermediate between the hot Mars and the cold Saturn, therefore its nature is mixed. (5) But I, ABRAHAM THE COMPILER, say that PTOLEMY did not compile this book, because there are in it **many statements devoid of science and against the weight of experience**,^(ᵞ,6,7) as I shall explain in the BOOKS OF JUDGMENTS.^(ᵞ,8) (6) {Moreover} others say that these natures ⟨of the planets⟩ were known by the method of experience and the truth, (7) because there is no star, **neither an upper one** [fixed stars] **nor an inferior one**^(ᵞ,9) [planets], **that is of a cold or hot nature**,^(ᵞ,10) because they are made **of a fifth substance**,^(ᵞ,11) as ARISTOTLE demonstrates with **good and complete reasons**.^(β,12) (8) However, inasmuch as the body of the Sun is large, for it is 166 times larger than the body of the Earth, and is not that distant from the Earth, consequently it generates by its motion a {warming} power in the air which makes it hot. (9) Since the Moon, although it is close to the Earth, {nevertheless} its body is smaller than ⟨the Earth's body⟩, {for that reason} it generates by its motion moisture in the air, because the nature of anything located on Earth, when it warms moderately **it retains heat**.^(ᵞ,13) (10) Since the Sun's heat is so intense it dries up ⟨the air⟩ right away, and {for that reason} the Moon generates a moisturizing power in species of plants and in the brain; and this has been tested experimentally. (11) {Therefore} the general rule is that no star and no luminary ⟨is found⟩ generating cold, but only heat, on account of the motion and the nature of the light emitted by it. (12) {But} they said^ᵞ that the Moon is cold only because it does not generate a heat that **is similar or appropriate**^(β,14) to the human temperament, just as the physicians said^ᵞ that the flesh of an ox is cold, and it is known that all flesh is hot, but with respect to the **temperament of the human mixture**^(ᵞ,15) ⟨the flesh⟩ itself is cold and

ergo Saturnus, quia valde remotus est a terra, et corpus eius ita grande non est ut corpus Iovis. (14) Idcirco **dixerunt**[γ] et ipsum esse frigidum, quando namque preest nativitati hominis, quia caliditatem convenientem non confert, significat super mortem. (15) De Iove {autem}, **dixerunt**[γ] quod calidus est et humidus, {sed non} secundum humane nature {modum}; rursus Venerem dixerunt esse frigidam et humidam, eo quod terre propinqua est et corpus suum minus terra quemadmodum et Luna; consimiliter quoque iudicium est de Mercurio. (16) Corpus {vero} Martis maius[1] est inferioribus planetis, et **Sole superius**,[γ] quapropter ipsum **dixerunt**[γ] esse calidum ad hoc et propter colorem[2] eius rubicundum. (17) Consimiliter etiam **dixerunt**[γ] de omnibus stellis supremis que *inquam* sunt rubicunde, ut est Oculus Cancri, et Cor Scorpionis, horum enim natura est ut natura Martis.

6 (1) **Dixerunt**[γ] {autem} de Sole quod est masculus, propter caliditatem magnam cum siccitate quam generat;[3] de Luna {vero} dixerunt contrarium, *scilicet quod est* femina. (2) Et dicunt etiam quod eius fortitudo nocturna est, et hec quidem res est manifesta; virtus {autem} Solis diurna est, de nocte enim sub terra est. (3) Sic {vero} de Iove **dixerunt**[γ] quod | de bonis stellis est, et huius ratio explanabo cum ad locum suum pervenero; ipse namque masculus est quod magnam generat caliditatem, et econtrario Venus. (4) De Saturno {autem} **dixerunt**[γ] quod masculus est et de **planetis diurnis**,[γ] **coincidere**[γ] namque facit naturam suam in calore diei; contrarium {vero} huius est in Marte, propter quod **dixerunt**[γ] ipse esse feminum ac de **planetis nocturnis**.[γ] (5) {Denique} Mercurius mutabilis est propter motus suos; eo propter dixerunt ipsum quandoque masculinus esse quandoque femininus. (6) **Ratio** {vero} **longitudinis Solis sive augis**[β] **est secundum respectum longitudinis eius**[γ] **est a terra;**[γ] **ceterum rationem de Dracone**[γ] explanabimus in loco suo.

---

[1]maius] M; L om.   [2]colorem] M; L calorem.   [3]generat] M; L generant.

harms him [man]. (13) The same applies then to Saturn, because it is so far from the Earth, and its body is not as large as Jupiter's body. (14) Therefore they said[Y] that it itself is cold, for when it rules over the nativity of some person, then, because it does not provide adequate heat, it indicates death. (15) {But} regarding Jupiter, they said[Y] that it is hot and moist, {but not} according to the {proper measure} of human nature; as for Venus, they also said[Y] that it is cold and moist, because it is close to the Earth and its body is smaller than the Earth in the same way as the Moon; and the same judgment applies to Mercury. (16) {Moreover} the body of Mars is larger than ⟨the body of⟩ the lower ⟨planets⟩, and ⟨it is⟩ **above the Sun,**[Y,16] therefore they said[Y] that it is hot, and also because its color is red. (17) The said[Y] the same about all the upper stars which, *I say*, are red, such as the Eye of Cancer [Aldebaran] and the Heart of Scorpio [Antares], whose nature is like Mars's nature.

6 (1) {But} they said[Y] that the Sun is masculine, because of the great heat with dryness that it generates; regarding the Moon the said {indeed} the opposite, *namely, that it is* feminine. (2) They also say that its [i.e., the Moon's] power is nocturnal, and this indeed is something that may be seen; {but} the power of the Sun is diurnal, because it is underneath the Earth during the night. (3) {Moreover} regarding Jupiter, they said[Y] it is one of the good stars, and I shall explain the reason for this when I come to the appropriate place; and that it is masculine because it generates great heat, and that Venus is the opposite. (4) {But} regarding Saturn, they said[Y] that it is masculine and one of the **diurnal planets,**[Y,1] because **it makes** its nature **coincide**[Y,2] with the heat of the day; the opposite {indeed} applies to Mars, and therefore they said[Y] that it is feminine and one of the **nocturnal planets.**[Y,3] (5) {Next,} Mercury is mutable because of its motions; they therefore said that sometimes it is masculine and sometimes feminine. (6) {Moreover} **the reason for the longitude or apogee of the Sun**[β,4] **is according to the relation of its longitude**[Y,5] [distance] **from the Earth;**[Y,6] we shall explain **the reason for all the rest about the Dragon**[Y,7] in its proper place.

§2

1 (1) Capitulum secundum.¹ Vocata fuerunt .6. signa **septentrionalia sive sinistra**,β quia Sol vadit per ipsis a parte sinistra respectu **equalis linee seu equinoctialis**,β et econtrario per meridionalia. (2) ⟨⟨...⟩⟩. **Quidam**γ {igitur} annum suum inceperunt a principio introitus Solis in signum Capricorni, eo quod ibidem incipiunt dies prolongari, postquam ad tantam abbreviationem pervenerunt quod minor esse non potest in omnibus **climatibus**.γ (3) Alii {autem} annum suum inceperunt {circa} principium introitus Solis in signum Arietis, tunc enim equatur dies e nox. (4) **Alii**γ {vero} annum eorum inceperunt quando ingreditur Sol in signum Cancri, quia tunc est in fine **septentrionali**, qui propinquior est **habitabili terre**.γ (5) {Item} **quidam**γ,² inceperunt {eum} quando Sol intrat in signum Libre, eo quod tunc equatur nox diei, et ⟨⟨...⟩⟩ iustus est incipere quando dies et nox equantur quam in aliis locis. (6) Quoniam {igitur} Sol, cum intrat in Arietem, appropinquat **loco habitabili**γ et renovatur mundus, et contrarius huius accidit quando Libram ingreditur, idcirco **iustus et rationabile**β est quod sit anni principium a signo Arietis, et **quia**γ caput est omnium signorum.

62va **2** (1) {Ideo} **dixerunt**γ | de ipso quod est signum igneum, prout commemoravi; item masculinum est propter caliditatem, et est nature diurne quia calida est dies, similiter et orientalis quia calida est eadem pars orientalis; et est **mutabile seu tropicum et mobile**β quia dies augmentari {super noctes} incipiunt, et noctes **minorari ser minui**;β {consimiliter} et hore augmentari incipiunt propter longitudinem arcus diurni, **ascensiones**γ {vero} **ipsius diminute**,γ id est, pars circuli.γ (2) **Estque obliqua**γ vocatur propter **diminutionem**γ **ascensionum**γ suarum; est {autem} de **signis bonis seu beneficis**β eo quod apparet in ipso fortitudo Solis; significat {autem} super tonitrua et fulmina propter mutationem temporis **a frigido**γ et adventum caliditatis. (3) Et hoc quod dixerunt, si est septentrionalis caliditatem generat, si {vero} meridionalis frigiditatem, hii quidem sermones SAPIENTIUM sunt INDORUM, sed PTOLOMEUS eos deridet. (4) Hoc {autem} quod dicunt ipsum figure super quadrupedia, ideo est quia arieti assimilatur. (5) Dixerunt etiam quod precisa sunt membra ipsius, eo quod ⟨⟨...⟩⟩ apparent eius membra **convenienter ordinata**,γ unum {videlicet} post aliud. (6) Item

---

¹Capitulum secundum] L (in margin); M om.   ²quidam] M; L quidem.

LIBER CAUSARUM SEU RATIONUM

§2

1 (1) Second chapter. Six signs were designated **northern or left-hand**,[β,1] because the Sun travels through them on the left side with respect to the **equal or equinoctial line**[β,2] [equator], and the opposite applies ⟨when it travels⟩ through the southern ⟨signs⟩. (2) ⟨⟨Aries⟩⟩. {Therefore} **certain people**[γ,3] began their year from the beginning of the Sun's entry into the sign of Capricorn, because in that very place the days begin to grow longer, after they reached, in all the **climates**,[γ,4] a shortness that none can be smaller. (3) {But} others began their year {around} the beginning of the entry of the Sun into the sign of Aries, because day and night are equal then. (4) {But} **others**[γ,5] began their year when the Sun enters the sign of Cancer, because then it is in the end of **the north**,[γ,6] which is closer to the **habitable Earth**[γ,7] [the ecumene]. (5) {Likewise}, **certain people**[γ,8] began {it} [their year] when the Sun enters the sign of Libra, because day and night are equal then, and it is ⟨⟨more⟩⟩ correct to begin when day and night are equal than in any other place. (6) {Therefore,} because the Sun, when it enters Aries, draws near to the **habitable place**[γ,9] [the ecumene] and the world is renewed ⟨then⟩, and ⟨because⟩ the opposite happens when it enters Libra, it is therefore **just and rational**[β,10] that the beginning of the year be in the sign of Aries, and **because**[γ,11] it [Aries] is the head of all the signs.

2 (1) {For that reason} **they said**[γ] about it [Aries] that it is a fiery sign, as I have mentioned; likewise, masculine because of the heat; and that it is of diurnal nature because the day is hot; and likewise eastern because the same eastern part is hot; and it is **mutable or tropical and changeable**[β,1] because the days begin to be increased {above the nights}, and the nights to be **reduced or become smaller**;[β,2] {similarly,} the hours begin to be increased because of the length of the arc of the day, and **its ascensions**[γ,3] {indeed} **are diminished**,[γ,4] **that is, the part of the circle**.[γ,5] (2) And it is called **oblique**[γ,6] because of the **diminution**[γ,7] of its **ascensions**;[γ] {but} it is one of the **good or benefic signs**[β,8] because the strength of the Sun is perceptible in it; {but} it indicates thunder and lightning because of the change of the weather **from cold**[γ,9] and the arrival of the heat. (3) And what they said, that if it is northern it generates heat, {but} if southern ⟨it generates⟩ cold, these are indeed the statements of the SCHOLARS OF THE INDIANS, but PTOLEMY laughs at them. (4) {But} what they said, that it is a four-footed form, this is because it resembles a ram. (5) They also said that its limbs are cut off, because its limbs are ⟨⟨not⟩⟩ **properly arranged**,[γ,10] {that is,} one after the other. (6) Likewise, they said that it indicates two

496   PART THREE

dixerunt quod super duos colores significat in apparentia ⟨⟨...⟩⟩, eo quod mutatur. (7) Dixerunt quod dimidiam vocem ipsum habet, eo quod est in figura bestie et non in figura humana. (8) Item dixerunt quod eius est cor orientis, propter caliditatem eius, et quia etiam in ipso equatur dies nocti; {ideo} dixerunt quod eius est cor orientis. (9) Et Leo quidem a sinistris orientis, quia Sol ibi est in parte sinistra; et {ideo} similiter fuit Sagittarius **meridionalis seu dexter orientalis**.^{β} (10) Dixerunt quoque caliditatem eius temperatam esse, propter tempus *anni*; et similiter eius est sanguis. (11) Et de saporibus dulcis; ac de coloribus rubeus, ⟨⟨...⟩⟩, eo quod de coloribus medius inter album et nigrum. (12) In parte {autem} eius de **animalibus seu bestiis**^{β} sunt pecudes, eo quod stelle eius sunt[1] tamquam ymago arietis; de **metallis** {vero} **seu mineralibus**,^{β} aurum, ferrum, argentum, et cuprum, eo quod hec omnia in ignem veniunt et natura eorum | ignea. (13) Dixerunt {autem} in parte eius est **clima**^{γ} tertium, **propter caliditatis eius temperamentum**.^{γ} (14) Et dixerunt quod **in pascuis**[2] **gregum seu ovium significationem habet**,^{βγ} propter ymaginem stellarum que in eo sunt; {similiter} et in locis ignium,[3] quia talis est eius natura; item eius sunt hospitia **latronum et siccariorum**,^{β} eo quod est domus Martis, ac etiam omnia **habitacula deserta, in quibus latrones et siccari**^{β} **habitare possunt**;^{γ} *insuper eius sunt* domus orationum, eo quod principium eius est in **linea equali**;^{γ} consimilis quoque ratio de locis **iudicium seu iudiciorum**.^{β} (15) De litteris, {vero} rationem ignoro. (16) Anni {autem} eius .15. sunt ⟨⟨...⟩⟩ Martis, ⟨⟨...⟩⟩, et similiter mensium (17) Rationem et dierum ac horarum, ego vidi IN LIBRO ALBUMAZAR, ⟨⟨...⟩⟩. (18) Ac {vero} quod dixerunt ibi ascendet mulieris ymaginem, et piscis caudam, et caput trianguli, atque ymaginem tauri, hoc ideo quia ascendunt stelle in quibus ymaginibus assimilantur. (19) Et consimilis quidem est ratio de omnibus que ibi ascendere dicit PTOLOMEUS, **non autem sic est de hiis super quibus locuti sunt INDI**,^{γ}

quia, ut dicit ALBUMAZAR *et alii* INTRODUCTORIO, INDI *crediderint quod non est stella nisi precise .9. sphere*[4] *ascendentibus diversis speciebus,*

---

[1]de animalibus seu bestiis sunt pecudes, eo quod stelle eius sunt] M; L in margin.   [2]pascuis] M; L piscibus.   [3]ignium] M; L igneum.   [4]quia ut dicit Albumazar et alii Introductorio Indi crediderunt quod not est stella nisi precise .9. sphere] M; L om.

colors in ⟨its⟩ appearance ⟨⟨and two shapes⟩⟩, because it is changed. (7) They said that it has half a voice, because it has the form of a beast and not a human form. (8) Likewise, they said that the heart of the east belongs to it, because of its heat, and because day and night become equal in it; {consequently} they said that the heart of the east belongs to it. (9) And ⟨they said that⟩ Leo is left-eastern, [i.e., in the northeast] because there the Sun is on the left-hand side [i.e., the north]; and similarly {for that reason} Sagittarius is **southern or right-hand eastern**.[β,11] [right-eastern] (10) They also said that its [Aries'] heat is mixed, because of the weather *of the year*, and in like manner the blood belongs to it. (11) Of the tastes, sweet; and of the colors, reddish, ⟨⟨and any saffron-colored⟩⟩, because of the colors it is intermediate between white and black. (12) {But} of the **animals or beasts**,[β,12] sheep are in its portion, because its stars are in the image of a ram; {moreover,} of the **metals or minerals**,[β,13] gold, iron, silver, and copper, because all of them come from fire and their nature is fiery. (13) {But} they said that the third **climate**[γ] is in its portion **because of the mixture of its heat**.[γ,14] (14) They said that **it has a signification about the pasturelands for herds or sheep**,[βγ,15] because of the image of the stars located in it; and {also} about the places of fires, because that is its nature; likewise, in its portion are the lodgings of **robbers and murderers**,[β,16] because it is the house of Mars, and also all **deserted dwelling places, where robbers and murderers**,[β,17] **can dwell**;[γ,18] *in addition in its portion are* houses of prayer, because its beginning is in the **equal line**[γ,19] [equator]; likewise is the reason for the places of **judges or judgments**.[β,20] (15) I do not know, {however,} the explanation for the letters. (16) {But} its years are 15, ⟨⟨like the number of the least years⟩⟩ of Mars, ⟨⟨as I shall explain in its proper place⟩⟩, and so too ⟨the reason for its⟩ months. (17) As for the reason for the days and hours, I saw it in the BOOK BY ABŪ MA'SHAR, ⟨⟨and I verified it experimentally⟩⟩. (18) {But} what they said, ⟨namely,⟩ that the image of a woman rises there, and the tail of a fish, and the head of a triangle, and the image of a bull, this is because stars that are similar to these images rise there. (19) The same reason applies to everything that PTOLEMY says rises there, **but this is not so regarding the things referred to by the INDIANS**,[γ,21]

because, as ABŪ MA'SHAR and others say in the INTRODUCTION, the INDIANS believed that there is no star except precisely when the different images of the ninth sphere are ascending,[22]

nos {tamen} **secretum illud**^γ ⟨⟨...⟩⟩ scimus. (20) Quod {autem} dixerunt illum, qui natus fuerit in ipso, erit corpus eius temperatum et aures eius laxe, hii quidem sermones per experientiam **veraces inventi sunt in manibus eorum.**^γθ

3   (1) {Porro} **signa**[1] **hec scilicet Taurus,**^γ Cancer, Scorpio, Capricornus et Pisces **orbationes**^γ significant et egritudines, sed non ita signum Leonis et Sagittarii, quia caliditas eorum fortis[2] est **sine defecto;**^γ et residua sunt signa que super figuram sunt humanam, et hec quidem **sanitatem** significant **corporis et perfectionem.**^β (2) **Signum** {igitur} **hoc initium est et caput**^β *in ceterorum divisione signorum,* eo quod caput est omnium signorum; quapropter et super caput significat, Taurus super collum, Gemini super humeros, brachia et manus, Cancer super costas et pectus, Leo super **ventrem superiorem seu stomachum,**^β Virgo super ventrem, Libra supra lumbos, Scorpio super pudibunda, Sagittarius super **femora seu coxas,**^β | Capricornus super genua, Aquarius super tibias, et Pisces super pedes. (3) Dixerunt {autem} Egyptii sapientes quod dolor Saturni ⟨⟨...⟩⟩ est in pectore, et Iovi in corde. (4) ⟨⟨...⟩⟩ Domus enim prima **planete**^γ respectu signi Arietis posita est tamquam signum Arietis[3] secundum se, et {ideo} dixerunt quod **dolor seu passio**^β Iovis in Sagittario, qui est eius prima domus inter suas domus, est in capite, quemadmodum et Aries significat super caput. (5) {Ideo} quod dolor Martis in Ariete est in capite, {eo quod initium est et caput}; ac per hoc in divisione Piscium sunt pedes respectu signum Arietis. (6) Et ob hoc etiam dolor Veneris in Arietis ad pedes spectat, proportio namque signi Arietis ad primam eius domus quod est Taurus, est[4] sicut proportio signi Piscis in Arietem. (7) Dixerunt quoque, secundum divisionem quam facere inceperunt ab Ariete, quod super pectus significat Cancer, qui signum quartum est ab Ariete, domus {autem} Saturni prima Capricornus est, et signum Arietis quartum est respectu domus illius; quare locum doloris Saturni in Ariete est pectus; hec {ergo} est ratio de omnibus doloribus in quolibet signo. (8) Hoc {autem} quod dixerunt in hac parte signi esse regnum, ideo est quia Solis **exaltatio**^γ est in hoc signo; rursus dixerunt quod significat super homines bellicosos et super occisionem, ignem, et sanguinem, quia domus est Martis.

4   (1) Opus {autem} habeo nunc *sermonem* ampliare. (2) Rimatus quidem enim iam sum libros sapientium astrologie^γ ad sciendum **rationem**

---

[1]signa] M; L scilicet.   [2]fortis] L; M fortis temperata.   [3]posita est tamquam signum Arietis] M; L om.   [4]est] M; L et.

{yet} we do ⟨⟨not⟩⟩ know **this secret**.^(γ,23) (20) {But} what they said, that ⟨regarding⟩ one born in it, his body will be mixed and his ears flaccid, these statements **came up in their hands to be correct**^(γθ,24) through experience.

3 (1) {In addition,} **these signs, namely, Taurus,**^(γ,1) Cancer, Scorpio, Capricorn, and Pisces, indicate **defects**^(γ,2) and diseases; but this does not apply to the sign of Leo and Sagittarius, because their heat is strong and **without defect**;^(γ,3) this leaves the signs with a human form, and these indicate **health and perfection of the body**.^(β,4) (2) **This sign,** {then,} **is the beginning and the head**^(β,5) *in the division of the remaining signs*, because it is the head of all the signs; for that reason it indicates the head, Taurus the neck, Gemini the shoulders and arms and hands, Cancer the ribs and chest, Leo the **upper abdomen or stomach**,^(β,6) Virgo the abdomen, Libra the hips, Scorpio the genitals, Sagittarius the **thighs or hips**,^(β,7) Capricorn the knees, Aquarius the lower legs, and Pisces the feet. (3) {But} the EGYPTIAN SCHOLARS said that the chest is the pain of Saturn ⟨⟨in it [i.e., in Aries]⟩⟩, and the heart ⟨is the pain⟩ of Jupiter ⟨in Aries⟩. (4) ⟨⟨This is the reason for it:⟩⟩ the first house of the **planet**^(γ,8) with respect to Aries was put as if it were the sign of Aries according to it; and {therefore} they said that the **pain or suffering**^(β,9) of Jupiter in Sagittarius, which is the first of its houses, is in the head, just as Aries indicates the head. (5) {Therefore} the pain of Mars in Aries is in the head, {because it [Aries] is the beginning and the head}; and consequently the feet are in Pisces' portion with respect to the sign of Aries [i.e., the feet are the pain of Mars in Pisces]. (6) Consequently the pain of Venus in Aries belongs to the feet, because the proportion of the sign Aries to its first house, which is Taurus, is like the proportion of the sign of Pisces to Aries. (7) They also said, according to the division they began to make from Aries, that the chest is indicated by Cancer, which is the fourth sign after Aries, {and so} the first house of Saturn is Capricorn; and the sign of Aries is the fourth with respect to its house; for which reason the place of the pain of Saturn in Aries in the chest; this, {therefore,} is the reason for all the pains in each of the signs. (8) {But} what they said, that kingship is in the portion of the sign, this is because the **exaltation**^(γ,10) of the Sun is in this sign; in addition, they said that it indicates warlike men and slaughter, fire, and blood, because it [Aries] is the house of Mars.

4 (1) {But} I need now to amplify *this statement*. (2) I have searched the BOOKS of the SCHOLARS OF ASTROLOGY^(γ,1) to know the **reason and cause**^(β,2)

et causam^β domorum, sed nullam inveni rem veritatem, nisi quod tantum dixerunt *sic fecimus* et experti sumus et **invenimus hoc verum.**^{γ} (3) Apud HERMETEM^γ vero rationem invenimus ⟨⟨...⟩⟩. (4) Qui ait quod signum Cancer mundi est, **ipse enim ascendens est cum Sole,**^{γ} **in principio Arietis existens in medio celi est**^{γ} **in loco equali linee sive spere recte,**^{β} et hoc est radix. (5) Quapropter aspiciunt ad coniunctionem Saturni et Maris in hoc signo quibuslibet .30. annis ad sciendum res mundi ab illorum coniunctione, secundum quod IN LIBRO CONIUNCTIONUM explanabo. (6) Quoniam {igitur} | signum hoc **septentrionale** est, ac etiam **habitabilis nostra**^{γ} **versus septentrionem,**^{γ} magis apparebit in ipso virtus **planete**^{γ} cuiuslibet ibidem existentis quam in ceteris signis; et quia Luna terre propinqua est, {ideo} signum hoc **est**^{γ} domus Lune. (7) Erit quoque signum sequens, quod est Leo, domus Solis, ibi enim apparet eius fortitudo in tota **habitabili**^{γ} fortior quam in ceteris signis, quia tunc **fortior est et multiplicatior est calor eius.**^{β} (8) Quia {vero} hec sunt luminaria, et Saturnus super **contrarium** significat **luminarium seu luminis,**^{β} ea propter fuerunt domus eius luminarium[1] domibus opposite. (9) Alii {autem} dicunt quod in divisione Saturni posuerunt Capricornium et Aquarium, eo quod in hiis signis augmentatur frigidus quando Sol intratus in ipsa. (10) Et quia Iupiter secundus est post ipsum in **spera,**^{γ} {ideo} **fuerunt domus Iovis secunde domibus Saturni, que sunt Capricornus et Aquarius,**^{γ} erit quoque domus Iovis una ante domus Saturni proportionaliter, **secundum quod domus Saturni una est respectu domus Iovis, et respectu unius domorum Saturni similiter.**^{γ} (11) Erat quoque conveniens domum tertiam ante domos Saturni ac etiam post eas Martis est domos, secundum quod eius **spera**^{γ} tertia est a **spera**^{γ} Saturni. (12) Sol {ergo}, quia in quarta **spera**^{γ} est a Saturno, et est aspectus inimicitie, secundum quod explanabo cum ad aspectus pervenio, conveniens est domum Solis est in aspectu inimicitie ad domum Saturni; et quia Luna in **spera**^{γ} septima est a **spera**^{γ} Saturni, domus {autem} septima[2] domus bellorum est, idcirco domus Lune opposita est domum Saturni.

5   (1) Dicit {igitur} HERMES^γ quod postquam scimus hec **signa**^{γ} domus esse luminarium, partiantur planetis aliis residua .10. **signa.**^{γ} (2) Et erit unicuique planete una domus in parte Solis et alia in parte Lune, sed una est ante et alia retro. (3) Quapropter dixerunt **SAPIENTES ASTRORUM**^{γ} quod a

---

[1]seu luminis, ea propter fuerunt domus eius luminarium] M; L om.   [2]et quia Luna in spera septima est a spera Saturni, domus autem septima] M; L om.

of the houses, but I found nothing correct except that they said that we *did this*, verified it experimentally, and **found it to be true.**ʸ,³ (3) But we found this explanation by **HERMES**ʸ,⁴ ⟨⟨and it runs as follows⟩⟩. (4) He said that Cancer is the sign of the world, **because when it** [Cancer] **ascends with the Sun,**ʸ,⁵ **it** [the Sun] **is at the beginning of Aries in midheaven**ʸ,⁶ **in the place of the equal line or upright sphere**,ᵝ,⁷ and this is a root. (5) For this reason they look for the conjunction of Saturn and Mars in this sign [Cancer] every thirty years to know the affairs of the world from their conjunction, as I shall explain IN THE BOOK OF CONJUNCTIONS. (6) {Therefore,} since this sign is **northern**,ʸ,⁸ and also **our habitable**ʸ,⁹ ⟨part of the Earth⟩ [the ecumene] **faces the north**,ʸ,¹⁰ the power of any **planet**ʸ that is in it [Cancer] is felt more than ⟨when it is⟩ in the other signs; and since the Moon is near the Earth, {therefore} this sign is ʸ,¹¹ the house of the Moon. (7) Also the sign that is next to it, which is Leo, will be the house of the Sun, because there its [the Sun's] power is manifest throughout the **habitable**ʸ ⟨part of the Earth⟩ stronger than in the other signs, because then its [the Sun's] **heat is stronger and more increased.**ᵝ,¹² (8) {Moreover,} because those are the luminaries, and Saturn indicates the **opposite of the luminaries or the light**,ᵝ,¹³ therefore its [Saturn's] houses are in opposition to the houses of the luminaries. (9) {But} others said that they assigned Capricorn and Aquarius to Saturn's division, because in these signs the cold increases when the Sun is in them. (10) Because Jupiter is next to it in ⟨its⟩ **sphere,**ʸ {therefore} **Jupiter's houses are next to Saturn's houses, which are Capricorn and Aquarius,**ʸ,¹⁴ and one house of Jupiter will precede Saturn's house, **to the extent that one house of Saturn with respect to the house of Jupiter is proportionally similar to one of Saturn's houses.**ʸ,¹⁵ (11) So it is also fitting that the third house, before or after Saturn's houses, is ⟨one of⟩ Mars's houses, to the extent that its **sphere**ʸ is the third ⟨counting⟩ from Saturn's **sphere.**ʸ (12) {Therefore} the Sun, since it is in the fourth **sphere**ʸ from Saturn, and this is an aspect of enmity, as I shall explain when I come to the ⟨subject of the⟩ aspects, it is fitting that the house of the Sun be in an aspect of enmity to the house of Saturn; and since the Moon is in the seventh **sphere**ʸ from Saturn's **sphere,**ʸ {but} the seventh house is the house of wars, therefore the house of the Moon is in opposition to the house of Saturn.

5 (1) {Therefore,} **HERMES**ʸ,¹ says that after we know that these **signs**ʸ,² are the houses of the luminaries, the remaining ten **signs**ʸ were distributed to the planets. (2) And to each planet there will be one house in the part of the Sun and another ⟨house⟩ in the part of the Moon, but one is forward and the other backward. (3) Therefore the **SCHOLARS OF THE STARS**ʸ,³ said that **from**

Leone^γ usque ad finem Capricorni est pars Solis, **et hec vocatus maior est.**^γ (4) Quia Soli fortitudo in hac parte sicut fortitudo **planete in terminis suis;**^γ et consimiliter est Luna in parte **minori,**^γ que est a principio Aquarii usque ad finem Cancri. (5) | Quocirca dicunt SAPIENTES EXPERIENTIE quod res omnis quam emerit homo, Luna in parte **minori**^γ existente, carius venditur quam empta fuerit, et contrarius huius est si fuerit in parte **maiori.**^γ (6) {Preterea} **si**^γ consideraveris proportionem circuli Saturni ad circulum Veneris, inveneris eandem proportionem domus huius ad domum illius, et proportio domus quidem unius ad domum secundam est sicut proportio domus secunde unius ad domum secundam alterius, et consimilis via est de Saturno cum Mercurio. (7) Hanc itaque domorum proportionem in omnibus inveneris domibus planetarum quod secundum proportionem circuli unius planetarum ad circuli alterius sit, et proportio domus prioris planete unius ad domum primam alterius, et sic etiam proportio domus secunde planete unius ad secundam domum alterius planete. (8) **Hec** {igitur} **res experta est et verax,**^β nec oportet hiis magis immorari. (9) Fuerunt {autem} domus Saturni luminarium domibus opposite quia contraria est eorum natura; et domus quidem Iovis, que est in parte Solis, est in aspectu trino ad domum Solis, eo quod **bona**[1] **est eius natura,**^γ secundum quod explanabo; et est domus eius in parte secunda que est Lune in consimili proportione ad domum illius, *scilicet Lune*. (10) Martis {vero} domus in aspectu quarto sunt {ad domus} luminarium, quia nocivus est ipse et aspectus quartus inimicitie est; Veneris {autem} domus ad domus luminarium in aspectu sunt sextili, eo quod stella bona est, sed non ita perfecte ut Iupiter, et consimiliter aspectus sextilis *a bonitate* deficit aspectus trinum. (11) Eritque domus Mercuri propinquus domui Solis quia ab eo non multum elongatur. (12) Ait {autem} PTOLOMEUS quod cum fuerit alicuius planete locus respectu loci Solis aut Lune sicut se habet proportio domorum eorum ad domus illorum, tunc erit planete fortitudo magna, et hoc est expertum.

6 (1) **Est** {igitur} **signum Arietis**^γ **domus honoris seu exaltationis**^β Solis, eo quod ibidem incipit **moveri** ad **partem habitabilis,**^γ et apparet eius virtus

---

[1]bona] M; L Luna.

Leo^{γ,4} to the end of Capricorn is the part of the Sun, **and this was called the larger**^{γ,5} ⟨part⟩. (4) For the Sun has power in this part like the power of **a planet in its terms**;^{γ,6} the same applies to the Moon in the **smaller**^{γ,7} part, which is from the beginning of Aquarius to the end of Cancer. (5) Therefore the SCHOLARS OF EXPERIENCE say that anything a person purchases when the Moon is in the **smaller**^{γ} part is sold more expensively than it was purchased, and the opposite occurs if it [the Moon] is in the **larger**^{γ,8} part. (6) {In addition,} if^{γ,9} you have observed the proportion of the circle of Saturn to the circle of Venus, you will find that the proportion of its [Saturn's] house to its [Venus's] house is the same, and that the proportion of the house of one ⟨of them⟩ to the second house is like the proportion of the second house of one ⟨of⟩ them to the second house of the other, and the same way applies to Saturn with Mercury. (7) Thus you will find ⟨that⟩ the proportion in the houses of all the planets is as the proportion of the circle of one of the planets to the circle of the other, and the proportion of the first house of one planet to the first house of the other planet is like the proportion of the ⟨first⟩ house of the second planet to the second house of the other planet. (8) {Therefore,} **this thing is known experimentally and is true**,^{β,10} and there is no need to dwell on it any longer. (9) {But} the houses of Saturn were in opposition to the houses of the luminaries because it [Saturn] is opposed to their nature; and the house of Jupiter, which is in the part of the Sun, is in the aspect of trine to the house of the Sun, because **its** [Jupiter's] **nature is good**,^{γ,11} as I shall explain; and its [Jupiter's] second house, which is in the part of the Moon, has a similar proportion [i.e., it is also in trine] to its house, *namely, of the Moon*. (10) {Moreover} the houses of Mars are in the aspect of quartile to {the houses of} the luminaries, because it is harmful and the aspect of quartile is of enmity; {but} the houses of Venus are in the aspect of sextile to the houses of the luminaries, because it [Venus] is a good star, but it not as complete as Jupiter, and likewise the aspect of sextile falls short *of goodness* in comparison to the aspect of trine. (11) The house of Mercury will be adjacent to the house of the Sun because it does not move far away from it. (12) {But} PTOLEMY said that when the place of a planet with respect to the place of the Sun or the Moon is as the proportion of its [the planet's] houses to their [the luminaries'] houses, then the planet will have great power; and this has been known experimentally.

6 (1) **The sign of Aries**,^{γ,1} {then,} is the Sun's **house of honor or exaltation**,^{β,2} because that is where it begins **to move**^{3} towards **the habitable part**^{γ} ⟨of the Earth⟩, and its [the Sun's] power becomes perceptible in the

in mundo. (2) SAPIENTES {autem} INDORUM aiunt quod gradus honoris sui est .19. signi, eo quod ibi stella est de complexione Iovis et Veneris; quod | si ratio et causa hec est,^{βγ} tunc mutabitur gradus, secundum quod de gradibus lucidis dicam et tenebrosis. (3) Dixerunt {autem} quod domus est odii Veneris, eo quod in aspectu est opposito domui sue; est etiam **locus humiliationis sive oppositum augis**^{β} Mercurii, et hoc quidem scitum est secundum **viam demonstrationum geometricarum**.^{γ}

63vb

7 (1) {Item} dixerunt quod domini triplicitatis eius sunt in die quidem Sol ⟨⟨...⟩⟩, quia domus eius et domus Iovis eiusdem nature sunt cum hoc signo. (2) Dederunt {autem} fortitudinem Soli de die, quia apparet de die eius virtus; et posuerunt Iovem de nocte, quia de nocte super terram esse potest, et omnis stella super terram existens maioris est fortitudinis quam illa que sub terra est. (3) Posueruntque participem Saturnum, eo quod frigidus est et signum calidum rectificat eius naturam; scire {autem} debes quod id quod dixi calidum et frigidum, non est nisi secundum id quod generant, **ut hoc universaliter de manibus nostris expediamus**.^{γ} (4) Martem {vero} ab hac participatione repulerunt propter **excellentiam**^{γ} caliditatis sue.

8 (1) **Alio quidem** {autem} **modo secundum sententiam**, *inquam*, SA-PIENTIUM EGYPTORUM, **Mars est primus quia ipse dominus domus est; secundus** {autem} **Solis, eo quod domus eius est secunda triplicitatis; tertius** {vero} **Iupiter, quia dominus tertius domus est huius triplicitatis.**^{γ,1} (2) Ac {vero} INDI facies distinguere inceperunt a Marte, domino domus, posueruntque secundam faciem Soli, secundum quod eius circulus Marti est secundus, et secundum hanc viam sunt omnes facies donec in fine Piscium revertantur ad Martem. (3) Sunt enim .36., que si per septem dividantur propter planetas, quia **revertantur iterum sive circulantur**,^{θ} et remanet una. (4) Consimiliter quoque si volueris scire, secundum viam numeri, quis est dominus faciei signi dati, scito **longitudinem sive distantiam**^{β} signi a principio Arietis, **et signa que fuerunt**^{γ} multiplicata per .3., et quod exierunt trahe .7. et .7. *sive divide per septem*. (5) Et in eo quod residuum fuerit, incipe numerare a Marte, qui dominus est domus, secundum ordinem **planetarum**,^{γ} et qua inter dominos facierum inveneris **ultimo**,^{γ} subsequentem **secundum circulationem**^{γ} ille dominus erit faciei, et cum

---

[1]tertius vero Iupiter quia dominus tertius domus est huis triplicitatis] M; L in margin

world. (2) {But} the SCHOLARS OF THE INDIANS say that the degree of its honor [exaltation] is 19° of the sign [Aries], because in this place there is a star with the mixture of Jupiter and Venus; **but if this is the reason or cause,**[β,γ,4] then the degree will be changed, as I shall explain ⟨when I discuss⟩ the bright and dark degrees. (3) {But} they also said that it is Venus's house of hate [house of detriment], because it is in opposition aspect to its [i.e., Venus'] house; and it is also Mercury's **place of humiliation or opposite the apogee**[β,5] [perigee], and this is known according to the **method of geometric demonstrations.**[γ,6]

7 (1) {Likewise}, they said that the lords of its triplicity are the Sun by day ⟨⟨and Jupiter by night⟩⟩, because its [the Sun's] house and Jupiter's house have the same nature as this sign. (2) {But} they assigned power to the Sun by day, because its power is perceptible by day; and they put Jupiter by night, because it can be above the Earth at night, and any star that is above the Earth exerts more power than one that is underneath the Earth. (3) They made Saturn ⟨its⟩ partner, because it is cold and the hot sign rectifies its nature; {but} you must know that when I said cold and hot, this is only according to what they generate, **as we ourselves explain this as a general rule.**[γ,1] (4) {Moreover} they left Mars out of this partnership because of **the extreme degree**[γ,2] of its heat.

8 (1) {But} **by another method, according to the opinion** *I say,* **of the EGYPTIAN SCHOLARS, Mars is first, because it itself is the lord of the house;** {but} **the Sun is second, because its house is the second of the triplicity;** {but} **Jupiter is third, because it is the lord of the third house of this triplicity.**[γ,1] (2) {But} THE INDIANS began to distinguish the faces [decans] from Mars, the lord of the house, and they assigned the second face to the Sun, inasmuch as its circle is second to Mars, and by this method all the faces were ⟨assigned⟩, until at the end of Pisces they [the faces] are again ⟨assigned⟩ to Mars. (3) For there are 36 ⟨faces⟩, which, if they are divided by seven because of the planets, since they **return back again or form a circle,**[β,2] one is left over. (4) Likewise, if you wish to know, according to the numerical method, which is the lord of the face of a certain sign, ascertain the **longitude or distance**[β,3] of the sign from the beginning of Aries, and multiply **the resulting signs**[γ,4] by three, and ⟨from⟩ the result extract seven and seven *or divide by seven.* (5) And in what remains, begin counting from Mars, which is the lord of the house, according to the order **of the planets,**[γ,5] and among the lords of the faces you will find **the last,**[γ,6] and the next

perveneris ad Lunam, semper reincipiendum est a Saturno. (6) Cuius exemplum est: invenimus nativitatem in .15. gradu signi Virginis, et iam scimus | quod facies est .10. graduum, et quod est in secunda signi facie. (7) Et transiverunt .5. signa a principio Arietis, que quidem multiplicentur per .3. et ascendunt .15.; apponamus {autem} unum propter primam faciem signi Virginis **perfectam seu pertransitam**,^{β} et sunt .16. per totum. (8) Trahantur {ergo} .7. et septem *sive dividantur per septem*, et remanebunt due; tunc incipiamus a Marte numerare, et Marti quidem et Soli erunt .2., convenit ergo faciem **illam**^{γ} esse Veneris, que sub Sole est consequenter.

9 (1) In terminis quidem {autem} quos PTOLOMEUS commemoravit **nullatenus est considerandum**;^{γ} dicit {tamen} quod sic invenit eos in **LIBRIS INDORUM ANTIQUORUM NECNON EGYPTORUM,**^{γ} **et ait**^{γ} ipsos expertos esse. (2) {Porro} numerus terminorum planete cuiuslibet in omnibus signis est tamquam numeris annorum eius magnorum.

10 (1) {Sane} quia triplicitas in nona domo terminatur, {ideo} distinxerunt **SAPIENTES**^{γ} signum quodlibet in novem partes, vocatas novenarias, item est et finis numeri novenarius. (2) Posuerunt {igitur} naturam prime novenarie signo primo, quod est Aries, secundam Tauro, ultimam Sagittario, qui **finis seu ultimus**^{β} est triplicitatis. (3) {Quod} si **ascendens**^{γ} fuerit Leo vel Sagittarius, ponunt primam novenariam Arieti et secundam Tauro, secundum modum signi Arietis, **qui**^{γ} principium est triplicitatis. (4) Universaliter {autem} semper incipiunt in triplicitate a signo mobili; propter quod in triplicitate Tauri incipiunt¹ a Capricorno, secundum viam signorum **dictam in Arietem**.^{γ} (5) Inceperuntque in triplicitate Geminorum a Libra qui est signum mobile, ⟨⟨...⟩⟩.

11 (1) Ratio {autem} virtutis duodenariarum est que partiti sunt quodlibet signum secundum naturam duodecim signorum, et dederunt partem primam domino signi ascendentis, et secundam partem domino signi secundi, et sic de omnibus. (2) Alio {vero} modo, deputaverunt .2. gradus et dimi-

---

¹in triplicitate a signo mobili propter quod in triplicitate Tauri incipiunt] M; L in margin.

one **in the cycle**[γ,7] will be the lord of the face, and when you reach the Moon, you must always begin again from Saturn. (6) An example of this: we find the ⟨ascendant of the⟩ nativity at Virgo 15°, and we already know that the face is ⟨at Virgo⟩ 10°, so that it is in the second face of the sign. (7) Five signs have passed from the beginning of Aries ⟨to Virgo⟩, which, multiplied by 3 yields 15; {but} we add one for the first face of the sign of Virgo, **which has been completed or has already passed,**[β,8] and the total is 16. (8) {Accordingly,} sevens are extracted ⟨from them⟩ *or they are divided by seven*, and two remain; then we begin to count from Mars, so that Mars and the Sun are the two, therefore it is fitting that **this**[γ,9] face be ⟨assigned⟩ to Venus, because it is underneath the Sun.

9 (1) {As for} the terms which PTOLEMY mentioned, **they must by no means be taken into consideration;**[γ,1] {yet} he says that he found them in this manner **in BOOKS OF THE ANCIENT INDIANS AND ALSO EGYPTIANS,**[γ,2] **and he said**[γ,3] that they were verified experimentally. (2) {In addition,} the number of the terms of any planet in all the signs is as the number of the great years.

10 (1) {Certainly,} because the triplicity ends in the ninth house, {therefore} the **SCHOLARS**[γ,1] divided any sign into nine parts, called *novenariae*[2] [ninths-parts], and likewise ⟨because⟩ the number nine is the end of the number [the last of the digits]. (2) {Therefore,} they assigned the nature of the first *novenaria* [ninths-part] to the first sign, which is Aries, the second ⟨*novenaria*⟩ to Taurus, the last ⟨*novenaria*⟩ to Sagittarius, which is **the end or the last one**[β,3] of the triplicity. (3) {But} if the **ascendant**[γ,4] is Leo or Sagittarius, they assign the first *novenaria* [ninth-part] to Aries and the second to Taurus, according to the method of the sign of Aries, **which is**[γ,5] the beginning of the triplicity. (4) {But} the general rule is that they begin the triplicity from a changeable sign; consequently in Taurus' triplicity they begin from Capricorn, according to the order of the signs **mentioned regarding Aries.**[γ,6] (5) They begin Gemini's triplicity from Libra, which is a changeable sign, ⟨⟨and ⟨they begin⟩ the last triplicity with Cancer, which is a changeable sign⟩⟩.

11 (1) {But} the reason for the power of the *duodenariae*[1] [twelfths] ⟨is⟩ that they divided up any sign according to the nature of the twelve signs, and assigned the first part to the lord of the sign of the ascendant, the second part to the lord of the second sign, and so on for all of them. (2) {But} by another method, they assigned two-and-a-half degrees to the power of the

dium virtuti domini signi primi, et sic¹ fecerunt **donec**ᵞ perficient virtutem {signorum} .12. in gradibus signum cuiuslibet, et hec est veritas. (3) Habetque magnam fortitudinem in revolucione {annorum} mundi.

12 (1) ⟨⟨...⟩⟩. (2) Scito quod antiqua ⟨⟨...⟩⟩ fuit dissensio que quidem adhuc perseverat **donec inveterati sunt** ASTRORUM SAPIENTES.ᵞ (3) Quidam enim ponebant **annum suum**ᵞ a puncto introitus **anni**ᵞ | in principio signi Arietis **ymaginati ab homine,**ᵞ **videlicet a coniunctione**ᵞ durorum circulorum magnorum, ubi equantur nox et dies. (4) Ait {autem} ABRACAZ quod annus solaris est .365. dies et quarta pars diei; dicit {tamen} quod aliquod deficit a quarta, sed nescit quantus est defectus; (5) nisi quod ⟨⟨...⟩⟩ dicit hanc diminutionem esse unius partis quarum .300. sunt in die; SAPIENTES {vero} SARRACENORUM SEU ARABUMᵝ scrutati sunt et invenerunt quod hic defectus est una .110. partium in die; et quidam dicunt parte .106.; veritas {autem} est quod hic defectus est pars una de .131. (6) {Verum} SAPIENTES INDORUM de coniunctione duorum circulorum non curant, sed est annus ipsorum a coniunctione Solis cum **stella fixa**ᵞ quousque revertatur iterum ad suam coniunctionem. (7) Est {autem} inter ANTIQUOS discordia, namque quidam aiunt quod poli **zodiaci**ᵞ ascendunt et descendunt .8. gradus; alii {vero} dicunt quod super caput Arietis et Libre sunt duo *parvi* circuli. (8) Sed INDI,ᵞ secundum ipsorum operationem, fecerunt unam viam rectam, dicunt enim quod stelle **orbis**ᵞ signorum non moventur. (9) ANTIQUI {vero}, et PTOLOMEUS cum ipsis, dicunt quod in .100. annis moventur uno gradu; posterius {autem} perscrutantes invenerunt quod motus est unius gradus in .66. annis. (10) **Verus et rectius**ᵝ est motum esse *unius gradus* in .70. annis. (11) {Igitur} si verum dicunt hii quod **transmutate seu mote sunt stelle supreme,**ᵝ tunc iam ingressus est motus eorum in numero anni solaris **secundum** INDOS;ᵞ si {autem} non fuerit eis motus secundum quod dicunt SAPIENTES,ᵞ tunc non erit contra SAPIENTES INDORUM. (12) Et hii quidem sermones prolixa indigent explicatione. (13) Universaliter {autem} INDORUM SAPIENTES partiti sunt signa equaliter secundum quod visui apparent, **et hoc est**ᵞ secundum ymagenes; PTOLOMEUS {vero} ET SUI SEQUENTESᵞ secundum congruentiam vie **probationum seu demonstrationum.**ᵝ (14) ASTROLOGUSᵞ {igitur} **extrahere seu accipere**ᵝ debet gradum ascendente

---

¹sic] M; L om.

lord of the first sign and they proceeded in this way until^(γ,2) they completed the power of the 12 {signs} in the degrees of any sign, and this is the truth. (3) It [the *duodenaria*] has a great power in the revolution {of the years} of the world.

12 (1) ⟨⟨The Indian scholars said that there are bright and dark degrees; here is the reason for them⟩⟩. (2) Know that there is an old ⟨⟨and great⟩⟩ disagreement which persists **as long as the SCHOLARS OF THE STARS are old.**^(γ,1) (3) For some people fixed **their year**^(γ,2) from the moment of the entry of **the year**^(γ,3) in the beginning of the sign of Aries **imagined by a human being,**^(γ,4) namely, from the **intersection**^(γ,5) of the two great circles, where the night and the day are equal. (4) {But} HIPPARCHUS says that the solar year is 365¼ days; {nevertheless,} he says that something is lacking from the quarter, but he did not know how much the deficit is; (5) but ⟨⟨Ptolemy⟩⟩ says that the deficit is the 300th part of a day; {moreover} **THE SCHOLARS OF THE SARACENS OR OF THE ARABS**^(β,6) investigated closely and found that this deficit is 110th of a day; and certain people said that it is 106th of a day; {but} the truth is that the deficit is 131th of a day. (6) {But} the SCHOLARS OF THE INDIANS pay no attention to the intersection of the two circles, but their year is from the conjunction of the Sun with a **fixed star**^(γ,7) until it [the Sun] returns once more to its conjunction [i.e., with the same upper star]. (7) {But} there is a disagreement among the ANCIENTS, for some say that the poles of the **zodiac**^(γ,8) ascend and descend eight degrees; {moreover} others say that there are two *small* circles at the head of Aries and Libra. (8) But the **INDIANS,**^(γ,9) according to their ⟨mode of⟩ working, designed a correct method, for they say that the stars of the **orb**^γ of the signs do not move. (9) {Moreover} the ANCIENTS, and PTOLEMY with them, say that they move one degree in 100 years; {but} those who investigated closely after them found that their motion is one degree in 66 years. (10) **True and more correct**^(β,10) is that the motion is *one degree* in 70 years. (11) {Therefore,} if those who say that **the highest stars change or move**^(β,11) were right, then their motion would have entered in the reckoning of the solar year **according to the INDIANS;**^(γ,12) {but} if they have no motion according to what the **SCHOLARS**^(γ,13) say, then this will not be against the ⟨theory of the⟩ SCHOLARS OF THE INDIANS. (12) These statements require a long explanation. (13) {But} as a general rule the SCHOLARS OF THE INDIANS divided the signs equally according to how they appear to sight, **and this is**^(γ,14) according to the images [the constellations]; {but} **PTOLEMY AND HIS FOLLOWERS**^(γ,15) ⟨divided the signs⟩ according to the fitness of the method of **proofs or demonstrations.**^(β,16) (14) {Therefore,} the **ASTROLOGER**^(γ,17) must

ac etiam loca planetarum secundum compotum TABULARUM SAPIENTIUM EXPERIENTIE; si {vero} iudicare voluit secundum viam ymaginum, et gra-
64va duum lucidorum et tenebrosorum ac etiam | putealium, qui videlicet sunt stelle quedam obscure multum, sicut homo casus passus in puteo, oportet quidem ipsum in hoc anno, qui {secundum HEBREOS} est .908., diminuere .8. gradus perfectos. (15) Denique loca stellarum magnarum in quolibet signo commemorata, accepta quidem sunt secundum viam SAPIENTIUM EXPERIENTIE in diebus istis.

13 (1) Taurus, quidem quia frigidus est, {ideo} dixerunt quod est signum femininum, atque nocturnum; et iudicaverunt ipsum esse **stabile seu fixum**,^{β} eo quod *in ipso* tempus *anni* **stat secundum viam unam**;^{θ} non oportet rememorari **alia, quia in signo Arietis commemoravimus illa**.^{γ} (2) Significat {autem} super **luxuriam aut prolis generationem**,^{θβ} eo quod domus est Veneris, **et universaliter caliditatem cum frigido temperatam**,^{γ} propter naturam suam et tempus *anni*. (3) Eius igitur est melancolia, eo quod frigidum *signum* est et siccum; de saporibus {autem}, ille qui dulcis est propter tempus *anni*, quod calidus est et humidus; ⟨⟨...⟩⟩. (4) De vegetalibus {autem}, in parte ipsius sunt **arbores alte et sublimes**,^{β} eo quod hec est de natura terre. (5) Et {quia} domus est Veneris, {ideo} dixerunt quod **virtutem habet**^{γ} in fructibus ac in omnibus **plantis seu arborum**,^{β} quarum sapor et odor **dulcis**.^{γ} (6) De **climatibus et regionibus**,^{β} quod in parte eius est, hoc invenerunt per viam experimenti. (7) Et anni eius octo sicut anni Veneris minores. (8) Dixerunt etiam de hoc signo quod est meridionale quia sic experti sunt; PTOLOMEUS {vero} discordans ab ANTIQUIS dicit signa ignea septentrionalia[1] fore, et signa aquea orientalia, sed bene confitetur quod signa terrea sunt meridionalia et signa aerea occidentalia. (9) IACOB {autem} ALKINDI ait quod signa ignea orientalia sed conversiva sunt versus septentrionem, et hoc est verum.

14 (1) Geminum itaque duorum dicunt esse corporum, eo quod **prima pars**[2] **eius seu medietas**^{β} est **de natura temporis anni calida**,^{γ} et medietas
64vb secunda **de natura temporis anni sicca**;^{γ} eademque est ratio de signo | Virginis et Sagittarii ac Piscium. (2) Et quia figure est hominis qui non est multum prolificus, idcirco dicunt quod est sterile; significat {autem} super omnem sublimitatem **et principes, duces, et prophetas, legislatores**,^{γ} eo quod est de natura aerea; et est in fine partis septentrionalis; et locus **augis**^{γ} Solis.

[1]septentrionalia] M; L om.   [2]pars] M; L om.

calculate or extract^{β,18} the degree of the ascendant and the positions of the planets according to the reckoning of the TABLES OF THE SCHOLARS OF EXPERIENCE; {but} if he wants to pass ⟨astrological⟩ judgment according to the method of the images [the constellations], of the bright and dark degrees, and also of those pertaining to a pit, namely, certain very dark stars, as if a man had fallen into a pit, this year, which {according to the HEBREWS} is ⟨4⟩908 [i.e. 1147/8 C.E.], it is necessary to subtract eight whole degrees. (15) Finally, the positions of the large stars mentioned ⟨in *Reshit Ḥokhmah*⟩ in any sign, are taken according to the method of the SCHOLARS OF EXPERIENCE in these days [i.e., in 1147/8 C.E.].

13 (1) Taurus, because it is cold, {therefore} they said that it is feminine, and ⟨one of the⟩ nocturnal ⟨signs⟩; and they judged that this sign is **stable or fixed**,^{β,1} because *in it* the season *of the year* stands in one way;^{θ,2} there is no need to call to mind **the other things, because we mentioned the other things in** ⟨**the section on**⟩ **the sign of Aries.**^{γ,3} (2) {But} it indicates **lust or generation of offspring**,^{θβ4} because it is the house of Venus, **and as a rule** ⟨**it indicates**⟩ **heat mixed with cold**,^{γ,5} on account of its nature and the weather of the *year*. (3) The black bile pertains to it, because it is a cold and dry *sign*; {but} of the tastes, the sweet, because of the season *of the year*, which is hot and moist; ⟨⟨and astringency and constipation because of its nature⟩⟩. (4) {But} of plants, **tall and lofty trees**^{β,6} are in its portion, because it is of earthy nature. (5) {Since} it is the house of Venus, {hence} they said that it **has power**^{γ,7} in fruits, and in all the **plants or trees**^{β,8} whose taste and smell **is sweet.**^{γ,9} (6) Of the **climates and regions**,^{β,10} they found what is in its portion by the way of experience. (7) Its years are eight, like the number of Venus' least years. (8) They said about this sign that it is southern because they found this experimentally; {but} PTOLEMY, while disagreeing with the ANCIENTS, says that the fiery signs are northern, and that the watery signs are eastern, but he accepts that the earthy signs are southern and the airy signs are western. (9) YAʿQUB AL-KINDĪ, {however,} said that the fiery signs are eastern but inclined to the north, and this is correct.

14 (1) Thus they said that Gemini is of two bodies, because **its first part or half**^{β,1} **is of the hot nature of the season of the year,**^{γ,2} and the second half **is of the dry nature of the season of the year;**^{γ,3} and the same reason applies to Virgo, Sagittarius, and Pisces. (2) Since it has the form of a man who is not very prolific, consequently they said that it is barren; {but} it indicates every highness, **and princes, dukes, prophets and law-givers,**^{γ,4} because it is of airy nature; it is at the end of northern part; and the place of the Sun's **apogee**^{γ,5} ⟨is there⟩.

15 (1) De Cancro quidem dixerunt quod est signum rectum, eo quod in omni **climate**ʸ **ascensiones eius**ʸ maiores sunt .30. gradibus. (2) {Unde} a principio huius signi usque ad finem Sagittarii sunt {omnia} signa recta, **ab initio** {vero} **seu a capite**ʸ Capricorni usque ad finem Geminorum sunt **obliqua**ʸ signa, cuiuslibet enim eorum **ascensiones**ʸ minores sunt .30. gradibus. (3) Iam {autem} **dictum est**ʸ ⟨⟨...⟩⟩ quare pectus huic signo deputaverunt, ipsi enim inceperunt distinguere a capite usque ad pedes; et {ideo} dixerunt quod Taurus super collum significat, et Geminum super manus et brachia, spectabit ergo cor ad signum Leonis. (4) Quapropter ait PTOLOMEUS quod omnis homo in cuius nativitate fuerit Venus in Leone, concupiscentiam habebit magnam erga mulieris, et huius ratio est quia Venus super **luxuriam**ʸ significat, et quia hic est in parte cordis {ideo} sic contingit. (5) Non oportet {igitur} de aliis loqui signis, quia ratio super ipsas secundum eandem viam est qua¹ in signo Arietis. (6) Dixerunt {autem} de Virgine quod super hominem significat et super volucres, eo quod de duabus est figuris; et dixerunt {etiam} quod significat super vegetabilia minuta, eo quod dominus domus est **stella parva omnium quidem stellarum minima;**ʸ quoniam igitur domus est Mercurii, {ideo} dixerunt quod super **scientiam**ʸ significat ⟨⟨...⟩⟩ et magisteria.

16 (1) **De domibus** itaque **honoris sive de exaltationibus**ᵝ nunc loquamur. (2) **Honor** {igitur} **seu exaltatio**ᵝ Lune est in tertio gradu Tauri, **secundum**ʸ sententiam SAPIENTIUM INDORUM. (3) PTOLOMEUS {vero} dicit quod totum signum est domus honoris eius, cuius quidem ratio est quia cum Soli coniungitur **in principio mundi**ʸ apparebit occidentalis **super orizonta**ʸ

65ra   in signo Tauri. (4) SAPIENTES {autem} INDORUM | dixerunt quod propter distantiam² loci **honoris seu exaltationis**ᵝ Solis **secundum quantitatem luminis seu radiorum**ᵝ **ipsius Solis,**ʸ {ideo} dixerunt quod gradus honoris Lune est tercius Tauri. (5) Et erit **casus**ʸ Solis in .19. gradu Libre, ⟨⟨...⟩⟩, et hinc ⟨⟨...⟩⟩ usque ad tercium gradum Scorpionis est **locus combustionis seu via combusta;**ᵝ dixerunt {autem} quod in hoc loco debilitatur virtus planete cuiuslibet; et vocaverunt locum combustionis tamquam si planeta combustus esset **in radiis sive lumine**ᵝ Solis. (6) {Item} dixerunt quod Libra domus est honoris Saturni, quia natura eius contraria est natura Solis, unde domus honoris est domus casus Solis, et domus casus eius est³ domus honoris Solis. (7) Dixeruntque ⟨⟨...⟩⟩ quod honor Saturni est in .21. gradu

---

¹qua] M; L quia.   ²distantiam] M; L instantiam.   ³domus casus eius est] M; L om.

15 (1) They said about Cancer that it is a straight sign, because **its ascensions**[γ] are more than thirty degrees in any **climate.**[γ] (2) {Therefore,} from the beginning of this sign until the end of Sagittarius {all} the signs are straight, {but} **from the beginning or the head**[γ,1] of Capricorn until the end of Gemini the signs are **oblique,**[γ] for the **ascensions**[γ] of each of them are less than thirty degrees. (3) {But} **it has been** already **said**[γ,2] ⟨⟨the reason of⟩⟩ why they assigned the chest to this sign, ⟨namely,⟩ because they began to classify from the head to the feet; {hence} they said that Taurus indicates the neck, and Gemini the hands and the arms, and consequently the heart will belong to the sign of Leo. (4) Therefore PTOLEMY said that every person in whose nativity Venus is in Leo will have a great erotic desire for women, and the reason of this is that Venus indicates **lust,**[γ,3] and since this [lust] is in the heart's portion, {therefore} it happens in this manner. (5) There is no need, {then,} to speak about the other signs, because the reason for them is according to the same way as for the sign of Aries. (6) {But} regarding Virgo, they said that it indicates human beings and birds, because it is of two forms [bicorporal]; and they {also} said that it indicates small plants, because the lord of its house [Mercury] is **a small star, the smallest of all the stars;**[γ,4] therefore, because it [Virgo] is the house of Mercury, {consequently} they said that it indicates **science,**[γ,5] ⟨⟨writing⟩⟩ and professions.

16 (1) Thus I shall now speak **about the houses of honor or about the exaltations.**[β,1] (2) {So,} **the honor or exaltation of the Moon**[β,2] is in the third degree of Taurus, **according to**[γ,3] the opinion of the SCHOLARS OF THE INDIANS. (3) {Moreover} PTOLEMY says that the whole sign is its house of honor, the reason being that when it is conjoined to the Sun **at the beginning of the world**[γ,4] it appears western **above the horizon**[γ,5] in the sign of Taurus. (4) {But} the SCHOLARS OF THE INDIANS said that ⟨this is so⟩ because the distance of the place of the Sun's **honor or exaltation**[β] ⟨is⟩ **according to the quantity of the light or rays**[β,6] **of the Sun itself;**[γ,7] {hence} they said that the degree of the Moon's honor is the third ⟨degree⟩ of Taurus. (5) The **fall**[γ,8] [dejection] of the Sun will be at Libra 19°, ⟨⟨and the degree of shame of the Moon is Scorpio 3°⟩⟩; hence ⟨⟨they called from Libra 19°⟩⟩ to Scorpio 3° **the place of burning or the burnt path;**[β,9] {but} they said that the power of any planet is weakened in this place; and they called "place of burning" as if the planet were burnt **in the rays or the light**[β,10] of the Sun. (6) {Likewise,} they said that Libra is the house of Saturn's honor, because its nature is the opposite of the Sun's nature; therefore ⟨Saturn's⟩ house of honor is the Sun's house of fall, and its [Saturn's] house of fall is the Sun's house of honor. (7) The ⟨⟨Indian scientists⟩⟩ said that

Libre, quia sic experimentati sunt. (8) ENOCH {autem} SIVE HERMES^β ait quod honor Saturni duobus gradibus distat ab opposito honoris Solis, quatenus Soli magnum non esset nocumentum. (9) Rursus dixerunt INDI^γ quod honor Capitis Draconis est in tertio gradu Geminorum, et ibidem est casus Caude; PTOLOMEUS {vero} deridet eos, eo quod Caput Draconis non est stella aliqua, et ipse ius habet, *et rationabiliter quia movetur*. (10) {Amplius} de Iove dixerunt quod domus honoris eius Cancer est, quia Iupiter super ventos significat **septentrionales**,^{γ} et quando ibidem est multiplicat ventos; INDORUM {vero} SAPIENTES dixerunt quod gradus honoris eius in medio signo est. (11) Mars {autem}, quia ventos generat meridianos, et cum es in signo Capricorni multiplicantur, dixerunt quod est domus honoris Martis; et quia ipse in aspectu opposito cum Iove est sicut Sol cum Saturno, {ideo} **in illo est contraria natura**^{γ} Martis nature Iovis. (12) Dixerunt {quoque} INDORUM SAPIENTES quod gradus honoris eius est in .28. gradu Capricorni, quia ibi est **exaltatio**^{γ} secundum naturam eius. (13) De Venere {autem} dixerunt quod domus honoris eius sunt Pisces quia sic experti sunt; et domus casus eius Virgo; et {ideo} significat omni **luxurioso malum**^{γ} quod non est conveniens. (14) Quoniam {utique} Venus significat super **delicias et delectationes seculi**,^{β} Mercurius {vero} super sermones sapientie, {ideo} dixe-

65rb runt | quod domus honoris Mercurii opposita est domui honoris Veneris, et domus **casus**^{γ} eius est domus honoris alterius. (15) Quod {vero} de signis aqueis dixerunt, **voce carent seu vocem non habent**,^{β} huius ratio est **de generatis in aqua sive in aquatilibus**,^{β} *quia*^{1} *carent voce*.

17 (1) Ratio quidem de domibus triplicitatis ignee iamque dicta est. (2) In triplicitate {vero} signorum terreorum, *dominum* triplicitatis **primum** in die posuerunt Venerem, ⟨⟨...⟩⟩. (3) Et dixerunt quod **in nocte incipiendum est a Luna**,^{γ} eo quod ipsa domina^2 honoris est huius domus, et **eius presentia et luminositas**^{β} de nocte magis apparens est quam de die. (4) Posueruntque Martem participem cum illis, eo quod super **partem**^{γ} significat meridianam, ⟨⟨...⟩⟩; et repulerunt Mercurium ac Saturnum, quia fortitudinem **in angulo meridiano**^{γ} non habent. (5) In signis {autem} aereis **dominum triplicitatis primum**^{γ} posuerunt Saturnum, eo quod dominus est

---

^{1}quia] M; L qua. ^{2}domina] M; L domus.

Saturn's honor is at Libra 21°, because they tested experimentally in this manner. (8) {But} ENOCH or HERMES[β,11] said that Saturn's honor is two degrees distant from opposition to the Sun's honor, so that great harm will not befall the Sun. (9) In addition, the INDIANS[γ,12] said that the honor of the Head of the Dragon is at Gemini 3°, and there [too] is the fall of the Tail ⟨of the Dragon⟩; {but} PTOLEMY laughs at them, because the Head of the Dragon is not any star; and **he is right**[θ,13] [lit. he has the law], *and this is in accordance with reason because it moves*. (10) {Besides,} regarding Jupiter, they said that its house of honor is Cancer, because Jupiter indicates the **northerly**[γ,14] winds, and when it is there it increases the winds; {but} the SCHOLARS OF THE INDIANS said that the degree of its honor is in the middle of the sign. (11) {But} Mars, because it generates southerly winds, and they are increased when it is in Capricorn, they said that it [Capricorn] is Mars's house of honor; and since it itself [Mars] is in opposition aspect with Jupiter as the Sun with Saturn, {therefore} **there is a nature in it** [Capricorn] **that is contrary**[γ,15] to Jupiter's nature. (12) The SCHOLARS OF THE INDIANS {also} said that the degree of its [i.e. Mars'] honor is Capricorn 28°, because there is **the exaltation**[γ,16] according to its nature. (13) {But} regarding Venus, they said that the house of its honor is Pisces, because they verified that experimentally in this manner; and the house of its fall is Virgo; {hence} it indicates any **luxurious evil**[γ,17] that is not proper. (14) Because {certainly} Venus indicates the **delights and pleasures of the world**,[β,18] {but} Mercury indicates statements of wisdom, {therefore} they said that the house Mercury's honor is in opposition to the house of Venus's honor, and that the house of its [Mercury's] **fall**[γ] is the house of honor of the other [Venus]. (15) {Moreover} what they said regarding the watery signs, ⟨namely, that⟩ they **lack a voice or do not have voice**,[β,19] its reason follows from **those generated in water or in aquatic animals**,[β,20] *because they lack a voice*.

17 (1) The reason of the houses of the fiery triplicity has been already mentioned. (2) {But} in the triplicity of the earthy signs, they made Venus the first *lord* by day, ⟨⟨because the sign of Taurus belongs to Venus [Taurus is the planetary house of Venus]⟩⟩. (3) They also said that **by night one must begin from the Moon**,[γ,1] because it is the lady of the honor of this house, and **its presence and luminosity**[β,2] is more noticeable by night than by day. (4) They made Mars their partner, because it indicates the southern **part**,[γ,3] ⟨⟨and the earthy signs are southern⟩⟩; and they excluded Mercury and Saturn, because they have no power **over the southern corner**.[γ,4] (5) {But} regarding the airy signs, they made Saturn **the first lord of the triplicity**,[γ,5]

signi Aquarii, et inceperunt ab ipso in die, quia masculinus est et virtus eius diurna. (6) **Dominumque triplicitatis secundum**^γ posuerunt Mercurium, eo quod dominus est Geminorum; et fortitudo eius de nocte maior quam de die, {ideoque} de nocte inceperunt ab ipso. (7) Repulerunt {autem} Venerem, **dominam**^γ signi Libre, a fortitudine triplicitatis, eo quod super **delicias** significat **et concupiscentias**,^β ⟨⟨...⟩⟩; unde loco eius Iovem **hiis signis** deputaverunt, eo quod **equalis seu temperatus**^β est in sua natura. (8) {Denique} **triplicitatis ultimam deputaverunt Venerem**,^γ quia **multiplicationem prolis**^θ significat, et hec est natura Veneris. (9) Inceperunt {ergo} ab ea de die, secundus {autem} dominus eius Mars est, dominus videlicet signi Scorpionis, posueruntque participem Lunam, dominam domus Cancri, et hec est ratio ANTIQUORUM.

18 (1) PTOLOMEUS {vero} dissentit in domibus triplicitatis; et nos quidem experientiam accepimus sermonum eius, sed **non sunt verificati in manibus nostris**;^θ quapropter sustentati sumus super sermones antiquorum. (2) Universaliter {autem} dico tibi quod omnes quod invenieris a PTOLOMEO cum loquitur de circulis *et que ad hoc spectant*, veri sunt et nullum veriores illis, sed **iudicia et | sententia sue**^β non sunt secundum eius scientiam;[1] omniaque inveneris in iudiciis que dixit DORONIUS REX aut MESSHEALLAH INDUS,^γ **sustentare super illa debemus**.^γ (3) Id quod dixerunt Antiqui de natura stellarum superiorum que sunt in signis, sic experimentati sunt. (4) Sed **non ascendat in cor tuum**^θ quod sint composite, **nisi quod nature que in terra generant similitudinem quandam habent**.^γ

65va

§ 3

1 (1) Capitulum tertium.[2] **Fundamentum** {quidem} **et radix**^β iudiciorum sunt aspectus. (2) Dicit IACOB ALKINDI quod postquam signa sunt duodecim, ipsa et[3] per medium[4] dividuntur, et est aspectus oppositus, similiter per tertias et quartas et sextas, non {autem} per alias partes sunt divise. (3) Dixerunt {autem} SAPIENTES IN[5] GEOMETRIA quod non dividitur circu-

---

[1]Universaliter autem dico tibi quod omnes quod invenieris a Ptolomeo cum loquitur de circulis et que ad hoc spectant, veri sunt et nullum veriores illis, sed iudicia et sententia sue non sunt secundum eius scientiam] Cf. De mundo, Prologus, 14: unam itaque generalitatem tibi dico quod omnes sermones quos invenies a Ptholomeo ubi de circulis loquitur veri sunt, et non ab ipso alii magis; iudicia vero sua scientie non conveniunt.   [2]Capitulum tertium] M; L om.   [3]et] L; M quoque.   [4]medium] L; M medium itaque.   [5]in] M; L om.

because it is the lord of the sign of Aquarius, and they began from it [Saturn] by day, because it [Aquarius] is masculine and its power is diurnal. (6) They made Mercury the **second lord of the triplicity**,ᵞ,⁶ because it is the lord of Gemini; its power is greater by night than by day, {and consequently} they began from it [Mercury] by night. (7) {But} they excluded Venus, the **lady**ᵞ,⁷ of the sign of Libra, from the power of the triplicity, because it indicates **pleasures and desires**,β,⁸ ⟨⟨and these signs are temperate⟩⟩; therefore instead of it they assigned Jupiter over these signs, because it is **equal or temperate**β,⁹ in its nature. (8) {Finally} **they considered Venus the last of the triplicity**,ᵞ,¹⁰ because it indicates **increase of offspring**,θ,¹¹ and this is Venus's nature. (9) {Therefore} they began from it [Venus] by day, {but} its second lord is Mars, namely, the lord of Scorpio, and they made the Moon, the lady of the house of Cancer, ⟨its⟩ partner; and this is the reason put forward by the ANCIENTS.

18 (1) {But} PTOLEMY disagrees ⟨with them⟩ about the houses of the triplicity; we have tested his statements but **they did not came up true in our hands**;θ,¹ hence we have relied on the statements of the ANCIENTS. (2) {But} as a general rule I say to you that all ⟨the statements⟩ by PTOLEMY, when he speaks about the circles [the orbs] *and what belongs to this*, are true and nothing is truer than them, but his ⟨astrological⟩ **judgments and statements**β,² do not befit his science;³ and everything you will find of the ⟨astrological⟩ judgments which KING DORONIUS and MĀSHĀ'ALLĀH **THE INDIAN**ᵞ,⁴ said, **we must rely on them.**ᵞ,⁵ (3) As for what the Ancients said about the nature of the upper stars that are in the signs, they were tested experimentally in this manner. (4) But **do not let to come up in your heart**θ,⁶ [i.e., do not let to come up in your mind] that they [the upper stars that are in the signs] are composite ⟨bodies⟩, **except that they have a certain similarity to the natures they generate on earth.**ᵞ,⁷

§ 3

1 (1) Third chapter. The aspects are {indeed} the **foundation and root**β,¹ of ⟨astrological⟩ judgments. (2) YA'QUB AL-KINDĪ says that since there are twelve signs, they are divided in the middle [into two parts], and this is the opposition aspect, likewise into three, four and six parts, {but} they are not divided into other parts. (3) The SCHOLARS OF GEOMETRY, {however,} said

lus nisi secundum hos aspectus, et huius probatio est quia omnis circulus per dyametrum dividitur; **a principio aut dyametri in finem**,[1] sive a ter**minis dyametri mutuo**,^β est aspectus oppositus. (4) {Item} quia[2] in omni circulo sunt duo dyametri *orthogonali se secantes*, et secundum hoc dividitur circulus in quatuor partes equales, quarum unaqueque in fine dyameter est, et vocate sunt **anguli sive cardines**,^β prout explanabo, et hic est aspectus quartus. (5) Rursus dividitur circulus per tres partes equales, nam cum positus punctum unum *in extremitate* tertie quarte dyametri, et extractus[3] sinum in[4] utraque parte, tunc dividetur circulus per tres partes equales, erit enim in circulo triangulus cuius omnia latera sunt equalia, ⟨⟨...⟩⟩, secundum hoc ergo est aspectus trinus. (6) {Item} cum posueris punctum **in medio**^γ diametri, fecerisque ibidem triangulum equilaterum, erit latus quodlibet medietas dyametri, et erit tunc sexta pars circuli; et hic est aspectus sextilis.

2 (1) Et EGO ABRAHAM perscrutatus sum etiam et **consideravi in equatione domorum aspectus.**^γ (2) Quod non oportet **immorari**^γ certa aspectum oppositum, nam ille quidem aspectus per viam exit circuli, tandemque quia tibi dicam rationem in domo septima per modum numerandi. (3) Ceteri {autem} | aspectus sic se habent. (4) Nos quidem invenimus quod **unum similitatem habet ad quinque**^γ ambo namque[5] se ipsa servant, *id est, in imparitatem suam*, et sex etiam .2. assimilantur, quia ambo paria sunt et per imparia dividuntur. (5) Consimiliter quoque .3. cum .7., nam ambo sunt imparia et sunt divisa per non paria, similiter etiam .4. cum .8., et sic de omni numero usque ad infinitum, incipiendo a quocumque volueris numero. (6) Conveniens igitur ad[6] domum quintam secundum naturam esse domus prime, et consimiliter nonam, quia ipsa etiam quinta quedam est licet **a posteriori vel retrorsum**;^β quapropter est **vocatus**^γ aspectus trinus **amicitie**^γ perfecta. (7) Unum enim et .3. ambo sunt imparia et non sunt **dupla seu duplicata**,^β qua admonum neque[7] .5. **duplicata sunt seu dimidiis aut sub duplis composita**.^β (8) Duo {vero} et quatuor ambo quidem paria sunt, **sed non secundum eandem paritatis perfecte naturam**,^γ nam hec in imparia dividuntur illa {vero} in paria. (9) Et hic quidem sextilis est aspec-

---

[1]finem] M; L fine. [2]quia] M; L om. [3]extractus] M; L extraheris. [4]in] L; M ab. [5]namque] L; M om. [6]ad] L; M om. [7]neque] L; M naturam.

that the circle is divided only according to these aspects, and its proof is that every circle is divided by the diameter; and the aspect of opposition is **from the beginning of the diameter to the end ⟨of the diameter⟩ or mutually from the extremities of the diameter.**[β.2] (4) {Likewise,} since in every circle there are two diameters {at right quadrants and intersecting each other}, consequently the circle is divided into four equal parts, each of which is at each end of a diameter, and they are called **angles or cardines,**[β.3] as I shall explain; and this is the aspect of quartile. (5) Also the circle is divided into three equal parts, for if a point is fixed at *the extremity* of three quarters of the diameter, and the sine is calculated for both parts, then the circle is divided into three equal parts, because inside the circle there will be a triangle all of whose sides are equal, ⟨⟨and the ⟨relative⟩ dimensions of any ⟨equilateral⟩ triangle are the same⟩⟩; therefore, according to this is the aspect of trine. (6) {Likewise,} when you put a point **at the middle**[γ.4] of the diameter, you will draw in that very place an equilateral triangle, ⟨the length of⟩ any of its sides is half of the diameter, and this will be the sixth part of the circle; and this is the aspect of sextile.

2 (1) And I, ABRAHAM, have also sought and **scrutinized the aspects in the equation** [correction] **of the houses.**[γ.1] (2) For there is certainly no need **to dwell on**[γ.2] the opposition aspect, because this aspect results from the method of the circle; and because I will tell you the reason later, in the seventh house [chapter] by the method of reckoning. (3) {But} the other aspects are in this manner. (4) We have found that **one bears a similarity to five**[γ.3] because both preserve themselves, *that is, in its quality of being an odd number*, and six resembles two because both are even numbers and when they are divided in two the result is an odd number. (5) Three and seven likewise, because both are odd numbers and are divisible by odd numbers, similarly four and eight, and in this manner any number ad infinitum, beginning from any number you would wish. (6) So it is fitting that the fifth house should be as the nature of the first house, and similarly the ninth ⟨house⟩ because it is also fifth but **from the rear or backwards;**[β.4] hence, the aspect of trine **is called**[γ.5] complete **friendship.**[γ.6] (7) Now one and three are both odd numbers and they are not **double or twofold,**[β.7] just as five is not **twofold or composed of halves or doubles.**[β.8] (8) {Moreover,} both two and four are even ⟨numbers⟩, **but not according to the same nature of complete parity,**[γ.9] because the former [i.e., 2] is divided into an odd number [i.e., when it is divided in half, the result is an odd number], {but} the latter [i.e., 4] into an even number [i.e., when the latter is divided in half, the result is an even number]. (9) This is the aspect of sextile; and

tus; propter quod dixerunt quod dimidie est **amicitie**.ᵞ (10) Unum {autem} ad quatuor **in inimicitia est**,ᵞ hoc enim radix numeri est ille {vero} compositus;¹ item hoc est impar ille {vero} par; consimili quoque modo .2. ad. .5. se habent, et erit totus numerus secundum hanc viam; hic {ergo} est aspectus quartus, qui inimicitie aspectus est. (11) **ARISMETICI**ᵞ {autem} de aspectibus locuti sunt sermones prolixos, et non oportet eos rememorari. (12) Aspectus {igitur} qui est ante **stellam seu planetam**ᵝ dexter vocatus, secundum viam exempli in hominibus. (13) Quod {autem} dixerunt aspectum oppositum esse **fortissimum**,ᵞ hoc quidem rectum est, eo quod circuli medietas est; aspectus {vero} quartus fortior est trino, quamvis minor est in numero, et hoc ideo est quia in **angulis**ᵞ eius est;² sextilis demum minus *fortis* est omnibus propter parvitatem *profecto* numeri sui.

3 (1) {Sane} eius quod dixerunt de **ascensionibus equalibus**,ᵞ rationem querere non oportet, quia {bene} scita est; similiter et de signis quibuscumque **quarum hore torte sunt**.ᵞ (2) **Equales signa aut recta**ᵝ bona sunt in omnibus rebus, quapropter est eis fortitudo maior quam **obliquis**,ᵞ ideo quod dicuntur esse **contraria**.ᵞ (3) **Et stelle | que sunt in ecliptica recte sunt**,ᵞ nam due stelle, ille loco unius **presulis sunt seu prepositi qui vocantur *almubtaz***;ᵝ Aries {vero} et Libra quamvis ambo sunt signa calidi et equalia **in qualitate activa**,ᵞ inimicitia {tamen} est inter ipsos, propter aspectum oppositum.

66ra

4 (1) Quod {autem} dixerunt, circulum quolibet *hore* memento dividi in quatuor **divisiones**,ᵞ hoc rectum est etiam, et est quarta circuli a linea medii celi usque ad gradum ascendentis orientalem, et hec quidem precedit. (2) Et assimilatur aeri, sanguisque sicut aer est *in complexione*, **visibilitas** {autem} **coloris**ᵞ eius est albedo, eo quod initium est colorum. (3) De quarta {vero}³ que inter linea medii celi est et gradum occidentem, dixerunt quod operationes eius sunt retrorsum, eo quod circuli medietas est que descendit; apparentia {autem} coloris eius rubedo est, propter copiam caliditatis sue. (4) Nec oportet residuas commemorare quartas, quia una est via in omnibus. (5) Color {autem} nigrum propter frigidum et siccum; viridis {vero} propter frigidum etᵞ humidum. (6) **Et omne id quod superius est sive omne quoque super orizontem elevatum est**,ᵝ appellaverunt

---

¹compositus] M; L oppositus.   ²quia in angulis eius est] L; M om.   ³De quarta vero] L; M natura.

for this reason they said that it is half **friendship**.ʸ (10) {But} one and four ⟨are⟩ **in enmity**,ʸ,¹⁰ because the former is the root of counting {but} the latter is composite; likewise, the former is odd and the latter is even; and the same pattern applies to two and five, and any other number will be in accordance with this method; {therefore} this is the aspect of quartile, which is an aspect of enmity. (11) The **ARITHMETICIANS**,ʸ,¹¹ {however} said very long statements about the aspects, and there is no need to recall them. (12) {Therefore,} the aspect that is before a **star or planet**ᵝ,¹² is called right-hand, to use a human metaphor. (13) {But} what they said, ⟨namely,⟩ that the aspect of opposition is **the strongest**,ʸ,¹³ this is correct because it is the half of the circle; {moreover} the aspect of quartile is stronger than the aspect of trine, although it is less in number [i.e., 90° is less than 120°], and this is because it [quartile] is in [coincides with] its [the circle's] **angles**;ʸ,¹⁴ finally, the aspect of sextile is less *strong* than all the others, because of the smallness *in the benefit* of its number.

3 (1) {Certainly,} as for what they said about the **equal ascensions**,ʸ,¹ there is no need to search for an explanation, because it is {well} known; and similarly for any of the signs **whose hours are crooked**.ʸ,² (2) The **equal or straight signs**ᵝ,³ are good for everything, therefore they have more power than the **oblique**ʸ ⟨signs⟩; this is why they were called **contrary**.ʸ,⁴ (3) **The stars that are in the ecliptic are straight**,ʸ,⁵ because two stars are in the place of one **ruler or chief, which are called *al-mubtazz*;**ᵝ,⁶ {moreover} Aries and Libra, although both are hot and equal **in active quality**,ʸ,⁷ there is {nevertheless} enmity between them, because of the opposition aspect.

4 (1) {But} what they said, ⟨namely,⟩ that at any moment *of the hour* the circle is divided into four **divisions**,ʸ,¹ this is correct, and the quadrant of the circle is from the line of midheaven to the eastern degree of the ascendant, and it goes ahead. (2) It is similar to air, and blood is like air *in mixture*, {but} its **visibility of color**ʸ,² is white, because it is the beginning of the colors. (3) {But} as for the quadrant between the line of midheaven and the descendant degree, they said that its workings are backward, because it is ⟨in⟩ the half of the circle that descends; {but} the appearance of its color is red, because of the abundance of its heat. (4) There is no need to mention the remaining quadrants, because they all have the same pattern. (5) The black color, {however,} is because of cold and dryness; {but} green because of cold **and**ʸ,³ moisture. (6) **Everything that is above or everything that is raised above the horizon**,ᵝ,⁴ they called ⟨⟨right-hand⟩⟩ **by way of example**

⟨⟨...⟩⟩ **via exempli seu per modum manifestationis**,^β eo quod isti medietati maior est **fortitudo seu virtus**^β quam relique medietati, et consimiliter de dextra est respectu sinistre; due igitur quarte masculine vocate dextere, propter magnam eorum fortitudinem. (7) Et quod dixerunt de **medietate circuli ascendente**,^γ hec scitum et discopertum, nam **ascensiones**^γ signorum in medietate descendente sunt ut **ascensiones**^γ signorum oppositorum illis, que sunt in **medietate circuli ascendente**.^γ (8) {Porro,} dicit MAGISTER NOSTER ABRACHAM, *VOCATUS PRINCEPS*, quod discordia est inter HUIUS MAGISTERII SAPIENTES, quidam enim aiunt quod a gradu ascendente usque ad **lineam anguli terre seu abyssi**^β est quarta orientalis, et a linea medii celi usque ad gradum ascendente meridionalis, et a **linea anguli terre**^γ usque ad gradum occidentes est sinistra, et a gradu occidente usque ad lineam medii celi occidentalis. (9) Ita distinxerunt omnes **MAGISTRI INSTRUMENTORUM SEU ASTROLABII**,^β et mea quidem | opinio ad¹ illos declinat.

66rb

5 (1) In sermonibus quidem de duodecim domibus rationes non inveni in LIBRIS ANTIQUORUM, quas commemorande dignum est, (2) nisi quod dixerunt: nullum esse dubium quoniam {hore} minuto quoliblet circulus in .4. partes dividitur, et sunt puncta secundum circuli dyametralitates {accepta}. (3) Et hoc est veritas, **quod gradus ascendentis gradui occidenti dyametraliter opponitur, et gradus medii celi infimo etiam opponitur angulo terre**.^γ (4) {Item} dixerunt quod res qualibet secundum tria distinguitur, **primo** namque augmentari incipit, deinde *in statu est* et **permanet secundum viam unam**,^θ postmodum diminuitur quousque nichil eius inveniatur; secundum hoc distinxerunt **id quod inter qualibet duo puncta est**^γ in tres divisiones, vocaveruntque .4. puncta **cardines seu angulos**.^β (5) Et **domos subsequentes, que consequentes ad hoc pervenient ut sicut anguli**, etiam vocaverunt **succedentes angulis**.^γ (6) Et eis fortitudo mediocris **angulis**^γ est enim fortitudo magna, conveniens {igitur} est ut sit fortitudo maxima **angulo**,^γ qui in linea medii celi est et **angulo**^γ primo, qui est gradus ascendens. (7) Dicit {enim} MESSEHALLAH quod hic fortior est eo qui in linea est medii celi; PTOLOMEUS {vero} dicit contrarium, et ipse quidem **ius habet**^θ **et verum dicit**;^β ***angulus*** {***itaque***} ***septime domus***^γ fortior est **quam angulus quarte domus**.^γ (8) In succedentibus {autem} nulla superior est unde-

---

¹ad] M; L ab.

or to make it clear,[β,5] because this half has more **power or strength**[β,6] than the other half, and likewise, what relates to the right-hand applies to the left-hand [i.e., the right-hand is stronger than the left-hand]; therefore, both masculine quadrants were called right-hand because of their great power. (7) What they said about the **ascending half of the circle**,[γ,7] this is known and manifest, for the **ascensions**[γ,8] of the signs in the descending half ⟨of the circle⟩ are as the **ascensions**[γ] of the opposite signs, which are in the **ascending half of the circle**.[γ] (8) {In addition,} OUR MASTER ABRAHAM,[9] CALLED THE PRINCE, says that there is a disagreement among the SCHOLARS OF THIS ART, for some say that from the ascendant degree to the **line of the angle of the Earth or of the abyss**[β,10] the quadrant is oriental, and from the line of midheaven to the degree of the ascendant ⟨the quadrant is⟩ southern, and from **the line of the angle of the Earth**[γ,11] up to the descendant degree ⟨the quadrant is⟩ northern, and from the descendant degree up to the line of midheaven ⟨the quadrant is⟩ western. (9) **All the MASTERS OF THE INSTRUMENTS OR OF THE ASTROLABE**[β,12] distinguished ⟨the quadrants⟩ in this manner, and my opinion inclines to theirs.

5 (1) As for the twelve houses, I have not found any explanations of them in the BOOKS OF THE ANCIENTS, which are worth mentioning, (2) except that they said: there is no doubt, because at any minute {of the hour} the circle is divided into four parts, and they are points {taken} according to the diameters of the circle. (3) And this is true; **for the degree of the ascendant is opposed to the degree of the descendant, and the degree of midheaven is opposed below to the angle of the Earth.**[γ,1] (4) {Likewise,} they said that anything is divided into three, for first it begins to increase, next it *keeps the ⟨same⟩ position* **and stands in the same way**,[θ,2] afterwards it diminishes until nothing of it is found; according to this they divided **what is between any pair of points**[γ,3] into three divisions, and the four points were called **cardines or angles.**[β,4] (5) The **subsequent houses, which follow and arrive at that ⟨place⟩ like angles**,[γ,5] were called **succedent to the angles.**[6] (6) They [the succedents to the angles] have intermediate power because the **angles**[γ,7] have great power; {therefore} it is fitting that the greatest power be the **angle**[γ] that is in the line of the midheaven, and to the first **angle**,[γ] which is the degree of the ascendant. (7) {For} MĀSHĀ'ALLĀH says that this one [the angle in the degree of the ascendant] is stronger than the one in the line of the midheaven; {but} PTOLEMY says the opposite, and **he is right**[θ,8] [lit. he has the law] **and he tells the truth;**[β,9] {thus} *the angle of the seventh house*[γ,10] is stronger **than the angle of the fourth house.**[γ,11] (8) {But} of the succedent ⟨houses⟩, none is superior to the eleventh, for it itself

cima, ipsa enim honorabili succedit angulo, et super terram existit, ac in aspectu sextili cum gradu ascendente. (9) Post hanc {igitur} est quinta domus: quamquam enim sub terra sit, in aspectu {tamen} trino est cum gradu ascendente; deinde secunda domus, eo quod aspectum[1] non habet ad *gradum* ascendentem. (10) **Sicut nec octava**[γ] {verum}, quia domus secunda succedens angulo nobiliori quam sit angulus occidentis, {ideo} dixerunt domum secundam octava **fortiorem**[γ] esse. (11) {Rursus} dixerunt cadentium meliorem esse nonam, eo quod super terram est, et in aspectu trino ad gradum ascendentem; | post ipsam {vero} tertiam, nam licet sub terra sit, in aspectu {tamen} est sextili cum gradu ascendente. (12) Residue {vero} domus sunt sexta et duodecima, peiores omnibus ipsarum, enim neutra aspectum habet cum gradu ascendente; domus {tamen} sexta peior est quam duodecima, eo quod est sub terra.

6 (1) Ait {itaque} ABRAHAM MAGISTER NOSTER quod quia gradus ascendens qui exit sub terra nato similis est qui exit de ventre matris sue, {ideo} dixerunt quod signum hoc super vitam significat et super corpus; et **est questio**[γ] super omnem cogitatum occultum qui **exit in lucem.**[β] (2) **Quoniam**[γ] {igitur} **angulus**[γ] iste primus semper **est in medio duorum angulorum,**[γ] quorum unus est **abyssi linea seu anguli terre**[β] alter {vero} **linea medii celi,**[γ] {ideo} dixerunt quod **hiis angulis**[γ] super parentes significant. (3) ANTIQUI {autem} dixerunt quod domus quarta super patres significat, et domus .10. super matres. (4) PTOLOMEUS {vero} dicit contrarium huius rei, et ius est ANTIQUORUM, conveniens enim[2] est ut signum super matrem significans **visui magis sit apparens.**[γ] (5) {Preterea} quia **domus ista**[γ] magis occulta est omnibus, {ideo} dixerunt eam significare super **res absconditas et occultas;**[β] {item} quia **finis est et ultimus angulorum,**[β] super finem significat omnis rei; amplius super terras significat et agros *ob eandem causam*. (6) Dixerunt etiam quod domus decima super **dominia** significat **seu principatus,**[β] et magnitudinem *status*, eo quod non est **angulus**[γ] **superior ipso aut honorabilior;**[β] et significat etiam super **magisteria et artificia,**[β] **famosa propter eandem causam.**[γ] (7) Quia {vero} domus septima in **angulo**[γ] est contrario prime domui, hec enim ascendit et illa descendit, idcirco dixerunt quod significat super femellas, que contrarie sunt masculis. (8) Et quia **descensiones**[γ] eius in omni loco equales sunt **ascensionibus**[γ] prime domus,

---

[1]aspectum] M; L in aspectu.   [2]enim] M; L tamen.

follows the honorable angle, and it is situated above the Earth, and is in the aspect of sextile to the ascendant degree. (9) After this, {then,} is the fifth house: for although it is beneath the Earth, it is {nevertheless} in the aspect of trine to the degree of the ascendant; next is the second house, because it does not have any aspect to the ascendant *degree*. (10) {Indeed,} **not like the eighth**^{γ,12} ⟨house⟩, because the second house follows the angle that is more honorable than the angle of the descendant; {therefore} they said that the second house **is stronger**^{γ,13} than the eighth. (11) {In addition,} they said that the best among the cadent ⟨houses⟩ is the ninth, because it is above the Earth, and in the aspect of trine to the ascendant degree; the third ⟨house⟩ is {indeed} next, for, even though it is underneath the Earth, it is {nevertheless} in the aspect of sextile to the ascendant degree. (12) {But} the sixth and twelfth houses are left over; they are worst of all, because neither of them is in any aspect to the ascendant degree; {Nevertheless,} the sixth is worse than the twelfth, because it is underneath the Earth.

6 (1) {Accordingly} ABRAHAM, OUR MASTER,¹ said that because the ascendant degree, which rises from below the Earth, resembles the native who emerges from his mother's womb, {therefore} they said that this sign indicates life and the body; and **it is the question**^{γ,2} about any hidden thought which **emerges into the light.**^{β,3} (2) {Consequently,} **since**^{γ,4} this first **angle** is always **in the middle of two angles,**^{γ,5} of which one is **the line of the abyss or angle of the Earth**^{β,6} [i.e., line of the lower midheaven] {but} the other is the **line of midheaven,**^{γ,7} {therefore} they said that **by means of these angles**^{γ,8} they indicate parents. (3) {But} the ANCIENTS said that the fourth house indicates fathers, and the tenth house mothers. (4) {But} PTOLEMY says the opposite thing, and the ANCIENTS are correct, because it is fitting that the sign indicating the mother **be more manifest to sight.**^{γ,9} (5) {In addition} because **this house**^{γ,10} is more hidden than all the others, {therefore} they said that it indicates **secret and hidden things;**^{β,11} {likewise,} because it is **the end or the last of the angles,**^{β,12} it indicates the end of everything; it also indicates landed property and fields *for the same reason*. (6) They said that the tenth house indicates **lordships or governances**^{β,13} and greatness *of rank*, because no **angle**^γ is **higher or more honorable**^{β,14} than it is; it also indicates **professions and arts,**^{β,15} renowned for this reason.^{γ,16} (7) {But} since the seventh house in its **angle**^γ is opposite the first house, for one ascends and the other descends, therefore they said that it indicates the females, who are the opposite of the males. (8) Since its **descensions**^{γ,17} [descending rising times] at any place are the same as the **ascensions**^γ of the first house, {therefore} they said that it indicates being

{ideo} dixerunt quod significat super adiutorium hominis, quod ei simile est **in parte**,ᵞ et | ob hoc etiam significat hec domus super comparticipantes; ac {vero} quia in aspectu opposito est domui prime, *ideo significat* super **bella et contrarietates**.ᵝ (9) Quoniam {autem} domus quinta de natura est domus prime, propter aspectum tertium qui **amicitie**ᵞ est perfecte, {ideo} significat super **filios seu prolem**,ᵝ et super **victum**ᵞ et vestitum, hec enim¹ necessaria sunt humane vite. (10) Domus {vero} undecima, quia de domibus succedentibus *angulis*, et est cum gradu ascendente in aspectu sextili, qui dimidie est **amicitie**,ᵞ {ideo} super **amicos**ᵞ significat; {item} et propter fortitudinem eius, quia succedens est **angulo**ᵞ honorabili, idcirco significat super **gratias et bonam fortunam**ᵝ ac honorem. (11) Domus quoque secunda quia succedens est ab **angulo** ⟨⟨...⟩⟩, qui super vitam significat, ideo dicunt quod super possessiones significat, et est domus auxiliorum nati. (12) Quia {vero} domus octava succedens est *angulo septime domus*,ᵞ que contraria est domui prime, nec est ei colligata aspectu aliquo, {ideo} significat quod est domus mortis. (13) **Q**UIDAMᵞ {autem} dixerunt quod dominus domus septime super mortem significat hominis, eo quod contrarius est vite, et hoc quidem bene sciebat **E**NOCH **qui est** **H**ERMESᵝ ac **D**ORONIUS et **B**AALIM ac **B**ABYLONII, sed quod rectum est hoc est istorum. (14) Domus {autem} nona, quia cadens est **angulo**,ᵞ et Sol cum est ibidem **mutatur et declinat**ᵝ a linea medii celi, que est **angulus**,ᵞ {ideo} dixerunt quod itinerum domus est, **et hoc magis super illum**ᵞ qui depulsus est a gradu suo; quia {vero} sapientia in anima est sicut corpus hominis, de loco ad locum euntis ⟨⟨...⟩⟩, {ideo} dixerunt quod est domus **scientie**;ᵞ {item} est et domus **fidei seu legis**,ᵝ fides enim **de scientia venit vel descendit**.ᵝ (15) Consimiliter quoque de domo tertia dixerunt quod etiam significat super omnem **scientiam propinquam**;ᵞ et quia ascendens aspicit aspectu sextili, {ideo} dixerunt quod significat super fratres, et propinquos, ac eis similes. (16) Domus {vero} | duodecima, quia cadens est, et **secundum qualitates signorum**ᵞ semper diversa a natura signi ascendentis in **qualitate** *inquam* **activa**,ᵞ que radix est, {ideo} significat super vituperationes ac rixas ac **iurgia seu obprobria**; et quia colligata non est ascendenti, {ideo} significat super **domum carceris**;ᶿ quia {vero} pars aliqua signi ascendentis in domo duodecima est, cum non fuerit gradus ascendens initium **signi vel domus**,ᵝ idcirco dixerunt quod significat super bestias que sunt hominem equitature. (17) Residua {autem} domus sexta; *videlicet* quia sub terra est significat

---

¹enim] L; M tamen.

a helpmate to a man, which is similar to it **in part**;ʸ,¹⁸ hence this house [the seventh] indicates partners; {but} because it is in opposition aspect to the first house, *therefore they said* **wars and conflicts**.ᵝ,¹⁹ (9) {But} since the fifth house is of the nature of the first house, because of the aspect of trine which is of complete **friendship**,ʸ,²⁰ {therefore} it indicates **sons or offspring**,ᵝ,²¹ and **nourishment**,ʸ,²² and clothing, because these are necessary for human life. (10) {Moreover} the eleventh house, since it ⟨is one of⟩ the houses that are succedent *to the angles*, and it is in the aspect of sextile to the ascendant degree, which is half **friendship**,ʸ {hence} it indicates **friends**;ʸ,²³ {likewise,} because of its strength, for it is succedent to the honorable **angle**,ʸ hence it indicates **favors and good fortune**ᵝ,²⁴ and honor. (11) The second house, too, since it is succedent to the ⟨⟨first⟩⟩ angle, which indicates life, hence they say that it indicates possessions, and it is the house of the native's helpers. (12) {Moreover} the eighth house, since it is succedent to the *angle of the seventh house*,ʸ,²⁵ which is opposite the first house, and is not bound to it by any aspect, {hence} they said that it is the house of death. (13) {But} CERTAIN PEOPLEʸ,²⁶ said that the lord of the seventh house indicates the man's death, because it is the opposite of life; and ENOCH, who is HERMES,ᵝ,²⁷ and DORONIUS, ⟨VETTIUS⟩ VALENS, and the BABYLONIANS knew this well, and they are right. (14) The ninth house, {however,} since it is cadent from the **angle**,ʸ and when the Sun is there **changes and declines**ᵝ,²⁸ from the line of midheaven, which is an **angle**, {therefore} they said that it is the house of journeys, **and this to a greater extent regarding**ʸ,²⁹ someone who has been degraded from his rank; {but} since wisdom in the soul is like the body of a man, going from one place to another ⟨⟨and seeking⟩⟩, {therefore} they said that it is the house of **science**;ʸ,³⁰ {likewise,} it is the house of **faith or law**,ᵝ,³¹ because faith **comes or derives from science**.ᵝ,³² (15) Likewise, regarding the third house, they said that it indicates any **near science**;ʸ,³³ and because it aspects the ascendant by the aspect of sextile, {therefore} they said that it indicates brothers, relatives, and the like. (16) {Moreover} the twelfth house, since it is cadent ⟨from the angle⟩, and **according to the qualities of the signs**ʸ,³⁴ it is always different from the nature of the ascendant sign in the **active quality**,ʸ,³⁵ *I say*, which is a root, {therefore} it indicates vituperation, quarrels, and **strife or dishonor**;ᵝ,³⁶ and because it is not bound to the ascendant, {therefore} it indicates **prison**ᶿ,³⁷ [lit., the house of prison]; {but} because some part of the sign of the ascendant is in the twelfth house, when the degree of the ascendant is not at the beginning **of the sign or of the house**,ᵝ,³⁸ therefore they said that it indicates animals that men ride on. (17) {But} the sixth house remains; *namely* because it is

super occulta bella, que profecto egritudines et orbationes. (18) Hec {igitur} in universali dicta sunt de domibus, que et ASTRORUM SAPIENTES^γ per viam experientie sibi dixerunt evenisse. (19) **Rationes**^γ {vero} de dominis triplicitatum, qui significant super hoc et super hoc, numquam vidi in aliquibus LIBRIS ANTIQUORUM, preterquam in LIBRO ANDRUZEGAR FILII ZADI PARUCH IUDEI, in cuius diebus ita sapiens in astris nullus erat ut ille, SAPIENTES quoque SARRACENORUM SEU ARABUM,^β qui post ipsum venerunt, eidem sunt concorde.

§4

1 (1) Capitulum quartum.[1] Inquit NOSTER MAGISTER ABRAHAM. Iam commemoravi **rationes et causas**^β de Iove et Saturno ac de aliis planetis, quare nocivi sunt. (2) PTOLOMEUS {vero} dicit quod per SCIENTIAM ARISMETICORUM^γ hoc extraxerunt, invenerunt enim Saturnum secundum numerum .32., et hoc quidem sumptum erat ex proportione circuli sui ad terre circulum; et dixerunt {etiam} quod Iupiter est secundum numerum .24.; Mars {vero} secundum numerum .21.;^{γ,2} et Sol secundum numerum .18.; Venus {autem} et Mercurius secundum numerum .16.; Luna {vero} sicut ⟨⟨...⟩⟩ .12. (3) Proportio {autem} Solis ad Iovem sesquitertia est, que **nobilis** est **proportio seu honorabilis proportio,**^β {vero} **proportio Iovis diei est, et enim honorabilis est.**^{γ,3} (4) Secundum hanc {autem} viam, non est proportio luminaribus cum Saturno et Marte, propter quod dixerunt quod ipsi sunt nocivi. (5) Dicit itaque **MAGISTER EMDEMINA**^γ quod Saturnus super corpus hominis significat quemadmodum {etiam} domus prima; Iupiter {autem} super **substantiam seu possessiones et divitias**^β quemadmodum et circulus eius secundus est post circulum Saturni; et Mars super fratres secundum viam domus tertius, eo quod circulus eius tertius est ad circulum Saturni; Sol {vero} super patrem quemadmodum ut domus quarta, eo quod circulus eius quartus est ad circulum Saturni;[4] et Venus super **prolem**^γ sicut et domus quinta circulus quidem eius quintus est ad circulum Saturni; Mercurius quidem super **servos et familiam**^β quemadmodum et domus sexta, quia circulus | eius sextus ad circulum Saturni; Luna {vero} super mulieres

---

[1]Capitulum quartum] M; L in margin. [2]Mars vero secundum numerum .21.] M; L om. [3]vero Iovis diei est, et enim honorabilis est] M; L in margin. [4]et Mars super fratres secundum viam domus tertius, eo quod circulus eius tertius est ad circulum Saturni; Sol vero super patrem quemadmodum ut domus quarta eo quod circulus eius quartus est ad circulum Saturni] M; L in margin.

underneath the Earth, it indicates hidden wars, which indeed are like illnesses and defects. (18) These ⟨things⟩, {then,} were said as a general rule about the houses, and the SCHOLARS OF THE STARS[γ,39] said that they came to them by the method of experience. (19) {But} I have never seen the **reasons**[γ,40] for the lords of triplicities—why they indicate that and that—in any of the BOOKS OR THE ANCIENTS, except for THE BOOK BY ANDRUZAGAR THE SON OF ZADI PARUCH, THE JEW, in whose days no one was as knowledgeable about the stars as him; and THE SCHOLARS OF THE SARACENS OR OF THE ARABS,[β,41] who came after him, agreed with him.

§4

1 (1) Fourth chapter. ABRAHAM, OUR MASTER,[1] said: I have already mentioned the **reasons and causes**[β,2] for Jupiter and Saturn and the other planets, why they are harmful. (2) {But} PTOLEMY says that they calculated that from the SCIENCE OF THE ARITHMETICIANS,[γ,3] for they found Saturn to correspond with the number 32, and this was obtained from the proportion of its circle to the circle of the Earth; and they {also} said that Jupiter corresponds to the number 24; {moreover} Mars corresponds to the number 21;[γ,4] the Sun corresponds to the number 18; {but} Venus and Mercury correspond to the number 16; {but} the Moon ⟨is⟩ as ⟨⟨the number⟩⟩ 12. (3) The proportion between the Sun and Jupiter, {however,} is one and a third, which is a **noble or honorable proportion**,[β,5] {but} **the proportion of Jupiter is of the day, for it is honorable.**[γ,6] (4) {But} according to this way there is no proportion between the luminaries and Saturn and Mars, hence they said that they are harmful. (5) Thus MASTER IBN ABI DAMINA[γ,7] says that Saturn indicates the human body in the same way as {also} the first house ⟨does⟩; that Jupiter in the same way ⟨indicates⟩ **goods, possessions and riches**[β,8] in the same way as its circle is the second after Saturn's circle; and Mars ⟨indicates⟩ brothers according to the way of the third house, because its circle is the third to Saturn's circle; {but} the Sun ⟨indicates⟩ the father in the same way as the fourth house, because its circle is the fourth to Saturn's circle; and Venus ⟨indicates⟩ **offspring**[γ,9] like the fifth house, indeed its circle is fifth to Saturn's circle; indeed Mercury indicates **slaves and retainers**[β,10] in the same way as the sixth house, because its circle is the sixth to Saturn's circle; {but} the Moon indicates women as the seventh house,

significat sicut est domus septime, quia circulus eius septimus est ad circulum Saturnus. (6) Et revertitur quidem Saturnus **ad serviendum seu ut operetur**^β in octava domo, quapropter super mortem significat quemadmodum est octava domus; **secundum hanc** {ergo} **divisionem ad Iovem redit domus nona**,^γ que super ⟨⟨...⟩⟩ **prophetias** significat **et servitium divinum**^β secundum naturam Iovis; et **spectat**^γ quidem ad Martem domus decima, quia super dominium {etiam} significat et **violentiam**;^γ domus {autem} undecima Soli **debetur**,^γ quia super *eufortunium* significat et honorem et gratiam sicut domus undecima. (7) Domus {vero} duodecima ad Venerem **pertinet**,^γ que in natura sua super **delicias** significat **et gaudium**;^β extrema {autem} gaudii **luctus** occupat **et erubescentia ac obprobrium**^β quemadmodum et duodecima domus significat.

2 (1) De Saturno quidem iam dixi rationem qualiter frigidus est et siccus; **radix** {autem} **et causa**^β mortis frigidum est cum sicco, et {ideo} significat super mortem et **dolorem et planctum**;^γ significat {etiam} res antiquas eo quod est planeta superius et motus eius tardus est. (2) In divisione {autem} ipsius est Indorum terra, quia **clima**^γ primum est; et significat super **Mauros seu Ethiopes**,^β propter eorum nigredinem; {item} super Iudeos quia signum eorum Aquarius est, que est domus eius; et super **gentes antiquas**^γ eadem quia superius est; et agricolas, eo quod in eius divisione terra est; et ob hoc {etiam} in divisione ipsius de corpore hominis est splen; et consimiliter **cerdones**[1] **seu coriorum separatores**,^β et **cloacarum purgatores**,^γ eo quod odor ad eius naturam spectans inmundiciam significat. (3) {Item} significat super plumbum eo quod ponderosum est et **valoris**[2] **modici**;^γ et est in parte eius omnis locus tenebrosus et turpis^γ ⟨⟨...⟩⟩. (4) ⟨⟨...⟩⟩ quia **pulchram figuram et formosam**^β non efficit melancolia; *et significat* **arborem seu plantam**^β *kenesesin*,^δ et omnem **rem toxicam et pocionem mortiferam**,^β eo quod super mortem significat; *etiam super* | *retentionem et restrictionem propter frigiditatem*, et significat super gelum propter constrictionem, que in eo est; de indumentis {autem} omnem pannum grossum, eo quod natura melancolia grossa est; et non diligat nisi rem grossam. (5) {Preterea} in parte ipsius est cogitatio, quia superius est; et consimiliter est de sciendo **consilia et secreta**,^β spoliationes quoque facere, **et irritare seu provocare alios atque conturbare**,^β eo quod nocivus est; {item} omnem **magisterium seu artificium laboriosum**;^β {rursus} significat super vias

---

[1]cerdones] M; L cardones. [2]valoris] M; L valores.

because its circle is the seventh to Saturn's circle. (6) Saturn turns back **to serve or to work**[β,11] in the eighth house, and therefore indicates death in the same way as the eighth house; {therefore,} **according to this division the ninth house returns to Jupiter,**[γ,12] which indicates ⟨⟨craft,⟩⟩ **prophecies and divine service**[β,13] according to Jupiter's nature; the tenth house **belongs**[γ,14] to Mars, because it {also} indicates dominion and **violence;**[γ,15] {but} the eleventh house is **due**[γ,16] to the Sun, {because} it indicates *good fortune,* honor and favor, like the eleventh house. (7) {Moreover,} the twelfth house **belongs**[γ,17] to Venus, which by its nature indicates **delights and joy;**[β,18] {but} **sorrow, disgrace and shame**[β,19] seize the extremes of joy in the same way as the signification of the twelfth house.

2 (1) As for Saturn, I have already mentioned the reason of the manner in which it is cold and dry; {but} **the root and cause**[β,1] of death is cold with dryness, {therefore} it indicates death and **pain and lamentation;**[γ,2] it {also} indicates ancient things because it is an upper planet and its motion is sluggish. (2) In its portion, {however,} is the land of the Indians, because it is the first **climate;**[γ] it indicates the **Moors or Ethiopians,**[β,3] on account of their blackness; {likewise,} ⟨it indicates the⟩ Jews, because their sign is Aquarius, which is its house; and ⟨it indicates⟩ **ancient nations,**[γ,4] likewise because it is an upper ⟨planet⟩; and farmers, because the earth is in its portion; and for this reason, {also} of the human body, the spleen is in its portion; and likewise **leatherworkers or skinners,**[β,5] and **privy-cleaners,**[γ,6] because the smell[7] belonging to its nature indicates filth. (3) {Likewise,} it indicates lead, because it is heavy and of **slight value;**[γ,8] **and in its portion is every dark and ugly place**[γ,9] ⟨⟨because it suits a melancholy nature to be in solitude and not to stay in an inhabited place⟩⟩. (4) ⟨⟨It indicates any animal that is big because it is uppermost, and any animal that is ugly⟩⟩ because black bile does not produce any **beautiful or handsome form;**[β,10] *it indicates* **the tree or plant**[β,11] **kenesesin,**[δ,12] as well as any **toxic thing or deadly poison,**[β,13] because it indicates death; ⟨*it indicates*⟩ *retention and constipation on account of the cold*, and it indicates frost because of the restrain that is in it; {but} of garments, any fabric that is thick, because the nature of black bile is thick and it loves only what is thick. (5) {In addition,} thought is in its portion, because it is uppermost; and likewise regarding knowledge of **intentions and hidden things,**[β,14] also plundering, and **irritating or provoking and disturbing others,**[β,15] because it is harmful; {likewise,} any **profession or laborious art;**[β,16] {in addition,} it indicates long journeys,

longuinquas, eo quod supremus; suntque in eius divisione ossa, quia frigida sunt et sicca, et sunt corporis **fundamentum**.ᵞ (6) Distinxerunt quoque septem **capitula**⁶ᵞ que tacta sunt prius super septem planetas, oculi {namque} sunt luminarium, et aures Saturni ac Iovis, eo quod superiores sunt, nares {vero} Martis et Veneris, sed linguam cum ore Mercurii; et hoc quidem experimentati sunt ASTRORUM SAPIENTESᵞ et verum invenerunt. (7) {Amplius} significat super **amentia seu alienationem et insaniam**,β ut plurimum enim sit ex melancolia; et consimiliter paralisis et lepra; significat quoque super **dolores aut egritudines diuturnas**,β eo quod **tardus est et morosus in motu suo**.β (8) Significat {etiam} super senium, secundum quod declaravit PTOLOMEUS, Luna namque .4. servit annis, et post ipsam Mercurius .10., postquam Venus .8., deinde Sol .9.,ᵞ postmodum Mars .7., deincepts Iupiter .12., et demum in fine annorum Saturnus; **adduxit** {autem} ad hoc **in modum probationis naturam humanam**.ᵞ (9) Et iam[1] dixi quod cum frigidus sit Saturnus, {ideo} rectificatus eius virtus in oriente, et ob hoc dixerunt quod orientalis est. (10) Scito {autem} quod initium dierum est a prima die; et SAPIENTES quidem ASTRORUMᵞ dixeruntᵞ quod in hac die est maior fortitudo Soli quam aliis diebus, et cum diem partiti sunt in horas duodecim, primam **utique**ᵞ dederunt horam Soli, domino *inquam* diei, et secundam Veneri, cuius circulus sub circulo Solis est; et {ideo} dixerunt quod dominus hore secunde in die prima | Venus est, et ipsa cum Sole domina diei est, hoc enim est plurimum virtutis quasi habet; et consimiliter alii planete quousque ad Solem octava revertatur hora, et secundum hanc viam eveniet in divisione Saturni dies quidem Saturni,[2] et de noctibus similiter nox quarta. (11) De causa {vero} figure et literarum eius, nullam *adhuc* vidi rationem; causa {quidem autem} annorum eius maximorum est quia in hoc numero revertitur Saturnus ad locum suum secundum sententiam SAPIENTIUM INDORUM; et causa magnorum eius annorum in numero consistit terminorum Saturni per signa secundum sententiam SAPIENTIUM EGYPTORUM; causa {vero} annorum eius minimorum est quia in fine triginta annorum revertitur fere ad gradum eius **pristinum vel primum**;β causa mediorum est quia accipiebant medietatem annorum magnorum et addiderunt ei medietatem minorum;[3] annos {vero} divisiones vocate *alfardar*, taliter quidem commemorabunt[4] SAPIENTES PERSARUM sine probatione. (12) Ratio {autem} quare[5] corporis eius **fortitudo seu virtus**β est .9. graduum, est[6]

---

[1]iam] L; M ideo. [2]Saturmi] M; L om. [3]causa mediorum est quia accipiebant medietatem annorum magnorum et addiderunt ei medietatem minorum] M; L om. [4]commemorabunt] L; M commemontur. [5]quare] L; M om. [6]est] M; L esse.

because ⟨it is⟩ uppermost; the bones are in its portion, because they are cold and dry, and they are the **foundation**γ,17 of the body. (6) They divided the seven **headings**βγ,18 [i.e., orifices in the head] that were mentioned above among the seven planets, {because} the eyes are of the luminaries, the ears of Saturn and Jupiter, because they are upper ⟨planets⟩, {but} the nose of Mars and Venus, and the tongue with the mouth of Mercury; and the **SCHOLARS OF THE STARS**γ,19 tested this experimentally, and found it to be true. (7) {Besides,} it indicates **madness, loss of reason and insanity,**β,20 because it is mostly from the black bile; and likewise paralysis and leprosy; it also indicates **chronic pains or diseases,**β,21 because it is **slow and deliberate in its motion.**β,22 (8) It {also} indicates old age, according to what PTOLEMY demonstrated, because the Moon serves [is in charge] for four years, after it Mercury for ten ⟨years⟩, then Venus for eight ⟨years⟩, then the Sun for **nine**γ,23 years, then Mars for seven ⟨years⟩, and then Jupiter for twelve ⟨years⟩; and finally Saturn at the end of the years; {but} in this regard he [i.e. Ptolemy] **adduced human nature in the way of a proof.**γ,24 (9) I have already said that since Saturn is cold, {hence} its power is made straight [turns temperate] in the east, and for this reason they said that it is eastern. (10) Know, {however,} that the beginning of the days is from the first day [the days of the week begin with Sunday]; and the **SCHOLARS OF THE STARS**γ **said**γ,25 that on this day the Sun's power is greater than on the other days, and since they divided the day into twelve hours, **certainly**γ,26 they assigned the first hour to the Sun, the lord, *I say*, of the day, and the second to Venus, whose circle is beneath the circle of the Sun; {therefore} they said that the lord of the second hour in the first day [Sunday] is Venus, and she is the lady of the day with the Sun, because it is as if ⟨she⟩ has most of the power, and similarly with the other planets until the eighth hour returns to the Sun; and according to this method the day of Saturn [the diurnal part of Saturday] comes out in the portion of Saturn, and likewise among the nights, the fourth night. (11) {Moreover,} as for the cause of its form and letters, I have not seen any reason *until now*; {moreover} the cause of its greatest years, in the opinion of the **SCHOLARS OF THE INDIANS**, is that in this number ⟨of years⟩ Saturn returns to its place; the cause of the great years, in the opinion of the **EGYPTIAN SCHOLARS**, consists of the number of Saturn's terms in the signs; {moreover,} the cause of the least years is because at the end of thirty years it returns approximately to its **original or first**β,27 degree; and the cause of the middle ⟨years⟩ is that they extracted half of the great ⟨years⟩ and added them to half of the least ⟨years⟩; {but} the years of the divisions called *al-fardār* were mentioned in this manner by the **PERSIAN SCHOLARS** without proof. (12) {But} the reason why the **power or strength**β,28 of its

propter magnitudinem corporis eius, quod[1] fere equale est corpori Iovis, et non est post Solem maior ipsis; unde dixerunt quod **lumen seu radii**[β] Solis .15. gradus ante ipsum et consimiliter post ipsum; Lune {vero} .12. *eo quod luminare minus est*,[γ] nec est aliqua stella qua tale et tantum lumen habeat quantum ipsa preter quam Sol; similiter quodque dixerunt quod lumen Iovis .9. gradus est quemadmodum est Saturni; et quia corpus Martis minus est eis ac {etiam} terre propinquus, subtraxerunt ei unum gradum, et dixerunt quod lumine eius est .8. gradus; Veneris {autem} et Mercurii .7. gradus; tales {autem} fuerunt ANTIQUORUM **rationes**,[γ] et experti sunt hec veraque reppererunt.

3 (1) Iupiter. Iam quidem commemoravi rationem super eius naturam; et quia stella benevola est, significat super omnis boni **multiplicationem, et fructum.**[β] (2) De **climatibusque**,[γ] attribuerunt ei secundum, quemadmodum a Saturno secundus est; de gentibus, quoque PERSAS, quia signum eorum est Pisces, similiter et BABYLONIOS, quia domus **honoris eius seu exaltationis eius**[β] in loco termini preest super eos. | (3) {Item} attribuerunt ei omnem locum mundum, ac[2] domos orationum, secundum quod iam commemoravi in naturis; de indumentis {autem}, **venusta et placida**,[β] propter mundiciam eius. (4) De coloribus {autem} corporum, album cum rubeo, quia hec est *eius* natura recta; estque de parte eius auris sinistra, sed iam dictum est hoc in capitulo de Saturni; similiter et sanguis, quia similis est eius nature. (5) De etatibus {autem}, *senectutem*,[γ] eo quod est sub Saturno; **de partibus** {vero} **mundi**,[γ] septentrionalem, nam ipse ventos generat septentrionales; ratio denique annorum maximorum sicut ratio iam dicta de Saturno.

4 (1) Mars, iamque commemoravi {similiter} **naturam eius**;[γ] **de magnitudine quidem caloris eius et super occisionem contentionibus, bellis et conturbationibus.**[γ] (2) In parte {autem} eius ex **climatibus**[γ] tertium, eo quod tertius est a Saturno; {item} in eius divisione **Britani seu Anglici**,[β] *et homines illarum regionum*, et hoc quidem secundum sententiam ENOCH SIVE HERMETIS,[β] sed ipse ad hoc probationem non adduxit. (3) Nec est opus commemorandi **causam, item ferrum rubeum, sulphur, et omnia armorum instrumenta.**[γ] (4) Ac **de bestiis silvestribus**,[γ] **nocive seu fere**,[β] hoc enim est eius natura, ⟨⟨...⟩⟩ consimiliter quoque **petrosillum**[γ] et synapis, eo quod calida sunt et sicca; {item quoque} **rapinam et latrocinium**,[β] quia

---

[1]quod] L; M quidem. [2]ac] M; L ad.

body is nine degrees, is because of the size of its body, which is approximately equal to Jupiter's body, and after the Sun⟨'s body⟩ none is greater than its [Saturn's body] is; hence they said that the **light or the rays**[β,29] of the Sun ⟨are⟩ fifteen degrees before it and likewise after it; {but} ⟨the light⟩ of the Moon twelve ⟨degrees⟩, *because it is the smaller luminary*,[γ,30] and there is no star which has such and so much light as it except for the Sun; likewise they also said that the light of Jupiter is nine degrees, in the same manner as Saturn's; and because the body of Mars is smaller than theirs and {also} close to the Earth, they subtracted one degree and said that its light is eight degrees; {but} ⟨the light⟩ of Venus and Mercury ⟨is⟩ seven degrees; of such a kind, {however,} were **the reasons of the ANCIENTS**,[γ,31] and they verified them experimentally and found ⟨them⟩ true.

3   (1) Jupiter. I have already mentioned the reason for its nature; and since it is a benevolent planet, it indicates **increase** of any goodness, **and fruit**.[β,1] (2) And of the **climates**,[γ] they assigned the second to it, in the same way as it is the second from Saturn; of the nations, also the PERSIANS, because their sign is Pisces, and likewise the BABYLONIANS, because the **house of its honor or its exaltation**[β,2] in the place of the term rules over them. (3) {Likewise,} they assigned to it any clean place, and houses of prayer, as I have already mentioned in the section on natures; {but} of garments, **the charming and pleasing**,[β,3] because of its cleanness. (4) Of the colors of bodies, {however,} white with red, because this is *its* straight [temperate] nature; and the left ear is in its portion, but this has been already mentioned in the chapter on Saturn; and likewise the blood, because it is similar to its nature. (5) Of the ages, {however,} *old age*,[γ,4] because it is underneath Saturn; {but} **of the parts of the world**,[γ,5] the northern, because it generates the northerly winds; finally the reason for its greatest years is like the reason already mentioned about Saturn.

4   (1) Mars. I have already mentioned {similarly} **its nature;**[γ,1] ⟨and spoken⟩ **about the magnitude of its heat, and** ⟨referred⟩ **to killing by disputes, wars and riots.**[γ,2] (2) {But} of the **climates**,[γ] the third is in its portion; {likewise} in its portion are **the Britons or the English**,[β,3] *and the inhabitants of these regions*, and this is according to the opinion of **ENOCH OR HERMES**,[β,4] but he did not adduce any proof for this. (3) And there is no need to mention **the cause, also red iron** [copper]**, sulfur, and all the instruments of weapons.**[γ,5] (4) **Of the wild beasts,**[γ,6] **the harmful or wild**,[β,7] because that is its nature, ⟨⟨and *al-baks* because it is red,⟩⟩ and so too **parsley**[γ,8] and mustard because they are hot and dry; {likewise, also} **plundering and robbery**[β,9] because

hoc est **latronum opus et pestiferorum ad hec**;^β *et cor hominis eo quod rubicundum est.* (5) Super {autem} rationes commemoravimus quare significat super fratres, et quare eius {etiam} est naris dextra; preterea in eius divisione sunt **pudibunda**,^γ quia dominus est domus Scorpionis, qui significat super ipsa. (6) **De hominibus** {vero} **etatibus**,^γ iuventus, eo quod tertius est a Saturno; et *de mundi quidem partibus*,^γ occidentalis, hic enim quia frigida est et humida, naturam rectificat illius; ratio quoque dierum et annorum est quemadmodum in Saturno.

5 (1) Sol. Ait quidem ALBUMASAR: non est planeta stellis ita nocivus ut Sol quando sibi coniungitur **stelle seu planete**,^β quia non relinquitur eis **fortitudo seu virtus**,^β nec possunt ita facere reliqui nocivi; ac {tamen} est multo 68rb melior quam[1] Iupiter aut Venus in aspectu trino et sextili ⟨⟨...⟩⟩. | (2) In eius {igitur} parte est *sensus tactus*,^γ cuius natura bene scita[2] est in LIBRO ARISTOTILIS DE ANIMA. (3) {Item} in divisione ipsius est **clima**^γ quartum, secundum quod circulus eius quartus est a Saturno; iterum in eius divisione de gentibus sunt **Romani**,^γθ eo quod signum eorum est Leo, qui est domus eius; de hominibus {autem}, reges, eo quod in mundo non est creatura maior neque melior ipso; {ideo} quoque in divisione eius habet aurum, et *bonos* lapides preciosos, et quicquid **eis assimilatur**.^γ (4) Et de animalibus, hominem, quia humana anima ab eius virtute[3] dependet; {item} equos habet, eo quod sibi triplicitas[4] est in Sagittario, ibidem enim est equi figura; et habet leones propter domum suam; adhuc et arietes magnos, quia signum Arietis domus est honoris sui. (5) Ipsius quoque est sapientia et prudentia, propter virtutem anime; et significat super leges et consuetudines secundum viam Iovis; ac {etiam} super patres, eo quod radix est omnium corporum; et consimiliter super fratres et **mediocres seu medios**^β nato quidem maiores, qui patri assimilantur. (6) {Item} in eius divisione est cor, quia ibidem **spiritus et vita**;^β rursus oculus dexter ⟨⟨...⟩⟩, quia radix est luminis; similiter et cerebrum capitis, quia requiescit animam; adhuc et medietas corporis dexter, namque diviserunt duobus luminaribus, et fortiorem parte ei attribuerunt. (7) **De angulis**^γ {vero}, orientalem, ibi enim initium est **virtutis eius et fortitudinis**;^β ratio {autem} diei prime, iam dicta est; ac {vero} maximorum

---

[1]quam] M; L quamquam. [2]scita] M; L sicca. [3]virtute] M; L om. [4]triplicitas] L; M triplicitatis.

it is the **work of robbers and destructive people for these things**;[β,10] *and the heart of man, because it is red*. (5) {But} we have already mentioned why it indicates brothers, and why the right nostril {also} belongs to it; in addition, the **genitals**[γ,11] are in its portion, because it is the lord of the house of Scorpio, which indicates them. (6) {But} **of human ages**,[γ,12] youth, because it is the third from Saturn; and *of the parts of the world*,[γ,13] the western, and this is because it is cold and moist, ⟨which⟩ rectifies [tempers] its nature; the reason, too, for the days and years is the same way as for Saturn.

5 (1) The Sun. ABŪ MA'SHAR said: No planet is as harmful as the Sun when a **star or planet**[β,1] is conjoined to it, because no **power or strength**[β,2] is left to them, nor can the other harmful ⟨planets⟩ do this in this way; {nevertheless} it [the Sun] is much better than Jupiter and Venus in the aspect of trine and sextile, ⟨⟨and than the Moon alone in any aspect⟩⟩. (2) {Therefore,} in its portion is *the sense of touch*,[γ,3] whose nature is well known in the BOOK ON THE SOUL BY ARISTOTLE. (3) {Likewise,} in its portion is the fourth **climate**,[γ] inasmuch as its circle is the fourth from Saturn; in addition, of the nations, in its portion are **the Romans**,[γ,β,4] because their sign is Leo, which is its [the Sun's] house; {but} of human beings, kings, because no creature in the world is greater or better than it [the Sun] is; {therefore} it has also gold in its portion, and *good* precious stones, and anything **resembling them**.[γ,5] (4) And of living things, a human being, because the human soul depends on its [the Sun's] power; {likewise,} it has horses ⟨in its portion⟩, because there is a triplicity for it in Sagittarius, since in that very place there is the form of a horse; and it has lions ⟨in its portion⟩ because of its house; besides ⟨it has⟩ large rams ⟨in its portion⟩, because Aries is the house of its honor. (5) Wisdom and prudence, too, belongs to it [the Sun], because of the power of the soul; and it indicates laws and traditions according to the method used for Jupiter; and {also} fathers, because it is the root of all bodies; and likewise **middle or intermediate**[β,6] brothers who are older than the native, who are similar to the father. (6) {Likewise,} the heart is in its [the Sun's] portion, because in that very place is **the spirit and life**;[β,7] besides, ⟨it has⟩ the right eye ⟨⟨by day⟩⟩, because it is the root of light; and the brain of the head, because the soul resides ⟨there⟩; in addition ⟨it has⟩ the right half of the body, because they divided the body between the two luminaries, and they assigned the stronger part to it [the Sun]. (7) {Moreover,} **of the corners**,[γ,8] ⟨it has⟩ the eastern, because in that place is the beginning of its **power and strength**;[β9] {but} the reason for the first day [Sunday] has been already mentioned; {but} the cause of the greatest years, according to the

annorum causa est quia in hoc numero coniungitur Lune **absque superfluo divisionis alicuius**^γ **et absque diminutione seu defectu**^β secundum sententiam SAPIENTIUM INDORUM; et ratio quidem annorum magnorum est quia hii sunt anni vite naturalis; sed ratio minimorum est quia in quibuslibet .19. annis coniungitur Luna Soli, et non est inter eos **diversitas seu distinctio nisi modica,**^β secundum sententiam SAPIENTIUM INDORUM; causa {vero} mediocrum est quia sumpserunt quartam magnorum et addiderunt medietati minimorum; ita quidem dixerunt illi et hii {etiam} sunt experti; virtus | {autem} corporis eius iam dicta est prius.

68va

6 (1) De Venere, quidem iam dictum est et de natura eius; **dixerunt**^γ {autem} quod significat super *concupiscentias et voluptates ac desiderium seu appetitum.*^γ (2) Et in eius divisione est **clima**^γ quintus, consimiliter namque est circulus eius quintus ad circulum Saturni; de gentibus {vero}, **illi qui de** SARRACENORUM **lege sunt** SEU ARABES,^β eo quod ipsorum signum est Scorpio ⟨⟨...⟩⟩, fuerit enim ibidem coniunctio Saturni cum Iove. (3) Et quia significat super **concupiscentiam et appetitum ac voluptates**^β posuerunt in eius divisione loca muliebria; et significat super figuram et formositatem; ac super ranas eo quod colorate sint; quia {etiam} significat super **appetitum et desiderium,**^β {ideo} significat super comestiones et **potationes seu commessationes;**^β {item} super matrem quia femina est, eius enim natura frigida est et humida; et hec enim est ratio de filiabus et parvis sororibus, maiores namque in divisione Lune sunt, quia corpus eius maius est corpore Veneris. (4) **De etatibus**^γ {vero} hominis, eius est adolescentia, nam ipsa in gradu tertio est versus terram; dies {autem} et horas iam commemoravi, ac {etiam} virtutem corporis sui similiter; et annos eius maximos, quia tunc revertitur ad locum pristinum, sine excrescentia **partis seu divisionis**^β alicuius et sine diminutione aliqua, secundum sententiam SAPIENTIUM INDORUM; **magni** {vero} **seu maiores,**^β et mediocres ac minimi, secundum viam currunt Saturni.

7 (1) Mercurius. Dixerunt omnes ANTIQUI quod Luna super corpus significat hominis et naturam *eius*; eo quod, si in nativitate hominis fuerit cum aliquarum **nocivorum seu malivolorum,**^β erit ei **egritudo**^γ secundum **naturam loci**^γ in quo coniunguntur. (2) Quia igitur Mercurius supra ipsam est, {ideo} significat super scientiam, et **sermonem seu locutionem,**^β et animam. (3) Dicit {namque} ARISTOTELES quod omnis planeta propinquus

opinion of the SCHOLARS OF THE INDIANS, is because in this number ⟨of years⟩ it [the Sun] is conjoined to the Moon, **without any excess division ⟨of time⟩**γ,10 **and without subtraction or deficit;**β,11 and the reason for the great years is that these are the years of natural life; the reason for the least ⟨years⟩, according to the opinion of the SCHOLARS OF THE INDIANS, is because every nineteen years the Moon is conjoined to the Sun, and between them there is only **a moderate difference or distinction;**β,12 {moreover} the cause for the middle ⟨years⟩ is that they took a quarter of the great ⟨years⟩ and added it to a half of the least ⟨years⟩; they spoke in this manner and they {also} verified ⟨it⟩ experimentally; {and} the power of its [the Sun's] body has been already mentioned above.

6 (1) Venus and its nature have been already discussed; {and} **they said**γ,1 that it indicates *lust, pleasure, and desire or appetite.*γ,2 (2) The fifth **climate**γ is in its portion, because its circle is like that [i.e., the fifth] to Saturn's circle; {moreover,} of the nations, **those who follow the law of the SARACENS OR ARABS**,β,3 because their sign is Scorpio ⟨⟨in the term of Venus⟩⟩, since in that very place the conjunction of Saturn and Jupiter took place. (3) Since it indicates **lust, appetite and desires,**β,4 they assigned the places of women to its portion; it indicates the form and beauty; and frogs, because they are colored; since it {also} indicates **appetite and desire,**β {therefore} it indicates eating, **drinking-parties or revels;**β,5 {likewise,} it ⟨indicates⟩ the mother, because it is feminine, since its nature is cold and moist; in fact, this is the reason for daughters and young sisters, since the elder ⟨sisters⟩ are in the portion of the Moon, because its body is bigger than Venus's body. (4) {Moreover,} **of the ages**γ,6 of human beings, youth belongs to it [Venus], because it is in the third level with respect to the Earth; {but} I have already mentioned the days and the hours, {as well as} the power of its body; the ⟨number of its⟩ greatest years ⟨is⟩ because then it returns to the original place, without any excess **part or division**β,7 ⟨of time⟩ and without any deficit, according to the opinion of the SCHOLARS OF THE INDIANS; {moreover,} the ⟨number of the⟩ **great or greater**β,8 ⟨years⟩, and the middle and least ⟨years⟩ is according to the method used for Saturn.

7 (1) Mercury. All the ANCIENTS said that the Moon indicates the body of a man and *his* nature; hence, if in a man's nativity it is together with one of the **harmful or malevolent**β,1 ⟨planets⟩, he will have a **disease,**γ,2 according to the **nature of the place**γ,3 where they conjoin. (2) Because Mercury is above it [the Moon], {therefore} it indicates science, **talk or speech,**β,4 and the soul. (3) {Because} ARISTOTLE says that any planet that is close to the Earth

terre plus significat super conditiones homines quam ille qui remotus est; {ideo} quoque dicit quod ille fortitudinem non habet in terra | que superior est Sole; nos {autem} ANTIQUOS omnes vidimus ac testantes **quod de coniunctione superiorum nostra quidem manus**[Y] **et operationis experientia est super universalia seu communia,**[Y] quia super illa magis significant quam super ea que significant in particulari. (4) Ac {vero} **in parte Mercurii**[Y] est **clima**[Y] sextum, talis enim circulus eius se habet respectu circuli Saturni; {item} in divisione ipsius sunt volucres **leves et agiles**[β] ⟨⟨...⟩⟩; et non oportet sortilegia quidem commemorare et res alias, scientie namque sunt omnes; significat {autem} super fratres parvos, eo quod non est in celo stella minor a ipso. (5) **De etatibus**[Y] {vero} hominis, pueritiam, quia terre propinquus est; sapor autem eius acetosus est, eo quod frigidus et siccus multum; (6) Modum dierum iam commemoravi; et ratio annorum eius est secundum viam Saturni; {item} fortitudo corporis eius **iam dicta est.**[Y]

8 (1) Luna. Super quidem rationem commemoravi de natura ipsius; et ipsa omnia **replet**[Y] corpora, propter magnam eius humiditatem. (2) In eius {autem} divisione est **clima**[Y] septimus, hoc enim modo circulus eius respectu circuli Saturni se habet; **de animalibus** {autem}, **pisces;**[Y] ⟨⟨...⟩⟩ quia signum eorum Cancer est, qui est domus eius. (3) De hominibus {autem}, naute, eo quod ipsa mari **preest,**[Y] {quia} frigidum est et humidum; {adhuc} et **peregrinantes seu itinerantes,**[β] propter velocitatem motus eius; similiter nuntii ac servi, eo quod infima est planetarum; {item} argentum et cristallus atque calx,[1] propter albedinem que in eis est. (4) {Rursus} in divisione ipsius sunt asini, eo quod **vilissima seu infima**[β] hominis est equitatura; {iterum} **cucurbite**[Y] et melones, propter humiditatem eorum, que augmentatur post inceptionem illuminationem eius, ⟨⟨...⟩⟩. (5) ⟨⟨...⟩⟩ Et consimiliter obliviositas, adhuc et **scientia narrationum et fabularum,**[β] eo quod scientia propinqua est, {et parata seu facilis}. (6) **Et sententia que mutabilis est secundum omnem naturam**[Y] eo quod infima est et virtutem suam confert omnibus planetis; *de etatibus* {autem} *eius est* **infantia,**[Y,2] eo quod in primo est **orbe**[Y] a terra; iam {autem} commemoravi rationem de matre et de sororibus. | (7) {Porro,} in eius divisione est pulmo, cor enim ad Solem spectat; **de angulis** {vero} **seu mundi partibus,**[β] dextra **pars**[Y] occi-

---

[1]calx] M; L calix. [2]infantia] M; L infima.

indicates more about human affairs than one that is distant; {therefore} he says that one that is above the Sun does not exert power on Earth; {but} we have seen that all the ANCIENTS, **regarding the conjunction of the upper ⟨planets⟩,** bear witness **about what our hands**,γ,5 **and the experience of ⟨our⟩ work says about universal or general affairs,**γ,6 because they [the upper planets] indicate more about them [the universal or general affairs] than they indicate about particular ⟨affairs⟩. (4) And {indeed} the sixth **climate**γ is **in Mercury's portion,**γ,7 because its circle is like that [i.e., the sixth] with respect to Saturn's circle; {likewise,} in its portion are **light and agile**β,8 birds ⟨⟨because it is a small planet⟩⟩; and there is no need to mention divination and the other matters, because all of them are sciences; {and} it also indicates little brothers, because there is no star smaller than it in the heavens. (5) {But} **of the ages**γ of man, childhood ⟨belongs to it⟩, because it is close to Earth; {but} its taste is sour, because it is very much cold and dry. (6) I have already mentioned the pattern of the days; the reason for its years is according to the same method used for Saturn; {likewise,} the power of its body **has already been stated.**γ,9

8   (1) The Moon. I have already mentioned the reason for its nature. It **fills**γ,1 all bodies, on account of its great moisture. (2) {But} in its portion is the seventh **climate,**γ because that is the relationship of its circle to Saturn's circle; {and} **of living beings, fish,**γ,2 ⟨⟨of countries, al-Ṣabia⟩⟩ because their sign is Cancer, which is its house. (3) Of human beings, {however,} sailors, because **it rules over**γ,3 the sea, {because} it is cold and moist; {in addition}, **wayfarers or travelers,**β,4 because of the swiftness of its motion; and similarly messengers and slaves, because it is the lowest of the planets; {likewise,} silver, crystal and lime, because of the whiteness that is in them. (4) {In addition,} donkeys are in its portion, because they are **the cheapest and lowest**β,5 of the animals men ride on; {in addition} **gourds**γ,6 and melons, on account of their moisture, which increases after the start of its giving light, ⟨⟨and the opposite when its light wanes⟩⟩. (5) ⟨⟨Of human nature, excessive thinking and dementia are in its portion, because it is deficient in light,⟩⟩ and similarly forgetfulness; in addition, **the science of stories and fables,**β,7 because that is a kindred science {and ready to hand and easy to do}. (6) **The opinion that it is changeable according to every nature**γ,8 is because it is the lowest ⟨planet⟩ and gives its power to all the planets; *but of the ages, infancy,*γ,9 because it is in the first **orb**γ,10 from the Earth; {and} I have already mentioned the reason for the mother and sisters. (7) {In addition,} the lung is in its portion, because the heart belongs to the Sun; {but} **of the corners or parts of the world,**β,11 the right-western [i.e., southwest-

dentalis, ibidem enim augmentari incipit lumen eius;[1] dies namque ipsius et hore sicut aliorum planetarum. (8) Rationem {autem} nescio annorum eius maximorum ⟨⟨...⟩⟩ nisi pro tanto quod ait ALBUMASAR quod anni Solis magni sunt .120., et non videtur Luna quousque a Sole **distet seu elongetur**[β] .12. gradibus; propterea subtraxerunt .12. annos ab annis naturalibus, et sic fuerunt *anni Lune*[γ] .108.; ratio {vero} de annis minimis **non est recta**,[γθ] et {ideo} non commemoravi eam; sed ratio de mediocribus secundum viam est annorum Solis mediocrum; et iam quidem dictum est de fortitudine corporis eius.

9 (1) Loca {autem} gaudiorum planetarum septem hec sunt; Mercurius quidem in domo prima, quia super animam significant ambo; Lune in domo tertia, ambe namque similiter itinera significant propinqui ⟨⟨...⟩⟩; Venus in domo quinta, nam ambe super **delicias** significant **seu delectationes**;[β] Mars in domo sexta, ambo enim super egritudines significant; Sol in domo nona, eo quod ambo super itinera significant longinqua et **fidem seu leges**;[β] Iupiter in domo undecima, quia ambo super bonam fortunam significant et gratiam et honorem; Saturnus {vero} in domo duodecima, nam ambo significant vituperium et contentiones et domum captivitatis.

§5

1 (1) Capitulum .5. Omnium quidem eorum quod memorata sunt de **bonitatibus seu juvamentis**[β] planetarum, et **nocumentis sive maliciis**[β] eorum, non est querenda ratio, quia nota sunt *multa*. (2) **Quare**[γ] Saturni fortitudo maior est in Aquario quam in Capricorno, cum econtrario rem se habere convenientius videatur, eo quod Capricornus *frigidus est et siccus* sicut est[2] natura ipsius, causa quidem huius non est nisi quia Saturnus frigidus est siccus, signum {vero} Aquarii calidum et humidum, quapropter eius natura ibi rectificatur et super bonum[3] significat. (3) Et consimilis est ratio de Scorpione pro Marte, **cuius natura**[γ] calida est et sicca, si {vero} | fuerit in domo sua prima, que est Aries, calidus existens et siccus, **augmentabitur dolor super dolorem**,[θ] **signum** {autem} **Scorpionis rectificat naturam suam**.[γ] (4) {Item} convenientius est Saturnus esse in Aquarius, quia masculus est sicut ipse; et consimiliter Marti Scorpio, quia femini *sunt ambo*. (5) Eadem quoque est ratio de fortitudine Veneris in signo Tauri; ratio {vero} de Mercurio in Virgine est quia domus est {etiam} honoris sui.

---

[1]eius] M; L om. [2]est] M; L om. [3]bonum] M; L locum.

ern] **part**,γ,12 because from that very place its light begins to increase; and in fact the days and hours ⟨are⟩ the same as for the other planets. (8) {But} I do not know the reason for its greatest ⟨⟨and great⟩⟩ years, other than in accordance with what ABŪ MA'SHAR said, ⟨namely,⟩ that the great years of the Sun are 120, and ⟨that⟩ the Moon is not seen until it is **distant or removed**β,13 12 degrees from the Sun; therefore *they subtracted 12 years*γ,14 from the natural years, and in this way *the years of the Moon*γ,15 are 108; {but} the reason for the least years **is not right**,γθ,16 {therefore} I did not mention it; but the reason for the middle ⟨years⟩ is according to the method used for the Sun's middle years; ⟨the reason⟩ for the power of its body has been already mentioned.

9 (1) {But} these are the places of the joys of the seven planets; Mercury in the first house, because both indicate the soul; the Moon in the third house, because both indicate close-by journeys ⟨⟨and religions⟩⟩; Venus in the fifth house, because both indicate **delights or pleasures**;β,1 Mars in the sixth house, because both indicate diseases; the Sun in the ninth house, because both indicate distant journeys and **faith or laws**;β,2 Jupiter in the eleventh house, because both indicate good fortune and favor and honor; {but} Saturn in the twelfth house, because both indicate shame and quarrels and prison.

§5

1 (1) Fifth chapter. There is no need to look for a reason for everything mentioned about the **goodness or assistance**β,1 of the planets, and their **harms or evils**,β,2 because they are *much* known. (2) ⟨As for⟩ **why**γ,3 Saturn's power is greater in Aquarius than in Capricorn, even though the contrary seems to be more appropriate, since Capricorn is *cold and dry* like its [Saturn's] nature, the cause of this is because Saturn is cold and dry, {but} the sign of Aquarius is hot and moist, and for this reason its [i.e. Saturn's] nature is rectified [tempered] in this place [in Aquarius] and it indicates goodness. (3) The same applies to reason of Scorpio with respect to Mars, **whose nature**γ,4 is hot and dry, {but} if it is in its first house, Aries, which being hot and dry, **pain will be added to pain**θ,5 {but} **the sign of Scorpio rectifies its nature.**γ,6 (4) {Likewise,} it suits Saturn better to be in Aquarius, because it is masculine like the latter; and this also applies to Scorpio with respect to Mars, because *both are* feminine. (5) This is also the reason for the power of Venus in Taurus; {but} the reason for ⟨the power of⟩ Mercury in Virgo is because it is {also} the house of its honor.

2 (1) Causa {autem} fortitudinis planete cum est ascendens **versus partem septentrionalem**ᵞ est quia **nostra habitatio**ᵞ est **in parte septentrionali,**ᵞ ⟨⟨...⟩⟩ tunc fortificantur **radii luminis eius,**ᵞ et erit ei fortitudo magna super terram. (2) Contrarium {vero} huius est cum est meridionalis, et hec quidem res probatur per Solem, cum **in parte meridionali est vel septentrionali.**ᵞ (3) De ratione {autem} cum ascendit planeta **in circulo augis ecentrico quidem a terra,**ᵞ **contentio est et dissonantia magna** inter Indorum sapientes et Ptolomeus; sapientes enim Indorum dicunt quod planeta, cum est in **loco augis,**ᵞ quod assimilatur homini super equum suum equitati, et cum est in augis opposito, assimilatur servienti qui *pedes* ambulat. (4) Ptolomeus {vero} dicit cum est planeta propinquus terre, tunc est ei fortitudo magna, et contrarium huius res cum est in **loco augis sue.**ᵞ (5) **Secundum meam** {vero} **conscientiam, ut arbitror,**ᵝ **utrorumque sermones veri sunt,**ᵞ nam cum planeta remotus est a terra, tunc recipit fortitudinem magnam a superioribus *stellis*. (6) Unde si prefuerit **stella seu planeta**ᵝ super res anime, que sublimis est res, tunc **multa** erit nato **scientia**ᵞ in omnibus maneriebus; si {autem} **presul** fuerit seu **almubtaz**ᵝ super res corporis, tunc erit statura **parva et brevis,**ᵝ et non erit ei **robur et fortitudo**ᵝ conveniens. (7) {Quod} si fuerit planeta **in loco depressionis sue seu in opposito augis**ᵝ et sic **presul**ᵞ super animam, tunc significat quod natus erit fatuus et ignorans; si {vero} **presul**ᵞ fuerit super corpus, | tunc significat quod[1] erit ei corpus magnum et robustum; et huius quidem sermonis *veritatem* expertus sum multis vicibus. (8) Causa enim *quare est* planete fortitudo in statione sua secunda, est quia a loco illo incipit esse directa in suo cursu.

69va

(1) *Ecce quomodo planeta, circa augem existens, fortitudinem significat circa res anime; in opposito vero augis, et hoc est cum motus eius velocior est contra motum generalem quantum ad deferentem eius, fortitudinem et bonum esse corporis significat. (2) Et hoc dicit ipse[2] expertum esse. (3) Et hoc autem adverti potest, quod simili modo debet esse ratione illius motus quem[3] vocant* astrologi *motum in epiciclo, scilicet, directionem et retrogradationem, ut quidem directio super bonam dispositionem et esse corporis significet, retrogradatio vero super esse anime, cum motus generalis, scilicet, hic qui est ab oriente in occidens, super esse et conservationem entium, virtutem habeat et*

---

[1]quod] M; L quo.   [2]ipse] L; M ipse.   [3]quem] L; M quam.

2 (1) {But} the cause for the power of a planet when it rises **towards the northern part**[γ,1] is because **our habitable region**[γ,2] [the ecumene] is **in the northern part,**[γ,3] ⟨⟨and when a planet is in the north⟩⟩ then the **rays of its light**[γ,4] are made stronger, and it will have a great power on Earth. (2) {But} the opposite happens when it is southern, and this thing is tested by means of the Sun, when it is **in the northern part or in the southern.**[γ,5] (3) {But} as for the reason for ⟨the power of⟩ a planet when it rises **in the eccentric circle of the apogee from the Earth,**[γ,6] there is a **great dispute and disagreement**[7] between the SCHOLARS OF THE INDIANS and PTOLEMY; for the SCHOLARS OF THE INDIANS say that the planet, when is at the **place of the apogee,**[γ,8] resembles a man riding his horse, and when it is at the opposite of the apogee [the perigee], resembles a slave who walks *on the feet*. (4) {But} PTOLEMY says that when the planet is close to the Earth, then it has great power, and the opposite when it is at the **place of its apogee.**[γ] (5) {But} **according to my knowledge, as I see it,**[β,9] **the statements of both are true,**[γ,10] because when a planet is far from the Earth, then it receives great power from the superior *stars*. (6) Therefore, if a **star or planet**[β] is in charge of something related to the soul, which is something high, then the native will have **great knowledge**[γ,11] of all kinds; {but} if it is **the ruler or *al-mubtazz***[β,12] of something related to the body, then he will be of **small or short**[β,13] stature and will not have adequate **physical strength and power.**[β,14] (7) {But} if a planet is **at the place of its depression or at the opposite of the apogee**[β,15] [perigee] and also the **ruler**[γ,16] of the soul, then it indicates that the native will be a fool and ignoramus; {but} if it is the **ruler**[γ] of the body, then it indicates that he will have a large and powerful body; I have verified *the truthfulness of* this statement experimentally many times. (8) The cause for *why there is* power to the planet in its second station, is because in this place it begins to be direct in its course.

(1) *Behold how a planet, situated near the apogee, indicates power with respect to something related to the soul; but in the opposite of the apogee [i.e., the perigee], and that is when its motion is quicker against [i.e., in the opposite direction] the general motion on its deferent. it [i.e., the planet] indicates power and well-being of the body. (2) And this, he [Ibn Ezra] says, has been verified experimentally. (3) Now this can be realized, ⟨namely,⟩ that in a similar mode must be the reason of the motion that the ASTROLOGERS call motion on the epicycle, namely, direct motion and retrogradation, so that direct motion indicates the body's good temperament and being, but retrogradation ⟨indicates the soul's good temperament and⟩ being, while the general motion, namely, the one which is from east toward west, has power and causal-*

causalitatem, ut vult PHILOSOPHUS, *motus vero in obliquo circulo, qui contrarius est primo, scilicet, secundum successionem signorum, generationis est causa et corruptionis.* (4) *Et quia generatio et corruptio proprie passiones sunt corporis, igitur huiusmodi causa fortis motus, scilicet directionis secundum* ASTROLOGOS, *qui secundum* ALPETRAGIUM *et secundum veritatem, potius deberet appellari retrogradatio, cum sit contra intentionem generalem, convenienter debet fortitudinem causare corporis, propinqui inquam generationis et corruptionis subiecti ex contrarietatibus elementorum constituti.* (5) *Motus vero ille, qui ab* ASTROLOGIS *retrogradatio vocatur, secundum hanc viam, corporis debilitatem et impedimenta significabit.* (6) *Unde quemadmodum 'fortes corpore', 'ineptos mente' videmus, sic iuxta* PHILOSOPHUM, *'molles carne et passibiles aptos mente' frequentius experimur.* (7) *Propter quod* DOGMA PLATONIS *et universaliter omnium* PHILOSOPHANTIUM *tenet hoc quod ad operationes intellectus libere[1] extendas: necessarium est corporales vires subigi et tamquam infortunatas in se serviliter captivari.* (8) *Unde et* PHILOSOPUS IN OCTAVO[2] POLITICORUM: *'labor quidem | corporis impediens est intellectum, qui autem huius corpus.'* (9) *Hoc idem quoque tamquam nature legem existimans tanto evenientem in maiori parte dixit 'ingenio pollet cui vim natura negavit.'* (10) *Hac vero de causa convenientius est, magis quod res divinior, motus, scilicet, ille qui primo similior est, virtutem habeat super illam partem hominis, per quam ad operationes divinas, que sunt ratione uti et intellectu,[3] aptius disponantur.* (11) *Rationis enim perfectio, ut dicit* PLATO, *et 'intellectus' est 'Dei propria et paucorum admodum' animalium, verbi gratia, 'hominum'.* (12) *Unde* PHILOSOPUS IN DECIMO ETHICORUM: *'vita' autem que 'secundum intellectum est melior vita quam hominem.'* (13) *'Non' enim 'secundum quod homo est, sic vivit, sed secundum quod divinum aliquod in ipso existit'.*[4] (14) *Consonum est ergo rationi quod planeta directus fortitudinem corporis et anime detrimentum significet, econtrario retrogradus, utendo nominibus ab* ASTROLOGO *usitatis, sicut satis apparere potest intuenti.* (15) *Sciendum autem est quod in proposito sustentatus sum super* PRINCIPIA PHILOSOPHIE ARISTOTELIS *non ponendo ecentricos et epicilos, ut dicatur planeta aliquando propinquior terre, aliquando remotior; sed modum motus planetarum considerantes solum quantum ad convenientiam eius cum motu primo, et differentiam velocitatis quoque eius secundum hoc et tarditatem* PRINCIPIIS PHILOSOPHIE *adaptamus.*

---

[1]libere] L; M libre.   [2]octavo] M; L octava.   [3]intellectu] corrected; LM intellectus.   [4]*exisitit*] L in margin.

ity over the existence and conservation of beings, as the PHILOSOPHER [*Aristotle*] *determines, but the motion in the oblique orb, which is contrary to the first* ⟨*motion*⟩, *namely, according to the sequence of the signs, is the cause of generation and corruption.* (4) *Since generation and corruption are qualities characteristic of the body, therefore of this sort is the cause of the strong motion, namely, of direct* ⟨*motion*⟩ *according to the* ASTROLOGERS, *which, according to* AL-BIṬRŪJĪ *and according to the truth, should rather be called retrogradation, since it is against the general sense, and more appropriately should cause the strength of the body which is close and subject to generation and corruption, and is constituted by the contrariety of the elements.* (5) *But this motion, which is called retrogradation by the* ASTROLOGERS, *according to this method, will indicate weakness and hindrance of the body.* (6) *Hence, just as we see that* ⟨*human beings*⟩ *'strong in body'* ⟨*are*⟩ *'inept in mind', so, according to the* PHILOSOPHER, *we find experimentally more frequently that* ⟨*human beings*⟩ *'weak in flesh and susceptible to pain are apt in mind.'*[17] (7) *Therefore the* DOCTRINE OF PLATO *and of all the* PHILOSOPHERS *asserts what you may extend freely to the operations of the intellect: the bodily powers must be subjugated and subdued as slaves in the same way as unfortunate* ⟨*things*⟩ *in themselves.* (8) *Hence the* PHILOSOPHER *in* THE EIGHTH ⟨BOOK⟩ OF THE POLITICS ⟨*says*⟩: *'the labor of the body hinders the mind, which however* ⟨*impedes*⟩ *the body.'*[18] (9) *Also, appraising the law of nature as it usually comes out, he said: 'he may be strong in intelligence to whom nature denies strength.'*[19] (10) *The motion, namely, the one which is more similar to the first* ⟨*motion*⟩, *is more appropriate for this reason, more than the thing that is more divine,* ⟨*and*⟩ *would have power over that part of a human being by which the things that are used by reason and the intellect are better suited to the divine operations.* (11) *Perfection of reason, as* PLATO *says, and the intellect is 'characteristic of God and to some extent of living beings', that is, 'of human beings.'*[20] (12) *Hence, the* PHILOSOPHER *in* THE TENTH ⟨BOOK⟩ OF THE ETHICS ⟨*said*⟩: *'life according to the intellect is a better life insofar as he is a man.'*[21] (13) *Not 'insofar as he is a man, as he lives, but insofar as there is something divine in him.'*[22] (14) *Therefore it is harmonious with reason that a direct planet indicate power of the body and harm to the soul, and the opposite regarding the retrograde* ⟨*planet*⟩, *using the names employed by the* ASTROLOGER, *as it seems sufficiently is possible to observe.* (15) *One must know that on purpose I rely on the* PRINCIPLES OF PHILOSOPHY *of* ARISTOTLE *when I do not posit eccentric* ⟨*circles*⟩ *and epicycles, when it is said that a planet is sometimes closer to the Earth, sometimes more distant; but when considering the motion of the planets alone for its suitability to the first motion, we adjust the* PRINCIPLES OF PHILOSOPHY *by the difference of its velocity and also its slowness according to this.*

(16) *Inquit* TRANSLATOR: *Bone quidem fortune ab* ASTROLOGIS *vocate*[1] *sunt prosperitates in bonis exterioribus secundum quandam excellentiam, prout etiam apud vulgares consuete sunt reputari.* (17) *Quamquam igitur opus sit aliquali prosperitate exteriori homini enti, nihilominus tamen communiter vocate prosperitates, secundum quod etiam ab* ASTROLOGIS *appellantur, impedimenta sunt ad speculationem, ut testatur* PHILOSOPUS *et rei veritas, et in hoc etiam sensu*[2] *omnes* PHILOSOPHI *convenerunt.* (18) *Unde* SEXTO ETHICORUM: *'Anaxagoram' inquit 'et' consimiles 'sapientes quidem, non prudentes autem aiunt esse, cum ignorantes videantur conferentia sibi ipsis, et superflua quidem et admirabilia et difficilia et divina scire ipsos aiunt; inutilia autem quoniam non humana bona querunt.'* (19) *Item*[3] IN QUARTO: *'et accusant', inquit, 'fortunam* | *quoniam maxime digni existentes nequaquam ditantur.'* (20) *Unde et fortune ymago ceca depingitur.*[4] (21) *'Contingit autem non irrationabiliter hoc', ut ait* PHILOSOPHUS, *'non enim possibile pecunias habere non curantem ut habeat*[5] *quemadmodum neque in aliis'.* (22) *Non solum autem hoc ita se habet in felicitate speculativa, sed etiam in*[6] *activa.* (23) *'Existimandum' namque 'non est multis et magnis indigere felicem futuram; non enim in superabundantiis*[7] *per se sufficiens, neque iudicium necque actio; possibile autem et non principes terre et maris bona agere.* (24) *Ydiote enim', ait* PHILOSOPHUS, *'potentibus non minus studiosa videntur agere, sed et magis'.* (25) *Idem quoque patet* QUARTO POLITICORUM. (26) *Quemadmodum igitur bona fortuna appetitui sensuali attributa planetarum directioni proportionaliter secundum* ASTROLOGOS, *secundum quod et inferior spera contra superiorem 'movendo aliquando vincit', ut innuit* PHILOSPHUS TERTIO DE ANIMA, *sic et bona fortuna beatitudinis, que in appetitu consistit intellectuali, planetarum retrogradationi proportionanda relinquitur, secundum quod inferior spera superiorem pro posse suo consequitur in motu.* (27) *'Natura autem que sursum semper principalior', ut ibidem ait* PHILOSOPUS. (28) *Et hoc quidem sensui consentaneum est, rationi etiam secundum mentem* ASTROLOGORUM, *prout hic apparet in textu.* (29) *Cum enim secundum* PRINCIPIA PHILOSOPHIE *impossibile sit ecentricos esse stellarum circulos, in quibus moventur, quid aliud esse potest locus augis et eius oppositum nisi loca in quibus contra motum supremum velocius aut tardius movetur stella.* (30) *Quanto autem movetur tardius, tanto supreme spere similius, et tunc, ut ait* ACTOR, *anime significat*

---

[1]vocate] M; L vocata. [2]sensu] corrected, LM sensui. [3]Item] L; M item et. [4]depingitur] L; M pingitur. [5]habeat] M; L hebeat. [6]in] L; M om. [7]superabundantiis] corrected; L superabundantiam; M superabundantia.

(16) *The translator says: good fortunes are called by the astrologers prosperities in external [i.e., worldly] good conditions according to a certain excellence, as they are also usually considered by the common people.* (17) *Accordingly, although a human being must have some sort of exterior [i.e., worldly] prosperity, likewise they are called nevertheless they are called prosperities in a general sense, as they were designated by the astrologers, they are hindrances to ⟨intellectual⟩ speculation, as the Philosopher and the truth of the matter bear witness, and in this meaning also all the philosophers agreed.* (18) *Hence ⟨Aristotle said⟩ in the sixth ⟨book⟩ of the Ethics: 'They say,' he [Aristotle] said, 'that Anaxagoras and similar wise men are not prudent, when they seem to be ignorant of what is to their own advantage and say that they know things that are unnecessary, admirable, difficult and divine; but useless because they do not seek human goods.'*[23] (19) *Likewise, ⟨Aristotle said⟩ in the fourth ⟨book of the Ethics⟩: 'They accuse,' he [Aristotle] said, 'fortune, because the worthiest by no means enrich themselves.'* (20) *Hence, fortune is portrayed as blind.* (21) *'But that this happens is not unreasonable,' as the Philosopher said, 'because it is not possible to have wealth without taking care to obtain it, in the same way as in other things.'*[24] (22) *This applies not only to contemplative happiness but also to active ⟨happiness⟩.* (23) *For 'one must not think that future happiness needs many and great ⟨things⟩; because it does not ⟨depend⟩ on having more than is sufficient, neither ⟨in⟩ judgment nor ⟨in⟩ action; and it is possible to do good deeds without being princes of dry land and sea.* (24) *Because the common people,' said the Philosopher, 'not only seem to do no fewer good deeds than the powerful, but even more.'*[25] (25) *Also this is clear in the fourth book of the Politics.* (26) *Therefore in the same way as good fortune that pertains to sensual desire is proportionally attributed to the direct ⟨motion⟩ of the planets according to the astrologers, according to which the inferior sphere in its motion sometimes prevails over the superior ⟨sphere⟩, as the Philosopher suggested in the third ⟨book⟩ of On the soul, so the good fortune of happiness, which consists of intellectual desire, remains in proportion to the retrogradation of the planets, according to which the inferior sphere follows the superior in its motion, according to its ability.* (27) *'Nature, which ⟨is directed⟩ upwards, is always more important,' as the Philosopher says in that very place.* (28) *And this fits the senses, but according to the astrologers, the soul, as this appears in the text.* (29) *Since according to the principles of philosophy it is impossible for there to be eccentric circles of the planets on which they move, what else can the place of the apogee and its opposite [perigee] be except the places where the star moves quicker or slower contrary to the superior motion.* (30) *To the extent that it moves more slowly, so it is more similar to the superior orb, and then,*

perfectionem. (31) *Cum itaque, per retrogradationem, planeta motum spere superioris perfectius consequatur, ac eidem magis assimiletur et melius quam per motum alium, relinquitur illam in rebus anime sublimitatem importare*[1] *non obstantibus tamen impedimentis que in rebus corporis adducit*. (32) *Unde quomodo tristitias et contradictiones et cetera impedimenta corporalia causat retrogradatio, sic et accidentia tribulant et conturbant beatum*. (33) *Tristitias enim inferunt et impediunt multis operationibus in quibus oportet esse virum 'tanquam tetragonum sine vituperio'.* | (34) *Et hinc alibi scriptum est 'verti me ad aliud vidique sub Sole, nec sapientium panem nec doctorum divitias nec artificium gratiam' et cetera*. (35) *Sed revertatur ad textum*.[2]

70rb

(9) Non oportet {autem} rememorari fortitudines planetarum masculinorum **et signorum masculinorum,**$^\gamma$ eo quod **diei assimilantur,**$^\gamma$ preter quam signum Libre pro Sole, quia **domus est vituperii seu casus.**$^\beta$

3 (1) Quod {autem} dixerunt, **malum planete seu nocumentum**$^\beta$ vel cum Capite Draconis aut Cauda eius hoc est, secundum INDORUM opinionem. (2) Et veritas quidem est quod ita est cum Cauda, sed in capite non est nisi bene. (3) Et quod dixerunt de existentia cum Capite Draconis Lune aut[3] in Cauda eius, ipsi non recte locuti sunt, et talis est {etiam} opinio PTOLOMEI, nam quod coniunctio **circuli Lune zodiaco similis seu deferentis Lune cum zodiaco seu ecliptica vel horum sectio noceat circulo planete qui zodiaco similis est seu deferens vocatur;**$^\gamma$ hoc est dictum, vani super sermones. (4) Consimiliter quoque Caput Draconis nocumentum {tamen} non affert[4] Lune nisi cum **eclipsatur.**$^{\gamma,5}$ (5) Quod {autem} dicunt INDORUM SAPIENTES,$^\gamma$ Caput *Draconis*[6] bonum esse cum bonis, **rectum est et verum;**$^\beta$ reliqua {vero} *mala* nota sunt, nec indigent rationis explanatione.

---

[1]importare] L; M imponere.   [2]Sed revertatur ad textum] L; M om.   [3]aut] M; L autem.   [4]affert] M; L aufert (in the margin).   [5]nocumentum tamen non affert Lune nisi cum eclipsatur] M; L in margin.   [6]Quod autem dicunt Indorum sapientes caput draconis] M; L in margin.

the AUTHOR [*Ibn Ezra*] *says, it indicates perfection of the soul.* (31) *Since thus, by means of retrogradation, the planet follows the motion of the superior orb more perfectly, and it is more similar to it and better than by the other motion, it remains that it brings about excellence in matters of the soul, notwithstanding the hindrances that it brings to the matters of the body.* (32) *Therefore, just as retrogradation causes sadness, disputes and other bodily hindrances, so the accidents afflict and disturb the happy person.* (33) *They induce sadness and impede many works in which a man must be 'foursquare without shame.'*²⁶ (34) *Hence it is written elsewhere, 'I have seen something else under the Sun, nor does food come to the wise or wealth to the doctors or favor to the learned;'*²⁷ *etc.* (35) *But let us return to the text.*

(9) There is no need, {however,} to mention the powers of the masculine planets **and the masculine signs**,ᵞ·²⁸ because they are **similar to the day**,ᵞ·²⁹ with the exception of Libra for the Sun, because it [Libra] is the [Sun's] **house of shame or fall**^β,³⁰ [house of dejection].

3 (1) {But} as for what they said, ⟨namely,⟩ that the **evil or harm of the planet**^β,¹ is when it is with the Head of the Dragon or with its Tail, this is the opinion of the Indians. (2) But the truth is that this is in this manner when it is with the Tail, but in the Head it is only good. (3) As for what they said about ⟨a planet's⟩ being with the Head of the Dragon of the Moon or its Tail, they did not speak rightly, and such is {also} PTOLEMY's opinion, for **how could the conjunction of the circle of the Moon [that is] similar to the zodiac or ⟨the circle⟩ of the deferent of the Moon with the zodiac or the ecliptic or their intersection afflict the circle of the planet [that is] similar to the zodiac or ⟨the circle that⟩ is called the deferent?**ᵞ·² ⟨About these things⟩ it has been said that they are foolish statements. (4) In like manner, the Head of the Dragon does not bring {in fact} harm to the Moon unless it is **eclipsed.**ᵞ·³ (5) {But} as for what the **SCHOLARS OF THE INDIANS**ᵞ·⁴ said, ⟨namely, that⟩ the Head *of the Dragon* is good with the good ones, **this is right and true;**^β,⁵ the rest, {however,} have been *wrongly* mentioned, and they do not require an explanation of the reason.

§6

1 (1) Capitulum sextum.[1] Quod quidem {autem} commemorabunt, lumen planete fortitudinem augmentare corporis eius, hoc est secundum oculorum visionem, nam cum terre propinquus est maior esse videtur quam appareat cum remotus est ab ea; et hec quidem res sciri potest **per portionem seu partem**$^\beta$ circuli **augis**$^\gamma$ cuius egressum est centrum a centro terre. (2) Residue {vero} res memorate note sunt.

2 (1) ⟨⟨...⟩⟩ quare {autem} **coniunctio**$^\gamma$ *cum Sole* in minori est minutis .16., hoc {quidem ideo} est quia hic numerus fere semidiametrum continet Solis; unde cum **est coniunctio partis vel per partem vel ad partem**,$^\beta$ {tunc} **est planeta in directo centri Solis et coniungitur centro Solis.**$^\gamma$ (2) Sed hoc non accidit planetis superioribus donec sint **in loco augis**$^\gamma$ **circuli parvi seu epicicli**,$^\beta$ et tunc erunt a terra elongati; si {ergo} cum hoc fuerint in **loco augis**$^\gamma$ magni circuli *videlicet deferentis*, tunc **in maxima erunt elongatione | a terra.**$^\gamma$ (3) Quod {igitur} diximus, planete fortitudinem esse cum in tali est coniunctione, hoc quidem est opinio SAPIENTIUM INDORUM; PTOLOMEUS {vero} deridet ipsos. (4) EGO {tamen} vidi **IN LIBRIS**$^\gamma$ DORONII, qui *apud nos* quidem est **princeps iudicum**,$^{\gamma,2}$ quod ipse SERMONES INDORUM$^\gamma$ expertus erat, et sic ait IN LIBRO SUO: si fuerit Mercurius coniunctus Soli, tunc in celo **secundus erit Mercurius sive duplex**,$^\beta$ et hoc est dictu quod[3] duplicatur **virtus eius seu fortitudo**,$^\beta$ et consimiliter alii planete. (5) Quod {autem} Saturnus et Iupiter de combustionis exeunt termino post sex gradus, causa quidem huius est propter magnitudinem corporum eorum, et {quia} corpus Martis tante magnitudinis non est ut illi, idicirco .10. gradus dederint Marti.; alie {vero} res note sunt.

3 (1) Divisa sunt {autem} iudicia de planetis inferioribus Sole et de superioribus. (2) Quia superiorum fortitudo in oriente est, ⟨⟨...⟩⟩, Sol enim tunc in motu suo velocior[4] sit superioribus; postquam eis coniunctus[5] fuerit, ipse **transiens reliquit eos**,$^\beta$ et illi quidem ascendunt orientales ab eo, et tunc augetur eorum fortitudo propter velocitatem {etiam} motus sui. (3) Inferio-

---

[1]Capitulum sextum] M; L in margin. [2]iudicum] M; L iudicium. [3]quod] L; M quia.
[4]velocior] M; L velociorum. [5]coniunctus] M; L coniunctum.

§6

1 (1) Sixth chapter. What they have mentioned, {however,} that the light of a planet increases the strength of its body, this is according to the sight of the eyes, for when it is close to the Earth it appears larger than when it is far from it; and one can know this **by the portion or the part**^(β,1) of the circle of the **apogee**^(γ,2) whose center is removed from the center of the Earth. (2) {But} the rest of the things that were mentioned are known.

2 (1) {But} ⟨⟨the reason⟩⟩ why **the conjunction**^(γ,1) *with the Sun* is less than 16 minutes ⟨away from the Sun⟩, this {indeed} is because this number contains approximately half the diameter of the Sun; hence when **the conjunction is of the part or by the part or to the part ⟨of the Sun⟩,**^(β,2) {then} **the planet is directly ⟨facing⟩ the center of the Sun, and it is joined to the center of the Sun.**^(γ,3) (2) This does not happen with the upper planets until they are in the **place of the apogee**^(γ,4) of **the small circle or epicycle,**^(β,5) and then they will be distant from the Earth; {therefore} if with this they were in the **place of the apogee**^(γ) of the great circle, *namely, of the deferent,* then they will be **at the greatest elongation** [i.e., distance] **from the Earth.**^(γ,6) (3) What we have said, {then,} that there a planet has power when it is in conjunction, this is the opinion of the SCHOLARS OF THE INDIANS, {but} PTOLEMY laughs at them. (4) {Nevertheless,} I have seen **in THE BOOKS**^(γ,7) BY DORONIUS, who *in our opinion* is the **leader of the judges**^(γ,8) [i.e., the astrologers], that he himself verified experimentally the STATEMENTS OF **THE INDIANS,**^(γ,9) and says as follows in HIS BOOK: if Mercury conjoins the Sun, then there will be **a second or double Mercury**^(β,10) in the heavens, and this says that its **power or strength**^(β,11) is doubled, and similarly with the other planets. (5) {But} that Saturn and Jupiter emerge from the boundary of burning at six degrees, the cause for this is because of the size of their bodies, and {since} Mars's body is not of such a size as theirs, for this reason they assigned Mars 10 degrees; {but} the other things are known.

3 (1) {But} the ⟨astrological⟩ judgments about the planets inferior to the Sun differ from the ⟨astrological judgments about the planets⟩ superior to it. (2) For the power of the superior ⟨planets⟩ is in the east, ⟨⟨whereas ⟨the power of⟩ the inferior ⟨planets⟩ is in the west⟩⟩, because then the Sun is quicker in its motion than the superior ⟨planets⟩; after it [the Sun] is conjoined to them [the superior planets], and it **passes and leaves them behind,**^(β,1) ⟨then⟩ they rise east of it, and then their power increases {also} because of the speed of its [the Sun's] motion. (3) {But} when the infe-

res {vero} quando Soli coniunguntur, quia velociores eo sunt, idcirco relinquunt ipsum et apparent occidentales ab eo, et tunc augetur eorum virtus quia tunc veloces {etiam}[1] sunt in moto suo. (4) {Preterea} accidit Veneri et Mercurio accidentes quale ceteris non accidit planetis, coniunguntur enim Soli directi existentes in moto suo, ac {etiam} coniunguntur eidem retrogradi existentes. (5) Hoc {autem} {ideo} est quia non **elongantur**ʸ a Sole nisi in certa distantia, et hoc quidem **elongatio**ʸ est propter **parvum circulum seu epiciclum**,ᵝ circuli {autem} ipsorum magni sunt equales.

Inquit TRANSLATOR: *vult* ACTOR *dicere de motibus eorum in suis differentibus quod illi sunt equales.*

(6) Claves {vero} Lune exemplabo in **LIBRO SECULI SIVE REVOLUTIONUM MUNDI**.ᵝ

§7

1   (1) Capitulum septimum.[2] ⟨⟨...⟩⟩. **SAPIENTES ASTRORUM**ʸ dicunt quod
70vb **applicationis**ʸ initium .15. graduum, PTOLOMEUS {vero} dicit quod initium | **applicationis**ʸ est secundum **fortitudinem**ʸ planete, ante et retro, et hoc quidem **verius**ʸ est secundum quod mihi videtur. (2) Quod {autem} dixerunt, leviorem **occultare seu eclipsare**ᵝ graviorem, hoc verum est cum fuerit coniunctio[3] equalis in longitudine quidem et latitudine, et quicquid tunc significatum fuerit ex hoc, verum est. (3) Facies {autem} sic: vide si fuerunt ambo planete **in ecliptica**,ʸ tunc erit coniunctio vera. (4) Si {ergo} scire volueris **fortitudinem seu dominium**ᵝ *cuius inquam* **est coniunctio**,ʸ considera quis eorum propinquior est loco **augis**ʸ **circuli magni seu deferentis**,ᵝ nam ille vincet **alium sive socium suum**.ᵝ (5) Et computa **fortitudinem**ʸ hanc quod est in numero .4. fortitudinum, qui {vero} illorum **propinquor** fuerit **loco**ʸ **augis**ʸ parvi circuli vincet **alterum**ʸ in tribus fortitudinibus. (6) {Item} qui horum **septentrionalis fuerit altero**,ʸ **sive septentrionali existente sive non**ʸ aut meridionali, **septentrionalis**ʸ vincet; si {vero} fuerunt ambo **septentrionales**,ʸ ille qui magis **septentrionalis**ʸ fuerit alterum vincet. (7) Et huius quidem dicti causa est quia omnis stella que propinquior est

---

[1]etiam] L; M om.   [2]Capitulum septimum] M; L om.   [3]coniunctio] corrected according to the Hebrew; LM longitudo.

rior ⟨planets⟩ are conjoined to the Sun, because they are quicker than it is, they pass it and appear [i.e., rise] west of it; and then their power increases because then they {too} are quick in their motion. (4) {In addition}, accidents occur to Venus and Mercury whose like does not occur to the other planets, for they [Venus and Mercury] are conjoined to the Sun when they are direct in their motion, and they are {also} conjoined to it [the Sun] when they are retrograde. (5) {But} this, {then,} happens because they are **elongated**$^{\gamma,2}$ only a certain distance from the Sun, and this **elongation**$^{\gamma,3}$ is because of **the small circle or epicycle,**$^{\beta,4}$ {although} their great circles [i.e., eccentric circles] are the same.

THE TRANSLATOR says: regarding their motions in their different ⟨circles⟩, THE AUTHOR [Ibn Ezra] means that they are the same.

(6) {But} I shall explain the keys of the Moon in the **BOOK OF THE AGE OR THE REVOLUTIONS OF THE WORLD.**$^{\beta,5}$

§7

1 (1) Seventh chapter. ⟨⟨"Application"⟩⟩. The **SCHOLARS OF THE STARS**$^{\gamma,1}$ say that the beginning of **"application"**$^{\gamma,2}$ begins at 15 degrees, {but} PTOLEMY says that the beginning of "application"$^{\gamma}$ is according to the **power**$^{\gamma,3}$ of the planet, in front of or behind it, and this seems **more true**$^{\gamma,4}$ in my opinion. (2) {But} as for what they said, that the lighter [i.e., quicker] ⟨planet⟩ **hides or eclipses**$^{\beta,5}$ the heavier [i.e., slower] one, this is true when the conjunction is the same in longitude and latitude; and then everything that is indicated by it comes true. (3) You will proceed, {however,} in this manner: observe whether both planets are **in the ecliptic;**$^{\gamma,6}$ then this will be a true conjunction. (4) {Consequently,} If you wish to ascertain **the power or dominion**$^{\beta,7}$ **to which,** *I say,* **this conjunction belongs,**$^{\gamma,8}$ observe which of them is closer to the place of **the apogee**$^{\gamma,9}$ **of the great circle or deferent,**$^{\beta,10}$ because this one will be victorious over **the other or its companion.**$^{\beta,11}$ (5) Reckon this **power**$^{\gamma,12}$ as if it were in the number of four powers; {but} the one of them which **is closer to the place**$^{\gamma,13}$ of the **apogee**$^{\gamma}$ of the small circle will be victorious over **the other**$^{\gamma,14}$ by three powers. (6) {Likewise}, for the one of them that is **north of the other,**$^{\gamma,15}$ **whether it** [the first planet] **is northern or not**$^{\gamma,16}$ or southern, the **northern**$^{\gamma,17}$ will be victorious; {but} if both of them are **northern,**$^{\gamma}$ the one that is more **northern**$^{\gamma}$ will be victorious over the other. (7) The cause of this mentioned

habitationi nostre,ᵞ maiorem habetᵞ fortitudinem. (8) {Quod} si fuerunt ambo meridionales, ille cuius latitudo minor fuerit alterum vincet cuius latitudo maior fuerit; si {autem} latitudo magna fuerit inter eos, non apparebit opus coniunctionis eorum nisi minus dimidio. (9) Et huic {quidem} victorie **in angulo**ᵞ *scilicet elevationis versus septentrionem* est fortitudo .2.; illi {vero} qui plus habet **dignitatis**ᵞ in loco coniunctionis est fortitudo una, et cum fortitudines computaveris, tunc scies quis est vincens.

2 (1) Si {autem} fuerint duo planete in aspectu opposito et fuerint ambo **in ecliptica**,ᵞ tunc est **aspectus integrus et perfectus**,ᵝ quia sunt inter eos .180. gradus equales. (2) Si {vero} fuerit eorum latitudo **in eodem angulo seu in eadem parte**,ᵝ *puta* si fuerint ambo **septentrionales**ᵞ aut meridionales, tunc non est oppositus aspectus perfectus, et huius causa est quia inter ipsos minus est .180. secundum quod est eorum latitudo. (3) Et si fuerit unius latitudo **septentrionalis**ᵞ alterius {vero} meridiana, fueruntque latitudines equales **altera alteri**,ᵞ aspectus oppositus perfectus erit, secundum enim quod ascendit alter sic et alter descendit.¹ (4) Si {vero} latitudines non habuerunt equales non erit aspectus perfectus,² et erit **defectus seu diminutio eius**ᵝ secundum superfuum alteri super aterum; | et si unus **in ecliptica**ᵞ fuerit alter {vero} **septentrionalis**ᵞ vel meridianus, non erit aspectus perfectus et erit defectus in aspectu secundum quod fuerit latitudo. (5) Adhuc {autem} loquar in decima parte de aspectibus.

71ra

3 (1) Quod {autem} dicunt **de gradibus, qui equalium sunt ascensionum**,ᵞ opus non est huius querere rationem, nota enim est. (2) **Similiter et de aliis quorum nomina sicut**ᵞ **solitudo**,ᵞ ⟨⟨...⟩⟩ collectio, redditus luminis, *refrenatio seu contradictio* et cetere; res exemplaris quidem dicte; in omnibus {autem} concordat Ptolomeus preter quam in ⟨⟨...⟩⟩ remunerationis *ratione*, et ego nescio illam.

---

¹erit, secundum enim quod ascendit alter sic et alter descendit] M; L in margin.   ²Si vero latitudines non habuerunt equales non erit aspectus perfectus] M; L in margin.

thing is because every star that is closer to **our habitable**[Υ,18] ⟨part of the Earth⟩ [the ecumene] **has**[Υ,19] greater power.[20] (8) {But} if both are southern, the one whose latitude is smaller will be victorious over the one whose latitude is greater; {but} if the latitude between them is great, less than half of the effect of their conjunction will be seen. (9) Two powers ⟨are assigned⟩ to this victory, {indeed,} **on account of the corner,**[Υ,21] *namely, the one raising with respect to the north*; {but} there is one power to the one that has more **dignity**[Υ,22] in the place of the conjunction; when you have calculated the powers you will know which of them is victorious.

2 (1) {But} if the two planets are in an opposition aspect and both are **on the ecliptic,**[Υ,1] then the **aspect is full and complete,**[β,2] because there are 180 equal degrees between them. (2) {But} if their ⟨ecliptical⟩ latitude is **in the same corner** [i.e., side] **or in the same part,**[β,3] *for example* if both are **northern**[Υ] or southern, then it is not a complete opposition aspect, and the cause is that there is less than 180 degrees between them according to what is their latitude. (3) If the latitude of one of them is **northern**[Υ] {but} of the other is southern, and the latitudes are **of one to the other**[Υ,4] are equal, this will be a full aspect opposition aspect, because just as one ascends, the other descends. (4) {But} if they do not have equal latitudes the aspect will not be complete, and its **deficit or shortfall**[β,5] will be according to the excess of the one over the other; if one is **in the ecliptic**[Υ,6] {but} the other is **northern**[Υ] or southern, the aspect will not be complete, and the deficit will be in the aspect in accordance with the latitude. (5) {But} I shall say more about the aspects in the tenth chapter.

3 (1) {But} as for what they said about **the degrees, which are of equal ascensions,**[Υ,1] there is no need to try to seek its reason, because it is known. (2) **The same applies to others whose names are like**[Υ,2] "**solitude**,"[Υ,3] ⟨⟨"desolation", "translation",⟩⟩ "collection," "reflecting the light," *"restraining or contradiction,"* and the others; they were said as an example [a metaphor]; PTOLEMY, {however,} accepts them all except for *the reason of* ⟨⟨"pleasantness"⟩⟩ ⟨and⟩ "recompense," but I do not know it.

§8

1 (1) Capitulum octavum.[1] Super universalibus quidem iudiciis memoratis, non oportet rationes querere, quia note sunt. (2) Ratio {autem} quare Luna particeps ascendenti ponitur, hec est quia **similitudinem habet cum signo ascendente**.ᵞ (3) Et ⟨⟨...⟩⟩ quod significant aspectus quartus aut oppositum malum est perfectum, hoc {autem} **rectum et rationabile**,ᵝ quia super inimicitiam significat; quia {vero} aspectus trinus et sextilis super amicitiam, {ideo} alleviant malum. (4) Quod {autem} dicunt, si **nocivus aut malus**ᵝ fuerit dominus rei quesite, significat retardationem super quesitum, verum quidem est de Saturno, eo quod tardus[2] est in moto suo, et non sic Mars. (5) Rursus quidem **dictum**[3] estᵞ de planeta, quod debilis est quousque[4] ad quintum gradum signi **pervenerit**,ᵞ et hoc quidem est secundum sententiam SAPIENTIUM PERSARUM. (6) PTOLOMEUS {vero} deridet eos et **ipse ius habet**,ᶿ *quia termini unius non sunt maiores terminis alterius;*ᵞ *apud illos autem contentio est si per considerationem intellectus signa distinguenda sunt*,ᵞ incipiendo quidem a principio **coniunctionis sive sectionis**ᵝ ⟨⟨...⟩⟩ magnorum circulorum, {equinoctialis videlicet et ecliptice,} aut ab ymagine que visui apparet in loco noto; secundum has {ergo} vias duas ⟨⟨...⟩⟩; quas ipsi dixerunt si fuerit planeta **in fine signi vel in ultima parte eius**,ᵝ ipse iam amisit virtutem signi prioris. (7) Sermones {vero} quos diximus, quod ⟨⟨...⟩⟩ sunt stelle tenebrose significantes super nocumenta, sic dicti sunt a SAPIENTES INDORUM. (8) {Item} dixerunt quod planeta bonus in octava domo existens neque bonum significat neque malum, | ⟨⟨...⟩⟩ quia nichil addit super vitam neque super **substantiam seu divitias**ᵝ *nisi quod super mortem significat mirabilem.*ᵞ (9) Quod {igitur} **hic commemoramus verum est;**ᵞ in LIBRO {autem} NATIVITATUM **de hiis loquar, que rectificant testimonia et de hiis etiam que talia non sunt.**ᵞ

71rb

---

[1]Capitulum octavum] M; L in margin.   [2]tardus] M; L tardius.   [3]dictum] M; L om.
[4]quousque] L; M usque.

LIBER CAUSARUM SEU RATIONUM 559

§ 8

1 (1) Eighth chapter. Regarding all the judgments mentioned ⟨in this chapter⟩, there is no need to seek the reason, because they are known. (2) {But} the reason why the Moon was made partner to the ascendant is **because of its resemblance to the ascendant sign.**ᵞ,¹ (3) And ⟨⟨what they said⟩⟩ that quartile and opposition indicate total evil, this {however} is **correct and based on reason,**β,² because they indicate enmity; {but} since the aspects of trine and sextile ⟨indicate⟩ friendship, {therefore} they mitigate the evil. (4) {But} as for what they say, ⟨that⟩ if the lord of the requested thing is a **harmful or bad**β,³ ⟨planet⟩, it indicates delay in the requested matter, this is true for Saturn because it is slow in its motion, but not so Mars. (5) Besides, what has been said ᵞ,⁴ about a planet, that it is weak until **it arrives at**ᵞ,⁵ the fifth degree of the sign, this is according to the opinion of the PERSIAN SCHOLARS. (6) {But} PTOLEMY laughs at them and **he is right**θ,⁶ [lit. he has the law], *because the terms⁷ of one* ⟨*sign*⟩ *are not larger than the terms of the other;*ᵞ,⁸ *but among them there is a dispute whether the signs should be separated by a consideration of the intellect,*ᵞ,⁹ starting from the beginning of the **conjunction or intersection**β,¹⁰ of the ⟨⟨two⟩⟩ great circles, {namely, the equinoctial and the ecliptical,} or from the image that appears to sight in a known place; {therefore} ⟨⟨the signs are not separated⟩⟩ according to these two methods, regarding which they said that if the planet is **in the end of the sign or in its last part,**β,¹¹ it [the planet] has already lost the power of the previous sign. (7) {But} the remarks that we have already said, that ⟨⟨the pits⟩⟩ are dark stars indicative of harms—that is what the SCHOLARS OF THE INDIANS said. (8) {Likewise,} they said that a good planet situated in the eighth house indicates neither good nor evil, ⟨⟨this is true⟩⟩ because it does not add to ⟨the length of⟩ life or to **wealth or riches,**β,¹² *but only indicates a marvelous death.*ᵞ,¹³ (9) **What we have mentioned here,** {then,} **is correct;**ᵞ,¹⁴ {but} **in the** BOOK OF NATIVITIES **I will speak about those things that set testimonies rightly and also about those that are not like that.**ᵞ,¹⁵

§9

1   (1) Capitulum nonum.[1] PTOLOMEUS quidem **affirmat**[γ] quod sors Lune **tamen**[γ] vera est, eo quod querit gradum qui in tali proportione sit *ad locum* Lune, que terre propinqua est, in *generali* proportione gradus ascendentis est ad Solem, et hoc est pars Lune; unde ait quod die et nocte accipiatur a Luna. (2) Quod {autem} dicunt tamquam Solis esse partem, illam que **pars est secretorum sive celati animi,**[β2] **totum**[3] **hoc ad confirmationem seu fortificationem illius est,**[β] hec enim est ipsamque pars Lune secundum PTOLOMEUS; ⟨⟨...⟩⟩; quia tamen alias vidi partes in **LIBRIS**[γ] DORONII, idcirco eas commemoravi. (3) Sors {igitur} Saturni super qualibet rem significat que de significatione ipsius est secundum naturam suam, et consimiliter de quolibet aliorum. (4) **In alia** {vero} **sorte sit coniunctio**[4] **cum Mercurio,**[γ] eo quod ipsius natura est **intellectu et sapientie ac scientiis**[β] immisceri et non rebus seculi. (5) Iupiter {autem} super divitias significat, secundum quod dictum est, quapropter dixerunt quidam quod quia domus Mercurii opposite sunt domibus Iovis qui super divitas significat, idcirco non sunt divitieque quam plurimis SAPIENTIUM. (6) Et hic quidem **sermo**[γ] qui propinquus est veritati, est quod quocumque[5] signo in orientali angulo ascendente in hora nativitatis, semper erit natus de natura domini signi, quamvis {etiam} de genere non sit convenienti **ad talem gradum**[γ] *puta dominandi*. (7) Et huius exemplum est homini quidem qui **servus**[γ] est; nascetur filius et erit signum eius Leo, quamvis {ergo} fuerit Sol in malo loco, in natura {tamen} nati erit dominari et **servos sibi subiciet seu habebit.**[β] (8) Consimiliter, quoque si fuerit dominus signi ⟨⟨...⟩⟩ Mercurius, quamquam in genere suo non sit sapiens et Mercurius {etiam} in malo loco, **erit natus prudens**[γ] in **sermonibus secula-**

71va   **ribus;**[γ] {quod} si in bono loco fuerit, sapiens | erit licet {etiam} sapiens non fuerit pater eius.

2   (1) Ratio {autem} partium ⟨⟨...⟩⟩, et **primo domus prime**[γ] quia domus prima super vitam significat. (2) Accipitur {autem} pars a **longitudine seu distantia**[β] que fuerit inter duos superiores planetas eo quod ipsi sunt **radix omnis,**[γ] namque alius planeta **presul**[γ] **existens**[γ] super vitam, **virtutem seu fortitudinem** suam alteri dabit illorum. (3) {Iterum} **est pars ascendentis**[γ] super corporis fortitudinem significans, et domus {etiam} prima super hoc

---

[1]Capitulum nonum] M; L in margin.   [2]animi] L; M om.   [3]totum] L; M < sunt.   [4]coniunctio] L; M commixtio.   [5]quod quocumque] L; M quoque.

LIBER CAUSARUM SEU RATIONUM 561

§9

1 (1) Ninth chapter. PTOLEMY **asserts**[γ,1] that the lot of the Moon **nevertheless**[γ,2] is true, because he seeks a degree which is in the same proportion to *the place of* the Moon, which is close the Earth, as the *general* proportion of the degree of the ascendant to the Sun, and this is the part [lot] of the Moon; therefore, he said that it [the lot of the Moon] is taken by day and by night from the Moon. (2) {But} as for those who say also that the part [i.e., lot] of the Sun is the one which is the **part of the hidden things or hidden soul**,[β,3] **this is completely for its confirmation or corroboration**,[β,4] **because it is**[γ,5] the lot of the Moon according to PTOLEMY; ⟨⟨and he laughs at all the other lots⟩⟩; yet because I saw the other lots in the **BOOKS**[γ,6] **BY** DORONIUS, therefore I have mentioned them. (3) {So,} the lot of Saturn indicates anything whose signification is in accordance with its nature, and the same applies to any of the others [the other planets]. (4) {But} **the conjunction with Mercury is in the other lot**,[γ,7] because its nature is to be involved in **intellectual activity, and wisdom and sciences**[β,8] and not with worldly affairs. (5) {But} Jupiter indicates riches, according to what has been mentioned, therefore certain people said that, given that the houses of Mercury are in opposition to the houses of Jupiter, which indicates money, hence there are no riches to most SCHOLARS. (6) This **statement**,[γ,9] which is close to the truth, is that for whatever sign is rising in the east at the time of birth, the native will always be of the nature of the lord of the sign, even if he is not from a family suited **for such a status**,[γ,10] *for example, ruling*. (7) An example of this is that of a man who is a **slave**;[γ,11] he begets a son whose sign is Leo [i.e., the planetary house of the Sun]; {then,} even though the Sun is in a bad place, {nevertheless} the native will have a lordly nature and **he will own or have slaves**.[β,12] (8) Likewise, if Mercury is the lord of the sign ⟨⟨of the ascendant⟩⟩, even though there is no wise person in his family and {also} Mercury is in a bad place, **the native will be wise**[γ,13] in **wordly statements**;[γ,14] {but} if it is in a good place, he will be wise {even} though his father was not wise.

2 (1) {But} the reason for the lots ⟨⟨of the houses stems from the reason of the houses⟩⟩, **and in the first place that of the first house**,[γ,1] because the first house indicates life. (2) This part [i.e., lot], {however,} is taken from the **longitude or distance**[β,2] which is between the two superior planets [Saturn and Jupiter], because they are **the root of everything**,[γ,3] because any other planet that **is**[γ,4] the **ruler**[γ,5] of life will give its **power or strength**[β,6] to one of them [Saturn and Jupiter]. (3) {In addition,} **the part** [lot] **of the ascendant**[γ,7] indicates the strength of the body, and the first house indicates

562 PART THREE

significat. (4) Extraxerunt {autem} illam a **longitudinem**ʸ que est inter duas partes, que sunt luminarium, eo quod ipsa super corpora significant, ut dictum est totum eius latus dexterum Solis est et sinistrum Lune.¹ (5) Sortem {autem} scientie acceperunt a **longitudinem**ʸ que inter Mercurium fuerit et Martem, eo quod Mercurius super **intellectum**ʸ significat² et Mars super accelerationem. (6) Consimiliter {igitur} modo se habet partes relique, unde non oportet eas rememorare.

3 (1) Partem itaque regni extraxerunt Persarum sapientes, **et secundum ipsa est**ʸ numerus dierum regum, sed Ptolomeus non consentit eis; due {vero} **sortes seculi seu revolutionis annorum mundi,**ᵝ que exeunt in domibus unius planete rationes quidem earum note sunt per viam numeri, (2) *quam utique*³ iam commemoravi, distantia namque domus planete cuiuslibet a domo Lune est sicut distantia alterius domus sue a domo Solis; non est {autem} locus a quo habet proportio equalis est semper nisi a .15. gradus utriusque domus luminarum. (3) Nam si fuerit planeta in principio Virginis, in quinque gradibus primis, exibit altera sors in quinque gradibus postremis signi Geminorum, oportet {igitur} a medio domorum distantiam esse .20 gradus, et consimiliter in omnibus. (4) Quod {autem} ait Enoch super sorte pluvie qualibet die, **verificatum est,**ʸ ratio {vero} huius est quia natura signi est tanquam natura dominus eius.

§10

1 (1) Capitulum .10.⁴ Dicit noster magister Abraham quod omnes Antiquorum et Sapientes moderni,ʸ omnes hii in aspectibus **erraverunt**.ʸ (2) Et nos quidem invenimus, in aspectibus qui sunt Enoch sive Hermetis,ᵝ **probationes bonas perfectas**ᵝ super illorum destructione; similiter et super equationibus domorum duodecim, ita quod ipse invenit quandoque in quinto **climate**ʸ domum unam .60. graduum et aliam .20.; secundum meam {autem} opinionem Enoch non dicit ita. (3) {Item} inventus est in
71vb **Libro quadripartiti**ʸ quod ait | Ptolomeus si fuerit stella in principio domus decime dandum est aspectui eius quarto .90. gradus, et trino .120.

---

¹ut dictum est totum eius latus dexterum Solis est et sinistrum Lune] M; L in margin.
²Sortem autem scientie acceperunt a longitudinem que inter Mercurium fuerit et Martem eo quod Mercurius super intellectum significat] M; L in margin. ³utique] L; M utique quidem.
⁴Capitulum .10.] M; L in margin.

that {too}. (4) {But} they calculated it from the **longitude**γ,8 [distance] between the two parts [lots], which are ⟨the lots⟩ of the luminaries, because they indicate the body, ⟨since⟩ as already said the whole of its [the body's] right side belongs to the Sun and the left to the Moon. (5) {But} they took the lot of science from the **longitude**γ,9 [distance] between Mercury and Mars, because Mercury indicates the **intellect**γ,10 and Mars ⟨indicates⟩ speeding up. (6) Similarly, {then,} with the rest of the parts [lots], hence there is no need to mention them.

3 (1) Thus the part [lot] of royal power was calculated by the PERSIAN SCHOLARS, **and in accordance with it is**γ,1 the number of days of kings, but PTOLEMY does not agree with them; {but} the two lots **of the age or the revolution of the years of the world,**β,2 which come out in the houses of a single planet, their reasons are known by the method of the number, (2) *which indeed* I have already mentioned, for the distance of the house of any planet from the house of the Moon is as the distance of its other house from the house of the Sun; {but} there is no place where the proportion is always equal, except at 15° of both houses of the luminaries. (3) For if a planet is in the beginning of Virgo, in the first five degrees, then the other lot will come out at the last five degrees of the sign Gemini, {therefore} the distance from the middle of the houses ⟨of the luminaries⟩ must be 20 degrees, and similarly with all. (4) {But} what ENOCH said about the lot of rain on any day **has been verified,**γ,3 and its reason {indeed} is that the nature of the sign is as the nature of its lord.

§10

1 (1) Tenth chapter. ABRAHAM, OUR MASTER,[1] says that all of the ANCIENTS and the **MODERN SCHOLARS,**γ,2 all of them **were mistaken**γ,3 about the aspects. (2) We have found, regarding the aspects which are ⟨designated⟩ by ENOCH OR HERMES,β,4 **good and perfect proofs**β,5 about their refutation; and likewise regarding the **equations**γ,6 [corrections] of the twelve houses, to such an extent that sometimes he found in the fifth **climate**γ,7 one house of 60 degrees and another house of 20 ⟨degrees⟩; {but} in my opinion ENOCH does not speak in this way. (3) {Likewise,} it has been found in the **BOOK OF FOUR PARTS,**γ,8 too, that PTOLEMY says that if a planet is at the beginning of the tenth house, one must give 90 degrees to its aspect of

de gradibus **directi circulo**;ʸ si {vero} fuerit stella in gradu ascendente, est eius aspectus trinus .120. gradus de **ascensionibus terre**. (4) Et hic est error magnus, nam si fuerit latitudo terre ⟨⟨...⟩⟩ .48. gradus, et fuerit gradus ascendens **primus**ʸ Capricorni, tunc erit aspectus trinus secundum hanc viam in principio Cancri, non est {autem} dubium secundum sententiam omnium SAPIENTIUM quod ibi sit aspectus oppositus. (5) Ad hec in aspectibus commemoravit MESSEHALLAH res que ita non sunt ut dicit; veritas {autem} est quam tibi dicam, quia conveniens est aspectus esse[1] secundum viam distinguendi domos, et ita dicit IACOB ALKINDI, sed non preparavit viam *rectam* extrahendi illos.

2 (1) **Apponas** {ergo} **cor tuum**ᶿ et scito quod **equationes**ʸ domorum secundum duas sunt vias. (2) Una est secundum gradus circuli signorum, qui sunt equales sive signum ascendens fuerit in **initium**ʸ Arietis sive medium, sive caput Cancri sive medium eius, in **climate**ʸ quocumque. (3) Et quidem hoc generale est quod cuilibet domui dabis .30. gradus, et incipias ab ascendente. (4) Secunda {vero} via est ut sint domus **equate**ʸ secundum terre latitudinem et **ascensiones**ʸ signorum super eam. (5) Si enim[2] fuerit signum ascendens **primus**ʸ Cancri in quinto **climate**,ʸ semper erit in medio celi minus medietate Piscium, que est domus nona, contrarium {vero} huius accidit si fuerit signum ascendens caput Capricorni; et erit ita propter hoc quod hec duo *signa* sunt finis septentrionis et meridiei. (6) Et omnes SAPIENTES ASTROLOGIEʸ hoc concedunt, ac {etiam} SAPIENTES INSTRUMENTORUM ET ASTROLABIIᵝ *sententiam habentes*, probationes et enim[3] **sufficientes** super hoc sunt. (7) Omnium {igitur} SAPIENTIUM ASTROLOGIEʸ concordat sententia[4] super quatuor **angulis**,ʸ qui sunt principium domus prime, et domus quarte, et domus septime, atque domus decime; dissensio {autem} est in **equatione**ʸ quatuor domorum que sunt secunda, et tertia, et quinta, et sexta; semper namque quatuor domus hiis opposite, *illarumque* super[5] terram, **equales**ʸ sunt eis in omnibus **equationibus**.ʸ

3 (1) Consimiliter quoque concors est omnium sententia[6] super directionibus quod similiter sunt secundum duas vias. (2) Una via quidem est directio secundum **gradus** circuli signorum **equales**,ʸ alia {vero} mutatur,

---

[1]quam tibi dicam quia conveniens est aspectus esse] M; L in margin. [2]enim] L; M tamen. [3]et enim] L; M et tamen; [4]sententia] M; L scientia. [5]super] M; L supra. [6]sententia] M; L scientia.

LIBER CAUSARUM SEU RATIONUM 565

quartile, and 120 of the degrees of the **direct circle**[γ,9] [i.e., sphaera recta] to ⟨its aspect of⟩ trine; {but} if the planet is at the degree of the ascendant, its aspect of trine is 120 degrees according to the **ascensions of the country**.[γ,10] (4) This is a great mistake, because if the latitude of the country ⟨⟨of the native⟩⟩ is 48 degrees, and the degree of the ascendant is the **first**[γ,11] of Capricorn, then the aspect of trine, according to this method, will be at the beginning of Cancer; {but} in the opinion of all the SCHOLARS there is no doubt that in that place is the aspect of opposition. (5) MĀSHĀ'ALLĀH, too, mentioned things about aspects which are not as he asserted; {but} the truth is what I shall tell you, because it is fitting that the aspects be according to the method of dividing the houses; YA'QUB AL-KINDĪ speaks in this way, but he did not provide a *correct* method to calculate them.

2 (1) {So,} **pay attention**[β,1] [lit. put your heart] and know that the **equations**[γ,2] [i.e., corrections] of the houses are according to two methods. (2) One is according to the degrees of the circle of the signs [the zodiac], which are equal whether the ascendant sign is at the **beginning**[γ,3] of Aries or ⟨its⟩ middle, or the head of Cancer, or its middle, in any **climate**.[γ] (3) It is a general principle that you will assign 30 degrees to any house, and begin from the ascendant ⟨degree⟩. (4) {But} the second method is that the houses should be **equated**[γ,4] [i.e., corrected] according to the latitude of the country and the **ascensions**[γ] of the signs there. (5) For if the ascendant sign is the **first**[γ,5] ⟨degree⟩ of Cancer in the in the fifth **climate**,[γ] less than the middle of Pisces, which is the ninth house, will always be at midheaven, {but} the opposite of this happens if the ascendant sign is the head of Capricorn; and this will be so because these two *signs* are the extremity of the north and of the south [the tropics]. (6) All the SCHOLARS OF ASTROLOGY[γ,6] acknowledge this, and {also} the SCHOLARS OF THE INSTRUMENTS AND OF THE ASTROLABE[β,7] *having an opinion* ⟨*on this*⟩, and because there are also **sufficient**[8] proofs of this. (7) {So,} the opinion of all the SCHOLARS OF ASTROLOGY[γ] agrees about the four **angles**[γ,9] [i.e., cardines], which are the beginning of the first, fourth, seventh, and tenth house; {but} the disagreement is about the **equation**[γ] of the four houses, which are second, third, fifth, and sixth; because the four houses that are opposed to them, and are above *their* Earth [i.e., horizon], **are** always **equal**[γ,10] in all the **equations**.[γ]

3 (1) Likewise, the opinion of all agrees regarding the directions that in a similar manner are ⟨reckoned⟩ by two methods. (2) One method is the direction according to the **equal degrees**[γ,1] of the circle of the signs, {but} the other ⟨method⟩ varies [i.e., follows several different procedures], for if

72ra quia si fuerit gradus que dirigere volueris, **aut alterum | luminarium**ʸ ibi existentum, in principio domus decime aut quarte, dirigendus est secundum¹ gradus **circuli directi**.ʸ (3) Si {vero} gradus quem dirigere volueris fuerit in ascendente, diriges ipsum secundum **ascensiones terre**.ʸ (4) Similiter quoque, si dirigere volueris gradum occidentem, semper diriges ipsum per oppositum gradus sui, qui est ascendens. (5) {Quod} si non fuerit gradus quem dirigere volueris in aliquo **angulorum**ʸ dictorum, considera distantiam eius a linea medii celi, si quidem erit gradus in quarta que est inter lineam medii celi et gradum ascendentem. (6) Non oportet {autem} directiones has *nunc* rememorari, iam enim commemoravit² eas MAGISTER ABRAHAM VOCATUS PRINCEPS IN LIBRO SUO.

4 (1) Aspectus itaque conveniens est similiter esse secundum duas vias. (2) Una quidem via secundum **gradus** circuli signorum **equales**,ʸ .60. *inquam* gradus pro aspectu sextili ante se et similiter post se, ⟨⟨...⟩⟩ pro trino {autem} aspectu .120. ante se et similiter post se. (3) Et iam declaravit PRINCEPS predictus viam ad extrahendum gradum stelle si ei fuerit latitudo. (4) Conveniens {autem} est volenti dirigere **aut³ principium domus aut aspectum stelle**,ʸ quod incipiat a domo, que divisa est secundum **gradus equales**,ʸ et dandum est cuilibet gradum annum unum; et erunt {etiam} aspectus eius secundum **gradus equales**.ʸ (5) Alia {vero} via est cum **equatur**ʸ aspectus secundum **equationem**ʸ domorum, si enim fuerit stella in gradu ascendente, erit aspectus eius quartus in principio linee medii celi et similiter in linea abyssi, que sunt principia domus decime et domus quarte, **equate**ʸ quidem secundum **ascensiones**ʸ signorum. (6) Universaliter {ergo}: si fuerit in principio **anguli**,ʸ aspectus eius in aliis **angulis**ʸ erit aspectus quartus et oppositus. (7) Et si fuerit in gradu ascendente, erit aspectus eius sextilis in principio domus tercie et ipse quidem est aspectus sinister, dexter {vero} in principio domus undecime; aspectus {autem} eius trinus sinister in principio domus quinte, dexter {vero} in principio domus none. (8) Universaliter {autem}⁴ oportet aspectum eius trinum dextrum oppositum esse aspectui sextili sinistro, ac *per hoc* aspectum trinum sinistrum oppositum est aspectui sextili dextro; si {autem} fuerit stella in medio domus **conve-**
72rb **niet vel oportet**^β aspectum eius esse in medio | **alterius**ʸ domus **equate**ʸ per **ascensiones**.ʸ

---

¹secundum] corrected; LM secundus. ²commemoravit] M; L commemoraverunt. ³aut] M; L autem. ⁴autem] L; M igitur.

the degree you wish to direct, **or ⟨the degree⟩ of each of the luminaries**ʸ,² that happens to be there, is at the beginning of the tenth house or the fourth, one must direct according to degrees of the **direct circle**ʸ,³ [sphaera recta]. (3) {But} if the degree you would wish to direct is at the ascendant, you will direct it according to the **ascensions of the country**.ʸ (4) In like manner, if you wish to direct the descendant degree, you will always direct it by the opposite of its degree, which is the ascendant. (5) {But} if the degree you would wish to direct is in none of the above-mentioned **angles**,ʸ determine its distance from midheaven, whether the degree is in the quadrant that is between the line of midheaven and the degree of the ascendant. (6) {But} there is no need to mention these directions *now*, because MASTER ABRAHAM, CALLED THE PRINCE,⁴ already mentioned them IN HIS BOOK.

4 (1) Thus it is fitting that the aspects be according to two methods. (2) One method is according to **equal degrees**ʸ,¹ of the circle of the signs, 60 degrees, *I say*, for the aspect of sextile before it or behind it, ⟨⟨90 degrees for the aspect of quartile before it or behind it,⟩⟩ {but} 120 degrees for the aspect of trine before it or behind it. (3) The aforementioned PRINCE already revealed a method for calculating the degree of a star, if it has latitude. (4) {But} it is fitting for one who wants to direct either **the beginning of a house or the aspect of a planet**,ʸ,² that he should begin from the house, which is divided according to **equal degrees**,ʸ and he should assign a year to each degree; {also} its aspects will be in **equal degrees**.ʸ (5) But the other method is when the aspect is **equated**ʸ,³ [i.e., corrected] according to the **equation**ʸ,⁴ of the houses, for if the star is in the degree of the ascendant, its aspect of quartile will be at the beginning of the line of midheaven and at the line of the abyss [the lower midheaven], which are the beginnings of the tenth and the fourth houses, **equated**ʸ [i.e., corrected] according to the **ascensions**ʸ of the signs. (6) {So,} this is the general rule: if it is at the beginning of an **angle**,ʸ,⁵ its aspect in the other **angles**ʸ will be the aspect of quartile and opposition. (7) And if it is in the ascendant degree, its aspect of sextile will be at the beginning of the third house, {but} the right ⟨aspect of sextile⟩ at the beginning of the eleventh house; {but} its left aspect of trine ⟨will be⟩ at the beginning of the fifth house, {but} the right ⟨aspect of trine⟩ at the beginning of the ninth house. (8) In general, {however,} its right aspect of trine must be opposite the left aspect of sextile, and *by this ⟨method⟩* its left aspect of trine opposite to the right aspect of sextile; {but} if the planet is in the middle of the house, **it is appropriate or necessary that**ᵝ,⁶ its aspect be in the middle of the **other house**,ʸ,⁷ **equated**ʸ [i.e., corrected] by the **ascensions**.ʸ

5 (1) Tradam {igitur} tibi viam extrahendi quatuor domorum **equationes**.ʸ (2) Considera quot¹ sunt **gradus equales**ʸ inter gradum ascendentem et **abyssi lineam seu angulum terre**;ᵝ et sume tertiam eorum, addasque super gradum ascendentem in **gradibus equalibus seu rectis**.ᵝ (3) Et quare in TABULA REGIONIS **horas tortas seu inequales**ᵝ que scripte sunt **contra gradum ascendentem sive in eius directo**ᵝ ubi numerus ille invenietur. (4) Duplica² {ergo} horas cum suis partibus et adde³ eas super **ascensiones**ʸ ⟨⟨…⟩⟩ que sunt **in directo**ʸ gradus ascendentis. (5) Et quare **aggregatum seu collectum**,ᵝ si ipsum quidem inveniatur **in directo**ʸ gradus in quo invenitur⁴ ille numerus, {quia} ibi⁵ principium est domus secunde. (6) {Quod} si **collectum seu aggregatum**ᵝ fuerit plurimi gradus quam gradus ubi numerus **exit seu invenitur**,ᵝ minue duos gradus aut unum, et scito quot⁶ sunt **hore torte seu inequales**ᵝ que sunt **in directo**ʸ gradus ubi invenitur ⟨⟨…⟩⟩ post aminutionem. (7) Et sic facias quousque gradum invenias, ac {etiam} partem eius, {quia}⁷ est principium domus. (8) Si {vero} collectum illud⁸ minus fuerit fac⁹ contrarium, addas {namque} gradum super gradum ubi¹⁰ numerus invenitur, et fac **secundum quod rectum fuerit**.ʸ (9) Oportet enim **longitudinem**,ʸ que est a principio domus secunde ad principium linee abyssi, in gradibus **recti circuli**ʸ esse quatuor **horarum tortarum**¹¹ **seu inequalium**ᵝ **in directo**ʸ gradus¹² qui principium secunde domus est, et *eius quidem oppositum* principium est¹³ domus octave. (10) Similiter quoque extrahes principium domus tertie, addendo duas tertias predictas super gradum ascendentem, et addes et minues donec invenias gradum et partem. (11) Et est {etiam} conveniens **longitudinem seu distantiam**ᵝ principii domus tertie secundum **ascensiones**ʸ signorum *IN TABULA TERRE VEL REGIONIS*,ᵝ a gradu ascendente, esse quatuor **horarum tortarum seu inequalium**,ᵝ que sunt contra gradum qui principium domus est, et {eius oppositum} principium est domus none. (12) Consimiliter, quoque conveniet longitudinem, que est a principio domus huius usque ad lineam abyssi, esse duarum **horarum inequalium seu tortarum**,ᵝ secundum gradus **recti circuli**.ʸ (13) Rursus ita facies ad extrahendum | principium domus quinte, quia tu quares **gradus equales**,ʸ qui sunt inter abyssi lineam et gradum occidentem, et divides ipsos in tres partes, addasque tertiam super gradum linee

---

¹quot] M; L quod.   ²Duplica] L; M multiplica.   ³adde] corrected; L addes; M addas. ⁴invenitur] L; M invenietur.   ⁵ibi] L; M ibi procul dubia.   ⁶quot] M; L quod.   ⁷quia L; M quia hoc.   ⁸illud] L; M om.   ⁹fac] M; L facias.   ¹⁰ubi] L; M ubi vel in quo.   ¹¹tortarum] M; L om.   ¹²in directo gradus] M; L correspondentium gradui.   ¹³est] L; M om.

5 (1) {So,} I will give you a method for calculating the **equations**ʸ [i.e., corrections] of the four houses. (2) Determine how many **equal degrees**ʸ there are between the ascendant degree and the **line of the abyss or angle of the Earth**^(β,1) [i.e., lower midheaven]; take one third of them and add it to the ascendant degree in **equal or straight degrees.**^(β,2) (3) ⟨Then,⟩ in the TABLE OF THE COUNTRY, search for **the crooked or unequal hours**^(β,3) [seasonal hours] which are written **against or opposite the ascendant degree**^(β,4) where this number will be found. (4) {Therefore,} double the hours with their minutes and add them to the **ascensions**ʸ ⟨⟨of the signs⟩⟩ **opposite**^(ʸ,5) the degree of the ascendant. (5) Then search whether the **total or result**^(β,6) is found in the degree **opposite**ʸ the one in which this number is found, {because} the beginning of the second house is there. (6) {But} if **the result or total**^β is more degrees than the degree where the number comes out or is found,^(β,7) subtract two degrees or one, and ascertain how many **crooked or unequal hours**^β are **opposite**ʸ the degree where is found ⟨⟨the number⟩⟩ after the subtraction. (7) Proceed in this way until you find the degree, and {also} its minute, {because} ⟨this⟩ is the beginning of the house. (8) {But} if this result is less ⟨than the degree obtained by the calculation⟩ do the opposite, add {certainly} a degree to the degree where the number was found and proceed **according to what is right.**^(ʸ,8) (9) For the **longitude**^(ʸ,9) [i.e., distance], which is from the beginning of the second house to the beginning of the line of the abyss [i.e., the lower midheaven] in degrees of the **upright circle**^(ʸ,10) [at sphaera recta] must be four **crooked or unequal hours**^β **opposite**ʸ the degree which is the beginning of the second house, and *its opposite* is the beginning of the eighth house. (10) In a similar manner you will also calculate the beginning of the third house, adding the aforementioned two-thirds to the ascendant degree, and you will add or subtract until you find the degree and the minute. (11) It is {also} appropriate that the **longitude or distance**^(β,11) of the beginning of the third house, according to the **ascensions**ʸ of the signs *IN THE TABLE OF THE COUNTRY OR REGION*,^(β,12) from the ascendant degree, be four **crooked or unequal hours**,^β which come out against the degree which is the beginning of the house, and {its opposite} is the beginning of the ninth house. (12) Similarly, also the distance, which is from the beginning of this house to the line of abyss [lower midheaven], should be two **unequal or crooked hours**^(β,13) according to the degrees of the **upright circle**ʸ [at sphaera recta]. (13) In addition, you will proceed in the same manner to calculate the beginning of the fifth house, for you will search for the **equal degrees**ʸ which are between the line of the abyss and the descendant degree and divide them into three parts, and add the third part to the degree of the line of

abyssi; et scito gradum ubi numerus illi **invenietur seu exibit;**[β] accipiasque **horas tortas seu inequales,**[β] ac eorum minuta, que sunt **in directo**[γ] gradus, et adde eas super gradus quos invenies in TABULA RECTI CIRCULI[γ] **in directo linee abyssi seu contra lineam abyssi.**[β] (14) Et tunc, si **exeat seu inveniatur**[β] numerus in gradu primo, ibi est principium domus quintus; si {vero} non, addas modicum vel minuas quousque invenies gradum et partem eius. (15) Oportet {autem} principium domus quinte a gradu occidente distare quatuor **horis tortis seu inequalibus,**[β] que quidem invente sunt **in directo**[γ] gradus qui principium est domus secundum **ascensiones**[γ] TABULE REGIONIS. (16) {Item} addas illas duas tertias que dicte sunt super lineam abyssi **ad extrahendum seu inveniendum**[β] *gradum qui* principium est domus sexte; convenietque distantiam eius esse ⟨⟨...⟩⟩ secundum **ascensiones**[γ] signorum in TABULA REGIONIS **duarum**[γ] **horarum inequalium seu**[1] **tortarum**[β] que sunt **in directo**[γ] gradus que principium domus ⟨⟨...⟩⟩ est. (17) ⟨⟨...⟩⟩; iterum[2] convenit {etiam} ut accipias **ascensiones**[γ] que sunt **in directo**[γ] gradus usque *ascendens*.[γ] (18) Generalis {autem} hec est regula quod **ascensiones**,[γ] si accipiende fuerunt in medietate circuli ascendente, semper accipientur secundum quod fuerunt; si {vero} in medietate descendente, accipientur[3] ab earum oppositum; ⟨⟨...⟩⟩. (19) Et hoc quidem commemoravimus in TRACTATU ASTROLABII;[γ] {unde} si instrumentum illud perfectum habueris non erit tibi opus hoc labore, secundum quod ibidem explanavimus.[4] (20) Amplius in LIBRO NATIVITATUM **super sermonibus revolutionum**[γ] aliam viam tibi tradam,[5] que quidem similis erit huic iam dicte.

6   (1) Aspectus {igitur} sic facies, non est {autem} opus facere nisi tres tamen, *quia oppositi gradus oppositorum signorum denotare potes aspectus dextros,* [6] et hos sinistros, *ut pote* aspectum sextilem et quartum ac trinum. (2) Considerabis[7] {itaque} quot[8] **graduum equalium**[γ] distantia | planete sit a principio domus,[9] et quot[10] fuerunt multiplica per triginta; et si fuerunt ultra[11] gradus minuta excrescentia, fueruntque plura quam[12] .30., *pro*[13] *illis* adde gradus, si {vero} minus **diminute ea**.[γ] (3) Aggregatum {ergo}

---

[1]inequalium seu] L; M om.   [2]Iterum] L; M item.   [3]secundum quod fuerunt, si vero in medietate descendente accipientur] M; L in margin.   [4]explanavimus] L; M explanavi.   [5]tradam] M; L tradamus.   [6]quia oppositi gradus oppositorum signorum denotare potes aspectus dextros] M; L om.   [7]Considerabis] L; M considera.   [8]quot] corrected; L quod; M quod igitur.   [9]domus] L; M domus sic enim se habent omnes gradus domus equaliter ad .30. scilicet gradus planete in domo illa ad gradus quoslibet cuius domus multi ⟨...⟩ melius sit sicut se habent omnis equaliter ad gradus planete sicut se habent .30. ad quot fuerit. This digression does not occur in the Hebrew text.   [10]quot] M; L quod.   [11]ultra] L; M om.   [12]quam] M; L quod.   [13]pro] M; L per.

the abyss; ascertain the degree where this number **will be found or come out**;β,14 and take the **crooked or unequal hours,**β and their minutes, which are **opposite**γ the degree, and add them to the degrees you will find in the **TABLE OF THE UPRIGHT CIRCLE**γ,15 [i.e., table of sphaera recta] **opposite the line of the abyss or against the line of the abyss.**β,16 (14) And then, if the number **comes out or is found**β in the first degree, the beginning of the fifth house in that place is; {but} if not, add or subtract a little till you find the degree and minute. (15) {But} the distance between the beginning of the fifth house from the descendant degree must be four **crooked or unequal hours,**β which are found **opposite**γ the degree that is the beginning of the ⟨fifth⟩ house, according to the **ascensions**γ of the TABLE OF THE REGION. (16) {Likewise,} add the aforementioned two-thirds to the line of the abyss [i.e., lower midheaven] **to calculate or find**β,17 *the degree that is* the beginning of the sixth house; its distance ⟨⟨in degrees of the circle of rightness from the line of abyss⟩⟩ according to the **ascensions**γ of the signs in the TABLE OF THE COUNTRY should be **two**γ,18 **unequal or crooked hours,**β,19 which are **opposite**γ the degree ⟨⟨of the beginning⟩⟩ of the sixth house. (17) ⟨⟨Likewise, it is appropriate that its distance, according to the ascensions of the signs on the table of the country, be two crooked hours, which are opposite the degree of the beginning of the sixth house⟩⟩; it is {also} appropriate for you to take the **ascensions**γ that are **opposite**γ the degree until the *ascendant.*γ,20 (18) {But} the general rule is that the **ascensions,**γ if they were taken in the ascending half of the circle, will always be taken as they were; {but} if in the descending half of the circle, they will be taken from their opposite; ⟨⟨in like manner, the crooked hours should always be taken from the degrees that are above the Earth⟩⟩. (19) I have already mentioned this in the **TREATISE OF THE ASTROLABE;**γ,21 {therefore,} if you have that complete instrument, there is no need to go to such great pains, as I have explained there. (20) Moreover, in the BOOK OF NATIVITIES I will give you another method **about the matters of the revolutions,**γ,22 which will be similar to the one already mentioned.

6 (1) {Accordingly,} you will make the aspects in the indicated manner, {but} it is necessary to make only three, *because you can specify the right aspects opposite the facing signs,* and these are the left ⟨aspects⟩, *such as* the aspect of sextile, quartile, and trine. (2) {Therefore,} you will observe how many **equal degrees**γ is the distance of the planet from the beginning of the house, and multiply as many as they are by 30; and if there is an excess of minutes beyond the degree, and they are more than 30, add one degree *instead of them,* {but} if less **subtract them.**γ,1 (3) {Therefore,}

divide per numerum graduum domus equalium qui fuerunt a principio illius domus **equate**ʸ usque ad principium sequentis, *inter principia duarum domorum equatarum illius videlicet*[1] *et sequentis*, quodque in numero exivit[2] serva. (4) {Deinde} accipias {etiam} numerum graduum domus in qua **cadit vel est**^(β,3) aspectus eius,[4] quecumque volueris,[5] et scito quantus est numerus graduum inter principium domus illius **equate**ʸ et principium domus **equate**ʸ que est post ipsam. (5) Et multiplica numerum hunc per numerum servatum, aggregatumque divide per .30.; quod {ergo} exivit in numero, illud adde super principium domus in qua cadit aspectus. (6) Et tunc invenies gradus illius[6] aspectus propinquus; addas {ergo} vel minimas donec[7] illum **equaris**.ʸ

7 (1) Facies {autem} sic:[8] considera si fuerit planeta inter lineam medii celi et gradum ascendentem, et scito quanta est eius distantia a linea medii celi, minues {enim} gradus qui invenientur in **TABULA RECTI CIRCULI**ʸ **in directo lineae medii celi a gradibus inventis in eadem tabula in directo gradus in quo est planeta;**ʸ et quod inventum fuerit inter hos duos vocabitur[9] **distantia sive longitudo**,^β (2) quam dividas per horas tortas, que sunt **in directo**ʸ gradus planete in **TABULA REGIONIS**, et quod exierunt sunt hore; si {vero} remanserit aliquod non divisum, illud multiplica per .60., et quod exiverit iterum multiplica per .60. secunda vite. (3) Et reduc {etiam} gradus hore torte in minuta ⟨⟨...⟩⟩, collectioque ex hiis minutis adiunge minuta *hore, si cum gradibus fuerint*, ac per ea divide numero priorem, et quod exiverit erunt **minuta hore torte seu partes de .60. minutis hore**,^β *scilicet inequalis*. (4) Addas {ergo} super has horas et partes earum, pro aspectu quidem sextili quatuor **horas integras seu perfectas**,^β pro aspectu {vero} quarto sex, et .8. pro aspectu trino. (5) Et si exiverit aspectus, *puta* sextilis, in 73ra eadem quarta in qua est planeta, quare gradum | que tibi dixi in quo quidem exivit[10]

Glossa:[11] *aut in propinquo secundum estimationem ut prius dictum est. Ait* TRANSLATOR.[12]

---

[1]videlicet] L; M sicilicet. [2]exivit] L; M exivitur. [3]cadit vel est] L; M adest. [4]eius] M; L om. [5]volueris] L; M volueris aspectum. [6]illius] L; M suo. [7]donec] L; M quousque. [8]Facies autem sic] L; M itaque sic facies. [9]vocabitur] L; M vocabitur quam vocat allibicius signatorem circuli directi. [10]exivit] L; M exibit. [11]glossa] L (above the line); M om. [12]aut in propinquo secundum estimationem ut prius dicuts est. Ait translator] L; M om.

divide the total by the number of equal degrees of the house that are from the beginning of this **equated**^γ,2 [i.e., corrected] house up to the following ⟨house⟩,—*between the beginnings of the two houses, namely, of this ⟨house⟩ and the following ⟨house⟩*,—and keep what resulted of the number. (4) {Next} take {also} the number of degrees of the house in which its aspect **lies or is**,^β,3 for any aspect you wish, and ascertain how great is the number of degrees between the beginning of the **equated**^γ [i.e., corrected] house and the beginning of the **equated**^γ [i.e., corrected] house that comes next. (5) And multiply this number by the number that you have kept, and divide the total ⟨number⟩ by 30; {therefore,} add the number that resulted to the beginning of the house where the aspect lies. (6) And then find the degree that is close to its aspect; {therefore,} add or subtract until you have **equated**^γ [i.e., corrected] it.

7 (1) {But} proceed as follows: observe whether the planet is between the line of midheaven and the ascendant degree, and ascertain how large is its distance from the line of midheaven, {because} you will subtract the degrees that were found in the **TABLE OF THE UPRIGHT CIRCLE**^γ,1 [i.e., table of sphaera recta] opposite the line of midheaven from the degrees found in this table **opposite the degree where the planet is**;^γ,2 and what has been found between these two will be called **distance or longitude**,^β,3 (2) which you divide by the crooked hours [i.e., seasonal hours] **opposite**^γ the planet's degree in the **TABLE OF THE COUNTRY**, and the result is the hours; {but} if something remains that is not divided [i.e., less than 60] multiply it by 60, and multiply the result by 60 again for the second time. (3) Convert {also} the degrees of the crooked hours into ⟨⟨equal⟩⟩ minutes, and add the sum of these minutes to the minutes *of the hour, if they are with degrees*, and then divide them by the first number, and the result will be **crooked minutes of the hour or parts of 60 minutes**^β,4, *that is, unequal* ⟨*minutes*⟩. (4) {Therefore,} add to these hours and its parts, four **whole or complete hours**^β,5 for the aspect of sextile, {but} six ⟨hours⟩ for the aspect of quartile, and eight ⟨hours⟩ for the trine. (5) {But} if the aspect, *for example* sextile, comes out in the same quadrant where the planet is, search for the degree where, as I have told you the aspect comes out,

Gloss: or close to it according to the aforementioned reckoning. THE TRANSLATOR *said.*

aspectus, et accipe **horam inequalem seu tortam**^{β} in TABULA REGIONIS, et considera, si fuerit **distantia seu longitudo**^{β} in **ascensionibus**^{γ} **circuli directi,**^{γ} a linea medii celi sicut¹ hore planete et insuper quatuor hore cum illis,

hoc est dictu, si eiusdem fuerint quantitates ita quod ibi² sit numerus.

tunc enim verus est numerus tuus, quia ibidem est aspectus. (6) Si {vero} non, addas³ unum gradum vel .2. aut minuas ⟨⟨...⟩⟩, namque forte statim non invenies ipsum. (7) Si {autem} exiverit aspectus in quarta que est inter gradum ascendentem et lineam abyssi, considera quot horarum conveniet esse distantiam a gradu ascendente.

8 (1) Exemplum {igitur} dabo tibi, ut si fuerit planeta distans⁴ a linea medii celi .1. hora et .17. **partibus hore**⁵ **seu minutis.**^{β} (2) Convenit {ergo} distantiam aspectus sextilis a linea medii celi esse quinque horarum ac .17. **partium seu minutorum hore;**^{β,6} si {vero} fuerit aspectus quartus, convenit esse distantiam eius a gradu ascendente, ⟨⟨...⟩⟩ unius hore ac .17. partium de horis *inquam* inventis **in directo**^{γ} gradus in TABULA REGIONIS; aspectus {autem} trini⁷ distantia a gradu ascendente .3. erit horarum ac .17. partium, secundum viam aspectus quarti iam dictam. (3) {Item} convenit gradum in quo est aspectus tertius distare a linea abyssi duabus horis et .43. **partibus hore seu minutis**^{β} in **ascensionibus**^{γ} **spere recte,**^{γ} sed accipiende sunt hore **in directo**^{γ} gradus in TABULA REGIONIS, semper enim inter **angulum**^{γ} et **angulum**^{γ} sex **hore torte** sunt **seu inequales.**^{β,8} (4) {Quod} si planeta cuius aspectus **equare**^{γ} volueris in quarta fuerit que est inter ascendens et lineam abyssi, scito quanta est planete distantia a gradu ascendente. (5) Et fac ita: minue gradus inventos in TABULA REGIONIS contra gradum ascendentem a gradibus inventis **contra gradum planete seu in directo eius,**^{β} et quod exivit seu pervenit^β divide per horas tortas inventas **in directo gradus planete seu contra planetam**^{β,9} in TABULA REGIONIS; et tunc invenies horas **distantie seu longitudinis;**^{β} horas {ergo} | has super **domos**^{γ} adde secundum viam quam in prima quarta addebas. (6) Et si aspectus in eadem quarta exi-

---

¹sicut] M; L sic. ²ibi] L; M idem. ³addas] L; M addas vel minuas. ⁴distans] L; M om. ⁵hore] L; M om. ⁶hore] L; M om. ⁷trini] M; L trinus. ⁸inequales] M; L equales. ⁹planetam] L; M tabulam.

and take the **unequal or crooked hour**^{β,6} in the TABLE OF THE COUNTRY, and observe whether the **distance or longitude**,^{β,7} in ascensions^γ of the **direct circle**^{γ} [at sphaera recta], is from the line of midheaven, like the hours of the planet, and, in addition, four hours with them,

this is to say, if its quantities were like the number in that place;

then your number is correct, because the aspect is in that place. (6) {But} if not, add or subtract one degree or two, ⟨⟨as much as you need⟩⟩, because you will not find it immediately. (7) If the aspect comes out in the quadrant between the degree of the ascendant and the line of the abyss, observe how many hours it is appropriate for the distance from the ascendant degree to be.

8 (1) {So,} I will give you an illustration, such as when the planet is one hour and 17 **parts of the hour or minutes**^{β,1} distant from the line of midheaven. (2) {Therefore,} t is fitting that the aspect of sextile be 5 hours and 17 **parts or minutes of the hour**^{β} distant from the line of midheaven; {but} if it is an aspect of quartile, it is fitting that its distance from the ascendant degree, ⟨⟨in degrees of the table of the country,⟩⟩ be one hour and 17 parts of the hour, *I say*, as found **opposite**^{γ} the degree in the TABLE OF THE COUNTRY; {but} the distance of the aspect of trine from the ascendant degree will be three hours and 17 parts ⟨of the hour⟩, according to the aforementioned method for the aspect of quartile. (3) {Likewise,} it is fitting that the distance of the degree in the aspect of trine is from the line of the abyss be two hours and 43 **parts of the hour or minutes**^{β} in **ascensions**^{γ} of the **upright sphere**^{γ} [sphaera recta], but the hours should be taken **opposite**^{γ} the degree in the TABLE OF THE COUNTRY, because there are always six **crooked or unequal hours**^{β,2} between one **angle**^{γ} and another **angle**.^{γ} (4) {But} if the planet whose aspects you would wish to **equate**^{γ,3} is in the quadrant between the ascendant and the line of the abyss [i.e., lower midheaven], ascertain the size of the planet's distance from the degree of the ascendant. (5) Proceed as follows: subtract the degrees found in the TABLE OF THE COUNTRY opposite the ascendant degree from the degrees found **against the degree or opposite of the planet**,^{β,4} and divide **what resulted or came out**^{β,5} by the crooked hours found **opposite the degree of the planet or against the planet**^{β,6} in the TABLE OF THE COUNTRY; then you will find the hours of the **distance or longitude**;^{β} {therefore,} add these hours to the **houses**^{γ,7} according to the method that you added for the first quadrant. (6) If the aspect came out in the same quadrant,

verit, sume in TABULA REGIONIS **ascensiones**ᵞ inventas **in directo**ᵞ gradus, et considera si fuerit **distantiam seu longitudinem**ᵝ in TABULA REGIONIS[1] a gradu ascendente eadem in[2] numero horarum distantie cum additione aspectus; {item} facies {etiam} hoc ipsum[3] cum horis que sunt **in directo**ᵞ gradus. (7) Si {vero} fuerit aspectus in quarta que est inter lineam abyssi et gradum occidentem, minue **ascensiones**ᵞ inventas in TABULA DIRECTI CIRCULIᵞ contra lineam abyssi de **ascensionibus**ᵞ inventis **in directo planete**,ᵞ et divide **residuum seu quod exiverit**ᵝ **contra gradum seu in directo eius.**ᵝ,[4] (8) Si {ergo} fuerunt hore sicut **longitudo seu distantia**ᵝ post **augmentum seu additionem**ᵝ aspectus, tunc erit ibidem aspectus secundum veritatem, si {vero} non, tunc adde ⟨⟨...⟩⟩ {etiam} minue *ut dictum est*, et invenies gradum aspectus confestim.[5] (9) Viam {igitur} commemoravi ad extrahendum aspectus si fuerit planeta aut alterum luminarium in medietate circuli ascendente; {verum} si fuerit in medietate circuli descendente **computa planetam ac si esset**ᵞ in opposito gradus sui, et fac secundum viam quam ostendi tibi, et tunc invenies aspectus. (10) Nec est differentia inter eos,[6] nisi quod hii sinistri exibunt erunt dextre, et qui dextre sinistri, eo quod gradum accepisti oppositum planete.

9 (1) Directiones {autem} **alias commemorate**,ᵞ que sunt .1000ᵒʳᵘᵐ. et .100ᵒʳᵘᵐ. ac .10ᵒʳᵘᵐ., hoc quidem est sententia SAPIENTIUM PERSARUM et INDORUM, sed PTOLOMEUS deridet eos. (2) **Praeterquam in directione**ᵞ vocata *alfardar*, hanc enim expertus est; adhuc ad directionem signi quolibet anno **in rebus scitis et expertis**,ᵞ omniumque ANTIQUORUM sententia huic concordat, et cum eis PTOLOMEUS. (3) Quod {autem} diximus, superiores duos mutari de triplicitate ad triplicitatem in .960. annis, hoc est secundum viam propinquitatis, nam quandoque plus est quandoque minus. (4) {Item,} quod dixi, eos coniungi .12. vicibus in .240. annis, **hoc quidem quandoque .13. quandoque .12.**,ᵞ et hoc utique contingit propter velocitatem motus duorum superiorum aut | propter eorum tarditatem; hoc {igitur} adhuc explanabo tibi in LIBRO SECULI SIVE REVOLUTIONUM MUNDI,ᵝ per adiutorium Dei seculorum.

---

[1]ascensiones inventas in directo gradus et considera si fuerit distantiam sue longitudienum in tabula regionis] M; L in margin.   [2]in] L; M cum.   [3]ipsum] L; M idem esse.   [4]eius] L; M eius planete scilicet.   [5]confestim] M; L om.   [6]est differentia inter eos] L; M diametro eas.

take the **ascensions**[γ,8] found **opposite**[γ] the degree in the TABLE OF THE COUNTRY, and observe in the TABLE OF THE COUNTRY whether the **distance or longitude**[β] from the ascendant degree is the same as the distance in number of hours with the addition of the aspect; {also} proceed {likewise} with the hours which are **opposite**[γ] the degree. (7) {But} if the aspect is in the quadrant between the line of the abyss [i.e., lower midheaven] and the descendant, subtract the **ascensions**[γ] found opposite the line of the abyss in the TABLE OF THE DIRECT CIRCLE[γ,9] [i.e., table of sphaera recta] from the **ascensions**[γ] **opposite the planet**,[γ,10] and then divide **the remainder or what resulted**[β,11] by the hours ⟨found in the table⟩ **against or opposite the degree**.[β] (8) {Therefore,} if the hours are like the **longitude or distance**[β] after the **increase or addition**[β,12] of the aspect, then the aspect will be truly in this place; {but} if not, add ⟨⟨a little⟩⟩ {also} subtract *as has been mentioned*, and then you will find the degree of the aspect immediately. (9) {So,} I have mentioned the method of calculating the aspects if the planet or one of the luminaries is in the ascending half of the circle [above the horizon]; {but} if it is in the descending half of the circle [below the horizon] **calculate the planet as if it were**[γ,13] the opposite of its degree, and proceed according to the method I have shown to you, and then you will find the aspects. (10) There is no difference between them, except that those that came out on the left will be right, and the right ones are left ones, because the degree that you took is opposite the planet.

9 (1) {But} the **other** directions **mentioned**,[γ,1] which are of thousands, hundreds and decades, this is the opinion of the SCHOLARS OF THE PERSIANS AND THE INDIANS, but PTOLEMY laughs at them. (2) Except for **the direction**[γ,2] called *al-fardār*, *because* this one has been verified experimentally; in addition, for the purpose of the direction of the sign in any year **in respect to things known and verified experimentally**,[γ,3] the statements of all the ANCIENTS agree about this, and PTOLEMY with them. (3) {But} as for what we have said, that the upper ⟨planets⟩ [Saturn and Jupiter] move from triplicity to triplicity in 960 years, this is by way of approximation, since sometimes ⟨this period⟩ is longer and sometimes shorter. (4) {Likewise,} as for what I said, that they conjoin 12 times in 240 years, **this is however sometimes 13 and sometimes 12**,[γ,4] and this certainly occurs because of the swiftness of the motion of the two superior ⟨planets⟩ or because of their slowness; {so,} I shall explain this further to you in the BOOK OF THE AGE OR THE REVOLUTIONS OF THE WORD,[β,5] with the assistance of the God of the Universe.

(1) *Dicit* TRANSLATOR: *advertendum quod etsi per documentum* ACTORIS HUIUS *in hac parte satis rationabiliter inveniri possit veritas in aspectibus equandis, et nihilominus vacillans additionis ac diminutionis per quam operandum esse docet, incertitudo regulari⟨s⟩ non est arti conveniens quale esse docet in hoc proposito.* (2) *Preterea, quod, ad habendam equationem aspectuum planete distantia ab angulo, per partes horarum gradus ipsius planete dividendum esse, dicit* ACTOR, *in hoc error est secundum quod notum est ac satis declaratum in glossa quadam super* INTRODUCTORIUM ABRAHE DUCIS, CAPITULO DE ASPECTIBUS. (3) *Quapropter ad huiusmodi defectus ad implendos erroresque vitandos et aspectus ipsos artificiosius equandos, ac regularius ibidem regulare, quoddam et artificiosum ac breve tradidimus documentum.*

Explicit LIBER RATIONUM et completus est, cuius translatio perfecta est a MAGISTRO HYNRICO DE MALINIS, DICTO BATE, in Urbe Veteri anno Domini .1292º. in octavis nativitatis Beate Marie Virginis.[1]

---

[1]Explicit *Liber rationum* et completus est, cuius translatio perfecta est a magistro Hynrico de Malinis, dicto Bate, in Urbe Veteri anno Domini .1292º. in octavis nativitatis Beate Marie Virginis] L; M Completus est hic liber, cuius translatio perfecta a magistro Hynrico de Malinis, dicto Bate, in Urbe Veteri anno domini .1292º. in octavis nativitatis Beate Marie virginis gloriose. Explicit Liber rationum Abrahe.

(1) THE TRANSLATOR *says: Attention should be directed to the fact that although it is possible to find a sufficient and reasonable truth for the equation* [*i.e., correction*] *of the aspects by means of the text by* THIS AUTHOR [*Ibn Ezra*] *in this part* [*i.e., the end of Te'amim I*], *nevertheless, the uncertainty of the rules about addition or subtraction that he* [*Ibn Ezra*] *teaches should be used does not correspond to what the art should be in this case, as he* [*Ibn Ezra*] *teaches.* (2) *Moreover, there is an error regarding what* THE AUTHOR [*Ibn Ezra*] *says,* ⟨*namely,*⟩ *that to equate* [*i.e., correct*] *the aspects of a planet by the distance from the angle, the degrees of the planet should be divided by the minutes of this planet, as has been noted and sufficiently explained in a certain gloss on the* INTRODUCTION BY ABRAHAM, THE PRINCE, IN THE CHAPTER ON THE ASPECTS [*the gloss that appears at the end of Iudicia*]. (3) *Therefore, to overcome defects of this kind, to avoid errors, to equate* [*correct*] *these aspects more skillfully, and more in accordance with the rules, we have transmitted a document that is skillful and brief* [*i.e. Bate's excursus after the gloss at the end of Iudicia*].

Here ends and is completed the BOOK OF REASONS, whose translation was finished by MASTER HENRY OF MALINES, CALLED BATE, in Orvieto, in the year of the Lord 1292, on the eighth day after the ⟨Feast of the⟩ Nativity of the Blessed Virgin Mary.

PART FOUR

NOTES TO *LIBER CAUSARUM SEU RATIONUM*

§ 1.1

[1]1: **The circle has 360 parts.** H: חלקו הגלגל לשלש מאות וששים מעלות = They divided the circle into 360 degrees.

[2]1: **So many fractions.** H: כל השברים = all the fractions.

[3]4: **Lunations.** H: לבנות = Moons.

[4]5: **So according to the division come out 30 degrees which correspond to each degree.** H: והנה עלה בחלק כל מזל שלשים מעלות = so 30 degrees came out in the portion of each sign.

[5]6: **First smaller parts.** H: חלקים ראשונים = first parts.

§ 1.2

[1]1: **In the girdle of the signs or of the ecliptic line.** H: קרובים לחשב אפודת הגלגל = close to the girdle of the vest of the circle. → See note on *Introductorius*, § 1.10:5, s.v., "in the girdle of the imagination of the circle of the signs".

[2]3: **At the end of the book, with God's help, I shall speak of to the secret of the change of the places and of the signs.** Surprisingly, this statement points to *Ṭeʿamim* II, § 8.7:1, 254–255, which begins as follows: "End of the book. I shall now reveal a secret to you." Finally, I shall disclose a secret advice to you. In *Ṭeʿamim* I, is not addressed at the "end of the book" but at § 2.12:1–15, 50–53. This suggests that the material related to the motion of the fixed stars was mixed up in the earliest renderings of the texts of *Ṭeʿamim* I and *Ṭeʿamim* II, prior to their crystallization in the second half of the thirteenth century, which is the date of the earliest extant manuscripts.

[3]3: **Longitude.** H: מרחק = distance.

[4]3: **Line of equality.** H: קו הצדק = line of justice.

[5]3: **Hermes.** H: חנוך = Enoch.

[6]3: **Book of Longitudes.** H: ספר הארך = Book of the longitude.

[7]5: **Are like the diverse likenesses of certain signs, actually of shapes according to diverse considerations.** H: הם כמו דמיונות להיותם סימנים שיודעו = are like images so that they can be recognizable signs.

[8]5: **Hastening or rushing.** H: שקד = almond/amygdala. → Here *Reshit ḥokhmah* reading is identical with that of *Epitome*, ed. Heller (1548), 10, Clv: "Est ibi Aquila Cadens ... quam Amigdalam Ptolomeus dicit." Bate's, of Hagin's, radical divergence from the Hebrew source text may be due to the fact that שקד, as a verb, means to be industrious, to persevere, to take pains, etc.

[9]5: **When he picks out a star from ⟨another⟩ star.** H: שיחבר כוכב אל כוכב = when he connects one star to another. → The Latin here is *eligens*, but the sense is *ligens* = tying together; therefore the meaning of this sentence is: "connecting a star to another star."

[10]5: **Sphere.** H: הגלגל = the circle (*or* the wheel).

[11]5: **And it [the sphere] is not a thing that has a natural place.** H: ואין בדבר תולדתו שיהיה לו מקום שיוחל ממנו = and there is nothing in its nature that requires it to have a beginning.

[12]5: **Certain and known.** H: ידוע = known.

[13]6: **Among the images which have been recorded by the Ancients.** H: על כן, נניח הדבר כפי הצורות שהזכירו הקדמונים = therefore let us leave the matter according to the shapes mentioned by the Ancients.

§1.3

[1]1: **Sphere.** H: גלגל = circle.

[2]1: **Orb.** H: גלגל = circle.

[3]2: **Planets.** H: משרתים = servants. → Meaning, planets. See note on *Introductorius*, §2:5, s.v., "planets".

[4]2: **In their elongations and approximations to the Earth.** H: בגבהותם ובשפלותם כנגד נקודת הארץ = in their heights (i.e., apogees) and lownesses (i.e., perigees) with respect to the point of the Earth.

[5]3: **The girdle of the signs or of the ecliptic line.** H: קרובות אל חשב אפודת הגלגל = close to the girdle of the vest of the circle. → See note on *Introductorius*, § 1.10:5, s.v., "in the girdle of the imagination of the circle of the signs".

[6]5: **Desired.** H: יכלו = were able.

[7]6: **Planets.** H: כוכבים המשרתים = the serving stars. → See note on *Introductorius*, § 2:5, s.v., "planets".

[8]6: **And by this.** H: בעבור זה = because of this.

[9]7: **However.** H: כי = for.

[10]8: **The light.** H: כח אור = power of the light.

[11]9: **It does not belong to this book to be busy with.** H: אין זה הספר מוכן לדבר = this book is not ready to speak about.

[12]10: **Scholars of astrology.** H: חכמי המזלות = scholars of the signs.

[13]10: **Masters of judgments.** H: בעלי הדינין = lords of judgments. → Meaning, experts in astrological judgments.

[14]11: **Elongate.** H: ירחקו = move away.

[15]11: **Do not ⟨move⟩ in this way.** H: לא ירחקו ממנה = do not move away from it.

[16]11: **Elongation.** H: מרחק = distance.

[17]12: **Wandering stars.** H: המשרתים = the servants. → Meaningm planets. See note on *Introductorius*, § 2:5, s.v., "planets".

[18]12: **Shine or are luminous.** H: מאירים = give light.

§1.4

[1]2: **The greater active ⟨agent⟩ or ⟨the active agent⟩ to a greater degree.** H: הפועל הגדול = the great agent.

[2]3: **Change.** H: התהפך = reversed, turned over.

[3]3: **Northern or left-hand.** H: שמאלי = left. → Meaning, northern.

[4]4: **Said.** H: גזרו = decreed.

[5]4: **Which are like images of heat or of hot things.** H: כי יש שם צורת סוס = because there is the shape of a horse there.

[6]4: *Great Introduction,* **namely the second book, seventh chapter.** see *Great Introduction*, ed. Burnett and Yamamoto (2019), II:7, pp. 212–219.

[7]6: **Said.** H: גזרו = decreed.

[8]6: See below §3.1:5.

[9]7: **Said.** H: גזרו = decreed.

[10]7: **According to the nature of air.** H: כתולדת האויר = like the nature of air.

[11]7: **Said.** H: גזרו = decreed.

[12]7: **Have such a nature.** H: הם ככה = are like that.

§1.5

[1]1: **Clouds or vapors.** H: האיד = the vapor.

[2]2: **Changes.** H: מתהפך = is reversed, is turned over.

[3]3: **Said.** H: גזרו = decreed.

[4]3: **Whose light or heat.** H: אורו = its light.

[5]4: **Said.** H: גזרו = decreed.

[6]5: **Many statements void of science and against the pondering of experience.** H: יש שם דברים רבים בטלים משיקול הדעת והנסיון = there are many things in it that have in them nothing of rational thought and experience.

[7]5: **But I, Abraham the compiler, say that Ptolemy did not compile this book, because there are in it many statements void of science and against the pondering of experience.** Cf. *De mundo*, prologue 12.

[8]5: **Books of Judgments.** H: ספר המולדות = Book of Nativities.

[9]7: **Neither an upper one nor an inferior one.** H: אין כוכב משרת ולא עליון = there is not a serving star (meaning a planet) and not an upper one. → See note on *Introductorius*, § 2:5, s.v., "planets".

[10]7: **That is of a cold or hot nature.** H: שהוא קר או חם = which is cold or hot.

[11]7: **Of a fifth substance.** H: מתולדת חמישית = of a fifth nature.

[12]7: **Good and complete reasons.** H: ראיות גמורות = incontrovertible proofs.

[13]9: **It retains heat.** H: יתפשט = it expands.

[14]12: **Similar or appropriate.** H: כהוגן = adequately.

[15]12: **Temperament of the human mixture.** H: ממסך האדם = the temperament of an human being.

[16]16: **Above the Sun.** H: קרוב מהשמש = close to the Sun.

§ 1.6

[1]4: **Diurnal planets.** H: כוכבי היום = diurnal stars.

[2]4: **It makes coincide.** H: תתישר = will be tempered.

[3]4: **Nocturnal planets.** H: כוכבי הלילה = nocturnal stars.

[4]6: **Longitude or apogee of the Sun.** H: המרחק מהשמש = the distance from the Sun.

[5]6: **Relation of its longitude.** H: המרחק = the distance.

[6]6: In the current sentence, Bate, probably following Hagin's French version, by putting "longitudinis Solis sive augis" in the genitive case with respect to "ratio," misunderstood the meaning of the Hebrew, which explains the reason for the alteration of Mercury's nature, referred to in the previous sentence. → The reason for the longitude or apogee of the Sun is according to the relation of its longitude from the Earth. H: והטעם, המרחק מהשמש וכפי המרחק מהארץ = The reason (for the alteration of Mercury's nature) is its distance from the Sun and in accordance with the distance from the Earth.

[7]6: **The reason for all the rest about the Dragon.** H: דבר התלי = as for the Dragon.

§ 2.1

[1]1: **Northern or left-hand.** H: שמאליים = left-hand. → Meaning, northern.

[2]1: **Equal or equinoctial line.** H: קו הצדק = line of justice. → Meaning, equator.

[3]2: **Certain people.** H: רבים = many.

[4]2: **Climates.** H: הגבולים = the territories, terms. → Meaning, climates. See note on *Introductorius*, § 2.1:17, s.v., "climate".

[5]4: **Others.** H: רבים = many.

[6]4: **The north.** H: השמאל = the left.

[7]4: **Habitable Earth.** H: הישוב = the settlement. → Meaning, the ecumene. See note on *Introductorius*, § 2.5:11, s.v. "the habitable."

[8]5: **Certain people.** H: רבים = many.

[9]6: **Habitable place.** H: הישוב = the settlement.

[10]6: **Just and rational.** H: ראוי = suitable.

[11]6: **Because.** H: על כן = consequently.

§2.2

[1]1: **Mutable or tropical and changeable.** H: מתהפך = reversing direction.

[2]1: **Reduced or become smaller.** H: לגרוע = decrease.

[3]1: **Ascensions.** H: מצעדיו = its steps, processions. → Meaning, ascensions.

[4]1: **Are diminished.** H: חסרים = are lacking.

[5]1: **That is, the part of the circle.** H: זה ידוע מפאת הגלגל = this is known on account of the circle. → Note, however, that whereas פאה means "part", מפאת means "on account of."

[6]2: **Oblique.** H: מעוות = crooked.

[7]2: **Diminution.** H: חסרון = lacking.

[8]2: **Good or benefic signs.** H: המזלות הטובים = the good signs.

[9]2: **From cold.** H: סור הקור = removal of the cold.

[10]5: **Properly arranged.** H: כהוגן = adequately.

[11]9: **Southern or right-hand eastern.** H: נגב מזרח = south east.

[12]12: **Animals or beasts.** H: החיות = the animals.

[13]12: **Metals or minerals.** H: המתכות = the metals.

[14]13: **Because of the mixture of its heat.** H: בעבור חומו שהוא ממוסך = because of its heat, which is temperate.

[15]14: **It has a signification about the pasturelands for herds or sheep.** H: בחלקו מרעה הצאן = pastureland for sheep is in its portion

[16]14: **Robbers and murderers.** H: הלסטים = the robbers.

[17]14: **Robbers and murderers.** H: הלסטים = the robbers.

[18]14: **Desert dwelling places, where robbers and murderers can dwell.** H: כל בית מקורה שיתקנו ככה בעבור הלסטים = any roofed house that was designed like that because of the robbers.

[19]14: **Equal line.** H: קו הצדק = line of justice.

[20]14: **Judges or judgments.** H: דיינים = judges.

[21]19: **But this is not so regarding the things referred to by the Indians.** H: רק כל מה שידברו אנשי הודו שיעלו בכל פנים = but as for everything the Indians said that rises in any of the faces.

[22]19: This corresponds to *Great Introduction*, ed. Burnett and Yamamoto (2019), VI 1:9, pp. 548–549.

[23]19: **This secret.** H: סודם = their secret.

[24]20: **Came up in their hands to be to be correct.** H: עלה בידם = came up in their hands. → Hebrew idiom meaning that they were successful. Here the Latin follows the Hebrew precisely.

§2.3

[1]1: **These signs, namely, Taurus.** H: זה המזל ושור = this sign and Taurus.

[2]1: **Defects.** H: מומים = blemishes, deformities.

[3]1: **Without defect.** H: בלא עיפוש = without mold.

[4]1: **Health and perfection of the body.** H: בריאות הגוף = health of the body.

NOTES TO *LIBER CAUSARUM SEU RATIONUM*   591

[5]2: **This sign, then, is the beginning and the head.** H: ושמו הראש בחלק זה המזל = they assigned the head to this sign.

[6]2: **Upper abdomen or stomach.** H: הקרב העליון = the upper abdomen.

[7]2: **Thighs or hips.** H: הפחדים = the thighs.

[8]4: **Planet.** H: כוכב = star.

[9]4: **Pain or suffering.** H: כאב = pain.

[10]8: **Exaltation.** H: כח = power. → Here Bate offers the common Latin technical term for the concept of "exaltation".

§ 2.4

[1]2: **Scholars of astrology.** H: חכמי המזלות = scholars of the signs.

[2]2: **Reason and cause.** H: טעם = reason.

[3]2: **Found it to be true.** H: עלה בידינו = it came up in our hands ⟨as correct⟩.

[4]3: **Hermes.** H: חנוך = Enoch.

[5]4: **Because when it ascends with the Sun.** H: כי בו היה = because it was there.

[6]4: **It is at the beginning of Aries in midheaven.** H: והשמש בחצי שמים בתחלת מזל טלה = and the Sun in midheaven at the beginning of Aries.

[7]4: **In the place of the equal line or upright sphere.** H: במקום ששם קו היושר = in the place where the line of straightness is there.

[8]6: **Northern.** H: שמאלי = left hand.

[9]6: **Our habitable.** H: הישוב = the settlement. → Meaning, the ecumene. See note on *Introductorius*, § 2.5:11, s.v. "the habitable."

[10]6: **Faces the north.** H: בפאת שמאל = is in in the left side.

[11]6: **Is.** H: שמו = they put.

[12]7: **Heat is stronger and more increased.** H: יגדל החום = the heat will increase.

[13]8: **The luminaries or the light.** H: הפך האור = opposite of the light.

[14]10: **Jupiter's houses are next to Saturn's houses, which are Capricorn and Aquarius.** H: היה ביתו של צדק שני לבית שבתאי, שהוא דלי = Jupiter's house is next to Saturn's house, which is Aquarius.

[15]10: **To the extent that one house of Saturn with respect to the house of Jupiter is proportionally similar with respect to one of Saturn's houses.** H: עד שיהיה ערך בית שבתאי האחד אל ביתו כערך בית צדק אל בית שבתאי האחר = so that the proportion of one house of Saturn to its [Jupiter's] house will be as the proportion of Jupiter's house to the other house of Jupiter.

§ 2.5

[1]1: **Hermes.** H: חנוך = Enoch.

[2]1: **Signs.** H: הבתים = the houses.

[3]3: **Scholars of the stars.** H: חכמי המזלות = scholars of the signs.

[4]3: **From Leo.** H: מתחלת אריה = from the beginning of Leo.

[5]3: **And this was called the larger.** H: והוא החלק הגדול = and this is the great part.

[6]4: **A planet in its terms.** H: המשרתים בגבולם = the servants in their terms.
→ Meaning, the planets in their planetary terms.

[7]4: **Smaller.** H: קטן = small.

[8]5: **Larger.** H: הגדול = the large.

[9]6: **If.** H: כאשר = when.

[10]8: **This thing is known experimentally and is true.** H: וזה דבר ברור = this is a clear thing.

[11]9: **Its nature is good.** H: יושר תולדתו = the straightness of its nature. → Meaning, its temperate nature.

§2.6

[1]1: **The sign of Aries.** H: זה המזל = this sign.

[2]1: **The house of honor or exaltation.** H: בית כבוד = house of honor. → See note on *Introductorius*, §1.6:1, s.v., "honor or exaltation".

[3]1: **Move.** H: לנטות = to incline.

[4]2: **But if this is the reason or cause.** H: אם הדבר כך = if the thing is like that.

[5]3: **The place of humiliation or opposite the apogee.** H: מקום שפלות = place of lowness. → Meaning, perigee.

[6]3: **Method of geometric demonstrations.** H: דרך החשבון והמדות = method of arithmetic and geometry.

§2.7

[1]3: **As we ourselves explain this as a general rule.** H: ולהקל על התלמידים יאמר ככה = and put it this way to make it easier for students.

[2]4: **Extreme degree.** H: רוב = great.

§2.8

[1]1: **But by other method, according to the opinion, I say, of the Egyptian scholars, Mars is first, because it itself is the lord of the house; the Sun is second, because its house is the second of the triplicity; but Jupiter is third, because it is the lord of the third house of this triplicity.** H: והפנים הראשונים על דעת חכמי מצרים למאדים כי הוא בעל הבית, והשניים לשמש כי

ביתה הוא שני לשלישיות, והשלישיים לצדק בעבור כי הוא בעל הבית השלישי מן השלישיות = The Egyptian scientists ⟨assigned⟩ the first face [decan] to Mars, because it is the lord of the house [i.e., Aries], the second to the Sun, because its house [i.e., Leo] is the second in the triplicity, and the third to Jupiter, because it is the lord of the third house in the triplicity [i.e., Sagittarius].

[2]3: **Return back again or form a circle.** H: חוזרים חלילה = return again and again.

[3]4: **Longitude or distance.** H: מרחק = distance.

[4]4: **The resulting signs.** H: ההווה = what is there.

[5]5: **Of the planets.** H: ש׳צ׳ם׳ ח׳נ׳כ׳ל׳ = S⟨aturn⟩, J⟨upiter⟩, M⟨ars⟩, S⟨un⟩, V⟨enus⟩, M⟨ercury⟩, M⟨oon⟩.

[6]5: **The last.** H: סוף בעל הפנים = the end of the lord of the face.

[7]5: **In the cycle.** H: בגלגל = in the circle.

[8]7: **Which has been completed or has already passed.** H: שעברו = which has already passed.

[9]8: **This.** H: השניים = the second.

§2.9

[1]1: **They must by no means be taken into consideration.** H: אין לסמוך עליהם = they are not to be trusted.

[2]1: **In books of the Ancient Indians, and also of the Egyptians.** H: בנסיחה קדמונית = in an ancient text.

[3]1: **And he said.** H: והנכון גבולי מצרים = the correct ones are the terms of Egypt.

§ 2.10

[1]1: **Scholars.** H: חכמי הודו = the scholars of India.

[2]1: **Novenariae.** H: תשיעיות = ninth-parts. → See note on *Introductorius*, § 1.12:2, s.v. "novenaria."

[3]2: **The end or the last one.** H: סוף = end.

[4]3: **Ascendant.** H: המזל הצומח = the ascendant sign.

[5]3: **Which is.** H: כי הוא = because it is.

[6]4: **Mentioned regarding Aries.** H: עד שיהיה הסוף לבתולה = until the end is Virgo.

§ 2.11

[1]1: **Duodenariae.** H: שנים העשר = the twelfths. → See note on *Introductorius*, § 1.12:2, s.v. "duodenaria."

[2]2: **Until.** H: כדי = in order to.

§ 2.12

[1]2: **As long as the scholars of the stars are old.** H: בין חכמי המזלות = among the scholars of the signs.

[2]3: **Their year.** H: שנתו = his year.

[3]3: **The year.** H: השמש = the Sun.

[4]3: **Imagined by a human being.** H: במחשבת הלב = by the skill of the heart. → Meaning, by the skill of the mind.

[5]3: **Namely, from the intersection.** H: והטעם בהכנסה אל מחברת = and the reason is when it enters the intersection.

[6]5: **The scholars of the Saracens or of the Arabs.** H: חכמי ישמעאל = Ishmaelite scholars.

[7]6: **Fixed star.** H: כוכב עליון = upper star.

[8]7: **Zodiac.** H: גלגל המזלות = circle of the signs.

[9]8: **Indians.** H: חכמי הודו = scholars of India.

[10]10: **True and more correct.** H: הנכון = The correct ⟨fact⟩.

[11]11: **The highest stars change or move.** H: יתנועעו העליונים = the upper ⟨stars⟩ will move.

[12]11: **According to the Indians.** H: של הודו = of India.

[13]11: **Scholars.** H: בעלי הסדנים = the masters of the poles. → Meaning, those who are knowledgeable about the theory of the poles.

[14]13: **And this is.** H: והטעם = and the reason is.

[15]13: **Ptolemy and his followers.** H: בטלמיוס וחביריו = Ptolemy and his colleagues.

[16]13: **Proofs or demonstrations.** H: הראיות = the proofs.

[17]14: **Astrologer.** H: בעל המזלות = expert in the signs.

[18]14: **Calculate or extract.** H: להוציא = extract.

§ 2.13

[1]1: **Stable or fixed.** H: עומד = stationary. → Meaning, not moving.

[2]1: **Stands in one way.** H: יעמוד על דרך אחד = will stand in one way. → Hebrew idiom meaning, is stable.

[3]1: **The other things, because we mentioned the other things in ⟨the section on⟩ the sign of Aries.** H: כל מה שהזכרנו במזל טלה = everything we have mentioned in the sign of Aries.

[4]2: **Lust or generation of offspring.** H: פריה ורביה = reproduction and multiplication. → Hebrew idiom meaning procreation. See note on *Introductorius*, § 2.2:4, s.v., "fertility and abundance."

[5]2: **And as a rule ⟨it indicates⟩ heat mixed with cold.** H: וכללו ממוסך, חום עם קור = and its rule is that it is mixed, heat with cold.

[6]4: **Tall and lofty trees.** H: האילנים הגבוהים = the tall trees.

[7]5: **Has power.** H: יש תועלת = there is utility.

[8]5: **Plants or trees.** H: עץ = tree.

[9]5: **Is sweet.** H: טובים = are good.

[10]6: **Climates and regions.** H: הגבולים = the territories, terms. → Meaning, climates. See note on *Introductorius*, § 2.1:17, s.v., "climate".

§ 2.14

[1]1: **Its first part or half.** H: חציו הראשון = its first half.

[2]1: **Is of the hot nature of the season of the year.** H: מתולדת זמן החום = of the nature of the season of heat.

[3]1: **Is of the dry nature of the season of the year.** H: מתולדת זמן הקיץ = of the nature of the summer season.

[4]2: **And princes, dukes, prophets and law-givers.** H: כמו השמים = like the heavens.

[5]2: **Apogee.** H: גבהות = height. → Meaning, apogee. See note on *Introductorius*, § 2.3:35, s.v. "place of the apogee."

§ 2.15

[1]2: **From the beginning or the head.** H: מראש = from the head.

[2]3: **It has been said.** H: הזכרנו = we have mentioned.

[3]4: **Lust.** H: המשגל = sexual intercourse.

[4]6: **A small star, the smallest of all the stars.** H: כוכב הקטן שבכל הכוכבים = the smallest of all the stars.

[5]6: **Science.** H: חכמה = wisdom.

§ 2.16

[1]1: **About the houses of honor or about the exaltations.** H: בתי הכבוד = houses of honor.

[2]2: **So, the honor or exaltation of the Moon.** H: אמרו כי כבוד הלבנה = they said that the honor of the Moon.

[3]2: **According to.** H: זה = this is.

[4]3: **In the beginning of the world.** H: בטלה, שהוא תחלת העולם = in Aries, which is the beginning of the world.

[5]3: **Above the horizon.** H: על הארץ = above the Earth.

[6]4: **Light or rays.** H: אור = light.

[7]4: **According to the quantity of the light or rays of the Sun itself.** H: כפי שתצא מאור השמש = as it leaves the Sun's light.

[8]5: **Fall.** H: מעלת קלון = the degree of shame. → See note on *Introductorius*, § 2.4:36, s.v., "fall or shame." Here Bate offers the common Latin technical term for the concept of "dejection".

[9]5: **The place of burning or the burnt path.** H: מקום השריפה = the place of burning.

[10]5: **In the rays or the light.** H: באור = in the light.

[11]8: **Enoch or Hermes.** H: חנוך = Enoch.

[12]9: **The Indians.** H: חכמי הודו = the scholars of India.

[13]9: **He is right.** H: הדין עמו = the law is on his side. → Meaning, he is right.

[14]10: **The northerly.** H: השמאליים = the left hand. → Meaning, northerly.

[15]11: **There is a nature in it that is contrary.** H: כי תולדת מאדים הפך = for Mars' nature is the opposite.

[16]12: **The exaltation.** H: כוכב עליון = an upper star.

[17]13: **Luxurious evil.** H: משגל רע = bad sexual intercourse.

[18]14: **Delights and pleasures of the world.** H: תענוגי העולם = pleasures of the world.

[19]15: **Lack of voice or do not have voice.** H: אין להם קול = do not have voice.

[20]15: **Those generated in water or in aquatic animals.** H: מהנולדים במים = from those born in water.

§ 2.17

[1]3: **By night one must begin from the Moon.** H: הלבנה תחל בלילה = the Moon begins by night.

[2]3: **Its presence and luminosity.** H: כחה = its power.

[3]4: **Part.** H: רוח = wind.

[4]4: **Over the southern corner.** H: ברוחות הדרומיים = over the southerly winds.

[5]5: **The first lord of the triplicity.** H: בעל השלישיות הראשונה = the lord of the first triplicity.

[6]6: **Second lord of the triplicity.** H: בעל השלישות השניה = the lord of the second triplicity.

[7]7: **Lady.** H: בעל = the lord.

[8]7: **Pleasures and desires.** H: תענוגים = pleasures.

[9]7: **Equal or temperate.** H: ישר = straight. → Meaning, temperate.

[10]8: **They considered Venus the last of the triplicity.** H: שמו השלישות האחרונה לנגה = they assigned the last triplicity to Venus.

[11]8: **Increase of offspring.** H: פריה ורביה = reproduction and multiplication. → Hebrew idiom meaning procreation. See note on *Introductorius*, § 2.2:4, s.v., "fertility and abundance."

§ 2.18

[1]1: **They did not came up true in our hands.** H: לא עלה בידינו = it did not came up in our hands. → Hebrew idiom meaning that they were not successful. Here the Latin follows the Hebrew precisely.

[2]2: **His judgments and statements.** H: דיניו ומשפטיו = his judgments and decrees.

[3]2: **As a general rule I say to you that all ⟨the statements⟩ by Ptolemy, when he speaks about the circles [the orbs] and what belongs to this, are true and nothing is truer than them, but his ⟨astrological⟩ judgments and decrees do not befit his science.** Cf. *De mundo*, Prologue, 14.

[4]2: **The Indian.** H: מארץ הודו = from the land of India.

[5]2: **We must rely on them.** H: סמוך עליהם = you should rely on them.

[6]4: **Do not let to come up in your heart.** H: אל יעלה בלבך = it should not come up in your heart. → Meaning, it should not emerge in your mind.

[7]4: **Except that they have a certain similarity to the natures they generate on earth.** H: רק טעם התולדת שיולידו בארץ כדמות אותה התולדת = The only reason for these natures is that they generate the same nature on Earth

§ 3.1

[1]1: **Foundation and root.** H: עקר = root.

[2]3: **From the beginning of the diameter to the end ⟨of the diameter⟩ or mutually from the extremities of the diameter.** H: מקצה האלכסון עד קצה האלכסון = from the end of the diameter to the end of the diameter.

[3]4: **Angles or cardines.** H: יתדות = pegs. → Meaning, cardines, i.e., the cusps of the first, fourth, seventh and tenth house of the horoscope. See note on *Introductorius*, § 3.4:2, s.v., "angles or cardines."

[4]6: **At the middle.** H: ברביעית = at the fourth part.

§ 3.2

[1]1: **Scrutinized the aspects in the equation of the houses.** H: ראיתי בחשבון בעצמו דרך המבטים = I saw a method for the aspects based on ⟨the use of⟩ numbers only.

[2]2: **To dwell on.** H: להזכיר = mention.

[3]4: **One bears a similarity to five.** H: אחד עם חמשה שהם שוים = one and five are the same.

[4]6: **From the rear or backwards.** H: אחורנית = backwards.

[5]6: **Is called.** H: היה = was.

[6]6: **Friendship.** H: אהבה = love.

[7]7: **Double or twofold.** H: מורכבים = composite.

[8]7: **Twofold or composed of halves or doubles.** H: מורכב = composite

[9]8: **But not according to the same nature of complete parity.** H: רק אין התולדת שלימה = but the nature is not complete.

[10]10: **In enmity.** H: משונה = at variance.

[11]11: **Arithmeticians.** H: בעלי חכמת הערכים = experts in the science of proportions.

[12]12: **Star or planet.** H: כוכב = star.

[13]13: **The strongest.** H: התקיף = the strong one.

[14]13: **Angles.** H: יתדות = pegs. → Meaning, cardines of the horoscope. See note on *Introductorius*, §3.4:2, s.v., "angles or cardines."

§3.3

[1]1: **About the equal ascensions.** H: על המצעדים שהם שוים = about the equal steps, processions. → Meaning, equal ascensions.

[2]1: **Whose hours are crooked.** H: ששעותיו המעוותות שוות = whose crooked hours are equal.

[3]2: **Equal or straight signs.** H: המזלות הישרים = the straight signs.

[4]2: **Contrary.** H: נגידים = governors. → See, however, *Introductorius*, §3.2:4, where these signs are called "dominus seu principans." This mistranslation is due to the fact נגיד without the *yod*, i.e. נגד, means contrary.

[5]3: **The stars that are in the ecliptic are straight.** H: ואשר הם בחשב האפודה נכונים = As for those that stand in the girdle of the vest. → See note on *Introductorius*, §1.10:5, s.v., "in the girdle of the imagination of the circle of the signs".

[6]3: **That is the ruler or chief, which are called** *al-mubtazz*. H: ממונה = overseer.

[7]3: **In active quality.** H: בתולדת הפועלת = in active nature.

§3.4

[1]1: **Divisions.** H: חלקים = parts.

[2]2: **Visibility of color.** H: מראה העינים = the appearance of the colors.

[3]5: **And.** H: עם = with.

[4]6: **Everything that is above or everything that is raised above the horizon.** H: כל מה שהוא למעלה מן הארץ = everything that is above the Earth.

[5]6: **By way of example or to make it clear.** H: דרך משל = metaphorically.

[6]6: **Power or strength.** H: כח = power.

[7]7: **Ascending half of the circle.** H: חצי הגלגל העולה = half of the ascending circle.

[8]7: **Ascensions.** H: מצעדים = steps, processions. → Meaning, ascensions.

[9]8: **Our master Abraham.** H: רבינו אברהם. → This reading is supported but the mayority of the checked Hebrew manuscripts. Two manuscripts, though, read: H: אברהם = Abraham, tout court.

[10]8: **The line of the angle of the Earth or of the abyss.** H: קו התהום = the line of the abyss.

[11]8: **The line of the angle of the Earth.** H: קו התהום = the line of the abyss.

[12]9: **Masters of the instruments or of the astrolabe.** H: בעלי כלי הנחשת = experts on the copper instrument, namely, the astrolabe.

§3.5

[1]3: **For the degree of the ascendant is opposed to the degree of the descendant, and the degree of midheaven is opposed below to the angle of the Earth.** H: כי המעלה ההווה כנגד הארץ והיא עולה, יש מעלה אחרת כנגדה שהיא שוקעת, ומעלה שלישית בקו חצי השמים, ורביעית בקו התהום = for there is one degree facing the earth, which is rising; and another degree

opposite it, which is descending, and a third degree at the line of midheaven, and a fourth at the line of the abyss.

[2]4: **Stands in the same way.** H: יעמוד על דרך אחד = will stand in one way. → Hebrew idiom meaning "will be stable."

[3]4: **What is between any pair of points.** H: כל נקודה מארבע הנקודות = every point of the four points.

[4]4: **Cardines or angles.** H: יתדות = pegs. → Meaning, cardines of the horoscope. See note on *Introductorius*, § 3.4:2, s.v., "angles or cardines."

[5]5: **Subsequent houses, which go after and arrive to that ⟨place⟩ like angles.** H: הבתים הסמוכים אליהם, שבמהרה ישובו גם הם יתדות = The houses that are adjacent to them, which will soon become pegs too.

[6]5: **Succedent to the angles.** H: סמוכים = close.

[7]6: **Angles.** H: יתדות = pegs. → Meaning, cardines of the horoscope. See note on *Introductorius*, § 3.4:2, s.v., "angles or cardines."

[8]7: **He is right.** H: הדין עמו = the law is on his side. → Meaning, he is right.

[9]7: **He has the law and he tells the truth.** H: הדין עמו = the law is on his side.

[10]7: **The angle of the seventh house.** H: היתד השביעי = the seventh peg. → Meaning, third cardo of the horoscope. See note on *Introductorius*, § 3.4:2, s.v., "angles or cardines." Bate's divergent translation is in fact a gloss correcting Ibn Ezra's concept of "seventh peg or cardo": since there are only four pegs or cardines, Bate explains that Ibn Ezra's "seventh cardo" refers to the cardo that coincides with the beginning of the seventh house, which corresponds to the third cardo.

[11]7: **Than the angle of the fourth house.** H: מהרביעי = than the fourth.

[12]10: **Not like the eighth.** H: וככה השמיני = the same applies to the eighth.

[13]10: **Is stronger.** H: טוב = is better.

§3.6

[1]1: **Abraham, our master.** H: רבינו אברהם = Abraham, our rabbi. → Meaning our teacher. This reading is supported at by two Hebrew manuscripts: Paris, Bibliothèque nationale de France, MS héb. 1056; Munich, Bayerische Staatsbibliothek, Cod. Hebr. 202. But the mayority of the checked Hebrew manuscripts read: H: אברהם = Abraham, tout court.

[2]1: **It is the question.** H: ובשאלות = and in ⟨the doctrine of⟩ interrogations.

[3]1: **Emerges into the light.** H: יוצאה לאור = emerges into the light.

[4]2: **Since.** H: והנה = so.

[5]2: **In the middle of two angles.** H: יכוננוהו השני יתדות = it is determined by the two pegs. → Meaning, two cardines of the horoscope. See note on *Introductorius*, §3.4:2, s.v., "angles or cardines."

[6]2: **The line of the abyss or angle of the Earth.** H: קו התהום = the line of the abyss.

[7]2: **Line of midheaven.** H: קו הרום = line of height.

[8]2: **By means of these angles.** H: אלה היתדות = these pegs. → Meaning, cardines of the horoscope. See note on *Introductorius*, §3.4:2, s.v., "angles or cardines."

[9]4: **Be more manifest to the sight.** H: הוא הנראה לעין = is visible to the eye.

[10]5: **This house.** H: הבית הרביעי = the fourth house.

[11]5: **Secret and hidden things.** H: כל מטמון = any buried treasure.

[12]5: **The end or the last of the angles.** H: סוף היתדות = the end of the pegs. → Meaning, cardines of the horoscope. See note on *Introductorius*, §3.4:2, s.v., "angles or cardines."

[13]6: **Lordshhips and governances.** H: השררה = the dominion.

[14]6: **Higher or more honorable.** H: גבוה = higher.

[15]6: **Professions and arts.** H: אומנות = art.

[16]6: **Renowned for this reason.** H:בעבורה שמו ונזכר בה נודע שהוא = on account of which he [i.e., the native] attains fame and his name is known.

[17]8: **Its descensions.** H: מצעדיו = steps, processions. → Meaning, ascensions.

[18]8: **In part.** H: מפאה אחת = from one side.

[19]8: **Wars and conflicts.** H: המלחמות = the wars.

[20]9: **Friendship.** H: אהבה = love.

[21]9: **Sons or offspring.** H: בנים = sons.

[22]9: **Nourishment.** H: והמאכל והמשתה = and the food and drink.

[23]10: **Friends.** H: האוהבים = the lovers.

[24]10: **Favors and good fortune.** H: חן = grace.

[25]12: **Angle of the seventh house.** H: היתד השביעי = the seventh peg. → Meaning, third cardo of the horoscope. See note on *Introductorius*, § 3.4:2, s.v., "angles or cardines." Bate's divergent translation is in fact a gloss correcting Ibn Ezra's concept of "seventh peg or cardo": since there are only four pegs or cardines, Bate explains that Ibn Ezra's "seventh cardo" refers to the cardo that coincides with the beginning of the seventh house, which corresponds to the third cardo.

[26]13: **Certain people.** H: רבים = many.

[27]13: **Enoch, who is Hermes.** H: חנוך = Enoch.

[28]14: **Changes and declines.** H: נטה = declines.

[29]14: **And this to a greater extent regarding.** H: ויורה = it indicates.

[30]14: **Science.** H: חכמה = wisdom.

[31]14: **Faith or law.** H: אמונה = faith.

[32]14: **Comes or derives from science.** H: מן החכמה = from wisdom.

[33]15: **Near science.** H: חכמה קרובה = near wisdom.

[34]16: **According to the qualities of the signs.** H: בדרך המזלות = in the way of the signs.

[35]16: **Active quality.** H: בתולדת הפועלת = in the active nature.

[36]16: **Strife or dishonor.** H: הקלון = shame.

[37]16: **Prison.** H: בית הסוהר = house of prison. → Latin: domus carceris = house of prison.

[38]16: **The sign or of the house.** H: המזל = the sign.

[39]18: **Scholars of the stars.** H: חכמי המזלות = scholars of the signs.

[40]19: **Reasons.** H: דברי = the things.

[41]19: **The scholars of the Saracens or of the Arabs.** H: חכמי ישמעאל = Ishmaelite scholars.

§4.1

[1]1: **Abraham, our master.** H: רבינו אברהם = Abraham, our rabbi. → Meaning, our teacher. This reading is supported at least by two Hebrew manuscripts: Paris, Bibliothèque nationale de France, MS héb. 1056; Munich, Bayerische Staatsbibliothek, Cod. Hebr. 202. But other checked Hebrew manuscripts read: H: אברהם = Abraham, tout court.

[2]1: **Reasons and causes.** H: טעם = reason.

[3]2: **Science of the arithmeticians.** H: חכמת הערכים = science of proportions.

[4]2: 21. H: 20.

[5]3: **Noble or honorable proportion.** H: ערך נכבד = honorable ratio.

[6]3: **But the proportion of Jupiter is of the day, for it is honorable.** H: וערך הלבנה אל צדק ערך כפל, גם הוא נכבד = and the proportion of the Moon to Jupiter is a double proportion, which is also noble.

[7]5: **Master Ibn Abi Damina.** H: אבן אבי דמינה = Ibn Abi Damina.

[8]5: **Goods, possessions and riches.** H: הממון = wealth.

[9]5: **Offspring.** H: פריה ורביה = reproduction and multiplication. → Hebrew idiom meaning procreation. See note on *Introductorius*, § 2.2:4, s.v., "fertility and abundance."

[10]5: **Slaves and retainers.** H: העבדים = the slaves.

[11]6: **To serve or to work.** H: לשמש = to serve.

[12]6: **According to this division the ninth house returns to Jupiter.** H: והנה היה בחלק צדק הבית התשיעי = so the ninth house is in Jupiter's portion.

[13]6: **Prophecies and divine service.** H: עבודת השם = divine service.

[14]6: **Belongs.** H: שב = returns.

[15]6: **Violence.** H: כח = power.

[16]6: **Destined.** H: שב = returns.

[17]7: **Pertains.** H: שב = returns.

[18]7: **Delights and joy.** H: תענוגים = pleasures.

[19]7: **Sorrow, disgrace and shame.** H: חרפה וקלון = shame and dishonor.

§ 4.2

[1]1: **But the root and cause.** H: ועקר = and the root.

[2]1: **Pain and lamentation.** H: עצבון ואבל = sadness and mourning.

NOTES TO *LIBER CAUSARUM SEU RATIONUM* 609

[3]2: **Moors or Ethiopians.** H: הכושים = the Ethiopians.

[4]2: **Ancient nations.** H: הזקנים = the elderly; cf. *Introductorius*, § 4.1:7: seniores = the elderly.

[5]2: **Leatherworkers or skinners.** H: מעבדי העורות = tanners. → Cf. *Introductorius*, § 4.1:7: cerdones coriorum.

[6]2: **Privy-cleaners.** H: מנקים בתי הכבוד = cleaners of houses of honor. → Meaning, privy-cleaners. Cf. *Introductorius*, § 4.1:7: cloacarum mundatores.

[7]2: **Smell.** H: המרה = the ⟨black⟩ bile.

[8]3: **Slight value.** H: אין בו תועלת אלא מעט = it is almost useless.

[9]3: **And in its portion is every dark and ugly place.** H: ובחלקו מהארץ המערות וכל מקום חושך = its portion of the Earth is caves and any dark place.

[10]4: **Beautiful or handsome form.** H: צורה יפה = handsome form.

[11]4: **The tree or plant.** H: אילן = the tree.

[12]4: *Kenesesin.* H: העפצים = the *'afaṣim* (the gall-oak). → Cf. *Introductorius*, § 4.1:13: אילן העפצים = arbor gallarum = gall-oak.

[13]4: **Toxic thing or deadly poison.** H: סם המות = drug of death.

[14]5: **Intentions and hidden things.** H: הסודות = the secrets.

[15]5: **Irritating or provoking and disturbing others.** H: ולעשות חמס ולכעוס ולפתות = to wreak violence, be angry, and seduce.

[16]5: **Profession or laborious art.** H: אומנות מיגעת הרבה = very exhausting craft.

[17]5: **Foundation.** H: עקר = root.

[18]6: **Headings.** H: שערים = gates, entrances, chapters of a book.

[19]6: **Scholars of the stars.** H: חכמי המזלות = scholars of the signs.

[20]7: **Madness, loss of reason and insanity.** H: השגעון = madness.

[21]7: **Chronic pains or diseases.** H: כאב עומד = standing (i.e. chronic) pain.

[22]7: **Slow and deliberate in its motion.** H: המתנתו בהליכתו = sluggish in its motion.

[23]8: **Nine.** H: תשע עשרה = nineteen.

[24]8: **Adduced human nature in the way of a proof.** H: הביא כדמות ראיות מתולדת האדם. = he brought something like proofs drawn from human nature.

[25]10: **Said.** H: נסו = verified by experience.

[26]10: **Certainly.** H: תמיד = always.

[27]11: **Original or first.** H: הראשונה = first.

[28]12: **Power or strength.** H: כח = power.

[29]12: **Light or the rays.** H: אור = light.

[30]12: **Because it is the smaller luminary.** H: בעבור שאורה פחות מהשמש = because its light is less than the Sun's. → Bate's divergent translation is in fact a gloss explaining why the Moon's light is less than the Sun's.

[31]12: **Reasons of the Ancients.** H: סברת הקדמונים = the opinion of the Ancients.

§4.3

[1]1: **Increase and fruit.** H: פריה ורביה = reproduction and multiplication. → Hebrew idiom meaning procreation. See note on *Introductorius*, § 2.2:4, s.v., "fertility and abundance."

[2]2: **House of its honor or its exaltation.** H: בית כבודו = house of its honor.

[3]3: **The charming and pleasing.** H: הנאים = the good-looking.

[4]5: **Old age.** H: בין הבחרות והזקנה = between youth and old age. → Bate's divergent translation is in fact a gloss specifying what is the stage of life between youth and old age.

[5]5: **Of the parts of the world.** H: מן הפאות = of the sides.

§4.4

[1]1: **Its nature.** H: טעם תולדתו = the reason for its nature.

[2]1: **About the magnitude of its heat, and ⟨referred⟩ to killing by disputes, wars and riots.** H: ומרוב חומו יורה על ההריגה ועל המריבות ועל המלחמה והכעס. = and because of its great heat it indicates slaughter, quarrels, war, and anger.

[3]2: **The Britons or the Englishmen.** H: אנשי אינגלא טירא = the inhabitants of Inglaterra (England).

[4]2: **Enoch or Hermes.** H: חנוך = Enoch.

[5]3: **The cause, also red iron, sulfur, and all the instruments of weapons.** H: טעם הברזל האדום והגפרית וכל כלי נשק = the reason of copper (lit. red iron), sulfur, and weapons.

[6]4: **Of the wild beasts.** H: ומרמש האדמה = of the creeping things on Earth.

[7]4: **The harmful or wild.** H: כל מזיק = every one that is harmful.

[8]4: **Parsley.** H: פלפל = pepper.

[9]4: **Plundering and robbery.** H: הגניבה = theft.

[10]4: **Robbers and destructive people for these things.** H: לסטים = bandits.

[11]5: **Genitals.** H: האבר = the member (i.e., the penis).

[12]6: **Of human ages.** H: משנות האדם = of human years.

[13]6: Of the parts of the world. H: מן הפאות = of the sides. → Bate's divergent translation is in fact a gloss specifying what are the "sides" referred to by Ibn Ezra.

§ 4.5

[1]1: Star or planet. H: כוכב = star.

[2]1: Power or strength. H: כח = power.

[3]2: Sense of touch. H: הנפש המרגשת = the sensitive soul. → Bate's divergent translation is in fact a gloss specifying one of the main attributes of the the sensitive soul.

[4]3: The Romans. H: אדום = 'Edom. → Here Bate translates a Hebrew word ('Edom = Idumea) that in medieval Hebrew is a code name for Rome. Cf. *Introductorius*, § 2.7:13: "the land of Edom {{or of the Christians}}," et passim.

[5]3: Resembling them. H: דומה לזהב = resembling gold.

[6]5: Middle or intermediate. H: האמצעיים = intermediate.

[7]6: The spirit and life. H: הרוח = the spirit.

[8]7: Of the corners. H: מהפאות = of the sides. → Cf. § 4.3:5 (Jupiter), § 4.4:6 (Mars), § 4.8:7 (Moon), where Bate denotes the same concept as "partes mundi = parts of the world"

[9]7: Power and strength. H: כח = power.

[10]7: Without any excess division. H: בלא תוספת חלק = without any added part.

[11]7: Without subtraction or deficit. H: בלא מגרעת = without subtraction.

[12]7: A moderate difference or distinction. H: רק חלקים מעטים = only a few minutes.

§4.6

[1]1: **They said.** H: ניסו = they found by experience.

[2]1: **Lust, pleasure, and desire or attraction.** H: הנפש המתאוה = the appetitive soul. → Bate's divergent translation is in fact a gloss specifying the main attibutes of the the appetitive soul.

[3]2: **Those who follow the law of the Saracens or Arabs.** H: מי שהוא על תורת ישמעאל = one who belongs to the religious system of Ishmael.

[4]3: **Lust, appetite and desires.** H: התאוה = lust.

[5]3: **Drinking-parties or revels.** H: משקה = drink. → Here, Bate, or Hagin, confused the letter ק with the letter ת, and read משתה (= drinking party) instead of משקה (= drink).

[6]4: **Of the ages.** H: משנות = of the years.

[7]4: **Part or division.** H: חלק = part.

[8]4: **Great or greater.** H: גדולות = great.

§4.7

[1]1: **Harmful or malevolent.** H: המזיקים = the harmful.

[2]1: **Disease.** H: חולי קבוע = chronic disease.

[3]1: **Nature of the place.** H: המקום = the place.

[4]2: **Talk or speech.** H: הדבור = speech.

[5]3: **Our hands.** H: ידינו = will pronounce judgment. → But the same Hebrew word, with different vocalization, means "our hands".

[6]3: **Regarding the conjunction of the upper ⟨planets⟩, bear witness about what our hands and the experience of ⟨our⟩ work is about universal or general affairs.** H: כי ממחברת העליונים ידינו על הכללים = because

[7]4: **In Mercury's portion.** H: בחלקו = in its portion.

[8]4: **Light and agile.** H: קל = light.

[9]6: **Has already been stated.** H: הזכרתיו = I have mentioned.

§4.8

[1]1: **Fills.** H: תבלה = will cause to decompose. → Here, Bate, or Hagin, confused the letter ב with the letter מ, and read תמלא (= will fill) instead of משקה (= will cause to decompose).

[2]2: **Of living beings, fish.** → This phrase does not occur in any of the Hebrew checked manuscripts.

[3]3: **It ruler over.** H: תורה = indicates.

[4]3: **Wayfarers or travelers.** H: הולכי דרכים = wayfarers.

[5]4: **The cheapest and lowest.** H: למטה = below.

[6]4: **Gourds.** H: הקישואים = squash.

[7]5: **The science of stories and fables.** H: דעת ההגדות = knowledge of legends.

[8]6: **The opinion that it is changeable according to every nature.** H: וטעם שהיא נוטה עם כל תולדת = The reason that it is inclined to any nature.

[9]6: **Infancy.** H: שנות הגמול = the years of weaning. → Bate's divergent translation is in fact a gloss specifying the stage of life when the child is weaned.

[10]6: **Orb.** H: רקיע = heaven.

[11]7: **Of the corners or parts of the world.** H: מהפאות = from the sides. → See note on § 4.5:7, s.v. "corners."

[12]7: **Part.** H: מהפאות = of the edges ⟨of the horizon⟩.

[13]8: **Distant or removed.** H: היות מרחקה = its distance is.

[14]8: **They subtracted 12 years.** H: חסרום = they subtracted them. → Bate's divergent translation is in fact a gloss specifying the amount of years that were subracted, which Ibn Ezra does not.

[15]8: **The years of the Moon.** H: שנותיה = her years. → Bate's divergent translation is in fact a gloss specifying the planet to which the years belong.

[16]8: **Is not right.** H: לא ישר בעיני = is not right in my eyes.

§ 4.9

[1]1: **Delights or pleasures.** H: תענוגים = pleasures.

[2]1: **Faith or laws.** H: אמונות = beliefs.

§ 5.1

[1]1: **Goodness or assistance.** H: טובת = goodness.

[2]1: **Harms or evils.** H: רע = evil.

[3]2: **Why.** H: וטעם היות = the reason for.

[4]3: **Whose nature.** H: כי תולדתו = because its nature.

[5]3: **Pain will be added to pain.** H: יוסיף מכאוב על מכאוב = pain will be added to pain.

[6]3: **The sign of Scorpio rectifies its nature.** H: ובמזל עקרב תתישר תולדתו = and in the sign of Scorpio its nature is rectified.

§5.2

[1]1: **Towards the northern part.** H: בפאת שמאלית = in the left side. → Meaning, in the northern side.

[2]1: **Our habitable regions.** H: הישוב = the settlement. → Meaning, the ecumene. See note on *Introductorius*, §2.5:11, s.v. "the habitable."

[3]1: **In the northern part.** H: בפאת שמאל = in the side of the left. → Meaning, in the northern side.

[4]1: **Rays of its light.** H: ניצוץ אורו = the spark of its light.

[5]2: **In the northern part or in the southern.** H: בפאת שמאל ודרום = on the northern side and on the southern.

[6]3: **The eccentric circle of the apogee from the Earth.** H: בגלגל הגבהות שמוצקו רחוק ממוצק הארץ = in the circle of the height (i.e., apogee) whose center is far from the center of the Earth.

[7]3: **Great dispute and disagreement.** H: מחלוקת = disagreement.

[8]3: **Place of the apogee.** H: מקום הגבהות = place of the height (i.e., apogee).

[9]5: **According to my knowledge, as I see it.** H: לפי דעתי = according to my opinion.

[10]5: **The statements of both are true.** H: דברי כולם נכונים = all of them are right.

[11]6: **Great knowledge.** H: חכמה יתירה = exceeding wisdom.

[12]6: **The ruler or *al-mubtazz*.** H: ממונה = overseer.

[13]6: **Small or short.** H: קצרה = short.

[14]6: **Physical strength and power.** H: כח = power.

[15]7: **At the place of its depression or at the opposite of the apogee.** H: במקום שפלותו = at the place of its lowness. → Meaning, at the place of its perigee.

[16]7: **Ruler.** H: ממונה = overseer.

[17]6: *De an.* II 9 421a25–26.

[18]8: *Polit.* VIII 1339a 10–11.

[19]9: *Disticha Catonis* II 9.

[20]11: *Timaeus* 51E.

[21]12: *Eth. Nic.* 1177b26–28.

[22]13: *Eth. Nic.* 1178a6–7.

[23]18: *Eth. Nic.* VI 7, 1141b4–8.

[24]21: *Eth. Nic.* IV 1, 1120b17–20.

[25]24: *Eth. Nic.* X 9, 1179a1–8.

[26]33: *Eth. Nic.* I 10, 1100b21–22.

[27]34: Eccl. 9:11.

[28]9: **And the masculine signs.** H: במזלות הזכרים = in the masculine signs.

[29]9: **Similar to the day.** H: דומים להם = similar to them.

[30]9: **House of shame or fall.** H: בית קלונו = its house of shame.

§5.3

[1]1: **Evil or harm of the planet.** H: רעת הכוכב = evil of the star.

[2]3: **How could the conjunction of the circle of the Moon [that is] similar to the zodiac or ⟨the circle⟩ of the deferent of the Moon with the zodiac or the ecliptic or their intersection afflict the circle of the planet [that is] similar to the zodiac or ⟨the circle that⟩ is called the deferent.** H: כי מה יזיק מחברת גלגל הדומה למזלות של הלבנה עם הדומה לגלגל המזלות של הכוכב לכוכב = how could the conjunction of the circle of the Moon that is similar to the signs with ⟨the circle⟩ that is similar to the circle of the signs of the planet with respect to a planet afflict the planet.

[3]4: **Eclipsed.** H: נקדרת = darkened.

[4]5: **Scholars of the Indians.** H: חכם הודו = one Indian scholar.

[5]5: **This is right and true.** H: הוא נכון = this is correct.

§6.1

[1]1: **By the portion or the part.** H: מפאת = from.

[2]1: **Apogee.** H: גבהות = height. → Meaning, apogee.

§6.2

[1]1: **The conjunction.** H: הדבק = the one joined to.

[2]1: **The conjunction is of the part or by the part or to the part ⟨of the Sun⟩.** H: דבק חלק בחלק עם השמש = joined part by part with the Sun.

[3]1: **The planet is directly ⟨facing⟩ the center of the Sun, and it is conjoined to the center of the Sun.** H: תהיה הנקודה האמצעית של כוכב דביקה עם הנקודה האמצעית של השמש = the middle point of the star [i.e., planet] will be joined to the middle point of the Sun.

[4]2: **Place of the apogee.** H: מקום הגבהות = place of the height.

[5]2: **The small circle or epicycle.** H: גלגלו הקטן = its small circle.

[6]2: **At the greatest elongation from the Earth.** H: במרחק הרחוק מהארץ = at the furthest distance from the Earth.

NOTES TO *LIBER CAUSARUM SEU RATIONUM*

[7]4: **In the books.** H: בספר = in the book.

[8]4: **Leader of the judges.** H: ראש לבעלי הדינין = head of the experts in judgments.

[9]4: **The Indians.** H: הודו = India.

[10]4: **A second or double Mercury.** H: שני כוכבי חמה = two Mercury.

[11]4: **Power or strength.** H: כח = power.

§6.3

[1]2: **Passes and leaves them behind.** H: תניחם = passes them.

[2]5: **Elongated.** H: ירחקו = are distant.

[3]5: **Elongation.** H: מרחק = distance.

[4]5: **The small circle or epicycle.** H: הגלגל הקטן = the small circle.

[5]6: **Book of the age or the revolutions of the world.** H: ספר העולם = Book of the World. → For an explanation of this doublet, see note on *Introductorius*, §2.4:34, s.v., "sign of the age or of the world."

§7.1

[1]1: **Scholars of the stars.** H: חכמי המזלות = scholars of the signs.

[2]1: **Application.** H: הקירוב = getting close.

[3]1: **Power.** H: כח אור = power of the light.

[4]1: **More true.** H: הנכון = the correct one.

[5]2: **Hides or eclipses.** H: שיסתיר = that will hide.

[6]**3: Ecliptic.** H: בחשב האפודה = in the girdle of the vest. → See note on *Introductorius*, § 1.10:5, s.v., "in the girdle of the imagination of the circle of the signs".

[7]**4: The power or dominion.** H:הכח = the power.

[8]**4: The power or dominion to which this conjunction belongs.** H: למי הכח מהנחברים = which of the conjoining ⟨planets⟩ has power.

[9]**4: Apogee.** H: גבהות = height. → Meaning, apogee.

[10]**4: The great circle or deferent.** H: גלגלו הגדול = its great circle.

[11]**4: The other or its companion.** H: חבירו = its companion.

[12]**5: Power.** H: הניצוח = victory.

[13]**5: Is closer to the place.** H: במקום = in the place.

[14]**5: The other.** H: חבירו = its companion.

[15]**6: Northern with respect to the other.** H: בפאת שמאל מחבירו = in the left side with respect to its companion.

[16]**6: It is northern or not.** H: באפודת הגלגל = in the vest of the circle. → See note on *Introductorius*, § 1.10:5, s.v., "in the girdle of the imagination of the circle of the signs".

[17]**6: Northern.** H: השמאלי = the left hand.

[18]**7: Our habitable.** H: הישוב = the settlement. → Meaning, the ecumene. See note on *Introductorius*, § 2.5:11, s.v. "the habitable."

[19]**7: Has.** H: יראה לו = it appears to have.

[20]**7: Every star that is closer to our inhabited ⟨part of the Earth⟩ has a greater power.** H: כל מה שיהיה הכוכב קרוב אל הישוב יראה לו יותר כח = the closer a planet is to the ecumene, the more power it appears to have.

[21]**9: On account of the corner.** H: בפאה = on account of the side.

[22]9: **Dignity.** H: ממשלה = dominion.

§7.2

[1]1: **On the ecliptic.** H: בחשב האפודה = in the girdle of the vest. → See note on *Introductorius*, §1.10:5, s.v., "in the girdle of the imagination of the circle of the signs".

[2]1: **The aspect is full and complete.** H: המבט הוא שלם = the aspect is complete.

[3]2: **In the same corner or in the same part.** H: בפאה אחת שוה = in one and the same side.

[4]3: **Of one respect the other.** H: שניהם = of both.

[5]4: **Deficit or shortfall.** H: החסרון = the deficit.

[6]4: **In the ecliptic.** H: בחשב האפודה = in the girdle of the vest. → See note on *Introductorius*, §1.10:5, s.v., "in the girdle of the imagination of the circle of the signs".

§7.3

[1]1: **The degrees, which are of equal ascensions.** H: על המעלות שהן שוות במצעדיהם = about the degrees which are equal in their steps, processions. → Meaning, equal ascensions.

[2]2: **The same applies to others whose names are like.** H: ואלה השמות = these are the names.

[3]2: **Solitude.** H: הילוך בדד = solitary motion.

§8.1

[1]2: **Because of its resemblance to the ascendant sign.** H: בעבור שהיא קרובה אל הארץ = because it is close to the Earth.

[2]3: **Correct and based on reason.** H: דין הוא = this is right.

[3]4: **Harmful or bad.** H: מזיק = harmful.

[4]5: **What has been said.** H: מה שאמרו = what they said.

[5]5: **It arrives at.** H: היותו = it is.

[6]6: **He is right.** H: הדין עמו = the law is on his side. → Meaning, he is right.

[7]6: **Terms.** → See above § 2.9:1–2.

[8]6: **Because the terms of one are not greater than the terms of the other.** H: כי אין המזלות נבדלים זה מזה = because the signs are not separated one from the other. → Bate's divergent translation is a gloss explaining why the signs should not be separated one from the other: the total sum of degrees of the planetary terms is the same in all of the twelve signs; i.e., 30°.

[9]6: **But among them there is a dispute whether the signs should be separated by a consideration of the intellect.** should be separated by a consideration of the intellect] H: כי מחלוקתם הם כפי מחשבת הלב = because their divisions are according to a mental construct. → Bate's divergent translation is a gloss converting the problem posed by Ibn Ezra regarding the division of the signs into a dispute among scholars.

[10]6: **Conjunction or intersection.** H: מחברת = conjunction.

[11]6: **In the end of the sign or in its last part.** H: בסוף המזל = in the end of the sign.

[12]8: **Wealth or riches.** H: ממון = wealth.

[13]8: **But only indicates a marvelous death.** H: רק יש לו טובה אחת, שינצל ממיתה משונה = but it has one benefit, that ⟨the native⟩ will be saved from a strange death. → Bate's divergent translation comments on Ibn Ezra by paralleling the latter's "being saved from a strange death" with "dying a marvelous death".

[14]9: **What we have mentioned here is correct.** H: והעדיות שהזכרנו הם נכונים = the testimonies that we have mentioned are correct.

[15]9: **In the Book of nativities I will speak about those things that set testimonies rightly and also about those that are not like that.** H: ובספר המולדות אדבר על הכשר לעדות ועל הפסול = in the *Book of Nativities* I will speak about what is qualified to give testimony and what is not valid.

§9.1

[1]1: **Asserts.** H: מודה = acknowledges.

[2]1: **Nevertheless.** H: לבדו = alone.

[3]2: **Lot of the hidden things or of the hidden soul.** H: גורל התעלומה = lot of the hidden thing.

[4]2: **This completely is for its confirmation or corroboration.** H: יותר חזק = stronger.

[5]2: **Because it is.** H: זה הוא בעצמו = it is itself.

[6]2: **Books.** H: ספר = book.

[7]4: **The conjunction with Mercury is in the other lot.** H: והיה גורל העוני דבק עם כוכב חמה = The lot of poverty is joined with Mercury.

[8]4: **Intellectual activities, and wisdom, and sciences.** H: חכמה = wisdom.

[9]6: **Statement.** H: דבר = thing.

[10]6: **For such a status.** H: למעלה גבוהה = to high status.

[11]7: **Slave.** H: משרת פורני = one who tends an oven.

[12]7: **He will own or have slaves.** H: ישים משרת תחתיו = he will have a servant under him.

[13]8: **The native will be wise.** H: יהיה מבין = will understand.

[14]8: **Wordly statements.** H: דברי העולם = worldly affairs.

§9.2

[1]1: **And in the first place that of the first house.** H: כי הנה לבית ראשון יש לו גורל החיים = for the first house has the lot of life.

[2]2: **Longitude or distance.** H: מרחק = distance.

[3]2: **The root of everything.** H: עיקרים = roots.

[4]2: **Is.** H: אם יהיה = if it will be.

[5]2: **Ruler.** H: ממונה = overseer.

[6]2: **Power or strength.** H: כח = power.

[7]3: **Part of the ascendant.** H: גורל המסעד = the lot of firmness.

[8]4: **Longitude.** H: מרחק = distance.

[9]5: **Longitude.** H: מרחק = distance.

[10]5: **Intellect.** H: חכמה = wisdom.

§9.3

[1]1: **And in accordance with it is.** H: וככה גורל = and similarly the lot.

[2]1: **Of the age or of the revolution of the years of the world.** H: לעולם = for ever. → Literally "to the world," and this is the reason for Bate's mistranslation, which involves "the world" in the expression "years of the world".

[3]4: **Has been verified.** H: הוא נכון = is correct.

§10.1

[1]1: **Abraham, our master.** H: רבינו אברהם = Abraham, our rabbi. → Meaning, our teacher. This reading is supported at least by two Hebrew manuscripts: Paris, Bibliothèque nationale de France, MS héb. 1056; Munich, Bayerische Staatsbibliothek, Cod. Hebr. 202. But the mayority of the checked Hebrew manuscripts read: H: אברהם = Abraham, tout court.

[2]1: **Modern scholars.** H: חכמי דורנו = scholars of our generation.

[3]1: **Were mistaken.** H: השתבשו = were confused.

[4]2: **Enoch or Hermes.** H: חנוך = Enoch.

[5]2: **Good and perfect proofs.** H: דברים שיש ראיות גמורות = things about which there are complete proofs.

[6]2: **Equations.** H: תקון = correction. See note on *Introductorius*, § 6.3:2, s.v. "equation."

[7]2: **Climate.** H: גבול = territory, term. → Meaning, climate. See note on *Introductorius*, § 2.1:17, s.v. "climate."

[8]3: **Book of four parts.** H: ספר ארבעה שערים = book of four chapters.

[9]3: **Direct circle.** H: גלגל היושר = circle of straightness.

[10]3: **Ascensions of the country.** H: מצעדי הארץ = steps/processions of the country. → Meaning, ascensions of the country.

[11]4: **First.** H: תחלת = beginning of.

§ 10.2

[1]1: **Pay attention.** H: שים לבך = put your heart = apponas ergo cor tuum.

[2]1: **Equations.** H: תקון = correction.

[3]2: **Beginning.** H: ראש = head.

[4]4: **Equated.** H: מתוקנים = corrected.

[5]5: **First.** H: תחלת = beginning of.

[6]6: **Scholars of astrology.** H: חכמי המזלות = scholars of the signs.

[7]6: **Scholars of the instruments and of the astrolabe.** H: חכמי כלי הנחושת = scholars of the instrument of copper.

[8]6: **Sufficient.** H: רבות = many.

[9]7: **Angles.** H: יתדות = pegs. → Meaning, cardines of the horoscope. See note on *Introductorius*, § 3.4:2, s.v., "angles or cardines."

[10]7: **Are equal.** H: מעלותם שוות = their degrees are the same.

§ 10.3

[1]2: **Equal degrees.** H: מעלות ישרות = straight degrees.

[2]2: **Or ⟨the degree⟩ of each of the luminaries.** H: או אחד המאורות = or one of the luminaries.

[3]2: **Direct circle.** H: גלגל היושר = circle of straightness.

[4]6: **Master Abraham, called the Prince.** H: ר' אברהם הנשיא = R' Abraham ha-Naśi'. → Meaning, Rabbi Abraham the Prince. This title refers to Abraham Bar Ḥiyya.

§ 10.4

[1]2: **Equal degrees.** H: מעלות ישרות = straight degrees.

[2]4: **Either the beginning of a house or the aspect of a planet.** H: תחלת בית אל מבט כוכב = the beginning of a house to the aspect of a star.

[3]5: **Equated.** H: מתוקן = corrected.

[4]5: **Equation.** H: תקון = correction.

[5]6: **Angle.** H: יתד = peg. → Meaning, cardo of the horoscope. See note on *Introductorius*, § 3.4:2, s.v., "angles or cardines."

[6]8: **It is convenient or necessary that.** H: ראוי = it is fitting that.

NOTES TO *LIBER CAUSARUM SEU RATIONUM*   627

[7]8: **Other house.** H: כל בית ובית = each and every house.

§10.5

[1]2: **Line of the abyss or angle of the Earth.** H: קו התהום = line of the abyss.

[2]2: **Equal or straight degrees.** H: מעלות ישרות = straight degrees.

[3]3: **Crooked or unequal hours.** H: השעות המעוותות = the crooked hours.

[4]3: **Against the ascendant degree or opposite to it.** H: לנכח המעלה = opposite the degree.

[5]4: **Opposite.** H: כנגד = against.

[6]5: **Accumulated or the result.** H: המחובר = what has been added up.

[7]6: **Comes out or is found.** H: יצא = came out.

[8]8: **According to what is right.** H: כמשפט = as the rule.

[9]9: **Longitude.** H: מרחק = distance.

[10]9: **Upright circle.** H: גלגל היושר = circle of straightness.

[11]11: **Longitude or distance.** H: המרחק = the distance.

[12]11: **In the table of the country or region.** H: בארץ = in the country. → Bate's divergent translation glosses Ibn Ezra's expression "in the country".

[13]12: **Unequal or crooked hours.** H: השעות המעוותות = the crooked hours.

[14]13: **Will be found or come out.** H: שיצא = will come out.

[15]13: **Table of the upright circle.** H: לוח גלגל היושר = table of the circle of straightness.

[16]13: **Opposite the line of the abyss or against the line of the abyss.** H: כנגד קו התהום = against the line of the abyss.

[17]16: **To calculate or find.** H: להוציא = to calculate.

[18]16: **Two.** H: ארבע = four.

[19]16: **Unequal or crooked hours.** H: השעות המעוותות = the crooked hours.

[20]17: **Ascendant.** H: הזורחת = the shining. → Bate's divergent translation glosses Ibn Ezra's expression "the shining".

[21]19: **Treatise of the Astrolabe.** H: ספר כלי הנחושת = Book of the instrument of copper.

[22]20: **About the matters of the revolutions.** H: בדברי על התקופות = when I speak about the revolutions.

§10.6

[1]2: **Subtract them.** H: הניחם = leave them.

[2]3: **Equated.** H: מתוקן = corrected.

[3]4: **Lies or is.** H: שם = there is.

§10.7

[1]1: **Table of the upright circle.** H: לוח גלגל היושר = table of the circle of straightness.

[2]1: **Opposite the degree in which the planet is.** H: כנגד קו חצי השמים = against the line of midheaven.

[3]1: **Distance or longitude.** H: מרחק = distance.

[4]3: **Crooked minutes of the hour or parts of the 60 minutes.** H: חלקי שעה מששים = minutes of the hour of 60.

[5]4: **Whole or complete hours.** H: שעות שלמות = complete hours.

[6]5: **Unequal or crooked hours.** H: שעות מעוותות = crooked hours.

[7]5: **Distance or longitude.** H: מרחק = distance.

§10.8

[1]1: **Parts of the hour or minutes.** H: חלקים = parts.

[2]3: **Unequal or crooked hours.** H: שעות מעוותות = crooked hours.

[3]4: **Equate.** H: לעשות = make.

[4]5: **Against the degree of the planet or opposite it.** H: כנגד מעלת הכוכב = against the degree of the star.

[5]5: **What was worked out or came out.** H: העולה = what arises.

[6]5: **Opposite the degree of the planet or against the planet.** H: לנכח מעלת הכוכב = opposite the degree of the star.

[7]5: **Houses.** H: המבטים = the aspects.

[8]6: **Ascensions.** H: מצעדי המזלות = steps/processions of the signs. → Meaning, ascensions of the signs.

[9]7: **Table of the direct circle.** H: לוח גלגל היושר = table of the circle of straightness.

[10]7: **Opposite the planet.** H: כנגד קו המבט = against the line of the aspect.

[11]7: **The remainder or what came out.** H: העולה = what arises.

[12]8: **Increase or addition.** H: תוספת = addition.

[13]9: **Calculate the planet as if it were.** H: חשוב כי הכוכב = assume that the star.

§10.9

[1]1: **The other directions mentioned.** H: שהזכרתי = which I have mentioned.

[2]2: **The direction.** H: ניהוג הזמן = the direction of time.

[3]2: **In respect to things known and verified experimentally.** H: דבר ידוע ומנוסה = is something known and verified by experience.

[4]4: **This is however sometimes 13 and sometimes 12.** H: שהם שתים עשרה פעמים שיתחברו, יש פעמים שיתחברו שלוש עשרה פעמים = for sometimes they conjoin 12 times, sometimes they conjoin 13 times.

[5]4: **Book of the age or the revolutions of the word.** H: ספר העולם = Book of the World.

Printed in the United States
by Baker & Taylor Publisher Services